TO PLAY THE GAME

A History of Flight 571

JOHN GUIVER

www.heddonpublishing.com
www.facebook.com/heddonpublishing
@PublishHeddon

Table of Contents

It's all in this to play the game
To win or lose and be the same
To take the blame, to smile the while
Oh! Help me Lord to play the game

For when the one great scorer comes
To write against your name
He'll ask not if you won or lost
But how you played the game

Old Christians prayer.

Preface

It is a measure of the widespread interest in the Andes story that, by the time the authorized account appeared in April 1974, ten unofficial books on the tragedy had already hit the shelves, the first of them appearing just one month after the survivors were rescued from the mountain. Piers Paul Read's *ALIVE*, commissioned by the survivors, is without doubt the seminal work on the subject, selling over five million copies in the years immediately following its publication. Universally praised for its compelling narrative (author Graham Greene said of it: "It is inconceivable to me that this story could have been better told"), the book remains essential reading for anyone interested in the story.

In recent years, the flow of books, which include several survivor memoirs, has started afresh. Notable amongst the general accounts is *Sociedad de la Nieve* by Uruguayan author Pablo Vierci, a friend and former classmate of the passengers. His 2009 account interleaves personal testimonies of each of the sixteen survivors with chapters describing events on the mountain. Vierci's book forms the basis of a new film of the same name by acclaimed Spanish director J.A. Bayona, due for release in 2023, following close on the fiftieth anniversary of the event.

Given that there are around forty books on the subject, numerous documentaries, two feature films, and countless articles and television interviews, the question arises as to why there is any further need to add to this already considerable body of work. To answer that, I have to say a bit about my own involvement with the story. Like many, my introduction to this extraordinary tale of survival was through Piers Paul Reads' book. My late mother-in-law gave me her own first-edition copy of *ALIVE*, sensing in her wisdom that the story would resonate with me. She was not wrong. For a year afterwards, the pristine copy that she gave me became increasingly tattered as I leafed through it every night, trying to extract every nugget of information, and imagining myself on the mountain.

It is difficult for me to analyse exactly what struck so deep a chord. I had some commonality with the passengers, having gone to a Catholic rugby-playing school, taught in my case by Benedictine monks rather than the Irish Christian Brothers of *Stella Maris College*. With an Italian mother, I perhaps also had a better appreciation of Latin sensibilities than the typical Anglo reader. And it was a true-life tale of endurance and survival – a genre that appeals to me. The anthropophagy[1], perhaps what the ordeal is most noted for, did not loom large for me – I saw it as a necessary decision, one of many that the survivors had to make in an extraordinary sequence of events.

The bond forged between the sixteen survivors by their experience, which brought them face-to-face with death on a daily basis, was enviable, but I was left with a nagging dissatisfaction after reading *ALIVE*. Several of the boys who died on the mountain were mentioned only by name, and I felt a certain injustice at their omission in a story that would raise the survivors to such heights of fame. I was interested to know more about their lives and their families. In those days before social media, it would have been difficult, and an invasion of privacy to pursue that curiosity, so I put my obsession on the back-burner and got on with my life.

Fast-forward twenty-five years to January 2013 when, for the first time, I had enough disposable income to afford an adventure holiday, and I signed up to mountaineer Ricardo Peña's expedition to the site of the accident, a trip on which I met survivor Eduardo Strauch. Through him I met another survivor, Pedro Algorta, whose memoir I offered to translate, despite knowing no Spanish at the time. Pedro, in turn, introduced me to Sandra Maquirriain, a sister of Felipe Maquirriain, one of the victims of the tragedy who received just a single mention in *ALIVE*. Sandra, who for many years had found it difficult to talk about the tragedy, seemed happy to speak to me, and share some memories of her brother. Over time, I met several other family members, including Graciela Parrado, who had lost her mother and sister in the tragedy but whose brother Nando survived as one of the great heroes of the story. One of the first things Graciela asked me was: "Why are you writing a book?" The question took me aback, as I'd not consciously considered embarking on such an arduous task, my day job as researcher in Machine Learning and Artificial Intelligence affording me precious little spare time.

But the idea nagged away at me, and, in October 2019, in a position to take a six-week sabbatical from my job, I headed out to Uruguay to test the waters, to speak to as many siblings of the tragedy's victims as I could, and to see if there was any appetite for such an endeavour. I started with those I already knew, and my introductory statement "I'm thinking of writing a book", very soon became "I am writing a book." As word of mouth spread about my project, my days rapidly filled up with one interview after another, though rarely arranged more than a couple of days in advance. The trust that the families

---

[1] 'Anthropophagy' is the word that the sixteen have always preferred to use over the more widely-used 'cannibalism' with its connotations of eating human flesh through choice and habit.

placed in a complete stranger from England was extraordinary, and I finally got to hear the stories that I'd wondered about all those years previously. That trust, and the way in which the families opened up, left me with little choice, and the wish to tell their stories became an imperative. I started writing as soon as I returned to England. My day job left me little time to focus on the task, although the onset of the global pandemic cut out my commute and gained me a couple of hours each day. So in April 2021, I made the decision to retire from the world of blue-sky research to devote all my time to writing.

I had originally conceived of the book as strictly an addendum to that of Piers Read, a continuation of his work, but I soon realised that, in order for it to be cohesive and self-contained, I would also need to cover old ground. I was reluctant to use the current memories of the survivors as the basis for retelling the story, because they have spoken in public about it countless times, and, as Pedro Algorta observes in his memoir: "We remember things as we last spoke about them… not necessarily as they really were, but as we have recounted them, and every time we tell a story we add to it and so build up our own story layer by layer." Instead, I made the decision to go back to the original archival material, whilst at the same time making an effort to try to bring new detail and fresh perspective to the story, hopefully going some way towards attaining the conflicting goals of completeness and complementarity. Piers Read was particularly supportive and helpful here, granting me special access to his archive at the Brotherton Library in Leeds, but I made use of other archives also: the Clay Blair papers in the American Heritage Center of the University of Wyoming, and several private archives.

The situation for the families of those who didn't return from the mountain was quite different from that of the survivors. They had rarely, and in a few cases never, spoken about their loved one outside the family, and so memories were fresh and more reliable. The result was that I left Uruguay in November 2019 with sixty-five hours of interviews, which were supplemented by many emails, text conversations, and further interviews over the following year and a half. Their testimony is the primary source for Part VI of this book, forming almost half of its content, and hopefully going a long way towards providing a more balanced history for future generations.

Early in 2022, I was contacted by Chilean researcher Guillermo Scott. He had heard that I was writing a book, and had been planning on writing one himself, also aligned with the fiftieth anniversary of the event. His was to be based on a comprehensive set of interviews he had conducted in Santiago, speaking with many of the original protagonists on the .Chilean side – Air Force and Army personnel, Andinistas, journalists, rugby players, and others. In April 2022, he made a trip to England, taking the opportunity both to visit Piers Read and to learn about my project at first hand. For a while, we discussed the possibility of joining forces and co-authoring a book, but I had already made significant headway on mine, and I was reluctant to change its emphasis in a way that would compromise the representation I had made to the families. On the other hand, part of the balance that I sought to achieve included telling the stories of the many Chileans who gave their time, and risked their lives, to help with the search and rescue. In the end, Guillermo made a suggestion: he would put his book on hold and give me full access to his archive, to be used entirely at my own editorial discretion. In return, he would receive exclusive Spanish-language translation and publication rights for my book. We signed an agreement, and the fruits of Guillermo's impressive research are clearly evident in my retelling of the story.

Before I went out to Uruguay in October 2019, Piers Read light-heartedly warned me to "take care: it is a seductive country". And it is indeed a beguiling place, with its courteous people, wonderful food, beautiful beaches, and rural heritage. With a literate population in which culture and education are prized, it still retains the wild underbelly of a young country settled by pioneers and inhabited by *gauchos*. Visiting in 1925, Einstein had nothing but good to say about Uruguay, praising its social institutions and its humanity, and singling out its relatively small population as a contributing factor. Certainly there is a sense of it being one big family, and it is perhaps this connectedness, alongside the practicality and endeavour of its people, that has allowed it to ride out the various crises in its history, maintaining a surprisingly stable equilibrium between order and chaos. This historical and sociocultural backdrop, which provides an important context for understanding the Andes story, is the focus of Part I of this book.

A brief note to my US readers: I have to ask your indulgence for having restricted this book to British English; the alternative would have been to create parallel versions of each English edition, something I was reluctant to do. Hopefully the less familiar spellings and word choices will not be a barrier to your enjoyment of the book.

And to all my readers: one of my goals is for this history to open your eyes to the human side of this famous tragedy. It is easy for outsiders to dismiss the story as something impersonal, distasteful, and distant – "the one about the rugby players who ate each other". But its unwilling participants came from a vibrant, intelligent, and closely-connected community, where its winners and losers still live side by side. Their humanity and kinship is typical of the Uruguay I know, and my hope is that this book will encourage more readers to visit this fascinating and welcoming country.

John Guiver
September 2022

I. Beginnings

At daybreak on Thursday 12th October 1972, members of a Uruguayan first-division rugby team, along with their friends and relatives, started making their way to Carrasco airport, for an early morning flight to Santiago. Most lived just a few kilometres away. Some sharing rides with friends or teammates, others being driven by family members or girlfriends, there was a palpable air of excitement as the passengers arrived and gathered in the departure lounge of Uruguay's main airport. The team was the *Old Christians*, comprising the alumni of *Colegio Stella Maris (Stella Maris College)* – also known as *The Christian*, after the Irish Christian Brothers who founded it. They were travelling to Santiago, to play a friendly game against a Chilean club of similar standing – the *Grange Old Boys*. But over the long weekend, there would also be ample opportunity to relax and enjoy the warm Chilean hospitality, the beaches of Viña del Mar, or the skiing at *El Portillo*; all at unusually favourable exchange rates.

The plane and its air force crew were chartered from the *Fuerza Aérea Uruguaya* (Uruguay Air Force, abbreviated FAU) for whom it was common practice to operate civilian flights. With a few days to go, it had looked like the whole thing might have to be called off, as not enough people had signed up to allow the advertised $40 ticket price. But in a leap of faith, the organizer of the trip – *Old Christians* captain **Marcelo Pérez del Castillo** –told his Chilean hosts that the trip would go ahead, enlisting the help of fellow *Old Christians* **Julio Martínez Lamas** and Pepe Pollak in a final push to fill the remaining places. Cajoling friends, teammates, friends of friends, and relatives, with enticing visions of a relaxing few days in Chile, they managed to sell the balance of the forty tickets with one day to spare.

Despite the careful planning, one boy – Gilberto 'Tito' Regules – had not turned up at the airport, causing his friends to joke that the plane would now crash, that they would die, and he would survive. But as they boarded the plane, none of them could have imagined that their departure would mark the start of one of the most extraordinary episodes in the history of human survival.

Friends and family watched from the wide viewing balcony as the white Fairchild FH-227D took to the air, remaining until it became a dot in the western sky before returning to their homes. No news that evening was good news; it meant that the boys had arrived safely in Santiago. The following evening, however, reports started coming through that a Uruguayan Air Force plane was missing in the *Cordillera* – the Andes mountain range. Most parents dismissed the story – it didn't make sense, because the boys should have arrived in Chile the previous day. What they didn't yet know was that the plane had been forced to stop overnight in Mendoza, on the Argentinian side of the Andes, due to dangerous conditions in the *Cordillera*. Eventually, it became apparent that it was indeed the *Old Christians* flight. The plane had vanished in the Andes without trace.

The intensive search and rescue efforts yielded no sign of any wreckage, and were called off after eight days due to dangerous conditions. Over the following two months, unofficial search expeditions conducted by the parents of the boys, with the help of an army of Chilean volunteers, were also unsuccessful. A renewed official search effort was just winding down for the Christmas holidays when, on 21st December, 71 days after *Flight 571* took off from Carrasco airport, startling and sketchy reports started to emerge... Two boys spotted by a cattle drover across a mountain torrent in a remote valley in the Chilean *precordillera*... A note wrapped around a stone thrown to the opposite bank, with a desperate plea for help: 'I come from a plane that fell in the mountains...'

Over the following hours, more details emerged. The boys were **Nando Parrado** and **Roberto Canessa**, who had hiked for ten days across the Andes, arriving in a place called *Los Maitenes*, pasture-lands where cattle drover Sergio Catalan spent the summer months. And there were fourteen more survivors on the mountain. The parents, the world's press, and the curious, rushed to San Fernando in Chile, the closest town to *Los Maitenes*. Helicopters were dispatched to rescue the others on the mountain. A list of survivors was broadcast. The story was dubbed 'the Christmas Miracle'. The surviving boys were fêted as heroes in the streets of Santiago, and their story would become the stuff of legend, to be recounted in dozens of books, movies, and documentaries over the years.

It wasn't long before their reception back into 'civilization' was sullied by tabloid sensationalism. Reports and photographs were leaked about what they had been forced to do to survive. *¡Canibalismo!* was the headline. The boys were reluctant to talk about the matter whilst still in Chile, and so when eleven of the sixteen landed back at Carrasco airport on 28th December, eleven weeks after their departure, their first order of business was an international press conference, arranged to take place at *Stella Maris College*. On a stage in their old gym, they took it in turns to talk about their ordeal, but it was **Alfredo 'Pancho' Delgado** who agreed to speak about the difficult topic of the anthropophagy. Describing the silence and majesty of the mountains and talking of "an intimate communion, not to be exploited or made light of...", his inspired words brought the conference to an end with a standing ovation. Even the journalists from around the world felt it indecorous to direct any more questions to the boys.

Although this marked their homecoming and the end of their ordeal, the impact of the tragedy on the community was just beginning. In the close-knit neighbourhood of Carrasco, where most of the boys were from, families of survivors lived side-by-side with the families of those who didn't return. The survivors instantly became heroes and well-known figures, widely interviewed and written about. Their international profile rose further with the publication of *ALIVE*, the official account of their ordeal, which shot to the top of the best-seller list in several countries. Contrasted against that, the parents of those who died didn't even have the solace of saying goodbye to their sons – their remains were buried on the mountain. And for all those parents, it was as though their sons had died twice – after coming to terms with their assumed death, hope had been briefly revived with news of survivors, only to be dashed again when the list was broadcast.

Despite this, the bereaved families didn't condemn the boys for what they had done to survive, and some went out of their way to actively support the survivors, to relieve the psychological pressures they faced. The father of **Carlos Valeta** spoke to the press with extraordinary generosity: "Thank God that the 45 were there so that 16 homes were able to regain their children." The mother of **Gustavo 'Coco' Nicolich** said, "We support the decision taken by the boys and we are trying to help them overcome this ordeal." The father of **Arturo Nogueira** wrote a letter to the *El Día* newspaper, inviting the citizens of Uruguay to meditate on "the immense lesson of solidarity, courage and discipline that these boys have left us, and may it serve to teach us to put aside our petty egotism, unbridled ambition, and lack of interest in our fellow man."

Over the years, the tragedy hung as a cloud over the community – always present, rarely mentioned. Within many households, the accident was never spoken about. Relations between the survivors and the families of their dead friends were sometimes strained, and there was a reticence amongst the former to mention the subject, in respect for the feelings of the bereaved families. The guilt that the survivors felt was not what they were forced to do, but the fact that they had survived whilst their friends had not. All in all, it was easier to talk about other things.

Whilst the story received unprecedented worldwide attention, the reception within the wider community in Uruguay was relatively muted. The story of the Andes had taken place against the backdrop of political events that were threatening to fracture Uruguay's long-practised and cherished democracy. The military had been involved in a wide-scale round-up of Tupamaros guerrillas, before and during the time that the boys were on the mountain, and were now turning their attention to a government unable to deal with Uruguay's economic ills. The military's demands for a greater say in the running of the country would eventually result in the authoritarian civic-military dictatorship of June 1973. The Andes story took a back seat to these events, and besides, there was little sympathy for the fates of these privileged boys amongst a populace suffering from fifteen years of economic strife. An appreciation of these political and sociocultural contexts, and their wider historical precedents, are an important part of understanding the history and legacy of the Andes story.

Carrasco airport is still the international gateway into Uruguay, although the terminal used by the Andes passengers has been replaced by an impressive modern building, with an expansive curved roof and light-filled atrium. But the drive from the airport to downtown Montevideo brings you close to the story and the history of those times at every turn. An immediate connection is made soon after turning out of the airport car park. Drive past the *Museo Aeronáutico* and join the main highway heading towards town. A few hundred metres on, in the restricted *Base Aérea No. 1* to the right, you can glimpse two of the retired planes of the FAU transport group. In the foreground is a C-47 – registration FAU 514 – a sister plane of the FAU 508 which took part in the search flights in the Andes. Further back, and more evocative, is a Fairchild FH-227D – registration FAU 572 – the replacement plane for the identical Fairchild that was lost in the Andes.

Fig. 1. *Fairchild FAU 572, replacement for FAU 571.*

At the next roundabout, a right turn would bring you to the old airport terminal building, where the passengers gathered on that Thursday in October 1972; instead, turn left onto the Avenida de las Americas. When the survivors returned from Chile, this road was lined with people, waving and cheering the heroes of the Andes as the ONDA buses, with their greyhound logos, drove by on their way to the press conference. A few kilometres further on, you cross the *Puente Carrasco*, the bridge over *Arroyo Carrasco*, the creek that marks the eastern boundary of the *barrio* of Carrasco, where most of the passengers lived, and where many of the families still live today.

Fig. 2. *Departure terminal of Flight 571.*

Instead of continuing west along Avenida Italia, loop over the highway and head south towards the *Rambla*, skirting Carrasco on the right. A few hundred metres on, you will reach the River Plate, the muddy estuary that looks like a sea, 150 km across to Argentina at this point. Turn right onto the *Rambla*, the wide boulevard that follows the shore of the estuary all the way to Montevideo's *Ciudad Vieja* – the Old City – twenty kilometres to the west. The *Rambla* is deeply embedded in Uruguayan consciousness; a vital artery connecting people, places, and history. Its wide sidewalks and bikeways run uninterrupted alongside miles of sandy beaches. It is filled with people exercising, strolling, or relaxing on the many benches, with unobstructed views of the water and the expansive skies.

As you start down the *Rambla*, you will soon pass the Naval School on your right. Looking directly out into the estuary at this point, you can glimpse some rocks, known as *Las Pipas*, a couple of kilometres offshore. In May 1969, approaching the winter months in Uruguay, in a break from their studies, four boys set out in a canoe designed for two people. Their destination, *Las Pipas*. Getting into difficulties in the cold and choppy waters, they capsized, and, with the wind sweeping away their canoe, they attempted to swim back to shore. Only one made it; suffering from exposure and exhaustion, he half crawled into the Naval School to raise the alarm. The three who died – Daniel Costemalle, Eduardo Gelsi, and José Luis Lombardero – all had close connections to the Andes story.

Fig. 3. *Ponce de Leon's house – the centre of communications during the seventy-two days.*

The boys had set out from Carrasco beach, opposite Dr Andrés Puyol street, a few blocks further along the *Rambla*, where Lombardero lived. Puyol has many connections with the story. Lombardero's sister Inés was the *novia* (steady girlfriend) of **Arturo Nogueira** who also lived on Puyol, across the street from **Enrique Platero** and a few houses up from **Javier** and **Liliana Methol**. Of these four passengers, only Javier would survive the Andes. Midway between the Nogueira and Methol homes, Rafael Ponce de León, a friend and contemporary of many of the boys, had set up a ham radio shack in the basement of his father's house. Before the trip, he had helped Marcelo with the logistics, communicating by ham radio with the team's Chilean hosts. During the 72 days on the mountain, many of the families would gather at the house to hear news of the search effort, and it was

there that many of the parents heard for the first time whether their son survived or not, when the list was relayed live from Chile.

And in one sense, Puyol is where the Andes story begins. When *Stella Maris College* opened its doors in 1955, it was temporarily located in a

Fig. 4. *The first building used by Stella Maris College in 1955 at the corner of Puyol street and the Rambla.*

converted hotel where Puyol meets the *Rambla*. Some of the older passengers – **Julio Martínez Lamas**, **Marcelo Pérez del Castillo**, and the four cousins **Daniel Fernández**, **Eduardo Strauch**, **Fito Strauch**, and **Daniel Shaw** – appear in the very first school photo taken at this corner, and twenty-six of the forty passengers received their formative education at *Stella Maris*, with several others having strong connections.

Continuing on past Puyol, you soon see the iconic Hotel Carrasco and Casino, built in the 1920s, when Carrasco was still just a seaside resort. Einstein stayed at this hotel in 1925, later writing of his reception in Uruguay: "I was received with a genuine cordiality as I rarely find in my life". He had only good things to say about the country, admiring its social institutions and liberal outlook. On the night before the flight in 1972, some of the boys tried their luck at the casino, hoping to win some extra spending cash; one of them, Tito Regules, overslept the next morning, and missed the flight. Less than a year later, a room in the hotel was set aside for the exclusive use of the *Biblioteca Nuestros Hijos*, the library founded by the bereaved mothers to help underprivileged children, and to keep alive the memories of their sons.

Continuing along the sweeping curves of the *Rambla* takes you past other neighbourhoods that line the estuary, all with interesting connections to the history of that time. At Punta Gorda, the main road briefly departs from the *Rambla*, cutting across the headland, which juts out into the river like the prow of a ship, and where three of the passengers lived, including survivors **Nando Parrado** and **Coche Inciarte**. But it was the family home of Andes victim **Felipe Maquirriain** that held pride of place, directly overlooking *Plaza Virgilio* at the apex of the promontory.

Fig. 5. *Hotel Carrasco and Casino 1980.*

Joining the *Rambla* again, as you leave Punta Gorda and approach the built-up neighbourhood of Malvín, you pass Dr Alejandro Gallinal street, where, on 31ˢᵗ July 1970, four young Tupamaros guerrillas pulled in front of the car carrying US police adviser Dan Mitrione, and abducted him at gunpoint, just a block from the home of Andes victim **Guido Magri**. Continuing through to the western end of Malvín, you pass Yacó street, close to its intersection with Almería, where a week after Mitrione's abduction, the military captured nine leading Tupamaros, including founder Raúl Sendic. Ironically, this major counter-insurgency success led to Mitrione's death, the leaderless young guerrillas having no compunction about executing him once their leadership's deadline had expired.

Fig. 6. *Rambla passing through Malvín and Buceo 1970.*

Past Malvín, the *Rambla* brings you into the neighbourhood of Buceo. On the left, Buceo beach; on the right, the graffitied walls marking the southern end of the tranquil Buceo cemetery where **Rafael Echavarren**, the only fatality of the Andes tragedy to return to Uruguay, is laid to rest. Next to Buceo cemetery, though not visible from the *Rambla*, is the British cemetery, which contains the common grave of the victims of another 1972 tragedy; in May of that year, the *Royston Grange*, a British cargo steamer, caught fire after a collision with an oil tanker in the River Plate. All 74 on board, mainly British, died in the conflagration.

Fig. 7. *Buceo Cemetery.*

The next bend takes you past Buceo bay, with the yacht club and marina in sight at the far end. As the road starts to climb away from the bay, you can see a small futuristic building on the right, dwarfed by the *Panamericano* building behind it. In recent years, it has served as the headquarters of *Océano FM Radio*, but in 1972 it housed the *Zum-Zum* nightclub; a popular destination for many of the boys to go dancing with their girlfriends.

Fig. 8. *Zum Zum nightclub.*

Continuing over the crest of the hill, you pass the large Montevideo sign, a popular photo spot with Pocitos beach in the background. But the location, known as Kibón, has a sombre history. In November 1971, less than a year before the Andes disaster, the Navy was celebrating its 154th anniversary, with search and rescue demonstrations in front of a packed crowd. As a helicopter turned towards the onlookers, the jeep it was lifting caught on an embankment, dragging the helicopter down. It crashed into another helicopter on the ground, and the blades and other flying debris wreaked devastation, leaving eight dead and dozens with horrific injuries. The military tribunal charged with investigating the accident found no violation of regulations, and the episode was conveniently neglected against a backdrop of political turmoil and the fight against the Tupamaros.

Past Kibón is the vibrant neighbourhood of Pocitos, home to a number of boys on the trip – **Gastón Costemalle**, **Juan Carlos Menéndez**, and **Rafael Echavarren**. By the

seventies, the elegant grand residences of the first half of the century had been replaced by high-rise apartments with views over the estuary, and the neighbourhood was promoted in one tourist publication of the time as "the little Copacabana of Montevideo".

Fig. 9. *Kibon accident 1971.*

Beyond Pocitos beach, the road curves around towards Punta Carretas, where, a couple of blocks up from the *Rambla*, is a large shopping mall and the *Montevideo Sheraton*. In the seventies this area was the site of the prison from which, in the early hours of 6th September 1971, over one hundred Tupamaros escaped through a tunnel. Amongst them were Pepe Mujica (future president of Uruguay) and founder Raúl Sendic, a little over a year after his capture in Malvín.

Fig. 10. *From a 1970's postcard of Pocitos.*

Continue on for a few kilometres, and then follow the signs to the right to reach the *Plaza Independencia*. On the west end of the square is the gateway to the *Ciudad Vieja*, the historic old city, which occupies a peninsula surrounded by the River Plate and Montevideo Bay. It saw extraordinary events in February 1973, less than two months after the survivors returned, when the Navy blockaded the peninsula in a stand-off against the Army and Air Force; one of the more dramatic of a sequence of events that would lead to the civic-military dictatorship in June 1973.

On the east side of the square is the distinctive *Palacio Salvo*, with its flamboyant tower, briefly the tallest building in Latin America. But the centre of attention is the towering statue of José Artigas on horseback, and the mausoleum that contains his bones. Artigas is the proclaimed father of Uruguay, and his story is

Fig. 11. *Punta Carretas prison.*

intimately bound up with the fates of indigenous peoples of the region, most notably the Charrúa and the Guaraní.

Fig. 12. *Artigas monument and Palacio Salvo (1929).*

1970'S MONTEVIDEO

POINTS OF INTEREST

1 FAU Base Aéreo No. 1
2 1972 Departure Terminal
3 Avenida de las Americas
4 Puente Carrasco
5 Stella Maris College
6 Naval School
7 Las Pipas
8 Location of original school building
9 Hotel Carrasco (now Sofitel) and Casino
10 Punta Gorda
11 Malvín
12 Buceo cemetery
13 Zum-Zum nightclub (now Océano FM Radio)
14 Kibon
15 Pocitos Beach
16 Punta Carretas prison (now shopping mall)
17 Plaza Independencia

PASSENGERS' HOMES

9	Abal	28	Methol
24	Algorta	18	Nicola
25	Canessa	23	Nicolich
10	Costemalle	27	Nogueira
4	Delgado	30	Páez
5	Echavarren	14	Parrado
8	Fernández	34	Pérez del Castillo
31	François	26	Platero
22	Harley	2	Sabella
3	Hounie	7	Shaw
16	Inciarte	19	Storm
13	Magri	6	Strauch
12	Mangino	1	Turcatti
15	Maquirriain	20	Valeta
17	Martínez Lamas	29	Vázquez
21	Maspons	33	Vizintín
11	Menéndez	32	Zerbino

Fig. 13

The Charrúa, the Guaraní, and the Birth of Uruguay

The first known European to set foot on the shores of what is now Uruguay was explorer Juan Díaz de Solís in 1516. He sailed up the River Plate estuary to the confluence of the Paraná and Uruguay rivers, where he and a small landing party were promptly attacked and killed by a native tribe. Solís was a Portuguese navigator in the employment of the Spanish; a foreshadowing of the two colonial powers, who, a century later, would clash through a protracted series of border wars, interspersed by treaties, continuing through to the nineteenth century.

The disputed land comprised two territories. The *Banda Oriental* ('East Bank') encompassing all of what would later become Uruguay and the southern tip of Brazil. And the *Mesopotamia* region between the Paraná and the Uruguay rivers, part of modern-day Argentina. The most prevalent peoples who occupied these two large regions were the fierce semi-nomadic Charrúa who roamed the southern parts, and the more settled, agricultural Guaraní, who were found further north, where, in the seventeenth century, the Jesuits established a broad swathe of missions.

The Jesuits catechized the Guaraní, with whom they formed a close relationship; a history loosely dramatized in the 1986 film *The Mission*. The missions became prosperous centres, and the Guaraní quickly assimilated the culture of the missionaries, gaining fluency in Spanish and Portuguese, adopting various trades, and becoming adept at the making and playing of classical musical instruments. The missions provided some protection for the Guaraní, but even so, they were under frequent attack from Portuguese slave traders, and large numbers were killed or taken into slavery. At their peak in 1730, around 140,000 Guaraní were living in 30 missions. But smallpox and measles epidemics, as well as the ceding of the *Banda Oriental* mission lands to the Portuguese in 1750, and the expulsion of the Jesuits by the Spanish Crown in 1768, decimated these communities, causing the Guaraní to disperse.

Four years before the Jesuits were expelled, the officially acknowledged hero of Uruguayan independence, José Artigas, was born in Montevideo. His grandparents were among some of the original European immigrants, and his grandmother's brother was Salvador Carrasco, who gave his name to the neighbourhood so closely connected with the Andes passengers. Rebelling against his schooling by the Franciscans in Montevideo, Artigas took to life in the countryside, working with cattle and horses on his father's farm on the *Arroyo Carrasco*, and in Sauce and Pando, north of Montevideo. Later, the call of the wild pulled him further north into the interior, where he started living the *gaucho* lifestyle.

The *gauchos*, so symbolic of Uruguayan and Argentinian culture, were skilled in taming and riding wild horses, and in cattle work. They roamed freely, fending for themselves, or doing seasonal work for the *estancia* owners who were involved in the lucrative trade for cattle hides. Uruguayan author Javier de Viana wrote of them in *La Biblia Gaucha*:

> *The gaucho's word was an indelible signature and his conscience an irrefutable witness.*

Charles Darwin, who visited a young Uruguay in 1833, and recorded their skills in detail, was also an admirer:

> *The Gauchos, or countrymen, are very superior to those who reside in the towns. The Gaucho is invariably most obliging, polite, and hospitable: I did not meet with even one instance of rudeness or inhospitality. He is modest, both respecting himself and country, but at the same time a spirited bold fellow.*

Darwin then goes on to lament the knife fights, gambling, drinking, and indolence. Knives were an important part of *gaucho* culture, and knife fights were a common response to the slightest provocation, though the purpose was to mark rather than kill. Knives were also essential for slaughtering and preparing the cattle, both for their hides, and for their meat. It was a daily task for the *gaucho* to carve up a carcass, and their fondness for the different cuts of beef, cooked over the slow-burning embers of wood from the *quebracho* tree, is something that lives on in modern-day Uruguay, where an *asado* (barbecue) is traditional at gatherings of families and friends.

Another tradition that has come down from the early *gauchos*, which they in turn adopted from the Guaraní, is the habit of drinking *yerba maté* – a concoction of bitter leaves (the *yerba*) infused in hot water in a gourd-like container (the *maté*) and sipped through a metal straw (the *bombilla*), which also acts as a strainer. It is a common sight to see modern-day Uruguayans carrying around flasks of hot water and the other *maté* paraphernalia needed to indulge their habit on the go.

The abundance of cattle that gave the *gauchos* their livelihood was the result of the action of an early governor, who released a few dozen head in the early seventeenth century. Viana wrote of this:

> *On the wooded riverbanks, in the hidden corners of the hills, and in the fertile pampas, the handful of cattle and horses that Hernandarias gave to our land had procreated prodigiously... The dark nature of the land that forged the unyielding*

*character of the Charrúa and his aboriginal brothers, formed the same
indomitable and combative temperament in the bulls and in the colts....*

In his sojourn in the interior in the 1780s and 1790s, Artigas befriended not only the
gauchos, but also other marginalized groups: scattered settlers, who were trying to eke
out a living on the land, runaway slaves, and the indigenous peoples. In the *Banda
Oriental*, he spent considerable time with the native Charrúa, for whom he formed a
lifelong affection, and he fathered a son by a Charrúa woman. He also visited the
missions across the Uruguay river, where he had his first contact with the Guaraní, whose
promise of resettlement, land, and cattle by the Spanish authorities had come to nothing.
His interactions with the poor and dispossessed, and the injustices that they faced,
instilled in him a lifelong mission to protect these people and to fight for their interests.

Artigas' rise to prominence started in 1797, when he joined the *Blandengues* – the rural
police force appointed by the Spanish authorities, whose mission it was to patrol and
sustain order in the increasingly lawless interior. He rose rapidly through the ranks,
earning the loyalty of his men – many of them *gauchos* – and the respect and confidence
of the rural communities for forestalling the threat of anarchy. He further cemented his
relationship with the Guaraní in the mission communities on the Uruguay river, by
taking up their causes. He also acquired a large tract of land, with the intention of
providing for the permanent settlement and protection of his beloved Charrúa.

The first act in the struggle for independence by the colonies of this region was the 1810
May Revolution, which saw the removal of the Spanish Viceroy in Buenos Aires and the
establishment of a local government. This was the trigger for Artigas to rally the
disaffected interior provinces, both east and west of the Uruguay river. The key early
success was the battle of Las Piedras, just north of Montevideo, in which Artigas and an
army of loyal ex-militia, *Blandengues*, and *gauchos*, defeated the Spanish and restricted
them to the coastal cities; a victory still celebrated today with a public holiday in Uruguay.

Increasingly, the conflict became less about the Spanish, and more about the
centralised authority imposed by Buenos Aires. Over the following years, Artigas
consolidated his support across the territories, basing his centre of operations on
the Uruguay river, and orchestrating his trusted subordinates to take control of the
various communities. Artigas' vision was for a federated territory, with local
government taking decisions for local affairs, equitable distribution of land, an end
to servitude, and protection for local trade. His care and support for the indigenous
communities gained him their unbreakable loyalty, and both Charrúa and Guaraní
willingly fought alongside him and his generals.

In 1816, the Portuguese invaded the *Banda Oriental* from the north, with the complicity of Buenos Aires, whose government had become increasingly alarmed at Artigas' radical vision. The Portuguese forces proved too powerful, and Artigas suffered a series of defeats over the next few years. Weakened by the capture or desertion of his trusted generals, several of whom would play major roles in the years to come, Artigas was finally forced into exile in Paraguay in 1820.

With their protector out of the way, the Guaraní suffered heavily. One of Artigas' former generals, Ramirez, actively participated in destroying the Guaraní missions to the west of the Uruguay river, slaughtering any Guaraní they came across. Similarly, the Portuguese looted and destroyed the Guaraní communities in the eastern territories. Unlike the Charrúa, the scattered and Christianized Guaraní were largely assimilated into an emerging population, through intermarriage with European settlers.

The *Banda Oriental* became part of Brazil after the latter won independence from Portugal in 1822. Three years later, in 1825, another of Artigas' former comrades-in-arms, Juan Antonio Lavalleja, and his band of *Treinta Tres Orientales* (33 Easterners) took up the independence struggle, setting out from their base in Buenos Aires and entering the *Banda Oriental* by stealth. They were joined by another general of Artigas, Fructuoso Rivera, who had stayed on in the *Banda Oriental* after the former's defeat. The incursion of the *Treinta Tres* marked the start of a conflict with Brazil that eventually drifted into a stalemate until 1828, when the British, with trade interests in mind, brokered an agreement to create a buffer state that was independent of both Brazil and the United Provinces of Buenos Aires; and so Uruguay was born.

Two years later, Rivera became the first president of the newly-formed country, winning out over Lavalleja. In one of his first acts, Rivera, who ten years earlier had led the evacuation of a few thousand Guaraní from the Eastern Missions, was to obliterate all vestiges of Charrúa culture. Encouraged by Lavalleja to take effective measures to protect the settler communities, Rivera ordered the slaughter of the remaining Charrúa male population, and the dispersion of the women and children into servitude. A statue memorializing 'the last Charrúas' – four of whom, in a final indignity, were shipped to Paris to be 'exhibited' – stands today in *Parque Prado* in Montevideo.

The bravery and tenacity of the Charrúa has endured in Uruguayan consciousness. The term *garra charrúa* (tenacity of the Charrúa), a phrase known to all Uruguayans, is used to describe fighting spirit against impossible odds, usually within the context of one of the national sports teams competing on the world stage. Uruguay, a country of around three million, has always punched above its weight, with the national football team – the Charrúa – winning two world cups and reaching several more semi-finals. The Uruguayan national rugby team, perennially well-stocked with *Old Christian* players, is also renowned for its fighting spirit, with home games played at the Charrúa stadium in Montevideo.

In 1886, the 'national poet of Uruguay', Juan Zorrilla de San Martín, wrote a 4736-verse epic poem *Tabaré* about the fate of the indigenous people, inspired by a legend that he had heard from a Jesuit priest in Chile, about a blue-eyed Tehuelche. Tabaré is a Guaraní name meaning 'village man' (a popular name in Uruguay, with recent two-time president Tabaré Vázquez a notable beneficiary), but the eponymous hero is the son of a Charrúa chieftain. The poem, fittingly for what might be considered a national *mea culpa*, amalgamates the two:

"Why do you wound him in his obscure soul?
He is already sick, then let him die!
You nurse against the Indian a dark hate,
The sorrowful cacique Guaraní."

Blanca felt in her eyes a heavy tear,
And in her soul an unknown bitterness.
"I have no hatred for you, Charrúa chief",
Gently she answers to the prisoner.[1]

In another epic poem, *La Leyenda Patria*, Zorrilla immortalizes Lavalleja and his *Treinta y Tres*. And, commissioned by the government, he wrote a poetic history, *La Epopeya de Artigas*, which served as inspiration for the large statue of Artigas on horseback that dominates *Plaza Independencia*.

Fig. 14. *Juan Zorrilla de San Martín in 1928.*

The Guaraní language provides Uruguay with its name. *Río Uruguay* has several possible translations, but Zorrilla, with some poetic license, provided the most colourful: 'Rio de los Pájaros Pintados' – the River of Painted Birds. Four generations later, his great-granddaughter Cecilia Regules, a pioneer in the development of rural tourism in Uruguay, created an itinerary entitled *Ruta de los Pájaros Pintados*, a phrase

---

[1] From the translation into English verse by Walter Owen.

18

later adopted as a brand name by the government tourism office. It was Cecilia's brother Gilberto 'Tito' Regules who famously overslept on that morning of 12th October 1972, missing the ill-fated flight to Chile.

That is not the only Zorrilla/Regules connection to the Andes story. Zorrilla de San Martín was a devout Catholic and had founded *El Bien Público* newspaper in 1878 to preserve the values of the faith in a largely secular country. In a similar vein, he and Tito's great-uncle, Dardo Regules (later a senator), were among the founding members of the *Unión Cívica* party. Formed in 1910, it represented Uruguay's Catholic community, from which many of the Andes passengers would come. A year later, Dardo established *Guyer and Regules* which would become, and still is, one of the most prominent law firms in Uruguay. Sixty years after its formation, his son Gilberto would became the legal representative of Lippincott, the US publishing company chosen by the Andes survivors to tell their story.

Fig. 15. *The Last Charrúas: Senaca, Vaimaca Pirú, Guyunusa, and Tacuabé.*

THE BLANCOS AND THE COLORADOS

The second president, Manuel Oribe, was also a military man, one of Lavalleja's *Treinta y Tres*. Oribe and Rivera were bitter rivals from their time in Artigas' army, and in 1836, they founded the two political parties that would go on to dominate Uruguayan politics for the next 170 years – respectively, the *Colorados* and the *Blancos* (the *Partido Nacional*).

The preponderance of generals was noted by Charles Darwin, visiting in 1832. Talking about the 'very ancient' town of Colonia, a tourist stop even then, Darwin wrote:

> It was the chief seat of the Brazilian war; a war most injurious to this country, not so much its immediate effects, as in being the origin of a multitude of generals and all other grades of officers. More generals are numbered (but not paid) in the United Provinces of La Plata than in the United Kingdom of Great Britain. These gentlemen have learned to like power, and do not object to a little skirmishing. Hence there are many always on the watch to create disturbance and to overturn a government which as yet has never rested on any stable foundation.

And, true to form, fractious and violent confrontations would continue between the two parties for the next several decades, sometimes descending into civil war, and with various foreign powers intervening to protect their own interests. When the dust settled, the *Colorados* emerged with their seat of power in Montevideo and the coastal areas, with the *Blancos* predominant in the rural interior. And this continues to be an important distinction between the two parties and their supporters to this day.

Darwin's parting thoughts as the *Beagle* headed south towards Tierra del Fuego are equally insightful. Commenting on the egalitarianism, the toleration of foreign religions, the press freedoms, and the means of education, he prognosticated: "It is impossible to doubt but that the extreme liberalism of these countries must ultimately lead to good results".

Widespread immigration from Spain, Italy, France, Britain, and Germany swelled the population from 75,000 at the birth of the country to around a million by the turn of the century. The hard work of these immigrants helped to shape the country and build a prosperity that relied largely on the cattle and sheep industries.

The new century also saw the final throes of the military conflict between the *Blancos* and *Colorados*. The *Blanco* revolutionary army, led by Aparicio Saravia, was defeated by the

Colorados at the Battle of Masoller on 10th September 1904, Saravia dying ten days later from his wounds. A young doctor who served in the Saravista army, José Pedro Urioste, survived the conflict and would go on to have a successful medical and business career. In later years, the large Urioste clan would gather at his dairy farm in the Florida department during the Easter holidays, for a bit of relaxation and horse-riding in the countryside. Amongst them were his grandchildren, **Eduardo Strauch**, **Adolfo Strauch**, and **Daniel Shaw**, cousins with Urioste mothers, and all three passengers on Flight 571.

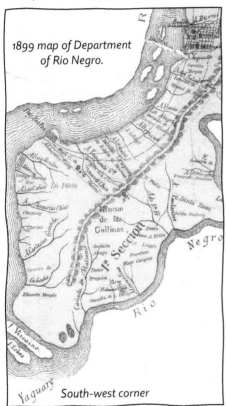

1899 map of Department of Rio Negro.

South-west corner

North-east corner

Fig. 16a. Rincón de las Gallinas, where the Rio Negro meets the Rio Uruguay, was the site of a major victory of General Rivera over the Brazilian forces in 1825.

Later, the Liebig factory was established there, producing meat extract and corned beef with the familiar brand names of Oxo and Fray Bentos, the name of the nearby river port.

Fig. 16b. Arroyo Salsipuedes was the location of the 1831 massacre of 40 Charrúa by troops under the command of General Rivera.

The settlement names reflect the varied origins of 19th century estate owners, Spanish, Portuguese, French, German, and English. These farms would provide the meat for the Liebig factory.

Saravia's defeat marked the end of civil war in Uruguay, and ushered in a period of stability under *Colorado* president José Batlle y Ordóñez, the most prominent in a line of Batlle politicians; his father had also held the office of president, as would his nephew, and, a century later, his great-nephew. José Batlle y Ordóñez served two terms and had the vision of transforming Uruguay into another Switzerland. Heavily influenced by Fabianism, he introduced many social, political, and economic reforms, including the eight-hour working day, free education up to university level, universal suffrage, a generous welfare state, some protection and state ownership of important industries, and the formal separation of church and state; though in practice, the presence and influence of the ecclesiastical powers had, from the beginning, been less prevalent in Uruguay due to its late colonization, the region lacking the precious natural resources of its near neighbours.

Fig. 17. *José Batlle y Ordóñez as a young man.*

The view of the opposition *Blancos* was that the European model that Batlle was trying to impose wouldn't work in a place like Uruguay, where there were many other influences. That it was an approach that favoured the city, and ignored the rural areas where much of the *Blanco* support was concentrated. The *Blancos* were also champions of the democratic process, fighting for secret ballots and proportional representation.

The bitter rivalry between the two parties is illustrated by the duel that took place in April 1920 between José Batlle y Ordóñez (at the time still active as a politician, but no longer president) and Washington Beltrán, a cofounder of the recently established *El País* newspaper. *El País*, the organ of the *Blancos*, published an article, entitled *¡Qué toupet!* ("What cheek!"), in response to Batlle's accusations of *Blanco* election fraud which had appeared in *El Día*, the newspaper Batlle had founded as a young man, and the organ of his faction of the *Colorados*. The *El País* article detailed the political misconduct of the *Colorados*, and then went on to say: "If anybody wants to know who has committed fraud, let them read *La Defensa*, *La Mañana*, and *El Día* in the months before the election. These columns distil the violent accusations of one faction of the *Colorados* against another, bringing out in bold relief the frauds they commit."

Batlle, labelled 'the champion of fraud' by the article, immediately challenged Beltrán to a duel. Beltrán favoured sabres, but Batlle, who had been injured in a recent duel with the other cofounder of *El País*, Leonel Aguirre, requested pistols. Beltrán sportingly agreed. The pistols were lent by the Uruguayan president of the day, Baltasar Brum, and on a rainy morning in a park in Montevideo, the duel took place with a casualness and gentility that belied the vitriol exchanged by the rival newspapers. It was raining, so they stood around chatting in the hope that it would stop. After 45 minutes with no end in sight, the master of ceremonies ordered that the duel should begin. Batlle requested that he be allowed to keep his hat on, as the rain was spattering his glasses; the master of ceremonies agreed, lending his own hat to Beltrán to make things fair. The duel was conducted at 25 paces and, after the first round of shots missed their target, Batlle's second shot hit Beltrán in the lung and heart, causing his almost immediate death.

Although duelling was illegal at the time, a bill to legalise it was passed soon after, and duels continued to be legal in Uruguay until 1992; an accepted way of resolving disputes of honour. Several prominent figures fought in duels over that period, including Batlle's great-nephew, Jorge Batlle, who would later become president of the country.

The 'factions' mentioned in the *El País* article are a characteristic feature of Uruguayan politics. To this day, both *Colorados* and *Blancos* have a confusing array of divisions – known as sectors – and until 1996 multiple candidates from the same party could stand for presidential election. And although the *Blancos* are traditionally seen more as the party of the right, and the *Colorados* as more centrist, each party has a spectrum of political stances, so that the parties hold overlapping views. Even the national newspapers were aligned by sector – whereas *El Día* was the mouthpiece of Batllismo on the left of the *Colorados*, *La Mañana* was aligned to Riverismo, more to the right of the party.

The following decades were a time of unprecedented economic growth. The post-war years in particular were a time of great prosperity, with the per-capita GDP on a par with most European countries, and a strong demand for Uruguayan exports. Uruguay continued to be a beacon of democracy and liberalism until, within the space of a few years, it went from being the most democratic country in South America, at the beginning of the sixties, to an authoritarian and sometimes brutal civic-military dictatorship in June 1973. It was against the backdrop of these unprecedented political events that the *Old Christians* set out on their ill-fated trip in October 1972.

The Seeds of Crisis

The starting point of the crisis can be traced to the mid-1950s, when an economic downturn, caused by declining exports, led to drops in the standard of living. This triggered a series of strikes, orchestrated by the powerful unions, that would continue on and off until 1973. Batlle's welfare state became too expensive to maintain in this environment, and both the *Blancos* (in power for the first time from 1958 to 1967) and the *Colorados* (in power thereafter until the start of the dictatorship), tried unsuccessfully to get the economy back on track.

Although the economic situation had drastically declined, the cherished freedoms were still intact at the start of the sixties. The communist and socialist parties were tolerated, and operated freely and democratically with their own newspapers, and participation in the elections. Che Guevara, speaking at the *Universidad de la República* in Montevideo in August 1961, acknowledged as much:

> I can personally claim that I know America, that in some way I have visited each of its countries, and I can assure you that under the present circumstances there is no country in our America where, as in Uruguay, expression of ideas is allowed. There will be one way of thinking or another, and that is logical; and I know that the members of the government of Uruguay are not in agreement with our ideas. However, they allow us to express these ideas here at the University and in the territory of the country under the Uruguayan government. So that is something that is not achieved in the countries of the Americas. You have something to look out for, which is, precisely, the possibility of expressing your ideas; the possibility of advancing through democratic channels as far as you can go.

Guevara, who in 1959 had fought alongside Castro in Cuba, was an iconic figure in Latin America, where there was widespread support for the Cuban revolution among leftists. The traditional socialist and communist parties in Uruguay, which were largely opposed to violence, and had operated within democratic boundaries, took Guevara's statement as a confirmation of their approach. But others on the left, disillusioned by the lack of action against the establishment, impatient with their failure to ever muster more than a few percent of the vote, and inspired by the Cuban revolution, favoured a call to arms. Various splinter groups arose, which eventually found a home in the urban guerrilla organization, the MLN-T, (the National Liberation Movement), popularly known as the Tupamaros.

It is likely that later, in 1966, Guevara used Uruguay as a refuge and staging post for his entry into Bolivia, where he would meet his death. And that the Tupamaros, who were skilled in disguise and forging of papers, provided Guevara with the Uruguayan identity and passport with which he entered Bolivia. One report claims that Guevara was briefly living clandestinely *en un chalet situado en la zona de las carnicerías de Carrasco*. The area of the *carnicerías* (butchers) was just over the *Puente Carrasco*, very near where the boys lived, and it was here that the Carrasco families would buy their meat. There may be some substance to this story. A Uruguayan Armed Forces summary of subversive activities of the time refers to a Tupamaro supporter codenamed 'Ansina', who was closely affiliated with the *Carnicería Tacuarembó*. The report goes on to say "His name and address ... appeared in Che Guevara's notebook, a fact of which he spoke with pride..."

As well as providing inspiration for the Tupamaros, the Cuban revolution also brought about the closer involvement of the US in Latin American affairs. Determined not to let the same thing happen elsewhere, the US rapidly increased their presence across the continent, both through the *US Agency for International Development* (USAID), and, more clandestinely, through the CIA. One part of USAID was the *Office of Public Safety* (OPS) which was a programme to train and equip police forces across the continent to deal with insurgency and riot control, and to place advisers, such as Dan Mitrione, in potential trouble spots.

In Uruguay, the conflicts between leftist groups and the police played out in an increasingly serious series of actions and reactions. Relatively benign and inconsequential at the beginning of the sixties, they became deadly by the end of the decade. In 1967, strongman Jorge Pacheco took over the presidency from his *Colorado* colleague, Óscar Gestido, who had died after a few months in office. One of Pacheco's first acts was to ban several radical parties and their newspapers, in particular those which were advocating violence to achieve their ends.

1968 saw unprecedented levels of unrest, with several hundred strikes called by the communist-dominated unions over the rapid deterioration in living standards caused by the economic crisis. University and high-school students also took to the streets in large numbers, mirroring similar demonstrations in cities and campuses across the world. They were demonstrating over student issues such as increased bus fares and the interference of the government in university affairs, and in support of the unions. In June of that year, Pacheco introduced a state of emergency to deal with the rampant inflation, the industrial action, and the student protests. These powers allowed him to freeze wages and prices, curb the labour unions, and restrict public gatherings.

In August of that year, in response to Pacheco's heavy-handed approach, the Tupamaros kidnapped Dr Pereira Reverbel, head of the state electricity company, and a personal friend and supporter of the president. Pacheco, suspecting Tupamaro presence on the *Universidad de la República* campus, responded by authorizing police raids of various university facilities. Although Reverbel was released unharmed four days later, the raids continued, and the day after his release, a police car came upon an impromptu demonstration of a few dozen students.

There are two accounts as to what happened next. In one account, the police vehicle intercepted the demonstration, and an officer began to open fire on the demonstrators, to intimidate the students; in the other, the demonstrators surrounded the police vehicle and began to attack it with stones and other objects, and a grounded policeman, separated from his fellow officers, drew his gun and fired a shot in self-defence. Whichever slant is put on the event, the result was the tragic death of a dental student, a member of the communist youth party. He had the iconic and curiously apt name of Líber Arce (a homophone of *liberarse* – to liberate oneself). The death of Arce, whose funeral was attended by a quarter of a million people in a city with a population of less than 1.5 million, notched up the tension further, and his name became a rallying cry; the Tupamaros would later name one of their commando cells after him.

THE TUPAMAROS

The Tupamaros were a uniquely Uruguayan phenomenon; a tight and well-organized urban guerrilla movement, comprising well-educated, often middle-class, adherents, who operated mainly in Montevideo. Disciplined and austere, they gained a reputation for carrying out meticulously planned and audacious raids. They would go on to influence the *Black Panthers* in the US, Germany's *Baader–Meinhof Gang*, and the *Symbionese Liberation Army*, famous for kidnapping Patty Hearst in 1974.

Founded by Raúl Sendic, who had been a leader of the sugar cane and sugar beet workers in Uruguay, the Tupamaros came to prominence in the mid-sixties, equipping themselves through a series of weapon heists, and funding themselves through several high-profile bank robberies. Their bomb and incendiary attacks on banks, government buildings, radio stations, businesses, and prominent residences, were planned to cause damage rather than loss of life. Their Robin Hood image gave them a measure of popular support. In one early action, they held up a delivery truck and distributed its cargo of Christmas food to the poor. In another, they stole the accounts of a loan company, and forwarded them to a judge, resulting in an official investigation.

Their mantra was action not ideology, which they played down, accepting recruits with a wide spectrum of views – Catholic, socialist, anarchist, and Marxist. The aim was to overthrow the status quo without giving too much thought as to what would come after. This lack of ideology, and their claim to be the heirs of Artigas, drew criticism from the traditional far left, who labelled them nationalists and adventurers.

Despite their broad-church approach, the Marxist leanings of the decision-makers is evidenced by the book *Surviving the Long Night*, an account by British Ambassador Geoffrey Jackson of his kidnapping and imprisonment for 244 days in 1971. Listening from his caged underground prison cell, he overheard his captors conducting a kangaroo-court trial in a nearby room. When a proposal was made to execute the prisoner, Jackson couldn't contain himself:

> *In horror and outrage, I heard myself shout ... that precisely as Marxist-Leninists they might not commit so irrational an atrocity. To my equal amazement I heard my outburst accepted with a laugh, and a mild invitation to continue. I asked if I could assume that all present ... were indeed Marxist-Leninists. They acknowledged that they were...*

Jackson went on to argue with them why they should not pass such a severe judgment; later, he speculated whether his intervention had had a small part to play in that prisoner's eventual survival.

Fig. 18. *Patricia Mary 'Evelyn' Jackson (left) leaving the British Hospital the day after her husband's kidnapping by the Tupamaros. She had been visiting his chauffeur and guards, who had been injured in the abduction. She is accompanied by close friend of the family, Marta Martínez de González Mullin, mother of Andes survivor* **Coche Inciarte**'s *fiancée Soledad.*

Jackson's long imprisonment gave him the opportunity to interact with many Tupamaros, as the team of guards changed every few weeks. He found a mix of people, almost all young, most university-educated, some humane and reasonable with a sense of humour, others more ruthless, and the occasional individual who was clearly ill-suited for the guerrilla lifestyle – one young guard spent the night crying for her mother. There were some tender moments also; Jackson wrote of a couple, who had finished their guard duties:

> They stretched their hands through the pig-wire and asked to take mine. "You will walk with us all our lives, Ambassador" were the girl's words. I return them with all my heart, to her and her young man, wherever they may be.

Some of the Andes passengers had first-hand experience of the urban guerrilla group. In September 1970, the Tupamaros blew up the Carrasco Bowling Club, situated at the corner of Mar del Plata and Pedro Figari streets. It was an attack against the 'privileged' families of Carrasco who frequented the club, but it was 48-year-old cleaning lady Hilaria Quirino Ibarra who was the most seriously injured. She was pulled from the rubble, moments before the building collapsed, by **Gustavo Zerbino**, who lived a block away and had acted immediately on hearing the explosion.

Another incident involved **Panchito Abal**'s family, who owned a grand house inside the perimeter of the botanical gardens in the Prado neighbourhood of Montevideo, a stone's throw from the official president's residence. A group of Tupamaros showed up one afternoon, tying up the grandmother and the maid, and daubing the walls and curtains with the Tupamaro emblem. They returned later that night to steal paintings, silver, and any other high-value items that could be sold to raise funds for the cause.

In 1969, two journalists, Antonio 'Manino' Mercader and Jorge de Vera, wrote a book, *Los Tupamaros – Estrategia y acción,* tracing the origins of the group, giving insights into their thinking and modus operandi, enumerating their actions to date, and featuring interviews with the guerrillas and with the police.

Mercader, who years later would become the Minster for Education and Culture in two governments, has an important connection to the Andes story. A contemporary and friend to many of the passengers and their circle, he handled the press communications as the story began to break in December 1972, providing professional support to the *Old Christians* committee set up to manage the reception of the survivors. Later, working with the same committee, he prepared a request for tender, inviting bids from around the world for the rights to publish the authorized account of the odyssey. He then acted as a researcher and adviser for the selected writer, Piers Paul Read, providing the young Englishman with background material on the families, and their local context.

Los Tupamaros is of special interest, because it provides a snapshot of the movement at the peak of their popular support. Up until the middle of 1969, even though there had been terrorism in the form of the bombings and raids, there had been no loss of life directly attributable to the Tupamaros. The *London Times* of 3rd December 1969 reported on this popularity: "Discovering in a Gallup poll that the Tupamaros, the urban guerrillas, enjoy considerable popular esteem in Uruguay, the Government of President Jorge Pacheco has now forbidden the Uruguayan press and radio to refer to them as other than common criminals".

An open letter, addressed to the police and replicated in the book, gives an insight into the thinking of the Tupamaros at that time:

> Our struggle is against those who use armed institutions and their members to repress the people and sustain their privileges... A struggle that will stop only with victory or death... Because we have deep faith in the Uruguayan people, from whom we have emerged and whom we have seen deceived and exploited with impunity. Faith that these people will soon rise up with us.... Because we no longer believe in the laws and institutions that the 600 privileged owners of the country – along with its political parties and bodies that manipulate public opinion – have created to defend their interests by starving the people and beating them if they resist.

The next three years would see a precipitous descent into violence, with more than 50 police, military, and civilians dying at the hands of the Tupamaros, the highest profile case being that of police adviser Dan Mitrione. The Tupamaros kidnapped him on 31st July 1970, because of his role in training the increasingly heavy-handed police, rather than due to the allegations starting to surface about his involvement in, or acceptance of the use of torture in interrogating radical suspects. A poll taken in Uruguay showed 20% 'For', 20% 'Against', and 60% 'No opinion' regarding Mitrione's execution, perhaps indicative of the unwillingness of a traditionally moderate people to take sides in an increasingly polarised and violent confrontation that was starting to threaten their country's long-cherished democracy. However, the later murder of innocent farm worker Pascasio Báez, who had inadvertently stumbled upon a rural hideout, evoked a more outraged reaction, and turned public opinion firmly against the Tupamaros.

In September 1971, the Pacheco government authorized the armed forces to conduct a campaign against them. By the end of 1972, around the time the Andes survivors were returning from their ordeal in the mountains, 3000 Tupamaros had been captured and several hundred others had fled the country. The captives would languish in prison until 1985, when democracy was restored, and a general amnesty put in place. Some, most notably José 'Pepe' Mujica, were singled out for special treatment and kept in harsh solitary confinement. The Tupamaros would later renounce their violence and join the *Frente Amplio*, the broad front of leftist parties, and, in 2010, Mujica became president of Uruguay; an office he held until 2015.

In 2016, three years before his death, Antonio Mercader had a chance to reflect on the legacy of the Tupamaros from the perspective of almost fifty years. Discarding the impartiality of his 1969 book, he expressed his retrospective anger at the Tupamaros' role in the events leading up to the dictatorship in an article entitled "Sobrevivientes y

Tupamaros". It was written in reaction to the Uruguay pavilion at the *Venice Biennale of Architecture 2016*, whose theme was 'using physical space in innovative ways to overcome adversity'. The exhibit drew a comparison between the Andes survivors' transformation of their battered fuselage and the Tupamaros' creation of urban hideouts and 'people's prisons'. Mercader wrote scathingly:

> In the Andes, it was the victims of an accident who did everything to survive, including the use of the aeroplane and its equipment as a refuge and instrument of salvation. The Tupamaros, meanwhile, chose their destiny, risking their lives and those of others while building the typical hideouts of the urban guerrillas of the time... Theirs was neither original nor a fight against adversity, for they executed a carefully conceived plan to destroy the fragile and permissive democracy of the time, which they would achieve a decade later as co-causers of military intervention and the coup d'état.

The 1971 elections

When Pacheco's presidency came to an end, he set his eyes on a second term, and ran again in the 1971 elections. Because successive incumbencies were not allowed by the constitution, a referendum to overturn this limitation was submitted to the electorate alongside the presidential vote. It failed to pass, although 491,680 people (41%) were in favour, almost 30% more than voted for Pacheco himself, suggesting considerable support for his handling of the crisis. As a consequence, Pacheco's running mate, Juan María Bordaberry, took his place, with Jorge Sapelli becoming the new vice-presidential candidate. Although the Bordaberry/Sapelli ticket did not win the most votes, the total *Colorado* vote narrowly exceeded the total *Blanco* vote, and Bordaberry became the next president, entering office in March 1972. Bordaberry's wife, Josefina Herrán, was the sister of an aunt of two of the Fairchild passengers, double cousins **Eduardo** and **Fito Strauch**. Accompanied by Brother McGuinness of *Stella Maris College*, she would be first in line to welcome back the returning survivors as they disembarked from the LAN-Chile Boeing 727 at Carrasco airport on 28th December 1972.

Fig. 19. *Jorge Pacheco and Juan María Bordaberry.*

In the close-fought election, the *Blanco*'s primary candidate was Wilson Ferreira Aldunate; a charismatic leader who had been agriculture minister in the sixties and was founder of the centrist *Por La Patria* sector of the *Partido Nacional*. He was a first cousin of Stella Ferreira, mother of *Old Christians* captain **Marcelo Pérez del Castillo**, the organizer of the 1972 trip to Chile. During the seventy-two days in the mountains, when the fate of the passengers was unknown, Ferreira would go several times a week to Stella's house to support the family.

Fig. 20. *Wilson Ferreira Aldunate who won the popular vote in the 1971 elections.*

The *Por La Patria* sector was the most popular *Blanco* faction among young liberals, and, like many others on the trip, Marcelo was an ardent supporter of his mother's cousin. **Julio Martínez Lamas** was also an active supporter, and a personal friend of Ferreira. Several of the boys actively campaigned through the *Movimiento Universitario Nacionalista* – the student movement aligned with the sector. A week after the plane disappeared, the *MUN* published a *nota angustiante* – a distressing notice – in which they expressed the hope that the boys would be found. The announcement went on to eulogise active members – **Gastón Costemalle, Numa Turcatti, Roy Harley, Gustavo Nicolich, Gustavo Zerbino,** and **Coche Inciarte**. Other supporters of the sector included **Daniel Fernández, Fito Strauch, Pancho Delgado,** and **Álvaro Mangino**.

Most of the passengers, through family tradition or considered political choice, favoured one or another sector of the *Blancos* or *Colorados*, which spanned a wide spectrum of political views. **Eduardo Strauch**, despite the *Blanco* tradition in the family stretching back to his grandfather's involvement in the Saravista army, felt that *Colorado* Jorge Batlle was the man to modernize and progress Uruguay; an opinion shared by

Roberto Canessa. **Antonio 'Tintín' Vizintín** and **Bobby François** backed the incumbent Pacheco. **Carlitos Páez** favoured the more conservative sector of the *Blancos*, represented by General Aguerrondo. Opinions within the **Methol** family were split; **Liliana** siding with Wilson Ferreira, and her husband **Javier** a Batlle supporter.

Voters in 1971 also had a new choice, with the participation, for the first time, of the *Frente Amplio*, a broad coalition of non-violent left-wing parties – the Socialist Party, the Communist Party, the Christian Democrats, and disenchanted politicians from the left-wing sectors of the traditional parties, particularly the *Colorados*. Most notable among the latter were reporter Zelmar Michelini and Afro-Uruguayan lawyer and poet Alba

Roballo, both of whom left the *Colorados* to found the coalition party. An exiled Michelini would later be assassinated in Buenos Aires in 1976. The party was led into the election by General Liber Seregni, a recently retired general, who would later be imprisoned by the dictatorship. The Tupamaros agreed to hold a ceasefire during the election campaign, to avoid any negative publicity that might transfer from them to the *Frente Amplio*.

Fig. 21. General Liber Seregni, leader of Frente Amplio.

Three of the boys had socialist views perhaps more typical of their generation at a time of student activism and demonstrations worldwide. **Fernando Vázquez** was a member of the *Juventud Demócrata Cristiana*, the youth wing of the centre-left Christian Democratic Party, which was part of the *Frente Amplio*. A month after the plane disappeared, the *Ahora* newspaper – the organ of the Christian Democrats, later banned by the military government – published a remarkably prescient poem he had written, *El Camino de un Hombre*, found by his family amongst his possessions. As a member of the party, Fernando would go with his friends to help out in the Barrio Marconi, an impoverished neighbourhood of Montevideo.

Pedro Algorta had spent several years in Chile, due to his father's job in the Inter-American Development Bank, and had seen, at first-hand, the living conditions of the urban poor, when working in the slums of Santiago. Influenced by some leftist teachers at school, he began to explore socialist ideas, and had been a class representative for MAPU, one of the parties that would help bring the Marxist government of Allende to power. Over the years, Pedro's ideas, influenced both by Marx, and by Jesuit philosopher Teilhard de Chardin, matured and mellowed, and when he returned to Montevideo, he started working at the grassroots level for the *Frente Amplio*. He would always argue for humanity over dogma, and, disaffected by the rigid mindset of his political companions, he put his activism behind him after the election and concentrated on his studies.

Arturo Nogueira was an idealist with a deep social conscience, and opposed to violence of any sort. Although a socialist, he had no allegiance to any of the parties in the *Frente Amplio*. He could argue convincingly and comprehensively about politics, and he and his sister Raquel would have heated discussions with their father, who was a Batlle supporter. Mr Nogueira, though he disagreed with their ideas, came to respect his son's clear arguments.

Arturo, along with others, such as **Gustavo Zerbino** and **Moncho Sabella**, often worked in the slums of Montevideo as part of the *Castores de Emaús*[1], a student group doing humanitarian work with the underprivileged. Moncho participated from an early age:

> *At weekends we would go to the poorest neighbourhoods of Montevideo to play football with the children who would be barefoot. We would bring food to share with them, and help them build their houses. I remember learning how to make bricks there; I was seven or eight years old at the time. That experience created a very strong vocation for solidarity in me, and that helped me to survive in the mountains.*

The results of the 1971 elections were very close. Summing the votes across sectors gave the *Colorados* 41%, the *Blancos* 40.2%, and the *Frente Amplio* 18.3%; the *Colorados* winning by a narrow margin of 12,000 votes despite the fact that, as an individual candidate, Wilson Ferreira had defeated Bordaberry by around 60,000 votes.

---

[1] Named after the New Testament story of two disciples who meet Christ on the road to Emmaus, after the crucifixion, failing to recognize him until he breaks bread with them in Emmaus.

THE ONSET OF THE DICTATORSHIP

Holding only 41 out of the 99 seats in the Chamber of Deputies, and 13 out of the 30 Senate seats, Bordaberry faced an uphill struggle to achieve any consensus to deal with the dire economic and social ills of the country. He had to work hard to build cross-party and cross-sector alliances in parliament in order to secure a working majority, sometimes in exchange for political favours.

An immediate problem that he faced was the renewed violence of the Tupamaros after the ceasefire of the election. The armed forces resumed their programme of rounding up the Tupamaros, and, later, targeting any individual or group that could be considered subversive. Businessman Jörg Thomsen, founder and curator of the *Museo Andes 1972* – the museum honouring the Andes story – likens the atmosphere of those days to that in East Germany, where everyone was under suspicion, and monitored by the Stasi. Montevideans were cautious when discussing political matters, because they were never quite sure if they were talking to a friend, or to an enemy who might make an anonymous denunciation.

Fig. 22. *Stop and search was a common occurrence in the quest to root out subversives.*

Thomsen, a teenager at the time, had first-hand experience of this. Early one dark winter morning, he and a friend were waiting for the school bus. They had been driven to the bus stop by his friend's mother, and they were sitting in her small Fiat 850. Suddenly, the street was flooded with blinding lights, and voices ordered them out of the car: "Hands up! Hands on the roof of the car! Legs apart!" Thomsen, already 6' 3", felt his knees quake as his mind struggled to comply with the conflicting instructions – placing his hands on the roof of the small car meant his hands were not 'up'! Although this particular episode didn't lead to an arrest, common occurrences of such incidents made for an uneasy atmosphere.

Passenger **Julio Martínez Lamas** experienced a surreal abduction. He was working in the imposing *Banco de la República* building in the Old City, when the military, as a scare tactic, entered and rounded up all the employees, initially holding them in the great entrance hall. The military were targeting banks because of ongoing strikes. Relying on an unwritten rule that the military could not apprehend you if you were singing the national anthem, the employees started singing en masse, until, one-by-one, they started to flag, and were taken away. Julio disappeared for a few days, along with 150 others. In the end, it was more traumatic for their families than for them, as they were being held under mild conditions in a large house in the department of Florida (north of Montevideo), free to play football and cards with one another.

The military were ruthlessly successful in rounding up the Tupamaros, who were interrogated, sometimes under torture, in order to extract information that could lead to further arrests. Subsequent conversations between the military and the guerrillas, created an awareness, in the former, of corruption and vested interests in the political and business elite. So once the Tupamaros had been dealt with, the armed forces, who had gained some public credibility and impetus, made it their mission to deal with other ills of society, stretching their remit to tackle cases of economic and political corruption.

In a first action on 28th October 1972, they arrested and imprisoned Jorge Batlle (great-nephew of José Batlle) who had led the *Unity and Reform Colorado* sector in the election. Batlle, in a radio broadcast, had criticized the military over their plan to reopen a 1968 case in which he had been acquitted of taking advantage of insider knowledge about a currency devaluation. The military took exception to his comments, and arrested him on a charge of slander; an action that prompted three ministers to resign, decimating the cabinet. The report of Batlle's arrest was heard by the boys on the mountain on their small transistor radio – some of the last news they received from the outside world before an avalanche engulfed the broken fuselage that served as their shelter, killing eight of them.

Behind the scenes, a document had been circulating among some senior military officers, outlining steps that could be taken to enable the armed forces to gain greater political control. The Minister of Defence at the time, Augusto Legnani, got wind of this, and wrote a letter on 19th October to the Commanders-in-Chief, reminding them of the limitations of their power under the constitution. On facing resistance to his ministerial authority, Legnani resigned the next day. The matter was taken up by *Colorado* Senator Amílcar Vasconcellos, who read Legnani's letter to the general assembly a few days later. Vasconcellos, who had led the left-wing sector of the *Colorados* in the election, has a small connection to the Andes story; his son – also Amílcar – is married to Cecilia Regules, sister of absent passenger Tito Regules. At the same time as Vasconcellos was addressing parliament, Tito's friends on the mountain were seeing sunshine for the first time in days, having finally managed to dig their way out of their frozen tomb.

Later that month, the military document itself was debated in parliament, and, in the New Year, as the military continued their indictments of the political establishment, Vasconcellos took the issue one step further, bringing the matter to the attention of the public on a national radio programme. His letter, broadcast to the Uruguayan people, was widely replicated in the press the following day. Whilst acknowledging that there were cases of corruption, Vasconcellos warned of the imminent and serious threat to the country's political institutions, and he accused elements of the military hierarchy of subversion themselves. Vasconcellos later expanded on the events of February 1973 in a book entitled *Febrero Amargo* (Bitter February).

The reaction to the Vasconcellos broadcast was swift. President Bordaberry responded immediately with his own open letter, chastising Vasconcellos for his damaging accusations, denying any campaign by the military to displace legal processes, and affirming his own commitment to defending the country's institutions. Meanwhile, the military commanders convened a hasty meeting, and a few days later the Army and Air Force issued their own response. Their joint communiqué, issued on 7th February and notably not signed by the Navy Commander-in-Chief Rear Admiral Zorrilla, accused Vasconcellos of trying to gain political capital on behalf of various factions that were seeking to discredit the armed forces. They reiterated the mission assigned to them by parliament – to restore internal order, and provide security for national development – and dismissed the document as merely a staff study which had not been made public because it had never been officially approved.

Events now cascaded in rapid succession. A flurry of ministerial and military resignations and appointments; the refusal of the armed forces to answer to the new defence minister; a televised presidential address, appealing to public opinion for the defence of the institutions; the take-over of television and radio stations by the army; a protective blockade of the Old City peninsula by the Navy, which declared itself loyal to the institutions; the resignation of the cabinet; communiqués by the Army and Air Force, detailing their political, social, economic, and administrative objectives in what amounted to a political manifesto; a request, by the president, for the Navy to stand down; the resignation of Rear Admiral Zorrilla; and a series of demands from the commanders of the armed forces.

Fig. 23. *Part of the Navy's blockade of the Old City peninsula.*

On 12th February 1973, the president, who by this time had lost a working majority in parliament, met with the armed forces at the Air Force's *Boiso Lanza* airbase in the north of Montevideo, and an agreement was reached that acceded to the demands of the Commanders-in-Chief to create a National Security Council, allowing the military to have a greater say in decision-making. Four months later, Bordaberry dissolved the legislature, replacing it with a State Council in which the military had a predominant role. It marked the start of the civil-military dictatorship.

EXILE

The next few years would see heavy censorship, banning of some political parties and newspapers, and an unprecedented round-up of leftists, trade unionists, and intellectuals, regardless of any proven or unproven activity. Tens of thousands were arrested, thousands were gaoled, and many tortured. This precipitated an exodus of politicians, journalists, academics, writers, activists, and sympathisers – around ten percent of the population in the seventies. Notable among the exiles were *Blanco* leader Wilson Ferreira, and founder of *Frente Amplio*, Zelmar Michelini. Both forged ties with international human rights groups, and campaigned against the regime from abroad. Michelini was assassinated in Buenos Aires in 1976, one of 180 Uruguayans who were killed or disappeared.

Those convicted as Tupamaros got 15- to 30-year sentences, although they were released in March 1985, when democracy was finally restored, and a general amnesty was agreed. But even those sympathising with leftist ideas might find themselves imprisoned for several years. Enrique Rodríguez Larreta, the husband of **Arturo Nogueira**'s sister Raquel, was arrested and gaoled in 1972, under the exceptional security measures in force at the time, his crime little more than to have been a student leader. On his release, he and Raquel and their young child went into exile in Argentina, still a democratic country up until March 1976. Three months after the Argentinian coup, Enrique went missing. His father, a journalist, travelled to Buenos Aires to try to find out what had happened to him. Raquel, now worried about her own son, aged 5, asked her father to collect his grandchild and take him to the safety of Montevideo whilst she and her father-in-law searched for Enrique.

It was a timely precaution. Within a couple of weeks, a group of armed men broke into Raquel's apartment. She and her father-in-law were handcuffed and hooded, bundled into a van, and driven to an abandoned workshop – the infamous Orletti garage – where they were thrown in with some other prisoners, among them Enrique. The next two weeks saw each of them, on multiple occasions, being taken 'upstairs' to undergo various tortures – beatings, hangings from the wrists, electric shocks, and water-boarding. The group of twenty-four prisoners, which included Margarita Michelini, whose father had been assassinated a few months earlier, was then transferred to Montevideo, in what became known as 'the first flight'. The airplane was a Uruguayan Air Force Fairchild, which landed at Air Base 1 in Carrasco. The fate of the twenty-two people on the 'second flight' is unknown to this day.

In Uruguay, the prisoners were first held in a house in Punta Gorda, then later in a Defence Intelligence Service building, closer to downtown. In both locations, interrogations, and in some cases torture, continued. Eventually, on 22nd December, Raquel was transferred along with Margarita Michelini to the Punta Rieles prison, a few kilometres north of Carrasco, and Enrique was taken to the Libertad prison in the department of San José. Enrique's father was released, and soon after – in January 1977 – presented a detailed testimony on the episode to the UN high commissioner. Raquel was freed at the end of 1977, and Enrique released on parole in 1981. With the government still under the control of the military, the family sought a safer haven and, with the help of the UN, started a new life in Sweden.

Amongst the many writers in exile was Cristina Peri Rossi, who had been a professor of comparative literature in Uruguay. She escaped the country in 1972, after her writings and any mention of her name were banned, and she was stripped of her professorship. During her first few years of exile in Spain and in Paris, she wrote a series of poems expressing her feeling of loss and alienation, the wound of separation poignantly delineated by the opening verse:

> I feel a pain here,
> on my homeland side.

These poems lay hidden for thirty years, until Rossi, observing other diasporas across the world, decided that they spoke for all exiles, and should see the light of day. They were published under the title *Estado de exilio* in 2003, and later in English as *State of Exile*[1].

---

[1] Copyright ©2008 by City Light Books. Translation copyright ©2008 by Marilyn Buck.

CARRASCO

At the end of the nineteenth century, Carrasco had been a wilderness of dunes and marshland, bounded on the south by the River Plate estuary, and on the east by *Arroyo Carrasco*. The name came from one of the early European settlers, Salvador Carrasco (the great uncle of José Artigas), whose *estancia* was in this area, fifteen kilometres to the east of the *Ciudad Vieja*.

In the early twentieth century, some entrepreneurs, among them Alfredo Arocena, purchased this land with the idea to develop it as a high-end *balneario* (beach resort). The project would reclaim and level the dunes, and create the necessary infrastructure to serve the professional classes looking to escape the more crowded beaches closer to town. Arocena hired French-Argentinian landscape architect Carlos Thays to design the resort. Land was levelled, streets laid out, trees planted, and 1918 saw the completion of the *Stella Maris* church built to serve the holidaymakers who would decamp to Carrasco for the summer months. A couple of years later, the luxurious and iconic *Hotel Carrasco* opened, overlooking Carrasco beach and the River Plate. These two buildings formed the north-south axis around which the *balneario* took shape, framed by Arocena and Divina Comedia streets to the west, and Costa Rica and Potosí streets to the east.

By 1930, a couple of dozen villas had been built, sparsely distributed within the four-street area, amongst them Arocena's house at the beach end of the street that bears his name. The following decades saw the appearance of dozens more, the one-time sandy wilderness gradually replaced by a green oasis, the streets and gardens lined with a profusion of jacaranda, wild olive, hibiscus, eucalyptus, and Chilean pine.

In the early fifties some professional families started to see the possibility of establishing a more permanent neighbourhood there. One of the 'crazies' who, in 1954, uprooted his family from the centre of Montevideo and transplanted them to the sparsely populated *balneario* was Dr Conrado Hughes. Hughes was a lawyer for the principal bus company in Uruguay, ONDA, which used the same buses as the US Greyhound Corporation and even adopted a greyhound logo, since, as Dr Hughes discovered, the original branding had not been patented or registered in Uruguay.

MONTEVIDEO – Balneario de Carrasco

Fig. 24. 1930 postcard of Carrasco. Hotel and casino in the foreground, Stella Maris church further back, Arocena's house front left at the beach end of the street bearing his name.

Fig. 25. 1950 aerial view of Carrasco. Stella Maris church on the right.

Dr Hughes had a family of four boys and a girl, and, with another boy on the way, there was the question of what to do about a school for their sons. Although other options were available, such as the secular British School a few kilometres away in the neighbourhood of Pocitos, or the Catholic *Seminario*, even further away, in the centre of Montevideo, there was a common desire, amongst the families moving to Carrasco, for a school that was both Catholic and bilingual. Mr Hughes had bumped into a cousin the previous summer at the *Stella Maris* church, and she had mentioned that her son went to just such a school in Buenos Aires. It was run by the Christian Brothers of Ireland. Other families knew about the Christian Brothers through their involvement in the *Movimiento Familiar Cristiano* – the worldwide Christian Family Movement.

Fig. 26. **Left**: *Stella Maris Church.* **Right**: *Ex Hotel Carrasco, restored to its former grandeur.*

The idea of such a school caught hold, and several parents got together to try to establish a similar one in Carrasco. A committee was formed, and after much work and lobbying of local religious leaders, some of the parents, including Manuel 'Manolo' Pérez del Castillo and his wife Stella Ferreira, travelled to Ireland to petition the Christian Brothers in person. The trip was successful, and on 2nd May 1955, *Stella Maris College* opened its doors in a temporary building on the *Rambla*, the first intake consisting of ninety-three boys in three classes, corresponding to the first three years of primary school, ages six to eight.

The faith of Dr Hughes and the other parents in the Christian Brothers would prove to be justified. Many of the boys would go on to have professional careers, including all five of the Hughes' sons, the oldest of whom – Conrado, popularly known as 'Connie' – went on to serve as minister of planning and budgeting in the cabinet of

44

President Luis Alberto Lacalle, and later became a well-known political commentator on the national TV debate show *Todas las Voces*. But it was the moral foundation, the moulding of character, that was most appreciated by the parents and, retrospectively, by the boys. Alongside the Catholic bilingual education, the brothers introduced Rugby Union as a way to instil discipline and teamwork, sacrifice and responsibility; life-values that would prove essential on the mountain.

The opening of *Stella Maris College* ('*The Christian*') was delayed for two months because of a polio epidemic, so some students are missing from the school photograph taken that day. But it is an image full of historical poignancy. The boys are flanked by the founding Brothers – Brother John O'Reilly on the left, responsible for the second-year class, and Brother McCaig and headmaster Brother Patrick Kelly on the right, responsible for the first- and third-year students respectively. Amongst the boys we already see several, who, seventeen years later, would be passengers on the ill-fated Andes flight: **Marcelo Pérez del Castillo**, son of Manolo and Stella and captain of the 1972 *Old Christians*, **Julio Martínez Lamas**, and four cousins, **Daniel Fernández, Eduardo Strauch, Adolfo 'Fito' Strauch**, and **Daniel Shaw**. Only three of the six would return from the mountain.

Many others in the photo would play important and diverse roles, during and after the tragedy. By 1972, Connie Hughes was an *Old Christians Club* board member, along with Adolfo Gelsi. With club president, Daniel Juan, and another classmate, Emilio Azambuja, they would form the committee hastily convened to organize the reception of the boys back into Uruguay, and to manage the rapidly escalating interest of the world's press. Adolfo Gelsi's brother Pablo, later to become an eminent psychologist, would act as the interpreter to the young English author Piers Paul Read, chosen by the survivors on the recommendation of the *Old Christians* committee to write the authorized account of their ordeal. Rafael Ponce de León, as a ham radio expert, would become the focal point of communication during the 72-day ordeal, providing daily updates between the parents in Carrasco and the ongoing search efforts in Chile. And José 'Pepe' Pollak, as a lawyer, would go on to represent the family of classmate **Julio Martínez Lamas**, left without a breadwinner, in an action against the Uruguayan Air Force.

As each year passed, a new generation of boys entered the school, **Guido Magri** joining in 1956 alongside **Nando Parrado** – the great hero of the Andes story – and Pablo Vierci. The latter, who at the age of ten wrote the words to the school hymn, would go on to become a journalist and author whose books include *La sociedad de la nieve* (*The Snow Society*) – an account of the Andes tragedy from the personal perspective of each survivor – and *Tenía que sobrevivir* (*I Had to Survive*), the co-authored memoir of **Roberto Canessa** who made the ten-day trek out of the Andes with Parrado in December 1972.

1957 saw the arrival of **Gastón Costemalle**, who transferred from another school and went straight into the class of '64. Gastón, Guido, and Marcelo, would become the early leaders on and off the rugby field, who would help to guide and develop the *Old Christians* rugby club.

Fig. 27. *Break time at Stella Maris College.*

By the beginning of the sixties, 26 of the 40 Andes passengers were being taught by the Christian Brothers at *Stella Maris College*. The school continued to grow until, in 1962, the oldest class had reached the end of the first stage of secondary education, the *Liceo*, and were ready to enter the second stage, the *Preparatorio* – the years preparing for university. As *Stella Maris* did not yet provide for this, the boys would typically go on to the private *Colegio Seminario* or in some cases to a top state school, *Instituto Alfredo Vásquez Acevedo* (IAVA), both located in the centre of Montevideo. The former had been a Jesuit seminary in the nineteenth century and became the *Colegio del Sagrado Corazón* – the *College of the Sacred Heart* – at the turn of the century, although it continued to be popularly referred to as the *Seminario*. Most of the boys from the Andes trip who were not at *The Christian*, specifically **Pancho Delgado**, **Rafael Echavarren**, **Ramón 'Moncho' Sabella**, and **Numa Turcatti**, did their entire schooling at the *Seminario*

As there was no space for coaching or practising sports at the temporary building on the *Rambla*, the Christian Brothers had to be patient with their plans to introduce the young students to rugby. While an ongoing search was made for a big enough site to house new buildings and rugby fields for the growing school, the *Carrasco Polo* Club came to the rescue, lending *The Christian* the use of their fields. Although originally a polo club, *Carrasco Polo* had diversified to include rugby, achieving some early success that saw the first fifteen sharing the 1952 Uruguayan club championship title with the *Old Boys*, the alumni club of the British school. In later years, *Carrasco Polo* and *Old Boys* would become perennial rivals of the *Old Christians*. The main school-age opponents of *The Christian* were the boys of the British school, whose secondary forms had relocated to Carrasco in 1958. It was a fierce rivalry, stoked by the Irish Brothers' aversion to all things British.

Eventually, a sizeable plot of land was found and purchased on Máximo Tajes street – a couple of kilometres north-east of the *Rambla* location – with funds coming from large individual donations, collections, loans, and fund-raising events. Building work was started with Manolo Pérez del Castillo as architect. The new premises were inaugurated on 12th March 1961, with the blessing of the Archbishop of Montevideo, Cardinal Barbieri.

When the first crop of sixteen boys left *The Christian* in 1962, they wanted to continue playing the game they had grown to love, and so a proposal was made to form an *Old Christians* rugby club. In 1964, the alumni team started competing in the second division of the Uruguayan Club Championship, using the school field to host home matches. They finished a creditable second place. The first fifteen was made up of familiar names from the classes of '62 and '63 – including **Daniel Fernández**, **Marcelo Pérez del Castillo**, **Eduardo Strauch**, Pepe Pollak, Adolfo Gelsi, Emilio Azambuja, and **Guido Magri**'s older brother Aldo, who would go on to have a pivotal role in the survival of the club after the devastation of the Andes tragedy. As there were not enough players from the *Old Boys*, the team was supplemented by members of the school's first-team squad, including **Gastón Costemalle** and **Daniel Shaw**.

By 1966, the *Old Christians* were playing in the first division, and their players were getting the attention of the national selectors. In 1967, Guido and Gastón, along with two other teammates, were selected to play for the national team in the Fifth South America Rugby Union Championship. They would be the first of many *Old Christians* to get the call. Team success would soon follow. In 1968, the club won its first Uruguay championship under the captaincy of Guido Magri, followed up by a second in 1970, this time led by Marcelo Pérez del Castillo.

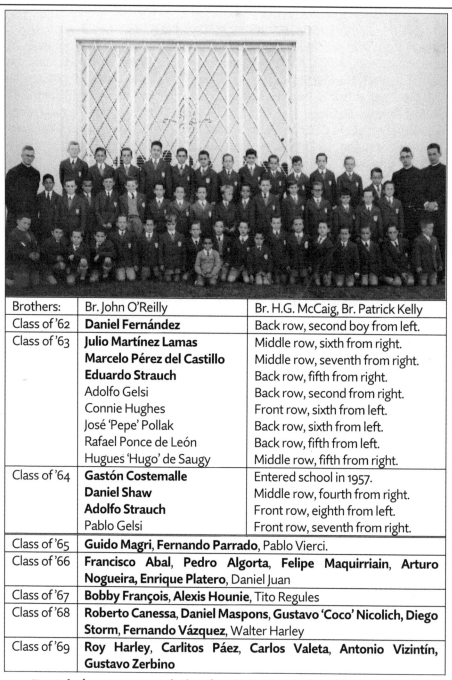

Brothers:	Br. John O'Reilly	Br. H.G. McCaig, Br. Patrick Kelly
Class of '62	**Daniel Fernández**	Back row, second boy from left.
Class of '63	**Julio Martínez Lamas**	Middle row, sixth from right.
	Marcelo Pérez del Castillo	Middle row, seventh from right.
	Eduardo Strauch	Back row, fifth from right.
	Adolfo Gelsi	Back row, second from right.
	Connie Hughes	Front row, sixth from left.
	José 'Pepe' Pollak	Back row, sixth from left.
	Rafael Ponce de León	Back row, fifth from left.
	Hugues 'Hugo' de Saugy	Middle row, fifth from right.
Class of '64	**Gastón Costemalle**	Entered school in 1957.
	Daniel Shaw	Middle row, fourth from right.
	Adolfo Strauch	Front row, eighth from left.
	Pablo Gelsi	Front row, seventh from right.
Class of '65	**Guido Magri, Fernando Parrado**, Pablo Vierci.	
Class of '66	**Francisco Abal, Pedro Algorta, Felipe Maquirriain, Arturo Nogueira, Enrique Platero**, Daniel Juan	
Class of '67	**Bobby François, Alexis Hounie**, Tito Regules	
Class of '68	**Roberto Canessa, Daniel Maspons, Gustavo 'Coco' Nicolich, Diego Storm, Fernando Vázquez**, Walter Harley	
Class of '69	**Roy Harley, Carlitos Páez, Carlos Valeta, Antonio Vizintín, Gustavo Zerbino**	

Fig. 28. **Andes passengers** *and others from Stella Maris College. (Photo: May 1955)*

LIFE IN THE SIXTIES

The community that developed in Carrasco in the fifties and sixties was one of like-minded professionals who wished to create an environment in which their children could grow and prosper, spiritually and intellectually. The large families were reflective of the Catholic faith that was central to many homes. Those who were fortunate enough to grow up in the neighbourhood, enjoyed an idyllic childhood, able to roam freely and safely. It was a place where everyone knew everyone, and the elegant detached houses, set back from the tree-lined streets, were invariably left unlocked. When Spanish diplomat Juan Ignacio Tena was posted to Uruguay in 1962, he and his family moved into a house close to the beach on Potosí street, one of the original central streets of Carrasco. They were warmly welcomed into the community, soon becoming part of a close circle of friends – the Fonseca, Nicolich, Regules, and Storm families, amongst others – all living nearby, and with similarly-aged children. The parents shared a rich social life, with frequent dinners, parties, *asados*, and informal get-togethers, and the children could wander at will, riding their bikes without supervision, and spending time with their friends on Carrasco beach. It was a life that was largely untouched by the growing political strife and economic hardships that were starting to affect the rest of the country.

Fig. 29. *Tito Regules' mother Isabel and Diego Storm's mother Bimba at a 1920s-themed fancy dress party.*

One of the Tena children, María, would go on become a successful author in later life, and wrote about those times in her prize-winning novel *Nada que no sepas*. The narrator in the novel, like María Tena, has spent the sixties – her school-age years – in Carrasco, and returns to Uruguay decades later, to resolve unanswered questions about the mysterious death of her mother, an event that triggered an abrupt departure back to her native Spain. This latter plotline places the book firmly in the realm of fiction, but the places are real, and there are parallels with the family's circle of friends.

Above all, it is the evocative memories exquisitely crafted by Tena that capture the atmosphere of the time and place. Reflecting on the sense of cultural freedom compared with Franco's Spain, the narrator recalls the mothers of her friends:

> They did not resemble the Spanish housewives of gazpacho and paella, who were dependent on their husbands... They were cultivated. The leading exhibitions, the latest books, the music that came from New York, from Europe... A world of beautiful people, very natural, very unimposing, bearing no relation to the formal and pretentious world of the Spanish rich. They were freer and more cultured, they had been living in a democracy for a long time, and it showed.

And she captures the sense of a charmed existence, the joy of life near the beach and the *estancias*:

> But freedom was also living near the countryside, near the sea. The bodies always relaxed, half-naked, in the air of those summers we spent there. A fascinating world for us children, lacking critical sense or social sensitivity, and still without political ideas. Those friends were not even the rich or the oligarchs of the country, but beings touched, we don't know why, by the hand of some god.

With Carrasco transitioning from *balneario* to a residential neighbourhood in the fifties, many families now owned or rented summer homes in the seaside resort of Punta del Este, where the turbid waters of the River Plate meet the Atlantic ocean. They would spend the summer months there, going daily to their favourite beach amongst the dozens lining the promontory, either on the rough ocean side or the calmer estuary side, popularly referred to as the *Brava* and the *Mansa* respectively. The fathers would join them when work permitted. It was another shared experience to bond the already close-knit community.

At Easter, the Tena children would head out to one or other of the *estancias*, more often than not *Las Cañadas*, the large farm owned by the Regules family on the eastern border of the department of Rio Negro, an estate with a rich history. Originally part of *La gran estancia de Yapeyú*, the vast expanse of grazing lands that served the Jesuit-Guaraní missions, it passed through a succession of owners, including the father of Julio Herrera y Obes, president of Uruguay from 1890 to 1894. An 1899 map shows the lands owned by Carmen Zorrilla de Lapuente, a first cousin of the national poet, Juan Zorrilla de San Martin. The estate briefly passed out of Zorrilla hands when it was bought by the owner of the neighbouring estate, Olga Behrens, granddaughter of *Liebig* factory president Franz August Hoffman, but Zorrilla involvement was restored when Olga's son, Gilberto Regules, married Isabel Zorrilla de San Martin, a granddaughter of the poet. Among the children of Gilberto and Isabel was Tito (the one who missed the flight) and his sister Cecilia, a best friend of María Tena.

Fig. 30. *Easter holidays at Las Cañadas.*

Left to right on gate: *Juan Storm, Mónica Nicolich, Carmen Regules, Ignacio 'Nanay' Fonseca, Cecilia Regules, Gustavo Nicolich (Coco's father), Coco Nicolich, Diego Storm, Tito Regules, Sarita Fonseca, and the son of a farm worker.*

Left to right below: *Isabel Regules, Pablo Fonseca, baby Carlitos Regules, Raquel Arocena de Nicolich (Coco's mother).*

A photo from the early sixties shows children of the Regules, Nicolich, Fonseca, and Storm families sitting on a farm gate at *Las Cañadas* together with the Nicolich parents. It captures a moment in time when life seemed perfect, no shadow yet of the times to come. But it is difficult to look at this picture of smiling children without reflecting on how they would be touched by the events of the coming decade and beyond, a microcosm of the history of Flight 571. **Coco Nicolich**, sitting next to his father, would die in the avalanche on the mountain ten years later, as would his friend **Diego Storm**, sitting next to him. Standing to the right is Coco's mother, Raquel, the granddaughter of Carrasco's founder Alfredo Arocena, and the last surviving founding mother of the *Biblioteca de Nuestros Hijos*, who celebrated her ninety-sixth birthday on 13th October 2022, the fiftieth anniversary of the accident. On the other side of Mr Nicolich is Cecilia Regules, the current-day owner of *Las*

Cañadas who has worked diligently to preserve the legacy and ecosystems of the *Estancias Gauchas*. Cecilia's brother Tito, who can be seen at the back right, would escape the accident in the Andes, and another plane crash in 1977, but would die in a car accident nineteen years after the death of his friends on the mountain.

Next to Cecilia is Coco's cousin, 'Nanay' Fonseca, looking more pensive than the others; he would become a Tupamaro, who, captured in the anti-subversive crackdowns of the early seventies, would languish in the infamous and ironically-named *Libertad* prison for 13 years, before being released in the general amnesty of March 1985. Ignacio's brother Pablo, standing below him, would become a painter, influenced by that most famous of Uruguay artists, Joaquín Torres García, and by Juan Storm – the father of his best friend Diego. Pablo's career would become increasingly hampered in later years by Parkinson's disease, an affliction shared by Diego's brother Juan, seen on the left of the photo. Juan would die in 2019, less than a year after the death of his and Diego's mother Bimba. Nanay, Pablo, and Sarita Fonseca (sitting on the fence next to Diego) would all die in 2022.

Fig. 31. *Goodbye to the Tena boys at Montevideo docks on the family's departure from Uruguay.*
Standing: *Diego Storm, Coco Nicolich, Caito Capurro, Nanay Fonseca, Juan Tena, Juani Caubarrere, Javier Tena, Miguel Campomar, Tito Regules.*
Below: *Carlitos Páez, Carlos Quagliotti, Pablo Fonseca.*

The themes of the Andes tragedy, the Tupamaros, and a paradise lost are summarised, in Tena's novel, by the fictionalized reflection of the mother of one of the Andes victims:

"Then came the boys' accident", she says, and starts to cry. "Like a divine punishment. And the Tupamaros. And the dictatorship. ... Nothing was ever the same again. But while we were living it we didn't know, we didn't accept that this excitement could end. It was impossible to imagine that we were on the brink of hell. Sticking it to God. And He punished us."

As the children grew into teenagers, their daily lives outside school and study were taken up with movies, dancing, the beach, parties, camping, rugby practice, and rugby games on Sunday. Friendships and connections were reinforced by boys going out with the sisters of their friends – girls from the *Colegio Sagrado Corazón* right next door to *The Christian*, or from the nearby *Colegio Jesús María*, a dozen blocks to the west.

Fig. 32. *Five of the gang in the grounds of the Harley family home in Carrasco.*
Coco Nicolich, Pablo Fonseca, Diego Storm, Roy Harley, Walter Harley, and Laika the dog.

One particular group of friends that emerged from this social circle was known, amongst themselves, as 'the gang' – **Coco Nicolich**, **Diego Storm**, Tito Regules, Pablo Fonseca, **Carlitos Páez**, **Bobby François**, **Roy Harley**, and Roy's older brother Walter. From different classes in *The Christian*, they remained firm friends after they left school and started university or agricultural school. They would meet regularly at one another's houses, to play cards, discuss politics, or reflect on life. After rugby, they would often get together at *La Mascota* – a small bar in Carrasco – to eat mozzarella, and chat. It was typical of the times that the boys' widely differing political views had no effect on their friendship, which remained loyal throughout the heightened tensions of the time. Coco and Roy were for Wilson Ferreira, Carlitos for Aguerrondo, Diego for Batlle, Bobby for Pacheco, and Pablo for the *Frente Amplio*, with Tupamaro sympathies. One event, however, did provoke a reaction. The military government, after the ousting and exile of leftist academics, asked Mr Nicolich to become Dean of Architecture and Rector of the *Universidad de la República*. He was reluctant to accept, but in the end, he was persuaded, much to the anger of Pablo and his brother Nanay, and even his own children. Nanay, who had been employed as a gardener by Coco's parents, later wrote a heartfelt letter to them from *Libertad* prison, to apologise for the rift that had grown between them.

Carlitos, like Diego, was the son of a renowned artist, Carlos Páez Vilaró, who would go on to play the central role in the parents' search for the boys. Vilaró and Carlitos' mother, Madelón Rodríguez, had divorced some years earlier, and the former now spent his time either travelling the world, or in his studio at Punta Ballena, where his eccentric "living sculpture" Casapueblo had gradually been taking shape. It consisted of a series of interconnected rooms and terraces, with curved, whitewashed walls built into the cliffs overlooking the sea, designed to resemble the mud nests of the native *hornero* bird. Conceived as a homage to women and to the sun, it was already a tourist attraction at the time of the accident.

The gang would often gather at Casapueblo, whether or not Páez Vilaró was there. One summer, the boys were staying there by themselves when a tourist appeared, asking to be shown around. Hesitant at first, the boys soon realized that they could charge for

Fig. 33. *Survivor Eduardo Strauch at Casapueblo, Jan. 2015.*

tours, and use the proceeds to fund their *asados* and wine for the summer. Tito became chief tour guide, hosting a steady stream of visitors throughout the season. On one occasion, Tito rounded a corner to find Carlitos Páez sprawled asleep on the floor. Without missing a beat, he pointed out 'the son of the owner' before moving on to the next item of interest.

In the years after the accident, Casapueblo would become a second home for not only the gang, but for all of the Andes survivors. Páez Vilaró's tireless efforts in searching for the boys had created a special bond, and they were always welcome at his house.

II. The Trip

THE PASSENGERS[1]

The success of the *Old Christians* rugby club in winning the 1968 and 1970 Uruguayan championships had fostered a desire to seek new challenges. Initially, this involved taking the boat over to Buenos Aires and playing their Argentinian counterparts – the old boys of their sister college *Instituto Cardenal Newman*. But by 1971, there was a desire to go further afield, and **Guido Magri** (23), who had captained the 1968 championship-winning team, set about arranging a trip to Chile.

Guido Magri

His contact was Ezequiel 'Chelin' Bolumburu, whom he had first met at the South America Rugby Union Championship in 1967, where they had both made their international debuts. Chelin's home club was the *Grange Old Boys*, a club based in Santiago with parallels to the *Old Christians*. The *Old Boys* had won the Chilean championship in 1969 and 1970, and, over the following decades, the two clubs, forever linked by the tragedy that was about to unfold, would have remarkably similar records. Waxing and waning over the decades, it was almost as if they were joined at the hip, with purple patches in the late seventies and mid-eighties, followed by a period of drought in the nineties, and scattered successes in the new millennium.

Guido had a more personal incentive to foster a connection between the two clubs. He had fallen in love with a Chilean girl, María de los Angeles Mardones, whose family had spent some years in Carrasco before returning to Santiago, and the trip would afford another opportunity to spend time with her. Chelin, and Guido's other contacts from his many trips to see Angeles, enabled him to make the necessary arrangements, and a Uruguayan Air Force plane was chartered, as a cost-effective means of transport.

The trip was successful, the *Old Christians* playing both the *Grange Old Boys* and a Chilean national team, winning one match and losing the other. The boys greatly

Marcelo Pérez

enjoyed their time in Chile, where they had been warmly received by their hosts, and they returned to Uruguay with the thought of getting together again the following year. One of the boys who was most enthusiastic about the idea was **Marcelo Pérez del Castillo** (25), and it was he who took charge of the 1972 trip. Marcelo, a highly respected leader who had captained the 1970 championship-winning team, was

---

[1] All portraits in this chapter are copyright © Museo Andes 1972. The artist is Daniel Vera.

the perfect man for the job, with the authority, drive, and organizational skills to bring the project to fruition.

He formed a committee consisting of former classmates Pepe Pollak and **Julio Martínez Lamas** (26) from the class of '63. The three of them would be responsible for filling the plane; 40 passengers were needed to guarantee a ticket price of 40,000 pesos, about $40. Pepe, a law student, was a strong rugby player, but made the decision not to go as he was saving up to buy a motorcycle – he had his eye on a 1947 Triumph. Julio, however, welcomed the prospect of a few days away from work. He had been the family breadwinner since age 15, starting as an apprentice at the *Banco de la República*, and working his way up through the ranks, popular with colleagues and customers alike. Exceptionally tall and

Julio Martínez Lamas

lean, Julio was an enthusiastic supporter and ambassador of the club, and had formerly been a captain of one of the *Old Christians* B teams, although he wasn't planning to play on this occasion.

Marcelo also enlisted the help of another old classmate, radio ham Rafael Ponce de León, who would prove invaluable in communicating with Chile to arrange the logistics around the game, including the boys' accommodation. Rafael didn't plan on going, as his wife was expecting a baby, a decision that would later allow him to become the primary point of contact between the parents in Montevideo, and those involved in search and rescue activities in Chile.

In the close-knit community of Carrasco, the news of the upcoming trip spread rapidly. The opportunity to spend a cheap extended weekend in Chile was balanced by the fact

that mid-term exams were coming up for many of them. The first task was to get the fifteen players needed for the matches. Guido Magri was not planning on going this time; he hadn't played rugby in 1972 as he had spent the year in Paysandú, and could ill-afford time off from his studies. So Guido's favoured position of scrum half would be filled by first-teamer **Alexis Hounie** (20), a compact and skilful player who had been part of the 1970 championship-winning team.

Alexis Hounie

Of the boys who had played the previous year, seven were able to go again: Marcelo, who could play in a number of positions; forwards **Nando Parrado** (22), Bobby Jaugust, and **Gastón Costemalle** (23); wing three-quarters **Roberto Canessa** (19) and **Panchito Abal** (21); and fly-half **Arturo Nogueira** (21) who had been one of the organizers of the previous year's trip. Bobby Jaugust, tall and blond, would be travelling by commercial airline, as his father was the Uruguayan representative of

KLM; he usually played in the number eight position at the back of the scrum or as lock forward in the second row.

Gastón Costemalle

Gastón Costemalle had played in the first team for several years, some of them as captain, and had been the first *Old Christian* to represent his country, playing prop against Chile in the Fifth South American Rugby championship. He was an avid sportsman, but his busy life – as a journalist, law student, and political activist – had left little time for rugby in recent months. Although he was out of training, he was keen to participate, and could play in the front row of the scrum or as a number eight.

Nando, who also played lock forward, would become one of the great heroes of the Andes tragedy. He shared his interest in motorcycles, cars, and rugby, with his best friend, Panchito Abal. Tall and shy, with thick-rimmed glasses and an uncomplicated nature, Nando was overshadowed by Panchito, who was strikingly handsome, and played rugby with a fluency and flair that

Panchito Abal

Nando Parrado

brought him to the attention both of the national selectors and the girls lining the touchline at the *Old Christians* games. Unlike many of the passengers who were pursuing university degrees or attending agricultural school, the two boys worked for their respective family businesses – Nando at *La Casa del Tornillo*, which dealt in screws and fixings, and Panchito at *Abal Hermanos*, a major Uruguayan tobacco and cigarette company. Fortuitously, the main offices were both on Paraguay street downtown, three blocks apart, and so they would meet each day for lunch.

Nando invited his mother **Eugenia Dolgay** (50), who had been born in the Ukraine, and his sisters Graciela and **Susana Parrado** (20). Eugenia and Susana jumped at the

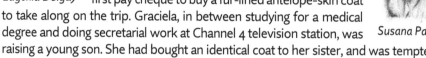

Eugenia Dolgay

opportunity, as they both enjoyed travelling. The two planned to go to the rugby games, and then visit friends or take advantage of the very cheap prices to go shopping. Susana ('Susy'), tall and blonde, was 20 and already a teacher of English and Economics at the Uruguayan American school – the youngest teacher in higher education. She used her first pay cheque to buy a fur-lined antelope-skin coat

Susana Parrado

to take along on the trip. Graciela, in between studying for a medical degree and doing secretarial work at Channel 4 television station, was raising a young son. She had bought an identical coat to her sister, and was tempted to sign up, but felt that she couldn't justify the additional expense of a trip to Chile.

Joining Panchito Abal as a three-quarter would be **Roberto Canessa** (19), one of the youngest on the team. Roberto was a maverick, never afraid to impose his opinion on

any situation, regardless of the consequences, his constant need to be active fuelled by a nervous energy. He was in his second year of medical school at the *Universidad de la República*. Nicknamed 'Musculo' by his teammates, his strength, fitness, and intelligence would make him the perfect companion for Nando on their famous ten-day trek through the Andes.

Roberto Canessa

Daniel Maspons (20), good-looking, stylishly dressed, and with a relaxed and straightforward personality, was a good friend of Roberto Canessa. He had recently broken into the first team, playing as a flanker, and was keen to go, but his father – despite his pride in his son's rugby achievements – was reluctant, saying that Daniel's studies should take priority. Mr Maspons ran the family business – importing English cashmeres and other fabrics – and Daniel was studying economics, with a view to eventually taking over from his father. It took a concerted effort by Marcelo, Julio, Roberto, and Daniel's sister Rosario to persuade

Daniel Maspons

Mr Maspons to give the go-ahead, but eventually he yielded, and gave his son the money for the ticket.

Roberto also invited his close friend and university study partner **Fernando Vázquez** (20), coincidentally born on the same day and year as Daniel Maspons. Although not a

rugby player, Fernando loved to travel, and had never been to Chile. A stand-out student at school and at university, he and Roberto were granted permission to miss an upcoming exam due to their excellent academic record. Fernando's father, a noted engineer, was concerned that they would be taking a chartered Uruguayan Air Force flight. He didn't trust their expertise to make such a trip over the Andes, and offered to pay for his son to join Bobby Jaugust on a scheduled commercial flight; but Fernando was adamant that it would be more

Fernando Vázquez

in the spirit of the trip and more fun to fly together as a group.

As Arturo Nogueira had travelled the previous year, his parents – with the financial burden of seven children in private school – gave his brother Daniel the first right of refusal for the upcoming trip. Daniel considered the invitation, but as none of his classmates were travelling, and he had some pending university entrance exams, he gave his older brother the go-ahead. Arturo, who played in the pivotal fly-half position, was studying economics at university. Highly intelligent and thoughtful,

Arturo Nogueira

he had a complex personality; loyal and open to his close circle of friends, but sometimes appearing brusque to outsiders in a way that belied his inner sensitivity.

Arturo recruited his friends **Pedro Algorta** (21) and **Felipe Maquirriain** (22). The three had been in the class of '66 at *The Christian*, and were now studying economics together at the university. For Pedro, it was a welcome opportunity to return to Santiago, where he had lived and studied for three years. He had many reasons to travel. He took a great interest in

Pedro Algorta

the political situation, as he had been a class representative for MAPU, one of the parties that had helped bring the Marxist government of Allende to power. He also had friends to visit from his time in Chile, including a girlfriend, Ana Luisa, with whom he needed to resolve unanswered questions about their relationship. Finally, it would give him the opportunity to stock up with university textbooks, which were much cheaper in Chile. Neither Pedro nor Felipe were rugby players,

Felipe Maquirriain

although Pedro had played a bit in Chile, but the two of them went along to a couple of the *Old Christians* rugby practices, to make themselves known.

Another passenger from the class of '66 was **Enrique Platero** (22), a neighbour of Arturo Nogueira, who was one of the prop forwards on the first team – nicknamed 'the bear' for his size and strength. Enrique's father had been against

Enrique Platero

the idea of his son going on the trip; he and Enrique had a difficult relationship, and he told him: "You don't study, you don't work... so you're not going to get any money." In the end, it was Nando Parrado who lent Enrique the funds. The other first-team prop, **Antonio 'Tintín' Vizintín** (19), also signed up. One of the youngest boys on the trip, Tintín's

Antonio Vizintín

great strength and fitness would prove to be essential on the mountain in his role as a porter, carrying the heaviest load during the two-day climb at the start of the final expedition.

Roy Harley (20), a strong and fast flanker, had almost gone the previous year, but had backed out when his close friends **Gustavo 'Coco' Nicolich** (20) and **Diego Storm** (20) had decided not to go. This year, all three were determined to travel, having heard what a wonderful experience it had been the previous year, and how *simpatica* were the Chilean girls. They had been making plans since June, and were amongst the first to sign up, although it took until a

Roy Harley

couple of weeks before departure for Coco to finally get the money together and confirm his place. Roy was an engineering student, who had developed his love of

engines, and all things mechanical, working with the trucks and tractors on his parents' farm in El Pinar. Coco, tall with dark, curly hair, was a self-confident boy, with a good sense of humour, who was studying to become a vet. He would fill the full-back position normally held by first-teamer Eddie Suarez – the

Diego Storm   *novio* of Arturo Nogueira's sister – who was unable   *Coco Nicolich*

to go. Diego, a first-year medical student, was slender and slightly built, and not a rugby player, but he had an adventurous spirit and enjoyed travelling, having hitchhiked the 2,500 km to Rio de Janeiro a couple of years previously, with Coco and two other friends.

Roy, Diego, and Coco encouraged other members of 'the gang' to travel: **Carlitos Páez** (18), Tito Regules (20), and the reluctant **Bobby François** (20). Carlitos had initially declined, saying that he had too many absences from the farm school, in Sarandí Grande, where he was studying agronomy, but later Coco convinced him to change his mind. Bobby was studying at a nearby farm school in Durazno,

Carlitos Páez   and had little interest in a trip to Chile, preferring

the quiet country life and a settled routine. But he was persuaded by the persistence of his friends, and by his family – his mother, who encouraged him to broaden his horizons, and his sister, who

gave him a wad of cash and a list of items to buy on the black market in Chile, where things were ten times cheaper. Tito, a former classmate of

Bobby François

Bobby at *The Christian*, was more easily persuaded. He played rugby for *La Cachila*, a team that enjoyed considerable success in the early seventies, and would be available to play in Chile if

Tito Regules   needed. In the end, the only members of the gang who declined to

travel were Pablo Fonseca and Roy's brother Walter.

Gustavo Zerbino (19) – another youthful first-teamer – was also quick to sign up. He had missed out the previous year, because he had been leading a camp in Tacuarembó for the *Castores de Emaús* – a Jesuit-led youth group that did social work in poor communities. He could play either as flanker or in the three-quarter line. Gustavo invited his friend **Carlos Valeta** (18). The two had been in the same

Gustavo Zerbino

Carlos Valeta

class at *The Christian* in the very early school years, until Gustavo had transferred to the *Seminario* in 1964, but they had been reunited at university, studying medicine together. At 18 years and 8 months, Carlos, not a rugby player, was the youngest of all the passengers. Both Gustavo and Carlos did voluntary work in the poor neighbourhoods of Montevideo, building houses and teaching skills. Carlos, with a special interest in psychiatry, also assisted the Jesuits with their work in the local psychiatric hospitals.

Eduardo Strauch (25) found out about the trip early on, as he and Marcelo Pérez del Castillo were partners in a joint architectural venture, and had been close friends from childhood, and classmates at *The Christian*. At school, Marcelo had given Eduardo the

Eduardo Strauch

nickname 'El Alemán' – the German – more for his attitudes than his looks. Eduardo, handsome and urbane, was well-travelled, having made a tour of Europe in 1969, with Gastón Costemalle and other friends. His family lived on the ground floor of a grand house in *Parque de los Aliados* (now *Parque Batlle*); a tree-lined, upmarket neighbourhood north of Pocitos. On the floor above, lived his double cousin **Adolfo 'Fito' Strauch** (24); their mothers were sisters – the Urioste side of the family –

Adolfo 'Fito' Strauch

and their fathers were brothers. The Strauch grandfather had owned a jewellery business, but that had been sold, and the fathers were now both ranchers. Fito was studying agronomy, though without the clear-cut vocation that Eduardo had for architecture. Although both cousins signed up for the trip, neither of them were planning to play rugby. Eduardo had been on the very first *Old Christians* team, but hadn't played for some years, and Fito currently played for another first division team, *Los Cuervos* ('The Crows', who played in black), and could stand in if needed.

Daniel Fernández (26) – a cousin on the Strauch side of the family – had heard about the trip from a friend at university, and later, Fito persuaded him to go. With a strike looming at the university, they wouldn't lose out academically, but the taciturn

Daniel Fernández

cousins had second thoughts when they heard that they would need to exchange $10 for each day they were in Chile – a requirement of the Chilean government to bring dollars into the country. However, the realization that too many people dropping out might lead to a cancellation of the trip, persuaded them to travel. Daniel had sold some pigs to get money for the trip. He was due to receive payment on the Monday before departure, but because he was travelling from the farm to Montevideo that day, he asked his father to collect the money and bring it the following day. Like Mr Vázquez, Mr Fernández was distrustful of the military pilots, and, not wanting his son to travel, he prevaricated and only appeared on Wednesday, the day before the trip – too late to purchase the requisite dollars. Daniel's sister came to the rescue, and lent him the necessary amount.

Daniel Shaw (24) – another cousin of Eduardo and Fito, this time on the Urioste side – was a late addition to the team – someone who could fill the three-quarter gap created by the absence of *Old Christian* first-teamer Eduardo Viera. Daniel – good-humoured and easy-going – had started working on his parents' farm a few months previously, having graduated from agronomy school in early 1972. Because the training regime was much less severe than that of the *Old Christians*, Daniel, like Fito, had been playing his rugby with *Los Cuervos* in recent months and would return from the interior every couple of weeks to participate. The

Daniel Shaw

first that Daniel's family heard about him going was when he returned unexpectedly from the farm two days before departure. Like several other parents, Mr Shaw didn't like the idea of his son travelling on a military plane, but was unsuccessful in his attempts to dissuade him from going.

Álvaro Mangino

As the net was cast wider in the attempt to fill the plane, boys with little connection to the *Old Christians* were approached. **Álvaro Mangino** (19), whose *novia*, Margarita Arocena Storm, was a sister of Marcelo's sister-in-law and a cousin of Coco Nicolich, was invited by *Old Christians* president Daniel Juan and first-teamer François Manchoulas. The son of a customs official, Álvaro had been to the *Deutsche Schule* and the Jesuit *Seminario*, where he had got to know Gustavo Zerbino. More recently, he had been attending a farm school.

Gastón Costemalle invited his friends **Pancho Delgado** (24) and **Coche Inciarte** (24) on the Saturday before the trip. The three boys and their *novias* would often get together to socialise, and that evening they were gathered at the house of Susana Sartori, Pancho Delgado's *novia*. Coche had been an early classmate of Gastón at the *Windsor School* in Pocitos, and they had remained lifelong friends. He had taken a road trip to Santiago in 1971, and had been very taken with the friendliness of the Chilean people. Despite not having gone to *The Christian*, he was friends with some of the boys – Gastón and Pancho of course, and Fito Strauch and Daniel Shaw from agricultural school.

Coche Inciarte

Pancho, who knew Gastón from his university law course, had gone to school at the *Seminario*. He had never been to Chile, and was initially reluctant to go, before Susana persuaded him otherwise. With little time to get together the money for the trip, Delgado went to his two grandmothers to ask for money – one lent money for the trip, the other the money for Chile.

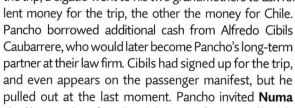

Pancho borrowed additional cash from Alfredo Cibils Caubarrere, who would later become Pancho's long-term partner at their law firm. Cibils had signed up for the trip, and even appears on the passenger manifest, but he pulled out at the last moment. Pancho invited **Numa**

Pancho Delgado

Numa Turcatti

Turcatti (24), who had been a close friend and classmate for most of his life – first at the *Seminario* and then at the Law Faculty. Numa was not a rugby player, preferring soccer, unlike his twin brother Daniel, who had played wing-three-quarter for Uruguay against Chile in 1969, in a team that included Guido Magri and Gastón Costemalle; it turned out to be Daniel's one and only game, resulting in a broken leg, which, despite several operations, was never quite the same again.

The final law student to sign up was Daniel Freiría, but like Cibils he found he was unable to travel after all. He offered the ticket to anyone of his study group who would be able and willing to go at such short notice, and **Juan Carlos Menéndez** (22)

took it off his hands. Juan Carlos – 'El Flaco' – was an intelligent, low-key individual, who was studying to become a public notary. Like Numa, his passion was soccer and he played for the Soriano Club in the University Soccer League. He had a casual acquaintance with some of the law students on the trip, from seeing them around the faculty, but in effect he was a complete outsider, having been to neither *The Christian*, nor the *Seminario*.

Juan Carlos Menéndez

By the time Marcelo got together with Julio on Sunday 8th October, four days before the trip, it was apparent that enough rugby players had signed up to allow the formation of a team consisting of first and second team players, and a couple of

former players. As an added bonus, **Dr Pancho Nicola** (40) agreed to go along as coach. Pancho had been an international rugby player, playing centre three-quarter for the Uruguayan national team, *Los Teros*, in the first South America Rugby Championship in 1951. His children – all boys – were current students at *The Christian*, and he had taken

Esther Horta

Pancho Nicola

on a coaching role with the *Old Christians*. He planned to travel with his wife **Esther Horta** (40), the couple leaving their children in the care of one of Esther's sisters.

64

It was a strong team – several had played or would go on to play for *Los Teros*: Gastón Costemalle, Bobby Jaugust, Roberto Canessa, Gustavo Zerbino, and Tintín Vizintín. It was also a balanced side, with most able to play in their favoured positions, though there would be some compromises in the final line-up. But despite the best efforts of the trip committee, there were still quite a few places to fill to cover the cost of the charter. With a go/no go decision required, Marcelo took a calculated risk – he was optimistic that a few more could be persuaded to travel, and he communicated with his Chilean hosts by ham radio, telling them that the trip would go ahead.

The full flat-rate for the plane was 1,600,000 pesos – approximately $1,600 on the black market – and the money was now due. When Marcelo told the Air Force that he hadn't yet sold all the tickets, they told him not to worry, that they would sell the extra tickets. Marcelo entrusted the money to Daniel Fernández to take to the TAMU office on the *Boiso Lanza* air force base in the north of the city. TAMU

1	Prop	Enrique Platero
2	Hooker	Gastón Costemalle
3	Prop	Tintín Vizintín
4	Lock	Nando Parrado
5	Lock	Bobby Jaugust
6	Flanker	Roy Harley
7	Flanker	Daniel Maspons
8	Number eight	Marcelo Pérez
9	Scrum-half	Alexis Hounie
10	Fly-half	Arturo Nogueira
11	Wing three-quarter	Panchito Abal
12	Centre three-quarter	Daniel Shaw
13	Centre three-quarter	Gustavo Zerbino
14	Wing three-quarter	Roberto Canessa
15	Full-back	Coco Nicolich
	Coach	Pancho Nicola

A possible line-up, 1972 Old Christians trip to Chile

(*Transporte Aéreo Militar Uruguayo*) was the commercial face of the air force, providing internal and international passenger and cargo flights on air force equipment. Any stragglers joining the trip in those last few days would have to go to the TAMU office to secure their ticket, which would now cost 5000 pesos more.

Those who had already signed up continued to push hard to fill the remaining places. One target was Connie Hughes, an *Old Christian* committee member and a cofounder of the club. Connie, who was studying engineering and business, earned a small wage – $100 per month – teaching mathematics at the university and at *The Christian*. He was soon to be married, and his fiancée earned not much more, working as a gastroenterology nurse. The couple had recently rented an apartment, which they were refitting in preparation for their life together, and the kitchen renovations and the purchase of a new refrigerator meant that finances were tight. The efforts to persuade

Connie to travel were typical of the conversations that were taking place across the community in the last-minute attempts to fill the plane:

SUNDAY 8TH OCTOBER

Marcelo calls Connie at his fiancée's house:

"Connie, are you coming on Thursday?"
     "No!"
"Why not?"
     "I haven't got the money."
"We can lend you the money."
     "No, I owe $250 for the kitchen and the fridge."
"How much are your instalments?"
     "$17 a month."
"The plane fare is only three months of payments."
     "No! I'm not going!"

MONDAY 9TH OCTOBER

Marcelo calls Connie again.

"Come on Connie, you're a board member, and a founder of the club!"
     "No."
"You know everyone will have a great time – four days in Chile is very cheap!"
     "No!"
"But the plane fare is only $50, that's a great deal!"
     "No! I'm not going!"

WEDNESDAY 11TH OCTOBER, 10:30 P.M., THE EVENING BEFORE THE TRIP

Connie is taking a bus home from town after teaching evening mathematics classes at the business school. He gets on the bus and is immediately greeted by a shout from the back. It is Gustavo Zerbino, returning from an evening meeting of *Castores de Emaús* at the *Seminario*:

"Hey Connie, why aren't you coming on the trip?"
     "I've given my reasons to Marcelo, I don't need to explain them to you also."
"Well, tell me anyway!"
     "I'm paying a $17 per month instalment for my kitchen renovations."

"If it's just a money problem, the club can give you a loan which you can repay in instalments. We offered Julito a loan."

> "Julito is single and can do what he wants; I can't just decide to spend three months' repayments to have fun with my friends."

"You're just under your fiancée's thumb."

> "No, we discussed it and we decided together. Besides, I'm no longer playing rugby these days, and I'm not in good shape!"

"You're so silly, you'll miss out on a wonderful occasion."

> "All the same, I'm not travelling."

"¡Pollerudo!"[1]

Another *Old Christians* committee member who decided not to go was the president of the club, Daniel Juan. From the class of '66, a former classmate of several of the passengers, Daniel had just returned from several days in Buenos Aires, where his sister had ridden in a horse show, and he couldn't afford another few days away. Both Daniel Juan and Connie Hughes would play prominent roles in the days following the return of the survivors to Montevideo.

Whereas the last-minute efforts to persuade Daniel Juan and Connie ended in failure, others were successful. Two days before the trip, Carlitos Páez and Bobby François invited **Ramón 'Moncho' Sabella** (21), who knew the former from high school, and the latter from agronomy school, and from the proximity of the families' farms. Tito Regules invited his

Moncho Sabella

friend **Rafael 'El Vasco' Echavarren** (22). Rafael was studying dairy farming at the *Escuela Superior de Lechería* in Nueva Helvecia, a town 120 km north-west of Montevideo. He had become enthused by cheese production, and had started a small dairy on his family's farm, putting into practice what he had learnt at the school. Of Basque heritage, he was hard-working and generous, with a love of the countryside and *gaucho* traditions. Like Tito, Rafael played rugby for *La Cachila*, but

Rafael Echavarren

although he enjoyed the ethos of the game, he wasn't a first-teamer, and wasn't planning on playing in Chile.

---

[1] Someone who's hen-pecked.

Meanwhile, on the Monday before departure, Panchito Abal invited his cousin **Javier Methol** (36), who worked with him at the family business – the *Abal Hermanos* cigarette factory in downtown Montevideo. At almost 37, Javier was older than most of the passengers, but he knew a few of them, and his son Pablo went to *The Christian*. Javier broached the idea with his wife **Liliana Navarro** (34) whose immediate reaction was,

"You're crazy – today is Monday and you want to travel on Thursday?!" More importantly, she didn't want to go because she was starting a course that day, picking up on her studies to become a notary, which she had put on hold since the birth of her first child. But arriving at the faculty that afternoon, she found that all classes were cancelled indefinitely, due

Javier Methol

Liliana Navarro

to a strike called in opposition to the Education Bill going through parliament, so when she arrived home, she gave Javier the go-ahead. Like the Nicola couple, Javier and Liliana would be leaving four young children at home; in the care of Liliana's parents.

The same strike that had led to Liliana's change of heart also led Guido Magri to reconsider. Although he wasn't planning on playing rugby, it was an opportunity to see Angeles one more time before their wedding in December, and to iron out any last-minute arrangements. He returned to Montevideo from Paysandú the day before the trip, with his friend and fellow student Alberto 'El Chileno' Rodríguez, and stopped by Marcelo's house to check that there were still tickets left. 'El Chileno' lent Guido the keys to his apartment in Santiago; a place where Guido had often stayed during his visits to see Angeles.

The final passenger to sign up was a middle-aged lady, **Graziela Augusto de Mariani** (42), who had no connection to any of the passengers. She and her husband Hector Mariani, a public accountant, had gone to the TAMU office in the hope of buying two tickets on one of the monthly flights to Chile, which were less than a third of the price of a commercial flight. They wanted to travel to see their daughter María del Carmen, who was living in Chile, and whose wedding would be at the end of October. Discovering that they would need to wait a couple of weeks until the next scheduled TAMU flight, they took the opportunity to buy the last remaining ticket on the *Old Christians*

Graziela Augusto de Mariani

charter flight. The couple decided that if only one could travel, it should be Carmen's mother, with Mr Mariani to follow at a later date.

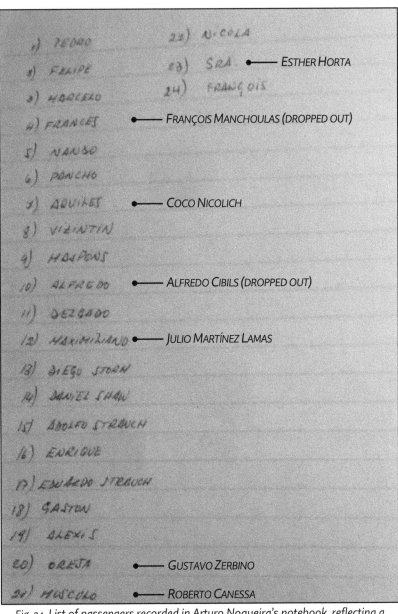

1) PEDRO
2) FELIPE
3) MARCELO
4) FRANCES •——— FRANÇOIS MANCHOULAS (DROPPED OUT)
5) NANDO
6) PONCHO
7) AQUILES •——— COCO NICOLICH
8) VIZINTIN
9) MOLPONS
10) ALFREDO •——— ALFREDO CIBILS (DROPPED OUT)
11) DELGADO
12) MAXIMILIANO •——— JULIO MARTÍNEZ LAMAS
13) DIEGO STORM
14) DANIEL SHAW
15) ADOLFO STRAUCH
16) ENRIQUE
17) EDUARDO STRAUCH
18) GASTON
19) ALEXIS
20) OREJA •——— GUSTAVO ZERBINO
21) MUSCULO •——— ROBERTO CANESSA

22) NICOLA
23) SRA. •——— ESTHER HORTA
24) FRANÇOIS

Fig. 34. List of passengers recorded in Arturo Nogueira's notebook, reflecting a moment in time in the attempt to fill the plane.

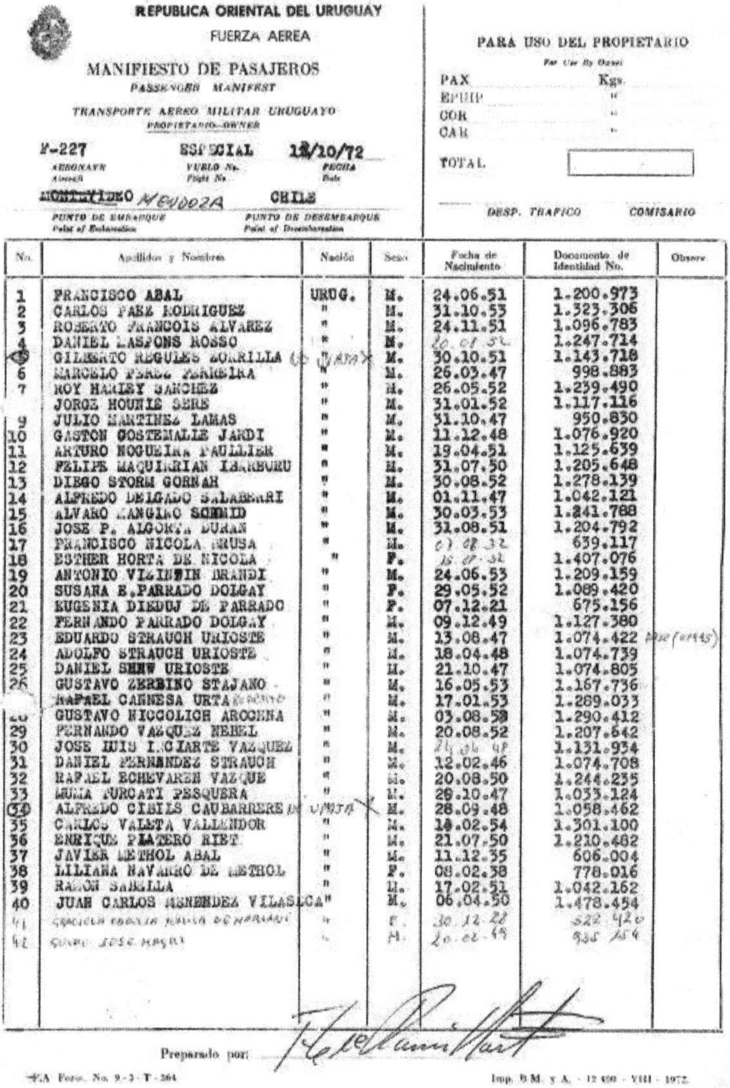

REPUBLICA ORIENTAL DEL URUGUAY

FUERZA AEREA

MANIFIESTO DE PASAJEROS

PASSENGER MANIFEST

TRANSPORTE AEREO MILITAR URUGUAYO
PROPIETARIO-OWNER

PARA USO DEL PROPIETARIO

PAX	Kgs.
EQUIP	"
COR	"
CAR	"
TOTAL	

F-227   ESPECIAL   12/10/72

AERONAVE   VUELO No.   FECHA
Aircraft   *Flight No.*   *Date*

MONTEVIDEO *MENDOZA*   CHILE

PUNTO DE EMBARQUE   PUNTO DE DESEMBARQUE
Point of Embarcation   *Point of Disembarcation*

DESP. TRAFICO   COMISARIO

No.	Apellido y Nombres	Nación	Sexo	Fecha de Nacimiento	Documento de Identidad No.	Observ.
1	FRANCISCO ABAL	URUG.	M.	24.06.51	1.200.973	
2	CARLOS PABE RODRIGUEZ	"	M.	31.10.53	1.323.306	
3	ROBERTO FRANCOIS ALVAREZ	"	M.	24.11.51	1.096.783	
4	DANIEL LASFONS ROSSO	"	M.	20.08.52	1.247.714	
5	GILBERTO REGULES ZORRILLA	"	M.	30.10.51	1.143.718	
6	MARCELO PEREZ PEREIRA	"	M.	26.03.47	998.883	
7	ROY HARLEY SANCHEZ	"	M.	26.05.52	1.239.490	
8	JORGE HOUNIE SERE	"	M.	31.01.52	1.117.116	
9	JULIO MARTINEZ LAMAS	"	M.	31.10.47	950.830	
10	GASTON COSTEMALLE JARDI	"	M.	11.12.48	1.076.920	
11	ARTURO NOGUEIRA PAULLIER	"	M.	19.04.51	1.125.659	
12	FELIPE MAQUIRRIAN IZARBURU	"	M.	31.07.50	1.205.648	
13	DIEGO STORM GORRAH	"	M.	30.08.52	1.278.139	
14	ALFREDO DELGADO SALABERRI	"	M.	01.11.47	1.042.121	
15	ALVARO MANGINO SCHMID	"	M.	30.03.53	1.241.788	
16	JOSE P. ALGORTA DURAN	"	M.	31.08.51	1.204.792	
17	FRANCISCO NICOLA RUSA	"	M.	03.08.32	639.117	
18	ESTHER HORTA DE NICOLA	"	F.	15.07.32	1.407.076	
19	ANTONIO VIZINTIN BRANDI	"	M.	24.06.53	1.209.159	
20	SUSANA E. PARRADO DOLGAY	"	F.	29.05.52	1.089.420	
21	EUGENIA DIEDUJ DE PARRADO	"	F.	07.12.21	675.156	
22	FERNANDO PARRADO DOLGAY	"	M.	09.12.49	1.127.380	
23	EDUARDO STRAUCH URIOSTE	"	M.	13.08.47	1.074.422	
24	ADOLFO STRAUCH URIOSTE	"	M.	18.04.48	1.074.739	
25	DANIEL SHAW URIOSTE	"	M.	21.10.47	1.074.805	
26	GUSTAVO ZERBINO STAJANO	"	M.	16.05.53	2.167.736	
27	RAFAEL CARNESA URTA	"	M.	17.01.53	1.289.033	
28	GUSTAVO NICCOLICH AROCENA	"	M.	03.08.52	1.290.412	
29	FERNANDO VAZQUEZ HEBEL	"	M.	20.08.52	1.207.642	
30	JOSE LUIS INCIARTE VAZQUEZ	"	M.	24.04.48	1.131.934	
31	DANIEL FERNANDEZ STRAUCH	"	M.	12.02.46	1.074.708	
32	RAFAEL ECHEVAREN VAZQUE	"	M.	20.08.50	1.244.235	
33	NUMA TURCATI PESQUERA	"	M.	29.10.47	1.033.124	
34	ALFREDO CIBILS CAUBARRERE	"	M.	28.09.48	1.058.462	
35	CARLOS VALETA VALLENDOR	"	M.	14.02.54	1.301.100	
36	ENRIQUE PLATERO RIET	"	M.	21.07.50	1.210.462	
37	JAVIER METHOL ABAL	"	M.	11.12.35	606.004	
38	LILIANA NAVARRO DE METHOL	"	F.	08.02.38	778.016	
39	RAMON SABELLA	"	M.	17.02.51	1.042.162	
40	JUAN CARLOS MENENDEZ VILASECA	"	M.	06.04.50	1.478.454	
41	GRACIELA... DE...	"	F.	30.12.28	522.420	
42	... JOSE MAGRI	"	M.	20.02.49	845.154	

Preparado por:

FA Form. No. 9-3 - T-364   Imp. D.M. y A. - 12 400 - VIII - 1972.

Fig. 35. *Passenger Manifest.*

The day before departure saw a flurry of preparation. Some returned from *estancias* and agricultural schools in the interior, in readiness for the early start; families got together to share a farewell meal; girlfriends and mothers helped pack; arrangements were made to share rides to the airport, and alarms were set for early the next morning. There was a transcendent air of anticipation and excitement for the upcoming trip.

For those living in Carrasco, the airport was only a fifteen-minute drive away, but for those coming from downtown or Pocitos, the journey was longer, and extra time was needed for those picking up friends. One of the earliest to rise was Mr Maquirriain, who set his alarm for 5:00 a.m., leaving his house in Punta Gorda an hour later, with his son Felipe. By 6:15 a.m., they had picked up Pedro Algorta at his uncle's house in Carrasco, and the three arrived at the airport at 6:30 a.m., one-and-a-half hours before the plane was due to depart. With plenty of time to spare, they went upstairs to the airport restaurant and had a leisurely breakfast. Afterwards, they mingled with the boys gathering in the terminal, with Felipe taking the opportunity to telephone his *novia*, Mercedes, before boarding the plane.

Mercedes coincidentally lived in the same apartment building as another passenger, Rafael Echavarren. Wearing a distinctive red jacket, Rafael arrived with his *novia* Ana, who had picked him up at his grandparents' house, where he had spent the night. Rafael had only got back from the *estancia* the previous day, and he and Ana had had a farewell dinner with his family the previous evening – his favourite meal of baked chicken and tomato salad, followed by a *dulce de leche* dessert. When Rafael had left after dinner, his mother had given him her customary blessing, making the sign of the cross over him. On arriving at the terminal building, Rafael looked around for his good friend Tito Regules, who had invited him, but he was nowhere to be found.

The gang had planned to go to the airport in two cars: Diego, Roy, and Coco in one, and Bobby, Carlitos, and Tito in another. On the night before departure, Roy – whose family rented out their large Carrasco home during part of the year – stayed over at Diego's house on Arocena Avenue, and early the next morning, Diego's mother, Bimba, drove them to the airport, stopping to pick up Coco on the nearby Divina Comedia street.

Carlitos and Tito both lived on Pedro Figari street, and had planned to walk the short distance to Bobby's house on Copacabana street on the morning of departure, from where Bobby's mother would drive them to the airport. Carlitos, anxious about the trip and determined not to be late, turned up very early. Bobby and Carlitos had breakfast, and waited for Tito to arrive. When he didn't turn up, they tried calling around; first his mother's house, and then his grandmother's house, but there was no answer. Eventually, they left for the airport, thinking that perhaps he had made his own way there. But when they arrived, they found the three who had gone in the other car, but no Tito. The boys joked that the plane would now crash and Tito would be saved, reflecting the superstition that someone missing a flight brought bad luck. In fact, in the days before the trip, the friends were always joking about the possibility of an accident, telling each other "We'll end up in the *Cordillera*." Carlitos even packed his winter boots, just in case that presentiment came true. His caution would be rewarded when, minutes after the accident, he spotted his suitcase in the snow and was able to retrieve them. They would serve him well in the Andes, as would the rosary that his mother had pressed on him when he had left his home that morning.

Tito, whose parents were divorced, had at the last moment decided to sleep at his father's house in *Parque de los Aliados*, rather than at his mother's house in Carrasco, and had slept through both the 5:30 a.m. wake-up call he had arranged, and the subsequent efforts of his sister Carmen to rouse him. There were several attempts to call him from airport, but inexplicably the phone had stopped working.

One more chance opened up to contact Tito. Eduardo and Fito Strauch were driven to the airport by Eduardo's brother, Ricardo. Fito almost contrived to make them late, sleeping through all attempts to rouse him, and ending up having to miss breakfast. The three stopped by to pick up their cousins: Daniel Shaw, who lived just round the corner from them, and Daniel Fernández. Arriving at the terminal, Eduardo reached into the pocket of the blue sports jacket he had bought for the trip, and realized, to his horror, that he had forgotten his money and documents. Ricardo was dispatched immediately to fetch them, and, as Mr Regules lived only a couple of blocks away from the Strauches, the boys asked him to stop by and check on Tito. Ricardo raced back, picked up Eduardo's documents and then drove to Mr Regules' house. Seeing the car in the driveway rather than in the garage, he assumed that they had crossed paths, and that Tito had already been dropped off at the airport. With time of the essence, Ricardo raced on past without stopping, arriving to give Eduardo his documents with just a few minutes to spare.

The boys living downtown had the furthest to travel. Alexis Hounie had called Moncho Sabella the previous evening, asking for a ride. The two of them were driven by Moncho's brother, Mono, who also stopped by to pick up Panchito Abal along the way. In Panchito's luggage were dozens of cartons of cigarettes, courtesy of the *Abal Hermanos* cigarette factory, as someone had mentioned that the ones in Santiago were neither so good, nor so readily available. As Moncho looked around on his arrival at the terminal, he found that he already knew quite a few of the passengers: Carlitos Páez and Bobby François, of course, who had invited him; former classmate Rafael Echavarren, who he hadn't realized was travelling; Daniel Fernández, whom he'd met at the Chilean embassy in Montevideo; and Numa Turcatti, who was a good friend of his brother, the two of them having shared a trip to Europe together a few years previously. Carlitos and Bobby introduced Moncho to the rest of the gang, and he soon felt at ease amongst them.

12th October was the start of a holiday weekend, and the terminal was packed, the airline counters jammed. As well as the *Old Christians* charter, there were several other flights leaving early that morning, including another TAMU flight leaving for the interior. In such a close community, it was inevitable that the boys would spot people they knew in the crowd of passengers going to other destinations. Moncho recognized two girls waiting for a flight to Buenos Aires, who gave him the address of a friend of theirs who lived in Chile. And Carlos Valeta, who was dropped off by his parents, bumped into a classmate from the faculty of medicine, who was on his way to Salto for the long weekend.

Like Carlos, other boys were driven to the airport by parents. Arturo Nogueira rode with his father, having said his goodbyes to his *novia*, Inés Lombardero, the previous evening, after exchanging keepsakes. Tintín was also driven by his father, who had originally thought about accompanying his son, before some last-minute business got in the way. Mr Vizintín waited with his son, chatting with Nando, Arturo, and others, until the boarding call came. Daniel Maspons's father had needed to head to his shop early that morning with his daughter Rosario, so Daniel's mother took him to the airport; he had said his goodbyes to Rosario the previous evening; an opportunity for her to slip her brother some extra spending money for the trip.

Others arrived in small groups. Marcelo Pérez, who planned to leave his car in the airport car park for the duration of the trip, drove himself, picking up rugby teammates Roberto Canessa and Gustavo Zerbino along the way. Coche Inciarte's *novia*, Soledad, driving her parents' Beetle, stopped to pick up Gastón Costemalle and Pancho Delgado en route to collecting Coche at his home in Punta Gorda; they arrived at the airport with time to spare, and Soledad stayed to see them off. Mr Parrado arrived in his olive-green Rover with Eugenia, Nando, and Susy; on the way, they had stopped by a friend's house who handed them a letter to deliver to his daughter who lived in Chile – Nando would eventually deliver it two-and-a-half months later. The family had breakfast together, and then mingled and chatted with the other passengers. The Methols arrived en masse in two cars, the children enjoying the rare treat of riding in the back of the pick-up truck, as the whole family came to see off Liliana and Javier.

With some passengers, there was a small presentiment of an accident. Esther Horta had a great fear of flying, and was worried about leaving her children for a few days, and what would happen if she didn't return. She had called her sister Cristina, to tell her that she hadn't made any legal arrangements for the care of her children should she die, and to ask her to look after the boys and not separate them should the worst happen. She had also spoken to one of the Brothers at the school, to ask him to take special care of her youngest son, who was just starting there.

The evening before the trip, Julio Martínez Lamas went out to eat with his mother and younger sister Ana Inés, at a restaurant in Carrasco. Ana Inés, who knew that Julio believed he would die young, had a sudden sense of the meal being a final farewell, and voiced this thought, causing her mother to react in alarm. Walking back home, they stopped by at Dr Nicola's house so that he could check up on Ana Inés, who was experiencing some earache. Whilst there, the Nicolas arranged with Julio to share their taxi ride to the airport the next morning.

Fernando Vázquez's *novia* Corina was visiting from Buenos Aires. She would always come by boat, as she didn't like flying, and she asked him if he were not afraid of crossing over the Andes. He teased her, saying that the plane would crash, and that he would survive, returning to Montevideo a hero. The evening before the flight, she helped him pack, and early the next morning Fernando went into his sister Teresita's room, which she was sharing with Corina, and kissed them both goodbye, before heading off to the airport. It was the last time they would see him.

As the time for departure approached, a final call was made for Tito Regules to come to the TAMU counter. When it was clear that he would not appear, Hector Mariani approached the Air Force representative to ask if he could fill the empty seat. But FAU red tape dictated that they were under strict orders not to accept anybody else, so Mr Mariani kissed his wife goodbye for the last time, before she disappeared through the boarding area, her suitcase laden with wedding presents for her daughter; gifts that would remain in the Andes.

With the passengers boarding, the relatives made their way up to the viewing balcony. Enjoying the unusually warm and clear spring day, they watched the passengers stroll across the tarmac towards the plane and mount the steps to the rear door. It was a Fairchild FH-227D twin-turboprop with wings mounted over the fuselage. Predominantly white, with FUERZA AEREA URUGUAYA written in large black letters on its grey belly, the registration number, 571, which would forever brand the tragedy, was prominently displayed on the nose, the tail, and by the door through which the passengers were entering.

THE FAIRCHILD[1]

The Fairchild was the latest and most modern addition to the FAU transport fleet. The use of military aircraft to carry civilian passengers was well established in Uruguay, with TAMU, formed a dozen years previously, operating both internal and external flights. The former connected the major provincial capitals by means of two circular routes: the Littoral (Montevideo – Paysandú – Salto – Artigas – Rivera – Montevideo) and the Eastern (Montevideo – Melo – Rivera – Artigas – Tacuarembó – Montevideo). These would each depart every other Friday, the Littoral schedule interleaving with that of the Eastern route. In addition, there were Monday and Friday flights to and from the central city of Durazno.

The external routes carried passengers and mail to the closest South American countries – Argentina, Brazil, Chile, and Paraguay – leaving on the first, second, third, and fourth Wednesday of the month respectively, the latter two operating only every other month. The FAU also offered charter flights as a way to raise additional funds – a fast and cheap method of group transportation for social clubs, schools, or sports teams.

Fig. 36. *The department capitals of Uruguay were connected by regular TAMU flights.*

The workhorse of the FAU transport fleet was the Douglas C-47, the military version of the DC3, also known as the Dakota. The complement of fifteen C-47s was supplemented by three more from *PLUNA* – the national carrier – after TAMU took over operating *PLUNA*'s routes to the interior in 1970. The C-47s were converted for passenger use, and were utilized on most of the

---

commercial routes. Later, in December 1972, a C-47 (FAU 508) would be used to search for the wreckage of the Fairchild, carrying some of the parents as observers.

In 1970, the FAU purchased two Fokker 'Friendship' F-27 planes, and a year later, two Fairchild FH-227D aircraft which were longer versions of the F-27s. In June 1971, a team of twelve –seven pilots, four technical specialists, and one navigator – travelled from Uruguay to the Fairchild factory in Hagerstown, Maryland, to learn about the plane. After an initial period of theoretical flight courses and technical maintenance training, practical flight instruction began on 20th July, continuing through to the second week of August.

Departing on 8th August, Chief of Mission, Colonel Wilder Jackson, and Colonel **Julio Cesar Ferradás**, captained the two aircraft, designated FAU 570 and FAU 571, on a multi-leg flight back to Uruguay. After overnight stops in Corpus Christi, Managua, Panama, and Lima, they crossed the Chilean Andes on 12th August 1971, and landed in Mendoza, foreshadowing the *Old Christians* flight that Ferradás would command fourteen months later. The next morning, Friday 13th, the two crews flew the final leg to Air Base 1 in Carrasco.

39-year-old Ferradás was one of the FAU's most skilled and respected pilots. He had logged over 5,000 flight hours, and had crossed the Andes dozens of times. He and Wilder Jackson, along with others such as Captain Enrique Crosa, were the most experienced pilots specializing in the Fokker and Fairchild aircraft. Both Jackson and Crosa would play a role in the aftermath of the accident, the former piloting FAU 570 as part of the initial search and rescue efforts, and the latter representing the FAU in the burial party that went to the mountain in January 1973.

Julio Ferradás

The copilot for the *Old Christians* flight was 41-year-old Lieutenant Colonel **Dante Lagurara,** who had around 2,000 flight hours under his belt, 500 of them in the F-27 and FH-27 cockpits. He had originally been a fighter pilot, and had been involved in a dramatic incident on 10th February 1963, in a practice session for an aerobatic display to

Dante Lagurara

celebrate the FAU's fiftieth anniversary. The team consisted of four Lockheed F-80s flying in diamond formation over the Lagomar beach resort, a few kilometres east of Carrasco. As the formation rolled left, the number 3 and 4 planes – piloted respectively by Lagurara and Lieutenant Gregorio Abella – came into contact, and plummeted to the ground. Both pilots were able to eject, but Abella, too close to the ground when his parachute activated, died on impact. To compound the disaster, Abella's plane crashed into a nearby holiday villa, killing a young girl who had just gone inside to fetch a coat whilst her grandfather waited outside. Lagurara, on the other hand, escaped unscathed, and was found hanging from a eucalyptus tree in his parachute harness. At the time of the *Old Christians* flight, Lagurara was married, with a baby girl, Valeria.

Joining the pilots was navigator First Lieutenant **Ramón Martínez**, aged 31, and married with no children. He had qualified in 1963, and had 1,700 flying hours. In the FAU, the role of navigating officer was multi-faceted, and included administrative tasks such as aircraft dispatch, passenger and baggage control, and even last-minute ticket sales. Some might participate in navigational tasks in the cockpit, but the ultimate responsibility for flight navigation rested entirely on the pilots' shoulders.

Ramón Martínez

The crew also included a technical specialist, **Carlos Roque**, who had worked as a mechanic for four years on C-47, Fokker, and Fairchild aircraft. Roque was only on

the flight through an act of kindness. He had just returned from another charter flight, carrying a group of retirees to Asunción in Paraguay, and to the Iguazú falls. The trip had included a visit to an indigenous Paraguayan community – the Maká people – in a reserve on the Paraguay river. By rights, Carlos Roque was not required to go on the next charter flight, but he stood in for a

Carlos Roque colleague who didn't want to miss his child's birthday party. Carlos, 24, was married with a young son Alejandro, just eighteen months old.

The final member of the crew was the steward – **Ovidio Joaquin Ramírez** – who was 26 and married, with two young boys, Juan Federico and Luis Alberto, the latter born just four months before the trip.

Ovidio Ramírez

As the passengers filed into the plane, they turned to the left, passing the lavatory compartment on one side and a small galley on the other, before entering through a doorway into the passenger cabin. The FAU configuration of the Fairchild for passenger use had twelve rows of four seats, a pair on each side of a central aisle, for a total of 48 seats. The seats were covered with a greenish-blue woven fabric, which would later be repurposed in the Andes for use as blankets, with the white antimacassars serving as bandages. The eleven windows on each side didn't align exactly with the seating, but they provided a clear view of the scenery below, unobstructed by the overhead wings.

A twelfth window on the right-hand side looked into the cargo area, which was reached from the main cabin via a door in the plastic wood-veneer bulkhead. The compartment had cargo nets on both sides, which would later serve as hammocks for the wounded;

and at the front left was the crew entrance, embedded in a larger cargo door. The pilot's cabin, with its flight deck slightly raised relative to the passenger deck, was through another door at the front of the cargo area.

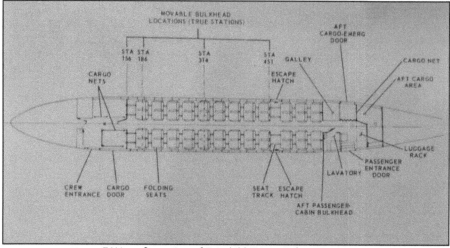

Fig. 37. *FAU configuration of Fairchild FH-227D for passenger use.*

Fig. 38. *Pilot's seat and main cabin of a Fairchild FH-227.*

The older passengers sat near each other, towards the front of the plane, introducing themselves, and getting to know one another. Behind them, the gang, augmented by Moncho Sabella and Rafael Echavarren, commandeered two rows of seats. A famous photo shows Coco Nicolich in the aisle, with his arm around Roy Harley, who is seated. Moncho and Rafael are across the aisle, with Bobby François and Carlitos Páez in the row behind. Further back, Coche Inciarte is seen sitting on the right of the photo, and Gastón Costemalle can be seen lighting Fito Strauch's cigarette. Standing in the aisle at the back, Álvaro Mangino faces the camera, and, at the front right, a bearded Julio Martínez Lamas surveys the scene.

Fig. 39. *A painting of a famous photo taken aboard the Fairchild. The artist is Fabián Varietti. The painting is owned by and displayed in the Museo Andes 1972.*

Not seen in the photo, Tintín Vizintín and Pancho Delgado were sitting in the very back row, having met that day for the first time. Nearby were Pancho's friends from the faculty – Numa Turcatti and Juan Carlos Menéndez. But the seating arrangement was not static; boys were standing up and moving around, chatting, joking, reading comics, and playing cards. At one point, some of the boys tried to rock the plane, by all piling onto one side, until they were severely reprimanded by the pilots.

There was an air of excitement, and a sense of freedom, about being away from home for a few days. There were animated conversations about the good time they'd have in

Chile, playing rugby, eating and drinking wine at some of fine restaurants in Santiago, or meeting and dancing with the pretty and *simpatica* Chilean girls. Aware of the temptations that might come their way, Gustavo Zerbino had confided to a Jesuit priest friend before leaving: "I'll go to Chile and behave well; that'll be my challenge." Gustavo was one of several who planned to rent a car, to go sightseeing in the coastal city of Valparaiso and the nearby resort of Viña del Mar, or to visit *El Portillo* ski resort, where a few would experience snow for the first time.

As the plane approached the Andes, the steward appeared in the passenger cabin, and announced that they were going to make an unexpected stop, due to conditions of severe turbulence and icing over the *Cordillera*. They made a bumpy landing at Mendoza's *El Plumerillo* airport. At first, the passengers thought that it would just be a short layover; perhaps an hour or so. Some passengers headed to the airport bar to enjoy a glass of wine, while others just milled around, waiting to see what was going to happen. The crew told them not to leave the airport, as their documents had to be processed.

The weather seemed fine in Mendoza, but the pilots explained that the Andes had a climate of its own, and that crossing in the afternoon could be dangerous, due to the treacherous currents created by the hot and cool air meeting. Eventually, to the disappointment of the boys, they were told that they would have to wait until the next day to cross the Andes. Not only would they have one less day in Chile, they would also miss the party that their hosts had arranged for them. The pilots told them to be back at the airport the next day at 1:00 p.m., which struck the boys as odd, given the earlier caution about an afternoon crossing of the *Cordillera*.

The pilots allowed the passengers to fetch overnight items from their luggage on the plane, before disappearing and leaving them to make their own arrangements. Realizing reluctantly that they would need Argentinian cash for food and transport, some took the opportunity to exchange money in the airport; others waited until they got into town, a few kilometres to the south-west.

The passengers split into small groups to get rides into town. Some of the boys hitchhiked. Moncho Sabella spotted a truck driven by someone his father knew from Montevideo, who agreed to take them into the centre. Others took taxis. Some passengers were taken, at no charge, to the door of the *Hotel Sussex* – an upmarket hotel in the heart of Mendoza.

Fig. 40. *The passengers at El Plumerillo airport, Mendoza.*

Above: *Canessa, Inciarte, Shaw, E. Strauch, Mangino, Fernández, Platero, Harley, Nicolich, Echavarren, Sabella, Páez, Storm, François, Parrado, Maspons, Menéndez, Algorta, Maquirriáin, Turcatti, Martínez Lamas.*
Below: *Nogueira, Pérez, Hounie, Magri, Zerbino, Abal, Vázquez, Vizintín, Valeta, Costemalle, Delgado, A. Strauch.*
Left: *Liliana Methol and Esther Horta chatting with Zenia Parrado (back to the camera).*

Mendoza is the capital city of the Argentinian province of the same name. Founded in the sixteenth century, it became, in the early nineteenth century, the headquarters of General San Martín, national hero and liberator of Argentina, Chile and Peru. Rather neatly, S. Martín is an anagram of Main Str., and there must be few towns in Argentina that don't have a major avenue bearing his name. That is certainly the case in Mendoza, where Avenida San Martín is the main shopping street. He also gives his name to the large park west of the downtown area, laid out at the end of the nineteenth century by the same landscape architect, Carlos Thays, who would design Carrasco twenty years later. To the west of the park, a road leads up to *Cerro de La Gloria*; a prominent hill with views over the city, where the imposing monument commemorating General San Martín's Army of the Andes is a popular tourist stop.

Fig. 41. **Left**: *Army of the Andes monument on the Cerro de la Gloria*. **Right**: *Plaza San Martín*.

In 1861, Mendoza suffered a major earthquake, which destroyed most of the buildings and killed several thousand people. The city was rebuilt from the ground up, with wide avenues and beautiful squares laid out in a pleasing urban design, the four lesser squares – *Plaza Chile, Plaza San Martín, Plaza España*, and *Plaza Italia* – symmetrically bounding the large central *Plaza Independencia*. The abundant trees that shade the squares and line the streets are irrigated by water channels, fed by melting snow from the Andes, making Mendoza a green oasis in the arid land east of the *Cordillera*. The city exudes an air of self-confidence and well-being, the numerous outdoor cafés and restaurants alive with locals, and with tourists visiting this national wine centre. Nowadays, there is also a steady stream of mountain adventurers, preparing or returning from their attempts to climb *Aconcagua* – at almost 7,000 metres, the tallest mountain in the Americas, and a rite of passage to the 8000-metre Himalayan peaks.

Despite their irritation at the loss of a day, the passengers, arriving in the centre of Mendoza on Thursday 12th October 1972, must have been pleasantly surprised at the beauty and vibrancy of the city, which showed no hint of the riots which had blighted it earlier that year. In protest against a 300% increase in electricity rates, workers and students had taken over the streets in a four-day standoff, which had ended in the death of three civilians, and the ultimate rescindment of the rate hike.

The *Hotel Sussex* at 250 Avenida Sarmiento, where many of the passengers were dropped off, was half a block from *Plaza Independencia*, right at the heart of the downtown area. It was one of a chain of luxury hotels in central and western Argentina, several of which – including the one in Mendoza – had an inhouse casino. Converted these days to an office building, *Edificio Sarmiento*, on what is now a pedestrian way, the *Sussex* was, at the time, one of the more expensive hotels in Mendoza. The passengers who could afford it, mainly the older passengers, checked in there – Dr and Mrs Nicola, Javier and Liliana Methol, Graziela Augusto, the Parrado family, and Panchito Abal, who shared a room with his friend Nando.

But the others who were dropped off there – Gustavo Zerbino, Coche Inciarte, Gastón Costemalle, Pancho Delgado, Numa Turcatti, Juan Carlos Menéndez, Daniel Fernández, Eduardo and Fito Strauch, and Daniel Shaw – went looking for a cheaper hotel. Stopping to eat at an Italian restaurant – which turned out to be more expensive than they'd anticipated – they asked the owner if he knew of a cheap hotel. He told them that

Fig. 42. *Ex-Hotel Sussex, now Edificio Sarmiento.*

they were about to open a *pensión* next door, in a former governor's house that had been converted to accommodate guests. They would allow them to stay there for 1000 pesos for the night; a third of the price of other hotels. The boys were joined at the *pensión* by Marcelo Pérez del Castillo, Julio Martínez Lamas, and Álvaro Mangino, and later by Guido Magri who, being short of cash due to his last-minute participation in the trip, switched hotels on discovering how cheap it was.

The *pensión* was the former house of governor Francisco Gabrielli, on the corner of Godoy Cruz and Patricias Mendocinas Street. The boys stayed on the upper floor, sleeping six or seven to a room. It is likely that the Italian restaurant where they had lunch was the long-vanished *O Sole Mio*, next door at 1642 Patricias Mendocinas.

Fig. 43. *'Casa de la Gobernador': former house of governor Francisco Gabrielli.*

Another group of boys – the extended gang – called around various hotels and made a reservation at the *Hotel San Remo*, also on Avenida Godoy Cruz; a hotel that exists to this day. Stopping for lunch before going to the hotel, they chanced upon a restaurant with a Uruguayan owner, the *Avenida* at Avenida San Martín 924. Emotional at seeing a large group of compatriots, he plied them with food and wine, whilst relating his life story. He refused to charge them, and sent them away with discount coupons to distribute to their fellow passengers. Tipsy from the wine, the boys leisurely made their way to the hotel, flirting with any girl unwise enough to cross their path. The *San Remo*, although hardly luxurious, was at least clean, and the rooms had private bathrooms. They split up into pairs to share the four rooms: on one floor, Bobby François with Moncho Sabella, and Alexis Hounie with Rafael Echavarren; on another floor, Roy Harley with Carlitos Páez, and Coco Nicolich with Diego Storm. They then settled down to a long siesta, to sleep off the effects of the food and wine.

A fourth group stopped at several hotels before choosing the *Hotel Horizonte* at 565 Gutiérrez street, 50 metres from *Plaza Chile*. Here, each room accommodated three boys: Pedro Algorta and Felipe Maquirriain shared with their former *Stella Maris* classmate Enrique Platero; Roberto Canessa roomed with his two friends Daniel Maspons and Fernando Vázquez; and Tintín Vizintín, Arturo Nogueira, and Carlos Valeta were in a third room. In later years, the hotel became a nursing home for elderly people, before being converted back to a guest house in 2003 as the *Hostel Malbec Plaza*.

Fig. 44. **Left**: *Hotel San Remo.*   **Right**: *Ex-Hotel Horizonte.*

Whilst the stopover in Mendoza was an annoyance for most of the passengers, it was an unexpected joy for Esther Nicola – an opportunity to visit her sister, Adela. The two siblings, each with four children, were very close. Adela's husband, Alberto Koninckx, was a biologist who, in 1970, had been offered a research position in Mendoza. For a year, he had lived away from his family, and on the couple of occasions that Adela had visited her husband, her four children would stay with Esther, joining their four cousins. By 1971, it was clear that this would be a long-term position for Alberto, and the whole family moved to the city, settling three or four kilometres north of the town centre.

Esther hadn't seen her sister since the move, so after checking into the *Sussex*, she and Pancho headed to Adela's house, hoping they'd be at home due to the national holiday. No-one answered the door when they arrived, but they spoke to a neighbour, who directed them back towards town to the local sports club – the Pacific club on Perú street – where the parents had gone to play tennis, and the children to roller-skate. After an emotional reunion, they made plans for the day. Adela wanted to show Esther some

85

of the nice places they had visited since moving to the city, so after arranging to leave the children at home, the two sisters and their husbands headed into the foothills north of Mendoza, to visit the thermal springs at Villavicencio. Later, back home with the children, they enjoyed a dinner prepared in their honour by their neighbours, and chatted long into the evening. To wrap up the day, Alberto and Adela drove the Nicolas back to the hotel via the *Parque General San Martín*, where they enjoyed a stroll through the lakeside rose garden.

Meanwhile, after lunch and siesta, the other passengers were making their own explorations of the city. Eugenia and Susy Parrado headed from the *Hotel Sussex* to the nearby Avenida San Martín, to do some shopping. Nando and Panchito went to see some stock car races on the outskirts of the city, and Graziela Augusto joined Javier and Liliana Methol in taking a bus to the *Cerro de la Gloria*, to see the monument and the view over the city. The destination was a popular one. Bobby, Moncho, Alexis, and Rafael took a taxi there after waking from their siesta, and Daniel Shaw and Daniel Fernández visited later in the evening, one stop on a tour of the city given by a local lady whom Shaw had befriended.

The two Daniels had, like the others in the *La Casa del Gobernador*, slept from 3:00 to 7:00 p.m. before going out walking in the town, where they had unexpectedly bumped into Guido Magri's aunt and uncle, Ana María and Adolfo Gelsi, who coincidentally were attending a conference in the city. The couple had been among the founders of the Uruguayan branch of the *Movimiento Familiar Cristiano*; an international Christian family movement that was also strong in Argentina, and possibly the focus of their visit to Mendoza. Fito Strauch and Coche Inciarte also came across the Gelsi couple and stopped to chat. The two boys were being shown around town by two Mendocinian girls – Lita Muñoz and Marta – whom they had met outside the tourist office on Avenida San Martín. Later, as the four of them were chatting idly at *La Casa de mi Abuela* coffee shop on Patricias Mendocinas street, Lita was suddenly hit by a strong premonition that the plane would crash. She kept silent about it.

In the evening, most of the other boys went out walking in groups, or sat drinking and chatting in one or other of the many cafés and bars. The two Daniels made use of the discount coupons that Carlitos Páez had given them for the *Avenida*, but several of the boys went without dinner, not wanting to waste their money in the expensive Argentinian restaurants.

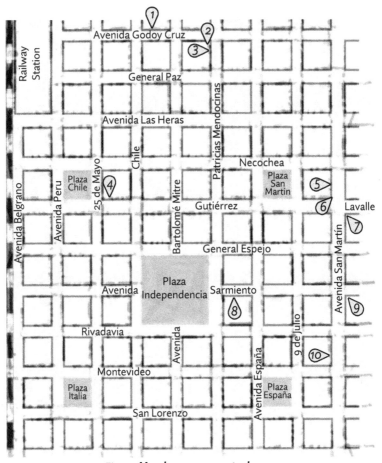

Fig. 45. *Mendoza 1972, central area.*

1. Hotel San Remo.
2. Casa de la Gobernador.
3. Restaurante O Sole Mio.
4. Hotel Horizonte.
5. Creaciones DAISY.
6. Streetcorner photograph.
7. Farmacia del Águila.
8. Hotel Sussex.
9. Edificio Gómez.
10. Restaurante Avenida.

In one bar, the boys met a group of girls from Concepción del Uruguay – an Argentinian town just across the River Uruguay from Paysandú. Some, such as Gustavo Zerbino, went dancing with them into the early hours of the morning. Others, such as Eduardo Strauch, Pancho Delgado, and Gastón Costemalle, just chatted over drinks, and had an early night. Pedro Algorta – who knew Mendoza quite well, having passed through it many times by train or car on his way to Chile – spent an enjoyable time dancing with one Argentinian girl, until his introduction of politics into the conversation put a rapid end to the evening. Tintín went out walking with Numa Turcatti and Juan Carlos Menéndez. They met and paired up with three Mendocinian girls and went sight-seeing with them throughout the city. Later, they treated the girls to dinner, finally getting back to their hotels at around 2:00 a.m.

Some briefly went to a dance on the roof-terrace of the iconic 13-floor *Edificio Gómez* building – the home of the local affiliate of the national Channel 13 TV station – before continuing on around the town. Moncho, arriving back at around 4:00 a.m. without a key, had to wake the owner, and also managed to wake his roommate Bobby, who had returned much earlier after exploring the city with Coco, Diego, and Alexis.

Marcelo, Julio, and Álvaro, after their siesta, took a bus around Mendoza, and stopped off to see the stock car races. Arriving late, they returned to the centre and strolled around, joining up with Panchito Abal and Nando Parrado to see the recently-released *What's up, Doc?* in one of the many cinemas near the intersection of Lavalle and Avenida San Martín. After the movie, they ate, and then returned to their hotels. Meanwhile, Nando's mother and sister met up for dinner with the Methols and Graziela Augusto.

At a time when international calls were prohibitively expensive, not many phone calls were made from Mendoza that evening. Guido Magri called his *novia* Angeles Mardones, who had been waiting in vain at *Los Cerrillos* airport in Santiago earlier that day; they reflected on the short distance – less than 200 km – that now separated them. Numa Turcatti called his older brother, who exhorted him to take special care of the camera he had lent him. And Graziela telephoned her husband late in the evening, to tell him that she was stuck in Mendoza, that everything was fine, and that everyone was happy. No-one in Carrasco received a phone call, so when the first news filtered through about the accident, there was widespread disbelief that it was the boys' plane, due to the assumption that they'd arrived in Chile the previous day.

On the next morning, the day of the accident, there was time to kill before heading out to the airport. Felipe Maquirriain and Pedro Algorta took the opportunity to visit the faculty of Economic Sciences at the local university – the *Universidad Nacional de Cuyo*, located at the north-west corner of *Parque General San Martín*. Arriving at around 11:00 a.m., they were greeted by Professor José Alberto Mora of the Economic Resources and Human and Industrial Relations department. Writing a letter of condolence to their parents three days later, Professor Mora remembered their short visit:

> They were aware of the existence in Mendoza of a Faculty of Economic Sciences, part of the National University of Cuyo, and they arrived there at around 11 o'clock on Friday morning. In my capacity as Head of Public Relations, I was happy to show them the facilities currently in operation as well as the soon-to-be-opened teaching area. They were impressed by the size and comfort of our buildings. They continually compared it with Montevideo and were very interested in the details of our curricula...

Mora went on to describe the tour of the facilities and the possibilities of collaboration that Pedro had raised. The tour was cut short by the need to leave for the airport, and the professor drove them himself:

> On the way, we made a detour so that they could see the Civic Quarter. José Pedro told me that, although somewhat 'peripheral', they were rugby players, so, with the prospect of remaining in Mendoza in the event of the trip being cancelled, I undertook to put them in touch with friends, and even, on the evening of that day, to invite them to a big party that the Mendoza Rugby Club was giving in an elegant "boîte" on the outskirts of the city. They planned, in case the flight to Chile was cancelled, not to return to Montevideo by plane but to stay a few days in Mendoza and even make a trip to San Juan. When I finally left them at the airport at 12.30 p.m., I think we all shared the exhilarating feeling that a friendship had been born between us.

The boys who had stayed at *La Casa del Gobernador* headed to Avenida San Martín in the morning and seated themselves at an outdoor café where they breakfasted on apple and banana juice, peaches, croissants, and coffee. As they were eating, the pilots walked by, uncertain still as to whether they were going to continue on to Chile, or return to Montevideo. Gustavo Zerbino jested with them, telling them that they had to cross the Andes at any cost. As the morning progressed, boys from other hotels started appearing, and many of them queued up to change a small amount of money for breakfast and for the bus to the airport. Some of the boys posed for a group photo – a poignant snapshot taken just hours before the impending disaster. Three of them would be dead before the end of the day, and only three would still be alive seventy-two days later, when they were finally rescued from the mountain.

Fig. 46. *Guido Magri, Numa Turcatti, Coche Inciarte, Gustavo Zerbino, Enrique Platero, Álvaro Mangino, Julio Martínez Lamas, and Carlos Valeta at corner of Av. San Martín and Gutiérrez St.*

In the background of the photo can be seen the *Farmacia del Águila,* which marks its location as the corner of Avenida San Martín and Gutiérrez street. The Parrados must have been close by, as they, along with Panchito Abal, stopped at the pharmacy that morning to buy a long list of supplies, several of which were difficult to get in Uruguay at the time, and some of which would prove to be essential on the mountain. The toothpaste in particular would serve as a dessert – a welcome variety in taste that Eduardo Strauch would later describe as "better than caviar". The Parrados also stopped at a shoe store – *Creaciones DAISY* – half a block from the pharmacy, where Nando bought some little red shoes for his two-year-old nephew Gaston. The shoes would feature – most prominently in the movie *Alive* – in a much-related anecdote in which Nando split up the pair before setting off on the final expedition. Taking one with him and leaving the other at the fuselage, he told the boys, "When I come back for you, we'll have a pair again."

The boys at the *Hotel San Remo*, several of whom hadn't gone to bed until the early hours, got up at around 11:00 a.m. They packed and settled the hotel bill before heading out for breakfast – their last meal before boarding. Rafael Echavarren, a cheese aficionado, bought a large chunk of Roquefort, from which they made sandwiches. After eating their fill, they headed to a nearby taxi rank, drinking beer as they walked. Roy Harley, wanting to use up his spare Argentinian money, stopped along the way to buy some chocolate and several 6-inch slabs of *turrón* (nougat) as a gift for his brothers and sisters. The confectionary that he and other passengers bought that morning would help stave off hunger during the first few days on the mountain.

Of the other boys at the *Horizonte*, Tintín rose at around 10:00 p.m. and joined Roberto Canessa, Daniel Maspons, and Fernando Vázquez in walking around town. When the others decided to have a full lunch, Tintín opted for just a sandwich and a Coca Cola, as he was saving his appetite for the seafood restaurants of Santiago. After eating, he took a bus to the airport, where other passengers were starting to arrive in groups. As organizers of the trip, Marcelo and Julio, together with Álvaro and Enrique, were amongst the earliest to make an appearance. Gustavo Zerbino and others who had breakfasted on Avenida San Martín arrived later, by bus, having stopped off to see an exhibition. The Parrados and Panchito Abal turned up by taxi at around noon, and the Methols also arrived early with Graziela Augusto, having eaten sandwiches in town. Adela and Alberto Koninckx picked up the Nicolas at the *Sussex* and drove them to the terminal, waiting with them to see if the flight would go ahead.

In fact, nothing much was happening at the airport. The passengers could see the plane parked a couple of hundred meters from the terminal, but none of the airport staff were around to check their papers, and the pilots had not yet arrived. With time to kill, the gang, a bit tipsy from the beer they had bought, amused themselves by checking their weight on the airport scales. Another distraction was the presence of a jovial, plump lady, dressed in a carnival-like manner with a voluminous skirt, multi-coloured stockings, and a small hat. Felipe Maquirriain discreetly drew a perfect caricature, which Gustavo Zerbino couldn't resist presenting to her. She was delighted, and insisted on a photo with the boys. When she told them that she was the godmother

Fig. 47. *Prior to boarding at El Plumerillo, 13th Oct. 1972. Coche Inciarte, Lita Muñoz, and Fito Strauch.*

of the pilots, they all claimed to be pilots in training, laughing and making horns with their fingers as they posed for the photo, with her at the centre.

Marta and Lita, the two girls who had shown Fito and Coche around town, turned up unexpectedly to see them off. They chatted with them and the other boys who had stayed at *La Casa del Gobernador*, whilst waiting for the pilots to arrive. Pancho Delgado jokingly invited them to accompany the group to Chile. Lita, mindful of the strong premonition she had had the day before, replied, half in jest, "No way! The plane is going to crash." Later, Lita was wracked with guilt over her silence about the premonition. During the seventy-two days that they were missing, she corresponded with Coche's family and with his fiancée Soledad, encouraging them to keep up their hopes. Like Soledad, and many of the *novias* and mothers in Carrasco, she was convinced that the boys were alive, and made a weekly pilgrimage to the sanctuary of Our Lady of Lourdes in nearby El Challao, to pray for their rescue.

Fig. 48. *Just before departure on 13 October.*
Foreground: *Javier, Esther, and Liliana.*
Back left: *Daniel Shaw, and Susy (in fur-lined coat).*
Back right: *Fito, Eduardo, and Daniel Fernández.*

When the pilots arrived at around 1:00 p.m., they were still doubtful whether conditions were safe enough to cross the *Cordillera*. They spoke to the pilot of a LAN-Chile cargo plane that had arrived in Mendoza and was on its way to Santiago. Experienced in crossing the Andes, his assessment was that there should be no problem for the Fairchild, with its modern navigation equipment. He was planning on taking the direct route over the *Cristo Redentor* pass, flying at an altitude of 26,000 ft, an option not open to the Fairchild FH-227 under the current meteorological conditions. Eventually, to cheers from the boys, the pilots decided to go ahead, submitting a flight plan that would take them on a longer but lower altitude route: 300 km south to Malargüe, then west across the Planchón pass to Curicó at an altitude of 18,000 ft, and finally north again to *Los Cerrillos* airport in Santiago. With the decision made, the passengers had their papers checked, and started boarding the Fairchild, which the pilots had taxied over to the front of the terminal building.

Several of the passengers had strong forebodings that the plane would crash. Gustavo Zerbino spoke to Esther Horta about his own misgivings, telling her that he was reluctant to board. He was looking for reassurance, but she told him that she had been having the same thoughts. Earlier, she had approached the pilot, telling him that she had four children at home, and that she wanted to get back safe and sound; she pleaded with them not to fly if conditions weren't right. The pilots reassured her. Adding to Esther's worries was the fact that it was now Friday 13th; a date on which she would never have planned to fly. Javier Methol told her not to worry, that for him, thirteen was a lucky number. Esther was not convinced, and took a sedative to calm her anxiety. When going up the steps to the plane, Pancho Delgado also had a strong premonition of impending disaster. He sat down in the back row, believing it to be the safest place in the event of an accident.

Fig. 49. *Col. Julio Ferradás in front of the Fairchild in Mendoza on the morning of the accident.*

As the boys waited in their seats, they saw the pilots approach the plane, and board with a large stash of wine; almost more than they could carry. There were laughs and whistles, and shouts of "Drunkards!" and "Smugglers!" The pilots took it good-humouredly. They stowed the wine in a compartment behind the copilot's seat, to be forgotten about until the boys would discover it several days later. They then started their pre-flight checks. As Ferradás was feeling a bit sick, Lagurara took command of the plane, which took off at 14:18 local time, 17:18 GMT – seventy-three minutes from disaster.

THE ACCIDENT

As the plane flew south towards Malargüe, the boys on the right-hand side had a spectacular view of the continuous wall of mountain peaks breaking through the clouds. Most prominent amongst them were the 6,960-metre *Aconcagua* – slightly behind them; and the 6,570-metre *Tupungato* volcano, into which a British South American Airways Avro Lancastrian, the *Star Dust*, crashed in 1947, famously leaving an enigmatic last radio transmission, its fate and whereabouts undiscovered for more than 50 years. Roberto Canessa, who had had a choice of seats when he boarded, rued the fact that he had chosen the left-hand side and was missing out on the sights; but he would have reason to be grateful later, as it was those on the right who would suffer the bulk of the fatalities, and the worst injuries.

As on the first leg, there was a lively atmosphere on the plane, with the boys laughing and joking, swapping places so as to get a better view, and walking up and down the aisle to chat with their friends or fetch a drink from the galley. Many of the boys had never seen snow-covered mountains before. The passengers were even allowed up to the pilot's cabin, two at a time, to see the instruments and the view from the cockpit. At 17:38 GMT, the pilots reported their first checkpoint – Chilecito – as required by the Instrument Flight Rules plan that they had filed. As they were approaching the next checkpoint of Malargüe, the pilot pointed out the salt flats below – perhaps the *Salinas del Diamante* – and visibility was good enough for the passengers to make out the tractor tracks against the white expanse.

At 18:08 GMT, aided by a tail wind of 20 knots, the pilot reported reaching Malargüe, and turned west towards Curicó. Flying at 18,000 ft, the Fairchild was now heading almost directly into a headwind estimated at 30 to 40 knots. Although it was cloudier over the mountains, visibility remained good, and passengers experienced no turbulence. Tintín stood in the galley, chatting with the steward, having temporarily given up his seat to allow two of the boys to play a game of *Truco* with the mechanic and the navigator. Once the game was over, he sat back down in his original seat, but the navigator soon asked the four boys in the back row to move forward, to better redistribute the weight in the plane. Momentarily annoyed that he had to give up his window seat, Tintín moved forward through the cabin, and to his surprise, found the right-hand pair of seats in the very front row unoccupied. He sat down there, across from Graziela Augusto, who was also sitting alone.

At 18:21 GMT, Ferradás established contact with the *Pudahuel* Air Traffic Control tower in Santiago. He reported being over Planchón – the approximate midpoint of the crossing between Malargüe and Curicó. With no beacon at Planchón, there wasn't a sure way to confirm the exact position of the Fairchild, and in fact it was some distance short of the checkpoint. Ferradás estimated Curicó at 18:32, but three minutes later, at 18:24, he inexplicably reported being over Curicó, and, with the authorization of *Pudahuel* to start a descent from 18,000 to 10,000 feet, Lagurara turned north towards Santiago. As the plane turned, the passengers could tell by the sound of the engines that it had started to decelerate. And whereas the flight up to that point had been completely smooth with good visibility, they now entered the clouds, and the plane started to shake. Gastón Costemalle gave the passengers a momentary scare, using the microphone at the back of the plane to announce: "Attention everyone! Please put on your parachutes, the plane has developed a fault and we're going to have to jump."

A short while later, the steward came out of the pilot's cabin, where he had been collecting the pilots' *maté*, and told them to fasten their seatbelts, saying, "Ahora viene lo bravo" – now comes the rough part. The passengers who were standing up sat down where they could, and fastened their belts. Their arbitrary choice of seat, made in an instance, sealed their fate. With everyone seated, the atmosphere became more muted in the plane, with people chatting quietly or reading. Eugenia Parrado, wearing her glasses, was engrossed in a book – possibly *Mujer Piloto* by Robert J Serling, which was found later in the plane; Guido Magri was reading a popular Argentinian comic magazine, *Patoruzú*; and Pedro Algorta was also leafing through a comic book – *Isidorito* –the Adventures of an Argentinian Playboy.

Soon after it turned, the plane was spotted from the ground below by a miner named Camilo Figueroa. He observed a white plane with broad wings slightly descending between the clouds on a north-westerly course. He was near a remote pass – *Paso El Tiburcio* – a few kilometres north-east of Planchón.

When the first air pocket hit, a chant of *Conga Conga Conga* arose from the front of the cabin, and the boys started throwing around a rugby ball in a show of bravado. Further back, shouts of *Olé, Olé* accompanied every bump. Pedro joined in, but he suddenly had no more appetite for his comic book, and handed it to Coche, across the aisle from him. Behind Pedro, Pancho Delgado was nervously remembering his feeling of dread when boarding the plane. Across the aisle from Pancho, Nando Parrado and Panchito Abal were engrossed in a conversation about a new business idea, selling fibre-based cleaning cloths in the interior of the country. Nando, an experienced flyer, took no notice of the air pocket, and carried on chatting, not even bothering to fasten his seatbelt.

Further forward, Roy Harley, who had never flown before, was wondering to himself if this violent buffeting of the plane was normal, and instinctively tightened his

95

seatbelt. Around the same time, an unknown namesake Charles Harley – an Englishman from Chesterfield Road in Barnet – was struggling through the deep snow of the Tinguiririca valley below. Although the poor conditions didn't allow him to see or hear the Fairchild pass by, his story, outlined in a letter to the *Observer* after the book *ALIVE* appeared, sets an atmospheric scene.

> On that Friday 13th October, I resumed an attempt to walk as far as possible a smugglers' and cattle drovers' track, which, roughly following the Tinguiririca river valley, eventually crosses from Chile into Argentina near Paso de las Damas. In the afternoon, walking then near to my knees in snow, I broke from the track, which there clings to the edge of the tree line, to climb a bluff on the slopes of the peak Aguilas del Chivato to obtain a clear view of the terrain ahead. From a high platform of rock I saw how the path, emerging from the burned-out oaks, continued through an ascending ravine, impassably under snow. I decided to call it a day.

> By then very tired, having struggled to the rock through snow thigh deep, I rested, huddling on the rock in a wind quite warm, from 3:30 to 4:00, regretting that I would not have opportunity to return that way later in Spring, when the snows would surely have melted. While I was resting, low cloud, driving over from the Argentine side of the mountains, hid several of the landscape features I had noted for compass reference...

> Given that few visit those rugged, glacial parts of the Andes in October, I wonder whether I ... was the closest potential witness to the crash.

In the clouds above the east end of the Tinguiririca valley where Charles Harley was huddling on the rock, the Fairchild was less than four minutes from disaster. Soon after, a second air pocket caused the plane to plummet even deeper than the first. As it dropped out of the clouds, the passengers saw that they were flying in a canyon with mountains to either side of them. Everyone suddenly fell silent, incredulous as to what they were seeing.

In the cockpit, Lagurara and Ferradás were desperately trying to recover the situation. Sitting in the jump-seat almost shoulder-to-shoulder with the pilots was Carlos Roque, the mechanic. Ahead of the three of them was a continuous 4,500 metre wall of snow and rock forming part of the high ridge of mountains separating Argentina and Chile. It was at a point where the ridge temporarily detours to the west, winding around a high valley before continuing north; a valley that would be the survivors' home for the next 72 days. As the plane approached the barrier ahead, the pilot aimed for a notch that was slightly lower, his only hope of avoiding a head-on collision. Frantically calling for more power, Lagurara pulled back on the stick, trying to ascend, in a desperate attempt to clear the ridge. The plane accelerated, but then started shuddering, as it approached its critical stall angle.

Back in the passenger cabin, everyone heard the cry for more power, and the sound of the engines straining at full throttle, and they were pressed back against their seats as the plane accelerated upwards. When the plane started shuddering, Tintín, sitting in the front row and seeking something firm to hold onto, grabbed the bottom of his seat. In the row behind, Javier Methol took hold of his wife's hand, and together they started to pray the *Our Father* out loud. Behind Javier, Roberto Canessa, who minutes earlier had been reassuring Esther

Fig. 50. *Approaching the impact point.*

Horta across the aisle about the buffeting of the plane, suddenly saw the rocks a few metres away; "¡Mira Chile!" he exclaimed, and prepared to die.

As the plane angled upwards, Roy Harley remembered a story Carlitos had told him about an incident in the Andes, involving a small plane. The pilot had come out of the clouds and, seeing a mountain right in front of him, had done a loop-the-loop to recover the situation. Roy momentarily wondered if the Fairchild's pilot was attempting a similar manoeuvre.

Throughout the cabin, people were bracing themselves for impact, cradling their heads in their hands, or holding onto the seat in front. After the initial burst of acceleration, the plane slowed and dropped down, the right wing hitting the ridge and separating from the fuselage, taking with it the roof and windows on the right-hand side, and severing the tail cone behind the passenger cabin. The force of the impact and sudden depressurisation tore some of the seats from their bearings, and out of the gaping hole at the back, flew the steward, the navigator and three of the boys – Alexis Hounie and Gastón Costemalle still strapped into their seats, and Guido Magri. A cloud of snow and frigid air filled the cabin as the belly of the fuselage hit the downward slope on the other side of the ridge, breaking off the left wing.

Incredibly, the fuselage stayed upright as it tobogganed down the mountainside, miraculously avoiding the jutting rocks, saved by that winter's unprecedented snowfall. The short time it took for the fuselage to travel the one-and-a-half kilometres to the bottom seemed like an eternity to the passengers. Expecting to die at any moment, the prayers and shouts of terror rose above the noise of the wind and of the fuselage hurtling through the snow. Some, like Roberto Canessa and Daniel Fernández, were quiet and philosophical, resigned to their fate. Tintín, believing that death was imminent, kept his eyes open in a desperate logic, telling himself that as long as he was seeing things, he wasn't yet dead. As the plane was sliding down, Gustavo Zerbino, anticipating everyone would be crushed by the seats when the fuselage finally came to a stop, took off his seatbelt and grabbed hold of the vertical stays supporting the luggage rack, bracing himself in the aisle. As he stood up, he saw first Daniel Shaw, and then Carlos Valeta, disappear out of the back of the plane.

As the slope levelled out, the fuselage, in another stroke of fate, hit a mound of snow on the glacier below, rather than continuing down the mountainside. It was enough to bring it to an abrupt halt, crushing the nose of the plane and the pilot's cabin, killing Ferradás immediately, and pinning Lagurara to his seat. In the passenger cabin, the sudden deceleration caused the seats, loosened by the impact, to pile forwards. Nando Parrado and Panchito Abal, still in their seats, were propelled from the back over everyone, and crashed against the front bulkhead. Panchito's head injury would prove to be fatal, and Nando wouldn't regain consciousness for another two days. In the cabin, there was a momentary hush before a shout of, "It's stopped, it's stopped!" broke the silence, soon followed by the cries of the injured, and the shouts for help emanating from the pile of seats and twisted metal. The fuselage had come to rest at a 45-degree slant to the right, and it was on that side that the passengers suffered the worst injuries, crushed by seats both from behind and from the left.

THE SEATING POSITIONS

Any attempt to reconstruct where everyone was seated at the point of the accident is complicated by conflicting statements, and by more recent memories inconsistent with the interviews of the time. It is possible, however, to build up a reasonably accurate picture from original statements – mainly from 1973 – summarised below, in which survivors recall whom they sat next to, or who was across the aisle or in the seat in front.

- Antonio Vizintín was sitting alone at the front right, having been asked to move from the back row. Graziela Augusto was across the aisle, also sitting by herself, at the front left.
- Javier Methol was sitting in the second row, to the left of the aisle, with Liliana by the window to his left; across the aisle were Esther Horta and Pancho Nicola.
- Roberto Canessa was sitting left of the aisle with Daniel Maspons to his left by the window, and Fernando Vázquez across the aisle. Roberto was chatting to Esther Horta across the aisle just before the accident, so this puts him in row three.
- The gang had commandeered two rows near the front of the plane, eight seats in all: Coco Nicolich was sitting next to Diego Storm in one pair of these seats, as Coco wrote in his letter to his *novia* before he died in the avalanche; Carlitos Páez was sitting on the right of the aisle next to the window, with Rafael Echavarren beside him, but they swapped positions before the accident; Roy Harley was sitting in the middle of the plane, to the left of the aisle, with Enrique Platero next to him; and Moncho Sabella was in the remaining pair of seats. Echavarren and Páez were in front of Moncho, and in front of them were Dr Nicola and his wife and Julio Martínez Lamas.
- Bobby François was sitting alone at the moment of the crash, towards the back left. Rafael Echavarren, who had been sitting next to him, had moved back to sit by Carlitos Páez before the seatbelt sign came on. The seat across the aisle from Bobby's was empty. Out of all the seats in the last few rows of the plane, his was the only one that stayed anchored, and when the fuselage came to an abrupt halt, he saw the seats slide forward past him, leaving nothing behind him.
- Gustavo Zerbino was sitting on the right-hand side, in the middle of the plane, under the wings. He and Álvaro Mangino separately claimed at the time that they were sitting next to each other at the moment of the accident. However, in *Sociedad de la Nieve*, written over 30 years later but based on detailed interviews with the survivors, Pablo Vierci writes: "Gustavo thought their heads would hit the roof of the plane. The stall alarm began to sound ... at which point Gustavo unfastened his seat belt, stood up, and held on with all his strength to the metal separators of the baggage compartments, to keep his balance. At that moment, the plane split in two, with a screeching metallic sound, and a gigantic gap opened up behind him; his seat flew out into the air, as did the adjacent seat where his friend Carlos Valeta had been sitting". It is unlikely that Carlos got sucked out of the plane at the point of impact; he was seen alive a few minutes later near the bottom of the slope. But we can take Gustavo's statement as evidence that Carlos was nearby him. Daniel Shaw, his seatbelt unfastened, was sitting across the aisle from Gustavo, and disappeared out of the back of the fuselage halfway down the slope.

- Daniel Fernández, by the aisle, and Fito Strauch, were sitting in the row behind Daniel Shaw. Earlier, Daniel Shaw had been asking to swap places with Fito, so that he could look at the mountains. Fito had been reluctant, and then the seatbelt sign had come on, and Daniel sat back down in his original seat.
- Eduardo Strauch was sitting further back from his cousins, on the right-hand side. He was by himself. He has a vague memory of Eugenia and Susana Parrado being nearby.
- Coche Inciarte was sitting left of the aisle, next to Juan Carlos Menéndez who was by the window; across the aisle from Coche were Pedro Algorta and Felipe Maquirriain. When the plane came to a halt, Coche looked back and saw nothing behind him.
- The four boys in the back row, who were asked to move further forward, were from left to right: Gastón Costemalle, Pancho Delgado, Numa Turcatti, and Antonio Vizintín.
- Having moved, Pancho Delgado was sitting next to Marcelo Pérez on the right. Coche was in the row in front of Pancho on the left.
- Nando Parrado was sitting next to Panchito Abal, about three rows from the back on the left-hand side. His mother and sister were a couple of rows forward of them, on the right-hand side. Guido Magri, Gastón Costemalle, and Alexis Hounie were nearby. In the accident, Panchito and Nando, still in their adjoining seats, were catapulted forwards to the front of the cabin. Roy Harley witnessed two seats flying over his head, and other seats were piling up behind him.
- Gastón Costemalle, after he moved, was sitting with Alexis Hounie, as their bodies were found next to each other on the mountain, still strapped into their adjoining seats.
- Guido Magri's body was also found nearby, although not in his seat.
- The navigator, Ramón Martínez, and the steward, Ovidio Ramírez, were in the back row, having asked the boys there to move forward. Martínez's body was still in its seat when found.
- Carlos Roque, the mechanic, was sitting on the jump-seat in the pilot's cabin.

These statements give an almost complete picture of where everyone was sitting, the only passenger unmentioned being Arturo Nogueira. It is important to note that there were no passengers or crew in the severed tail, which, as several photographs show, broke fairly cleanly behind the passenger cabin. And, despite the roof and fuselage wall on the right-hand side being ripped off from around row six, the floor was still intact much further back.

Whilst the back rows were the most severely impacted, with the sudden decompression ripping out the last row and at least one side of the penultimate row, almost all the seats broke loose from their bearings, and it was not just boys at the back who disappeared out of the back of the plane. And when the plane came to an abrupt halt, the momentum of the seats brought them all crashing forwards, destroying the bulkhead, and resulting in a dense, tangled pile at the front of the cabin. So, looking behind them, several of the boys had the sense of being in the last row before the break.

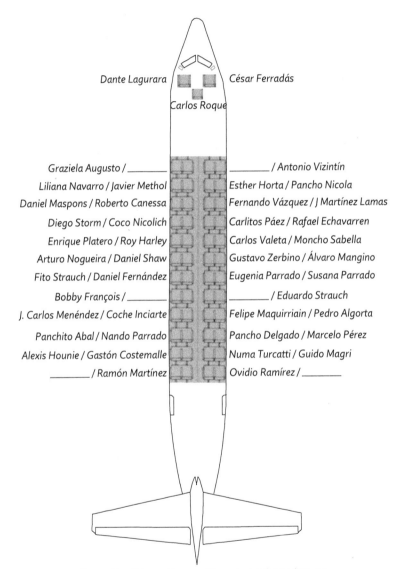

Dante Lagurara   César Ferradás

Carlos Roque

Graziela Augusto / _____   _____ / Antonio Vizintín
Liliana Navarro / Javier Methol   Esther Horta / Pancho Nicola
Daniel Maspons / Roberto Canessa   Fernando Vázquez / J Martínez Lamas
Diego Storm / Coco Nicolich   Carlitos Páez / Rafael Echavarren
Enrique Platero / Roy Harley   Carlos Valeta / Moncho Sabella
Arturo Nogueira / Daniel Shaw   Gustavo Zerbino / Álvaro Mangino
Fito Strauch / Daniel Fernández   Eugenia Parrado / Susana Parrado
Bobby François / _____   _____ / Eduardo Strauch
J. Carlos Menéndez / Coche Inciarte Felipe Maquirriain / Pedro Algorta
Panchito Abal / Nando Parrado   Pancho Delgado / Marcelo Pérez
Alexis Hounie / Gastón Costemalle   Numa Turcatti / Guido Magri
_____ / Ramón Martínez   Ovidio Ramírez / _____

Fig. 51. Possible seating positions just prior to impact.

MEDICAL TRIAGE

The first to take action after the fuselage came to a halt were two of the medical students – Roberto Canessa and Gustavo Zerbino – both of whom were uninjured and able to easily extract themselves. The pair set about freeing the other passengers. They were soon joined by Marcelo, who, sitting at the back, had escaped with relatively light injuries compared to those suffered by others on the right-hand side. Although in pain, Marcelo took care of organizing the work as the boys were freed one by one, whilst the two 'doctors' saw to the injured.

Roberto immediately checked on his two close friends: Daniel Maspons, who had been sitting next to him, was uninjured and easily freed; and Fernando Vázquez, who had been sitting across the aisle from him, had an injured leg, but was conscious and communicative, and seemed alright. Roberto left Fernando to attend to others, but an artery in his leg had been cut, and by the time Roberto returned, Fernando was dead.

The extended 'gang', sitting in the rows behind, were also remarkably free from injury – both those on the left and the right – only Rafael Echavarren had sustained a significant wound, and it didn't seem immediately life-threatening. The friends called out to one another, to check they were each still alive. Carlitos Páez had somehow landed over the seats of Coco Nicolich and Diego Storm. He asked them how they were, and they answered that they were fine, because he was there above them. He asked them to wait whilst he extracted himself from between two seats, which he eventually managed to do with some difficulty. Coco and Diego, another 'doctor', soon followed, their injuries relatively minor; Coco with a cut on his chin, and Diego with a bruised face. They immediately started helping Roberto and Gustavo.

Once Rafael was free from the seats, his friends saw that his trousers had been ripped to shreds, and his calf was hanging loose, separated from the bone. Rafael was more composed than all of them, refusing to complain, insisting it was merely a cut. He asked Gustavo what he could do about it. As an initial attempt at first aid, Gustavo put it back in place, disinfecting it with eau de Cologne, and wrapping it in a clean shirt. Terrible though the injury was, his friends believed that they would be rescued soon, at which point it could be properly seen to.

Unlike his friends, Moncho Sabella wasn't trapped in the pile-up at the front of the cabin. When his own seat had started sliding forward, Moncho had undone his seatbelt, and had been thrown clear. He found himself in the snow, completely uninjured. His first instinct was to try to speak to the pilot. Unable to reach the cockpit from the inside, due to the wreckage of the seats, he made the trip along the outside of the fuselage, using seat cushions as stepping stones over the deep snow. He found Ferradás dead, and Lagurara in great pain, with the control panel crushing his chest. Carlos Roque, who had been sitting further back in the jump seat, was nowhere to be seen, but appeared later in the main cabin, after some of the wreckage blocking the cockpit entrance had been cleared. Lagurara instructed Moncho how to set the radio's frequency to call for help, but he met with no success. Nevertheless, in order to keep everyone's spirits up, Moncho told them that he had made contact with Santiago. And, despite their desperate situation, no-one had any doubt that they would be rescued within a day or two. Later, others went to speak to Lagurara. Roberto tried to relieve the pressure on his chest by removing the seat cushion from behind his back, but it made little difference. Lagurara begged them to fetch his revolver, so that he could put an end to the pain, but even if they had been able to find it, they had no intention of giving it to him. Through all this, Lagurara kept repeating, "We passed Curicó, we passed Curicó." His words would have a lasting effect on the group's discussions and decisions over the following couple of months, orienting their whole thinking towards the west.

Roy Harley found himself with a metal bar in front of his neck, with his head pressed against the back of his seat. He managed to wriggle out to his waist, but he couldn't progress further, because his leg was trapped. Scared that the plane would start moving down the mountain again, or catch fire, he frantically tried to release his leg, and after several unsuccessful attempts, gave it a final tug, and broke free. He made his way back over a mass of seats, metal, and bodies, brushing away a hand that grabbed at his trousers, desperate to escape the fuselage and see what was outside. When he emerged at the back, he saw Bobby François sitting hunched on some suitcases in the snow, calmly smoking. "Hey Gordo[1], where are we?", Roy asked him. "I don't know," was Bobby's reply, "but we're here to stay." Bobby's seat had been one of the few to hold fast, and from his position near the back of the plane, he had watched the whole sequence of events unfold, as seats to the front and back of him slid forward, leaving

---

[1] Literally 'fatty', but widely used as a term of endearment in Uruguay for friends who are slightly on the chubbier side. Similarly *Flaco* ('skinny') is used for a thinner person. Both terms can also be given a feminine and/or diminutive ending: *Gorda, Gordito, Gordita,* and *Flaca, Flaquito, Flaquita.*

Bobby as the furthest back on either side. He had been the first to undo his seatbelt and hurry out of the plane, afraid that the fuselage might catch fire.

Carlitos had also made his way to the back. To his amazement, he saw that one of the handful of suitcases that had been scattered from the forward luggage compartment was his, the rest of them having been stored in the missing tail cone. He immediately opened it, taking out and putting on the boots which he had packed as a precaution. The clothes in the various suitcases were rapidly distributed, Roy putting on an extra pair of trousers and a rain jacket, and Moncho taking an extra sweater. Bobby François was given some trousers and a waistcoat, which he supplemented by stuffing insulation under his shirt.

One of the suitcases belonged to Álvaro Mangino, and he readily agreed to share out his own clothes. During the accident, Álvaro had been crouching with his feet on the seat in front of him, but his left leg had dropped down at the wrong moment, and the impact had driven his fibula into his knee cavity. Unable to walk, he was helped by Gustavo to the open

area at the rear of the fuselage, where the injured were being placed whilst work continued in the cabin. Although the roof and side had been ripped off from row six on the right-hand side, the floor extended back, creating an open 'porch' area, partially covered by the roof canopy on the left-hand side. It was here that Álvaro was left. He found himself next to Panchito Abal, who had

Fig. 52. *Right side of fuselage Jan 1973 after the rescue, with the 'back porch' on the left and the crushed nose cone on the right.*

been moved there earlier by the doctors. Panchito, with a horrific head injury, was in great distress, pleading not to be left alone, and Álvaro did his best to comfort him. Two other boys suffered broken legs: Pancho Delgado, and Arturo Nogueira. As he had done with Álvaro, Gustavo freed Pancho, and helped him to the back. Arturo was found by Roberto beneath a seat and, although Arturo insisted that he was alright, Roberto could see that his foot was badly twisted, and his leg seemed broken.

Those at the back suddenly became aware of someone half-striding, half-falling down the slope behind them. The figure was close enough for them to make out that it was Carlos Valeta. Marcelo and Bobby set off towards him, to try to guide him to the plane, but they immediately sank to their waists in the snow, and couldn't make any headway. Instead, the boys shouted to Valeta, trying to get his attention and direct him to the fuselage, but suddenly he started tumbling down the slope, and disappeared off to one side. His body would be found in December, after the final expedition had set out.

Fig. 53. *Moments after the accident, drawn by Coche Inciarte on his return to Uruguay.*

Another bit of drama occurred when Fito Strauch appeared at the back, and tried to wander off, sinking into the snow before his cousin Daniel Fernández pulled him back. Fito, aside from a swollen knee and ankle, had been concussed and unconscious for ten minutes after the accident, and couldn't remember anything about the flight. Eduardo had also received a blow on the head, as his seat had flown forward in the final impact, and he had been unable to understand what he was doing there. Daniel, who had emerged almost unscathed, explained to his cousin what had happened as he endeavoured to release Eduardo's foot. As he was working to free people, Daniel Fernández kept looking around for Daniel Shaw, who had been sitting in front of him, unable to understand how he could have just disappeared from the plane.

Further back, on the left-hand side, with no seats behind to crash into them, Coche Inciarte and Juan Carlos Menéndez had also escaped with minor injuries. Coche, with just a small nick on his knee, suffered more damage to what he was wearing than to his person; his tie completely shredded, and the glass of his Omega watch broken. From where his seat came to rest, Coche saw the full extent of the devastation laid out in front of him. Near his feet, trapped between some seats, was the body of Eugenia Parrado, who had died immediately. Beside her, Susana, though still breathing, had severe wounds to her head, her face bloodied and bruised. She was placed at the back, with the other injured passengers. Across from Coche, Felipe Maquirriain was also in a bad way, his leg twisted, and the blood coming from his mouth evidence of an internal injury. Felipe barely regained consciousness, and died in the night. Next to Felipe, Pedro Algorta had been heavily concussed, and couldn't remember anything about the trip or the accident, but was otherwise unhurt. Despite his amnesia, he was a willing worker, following Marcelo's orders like an automaton.

At the front of the cabin, Roberto and Gustavo were continuing their triage. Of those in the front row, Graziela Augusto was trapped, her broken legs caught in the twisted metal of her seat. Try as they might, the boys could not release her. On the right-hand side, Tintín had found himself lying on the floor, his seatbelt broken, buried beneath a mass of other seats. He wasn't yet aware of the bad injury to his arm, but his chest was compressed, and he was having difficulty breathing. He tried to shout for someone to help him, but no words would come out. As he lay there, waiting to be rescued, he heard the disembodied voices of Roberto Canessa and Coco Nicolich as they went about helping the wounded, discussing the need to take out the dead bodies.

Behind Tintín, Esther and Pancho Nicola had died immediately, crushed against the bulkhead by the barrage of seats. Across the aisle from the Nicolas, Javier and Liliana escaped with just minor injuries, Liliana suffering bruising to her face, and Javier with a cracked rib. But as Javier tried to get up, he felt overcome by a debilitating lethargy, which kept him rooted to his seat. The Fairchild had come to rest at about 12,000 feet, and he was feeling the effects of altitude sickness. As Javier tried to summon up the strength to get out of his seat and help, he became aware of a boy on the floor by his side. Javier helped him up, and allowed him to rest on his leg, the blood from the boy's injuries seeping over Javier. Behind the Nicolas, Julio Martínez Lamas had suffered injuries to his chest and head, and he would also die before the night was out.

When Enrique Platero appeared from under a seat, Gustavo was shocked to see that his belly had been impaled by an iron rod. Gustavo controlled his immediate panic, and, remembering from a medical psychology course the importance of reassuring the patient, he told Enrique that he was fine, and asked him to help with the other injured passengers. As Enrique turned, Gustavo wrenched out the rod, pulling out with it a few centimetres of intestine and peritoneum. Worried about infection, he didn't try to push it back into the wound; instead, as a temporary measure, he wrapped it against the outside of Enrique's stomach with a clean shirt. Enrique then set to work without complaint, continuing to help until there was no longer sufficient light.

Darkness came much sooner than expected. They had crashed just after 3:30 p.m. local time, but it had started snowing soon after, and the grey skies and the towering wall of mountains surrounding them combined to hasten the onset of dusk. Under Marcelo's leadership, the able-bodied had tried to clear space in the cabin, in anticipation for the night ahead, but many of the seats could not be moved, and some bodies were still trapped. And the fuselage still contained a considerable amount of snow, which had entered during its slide down the mountain. As the temperature dropped precipitously to 30° below, the surviving passengers crowded into the limited space in the wreckage of the fuselage, hoping to survive the night, and confident of a rescue the next day.

Some of the injured were placed in the forward baggage compartment, where it was marginally warmer, though the partition between it and the main cabin had been destroyed, and the cargo door had been twisted, creating large gaps through which the frigid wind could enter. The seat covers used as makeshift blankets provided scant relief from the cold.

At the other end of the fuselage, exposed to the elements on the back porch, were the most injured – those whom the boys felt wouldn't survive – Panchito Abal, Susana Parrado, and Nando Parrado. Close by, Marcelo and a group of friends from the gang – Carlitos, Bobby, Roy, and Diego – huddled together for warmth. The five spent the night on their feet, struggling to avoid sliding down the sloping floor. A demijohn of wine was passed around, providing some small comfort, but it was soon finished. Roy built a small wall out of seats and suitcases, but it had little effect in stopping the wind and driving snow. At one point, Diego felt that Nando wasn't as badly injured as they'd first thought, and they pulled him into the middle of the group; an intervention that would prove crucial in the weeks to come.

The remaining passengers stood, sat, or lay piled one on top of the other in the small space they had been able to clear between the porch and the baggage area, intertwined and side-by side with the injured and the dead. There was little room to move, and nobody slept. Álvaro spent the night going from a standing to sitting position and back, in order to straighten his leg, but every time he stood up, he would tread on those next to him. Eduardo sat down on Carlos Roque's head, thinking it was a cushion; Carlos, believing he was being attacked, demanded, military-style, that Eduardo identify himself. The night was punctuated by the moans and cries of the injured, and the ramblings of the semi-conscious. Lagurara, in the pilot's cabin, continued to shout out, "We passed Curicó, we passed Curicó." At the back, Susana Parrado was heard praying in English. It was especially terrible for Graziela Augusto, alone and unknown to the group, her legs still trapped in the metal support of her seat. Moncho Sabella and Coco Nicolich tried to console her. The two boys hadn't known each other before then, but they formed an instant bond, Coco lying on his stomach, and Moncho, who found he was able to withstand the cold better than most despite his scant clothing, lying on top of Coco to give him warmth. Together, they held Graziela's hand, but, she was scared and in severe pain, and her cries persisted throughout the night. Coco described the hellish situation in a letter written a week later:

> Soon it got dark, and it was the longest, coldest and saddest night of my life; it seemed like the descriptions of Dante's inferno. There were screams upon screams, an infernal cold that entered from all sides, since we were unable to cover anything, and some passengers whom we had not been able to free had to sleep hooked in their seats, and unfortunately the next morning several died.

A couple of dozen kilometres away, Englishman Charles Harley had descended below the snowline in the Tinguiririca valley, and, as he settled down to sleep, he observed a curious phenomenon, his account of which gives a preternatural air to that fateful night.

> At around 3:00 a.m., a vaporous glowing disc – seemingly twice the size of a dustbin lid, appeared from the west, and passed quite low through the misty sky until, having traversed some 140 degrees within five minutes, it stopped somewhat east of the line on which the Tinguiririca volcano lay. Within minutes of its stopping, the disc had been blotted out by thickening mist.

Those who died overnight included Julio Martínez Lamas, Felipe Maquirriain, the pilot Dante Lagurara, and Panchito Abal who had been found lying over Susana Parrado, in an attempt to keep her and himself warm. Susana was still breathing, but her toes were frozen, and she was only half conscious. She was moved to a warmer part of the plane. Graziela survived until the morning, but died just as the boys managed to free her. Taking stock, the surviving passengers counted five dead on impact, five who died overnight or at first light, seven who had disappeared out of the tail, and twenty-eight alive in the fuselage. It was the start of day two on the mountain.

III. Analysis of an Accident

There has never been a fully satisfactory explanation of why, at 18:24 GMT on Friday, 13th October 1972, the pilots of Uruguayan Air Force Flight 571 changed course early, heading north into the middle of the Andes. The modern one-year-old Fairchild FH-227D had the latest navigational equipment on board, a detailed flight plan that took into account wind speeds and directions at various altitudes, and an experienced pilot, who had crossed the mountain range dozens of times.

Existing explanations of the accident assume that the pilots mistakenly believed they were over Curicó, in the Central Valley of Chile, far from any peaks. From there, they would have had a clear run to Santiago. The pilots' apparent miscalculation has been attributed to a variety and combination of factors – underestimation of wind speed, failure of instruments, beacons off-line, magnetic distortions, and turbulence. More difficult to comprehend is the lack of attention to flight timings that ignored the impossibility of taking just sixteen minutes to cross from Malargüe on the Argentinian side of the range to Curicó on the Chilean side, even in the absence of a headwind. But there are theories for this also.

This chapter assembles and comments on many of the reports relating to the accident, providing a context for understanding them, and offering further analysis to complement existing theories.

THE FLIGHT PLAN

The Uruguayan Air Force traditionally used one of two routes to cross the Andes to Santiago – the direct *Cristo Redentor* pass to the north, so-called because of the large statue of Christ the Redeemer on the border of Argentina and Chile; or the Planchón pass, further south. On the previous day – Thursday, 12th October 1972 – both passes had been closed to the Fairchild, necessitating an overnight stop in Mendoza. By the 13th, conditions had improved slightly, but the required minimum altitude of 26,000 ft under Instrument Meteorological Conditions still precluded the *Cristo Redentor* pass from the pilots' consideration. The Planchón pass, on the other hand, with a required minimum altitude of only 18,000 ft, was well within the Fairchild's capabilities.

The pilots submitted an IFR (Instrument Flight Rules) plan, which would take the Fairchild south from Mendoza to Malargüe on airway A-26, west across the Planchón pass to Curicó in Chile on airway G-17, and then north to Santiago on airway A-3. The flight plan specified estimated times, taking into account meteorological conditions, for arriving at various checkpoints along the way – Chilecito, Malargüe, Planchón, Curicó, and Angostura – thé final checkpoint before entering Santiago airspace. The three airways were marked out by radio beacons at Mendoza, Malargüe, Curicó, and Maipú in the south-west of Santiago, enabling instrument flight from start to end.

The Fairchild was equipped with the latest in navigational aids, possessing two VOR and two ADF receivers. ADF (Automatic Direction Finding) is the older technology, which relies on an NDB (Non-Directional Beacon) emitting a fixed signal in all directions. The more modern VOR (VHF Omnidirectional Range) relies on the ground station emitting both a reference signal and a signal that varies by direction; the onboard instrument then converts these readings to display the bearing from the VOR station to the aircraft – known as the 'radial'. The VOR system is generally preferred by pilots, requiring less manual intervention, being less susceptible to diffraction around terrain or interference from storms, and providing an absolute bearing from the ground station that is encoded in the signal and unaffected by wind, direction of flight, or magnetic fluctuations. Importantly, both systems require a clear line of sight to the beacon.

An ADF receiver provides only the relative bearing of the aircraft from a ground station and, in isolation, says nothing about whether the plane has drifted out of the airway. The relative bearing can be used as a homing signal. The pilot adjusts the course so that the needle on the display points along the radial, but once the plane has passed over the ground station, the needle swings around to point in the other direction. The relative bearing can be combined with information from the magnetic compass to compute an absolute bearing, but a Radio Magnetic Indicator (RMI) obviates the need for the pilot to do this. The RMI combines the VOR and ADF into one instrument, showing needles for both. In its analysis of the crash site, the Uruguayan Air Force report refers in passing to just such an instrument: "considering the position of the needles of the pilot's RMI (both pointed towards the tail), it's possible to deduce that the selection of frequency in VOR and ADF were correct." So whether the pilots were utilising VOR, ADF, or both, they would have been aware of the absolute bearing of the Fairchild from the ground station, though it is conceivable that magnetic fields in the Andes might affect the latter.

It is not enough to just home in on the beacon. In the presence of winds, the pilot must constantly calculate course corrections, to compensate for the resulting drift. Correcting for the wind is more straightforward with a VOR; if the aircraft drifts off a radial, the pilot just needs to change course to intersect it again, an adjustment that is immediately evident on the display. When an aircraft is equipped with two VOR receivers – as was the Fairchild – the pilot can use one to follow the radial for the current airway, and the other to monitor the radial of another; in that way, the intersection of two airways can be determined accurately and unambiguously. For example, when heading towards Curicó on airway G-17, the Fairchild could simultaneously monitor the radial from the Maipú VOR station, and then turn into the A-3 airway when that reading was 186° – the radial from Maipú to Curicó, all radial angles being calculated clockwise from due north.

In the Uruguayan Air Force transport group, the pilots had ultimate navigational responsibilities, with the role of a navigating officer being largely administrative. The commander of the Fairchild, Colonel Julio Ferradás, was highly experienced, having made almost 30 crossings of the Andes. However, it was the less experienced Lieutenant Colonel Dante Lagurara who took the pilot's seat, with Ferradás taking charge of the communications. One witness at Mendoza airport reported that Ferradás was not feeling well on the day; others have claimed that Lagurara was in the pilot's seat to gain experience of such a crossing.

At approximately 17:10 GMT (14:10 Mendoza time), the pilots informed Air Base N° 1 in Montevideo that they were taxiing to take-off position, and that they were going to be crossing over the Planchón pass. Lagurara took off at 17:18 GMT with full tanks – enough for a five-hour flight – and headed south on airway A-26. Ferradás reported Chilecito at 17:38, and Malargüe at 18:08, two minutes behind schedule. At this point, the Fairchild turned west onto airway G17, heading into the Andes towards Curicó on the 283° radial from Malargüe.

When Ferradás made first contact with the *Pudahuel* control tower in Santiago at 18:21, there was no indication that anything was amiss. The flight had been smooth, with the plane cruising above the clouds at 18,000 feet, with good visibility. But 10 minutes later, the plane would vanish.

COMMUNICATIONS WITH PUDAHUEL AIR TRAFFIC CONTROL

Although the destination was Santiago's second airport, *Los Cerrillos*, the flight was being monitored by *Pudahuel*. The communications between the tower and the Fairchild were replicated in the book *Para que otros pueden vivir* by Chilean author Colonel Rodolfo Martínez Ugarte, which was published in 1973. As a FACH officer who had written extensively about the history of the Chilean Air Force, Ugarte was well placed to give accurate information about the Chilean side of things.

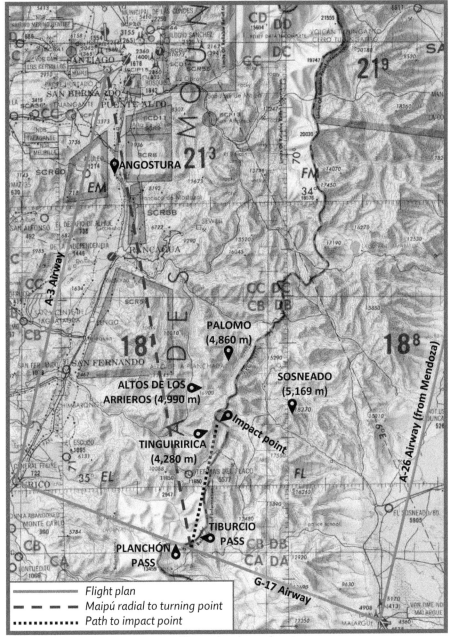

Fig. 54. *Planned and actual routes.*

113

Richard Cunningham, a US author living in Chile at the time of the accident, interviewed the *Pudahuel* air traffic controllers as part of the research for his 1973 account of the tragedy – *The Place where the World Ends*. There, he also provides, with commentary, an English version of the dialogue, which is consistent with Ugarte's.

Initial contact was made at 18:21 GMT:

FAU 571:   *Control Santiago, Uruguayan Air Force 571.*

SANTIAGO: Uruguayan 571 Santiago...

FAU 571:   *Santiago, Uruguayan 571 good afternoon, 21 Planchón 180 VM at the top Curicó 32.*

SANTIAGO: Uruguayan Air Force 571 received, authorized to the VOR of Maipú, to the VOR of Maipú UG-17 Curicó A-3 intersection Angostura, intersection Angostura direct flight to Maipú, radial 186 maintain 180 for the moment...

FAU 571:   *Uruguayo 571 received, from Curicó to Maipú by Amber 3 maintains 180...*

SANTIAGO: To the VOR Maipú VOR affirmative...

This exchange requires some explanation. After the initial greeting, the first message from the Fairchild gives the time as 18:21 GMT ('21'), the location as 'Planchón', and the altitude as 18,000 ft ('180'). 'VM' refers to Visual Meteorological Conditions – in other words, visibility good enough to fly without instruments. And the last bit of the message estimates them being over the top of Curicó at 18:32 GMT.

In fact, it was difficult for pilots to pinpoint Planchón exactly. There are two lakes – the *Lagunas de Tenas* – that can be used as visual landmarks in the summer. But typically, pilots would use the estimated time on the flight plan to switch communications from one operation centre to another. Based on the meteorological report ("five eighths of strong cumulus with a ceiling of 900 meters over the pass; winds oscillating from 280 to 300 degrees, at a speed of 40 to 60 knots"), the Chilean Air Force report estimated that in reality the Fairchild was still 14 nautical miles short of Planchón at the time of this communication.

The response from the controller authorises the use of the Maipú VOR. There is no instruction to turn, merely to maintain an altitude of 18,000 ft and monitor the radial from Maipú. A reading of 186° would indicate when the plane would intersect the Curicó-Angostura-Maipú airway. Much before Planchón, the line of sight to Maipú would have been blocked by peaks reaching up to 5000 metres or 16,400 ft, and it would not be possible to tune into the Maipú VOR.

The communication picks up again at 18:24 GMT, three minutes later (Ugarte reports 2 minutes and 6 seconds):

FAU 571:   *Santiago Uruguayo 571...*

SANTIAGO: Go ahead...

FAU 571:   *At 24 checking Curicó Victor Mike, setting course for Maipú, will report Angostura; estimating Angostura at 40...*

SANTIAGO: Uruguayan Air Force 571 received estimate Angostura 40, four zero...[pause] Uruguayan Air Force 571 is authorised to maintain flight level 100 notify leaving 180 for 100, change...

FAU 571:   *571 received for one zero zero will notify reaching that altitude...*

SANTIAGO: Received...

This is a surprising turn of events. Ferradás is reporting that the Fairchild has, impossibly, taken three minutes to fly the 40 nautical miles from Planchón to Curicó, and is now setting course for Maipú. If the pilot is using Maipú BDN and/or VOR to make this course change, then the displayed radial will clearly show that it is too early to turn.

With no radar coverage, the controller, perhaps assuming that the Fairchild was much closer to Curicó than the pilot estimated on the previous communication, takes the pilot's declaration at face value, and acknowledges the change of course. With no high peaks in the A-3 corridor, he authorises the Fairchild to descend to 10,000 ft, with an 18:40 estimated time of arrival at checkpoint Angostura.

The final acknowledged communication is at 18:30:

SANTIAGO: Uruguayan 571 can you confirm your current level?

FAU 571:   *Level 150...*

SANTIAGO: Received...

The Chilean Air Force later reported that all radio calls were made by Ferradás with his natural voice, with the exception of this last response, which was made hastily in response to the request from *Pudahuel*. The flight level of 15,000 ft was surprising; the Chilean Air Force report indicates that the expected rate of descent from 18,000 ft was 1,000 ft per minute, implying an expectation that the Fairchild would be levelling out at 10,000 by the time of this communication. This despite the knowledge in hindsight that the Fairchild had plummeted thousands of feet in two large air pockets.

Pudahuel contacted the Fairchild again two minutes later, at 18:32:

SANTIAGO: Uruguayan Air Force 571 Santiago...

An increasingly desperate series of attempts to contact the Fairchild were met with silence. We know now that sometime between 18:30 and 18:32, the pilots were focussing all their skill and attention on a desperate attempt to clear a mountain ridge on the Argentina-Chile border. They almost made it, although, had they succeeded, the stall condition of the aircraft makes it unlikely that they would have been able to recover the flight. As it was, the right wing clipped the ridge and broke off from the fuselage, in turn severing the tail cone. The other wing also broke off, and the fuselage careered down the slope on the other side of the ridge, coming to a stop on the glacier below. Its whereabouts and the fate of the passengers would be unknown for another seventy-two days.

THE CHILEAN AIR FORCE REPORT

The *Fuerza Aérea de Chile* (FACH) issued a report on 8th November 1972, 4 weeks after the accident, and 6 weeks before the wreckage was discovered. It serves as an essential baseline for any further analysis of the accident, and is given in verbatim translation below, supplemented by footnotes to clarify technical terms.

CHILEAN AIR FORCE
GENERAL STAFF
OPERATIONS DIVISION
AEROSPACE SECURITY COUNCIL

INVESTIGATION OF THE AIR ACCIDENT INVOLVING THE URUGUAYAN AIR FORCE PLANE No. 571/(Fokker 27)

(Occurred 13-Oct-1972 presumably in Chilean territory, on the Andean border with Argentina at the Planchón pass in the province of Curicó.)

I.   *HISTORY OF THE FLIGHT*

The Uruguayan Air Force plane No. 571, a two-motor, turboprop, FOKKER 27 plane[1], with 45 persons on board (5 crew members and 40 passengers) took off from Mendoza on 13th October 1972 at 17:18 GMT, with a IFR[2] flight plan to Santiago de Chile.

ATC[3] Mendoza authorized it to fly toward Santiago de Chile via Mendoza-Malargüe-Curicó-Maipú (via Angostura).

The plane first came into radio contact with Santiago-Centre reporting Intersection Planchón at 18:21 GMT over the top, estimating Curicó at 18:32. However, three minutes afterwards, it reported being over Curicó, at 18:24 GMT flying at 18,000 ft, Victor Mike[4], and estimating Angostura at 18:40. At this point, the Control Centre in Santiago authorized it to descend in airway A-3 from 18,000 ft to 10,000 ft. The pilot, when asked by the Control Centre in Santiago, approximately at 18:30 GMT, reported crossing at 15,000 going down. Subsequently nothing was known about the plane.

---

[1] Actually a Fairchild FH-227.

[2] Instrument Flight Rules (as opposed to Visual Flight Rules VFR), a set of regulations used for flying by instrument. An IFR flight plan is required under Instrument Meteorological Conditions (IMC).

[3] Air Traffic Control

[4] Visual Meteorological Conditions – VMC often abbreviated to "Victor Mike" over the radio.

II. INVESTIGATION

A. Authorization and take-off.

The plane took off at 17:18 GMT from Mendoza and went up to 18,000 ft via Chilecito-Malargüe, reporting Chilecito at 17:38 and Malargüe at 18:08 (having estimated Malargüe at 18:06). According to these data, during the ascent up to 18,000 ft, the plane flew with a V.T.[1] of 190 knots[2], which is approximately correct, because there were 30 to 60 knots of wind at 300 degrees (predominantly in the tail)[3].

B. Malargüe position.

Malargüe position at 18:08 corresponds to a V.T. of 210 knots which is estimated to be correct because during that section the FAU 571 was affected with a tailwind with a mean component of 20 knots.

C. Planchón Position.

The position "Planchón over the top – 18,000 feet V.M. at 18:21" reported by the pilot to the Control centre in Chile does not correspond to any possible reality, because between the radio beacon at Malargüe and the Intersection Planchón, there is a distance of 53 nautical miles and if we assume that the plane flew at 180 knots of V.T. (there were 30/40 knots of opposing wind in this section), at 18:21 the plane was 14 nautical miles from Planchón.

D. Curicó Position.

At 18:24 the plane reported "24 checks Curicó – V.M. heads for Maipú (004°)". This would mean that when the plane had, in reality, still 5 miles left to reach Planchón, the crew considered that they had passed Curicó and turned right, heading towards Maipú-VOR, in agreement with what had been authorised by ATC Santiago.

E. Descent from 18,000 feet.

Once the ATC-Santiago received the notification that the plane had passed Curicó, it authorised it to descend in airway A-3 from 18,000 feet to 10,000 feet, to which the pilot agreed.

At 18:30, ATC-Santiago consulted the FAU 571 on the level it was flying, and the pilot answered: "level 150". This means that over 6 minutes, the plane came down

---

[1] Velocidad Terrestre or groundspeed (VT or GS).

[2] 1 knot = 1 nautical mile per hour = 1.15 miles per hour = 1.84 km per hour.

[3] The southerly component of 300-degree wind would be half the value of the wind-speed.

3,000 feet, which is not a normal descent route for this kind of plane, which is 1,000 ft/min (background information supplied by pilots of the Uruguayan Air Force).

Subsequently, at 18:32, 18:33, and 18:35, ATC called the FAU 571 without answer.

III.   *VERIFIED FACTS REGARDING THE ACCIDENT.*

   A.   *Meteorological conditions 17:00 – 18:00 GMT.*

      1.   *High winds supplied by Mendoza.*
         5,000 m   300°/50
         7,000 m   290°/60

      2.   *High winds supplied by Santiago.*
         18,000 ft   250°/25
         12,000 ft   300°/20
         10,000 ft   300°/25

      3.   *Weather in Curicó.*
         South wind 6 knots, visibility 20 km. 3/8 cumulus at 600 m.

   B.   *Radio Navigation Aids.*

      1.   *From Malargüe. Conjecturally they were on the air because the FAU 571 had an ETA over the radio aid and corrected it by 2 minutes.*

      2.   *From Curicó: At 24:00 GMT a DC-68 of the Chilean Air Force verified that the radio navigation aids from Curicó were on the air. There are no previous verifications, but there are no reports of anomalies in the ground monitors.*

   C.   *Procedures of the ATC.*

      1.   *From the ATC-Mendoza: unknown*

      2.   *From ATC-Santiago: the tape recorded in the Santiago Control Centre testifies that there were no mistakes in the radio-telephonic procedures relating to the control of aerial transit (either from the part of the pilots, nor the control in Santiago).*

IV.   *INFORMATION SUPPLIED BY THE URUGUAYAN AIR FORCE*

   A.   *Crew*

      1.   *Pilot: Approximately 2000 flight hours, and experience in crossing the Cordillera – Qualified IFR.*

      2.   *Copilot: Approximately 5000 flight hours, and substantial experience in crossing the Cordillera – Qualified IFR.*

B.   The plane:

Plane with the following navigational equipment:
1.   2 VHF Navigation[1]
2.   2 ADF[2]
3.   1 DME[3]
4.   1 meteorological radar
5.   1 automatic pilot
6.   1 flight director
7.   2 magnetic compasses gyro-stabilized

C.   Other antecedents

1.   From the tape it follows that the radio-telephone calls were made by the copilot
2.   All radio calls were made by the copilot[4] with his natural voice as his companions knew it. Only the last call was made hastily, on request of ATC-Santiago.

V.   CAUSE OF THE ACCIDENT

It is not possible to determine the cause of this accident, because the plane has disappeared despite the thorough search by air that went on for 15 days.

VI.   ESTIMATION OF THE INVESTIGATOR OF THE ACCIDENT

A.   Conjecturally, the pilot, due to some radio-electric abnormality or to the application of mistaken procedures of IFR navigation, flying VMC over the top estimated he had crossed over one of the radio navigation aids in Curicó (a radio beacon and a VOR), which in neither case corresponded to reality, because of the strong wind that existed at 270° (30 to 40 knots). The airway has a direction of 283°.

Actually, at 18:24, the plane being approximately in the Planchón zone headed 004° towards Maipú. He was authorised to come down to 10,000 feet, reporting 15,000 at 18:30. No contact was then made with the Uruguayan plane because it did not answer to the persistent calls the ATC-Santiago made to it starting at 18:32.

---

[1] VOR (VHF Omni-directional Range).

[2] Automatic Direction Finding.

[3] Distance Measuring Equipment. Radio navigation technology that measures the slant distance between an aircraft and a ground station.

[4] Ferradás.

B. When it crossed clouds coming down from 18,000 feet, in some place near Planchón (the Argentinian-Chilean border), the plane must have crashed in the Cordillera at a height of 15,000 feet or less.

C. A non-qualified witness (a miner) said he had seen at approximately 19:00 GMT a plane flying low or between the clouds, to the north, and to the zone of the Tinguiririca volcano (Mount Palomo, Mount Sosneado). It was snowing at that time in the zone.

D. The zone in which the FAU 571 probably is, is north of the Planchón Intersection, exactly on the Argentinian-Chilean border; it is all covered with snow, and the search has been made difficult because of the altitude (4,000 to 5,000 meters).

E. Evidently, the crew made mistakes in the procedures of planning the flight and of radio navigation because:

1. They did not take into account in their calculations the high winds, supplied by Meteorology for the Malargüe Planchón leg.

2. They did not take into account the meteorological report, which at the time they are supposed to have passed by that place was practically CAVOK[1].

3. The passing over the radio-aids in Curicó does not bear the minimum scrutiny because there exists both a VOR and a radio beacon (RBN)

4. It is thought impossible four items of aerial navigation equipment (two VORs, two radio compasses) failed simultaneously, unless in an electrical emergency, a situation that was not reported by the crew.

VII. RECOMMENDATIONS

A. General

Inform pilots about this accident, emphasizing the importance of:
1. Dead reckoning
2. Applying the correct existing radio-navigation procedures in order to consider a radio aid passed.
3. Meteorological flight planning

B. For the Uruguayan Air Force.

Analyse the report, contributing other antecedents, if available, in, in order to contribute to flight safety and the prevention of future similar accidents.

---

[1] Ceiling (or Clouds) And Visibility [are] OK

C. *For SAR-Chile.*

> *Inform the Aerospace Security Authority of any antecedents received relating to the location of the wreck of the aircraft. This would allow the accident investigator to expand the current expert report.*

JULIO CERDA PINO
Squadron Commander (A)
EXPERT INVESTIGATOR

DISTRIBUTION

1. *Operations Management*
2. *Uruguayan Air Force*
3. *SAR Cerrillos*
4. *The 15 Operational Units*

A NON-QUALIFIED WITNESS

Section VI-C of the FACH report mentions a non-qualified witness who said he had seen, at approximately 19:00 GMT, a plane flying low or between the clouds, to the north, and to the zone of the *Tinguiririca* volcano (*Mount Palomo, Mount Sosneado*).

The witness was Camilo Figueroa, but initial press reports of his statement were inaccurate. For example, *Ahora* stated in its 16th October edition, three days after the accident, "The patrol of carabineros entered the *Jaula* ravine yesterday, on the back of mules and horses, to try to go over the *Paso Tiburcio*, where a miner, Camilo Figueroa, claimed to have seen a plane plunging to the ground with its engines on fire on Friday."

Interviewed later by Uruguayan reporters, Figueroa corrected those reports: "I saw the plane, it's true, but not losing altitude, nor wrapped in flames. Last Friday, around three in the afternoon, a white plane, with broad wings, was flying normally on a slight descending course over the area known as *Quebrada del Tiburcio*. I only saw the plane flying, and nothing more. It was heading towards Rancagua, north of Curicó."

Figueroa's report was considered credible enough that early searches by helicopter and on horseback were made in those areas. And his statement is consistent with what is known about the Fairchild's manoeuvres.

THE URUGUAYAN AIR FORCE REPORT

The *Fuerza Aérea Uruguaya* (FAU) delivered its report on 10th April 1973, holding a press conference at 5:00 p.m. on the same day to present its findings. The conference was chaired by Colonel Luis Charquero – the FAU's Director of Flight Safety and the leader of the investigation. Members of the investigating committee took turns to present different aspects of the report to a packed audience at Air Base 1 by Carrasco airport. It largely concurred with the FACH report, citing pilot miscalculation, the underestimation of the strong winds, and the possibility of magnetic effects in that part of the Andes affecting the onboard instruments.

The report also included statements by the pilots of the Uruguayan search planes – Colonel Wilder Jackson, who piloted the Fairchild's sister plane FAU 570 in the October search, and Major Ruben Terra, who piloted the C-47 FAU 508 in the December search. Both pilots indicated that their VOR and ADF instruments had operated normally in the Planchón region.

Unlike the FACH report, the FAU investigation had the benefit of knowing the location of the wreckage, and included an analysis of the crash site. The report described the break-up of the plane at the point of impact, and its subsequent slide down the north side of the mountain. The right wing hit the ridge first, breaking away from the fuselage and severing the tail cone. The subsequent decompression was responsible for tearing the seats from their bearings, though the impact of the base of the fuselage with the ground would surely also have contributed to that. The abrupt deceleration of the fuselage as it came to a halt after tobogganing down the mountain caused the seats and passengers to crash to the front of the cabin, destroying the bulkhead screen. These descriptions largely confirmed survivor accounts of the accident and so don't contribute much to the investigation.

As a military plane, the Fairchild carried no black box or voice recorder, but the report did make one deduction relating to the flight:

> *Following statements made by the survivors – considered as 'non-qualified witnesses' – and considering the position of the needles of the pilot's RMI (both pointed towards the tail), it's possible to deduce that the selection of frequency in VOR and ADF (radio compass) were correct.*

Trips to the site over the years by enthusiasts of the story have yielded new information and insights. In December 2005, Mexican-American mountaineer Ricardo Peña and

Argentinian guide Mario Peréz were exploring close to the top of the ridge. There they discovered a number of artefacts – including famously the jacket of survivor Eduardo Strauch – which pointed to a much narrower gully than had been originally assumed as the initial path of the fuselage down the mountain. The right wing apparently hit one of the several rock-pillars (referred to as gendarmes), the specific one having disintegrated in 2014, but the others further to the east still imposingly guarding the ridge.

Fig. 55. One of the Fairchild's engines, found March 1973.

One of the most interesting artefacts that still lay scattered on the mountain is a feathered propellor from the Fairchild. Feathering is an abnormal configuration of the propellor, in which the blades are pitched to minimize drag. The Fairchild FH-227D pilot's manual states:

> Automatic feathering occurs whenever a power lever is advanced above 13,000 rpm, but torque pressure is below 50psi, provided the opposite propeller is not already feathered.

From this, it can be deduced that the engines were revved up to beyond 13,000 rpm in the last moments, in a desperate attempt to clear the ridge; this is consistent with the accounts of some survivors of hearing shouts from the pilot's cabin: "Give me power," and the sounds of the engines revving to their maximum.

This observation about the feathered propellor originates from Hugo Igenes and Jörg Thomsen, and is one of several discussed in *Touched: The Story behind the Museum of the Andes 1972 Ordeal* by Jörg Thomsen and Patricia Maher-Affeldt. Thomsen – a Uruguayan industrialist with expertise in thermal insulation – is the founder and curator of the *Museo Andes 1972*, possessing in-depth knowledge of the story. Igenes is a former FAU navigator, who had flown in that role on the FAU 571 on the charter flight directly preceding the *Old Christians* trip; his extensive exploration of the site, combined with his experience of the Fairchild, make him one of the most credible investigators of the accident.

Fig. 56. *Feathered propellor from the Fairchild; the leading edges of the blades point forwards.*

In *Touched*, Thomsen also talks about the plane being in a state of aerodynamic stall, corresponding, according to the manual, to a speed of 157 km/h. He expresses the opinion that this condition caused the high wing of the Fairchild to hit the *gendarme* from above rather than front-on, the resulting fracture helping to absorb the energy of the impact. He comments further that had the plane cleared the ridge, the stall condition would have made it impossible to recover the flight and escape the valley.

In 2016, an FAU officer, emailing a relative of a passenger who died in the accident, wrote of the Uruguayan Air Force report: "In my search for this research, it seems that many years ago, a senior officer removed it from his folder at the request of the Ministry of National Defence, and it was never heard of again." The summary of the report given below was put together by journalist Eugenio Hintz in 1973 for author Piers Paul Read.

History of the flight:

➢ *Departure from Montevideo, Oct. 12 at 11.00 GMT.*

➢ *Overnight in Mendoza due to bad weather.*

➢ *Take-off from Mendoza: Oct 13 at 17.18 GMT, scheduled to cross the Andes through the Malargüe-Curicó pass. The route called to fly air corridor A-26 from Mendoza to Malargüe, G-17 from Malargüe to Curicó, and A-3 from Curicó to Santiago.*

➢ *The Fairchild reported Chilecito at 17.38, estimating Malargüe at 18.06.*

➢ *Reported Malargüe at 18.08, estimating Planchón at 18.21 flying at 18,000 feet above clouds in visual conditions.*

➢ *At 18.21 starts communicating with Santiago to report Planchón, estimating Curicó at 18.32.*

➢ *Reported Curicó at 18.24, and a change in direction, proceeding to Maipú – (according to instructions previously received from control tower), estimating arrival to Angostura at 18.40.*

➢ *Minutes later the ATC in Santiago authorized the Fairchild to come down to 10,000 feet and requested to report when reaching that altitude.*

➢ *At 18.30 Santiago called the Fairchild to check the altitude; the answer was 15,000 feet.*

➢ *At 18.32 Santiago called again and received no answer.*

Statements:

The pilots of the two FAU planes which participated in the search – the Fairchild FH-227 number 570 and the Douglas C-47 number 508 – were questioned by the investigators in Montevideo about the difficulties they might have had to receive radio signals in the area between Malargüe and Curicó. Both stated they had no reception troubles.

The Fairchild pilot said that only on his way back, Malargüe was not on the air, neither on VOR nor the beacon. Otherwise, the VOR and the radio gave no erroneous indications.

The C-47 pilot made the same statement (no difficulty in the reception of radio signals), although he added that his radio compass was continuously spinning and gave erroneous information on several occasions.

Conclusions:

After a detailed account of the route of the Fairchild followed by the Fairchild, the meteorological conditions, and the communications between the craft and the control tower – which adds nothing to whatever has been already reported – the UAF reaches the following conclusions:

a) *Based upon the analysis of the route made by the airplane, its performance, and the high winds existing in the area, we can deduce that it could never have blocked Curicó's VOR at 18.24 GMT as the crew reported (throughout the report the investigators use the term 'blocking' a VOR, seemingly the moment when the instrument shows that the plane is over a certain point). At that time the plane was over Planchón; therefore, according to the pilot's report, when he directed the bow towards VOR Maipú, the plane was in the middle of the range.*

b) *Taking into account the communications made by the pilot, the plane must have flown from six to eight minutes more after reporting Curicó, since he didn't answer a request made by the Santiago Control Centre made at 18.32 GMT.*

c) *If we take into consideration that the plane started to descend immediately after the apparent blocking of Curicó's VOR, and considering its performance and existing winds, as well as the pilot's report about his flight level six minutes after directing bow to VOR Maipú, it is possible to deduce that the craft could never have crossed over the Cerro Palomo, whose height is 16,800 feet.*

d) *It's evident that while flying between Malargüe and Curicó, the strong headwind existing in the area wasn't taken into consideration.*

e) *It's not possible to determine the cause which made the pilot think he was over Curicó.*

The wreckage of plane was found three miles north-east from the Tinguiririca volcano, and eight to ten miles south-east from the Cerro del Palomo.

No information could be drawn from the inspection of the plane's cabin, because the survivors took out all the radio navigation equipment, intending to broadcast their position.

Following statements made by the survivors – considered as 'non-qualified witnesses' – and considering the position of the needles of the pilot's RMI (both pointed towards the tail), it's possible to deduce that the selection of frequency in VOR and ADF (radio compass) were correct.

The influence of the magnetic fields in that area, due to seismic movements, could have altered the radio signals. This possibility is subject to scientific research, but it has been mentioned that in the last ten years there have been nine crashes in that area, and that Chilean Air Force pilots have reported some erroneous markings in the VOR and ADF stations.

Analysis of the wreckage:

➤ The wings separated due to the impact. The right wing was the one that hit against a rock.

➤ The fuselage was cut by the wing. The tail didn't hit the ground; it separated from the fuselage severed by the wing.

➤ The seats were torn out from their places due to the decompression in the cabin, followed by the speed and inertia of the downslide, and piled up against the pilot's cabin destroying the screen that separates the crew and passenger sections.

➤ The nose was crushed by the downslide on the snow and compressed against the pilot's seats. The windshield folded towards the interior without breaking.

➤ Only the front wheel stayed in place.

➤ The state of the bodies prevented to establish the cause of their deaths. According to the statements of the 16 survivors, 4 members of the crew and 8 passengers died the day of the accident; later due to the wounds, one member of the crew and six more passengers died; finally 10 passengers died in the avalanche.

Discrepancies:

a) Equipment: No observations

b) Proceedings:

1. A mistake in the calculation of the estimated time between Malargüe-Planchón-Curicó, a distance of 92 nautical miles, was made, as it was calculated in 16 minutes, that is to say, a speed of 345 knots.

2. The almost headwind in this area was not estimated; according to Control Mendoza, at 18,000 feet it blew from 290 degrees with a speed of 60 kilometres, while the investigator of the Chilean Air Force evaluated it came from 270 degrees with 30 to 40 kilometre strength.

c) Operations: The flight schedule in Mendoza was filled in with some mistakes, but the navigation miscalculations made later cannot be attributed to these mistakes.

d) Maintenance: no observations.

e) Supervision: no observations.

Final conclusions:

Probable main cause off accident: human factor. Probable contributing factor: influence in the magnetic field could have originated erroneous markings and indications in the radio-aid instruments, which convinced the pilot he was in Curicó.

THE ROLE OF AIR TRAFFIC CONTROL

Richard Cunningham writes of the critical communication at 18:24 GMT:

> *For a few agonizingly short seconds ... everything hung in the balance. If the control tower operator had requested the copilot to recheck his position; if he had demanded a visual confirmation of Curicó; if he had simply questioned the missing eight minutes – the catastrophe might have been averted. Tancredo Ortuvia (Codirector of Operations at Pudahuel) later suggested that the young man probably assumed that the plane had been closer to Curicó than the copilot initially thought.*

Commander Jorge Massa, a Chilean pilot who took part in the initial search and rescue mission, and in the helicopter rescue on the mountain, also exonerated the controller, explaining that he was required to accept the FAU pilot's statement of position as correct, having no way of verifying it in the absence of radar.

The Directorate of Aviation in Chile went one step further, by not only exonerating the air traffic controller, but also claiming that the Fairchild had actually reached Curicó and therefore, by implication, must have doubled back into the Andes. They issued a communiqué stating, "the Santiago control centre acted correctly, in full compliance with the procedures governing aeronautical regulations in the case under analysis, by not interfering with the sequence of the flight course followed by the aircraft, whose position at the time it began its descent was undoubtedly Curicó, as verified by the indication of the instruments and by the pilot's own observation of the terrain". The improbable last part of this statement directly contradicted the FACH report, which had concluded that "passing over the radio-aids in Curicó does not bear minimum scrutiny because there exists both a VOR and a radio beacon".

The communiqué appeared to be in reaction to an article that had appeared in Uruguayan newspaper *La Mañana* on 7th March 1973, which reported on the various theories and lines of investigation. One of the points it touched on was the failure of the controller to question the impossibility of reaching Curicó three minutes after it passed Planchón, and it was suggested that the accident might be a joint error, implicating both the control tower and the pilots. The FAU declined to comment on the issue, pending the completion of their investigation and the publication of their report. When it appeared more than a month later, it placed no blame on the air traffic controller.

THE VIERCI REPORT

Many years after the accident, Uruguayan author Pablo Vierci, working with retired FAU Colonel Carlos Horacio Muñoa, published an analysis of the accident which conjectured what might have happened. Muñoa knew both pilots, and spoke warmly about them in a sidebar to the main article. He referred to Ferradás as being one of the best pilots in the FAU, the most experienced Fairchild pilot, and the pilot who had flown the most Andes crossings in a Fairchild. Muñoa had also flown with Lagurara, and had been part of the four-man Lockheed F-80 formation team which had been involved in the 1963 accident.

Vierci's article appeared in *Bon Jour*, the Sunday colour supplement of the now-defunct Uruguayan newspaper *El Día*. It is replicated in translation below – with some minor corrections – with the permission of Vierci, a former director of the newspaper. This report is useful in providing detailed background information and explanations of some of the complex navigational details. Its conclusions will be discussed at the end.

Why did the Fairchild 571, flown by one of the Air Force's most experienced pilots, crash in the Andes Mountains on 13th October 1972? What exactly happened at the Malargüe-Curicó Pass when the plane turned north and began to descend into the mountain? To answer these questions – which have never been answered – we interviewed aeronautical specialists and those familiar with the Malargüe-Curicó pass, including the Air Force pilot who was flying the Fairchild 571 before the accident.

On the afternoon of 13th October 1972, more precisely between 15.20 and 15.35 hours, something happened on board the Uruguayan Air Force Fairchild 571 crossing the Andes on the Malargüe-Curicó airway that left 29 dead, changed the course of the lives of the 16 survivors, and shook the world.

What exactly happened? Until now, it has never been precisely explained.

Twenty years later, with the issue and the controversy reignited by the film Alive, El Día magazine first turned to the Uruguayan Air Force for its version of events. After several comings and goings, in which we were treated with particular deference, the Air Force preferred to remain silent, citing reasons that were more than acceptable.

Bon Jour then questioned those who could contribute elements to understand what happened: aeronautical specialists, pilots, friends and colleagues of the Fairchild 571 pilots, radio experts and those who know, like the back of their hands, the Malargüe-Curicó airway, where the circumstances that led to the tragedy took place. Among those consulted was retired Colonel Carlos Horacio Muñoa, who not only made the same trip on several occasions with the Fairchild 571, but also began flying it from the moment it arrived in our country in 1971.

This speculation is based on all this information.

Aeronautical charts

To understand what happened on 13th October, some aeronautical concepts must be understood.

Aircraft are guided by what are called aeronautical charts, i.e. maps that show the predetermined air routes, where they can fly. Such charts, as can be seen in Figure 1, show mainly radio aids rather than the cities and other elements recorded on conventional maps. These are stations that broadcast signals on a certain frequency, like radio stations, in order to guide the aircraft in flight.

The on-board instrument, which is called ADF, ('Automatic Direction Finder'), is tuned to the characteristic frequency of the next radio-aid that will appear on the route, and then the needle on the instrument panel will rotate until it points to exactly that point, from where the antenna of the radio-aid emits the signal. The aircraft then corrects course to where the needle indicates, and heads towards the radio-aid.

En route

The Fairchild 571, like all aircraft in the same circumstances, had to search the aeronautical chart for a series of radio aids that would allow it to reach Santiago. The aircraft's radio equipment was tuned to the radio aids in stages, because it did not have sufficient range to connect directly to the radio aids at the flight's destination, in this case Santiago. From Mendoza, the radio aids sought by the Fairchild 571 were those of Malargüe, Curicó, and Maipú, on the outskirts of the Chilean capital.

All these elements are fundamental to understanding what happened on the afternoon of 13th October 1972.

The other essential element to understand what probably happened is what is called the 'cone of silence'. When the aircraft passes over a radio-aid, i.e. over the antenna from which the broadcast starts, the needle of the on-board equipment turns 180 degrees and points backwards, i.e. towards the radio-aid that the aircraft has just passed. This is the conclusive proof that a certain point has been passed. But when the radio-aid is of the type like the one in Curicó, the phenomenon known as 'cone of silence' can occur: when passing over the antenna of the radio-aid, there is a fluctuation in the needle of the on-board equipment, as if it did not register or did not receive the requested frequency, or as if there had been an intermittent power cut in the radio-aid, since the on-board equipment receives the signal but immediately loses it, only to receive it again and lose it again a moment later. This fluctuation of the on-board equipment needles resulting from the 'cone of silence' may have been the key element in what happened to the Fairchild 571.

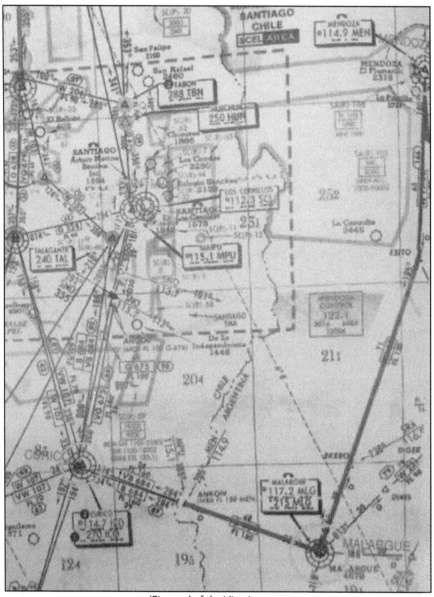

'Figure 1' of the Vierci report.

These fluctuations in the needle of the on-board receivers can also occur even if you are not passing over the antenna, i.e. over the 'cone of silence': it is the case that, for some reason, the radio-aid transmits intermittently, which causes the needle of the on-board equipment to fluctuate, even if you are many kilometres away from the radio-aid.

In the clouds

Another important element to take into account in order to understand the causes of the accident is that the flight of Fairchild 571, during most of the flight from Mendoza, was in the clouds, that is to say, it was an instrument flight.

You can fly in the cloud, with zero visibility, by instruments, or you can fly in VMC (Visual Meteorological Condition), i.e. with good visibility.

When you are in IMC (Instrument Meteorological Condition), i.e. without visibility, the aircraft must communicate with the reporting points specified in the flight plan, indicating at what altitude you are travelling and when you pass through the different points. This is what the Fairchild 571 was doing until it lost contact with Santiago.

The flight plan

The fourth element to be taken into account when analysing the Fairchild 571 accident is the navigation log. The chart is a sheet with several columns where information essential to guide a flight is recorded. Thus, in one column you write down the points through which you will pass; in another column you write down the distances, in miles, between the different points; in a third column you record the time it would take to get from point to point, taking into account the miles in the previous column and the speed of the plane; the fourth column records the estimated time of passing through the different points, which is calculated by adding the times in the previous column, while the last column records the actual time as it passes through the different points, correcting, where necessary, the estimated time in the third column.

Worst-case scenario

The Malargüe-Curicó passage is, from an air navigation point of view, one of the most difficult places imaginable. It is an airway through the mountains, where you fly at a minimum altitude of 6,000 metres, but surrounded by much higher mountains.

To complicate matters further, it is a passage with strong winds blowing from west to east – in other words, in the opposite direction to the Fairchild 571 flight – winds that are so strong that a flight to Santiago by jet takes two and a half hours to get there, while it takes just an hour and a half to get back, because it is downwind.

However, it is a pass that is not only crossed by large aircraft or turboprop aircraft such as the Fairchild, but can also be crossed by single-engine planes, provided there is good visibility.

The Fairchild is also considered a true champion of air navigation, so much so that it is a design of which new, modernised versions are still being built, despite the fact that it is now 30 years old.

On the afternoon of that 13th October, Fairchild 571 was not only flying on instruments, it was flying in very uncomfortable conditions. Strong winds and turbulence were, it is speculated, contributing factors in triggering what happened in the middle of the route.

Passing Malargüe

At 14.18 the plane took off from Mendoza heading south to Malargüe, because the direct flight to Santiago has a minimum en-route altitude of 26,000 feet, which is not suitable for this type of aircraft.

The Fairchild got the indication from the Malargüe radio-aid that they had passed, turned 90 degrees west, and continued towards Curicó. They noted the time and re-estimated Curicó on the chart.

After turning at Malargüe they set off on radial 285. If you look at the flight chart in Figure 1, you will notice FL 180, on the Malargüe-Curicó airway. This means that the minimum altitude level on this route is 18,000 feet, or about 6,000 metres. But if you look at the sector next to the airway, on the same chart in Figure 1, you will read the indication 204, which means that there, next to the airway where the Fairchild 571 was supposed to pass, the minimum altitude level is 20,400 feet, or 6,800 metres, and beyond that, the minimum level, according to the same air chart, rises to 21,100 feet.

86 miles

The distance between Malargüe and Curicó is 86 miles, 48 miles to Ankón, which in 1972 was called Planchón, and 38 from Planchón to Curicó. This distance, at a speed of 220 knots, or 400 kilometres per hour, should be done in 25 minutes. This is under normal conditions. But if you take into account the strong headwind that afternoon, the speed was not 400 kilometres per hour, because you have to subtract the headwind from that value.

So what happened?

What follows, of course, is conjecture. The plane tuned into Curicó and pointed towards that radio-aid station. But when it was barely halfway, or approximately 48 miles, the unthinkable happened: the pilots thought they were in Curicó, and at 15:24. they asked for permission to descend. The Santiago base authorised the descent, because if they were indeed in Curicó, as they said they were, they had to descend. Santiago could not know that they were not yet where they said they were, because at that time they had no radar, and could not see them.

So the Fairchild turned right, to the north, 38 miles before Curicó, and began to descend.

But they were not actually in Curicó, with a flat landscape, populated only by hills, but were in the middle of the Andes, where not only could they not descend, but they had to climb rapidly to reach the minimum flying altitudes.

What happened? Here the phenomenon of the 'cone of silence' mentioned above reappears. As mentioned, the moment you pass over a radio-aid, the indications on the instrument panel can be erratic, fluctuating, like when you don't receive a good signal.

What probably happened, then, at that fateful moment, is that on board the Fairchild 571, they may have mistaken a fluctuation of the aircraft receiver needle, caused by an intermittent oscillation at the Curicó station, for what they believed to be the erratic indication of the Curicó 'cone of silence', i.e. the indecisive indications of the needle when passing over the transmitter, exactly above the antenna of the radio-aid, in this case the antenna of the Curicó radio-aid.

In other words, an intermittent oscillation in the ground radionavigation equipment that caused a fluctuation in the on-board display was mistaken for the erratic display characteristic of the radio-aid's 'cone of silence', leading the pilots to believe that they were flying over Curicó.

The fluctuation in the on-board indication may also have been caused by the fact that, as the radio-aid equipment of the time was VHF, i.e. they always work with the receiver in sight of the transmitter, if a mountain or something comes between the ground equipment and the aircraft, the signal is lost. Because of the altitude they were flying at, it is likely that at some point they lost the signal and got that erratic needle indication, which made them think they were over the Curicó 'cone of silence'.

The question that arises, then, is the following: if only half the distance to Curicó had been covered, why did this error not appear in the navigation sheet in the fourth column, where the estimated time to reach Curicó is recorded? Because if the 86 miles had not been covered, but only 48, the estimated time in the fourth column could never correspond to the time that had actually elapsed. In other words, the 48 miles, at 220 knots, would have taken 15 minutes of flight time, and not the 25 minutes required to reach Curicó.

Here the other element mentioned above arises: the strong west-easterly winds characteristic of the Malargüe-Curicó passage, which on that day were probably 100 kilometres per hour. If a hypothetical plane flies at 100 kilometres per hour, the speedometer reads 100, because the air speed (True Air Speed) is 100. But if there is a headwind of 100 kilometres per hour, that hypothetical plane stops in space...

Retired Colonel Carlos Muñoa, a personal friend and colleague of the pilots who flew the Fairchild 571, even believes that it is very likely that the pilots calculated the wind, i.e. they assumed a certain wind, and with that wind they calculated the delay time. But despite the calculations, the journey had been even slower than they thought.

And here it becomes necessary to add technical details specific to the aircraft. When the aircraft flies at an altitude very close to its maximum limit, the aircraft slows down. To this we must add that the aircraft was very demanding, not only because it was obliged to fly at that altitude due to the minimum limit, but also because it was very heavy, so that much of the aircraft's power was used to stay in flight and not to move forward, as when a car is put in fourth gear at 30 kilometres per hour.

At the same time, the speed indicated on the speedometer is not necessarily the speed at which the plane is flying, because at 6,000 metres above sea level the speed indicated is different from the real speed. And, flying by instruments, there is no reference on board to the speed at which you are travelling.

It is likely that the pilots of the Fairchild 571 did what they had to do, that is, they checked the erratic information coming from the radio-aid against the estimated time in the fourth column of the spreadsheet, which gave them a coincident value, that is to say that approximately 25 minutes had elapsed that should have taken them to reach Curicó. But because of the violent headwind at that pass, added to the reasons mentioned in the previous paragraphs, in the 25 minutes of flight they had barely covered the 48 miles to Planchón... and there were still another 38 to go to reach Curicó.

Possibly the turbulence and the discomfort of the flight did the rest: more than attending to navigational details, the priority, at that hour, was to fly the aircraft.

The Fairchild 571 turned north, entered into liaison with Santiago, began to descend, and when they descended to 15,000 feet, between seven and ten minutes after turning, they crashed into the Tinguiririca volcano.

Those few seconds, when several adverse factors combined simultaneously, sealed the fate of Fairchild 571.

When the decision was made to turn right and descend into the highest part of the Andes Mountains, the die was already cast. Not only for those who perished in the accident, but also for the survivors, who in their desperate expeditions always assumed that the aircraft had passed Curicó.

A surprising omission in the report is that it only refers to the ADF receiver. The pilots would almost certainly be utilizing VOR in addition or in preference to ADF. Not only is VOR easier to use, it is less susceptible to interference from the conditions and environment. It is likely that the pilots were tuned in to both VOR and ADF beacons, and observing both needles on the RMI display.

A couple of statements in the report bear further comment. Firstly, the analysis talks of the possibility that "turbulence and the discomfort of the flight" might have added to the mistaken assertion by the pilots that they were over Curicó. But at the time they were flying with good visibility, and later statements by the survivors agree that the flight was smooth, and experienced no turbulence until they turned north into the clouds. It is likely to have been a factor closer to the point of impact, when two major air pockets were experienced, but this was after the plane turned north.

Secondly, the statement that the Fairchild "did not have sufficient range to connect directly to the radio aids at the flight's destination, in this case Santiago" was only the case in the first part of the flight up until Planchón. But after Planchón, there would have been a clear line of sight to the high-frequency radio beacon in Santiago.

Despite the thoroughness of the report and its methodical enumeration of the issues, its conclusion seems suspect. To justify the discrepancy between the flight plan and the pilot's communication that they were over Curicó, it posits a 25-minute flight period from Malargüe to when the Fairchild turned north. But it is clear from the checkpoint communications that this was only a 15-minute period.

AFTER THEY TURNED NORTH

Most of the theories attempting to explain the accident concentrate on the question of why the pilots supposedly believed they were over Curicó. Very little attention has been directed to what happened once they turned north.

Despite the unlikelihood of the pilots getting lost, given the navigational aids and ground-stations available to them, it is still within the realms of possibility. If they were using only the beacons from Malargüe and Curicó (in other words, the beacons along the G-17 airway) then they would know their bearing from the ground station, but not necessarily their distance. In such a situation, the cone of silence theory in the Vierci report might come into play. Such theories are supplemented by speculations about the pilots' confusion over the timings; for example, Hugo Igenes proffers a theory that the reporting of Curicó at 18:24GM was somehow identified in the pilot's mind with the 24 minutes it would take to cross the mountains.

But whether or not the pilots were lost along the G-17 airway, the situation changes once they turn north. The angle of trajectory from their turning point to the impact point almost exactly matches the bearing of 186° from Curicó to Santiago, so it is tempting to assume that the pilots deliberately took that heading, thinking that they were over Curicó. But the pilots will have locked on to the Maipú beacons before or after turning, and the instruments would have shown a heading of around 168° – the radial from Santiago to the Planchón area.

There are only two scenarios in which the pilots would not know in which direction the plane was heading after the turn; the first being that no navigational aids were being used (through instrument failure or beacons being offline), the second being that ADF alone was being used and an absolute bearing was not available due to the effect of local magnetic fields on the compass reading.

In the former case, ignoring the rashness of changing course without paying close attention to the flight timings, the pilots would have had to manually calculate a bearing, compensating for the wind to give the desired direction relative to the ground. Given that the pilots had, according to the FACH report, significantly underestimated the wind speed when flying between Malargüe and Planchón, it is difficult to believe that they would suddenly start compensating for it so perfectly after they turned north; it is more likely they would have drifted many kilometres to the east of the impact point.

The second case is possible, but it is unlikely, considering that when the Fairchild first made contact with Santiago control tower 3 minutes earlier at 18:21 GMT, the controller gave explicit instructions to tune into the Maipú VOR. The purpose of this was not to start heading towards Santiago immediately, but to monitor the radial – the bearing from Maipú – so that when it reached 186°, the pilots would know that the plane was over Curicó. Presumably, the pilots were using the other VOR and/or ADF to continue towards Curicó. Reaching the specified radial would indicate that the plane had intersected the A3 corridor, and could now turn north towards Santiago.

The implication of the communication at 18:24 GMT is that not only was the Maipú VOR online, but that it could be connected to from near Planchón, on the G17 air corridor between Malargüe and Curicó. In reality, they were not at Planchón by then; the FACH report estimated that they were still at least 14 nautical miles short – around 25 km to the east of Planchón. At that point, the line of sight to Maipú would have been blocked by the 4,860-metre *Mount Palomo* 75 km away, or by the 4,990-metre *Altos de los Arrieros* in the *Sierra del Brujo* range 60 km away.

If the FACH estimate of the Fairchild's position at 18:21 GMT is correct, then it would still have been several kilometres short of Planchón at 18:24, the time of the next communication, when the pilots report being over Curicó. Again, the FACH report agrees, stating that "the plane had, in reality, still 5 miles left to reach Planchón". The controller, after some hesitation, accepted the copilot's assertion that they were over Curicó. But if they had successfully tuned into the Maipú VOR by then, they could have no uncertainty as to where they were. The VOR beacon encodes radial information in its VHF signal and so could not be affected by local magnetic fluctuations. The FAU report even concludes that "the selection of frequency in VOR and ADF were correct". Despite this, the Fairchild turned north, presumably tracking Maipú along the 168° radial, outside the official airways.

The statement of the miner Figueroa is entirely consistent with this manoeuvre. He claimed to have seen "a white plane, with broad wings, flying normally on a slightly descending course over the area known as *Quebrada del Tiburcio*, heading towards Rancagua". *Tiburcio* is a mountain pass, only accessible by foot, a few kilometres north-east of Planchón; and Rancagua is a town 120 km to the north-west. So Figueroa is saying that the plane was flying in a roughly north-westerly direction from a point a few kilometres east of Planchón – a description which corresponds exactly to the trajectory outlined above.

If the Fairchild had continued along this radial, seven minutes later it would have passed about 15 km due west of the impact point, no doubt successfully continuing along that radial to Maipú, with the highest intervening mountain around 10,000 ft. To compensate for the strong winds coming from the west, the pilot would have had to make adjustments, taking a more westerly course to intersect the radial again and keep the needle centred. Even if the wind were stronger than estimated, with the instruments working correctly the deviation would still have been straightforward to correct.

But now let's hypothesize that in the first minute or two of changing course, the connection to the Maipú VOR was suddenly lost. The pilots, by then flying in thick cloud, with severe turbulence that caused the plane to plummet in two massive air pockets, would have had to resort to manual navigation. Richard Cunningham, in *The Place where the World Ends*, wrote: "By 18:00 GMT, the jet stream had fallen to near 18,000 feet, which meant that the current ... was blowing at 120+ miles per hour." The source for Cunningham's claim is unknown, but if true, it equates to 105 knots, 70 knots stronger than the assumed 30-40 knots. If the pilots were then adjusting for 30-40 knot winds, the net eastward drift of 70 knots would have brought the Fairchild exactly to the impact point.

What could have caused such a loss of VOR? If the pilots had tuned into Maipú at the earliest possible opportunity, it is likely that the larger than expected drift to the east, coupled with the loss of altitude from the first air pocket, rapidly took them back out of the line of sight to Maipú. Whatever the reason, the Fairchild would then have been flying blind, and by the time the aircraft finally dropped out of the clouds 7 minutes later at 15,000 ft, it was too late to recover. It found itself flying along a canyon with peaks at either side, and a mountain ridge straight ahead.

This hypothetical chain of events is premised on the assumption that the pilots had tuned into the Maipú VOR by the time of the 18:24 communication with the tower, and that the VOR was functioning accurately. If true, it begs the question of why the pilots, if they knew their location, turned north at that point. One explanation is that the pilot misconstrued the A3 radial from Maipú as 168° rather than 186°, mentally transposing the two digits; after all, there was no verbal cross-checking by the pilots with the tower. But this suggestion, although plausible on the face of it, is made less likely when one considers the experience of Ferradás in crossing the Andes. Another explanation is suggested by a conversation Richard Cunningham had in early 1973 with a *Pudahuel* air traffic controller, who remarked: "I don't think he was caught in strong turbulence. The plane was flying over the clouds with visibility and had many beacons to check its position. A pilot cannot get lost. Maybe he decided to leave the air corridor he was flying. Maybe he lost respect for the *Cordillera*, and decided to take a shortcut." If this were the case, we can only speculate as to whether it was a personal decision of the pilot, or a more standard practice of military planes flying this route at the time.

IV. The Mountain

Fig. 57. *The Valley of Tears – view from the south-west.*

As the boys emerged from the broken fuselage on the morning of 14th October, they were able to take in the full extent of their situation. The plane was lying tilted to one side on a glacier, its nose crushed and buried in the snow. Behind, to the south, they could see the steep slope of the Fairchild's descent, its track still visible in the snow. High above, the mountain ridge extended round in a chain, encircling them and trapping them on three sides. Only the east was open to them, but in the distance, an even taller mountain seemed to block the way. The boys were certain that they must be in Chile, as the plane had supposedly been descending to Santiago. The altimeter indicated 7,000 ft, and they concluded that they were in the Chilean *precordillera*.

In fact, they were at almost 12,000 ft on the Argentinian side of the border, the 15,000 ft continuous ridge being the boundary separating them from Chile. A few kilometres to the south-west of them, although not visible from the glacier, was the 14,042 ft *Tinguiririca* volcano; and the mountain the boys could see in the distance to the east was the 16,959 foot *El Sosneado*. The glacial valley that they found themselves in was the *Valle de las Lágrimas* – the *Valley of Tears*; the source of the *Lágrimas* river. It was an area of the Andes that was rarely if ever visited, even in summer. Some neighbouring valleys had unofficial high passes used by Argentinian and Chilean cattle traders, but the *Lágrimas* valley was impassable, and the fuselage lay far above the summer pastures used by the Argentinian *puesteros*.

For the indigenous Mapuche people of the southern Andes, the mythical *River of Tears* separates the land of the living from that of the dead, the ancestors awaiting their loved ones on the opposite bank. For Catholics, the *Vale of Tears* represents the trials and tribulations of this world, most famously mentioned in the prayer *Hail Holy Queen*: "To thee do we cry, poor banished children of Eve, to thee do we send up our sighs, mourning and weeping in this Vale of Tears". For the survivors, who had every confidence that all twenty-eight of them would be rescued before long, these two allegories would prove to have tragic resonance.

The first tasks at hand were to take care of the casualties, and to clear the cabin in case they had to spend another night there. Roberto and Gustavo assessed all the injured, tending to them in order of severity. Marcelo arranged that the wounded should be placed at the front of the fuselage where it was warmest, and that area became the de facto hospital wing where they were treated. The luggage racks at the front left, which were screened by a large net, served as a sort of bunk bed for some of the injured. There, they put Tintín and Arturo. Tintín felt so weak that he could barely move. He had hurt his left arm in the accident, but the full extent of the injury was not yet apparent. He had been concussed on the rugby field a couple of weeks before the accident and he attributed his weakness to that. It was only a couple of days later that Gustavo realized the seriousness of Tintín's injury. Blood had been soaking his dark jacket, and had gone unnoticed, until it had started dripping onto Enrique. When Gustavo cut the sleeve of Tintín's jacket, the blood, which had congealed and clotted, started gushing from his artery. Gustavo called Roberto over, and, together, they gave him a tourniquet to stem the flow. Tintín stayed in the luggage rack for several days, sitting up and chatting with the others when he felt well enough. Gustavo would attend to his medical needs, and Marcelo would bring him water and food.

Gustavo also took another look at Enrique's wound. He made a small cut where the length of intestine was attached to the peritoneal membrane, in order to more easily effect a repair, but he still didn't feel confident that it was safe to push the protruding tissue back in. He bandaged it again, expecting that it would be dealt with by the professionals, once they were rescued. Susana was also moved to the hospital wing, where she lay semi-conscious, calling for her mother. Nando was left where he had been originally placed, at the back of the fuselage, still unconscious; but one of the boys dressed him in a mechanic suit, to give him an extra level of protection against the cold.

Morane Saulnier MS760 Paris jet, serial number FAA E-220.

FACH 479 (here with original S/N 918), sister plane of Beechcraft Twin Bonanza FACH 478.

Fig. 58. *Argentinian Air Force jet FAA E-220 and Chilean Air Force twin-engine FACH 478 were two of eight aircraft searching for the lost Fairchild on Sunday 15ᵗʰ October 1972.*

Marcelo, with his natural leadership abilities, organized the clean-up of the cabin. In the process of removing the mangled seats, the boys came across a box of luggage straps, and they used these to haul out the bodies of those who had died, placing them face-down in the snow outside the fuselage. There was also a large quantity of snow still to remove from inside the plane. Their concerted efforts created enough space for the survivors to squeeze into the covered part of the fuselage by the time evening came around again.

The second night was a marked improvement on the first. The extra space allowed the survivors to block the back of the plane with a wall built from suitcases, the plastic wood-veneer bulkhead panels, and a cabin door. Clothes were used to stuff and cover the gaps. Cushions were placed on the floor, and seat covers were used as makeshift blankets. The night was still punctuated by the cries of the injured, who suffered every time someone moved, and by the confused shouts of boys half asleep. Several dreamt or imagined that a rescue party had arrived, only to awake to the harsh reality of their situation.

They arose the next morning to a beautifully clear, though cold, day. They continued the work on the cabin, and started to put their minds to solving the immediate problem of food. Marcelo took an inventory of the available supplies, much of which had been fortuitously bought in Mendoza. A few chocolate bars, some chocolate medallions and other assorted candy, the eight bars of *turrón* bought by Roy, a couple of tins of canned mussels, some biscuits, a bottle of *Guindado* cherry brandy, a bottle of whisky, some crème de menthe, and several bottles of wine, a few of which had been drunk on the first night. Later, when combing the cabin, Coco and Roy found another bottle of whisky, three pots of jam, and some dried fruit. It wasn't much, and as a precaution, Marcelo took control of the rations and distributed the daily portions: a small piece of chocolate, and a sip of wine or liqueur, served in the cap of a deodorant spray can. The supplies were kept in a cosmetic bag, which was initially stored on the luggage rack at the back of the fuselage, and later – after some items went missing – in the bunk area in the forward cabin.

The day was interrupted by a welcome sight – planes overhead. First, a jet flying high, crossing from east to west and then north to south. Later, a twin-engine plane flying lower. The two planes were part of a trinational search and rescue effort coordinated by the Chilean Air Force's *Servicio Aéreo de Rescate* (SAR). The first sorties had gone out on the evening of the accident, taking advantage of the small amount of daylight left – four aircraft overflying the mountainous terrain between Curicó and the Argentinian border. On the Saturday, the aerial search started early with 12 aircraft – including three Argentinian F-86 Sabre jets – logging a total of 36 hours of flight. Ground patrols were also sent out, comprising the *Cuerpo de Socorro Andino* (the Andean Rescue Corps), the *carabineros*, and the army. On Sunday 15th October, the day on which the boys saw the planes, there were eight aircraft involved. With no sign of wreckage in the mountains immediately north of Planchón, the search zone was extended further north, to the area between the Tinguiririca volcano, close to where the boys were, and Mount Palomo. The Argentinian Air Force *Morane Saulnier MS760 Paris* jet – serial number FAA E-220 – was probably the first plane that the boys saw; with a two-hour sortie in the late morning, it was the only jet involved in the search and rescue mission that day. The second plane may have been Chilean Air Force *Beechcraft Twin Bonanza*, serial number FACH 478, which did a 4-hour stint around midday, and another, 2½ hours later in the afternoon, although officially the Chilean aircraft were not authorised to stray into Argentinian territory.

In preparation for alerting any rescue craft that might fly overhead, the boys had made a cross in the snow, and had extracted the metal plates from the seatbacks, with which they planned to reflect the rays of the sun. Coco's raincoat, with its bright red lining, was also readied as something that might attract attention. When the second plane dipped its wings, everyone was convinced that they had been seen. Roberto went into the fuselage to the hospital wing, to let the patients know. They had heard the noise of the plane and the shouts of the boys. Roberto told them that he expected a rescue within a couple of hours. To celebrate, he took a bottle of wine from the supplies, and shared it with his patients. He was roundly chastised by the others, and when the rescue didn't come that evening, he acknowledged that it had been a rash thing to do.

Over the following days, increasingly elaborate theories were proposed as to why the rescuers hadn't appeared. Their first thought was that it was perhaps too difficult a place for helicopters to reach, so that the rescue would come by land. When that didn't appear, they rationalized that it might take a few days to prepare. When some asked why food and medicines hadn't been dropped by parachute, it was suggested that perhaps the rescuers believed that the supplies would sink into the soft snow and be irrecoverable. The realists among them soon came to realize that they hadn't been spotted, but several clung onto the hope that a rescue was coming.

Meanwhile, the boys continued to adapt to life on the mountain. On the face of it, water was not a problem, as there was snow all around, but the boys soon found that sucking on ice was not an efficient way to stay hydrated, and it created sores in their mouths. The first attempt at a solution was to put snow into one of the empty wine bottles and shake it vigorously for an hour; a number of boys set about this task. Later, Fito invented a process that made use of the seatback metal plates which the boys had used to signal to the rescue planes. He bent the plate to produce a notch that served as a spout. Snow was heaped onto the plate, which acted as a reflector, intensifying the effect of the sun to melt the snow. On sunny days, the boys would spend the morning making water this way, splitting up into pairs; one boy to hold the plate, the other to hold the bottle. Much later, when the sun was plentiful, and a large container had been found, they perfected and automated the technique so that it required almost no human intervention. Another water-making system was set up inside the fuselage, where melting snow dripped through holes in the roof, although the water produced this way tasted awful, as it filtered through the insulating material. To collect it, the boys rigged up a system of conduits to direct the water to a bottle held by one of them, typically Arturo as this was the part of the plane where he rested.

Whilst some occupied themselves making water or sewing blankets from the seating material, Coco Nicolich and his 'cabin crew' were tasked with clearing out the fuselage, removing the wreckage of the seats and cleaning out the rot and the stench. Although this created additional sleeping space, the injured boys lying on the crowded floor of the fuselage faced agony every night, as their broken or wounded limbs were inadvertently trodden on or kicked. Their plight prompted Roberto to consider constructing an upper floor. After getting the go-ahead from Marcelo, he and Daniel Maspons set to work, making use of the equipment designed to secure cargo. Taking advantage of the tilt of the plane, they fixed two six-foot struts to protrude horizontally from the left side of the fuselage, the free ends suspended by straps attached to anchor points above. A cargo net was then stretched between the two struts. The result was a hammock, which would take two of the injured and free up space on the floor. Cushions were put over the net for comfort, although when they fell out of place, as often happened, the webbing quickly became painful to lie on.

Marcelo, who had been sceptical at first, commended Roberto for having the idea and for following through on it, but Roberto wasn't finished yet. He and Daniel also rigged up a hanging bed made from a pair of conjoined seats. It was positioned adjacent to the hammock near the back of the fuselage, the part of the plane that the boys referred to as La Punta. Hanging higher than the hammock, it faced towards the front of the fuselage, so that whoever was sitting in it could rest their feet on the hammock; an arrangement that led to some arguments, as the boys jostled for a comfortable position.

Rafael and Álvaro would sleep on the hammock, the former with his injured leg dangling over the side. Later, after the avalanche, when Coche's leg was bad, he joined Rafael there for a few days. They hadn't known each other prior to the trip, but they soon became friends, united by a passion for dairy farming. Arturo would sleep in the hanging seat, occasionally accompanied by Pancho or Pedro. Positioned as they were in La Punta, the boys on the upper floor suffered miserably from the cold wind which now penetrated not only from the back, but also from below. They also lacked the human warmth that benefited the closely packed group of boys sleeping on the floor. As a result, those above were given extra blankets.

A hanging door also briefly formed part of the upper storey, though positioned further forward in the cabin. Enrique Platero slept on it for a while, and Roberto used it as an operating table a few days after the accident, when he cut away the dead peritoneal tissue that was protruding from Enrique's abdominal wound. The hanging door didn't leave much room below, and was claustrophobic to sleep under, so it was removed as soon as Enrique's wound had healed sufficiently for him to sleep on the floor. The door then became part of the makeshift wall at the back.

The final component of the upper floor was at the front left, where the luggage rack had been. It had been used for the wounded in the early days, but after the hanging beds had been put into operation, it was mainly Tintín who continued sleeping there.

The resulting configuration afforded the survivors a bit more comfort. Those on the left slept with their backs resting on the floor of the plane and their legs on the chests of the person or people opposite them, whilst those on the right sat leaning back on the right-hand wall, their legs sloping up. To avoid getting wet from the snow and sludge, the boys used big pieces of cardboard and the luggage racks as slats to line the floor, so that water from melting snow would run underneath them. It was still tight and uncomfortable, and led to flare-ups whenever one boy inadvertently kicked another, but it was a big improvement on the first few nights, when some had needed to stand.

An Intimate Communion

As the days passed with no sign of rescue, the boys mounted an initial expedition, to get their bearings, and to see if they could find the tail of the plane, which contained the batteries. The mechanic, Carlos Roque, the only member of the crew still alive, had suggested that they could be used to power the plane's radio, which would allow them to make contact with the outside world. The expeditionaries who made that first foray into the mountain were Fito, Roberto, Carlitos, and Numa. Marcelo, in charge of the rations, gave them a portion of chocolate, two bonbons, and half a bottle of liqueur.

Setting off at 7:00 a.m., they headed up the slope towards the impact point, under the assumption that the tail had come to rest near there. Wearing socks for gloves, and cushions strapped to their feet to avoid sinking into the snow, their progress was slow, and it soon became apparent that they had vastly underestimated the distances. When it became clear that they weren't going to get close to their goal of reaching the top, they stopped to discuss whether to continue. Roberto argued for a return to the fuselage, and Carlitos was also reluctant to take undue risks; he was mindful of the gang's parting admonition to turn back if it became difficult or dangerous, that if they were going to die, they should do so all together. Fito had narrowly avoided falling into a crevasse between two rocks, and it had unnerved the four of them. Numa alone wanted to climb further, and they pressed on for a while, but on reaching a plateau and not finding anything of note, they felt it was pointless to continue, and began their descent.

Arriving back, exhausted, in the early afternoon, they were welcomed by the boys at the fuselage, who massaged their feet to get their circulation flowing again. The expedition had emphasized the difficulty of their plight, and had prompted the thought in the minds of both Roberto and Fito of what they might eventually have to do to survive if a rescue failed to materialise. They had been very conscious of how weak they had felt; how sapped of strength and energy as they had struggled just a few hundred metres up the mountain. And they had taken the opportunity to see their surroundings from a higher vantage point, and realized that they might be deeper in the Andes than they had at first assumed, although Fito, looking at the imposing mountain that seemed to block their way to the east, noticed that it was surrounded by lower mountains, with less snow.

The same thought that occurred to Roberto and Fito had already been suggested to Carlitos by Nando the previous day. Seeing their mountainous surroundings for the first time after he miraculously awoke from his coma, Nando had resolved that he would walk out of there at any cost, if necessary using the bodies of the dead. The death of his sister Susana from her injuries a few days later only increased Nando's determination.

As the meagre supplies dwindled, and the boys grew weaker, private conversations started taking place amongst groups of friends. Fito whispered to his cousin Daniel Fernández one night: "I think that we're going to have to use the bodies – am I going crazy?" Daniel assured him that he had been thinking the same; the two then drew Eduardo into the discussion. Roberto had already spoken about it to Gustavo Zerbino, who had had the same idea, and to Daniel Maspons, who was astonished more than horrified. Roberto and Fito separately broached the subject with Marcelo. He was shocked initially, although later admitted that the arguments were sound. But he was reluctant to dishearten those who still maintained hope of an impending rescue.

By the weekend of 21st-22nd October, it was clear to the realists amongst the group that no rescue was coming. It had been close to a week since they'd seen or heard any rescue planes, and if anyone had spotted them, they would surely have dropped food by then. Roberto broached the subject in an afternoon meeting inside the fuselage. He and Gustavo Zerbino explained that, without vitamins and proteins, they would grow progressively weaker, and die on the mountain. The only way to survive, and moreover, to escape from their predicament, was to use the bodies of their dead friends. For some, the proposition came as a complete shock. Others, who had thought about it fleetingly before dismissing it, were now compelled to face the reality. For everyone, the prospect was horrific to contemplate, but the dilemma they faced was that no action was a death sentence – and the longer they waited, the less strength they would have to act.

The meeting lasted some hours, with each person given the opportunity to have their say. Philosophically, everyone agreed, but some felt that they wouldn't be able to carry through with it physically. Liliana Methol, in particular, felt that she could never do it, but was supportive of the others' decision. Most of the boys stayed put in the fuselage, as a small group made their way out to where the bodies lay at the front of the plane. Coco Nicolich captured the moment in a letter dated 22nd October:

> One thing that will seem incredible to you – it also seems so to me – today we started to cut the dead in order to eat them, there is nothing else to do. As for me, I asked God in all that is possible that this day would never come, but it came and we have to face it with courage and with faith. Faith because I came to the conclusion that the bodies are there because God put them there and, as the only thing that matters is the soul, I don't have any remorse – and if the day came and I could save someone with my body, I would gladly do it.

Gustavo Zerbino had made the same argument in the meeting, saying, "What more do I want once I'm dead other than to help you guys to keep on living." He injected some humour into the tense situation, adding, "If I die tomorrow for whatever reason, and you don't eat me, I'll come back and give you a good kick up the backside," to which Roberto replied, "Gus, don't be so inconsiderate, who's going to eat you? You'd poison us all!" But the sentiment was shared by the others. Everyone agreed that they would be happy for others use their body if it would help them to live, and that formed the basis of a pact, and provided a moral justification for them to proceed.

It was Fito who took the initiative. He made his way out of the fuselage, almost knocking down Álvaro as he strode with fixed purpose towards the nearest body, mentally steeling himself for the task ahead. Unwilling to ask Marcelo for the penknife, he grabbed a shard of glass, and, with Roberto and Gustavo at his side, he made the first cut. Telling them to think of it as a piece of cured meat, he ate a small piece, the first to break the taboo.

As Fito went back into the fuselage to inform the others, Gustavo and Roberto took over, cutting several slivers, which they placed on the roof of the fuselage. They, along with one or two others standing close by, also took a small piece. Pedro impressed on them the seriousness and intimacy of what they were doing, and made an analogy with Catholic communion. Through Christ's death, God had given spiritual life as celebrated in Holy Communion, and now the bodies of their companions were being used to give physical life to the survivors. Marcelo would later use those words to persuade some of those more reluctant to eat.

Very few ate that first afternoon. Daniel Fernández came out of the fuselage in response to Fito's prompting, and took a small piece. Like the others that day, he didn't do it to assuage his hunger; rather, he felt it was an obligation, to see if he could pass the test necessary for survival. For Pedro also, the act was an imperative, and there was no question that they were doing the right thing. In his memoir *Into the Mountains*, Pedro recalled his feelings:

> We were not convinced by rational arguments, we were convinced by our stomachs, by the hunger and weakness that we all felt. We ate with curiosity, with emotion, breaking a taboo, knowing that we were doing something significant, but that it was all we could and should do to continue living. Rational explanations only gave a framework for something that was born deep inside us. We had no need of further justification. We were hungry and we wanted to live. It was the only thing we could do....

From Coco's letter of 22nd October, it is apparent that the survivors had not yet heard the news about the suspension of the search efforts. He wrote:

151

Today we were able to repair a transistor radio that we found the other day in the plane, Roy fixed it and tomorrow we hope to have news of the rescue on some Chilean or Argentinian news programme... If they have called it off, which I don't believe and at this stage would seem incredible to me, in three or four days when we regain some strength, I think a group of us will set off to cross the part of the Cordillera that's still remaining, which I hope will be a short distance...

Initially, the boys had only been able to listen to Chilean stations, but then they had found a good battery and Roy had hooked up a long piece of wire for an aerial so that, for the first time, they were able to get the Uruguayan radio station *El Espectador*. Marcelo and Roy went out of the fuselage early on the morning of 23rd October to listen to the 7:00 a.m. news bulletin, hoping to hear a report on the search efforts. With Roy standing some distance away holding the end of the aerial, Marcelo leant back against the plane and tuned in to the station. To his dismay, the first thing he heard was that the search had been officially suspended, and wouldn't resume until February.

Coco, hearing their shouts and seeing their faces, realized what had happened, and ran into the fuselage to tell the others. His optimism helped prevent a total loss of hope, rallying the boys and raising their spirits after the initial shock. He told them that the news was a good thing, because now they would be forced to get out by their own efforts. Coco wasn't the only one who realized that this was a defining moment, a call to action. When Tintín heard the news, he too became invigorated, shouting out, "Come on, guys! It's up to us to get out now." The attitude of the group changed from one of waiting to one of action. For the realists, such as Fito, Roberto, and Pedro, the news came as no surprise.

The new urgency of their predicament prompted a call for an immediate exploratory expedition up to the impact point, to try to find the tail, and to assess their surroundings from a much higher vantage point. Numa, Gustavo Zerbino, and Daniel Maspons set off up the mountain early the following morning, 24th October. The three climbed all day, a couple of dozen steps at a time before stopping to rest. They skirted around to the west of the fuselage track, and were little more than halfway to the impact point by the time darkness fell. Not wanting to give up their hard-gained altitude, they took the risk of spending the night out, despite wearing just light clothes and shoes. The three sheltered between two rocks, beating each other throughout the night to keep their circulation flowing, and, miraculously, and to their surprise, they were still alive when the first rays of sunshine hit them the next morning. They wrung out their socks, wet from the frost, and continued on up the slope, hitting one false summit after another before eventually reaching the impact point, where they spotted a broken pinnacle with rocks scattered around it. Nearby, they found the wing of the plane. Below, scattered along the track of the fuselage were bits of wreckage – an engine, a wheel, a panel, and other assorted debris.

Before heading down, they surveyed the scene from the crest, scanning the horizon all around, and saw nothing but mountains in every direction, with no hint of an escape route. And the fuselage, over a kilometre below, appeared as a tiny dot, invisible to any search plane. They agreed not to say anything about this once they got back, so as not to disillusion the others. They headed back down, now following the path of the fuselage, stopping to examine each piece of wreckage. After a while, they came across a seat upside down in the snow, and, turning it over, they saw that it was Ramón Martínez, the navigator. Further down, they found Gastón and Alexis, still strapped into their conjoined seats, face-down in the snow; then Guido, although not in his seat. None of them had visible signs of injury. Each time they found a body, Gustavo would collect the identity card, wallet, and any chain or watch. Next, they found the steward, Ovidio Ramírez, and, much further down, they came across Daniel Shaw. As they continued their descent, they spotted parts of the tail and the lavatory, and, from that, they deduced that the tail cone must be further down the mountain.

The boys at the fuselage, who had feared the worst when the three expeditionaries hadn't returned on the first night, embraced them when they finally made it back. Sapped of energy, with their retinas burnt by the reflection of the sun off the snow, the three sat down, exhausted, in the seats that had been lined up against the outside of the plane. The others brought them some cooked meat.

Soon after the expeditionaries had set off, Fito and Roberto had set about cutting some more meat. Roberto had swallowed a piece in front of everyone, as an example to the others, telling them, "This is not your companion – your companion is gone. His soul is with God. Here is a piece of meat, as if from any animal. You have to try your best." Many were persuaded to eat over the next couple of days, each boy acting individually, according to their conscience, until only Coche and the Methols were left. Even they succumbed eventually. Coche and Javier were persuaded by Marcelo, who spoke to them gently and encouragingly, relaying Pedro's theological analogy. Liliana, the last to break the taboo, was persuaded by the need to return to her children, and ate despite her repugnance.

Marcelo, who had been devastated by the turn of events, and the need to use their companions' bodies, put aside his personal distress, and took a leading role in the following days, cutting the meat, and distributing the pieces from a tray. He was scrupulously fair in allocating the rations, even going without food himself if necessary, but even then an occasional argument would flare up about the relative size of the portions.

On the first day, the boys had swallowed the meat raw and with difficulty, using snow or water to help it down. But they soon realized that cooking it made it marginally more palatable, and they made a fire when the wind would allow. Only lack of wood or paper for fuel precluded more regular cooking, the limited supply coming from Coca-Cola crates, a wooden toolbox, the wooden chocks for the aeroplane wheels, and a book of poetry. There was also a limited supply of balsa wood lining the floor of the plane, which could be extracted with difficulty, using the plane's axe to cut through the sheet metal. Roy took on the role of cook, making the fire below a metal sheet placed on a seat frame. Some of the boys who could barely tolerate the raw meat – Roy, Coche, Arturo, and Numa – ate more on those occasions.

Fig. 59. 'Breaking a taboo'. Drawn by Coche on his return to Uruguay.

Along with the personal belongings of the victims, the expeditionaries had brought back other items that they thought might be useful – a coat, some clothes, a bottle of drink, and a penknife. The latter, decorated with a Chilean shield, had been a gift to Guido from his *novia* Angeles Mardones. It was one of three penknives that the group possessed, a second provided by Javier. Along with a good supply of razor blades and the plane's axe, they were used as the implements for cutting the meat. Those cutting directly from the bodies faced a horrific task, which never got easier, and it was done out of sight of the others. But for those who weren't faced with that daily horror, what had been repulsive at the beginning became normal over time, though many still balked at the raw meat.

EARLY SEARCH EFFORTS

The body responsible for the search and rescue missions was the *Servicio Aéreo de Rescate* or SAR, which operated out of *Los Cerrillos* airport in Santiago, part of FACH *Group 10*. The head of the service, Squadron Commander Jorge Massa, used the information at hand to map out a search area; a wedge of territory stretching from Planchón in the south to Mount Palomo in the north-west, and Mount Sosneado in the north-east, the latter in Argentina. An intense search was conducted over eight days, with almost everyone from *Group 10* participating in the fifty-four missions, which utilised planes from the three national air forces – seventeen from Chile, six from Argentina, and one, the Fairchild's sister plane FAU 570, from Uruguay. Additional sorties were conducted by carabineros and private aircraft. *Group 10* Airman Juan Carlos Polverelli, who would later be involved in the rescue on the mountain, described the process:

> *Mountain searches for accidents worked in the following way: first, planes would go out on patrol, and when they had more or less located the point, a helicopter would be sent. Massa was in charge of SAR, but he had the particularity that he was a helicopter pilot. His triangulation of the maps, where the plane could possibly be, was perfect, but the problem was that we were looking from border to coast, we never crossed into Argentina. Every piece of information that came in was analysed and we flew to the sector to search. We never found anything.*

Daily reports were filed, outlining the activities of the day, the summary for 16th October being typical:

> *Early in the morning, air and ground activities began, especially in the area of Mount Palomo and the Tinguiririca volcano, the most likely zone, patrolling extensively in the foothills and the central mountain range. Land patrols of the Andean Rescue Corps and carabineros made enquiries with locals, farmers and miners in the area without positive results. The weather conditions are favourable, with no rain or snowfall. From Montevideo, Uruguay, an aircraft identical to the one that had gone astray was sent to Los Cerrillos, following the same route in order to check positions and discover any abnormality that might have caused the FAU-571 to stray from the route. The aircraft's itinerary was followed normally, without any abnormality being observed, arriving at its destination at the estimated time, which was immediately communicated to Montevideo. ... This day, 24 missions were completed. Photographs were again taken of Mount Palomo, to be examined in the laboratory.*

That day would represent the peak of the search activity, with deteriorating weather limiting flights to just a handful per day thereafter, until, at 15:00 Chilean time on 21st October, the air search was officially suspended, two days ahead of what had been planned. The purpose of the search had been to look for wreckage, with no thought that there could be anyone alive, so the decision was sensible in view of the dangerous conditions, as later related by Polverelli:

> Massa gave the following example: imagine flying at about 100 metres over the national stadium, completely snowed in, and you are asked to find a ping pong ball. The logic was to wait for the thaw, and then look again.

The decision shocked the relatives, especially the mothers, many of whom believed their sons to be alive. A large group of family members and close friends had immediately travelled to Santiago on news of the accident, but most had since returned home. The very first to arrive had been renowned artist Carlos Páez Vilaró, the father of Carlitos. As the official search started to lose impetus, he began planning his own sorties on foot and by plane, enlisting the help of Dr Canessa and Dr Surraco, the fathers of Roberto and his *novia* Lauri respectively.

Páez Vilaró's intention was to scour the area around the Tinguiririca volcano, where the experts believed the plane had gone down. He travelled tirelessly through the communities south of Santiago, using his charisma to assemble a large army of contacts and volunteers. Inspired by the artist's single-minded determination to find his son, they freely pledged their time and resources. The Aero Club of San Fernando lent planes and pilots, the Colchagua regiment based in San Fernando conducted ground patrols, and a network of ham radio operators were ever at hand to communicate the latest news to Montevideo.

At the Uruguayan end of this communication channel was Rafael Ponce de León. He had been a classmate of Marcelo, Julio, and Eduardo at *Stella Maris College*, and had been instrumental in helping with the logistics of the trip, calling Chile several times to make arrangements. He himself had not been able to go on the trip, as his wife Chela had been in her third trimester of pregnancy, but he had sprung into action at first news of the accident.

He made use of the Collins KWM-2 transceiver in the basement of his father's house on Puyol street in Carrasco, less than a block from the homes of several passengers – the Methols, Arturo Nogueira, and Enrique Platero. Rafael had his own equipment at home, but due to some redecoration, it was temporarily out of commission. At the time, ham radio was the communication mechanism of choice for making international phone calls, which otherwise would have been prohibitively expensive. Although illegal, the method was widely used. A ham radio operator in one country would contact a counterpart in the destination country, who would then patch in a local phone call.

Rafael was a ham radio aficionado *par excellence*. Following in his father's footsteps, he had started as a preteen, cutting his teeth on the story of the Uruguayan floods of 1959, when the waters of the *Rio Negro* had overflowed the *Rincón del Bonete* dam. In later years, long after the drama of the Andes, he would become an amateur radio world champion four times, the latest in 1978. The format of the contest was to talk to as many contacts as possible over a 48-hour period, with scores weighted higher if the contact was out of country, and higher still if out of continent.

1978 – PHONE

WORLD WIDE DX CONTEST

RAFAEL PONCE de LEON, CW3BR

winner

K2HLB MEMORIAL AWARD

(N. JERSEY DX ASSN.)

Score: 1,662,718

28 MHz World Record

Fig. 60. *Rafael's 1978 world record score of 1,662,718 was 220,000 higher than the next best contestant.*

Rafael's world record session saw him make 4028 contacts across 104 countries; a rate of 84 contacts an hour over the two days.

Rafael's very first action when the Andes story broke was to scotch a rumour that the boys had safely landed in a small town in Chile. He contacted Angeles Mardones, the *novia* of Guido Magri, and the supposed source of the rumour. She categorically refuted it, and Rafael sent a recording of their conversation to the local media, to prevent any further propagation of the misinformation.

Over the following ten weeks, he would work tirelessly, maintaining regular contact with Páez Vilaró and the search teams, exchanging information with them morning and evening. Even at work, he had access to a ham station that would allow him keep up communications throughout the day. One of the defining scenes of the Andes story was the nightly gathering, at 8:00 p.m., of mothers and girlfriends outside the house on Puyol street. Mecha Canessa, Roberto's mother, was always the first to arrive, and others would soon follow, eager to hear the news of the day's progress.

Páez Vilaró's initial sorties were in the area of the Tinguiririca, close to the boys' actual location. He started by seeking, successfully, the cooperation of Joaquín Gandarillas, who had owned much of the land in the territory before it had been expropriated by the

Allende government. Later, a police sergeant at the *carabinero* checkpoint in Puente Negro suggested that Páez Vilaró should set up a base camp in *Los Maitenes*, and use the expert local knowledge of a certain muleteer named Sergio Catalán. From there, expeditions could be made along the *Portillo* and *San José* river canyons. Páez Vilaró was tantalizingly close to searching in the right areas. In their escape from the Andes, Roberto Canessa and Nando Parrado would trek down these canyons, and end up in *Los Maitenes*, where Catalán would be their first contact with civilization.

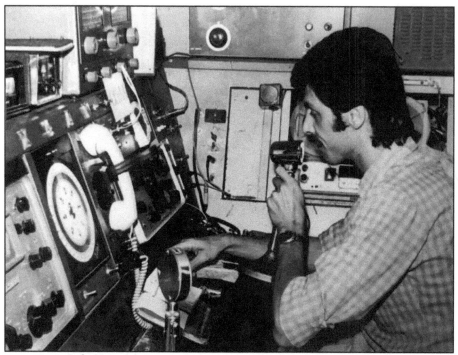

Fig. 61. *Rafael Ponce de Leon in the basement of his father's house on Puyol street.*

But events would transpire to move the search away from those lands. It started not long after the accident, when the two sisters-in-law of Javier Methol found out about a rhabdomancer, Claudino Frigeiro, who claimed to know where the plane was. In time, he would be proved correct. Using a divining rod, he identified a point 20 km north of Termas del Flaco on the Chilean-Argentinian border – near the *Tinguiririca* volcano. He also claimed to see survivors – at least five, but possibly more. The next day, the sisters-in-law went to see Rafael, and spoke by ham radio to Páez Vilaró, who told them that the SAR had already thoroughly searched that area. The matter was dropped, but Madelón Rodríguez – ex-wife of Páez Vilaró, and mother of Carlitos – took inspiration from Frigeiro's pronouncement, and decided to seek out a more famous seer. On the advice of Uruguayan mystic Boris Cristoff, she contacted parapsychologist Gerard Croiset in the Netherlands, who had had some success working with Dutch police.

Croiset delegated the work to his son, who was said to have similar powers. His initial statement would turn out to be uncannily accurate:

> I try to gain altitude. I climb sharply. Just when I think I've succeeded, I crash. One of the wings hits the projecting rocks. It falls off before my eyes. I'm falling. The tail crashes against the ridge and separates. The body of the plane, carried by its momentum, slides like a worm. It toboggans down the other side of the slope. It decelerates. The plane finally comes to a stop against a mound of snow, and because it is white, it blends in with it

And then:

> I see eight people coming out of the plane, I see darkness, death, hurry up and search. There are survivors!

The pronouncements on the location of the plane, however, would lead to weeks of fruitless searching. The place identified by Croiset was south of Planchón, diametrically opposite to the true location of the fuselage. Desperate to leave no stone unturned, and grateful to have a well-defined focus for his search, Páez Vilaró turned his attention to the area east of Talca, arriving on 23rd October. There he was met with the same welcome and hospitality that he'd encountered elsewhere in Chile, with offers of free help and resources from guides, boy scouts, muleteers, pilots, ham radio operators, priests, teachers, and other assorted citizens. Despite the dubious source of his information, he was also able to secure the help of the local *Chorrillos* regiment in Talca and the ongoing support of the Chilean Air Force, the former organizing foot patrols, and the latter providing continued use of FACH 478 to conduct air searches in coordination with two planes from the *Talca Aero Club*.

Communications were also freely provided by the *Talca Radio Club*, whose fleet of *Citronetas* (Citroen 2CVs) served as mobile ham radio stations. By this means, Páez Vilaró was able to keep in continual touch with Croiset and Ponce de León, as he travelled far and wide to the various search areas. He was effusive in his praise of the radio club members, who put aside work and family obligations to help with the search, and he singled out his frequent companions, Adolfo Burgos, Eduardo Fuster, and César Carrión, in his chronicle of the ten weeks he spent in Chile, written ten years after the accident.

Fig. 62. *Powerful antennas on the Talca ham radio club Citronetas allowed for communication on the go. The radio hams gave their time and resources freely over the period of the search.*

Páez Vilaró's account, entitled *Entre mi hijo y yo, la luna* ("Between my son and me, the moon"), is a richly poetic work that captures the depth of his emotions – the desperation and hope, the loneliness and comradeship – as he pursued his improbable cause. He became an instantly recognizable figure in the local communities, where people would refer to him as "The crazy father searching for his kid who's lost in the mountains", and his debt to the people of Chile is acknowledged in the opening lines of his book:

> *I come from a strange history of planes and volcanoes. Of tears and defeats. I come to touch a people who were born to give themselves, to open up in generosity like a flower, the people who inhabit the strip of land that is Chile, between the snow and the sea.*

Páez Vilaró's unwavering devotion to finding the lost plane was widely admired by the mothers who gathered each evening at Ponce de León's house, eager to hear his daily reports. Madelón, who had been the first to contact Croiset, and who was convinced by his visions, arrived in Talca the day after her ex-husband. With her was Bimba Storm, the mother of Diego. Whilst Páez Vilaró was coordinating ground searches, the two mothers took to the air in a small plane, exploring some of the areas indicated by Croiset. By 29th October, the weather had become overcast and rainy, causing the two mothers to curtail their search efforts and make plans to return to Montevideo. That day, Bimba felt an inexplicable sadness come over her, and she was unable to stop crying; a mother's presentiment, perhaps, of the events on the mountain that evening, which would take the life of her son.

THE AVALANCHE

With the official search called off, and the decision taken to use the bodies of their friends for food, the upcoming expedition became the boys' main focus. There were various options to consider: a large group versus a small group, in which direction to head, and whether or not to wait until the middle of November, when the risk of snowstorms was less.

Enrique, now fully recovered from his wound, and one of the fittest boys due to his rugby training, was the keenest proponent of an early expedition. Tintín and Bobby were his allies, and they envisaged walking to the west with a group of twelve, which included the gang and several others. Marcelo and Fito cautioned them that it was madness to set off so early, that they should wait until the thaw, but the thought of delaying for another few weeks didn't sit well with them, and they started making preparations. On 29th October, mindful of how Gustavo Zerbino had been affected by snow-blindness on his expedition, the three spent the day making sunglasses, cutting and filing some coloured plastic material that they had found. Events later that evening would render this preparation futile.

The hard work of Coco and his cabin team had considerably improved the sleeping conditions by the last week of October, freeing the fuselage of snow and debris. Every night, cushions were placed on the floor before everyone filed in to take their interleaved position on the left or right, after which Carlitos would construct the wall. Clothes were used to stuff any gaps in the wall and other parts of the fuselage. Before drifting off, the boys would chat and smoke, play cards when there was still light, and pray. By and large, the survivors slept near their own group of friends, and the conversations at night were often about their families, and life back home, imagining what everyone would be doing. Those who were studying agronomy, or whose families had farms, would talk about cattle, dairy production, and agriculture. Other discussions related to architecture – how to design better houses and *estancias*; Eduardo, Marcelo, Daniel, and Carlitos were at the centre of those conversations. More general topics, that included everyone, centred around food, or on planning the expedition.

In the early days, Marcelo had tried to raise everyone's spirits by encouraging them to sing, leading by example with a rendering of hits from his teenage years, such as *Blue Moon*. Inside the fuselage, Rafael, who had a passion for all things rural, led them in some traditional and emotive folk songs such as *El Indio Muerto*, about the death of a native Argentinian poet, and *Si vas para Chile* – "If you are going to Chile, I beg you to pass by where my beloved lives". Other songs such as *Clementine* and *The bear went over the mountain* were already well-known, the latter, in retrospect, being particularly apt:

> *The bear went over the mountain...*
> *To see what he could see...*
> *The other side of the mountain...*
> *Was all that he could see.*

Liliana especially enjoyed joining in on these occasions, conspicuous as the only female voice. Her tenderness and affection were a source of comfort and encouragement to the boys, and she would keep them believing that they'd get out of there, describing the meal that she was going to cook for them when they all got back to Montevideo. As the only surviving woman, she wouldn't countenance any favours, taking her turn sleeping in the coldest spots and working hard during the day, making water, and sewing gloves from the seat fabric.

On the night of Sunday 29th October, she took her place on the right-hand side, midway along the fuselage, with Javier opposite her. It would be a fateful choice for Liliana. It had been a beautiful day, but the survivors had bedded down early, as the temperature had dropped in the late afternoon. The previous two days had seen considerable snowfall, creating dangerous conditions on the slope behind them. The boys were well aware of the danger of an avalanche, and had seen several in other parts of the valley, but thus far nothing had come close to them. Javier had even suggested building a shelter away from the potential avalanche path, but they had neither the means nor the material to do that.

Roy, to Liliana's left, was chatting to his close friend Coco who had been confiding to him about how much he wanted to see his *novia* again, and his mother and sister; how little attention he had paid them sometimes. The conversation was interrupted by another of Roy's close friends, Diego, who was lying opposite, but who was suffering from a painful sore on his tailbone. Convinced that he would be more comfortable sleeping sitting up, Diego asked Roy to swap positions with him. There was still some daylight left as the two boys changed places. Roy lay on his back, with a shirt covering his head to protect himself from the cold. He was thinking about the conversation he had been having with Coco when he felt a vibration, then the noise of metal being knocked down by the snow, then snow pressing against his face. Hearing a second noise, he instinctively leapt up. Those who survived later likened the noise to that of a pistol shot with a silencer, or a magnesium flashbulb from an old camera.

It took a moment for Roy to understand what had happened. Everything had been covered by snow, and he could just hear faraway, muffled voices. Only the four on the upper floor remained unburied. Roy immediately dug for Carlitos beside him, half uncovering him, but the snow was already beginning to harden as he searched for Diego opposite him. Unable to find his friend, he scrambled through the collapsed wall at the back of the fuselage, thinking in his desperation to try to remove the snow from the back. Realizing the impossibility of the task, he went back in.

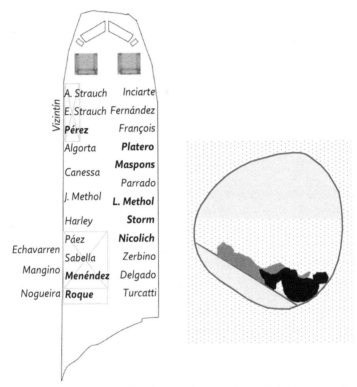

Fig. 63. *Sleeping positions at time of avalanche (dead marked in bold). Those on the right were buried deeper due to the tilt. The second avalanche covered the top of the fuselage.*

Tintín, sleeping on the upper level with a blanket over his head, had been covered by only a thin sprinkling of snow, and his first thought was that some of the other boys were playing a joke on him. He swore at them, but when he looked, he saw that the inside of the fuselage was completely covered with snow. Hearing the voices of the Strauch cousins buried beneath him, calling for help, Tintín started digging from his bed. Roy, on re-entering the plane, had seen Fito's hand sticking out from the snow, and set about releasing him. Fito, once free, started digging for Eduardo, who, after the initial terror of being buried, was experiencing a feeling of intense happiness and indescribable peace in the face of his impending death. He was abruptly brought back to the land of the living when Fito scooped the snow from his face. Fito told him to stay calm whilst he attempted to reach Daniel Fernández, who was deeply buried, opposite his cousins. Daniel had been able to hear voices from under the snow, and had struggled in vain to free his hands. He had relaxed and prepared himself to die, when he heard the sound of a hand digging, and felt a sudden rush of air. Daniel was then able to tunnel through to the space that Fito had just vacated. Lying next to Daniel, Coche had also resigned himself to dying and, like Eduardo, had felt an extraordinary peace, something he later described in his memoir:

> Anguish and desperation is transformed, in a split second, into the most genuine peace that I have ever felt in my life. I am reuniting with my father, whom I missed so much. There, dying happy and at peace, I am about to embrace my dear Dad.

But the movement of Fito's foot near his face had released a sudden flow of air, and Coche, born again, was able to follow Daniel out through the tunnel. As he escaped from under the snow, he shouted to Bobby to follow him out. Unable to extricate himself, Bobby needed the help of the others to pull him out. Contorting his body to squeeze through the tunnel, he felt something snap in his back, and found he could no longer move his legs; a condition that lasted half an hour, and precluded him from helping with the rescue.

After fully freeing Eduardo, Fito next turned his attention to Marcelo. He was helped by his cousin, and by Tintín, who had continued digging from above and calling out to Marcelo. When they finally uncovered him, they saw that he was dead, his arms over his head, and a look of resignation on his face. Moving up the line, Fito next uncovered Pedro, who, like several others, had resigned himself to die, and had taken comfort in the thought that his body would now serve to save his friends.

While Fito was digging at the front end of the fuselage, Roy was concentrating on the boys further back, removing the snow from Roberto's head and chest, before turning his attention to the deep snow across from him. Fortuitously, his hand found Nando's face, and created an air passage; Nando later estimated that he only had 10 or 15 seconds of life remaining. The boys who were already free had a desperate calculation to make over the next couple of minutes: whether to spend valuable time digging to completely free someone, thereby adding an extra pair of hands, or whether to just uncover the faces. Pedro, Javier, and Nando were left stuck in the snow, but Roy returned to free Roberto, who immediately started digging for Daniel Maspons. He found his friend already dead, looking as though he were just sleeping. With time running out, Roberto had no time to pause as he set about freeing Nando, who had become covered again.

Next to Roberto, in the moments after the avalanche, Javier had been able to get an arm out, and move the snow from his face. His feet were on Liliana's chest, and he shouted at her to hold on, to breathe slowly, that he would reach her. Rafael, on the hammock above, reached down to help him, but wasn't able to fully free him, and as Javier was in no immediate danger, the other boys moved on to search for their friends. Javier shouted for the boys to rescue Liliana, but by the time Gustavo had helped him get free, and the two of them had dug for Liliana, it was too late. Next to Javier, Carlitos had managed to free himself after Roy had removed the snow from his face and chest, and had immediately started digging for Diego and Coco opposite him. Finding it impossible to dig with his bare hands in the compacted snow, he covered them with a blanket and kept digging until he came across his two friends – both dead.

The boys on the upper floor had not been covered by snow, but the hammock had been crushed by debris from the wall, and by the hanging seat on which Arturo had been sleeping. Álvaro, sleeping on the hammock, was not in any danger of suffocation, but, being completely trapped, he had to wait until the end to be freed. Next to him, Rafael was able to provide some assistance to the boys below, reaching down to dig out Moncho who, with one arm free, had managed to scrape the snow from his face. Arturo's first instinct had been to scramble outside to see what was happening, but on coming back inside, he seemed in shock, unable to help.

Gustavo Zerbino's face had been uncovered by Carlitos in his search for Coco and Diego, and that had helped him survive until he was freed by other boys – Coche, Moncho, Roy, and Tintín – who were now digging at the back of the plane. To Gustavo's left, at the very back of the plane, were Pancho and Numa. Having heard them talking, Gustavo knew they were alive, and shouted at them to be patient, to wait until he was free. The curved emergency door, which had formed part of the wall had come down on them, giving Pancho a blow on the head, but allowing the two of them to breathe. Once Gustavo was free, they followed him out, the last to be rescued. Opposite Pancho and Numa had been their colleague from the law faculty – Juan Carlos. He and mechanic Carlos Roque beside him had been killed in the first moments, sustaining the full force of the avalanche as it had swept into the fuselage and buried them.

Once everyone still alive had been freed, the boys took stock. Along with Roque and Menéndez, six others had died. Five on the right-hand side, where the snow was deepest: Enrique, who had been the main proponent of an early expedition, Roberto's close friend Daniel Maspons, Javier's wife Liliana, and two members of the gang – Diego and Coco; only Nando had miraculously escaped from that contiguous row of six people. The final fatality was Marcelo; an anomalous death in a long row of survivors, he had succumbed quickly, despite early efforts to uncover him.

The remaining nineteen survivors, shocked, and now crammed into the cramped and claustrophobic space that remained between the snow and the roof of the fuselage, braced themselves for the night ahead. They dug and rearranged the snow as best they could, so that everyone had a place to sit or lie. Wet, without shoes, they had to keep moving throughout the night, and sleep one on top of the other, directly on the ice. Several of the boys were suffering from exposure, from having been lodged in the snow for so long. Nando, who had been buried the deepest, was pummelled by Eduardo and Carlitos all night, to keep his circulation flowing. Pedro, who had also been in the snow a long time, and was not only freezing, but also jaundiced and feeling quite unwell, was kept warm throughout the night by Pancho.

Around midnight, a second avalanche came, covering those lying at the back, although lightly enough that the snow was easily shaken off. It completely sealed the fuselage, however, and the boys soon realised that no air was entering the cabin. Roy dug his hand up through a gap in the cargo door, but was unable to reach to the surface. Fortuitously, the boys found an iron rod, unburied by the avalanche, that was long enough to break through and create an air passage.

It was the beginning of three days of misery and extreme isolation for the survivors; not only abandoned on the mountain, but now captives inside the fuselage, which itself lay under the snow. Whatever discomfort they'd experienced before seemed a distant luxury. The next morning, with the back entrance to the fuselage completely blocked by a tightly-packed wall of snow, the boys dug a tunnel through to the pilot's cabin. Wearing a woollen hat, some gloves, and Álvaro's waterproof jacket, Gustavo crawled through, past the dead pilots, and attempted to force open the upward-facing window on the left side of the cockpit, but was unable to budge it. Roberto, wearing the same equipment, also tried and failed, and it took Roy's strength to finally break through. Digging through to the surface, he found a blizzard raging that would continue for the next two days, and condemn the boys to remain in their tomb.

On the second day, to preserve their strength for any upcoming expedition, they decided to eat, but now, in their cramped quarters, there was no avoiding the horror of what needed to be done to sustain themselves. By the third day, 1st November, the blizzard had stopped, and the clouds had cleared, but it remained bitterly cold. A few of the boys ventured out, emerging from the tunnel into a pristine landscape. Laying out the blanket that had belonged to Nando's mother, they sat on the roof of the fuselage for a while, enjoying the sun and taking the opportunity to smoke, and to make water.

THE TAIL AND THREE DEATHS

All the work that had been undertaken in the first two weeks to clear the fuselage had been undone, putting paid to any hope of an early expedition, which had lost, in Enrique, its most active proponent. The next ten days were devoted to making the fuselage habitable again, and to recovering the bodies, the clothes, and the water-making equipment, which were now buried under the snow. Pedro and Carlitos did the bulk of the work, digging a tunnel from the back, using bits of metal from the plane as shovels. Every day or two, a body of someone who died in the avalanche would be released and dragged out through the tunnel, although those of Juan Carlos and Carlos Roque were too deeply embedded, and stayed in the wall of snow.

Everyone had been deeply shaken by the avalanche. Not only had the survivors lost close friends and leading members of the group, but there had also been an unspoken belief that having survived the plane crash, they would all get out of there alive. Although there was a constant worry of further avalanches, the wall of snow at the back served to protect them at night, and the igloo-like entrance was sufficiently narrow to prevent any significant quantity of snow from entering. With Coco dying in the avalanche, Daniel Fernández now took charge of the cabin, putting in place some simple procedures to keep things organized. The last one out of the plane in the morning had to pick up all the blankets and stow them on the hammock in order to dry them out and to prevent people from stepping on them. The wet cushions were taken outside, to sit on during the day. When they retired to the fuselage at night, Daniel would go in first, and the others would hand him the cushions to line the floor. Everyone else would then file in, taking off their shoes and placing them on the luggage rack. Finally, Carlitos, the last to enter, would build the wall before taking up his sleeping place in the warmest part of the fuselage, opposite Coche. Others also had preferred sleeping partners – Fito with Eduardo, Daniel with Gustavo, Bobby with Roy, Javier with Álvaro, and Roberto with Nando. The remaining boys would change around, or might decide to sleep by themselves now that there was a bit more space available.

The survivors had a common Catholic background and held similar beliefs, although there were different views on what faith meant, and whether God intervened directly in events or acted through human endeavour. The near-death experiences in the avalanche had sharpened their religious sensibilities, and there was now communal prayer every night, led by Carlitos, using the rosary that his mother had handed to him on his departure. The *Holy Rosary* in the Catholic church celebrates various events from the life of Christ, each event or 'mystery' meditated on whilst praying a 'decade' of the rosary, consisting of ten *Hail Marys* – one per bead – preceded by an *Our Father* and succeeded by a *Glory Be*. The five mysteries are followed by concluding prayers, including *Hail Holy Queen*, with its reference to the *Vale of Tears*. Each night, Carlitos would lead off, introducing and praying the first mystery before handing over to Coche, opposite him, who would follow with the second. The beads would then pass down the line, until the entire set of mysteries had been completed. This nightly mantra became an important and calming ritual, and several of the boys found it soporific, helping them to fall asleep well before its conclusion.

One of the common distractions before settling down to say the rosary was to talk about food. The boys made lists of food in all manner of different categories: home cooking; food that you or your girlfriend could prepare; sweet versus savoury dishes; exotic and international cuisine; rural fare, and invented recipes. A parallel discussion was to list all the restaurants in Montevideo, and their specialities; Coche recording them in Coco's diary, which he had found after the avalanche, and Nando noting them down in his sister's address book. As time passed by, however, the boys became increasingly frustrated and homesick by such discussions, and the topic was gradually dropped.

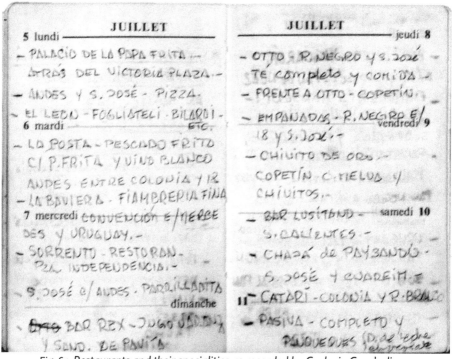

Fig. 64. *Restaurants and their specialities as recorded by Coche in Coco's diary.*

The loss of Marcelo in the avalanche forced a change of leadership, and the three cousins, Daniel, Fito, and Eduardo took on that role. Most importantly, they took charge of the cutting, and dictated the distribution of the food. The three sought to protect the younger boys from the horror of cutting directly from the corpses, so that no-one except them knew which body was being used. Supporting the triumvirate was a group of secondary cutters – primarily Gustavo, Carlitos, and Pedro – who would slice the large chunks into smaller pieces, allowing for more equitable distribution of the food. Eduardo would hand out the portions, the nominal ration being one thermos cap per person, once a day, at midday. Expeditionaries, however, could take what they wanted, and those doing the cutting also had the opportunity to take more; a practice that was accepted by the group.

The expedition was planned for 15th November, and would comprise a small group of the fittest. Roberto, Nando, Numa, and Fito were accepted without question by the group as the prime candidates, and a one-day trial expedition involving Tintín, Roy, and Carlitos was arranged to select other possible expeditionaries. After the three returned, Roberto, Nando, and Fito had a meeting to finalize the expedition team, and chose Tintín to take the place of Fito, who had had to drop out due to haemorrhoids. The expeditionaries were given privileged status, receiving the biggest portions of food, the warmest clothes, and the most comfortable places to sleep. The night before they set out, three of the boys – Gustavo, Eduardo, and Roy – slept standing up, so that the expeditionaries could have more room to stretch out and rest. Other boys gave up their cherished sweaters or socks, or their Ray-Ban sunglasses. And the cutters prepared a large supply of meat, which was packed, frozen, into rugby socks.

Any illusion that those who had survived the avalanche would eventually be saved was shattered by the death of Arturo on the planned day of departure. In the early days on the mountain, Arturo would crawl out of the fuselage to make water, unable to stand on his injured legs. But after the avalanche, in which he lost his good friends Marcelo and Enrique, he isolated himself, resting inside the damp fuselage. There were some fractious arguments, in particular one with Carlitos, who had been talking about the celebrities who had visited his father at Casapueblo. Arturo told Carlitos that he didn't want to be part of that world, in which people were materialistic but forgot about the human heart. But when Roberto berated him for his outburst, Arturo took Carlitos' hand, and begged him for forgiveness.

Despite his introspection, everyone realized what a special character Arturo had, and one day he led the rosary in such a profound and sincere way that everyone was deeply moved. Afterwards, Arturo cried at the emotion of it all, and confided in Pedro that for the first time since he had lost his faith, he had felt God again. Afterwards, he wrote a letter to his parents and *novia*, talking about his renewed belief: "I have never suffered as now, physically and morally, though I have never believed in Him as much as now".

Towards the end, Arturo stopped eating, going several days without food, but he developed a pathological thirst that couldn't be satisfied. In the last few nights, as Arturo became progressively weaker, Pedro slept next to him, talking to him about his family and girlfriend, about Argentinian football, and about the exams they were going to take when they got back home. With time, Arturo became feverish, and sank into a delirium. On the last night, which was exceptionally cold, the boys took him down from the seat to the floor, and Pedro slept holding him. In the night, Pedro awoke to find Arturo stiff beside him. Gustavo gave him artificial respiration, but Pedro knew he was dead, and he cried for the loss of his friend, sad that he had been unable to do more for him.

The cold night foreshadowed a snowstorm the next day, delaying the departure of the expeditionaries. They set off a couple of days later, but without Numa, who had developed an infection in his foot. Numa was distraught at not being able to go, and it marked the start of his rapid decline. The remaining three headed northeast, towards where the mountains seemed lower, with the thought that the valley might curve around to the north, and then to the west towards Chile, bypassing the intimidating headwall at the west end of the valley. Although a few, such as Pedro, felt that the way out was to the east, the predominance of opinion – informed by the dying words of the pilot – was that they were in the Chilean *precordillera*, and that to go east would take them deeper into the Andes. As if to confirm that, the way to the east seemed blocked by an imposing mountain that was higher than those that immediately surrounded them. Although they didn't know it at the time, it was the 5,189m *El Sosneado*, the southernmost 5000-metre peak in the world. A final consideration was that the Chilean *precordillera* was narrower, and closer to civilization, than that on the Argentinian side.

To carry their supplies, they used half of a Samsonite fibreglass suitcase as a sledge, loading it with blankets, food, two pairs of shoes each, spare socks, and a glass bottle of water. Each boy also had a homemade backpack, fashioned from trousers and straps; something Roberto had read about in a boy-scout manual. In these, they carried the supply of meat, spare clothes, straps, a bottle of cognac, and the revolver. A duffel bag held blankets, including the one that had belonged to Nando's mother. They took cushions to strap to their feet for when the going got soft in the afternoon sun, and aluminium poles to use as hiking sticks. On their hands, they wore mittens sewn by Tintín from seating material. They set out to shouts of encouragement from the boys, Nando and Tintín pulling the sledge, and Roberto dragging the cushions behind him.

After two hours of walking predominantly downhill, Roberto went over a crest and, to his surprise, spotted the tail cone below him. The three picked up their pace and, on arriving, dropped their packs and immediately set about opening the suitcases that were scattered all around. They found an ample supply of woollen socks and sweaters, and other good-quality clothes to replace those that they'd been able to scrounge back at the fuselage. Tintín was particularly pleased. He had brought along a pair of oversize boots belonging to Coco Nicolich, and, using four pairs of the newly discovered woollen socks, they now fit him comfortably.

Fig. 65. *El Sosneado, looking east from the Valley of Tears. January 2015.*

The boys also scoured the contents of the suitcases for food, finding a box of chocolates to add to the three *empanadas* and the bag of sugar they found on the galley shelves. In the luggage of Panchito Abal and Javier, they found over a dozen cartons of cigarettes, each carton containing ten packs. Most significantly, they found the batteries that Carlos Roque had told them about; a discovery which would have a marked effect on their plans to escape.

Despite having walked for only a couple of hours, the boys remained at the tail, resting and spending the night there, in far more comfortable conditions than they'd become accustomed to up at the fuselage. They found a metal receptacle with a closing door, in which they could burn wood. Using it as a stove, they were able to cook the meat they had carried with them. And the discovery of another transistor radio, for which they made an antenna by stringing a length of metal cable to a high rock, allowed them to listen to music as they settled down for the night.

Fig. 66. *The tail, March 1973.*

Reclothed and replenished, they set off again early the next morning, walking until midday, at which point the sun became too hot. Again, they decided to rest all afternoon, and stay overnight at their stopping point, but unlike the previous night, the temperature plummeted after sunset, and, even with the multiple layers of clothing, and four blankets, the boys had to resort to sleeping one on top of the other. With no sign of the valley curving around to the north and west, and a fear that things might have been a lot worse if they had been caught in a storm, Roberto felt it would be imprudent to continue, suggesting instead that they take the batteries up to the fuselage, and attempt to get the plane's radio transmitter to work. Against Nando's determination to press on, and Tintín's indecision, Roberto's arguments won the day, and the boys hiked back up to the tail, where they spent another night.

The next morning, they filled the sledge with clothes and cartons of cigarettes for the boys at the fuselage, along with some large cigars, the transistor radio, and a comic book. But the two black 24-volt batteries were problematic. They were huge – about half a metre long, and weighing around 50 kilograms each – and the boys quickly realized that it would be impossible to transport them even a short distance. The only alternative was to bring the radio to the batteries. Setting off at 9:00 a.m., they arrived back at the fuselage around midday. They were greeted with mixed emotions by the other survivors: disappointment at the failure of the expedition to reach Chile, but excitement at the news of the tail and the batteries, and by the large supply of clothes and cigarettes that would make life a little bit more tolerable. By and large, the boys were in agreement with the decision to get the radio to work, although one or two remained sceptical.

There had been another death whilst the expeditionaries had been away: Rafael had succumbed a few days after Arturo. He had been universally liked and admired by the others for his courage in the face of his injuries. With the flesh torn to the bone in one leg, and gangrene developing in the other, he never complained, and was irrepressibly optimistic and determined to escape from the mountain. Always joking, he infected everyone with his passion for dairy farming, speaking at length about cheese production. Only once did he get depressed, gathering everyone around him, and telling them, "Look guys, don't be sad, I know I'm going to die." He told them that he was leaving his motorcycle to his partner in the *tambo*, and his jeep to his girlfriend. They all started joking with him, asking him to also leave things to each of them, and to arrange for everyone to receive cheese. It would be a while after that before he died, but one day, like Arturo a few days previously, he became delirious, and started to have difficulty breathing. Despite Gustavo's best efforts to revive him, he died soon after.

Now began a long period of tedium as Roberto, with the help of Roy, set about dismantling the radio system. They had a few tools at their disposal – a screwdriver, some pincers, and an axe – but the task was complicated by the many components and the large number of wires that needed to be cut. Roberto spent several days pondering how it would all fit back together, before the rest of the boys lost their patience and started pressuring him to set off for the tail again. But it was the end of November by the time the three boys left with the radio components, this time accompanied by Roy, who, despite his weakened condition, was persuaded to join them, being the only one with any knowledge of electronics.

They spent a week at the tail, trying to hook up the radio to the batteries. There was momentary excitement when Roberto found the Fairchild repair manual. The index showed "Chapter 34: Communication", but when they went to those pages, they found they were missing, perhaps torn out by the strong wind that often swept through the valley. Roy did have a few successes, getting the dial and fan motors to work, but in fact the exercise was doomed to failure, the transmitter needing a 115-volt AC supply, rather than the 24-volt DC supply provided by the batteries.

They returned to the fuselage on 8th December, the day before Nando's twenty-third birthday. The boys at the fuselage weren't overly disappointed by the news that the radio couldn't be made to work, as they had heard on their transistor radio that the rescue efforts were going to start again, with the FAU sending out a C-47.

The trip to the tail hadn't been totally wasted, as Tintín had found insulating material that could be used to sew a sleeping bag for the next expedition. And Nando had found his luggage, in which were two large bottles of spirits – one of rum, and the other of *Espinillar* (a Uruguayan 76-proof whisky substitute) which they would take on the final expedition. He also found the pair of little red shoes bought in Mendoza for his nephew Gaston, which would become so symbolic of his walk to freedom.

With all sights now set on walking to the west, the three expeditionaries prepared for what they hoped would be the final expedition. Several boys, led by Carlitos, worked on sewing the 3-person sleeping bag. More meat was prepared, equipment and clothes chosen, and makeshift rucksacks packed. Nando and Tintín were eager to leave, but Roberto was more reluctant, weighing up the risk of the expedition against the probability that the new search efforts would find them. It took the death of Numa to tip the balance in favour of leaving. Numa had been one of the strongest from the beginning, taking part in the two main expeditions of the first ten days, and a later, shorter one with Pedro. Wearing Rafael's boots, which were slightly too large for him, he had developed two sores – one on his foot, and one on his ankle. Later, his leg became infected, and, unable to go on the subsequent expeditions, he became despondent, and stopped eating, despite the best efforts of Pancho, Coche, and the Strauches to persuade him otherwise. His deterioration was rapid. Roberto tried to stem the infection, lancing two large boils to remove the pus, and giving him antibiotics that he'd found in the tail, but Numa continued to go downhill. It was only when he complained of a sore on his tailbone and the doctors examined it that they realized how thin he had become; all skin and bones.

On 11th December, Numa became uncommunicative, his gaze fixed open. His friend Pancho sat beside him and prayed the rosary with him, and then Numa stopped breathing, dying in Pancho's arms. Coche later said of Numa that he was the purest, most honest man he had ever met, and all of the boys agreed that he had selflessly given everything to the group, at the cost of his own wellbeing.

Coche himself seemed to be going the way of Numa, with large boils on his legs, and a reluctance to eat; and Roy also was rapidly growing weaker. The prospect of another death persuaded Roberto of the urgency to leave immediately, and the three expeditionaries set off the next day at dawn, heading west towards the headwall.

THE TREK TO FREEDOM

Nando and Roberto's epic trek across the Andes has been documented and fêted many times, not least in Piers Paul Read's account of which *Lord of the Flies* author William Golding said, "His telling of the journey the young men undertook to get help could not be bettered." Nando later gave a personal account in his much-acclaimed 2006 memoir *Miracle in the Andes: 72 days on the mountain and my long trek home*, in which he credits his single-minded determination to step into the unknown to the desire to see his father again:

> *For a moment I felt his presence beside me and an eerie calm settled over me. I stared at the huge mountains to the west and imagined that there was a path leading over them that would take me back home. I felt my love for him tugging at me like a lifeline, drawing me towards those barren slopes. With my sights set on the west, I made him a silent promise: "I will fight. I will return home. I will not let the bond between us be broken. I promise you, I will not die here! I will not die here!"*

Roberto devoted nine chapters to the trek in his 2016 memoir *I had to Survive*. Like Nando, he spent hours contemplating possible routes up the headwall, trying to determine the best point of attack.

> *I spent two days before we struck out studying the enormous wall of ice we were about to scale. I'd scrutinize its details, section by section, trying to determine the best path across it... We could try to imagine the rock outcroppings, the peaks, the drops, the twist and turns, and the narrow gorges. We decided to attack it head-on, hiking directly west over the tallest part because it was also the shortest route.*

Although Roberto and Nando rightly receive credit for the ten-day trek into the unknown, it was the third expeditionary, Tintín, who helped make it possible. When the three set out on 12th December, it was Tintín who was carrying the biggest load, acting as a porter for the expedition. As well as his personal items, such as spare clothes and shoes, and cushions for his feet, he was carrying the bulk of the shared equipment and supplies: half the meat, a bottle of water, the bottle of *Espinillar* that they'd found at the tail, the revolver, the maps and compass, some straps, and a selection of items from the plane's first aid kit. He set out without questioning his role, with the same uncertainty as his more lauded companions, and with the same expectation that he could well lose his life in the attempt.

The boys left early on the morning of 12th December, heading west up the valley, with mountains either side of them. It quickly became apparent that the distances were much greater than they appeared, and that any hopes of reaching the top in one day were wildly optimistic. As they approached the base of the headwall, wary of the avalanche risk from the large serac overhanging the northwest end of the valley, the softening snow necessitated use of the cushions underfoot. Even then, the boys would sink to their knees at every step, and their makeshift snowshoes, attached with straps sewn to the cushions, became sodden and heavy, sapping their energy and slowing their progress to a crawl.

Fig. 67. The 1000-metre headwall blocking the way to the west.

At midday, they stopped for lunch, sitting on some stones, before continuing the painful struggle up the mountain, resting every few steps as the slope and altitude became increasingly vertiginous. At one point, Tintín came dangerously close to toppling over, pulled back by the weight of his backpack, before managing to twist around and save himself. As darkness approached, they started looking out for a place to sleep, becoming increasingly desperate as they continued climbing in the dying light, until Roberto spotted, next to a rock, a hollow carved out by the wind. Although far from level, it would afford them protection from sliding down the mountain. They climbed into their sleeping bag, lodging their sticks in the snow at their feet for extra security. After eating their ration of meat, washed down by a small quantity of *Espinillar*, they settled down to rest, with Roberto taking the warmer middle position on a cold, clear night. Lying at a steep angle, they barely slept, but their view from high above the snow-covered valley, illuminated by the bright stars and a half moon, was spectacular.

The next day's progress was equally slow and painful. The slope became noticeably steeper, and more slippery, and a succession of false summits added to their frustration. Unwilling to get caught out again, the three boys set up camp well before it got dark, still short of the summit, and with no clear idea of how much further it would be. The early stop gave them the opportunity to examine a line in the distance that Roberto had spotted as they had risen higher up the headwall, allowing an extended view to the east. Roberto was convinced it was a road, and it appeared to run through the middle of a green area that they assumed to be grass. Tintín was inclined to agree, but Nando was unconvinced, and he remained adamantly opposed to Roberto's suggestion that they change plans and head east again.

Fig. 68. *View to the north from high on the headwall, above the level of the serac.*

Roberto's eyes weren't deceiving him. The line he saw 20 km in the distance was actually *Provincial Route 220*; a gravel road leading to the *Sominar* sulphur mines and refinery, on the slopes of the *Overo* volcano, whose operations were active in the summer months of December to February. There were other pockets of civilization nearby: a long-closed hotel that had once served visitors to the *Termas del Sosneado* thermal pools; a police checkpoint for vehicles going to the mine; and the horse posts of *puestero* Antonio Araya and other families. The latter would have been manned in the middle of November, when the boys had aborted their expedition to the east. If they had continued on, and if they had managed to safely negotiate the ravines, crevasses, and torrents – by no means certain in the dangerous conditions of the spring thaw – they would have reached habitation within a couple of days.

As the boys lay down to sleep on the second night, Apollo 17 astronauts Eugene Cernan and Harrison Schmitt were making their final excursion on the moon 384,000 km above them; the last time man would set foot on the surface of the moon for the foreseeable future.

In the morning, Roberto remained with the backpacks at the camp, whilst Nando and Tintín scouted on ahead to see how close they were to the top. Roberto wanted to study how the landscape to the east changed with the sun, in case the line he had spotted was a trick of the light; but the more he looked, the more convinced he became that it was a road, with grass and a river beside it, and he thought he could make out other small roads in the mountain. Tintín arrived back two hours later, with the news that Nando had reached the top, and wanted Roberto to see for himself. It took him an hour to make the ascent, and the sight that greeted him was disheartening – mountains in every direction, as far as the eye could see. By then, Nando had recovered from the initial shock of the view to the west, and had been studying the landscape. He pointed out to Roberto a possible exit to the west, although it was guesswork as to what lay behind the mountains directly blocking their view.

Eventually, the two boys headed back down to where Tintín was waiting with the equipment, and as they lay in the sleeping bag that evening, they discussed what they should do. Nando suggested that Tintín should head back to the fuselage, and the other two should take his food ration and continue on to the west. He felt it was madness to return to investigate a possible road to the east. If it turned out to be a false lead, then they would have wasted another ten days, time they could ill afford, given the decline of Roy and Coche. Nando's proposal would allow Tintín to tell the others that there was a possible way out to the east, in case they needed to mount another expedition. There was also the prospect that the boys at the fuselage might be found by the search plane, which they had heard earlier that day, in which case Tintín would then be able to give the rescuers details as to Nando and Roberto's direction and plan of action.

By morning, Roberto had decided to go along with Nando's plan. He reflected that he had already wasted two weeks in the attempt to get the radio working, and he didn't want to be responsible for another ill-judged procrastination. Tintín handed over his rations and the best of his clothes, and headed back towards the fuselage, sliding down the headwall on a cushion. It took him less than an hour to retrace the route that had taken two days to climb. The other two decided to rest for the remainder of the day, to regain some strength before setting off the next morning.

Fig. 69. *View to the west from the summit. It would take Nando and Roberto two days to descend the 2000 metres to the bottom of the gulley.*

The climb up to the summit was much harder, now that they were carrying their full load; taking three hours compared to the one hour of two days previously. Once at the top, they headed down the gully to the west. It's hard to overstate the courage it took for Nando and Roberto to take this step into the unknown. They knew that there could be no way back, that in all likelihood they would be walking to their deaths. And if they found another mountain blocking their way, it was unlikely that they would have the strength to climb it. Either they would find a way out, or die in the attempt.

After two days of careful and sometimes hazardous descent through 2000 metres of rock and snow, they appeared to be close to the entrance of the valley at the bottom of the gully. As they lay in their sleeping bag that evening, they noticed that the sun was continuing to shine on the face of the mountain across the valley from them until late into the evening. It was cause for optimism, giving them hope that the way was open to the west. They were looking at the 4,360-metre south summit of *El Brujo*, the southernmost spur of the *Sierra del Brujo* mountain range.

Fig. 70. *The bottom of the gulley in sight. The evening sun on El Brujo across the San Andrés river valley suggested to the boys that the way might be open to the west.*

On day seven of the trek, they finally entered the valley. Wide and long, it stretched downwards into the distance towards the southwest. After making some headway down the valley, they were elated, in the early afternoon, to come across a river emerging from under the snow. It was surrounded by a profusion of life – greenery, mountain flowers, birds, and lizards. The boys stopped to celebrate and savour the moment, praying out loud in their gratitude, and confident that they would now survive. They had come across the *San Andrés* river, also known as the *San José* to the few locals who ventured there. Today it is the site of the 40-megawatt San Andrés hydroelectric plant, which was commissioned in 2014 as part of a wider project in the Tinguiririca basin. The road that links the plant to civilization follows the *San Andrés* river down the valley, past its confluences with the *Portillo* and *Azufre* rivers before finally joining the I-45 gravel road that runs parallel to the Tinguiririca river; a distance of 25 km and a total descent of 1,300 metres. From there, it is still another 35 km to the nearest village.

Fig. 71. *There is now a road that leads to the 2014 San Andrés hydroelectric plant. When Nando and Roberto started hiking down this valley on day seven, it was devoid of human presence.*

For Roberto and Nando, the boulder-strewn valley appeared vast and isolated, untouched by human presence. Progress was difficult and, in their weakened state, they weren't able to manage more than four or five kilometres a day, with Nando impatiently forging on ahead and then having to wait for Roberto to catch up. The landscape became increasingly verdant, however, and on day eight they came across signs of human activity. The first thing they saw was a rusty *Maggi* soup can, then a horseshoe, and finally some cows. That night, they were able to build a fire, and slept comfortably and soundly for the first time in months. The easy availability of firewood, and the warmer temperatures, convinced them to leave behind the sleeping bag and their unneeded clothing before setting off the next day. By early afternoon, Nando and Roberto came across a cattle trail next to the river, which made for easier going, and they headed towards a plateau they could see in the distance, topped by a corral. Unknown to the boys, their halting progress had already been noted by *arriero* Sergio Catalán and his two sons Cucho and Checho, who were herding cattle on the other side of the river. Catalán didn't pay too much attention to it at the time, assuming that they were tourists hiking in the *precordillera*. But the events of the next hours and days would propel him from the anonymity of his cherished way of life to one of unwelcome international fame.

By early evening, Nando and Roberto had reached their destination, and it seemed a perfect place to stop. The vegetation was lush, the trees plentiful, and there was fresh water nearby from the river. The stone-walled, gated corral was a reassuring sign that they were close to civilization. It was in fact a grazing area known as *Potrero de La Loma*,

situated on high ground above the confluence of the *Azufre* and *Portillo* rivers. The boys found a place to sleep under some trees, and Roberto rested whilst Nando went to explore their immediate surroundings. He soon returned, with the news of a second river joining the one that they'd been following. He couldn't see any way forward across the rivers, and the two boys spent some time pondering what to do, before deferring any decision to the morning.

As Nando went searching for brushwood to make a fire, Roberto suddenly spotted a man on horseback across the river. He shouted to Nando, pointing out to him the direction in which to run, and following him the best he could. Reaching the edge of the *Portillo* river gorge, they scanned the opposite bank, but there was no one to be seen.

Fig. 72. *Nando and Roberto in 1997 at the overhanging rock under which they had slept on day seven of their trek. Roberto is flanked by Gustavo and Moncho who accompanied him on the retracing of their route.*

Disappointed, Roberto resolved to return to the same spot early the next morning, in case the rider should reappear, and they were on the point of walking back up to their camp when they heard a shout.

Turning around, they saw three people on horses, driving cows and sheep along a path about 50 metres across the river. It was Catalán and his sons, returning from their day's work. They had noticed a disturbance amongst the horses on the plateau, perhaps caused by Roberto's shout to Nando, and had spotted the two boys again. Roberto and Nando started jumping and gesticulating, and shouting out for help, in their fear that the *arriero* would mistake them for hikers, but it was impossible to convey anything above the roar of the torrent. Catalán shouted back to them before continuing on his way. There was only one word that they could make out, and it filled them with optimism – *¡Mañana!*

Sergio Catalán, distinctive in his wide-brimmed *chupalla* hat, was an *arriero* of some repute in the area. He would spend the whole summer in the *precordillera*, not returning home until March or April. He leased land on the west side of the *Azufre* river, in a location called *Puesto Los Negros*, where he and his sons stayed the season, living in a crude wooden ranch. Their summer work began in November, with sheep-shearing at Catalán's winter base, in the village of Roma near San Fernando. Then they would load up the mules and horses with supplies, before embarking on a four-day trek, Catalán driving his large herd of sheep and cattle the 60 kilometres to their summer pastures.

When Nando went to the same spot in the morning, he found Catalán already waiting across the river. The muleteer gestured for Nando to go a couple of hundred metres upstream, where the sides of the gorge were less steep, and where they could both descend to the water's edge. There, Catalan took out a piece of paper and wrote a brief note on it. Wrapping the paper and pen with a stone in his white-and-blue checked handkerchief, he threw it across the river. His note read:

A man is on his way, whom I have sent there. Tell me what you want.

In reply, Nando wrote his famous plea for help:

I come from a plane that fell in the mountains. I am Uruguayan. We have been walking for ten days. I have a friend up there who is injured. In the plane there are still fourteen injured people. We have to get out of here <u>quickly</u> and we don't know how. We have no food. We are weak. <u>When</u> are you going to come up here to rescue us? Please. We can't even walk anymore. Where are we?

The message almost didn't make it to the other shore, landing at the water's edge before being retrieved by Cucho. Before leaving, Catalán threw over some pieces of bread to Nando, who climbed back up to the camp, and gave one to Roberto. The story of the bread has been a source of great mirth in recent years. In the original telling of the story in *ALIVE*, Piers Paul Read refers to a single piece of bread; Nando climbs back up to the plateau and breaks it in two, offering half to Roberto, who tries to refuse it. Many years later, Catalán recalled in passing that he had thrown five pieces of bread over the river. Some of the survivors have been merciless in ribbing Nando about this discrepancy, suggesting that he ate four of those pieces, leaving just one for Roberto. The truth is doubtless somewhere in between, and in a 1973 interview, Nando claimed to have received three pieces of bread, one of which he gave to Roberto.

Fig. 73. *The mule track leading from Los Maitenes to the l-45 gravel road.*

The man that Catalán was sending to the two boys was sixty-four-year-old Armando Cerda; a muleteer who had once worked for Catalán, but who was now working for landowner Jaime Gandarillas. Cerda and another muleteer, Enrique González, were based downstream of the confluence, on the east side of the *Azufre* river, in a place called *Los Maitenes*. Catalán had thrown a note to Cerda earlier, telling him to look out for the two crazy guys in *Potrero del Loma*, to see if they needed help. The grazing area was easily reached from *Los Maitenes*, across a small bridge which Nando had missed in his recce of the previous night, and Cerda's morning work involved him passing that way.

Meanwhile, Catalán, who understood the urgency of the situation, set off on his mule to alert the authorities in Puente Negro, fifty kilometres away; ten kilometres down a mule track, and then another forty along the I-45 gravel road. By the time Catalán reached the end of the mule track and crossed the Tinguiririca river, it would still take several hours to reach the town, but, by good fortune, he chanced upon a road crew just three kilometres down the road. His reputation, and the note he was clutching, convinced the foreman to allow the use of the crew's truck to transport Catalán to the carabinero checkpoint in Puente Negro. There again, it was Catalán's reputation that convinced the duty officer to take him seriously, and to escalate the matter to the main police station in San Fernando. A squad of carabineros was immediately dispatched to *Los Maitenes*.

Fig. 74. *Los Maitenes.*

Meanwhile, Cerda had located the two boys, their first external human contact since leaving Mendoza ten weeks earlier. Cerda gave them food, and asked them to wait whilst he completed his morning tasks. As they awaited his return, Nando and Roberto were approached by another group of local men, including Cucho and Checho. Curious to see these strange arrivals to their domain, they attached themselves with ropes and braved the *Portillo* river, crossing the torrent at the narrowest point. Heading up the slope of the gorge at the other side, they located the boys, and chatted with them for

185

some time, before Cerda returned from his chores. Helping Roberto to mount his horse, Cerda led them across the small bridge over the *Azufre*, to *Los Maitenes*.

There, they found a paradise compared to the barren landscapes of the previous weeks, with grass and trees all around, wild roses, and free-roaming animals. After being introduced to Enrique González, Nando and Roberto were led to a table, where they proceeded to devour everything that was put in front of them. Homemade bread, cheese, fried pork rinds, and *Porotos Granados* – a rustic vegetable stew. For dessert: bread with *dulce de leche*. All washed down with ample supplies of milk, coffee, and clean fresh water from a nearby stream. Fully sated, the two boys were led to a wooden cabin with a door and two beds, which Gandarillas would use on his visits to the ranch. There, they fell asleep immediately, exhausted by the physical exertions, emotional stress, and uncertainties of the previous ten days.

Waking at around 7:00 p.m., they felt ready for yet more food, which was provided unhesitatingly by their generous hosts. After dinner, they stayed chatting with the

arrieros late into the evening, before the arrival, in quick succession, of an army patrol led by Sub Lt. Francisco Cuadra of San Fernando's Colchagua regiment, a squad of carabineros wearing the distinctive thick green woollen coats issued to Chilean mountain forces, and finally Catalán himself, riding the mule which he had left tethered by the I-45 earlier that day. Nando and Roberto thanked him profusely, but he remained reticent, smiling shyly, and telling them that he had just done his duty to God

Fig. 75. *Seatbelt which formed part of Nando's backpack on the final expedition, presented by him to Francisco Cuadra.*

and country. Cuadra, on realizing that it would be impossible to reach the other fourteen survivors by land, sent two of his men back to San Fernando, to confirm the need for helicopters.

The boys chatted with the new arrivals into the early hours of the morning, before snatching another few hours' sleep. At daybreak, their rest was interrupted by an army of journalists and cameramen, who had made their way up the valley from the I-45, eager to get the scoop on this extraordinary story. The news had leaked when someone reporting a stolen bike at the San Fernando police station had got wind of what was happening. He had alerted journalist Archibaldo Morales, a well-known local personality, and somewhat of a maverick. After examining the note, Morales had taken a gamble. Convinced of its authenticity, he had contacted *Radio Portales* – the national parent network of his local radio station – and reported the news to them as confirmed fact. As a result, he was put live on air in the early afternoon of 21st December, several hours before the official confirmation. The gripping opening words of his bulletin – *SAN FERNANDO. CHILE. URGENTE* – would later form the title of one of the earliest books on the story.

The broadcast was heard in newsrooms around the country, and the reputation of *Radio Portales* convinced them to dispatch journalists and cameramen to San Fernando without delay. The national television station, *TVN*, sent Alipio Vera, who would conduct the very first interview with the survivors. He travelled with Ernesto Zelada, a journalist from the weekly magazine *Revista Vea*. The *El Mercurio* newspaper sent reporter Pablo Honorato, and Channel 13 – the Catholic TV station – sent Claudio Sanchez. They arrived in San Fernando in the late afternoon, and then, with directions from the carabineros in Puente Negro, drove as far as they could, before continuing on foot, just as the sun was setting. Carrying heavy equipment, and struggling in the dark, the group of journalists got lost, and were further delayed by the logistics of getting the expensive TV cameras across a torrent swollen by the thaw.

Fig. 76. *The journalists who made it to Los Maitenes.*

Their struggles were worthwhile – they were the only journalists to make it to *Los Maitenes*, beating the roadblock put up by the military later in the day. Hundreds of journalists were forced to remain in San Fernando, to await the arrival of the survivors. The only story that aired that day was due to Alipio Vera, who interviewed Catalán and the boys, asking Nando about his family, and Roberto about the food; a question carefully sidestepped. Eager to file the story, and make the footage available to the TV station, Vera set off back to San Fernando without waiting for the arrival of the helicopters with the first batch of survivors.

Fig. 77. *Journalist Alipio Vera interviewing Nando Parrado in Los Maitenes.*

The worldwide interest and the intrusion of the press came as a great shock to Catalán, and would become a lifelong burden. In his affectionate biography of Catalán – *Corazón de Arriero* – Ariel Osvaldo Torres wrote:

He couldn't avoid being singled out for what he had done. Strangers would come up to shake his hand, like a conquering hero, the honour of Chile. In fact, he had become a source of pride, both for his region, and the rest of the country.

His son Gonzalo, who was eight years old at the time of the rescue, says: "He attained such a high level of popularity that it overwhelmed him." The muleteer was grateful for so many compliments and acknowledgements, but he didn't know how to explain that it had been nothing more than a good deed on his part.

What irritated him most, however, was not the recognition of the people, but the harassment of the press. The door of his house would fill up with reporters who would pounce on him and his family, looking for statements... They would make him get on and off his horse, take off and put on his hat, look, smile, take out his handkerchief and wave.... He could not go about his normal activity without microphones and cameras in front of his face. At first he was happy to accept the questions, but as the days went by, he became increasingly uncomfortable with the attention he aroused.

Catalán was fêted not only in Chile, but also in Uruguay. In June 1973, he travelled there with his wife Virginia, spending several days in Montevideo, where there was an emotional reunion with fourteen of the survivors at Javier Methol's house. His fame would stay with him throughout his life, and he would receive frequent visits at his house in Roma from the survivors, and from fans of the story.

Fig. 78. *Roberto Canessa with Sergio Catalán.*
Left: *At Los Maitenes in 1972.* **Right**: *At Sergio's house in Roma near San Fernando in 2018.*

Torres embarked on his biography of Catalán in November 2017, with the support and authorization of the family. It is a fascinating and warm account that gives unique insights into the life of a muleteer, and chronicles how international fame intersected the world of this reticent and humble man. Torres was on the point of going to press, when he received the news of Catalán's death, age 91, on 11th February 2020.

CONCLUSION OF THE SEARCH

As Madelón and Bimba were concluding their trip to Chile at the end of October, they crossed paths with Dr Luis Surraco and Dr Jorge Zerbino – father of Gustavo – who, despite their scepticism at Croiset's reports, were on their way to help Páez Vilaró in his search efforts, and to provide him with some moral and practical support. With them was Guillermo Risso, the brother-in-law of Gastón Costemalle's novia. Over the next ten days, they continued the search, taking part in excursions on the ground and by helicopter before returning to Montevideo, convinced by then that the plane was not in the Talca area.

Fig. 79. *Parents' search in the first half of November.*
Left: *Zerbino (left) and Surraco (right).* **Right**: *Páez Vilaró (left) and Zerbino (right).*

By the middle of November, Páez Vilaró also needed to leave Chile for a few days, to deal with some pressing business relating to an exhibition of his art in São Paulo. Before leaving, he arranged for thousands of leaflets to be printed, offering 300,000 Chilean escudos for anyone who found the plane, the money raised by the parents in Montevideo. He was once again overwhelmed by the generosity of his Chilean hosts, with the printer refusing to take any money, and a large army of volunteers helping to distribute the flyers far and wide.

The gap left by Páez Vilaró's departure was filled by another group of relatives, which once again included Madelón. This time, she was joined by Rafael Echavarren's father, the mother and brother of Marcelo Pérez del Castillo, and Madelón's uncle, Raúl 'Rulo' Rodríguez Escalada. The latter was a commercial pilot for the Uruguayan national airline PLUNA, with decades of experience. In 1950, when Uruguay won their famous World Cup victory by beating the hosts Brazil in their newly-constructed 200,000-seat Maracanã stadium, Rodríguez Escalada had piloted one of the two *PLUNA* DC3 aircraft

190

dispatched to Rio to bring home the national heroes. His participation in the Andes search brought a reassuring presence and an element of authority to the parents' efforts. The newly-arrived group continued to search in the Talca area, making expeditions deep into the mountains on muleback, and concentrating their efforts on *Descabezado Grande*, the 'headless' peak that most closely matched Gerard Croiset's visions. They also rented a small plane to search the same area, but after several days with nothing to show for their efforts, they too returned to Montevideo. For the first time in almost two months, no-one was actively searching for the boys.

By the first week of December, it was clear that nothing more could be gained by continuing the search in the Talca area. Unhappy with the influence that Gerard Croiset had had on the search, some of the fathers got together on 5th December, in an attempt to persuade the Uruguayan Air Force to resume the search. The Chilean authorities, believing it was impossible that there could be any survivors, had already ruled out further sorties before February 1973. Even though the fathers also believed their sons to be dead, unresolved questions remained, and they wanted to turn their attention back to the original search area marked out by the SAR.

The group met with Brigadier José Pérez Caldas at the *Boiso Lanza* air force base. The Brigadier was sympathetic to their request and not only made available a C-47, but also authorised the participation of a limited number of the parents to act as observers on the flights. It was decided that Gustavo Nicolich, Juan Carlos Canessa, and Walter Harley would go to Chile, whilst the wider group of parents would provide monetary and logistical support.

300.000 ESCUDOS

DE **RECOMPENSA**

A la persona que encuentre el Avión Uruguayo perdido el día 13 de Octubre en horas de la tarde, con 47 pasajeros.

CARACTERISTICAS DEL AVION
COLOR BLANCO LETRAS F. A. U. - 571

Se presume que el avión cayó en los alrededores del cerro el Peine, Laguna del Alto, cerro de la Hornilla, Laguna del cerro Tres Cuernos.

La persona que lo encuentre deberá dar su información a Radio Club Talca - 2 Sur 859 3er Piso Of. 23 única autorizada para confirmarla.-

Dicha Recompensa esta depositada en la Embajada del Uruguay en Santiago de Chile, y es válida hasta el 31 de Diciembre de 1972.

Fig. 80. *Flyer offering a reward for locating the plane.*

On 10th December, there was a long follow-up meeting at Nicolich's house. The three going to Chile would be joined by Luis Surraco and Rulo Rodriguez Escalada. With Surraco acting as cartographer, the maps of the possible search areas were laid out on the dining room table. The group was well-equipped to bring an analytic approach to the task: Surraco and Canessa were both doctors, Nicolich an architect, Harley an engineer, and Rodríguez Escalada a pilot. They methodically went through all the SAR reports, the flight data, the weather conditions, the topography, and came to the conclusion that the plane must lie between the *Tinguiririca* and the *Sosneado* volcanoes.

After a delay due to an engine failure, the C-47 flights got going on 13th December, with Major Ruben Terra at the controls, and Nicolich and Rodríguez Escalada on board – a four-hour early morning flight over the Planchón pass. The following day, the C-47 flew at 16,000 feet over the region between *Tinguiririca* and *Palomo*; a flight that was heard both by the boys at the fuselage, and by the expeditionaries scaling the headwall. On 15th December there was a false alarm, as Nicolich spotted a cross on the Santa Elena mountain, below the assumed route of the Fairchild; photographs were taken and analysed, but it turned out to be part of a geological survey. As Christmas approached, the search was paused to allow the participants to spend time with their families over the holidays. Although they had not found the Fairchild, their actions had not been completely in vain; they had convinced the Chilean rescue services to resume their search, and the boys on the mountain had been injected with a renewed optimism by the sound of the C-47 methodically combing the mountains.

Fig. 81. *FAU 508, the C-47 which took part in the December search.*

On 20th December, Nicolich, Canessa and Harley boarded the C-47 to return to Montevideo, but it experienced yet another engine failure, and they were forced to make an emergency landing in San Rafael, on the Argentinian side of the Andes, where they spent the night. The next day, Canessa took a bus to Buenos Aires, but Nicolich and Harley decided to wait for the repair of the C-47, whose pilots were friends of the Fairchild crew. Late that night, communicating with Ponce de León via ham radio, the two heard the startling news that two boys had appeared in the Chilean *precordillera*, claiming to be from the Uruguayan plane. They left immediately for Mendoza, driven in the mayor's car by the local ham radio operator. From Mendoza, they hitched a ride to Santiago on a cargo plane, and then took a taxi, reaching San Fernando on 22nd December, just before the helicopters arrived with the first batch of survivors.

Páez Vilaró and Rodríguez Escalada had stayed on a bit longer in Chile before making their way back home. There had been a moment of excitement a couple of days earlier when Páez Vilaró, flying in a private plane owned by pilot André Muzard, had spotted footprints in the snow. A fellow passenger, Andinista Claudio Lucero, knowing the reality of the Andes, had discouraged him from believing that they could belong to the boys. Páez Vilaró was on the point of boarding a flight back to Montevideo on 21st December when he was paged on the airport intercom. He was summoned to receive a call from Colonel Morel in San Fernando. The regimental commander broke the astonishing news to him... a note had been delivered with the words "I come from a plane that fell in the mountains. I am Uruguayan..." The colonel requested that he return to San Fernando, to see if he could authenticate the note. Páez Vilaró and Rodríguez Escalada immediately exited the terminal building and hailed a taxi. Having spent the last of their Chilean escudos in preparation for their return to Montevideo, they explained their predicament to the driver. When he realized that it was the 'the crazy father looking for his lost kid', he told them not to worry, he would lend them the money and drive them the 150 kilometres from Santiago to San Fernando.

The driver, Tulio Carozzi, dropped them outside the Colchagua regiment at midnight, with a promise to return the next day, in case he could be of further service. Morel was at the gate of the barracks to meet Páez Vilaró, and immediately handed him the note. On examining it carefully, he told the commander unequivocally that it was genuine, keeping any doubts to himself. He was fearful that it might be dismissed as a hoax if he prevaricated.

Morel had been busy from the moment he had received a telephone call from the carabinero prefecture in San Fernando at around 3:00 p.m., a full three hours after Catalán's initial arrival. His first step had been to go to speak to the muleteer himself, to hear the facts at first hand, and to look at the note, to convince himself that the report was genuine. Assured by the carabineros that Catalán was a serious man, one to be trusted, Morel returned to the barracks, and started coordinating the rescue efforts. He first organized an army patrol, to be headed by Cuadra, whose mission was to make the first contact with the two survivors, and assess the situation. Equipped with food and medicines, the six-man team included high mountain specialists. The group left the barracks at 17:35 in a 4-wheel drive vehicle, reversing Catalán's route along the I-45, before heading on foot up to *Los Maitenes*.

His next task was to convince the initially sceptical Air Force Operations group that the emergency was genuine. In fact, the stars aligned in an extraordinary way, as described by Lieutenant Mario Ávila:

> On Friday 21st, Group 10 Commander Carlos García, head of SAR Commander Sergio Massa, and I, were having a preparatory meeting as the flight crew of a DC-6 cargo flight, due to depart at 7:00 a.m. the next morning for Punta Arenas. At 16:45, Massa received an urgent telegram from Operations, addressed to SAR, which read: "They are saying that two people have been found from a plane that had crashed in the mountains near San Fernando. The rescued say that there are 14 more people and SAR support is requested." García made the immediate decision to cancel the Punta Arenas trip, and gave the order to prepare the helicopters. It was a remarkable coincidence that the three pilots for the DC-6 flight were also helicopter pilots – that doesn't happen very often. Moreover, two of them were very experienced, and one of them was the Commander of the SAR, a person very closely related to the history of the accident.

In fact, García was also intimately familiar with the incident, having worked alongside Massa in directing the original search. With not enough daylight left to effect a rescue that evening, plans were made to leave early the next morning, the three pilots each set to command one of the SAR's modern 'Huey' rescue helicopters. Finding the remaining crew members at short notice was complicated by the annual Christmas party, which the FACH put on for officers with young children. Corporal Ramón Canales was one of those attending with his family:

> I was on duty that day, but as I was married and had children, our NCO appointed a single man to replace me, in this case Polverelli, so that I could be with my wife and children at the annual Christmas celebration. Afterwards, at about 6:00 p.m., I went to see Polverelli to see if anything had happened on the shift, but then Colonel Garcia arrived and said to me, "Canales, prepare three helicopters and assemble some crews, because it seems that the Uruguayan plane has appeared." As there were only single personnel on base, and Polverelli was right next to me, I told him to be there the next day at 5:00 a.m., and I started looking for two more crew members.

The two that were found were Juan Ruz and Abel Galvez, both single men, and like Polverelli they were assigned to the crew and instructed to be ready to depart early the next day. There was also the question of arranging for members of the volunteer *Cuerpo de Socorro Andino* to join the rescue party. Osvaldo Villegas, who would be joined by Sergio Díaz, and team leader Claudio Lucero, got a call at 10:00 p.m. that evening:

> I hadn't heard about it yet. That night Guillermo Silva, the National Chief of the Corps, called me and told me the news of the boys' appearance, that there was a letter and apparently it was all true. He told me that I had to be at the barracks the next day at 05:00 hrs. In the morning we were picked up at the CSA, and taken to the SAR in Group 10, from where we left in the helicopters.

The final passenger was Air Force nurse Wilma Koch, who belonged to a pioneering squadron of volunteer nurses that had been formed to help in natural disasters across the country, in the aftermath of the great Chilean earthquake of 1960. They were trained at the military academy, receiving specialized instruction in aerospace medicine, and were the very first women to enter the Chilean Air Force, having to contend with a mentality that considered it bad luck to have a woman as a member of the crew. Koch had turned up early in the morning in her Air Force uniform, expecting to join the flight to Punta Arenas. Instead, she was spotted by Garcia and Massa, who told her about the change of plan.

She was quite familiar with the saga of the Uruguayan plane crash and the search efforts because, on several occasions in the previous weeks, she had shared a ride in the Air Force 'hare' with both Carlos Páez Vilaró and Major Ruben Terra. The hare was a private van used to shuttle officers from town to the base and back, and Páez Vilaró had been staying in town at the *Hotel Crillón* for the duration of the Santiago-based search missions:

> We would pick him up from the hotel in the morning, and drop him off at the end of the day, so we talked a lot and became friends. As the only woman among many men in the hare, I wanted to keep him company, knowing the personal drama he was going through. I would ask him about his son and the search. He would answer me with tears in his eyes, telling me that he knew his son was waiting for him, that he would continue to search for him through land, sea, and sky. They were very intimate and intense moments.

Despite her knowledge of the accident, it was only when she spoke to her friends Sergio Díaz and Corporal Canales on board the helicopter that she realized it was the Uruguayan boys who needed to be rescued.

Two of the three helicopters – H-89 and H-91, commanded by García and Massa respectively – took off at 7:00 a.m. The departure of the third – H-90, piloted by Ávila – was delayed by a failed generator, and followed on, an hour or so later, carrying spare fuel drums to support the operation. The first destination was the Colchagua regiment in San Fernando. The foggy conditions forced the helicopters to fly low, as Ramón Canales recalled:

> We took off and flew a little above the high tension cables, guided by the cars driving along Route 5 south. By the time we got to Angostura we could barely see anything, and, spotting the tunnel, I joked to Commander Garcia, "let's go through it instead." Arriving in San Fernando, García said to me, "what do we do now, where is the Regiment?" and that's where I was able to save the situation. I was born and raised in San Fernando, and my grandparents lived next to the 19th Colchagua, so I guided them through the little streets of my childhood.

In San Fernando, Morel had been making plans for the reception of the survivors, both within the regimental compound where an emergency ward was set up in the infirmary, and at the local hospital. Basing the operational command centre in his office, he had met at 6:00 a.m. that morning with the local mayor, the Uruguayan chargé-d'affaires, the head of the carabineros, and the director of the *San Juan de Dios* hospital in San Fernando, to work through the details.

The helicopter crews were greeted by Colonel Morel and Páez Vilaró, the latter giving them letters to take to his son, in case he was one of the fourteen still alive on the mountain. Morel, one of three who would accompany the rescue team to *Los Maitenes*, provided them with a bag of *churrascos* and *hallullas*[1]. Also joining the helicopters in San Fernando were regimental doctor Eduardo Arriagada and army nurse José Bravo, the former having been summoned by Morel the previous evening:

> When I arrived at the regiment I read the note that had been thrown to the arriero, and knew immediately that it was genuine. Despite the few words, there was an anguish about it, and the message was very precise. Morel communicated that he was coordinating a rescue mission with the Air Force, that the helicopters were arriving the next day, and that they would need my services. He told me that by order of the Commander-in-Chief, an army doctor was required to go in the helicopters, and that they were expecting me the next morning at 8:00 a.m. at the

---

[1] Grilled meat and Chilean flatbread.

regiment. I thought it was a special adventure, and I would have gone even if I had not been assigned. I was the only doctor in the regiment, so there was no other option anyway, At the hospital I asked for some serums just in case, as I didn't know what I was going to find up there. I packed a bag and asked a field nurse (José Bravo) to accompany me, and by 7:45 a.m. we were at the Regiment, the sky completely overcast with a heavy low fog. The helicopter convoy arrived around 9:00 a.m. from Santiago and landed on the regiment's training field.

The helicopters arrived at *Los Maitenes* – now designated *Camp Alpha* – late in the morning, landing in thick fog. Their appearance was just in time to forestall the departure of Nando and Roberto, who were already on horseback, and preparing to head down to the I-45. The two boys dismounted, and greeted the rescuers enthusiastically. Roberto, who was in much weaker condition than Nando, was then led by Wilma Koch to the green medical triage tent, which had been erected by the army patrol. There, she examined him, checking his pulse and blood pressure whilst he told her about what had happened on the mountain, and how they had used the bodies of their friends to survive. Debriefed later in the cabin of H-89, the boys again spoke openly about what they had done to survive, and what the crew could expect to find on the mountain. The pilots then laid out a map for them, asking them to point out the route they'd taken on their ten-day trek.

Fig. 82. *FACH H-89 arriving in Los Maitenes.*

Realizing that they'd need one of the boys on board to help locate the plane, they asked Nando to accompany them. The Huey helicopters had ample space, but the thin air at the altitudes needed to reach the fuselage dictated that only essential personnel could travel: the two pilots, each with two crewmen, the three Andinistas, Parrado, and the army medical team of Dr Arriagada and Nurse Bravo. Some journalists who wanted to witness the rescue were refused permission to board, but that didn't stop the *El Mercurio* team, headed by reporter Pablo Honorato, from handing a camera to Polverelli, who would take one of the iconic photographs of the rescue: that of the boys welcoming the helicopters with upraised arms.

It was not the only camera at hand to record the historic rescue. Cuadra handed his own *Yashica J* 35mm rangefinder camera to José Bravo to capture colour stills of the site on behalf of the army. Commando Massa propped his personal Super 8mm camera on top of the cockpit's instrument panel, and set it to record. The SAR team had been provided with a World War Two era *Bell and Howell* newsreel camera, selected for its simple single-button operation. It had been rushed over to *Group 10* the previous day, from the government-owned TVN, due to the quick thinking of Alipio Vera before he left for *Los Maitenes*; and García had handed it over to Canales to operate. Finally, the CSA had a camera which had been provided by their public relations officer, Juan Gabriel 'Chiporro' Bustos, whose day job as the local news editor at *El Mercurio* newspaper meant he had been one of the first to hear the news of survivors.

Fig. 83. *Nando, on horseback with carabinero Vicente Espinoza Muñoz, had been on the point of leaving Los Maitenes when the helicopters arrived. Muleteer Enrique González in foreground.*

By 12:30 p.m., the fog had lifted sufficiently to allow the rescue team to leave. It was a close call. If they'd had to wait much longer, the mission would have needed to be postponed until the following day, due to the treacherous afternoon currents in the *cordillera*. The two helicopters took off, with García's H-89 taking the lead; Canales took the copilot's seat with Polverelli, Díaz, Arriagada, Bravo, and Parrado in the back, the latter equipped with a headset so that he could communicate with García. Following on their tail was H-91, with Massa and Ruz up front, and Galvez, Lucero, and Villegas behind them. Parrado started directing García up the valley, retracing the route which had led him and Canessa to safety.

Fig. 84. *Ramón Canales, Wilma Koch, Roberto Canessa, and Sergio Diaz in Camp Alpha in the late morning of 22ⁿᵈ December. Francisco Cuadra back centre.*

199

THE RESCUE

Following the expeditionaries' departure on 12th December, the boys at the fuselage had sat watching their slow progress up the headwall, until they eventually disappeared from sight. On the second day, they heard the C-47 rescue plane, and on the day after, they even caught a glimpse of it crossing the mountains to the west. The boys had practised an elaborate procedure for the eventuality of a plane flying over them, with positions marked out in the snow, to which they would run when a plane was heard. The injured boys would stand stationary in a cross shape, and the mobile boys would move around in an circle, waving pieces of red cloth. They extrapolated that on the fourth day the C-47 would fly directly over them, but then they heard on the news that the plane had been grounded with engine failure. That morning, however, they saw a dot rapidly descending the headwall, and soon realized that it was one of the boys. They pondered whether the expeditionaries had found a town or a road, and were sending someone back to tell them, or whether perhaps two of them had died. When Tintín arrived at the fuselage, he broke the news to them that there were just more mountains and snow to the west, but that Roberto and Nando were pushing on regardless.

The absence of the expeditionaries made life a bit more relaxed at the fuselage. The anxiety hanging over everyone in anticipation of their departure had dissipated, and there was a relief that something positive was being done. The days were now hot, and they even began to see signs of life – some flies, a bee, and some small birds. Most of the boys took it easy, sitting outside in the sun on the cushions and seats, but some stayed active, acutely conscious of their precarious situation. One of the concerns was the supply of food. They estimated that, with careful management, the bodies might last until the end of January. As a precaution, Fito and Gustavo Zerbino made an expedition up the mountain behind them, to try to find Daniel Shaw's body. Fito didn't want his cousin's body to be used, but if their stay on the mountain were to extend into the new year, it might become necessary, and the boys were worried that the intense sun would render his body unusable. Gustavo was the only one who knew where Daniel's body was lying, so he went along with Fito, the two of them waking at 5:00 a.m. in order to make an early start on firm snow.

The two boys found Daniel's body without too much difficulty, and started dragging it down with straps. But coming across one of the tailplanes, they tobogganed down on top of it, ending up on the opposite side of the valley. There, they were met by Pedro and Carlitos, but the snow was too soft to bring Daniel's body back to the fuselage. The four of them returned the next day, to complete the job. At the same time as Fito and Gustavo had been heading up the mountain, Pedro and Carlitos had gone down towards the east, and had found Carlos Valeta's body face-up in the snow. Even further down, they had found the other tailplane, and some baggage and seats.

The boys were hoping that the expeditionaries would reach civilization before the rescue plane found them, so that they would be able to say they did it alone. They liked to imagine the look on the first person's face when Nando and Roberto approached them saying, "We are from the Uruguayan plane." But after a week with no news, they began to accept the idea that the two expeditionaries were dead, and Fito realized that they might need to plan another expedition. The initial thinking was that it would leave in the first or second week of January, and comprise Fito, and one or more of Gustavo, Tintín, Daniel Fernández, Pedro, and Carlitos. Whether it would go east or west was still under discussion, and, to that end, there was some debate as to whether they should trek up one of the side mountains, to see if they could spot Roberto's road. The weaker boys accepted the reality that the stronger boys would need to save themselves, and that the others would be left behind. Roy, in particular, was starting to believe that he would never make it off the mountain, and Coche made the decision that he would give up his daily fight for survival on Christmas Eve.

On 21st December, the feeling of pessimism took an upturn. Both Daniel Fernández and Carlitos independently had strong premonitions that Nando and Roberto had made it to safety, and after praying the rosary that evening, Daniel stated his conviction to the others. The next day, before he went out to listen to the morning news on the radio, Daniel told the others: "I bet you that they now say two Uruguayans have appeared." Most of the boys stayed in the fuselage, but Eduardo and Pedro went out with him. Each morning, Daniel would tune into the half-hourly news reports on *Radio El Espectador*, and on this occasion, as soon as he turned on the radio, he heard a snippet saying, "We'll give more detail on the survivors in the *Cordillera* a bit later." Unwilling to announce the news to the boys in the fuselage immediately, in case it turned out to be another false dawn, they fiddled with the dial, hoping to hear some confirmation. On one station, they heard Gounod's *Ave Maria*, which Eduardo took as a sign from above. Finally, a few minutes after 8:00 a.m., they heard the names Parrado and Canessa, and there could no longer be any doubt. The atmosphere on hearing the news was explosive. Everyone started jumping up and down and hugging each other, almost unbalancing the fuselage on its by-now precarious pedestal of snow. There was a chorus of "We're saved!" and the boys broke into the stash of Cuban cigars that they'd been saving for Christmas.

After the first emotions started to subside, the boys began to prepare themselves for the arrival of the rescue helicopters, combing their hair, brushing their teeth, and sprucing up their clothing. Those who were wearing three pairs of trousers discarded the inner and outer pair. Then they sat down, and waited for the helicopters, talking excitedly, and joking about what they'd do when the rescuers arrived. One idea was that they would shut themselves inside the fuselage, and when the rescuers came knocking, they would feign ignorance and indifference. Another thought was that they would refuse any Chilean cigarettes offered to them by the rescuers, and instead offer their own; both Moncho and Gustavo ended up doing this. Fito and Moncho still had some cigarettes left, and now that the finish line was in sight, they offered them freely to the others. One preoccupation was what they should do about the bodies. They had planned to bury the remains before the helicopters came, but the rock-hard snow made it impossible to dig a sizeable hole, so they were forced to abandon that idea.

Only Pedro was unconvinced that the helicopters would arrive that day, and continued his normal activities. As the hours went by, it looked like he was right to be sceptical, but eventually they heard the distinctive thrum of helicopter blades. Surprisingly, when they finally spotted the two choppers just past noon, they were coming up the valley from the east. They circled above them several times, dropping smoke cannisters to assess the wind, and the boys could see that Nando was in one of them.

Nando had successfully guided the helicopters up the *San Andrés* valley, and then up the gully, only for them to be thwarted at the summit. Despite several frightening attempts, they had been unable to clear the ridge, and García, piloting the lead helicopter, was forced to seek a different way. Circling around to the right, he approached the *Lágrimas* valley from the south, entering it to the east of where the fuselage lay. The change of route had disoriented Nando, and it was a while before the fuselage and the tiny black dots of the survivors were spotted in the distance.

As the helicopters approached, they started circling above the boys, the deafening noise making them fearful that it might trigger an avalanche; a situation made more fraught by the mass of snow being thrown up by the blades. But it was an essential preliminary to landing, as explained by Ávila:

> *The plane was at 3,800 metres, but at around 2,200 metres, the tail rotor control starts to become critical, which means that the pilot is forced to position the helicopter on approach, and land it directly upwind. If he makes a mistake in this manoeuvre, he crashes, it's as simple as that. So, we would employ a method used in the Alps, which is to orbit a full 360 degrees at constant speed above the landing point, and then use the movement in the geometry of the turn to determine the ground-level wind direction.*

As H-89 came into land, there was almost disaster as Canales later recalled:

Nobody knows that we fell about 10 metres as we came in to land, when we experienced a compressor stall. We fell hard against the ground, and both skis were completely buried; it was so hard that the floor of the helicopter was filled with snow. Luckily we didn't touch any rocks because, if we had, we would have all been killed. So, for a few seconds, H-89 was at ground level, and that made it easier for the guys to get in.

The release of the three Andinistas and José Bravo onto the snow, the latter in shirt sleeves, gave the pilots a bit more control, allowing them to hover with one ski touching the slope. The boys were instructed to go towards the helicopters two by two. Daniel Fernández, with Álvaro hobbling behind him, had already managed to make it onto H-89, and with Arriagada and Parrado already in the cabin, García could take on no more weight, and left with the first two survivors. H-91, which had started with two fewer people, was able to take on four survivors, the places quickly filled by Eduardo, Pedro, Carlitos, and Coche, who all ran towards the cabin, and were hauled aboard by Galvez. The boys had assumed that everyone would be able to embark and leave, so, in the chaos of the first moments, there was no priority given to the weakest. In hindsight, the boys realized that they should have allowed Roy to go first. As it was, he had been blown to the ground by the turbulence from the blades, as Bobby and Fito had tried to lead him to one of the helicopters.

The six who had managed to make it on board were soon regretting it. The flight out was terrifying, the helicopters juddering violently as they tried to clear the ridge, before being buffeted back down. Eventually, both craft made it over, and despite his fear, Carlitos felt a tinge of sadness to be leaving their desolate but beautiful home of the last ten weeks.

The remaining eight boys expected the helicopters to return within the hour to pick them up, and the Andinistas prepared a makeshift landing pad, using the pilot cabin door, some partitions, and some pieces of metal – the same material that the survivors used each night to build the wall at the back of the fuselage. An immediate preoccupation of the boys was to eat something normal. Two bags of food had been thrown out of the helicopters, and this was supplemented by the Andinistas' own supplies. Whilst the boys were gorging themselves on *Pan de Pascua*, the Andinistas prepared steak sandwiches, using the provisions supplied by Morel, cooking the meat in butter. Some of the boys ate like gluttons, Moncho and Pancho wolfing down several of the sandwiches in quick succession. Fito showed more self-restraint, limiting himself to just one, saving his appetite for his return to civilization. He was unaware as yet that he would have to wait another day.

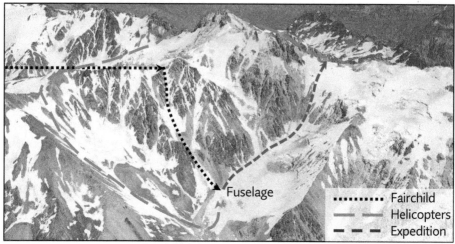

Fuselage

.... Fairchild
— — Helicopters
▬ ▬ ▬ Expedition

Fig. 85. *Fairchild, helicopter, and expedition routes.*

As the afternoon progressed, it became clear that the helicopters wouldn't be returning, due to the difficult afternoon conditions in the mountains. Any annoyance that the boys felt at having to spend another day on the mountain was more than compensated for by the generosity and high spirits of their rescuers. Sergio Díaz had been the first off the helicopter, their first human contact, and he had been visibly moved as he embraced the boys. A father of three and a grandfather, he was well-predisposed towards them, as his daughter was married to a Uruguayan, whom she'd first met in the mountains of the Chilean Lake District. Díaz even lived on Uruguay street in Puente Alto, a suburb of Santiago. He was a long-time member of the CSA, a volunteer organization, entirely reliant on donations, that specialized in high mountain rescue.

All the CSA members had full-time jobs, and were called up when needed. Díaz, who was a technical draughtsman and teacher by day, would frequently find himself having to work extra hours to make up for time spent in the mountains. Villegas worked as a photo-mechanic in a printing company, and, when not on CSA duty, would act as a mountain instructor, accompanying foreign expeditions conducting geological and mineral studies in Chile. The leader of the team, Claudio Lucero, was a firefighter, and had been climbing Andes peaks from an early age. Receiving his training, as a mountain instructor, in the Caucasus, he would go on to become one of Chile's most celebrated mountaineers.

The delay in rescue gave Gustavo Zerbino the opportunity to tell the Andinistas about the remains surrounding the fuselage. He went around with Lucero, showing him where the different bodies were buried, and naming each one. He also described the situation on the top of the mountain, and made a rough map for Lucero's reference, which would come in useful a month later, when the CSA would be involved in helping to move the dead to a shared grave.

The Andinistas set up a tent some distance from the fuselage, out of the path of any potential avalanche, and once they got organized, they started taking photographs of the boys and the site; black-and-white ones, using the camera handed to Lucero by Bustos, and colour ones with Cuadra's rangefinder.

Fig. 86. *The survivors enjoying steak sandwiches. Photo taken by José Bravo.*
Standing: *Villegas, Díaz, Tintín, Lucero, Pancho.*
Seated: *Javier, Roy, Bobby, Gustavo, Fito, Moncho.*

When evening came, there was a call for food again, and Lucero set about preparing beans, and various varieties of soup. As they ate, the Andinistas told anecdotes and stories about their group. And when they settled down for the night, Díaz joined them in the fuselage. It was the eve of his forty-ninth birthday. They spent the night joking, singing, and munching on biscuits, and when midnight arrived, they all joined in a chorus of *Happy Birthday*.

The next day, three helicopters arrived at mid-morning after the boys had breakfasted on fruit, bread, and biscuits, washed down with coffee, *maté*, and tea. Whilst H-90 observed from above, the remaining two craft descended as on the previous day, resting one ski on the snow. The Andinistas had gathered the boys together in preparation, and the rescue proceeded in a more orderly manner than that of the day before. H-89 picked up Moncho, Fito, Bobby, and Gustavo, the latter given permission to take on board the suitcase of personal effects, which he and Daniel Fernández had so conscientiously collected from their dead companions. The remaining four boys, Pancho, Tintín, Javier, and Roy clambered aboard H-91.

Although there was considerably less turbulence than on the previous day, the boys were still petrified by the manoeuvres needed to exit the valley, the helicopters circling and shuddering as they inched upwards. Moncho felt that they wouldn't make it, and was hugely relieved once they had cleared the summit. As they headed towards *Los Maitenes*, he was delighted to discover that García's second-in-command – Corporal Ramón Canales – shared his first name.

Canales, along with García, Massa and the other three crew members, would receive the prestigious *Medalla al Valor* for their participation in what was considered the most dangerous rescue mission that the SAR had ever conducted. Fate would bring García and Canales together again in more tragic circumstances in July 1977. García was the pilot of a DC6, transporting mainly military personnel from Punta Arenas to Puerto Montt in Chile's Lake District. Coming in for a manual landing, the plane experienced severe vertical windshear, and crashed to the forest floor, killing García and 37 others as the fuselage broke in two. Canales was sitting at the back, and, although injured, personally supervised the escape of 14 passengers from the rear part of the plane. For his bravery, he was awarded a second *Medalla al Valor*; the only officer ever to have been so honoured in the history of the Chilean armed forces.

THE LIST

The six boys rescued on the previous day, 22nd December, had first been flown to *Los Maitenes*, where on arrival they were helped out of the helicopters by the welcome party. They were euphoric at finding themselves in such a paradise, exhilarated by the greenery and the sweet smell of clover, and the signs and sounds of life all around them. Seated on the grass, they were examined by Dr Arriagada and Nurse Koch, with only Coche's leg infection a cause for concern. As they awaited their turn, the boys were handed cups of coffee – the first they'd had in seventy-two days – accompanied by chocolate and *galletitas*[1]. Under the strict orders of Arriagada, there was to be no protein yet, but that didn't prevent Álvaro Mangino from sampling the cheese made by the *arrieros* – it seemed to him the most delicious food he had ever tasted.

With the press cordoned off by the military, the boys spoke openly about what they had had to do, prompting Commander García to call them to one side, and caution them about the intense reaction that would likely result from the revelation. Worried about the psychological impact that the media frenzy would have on the boys, he encouraged them to act prudently and keep a low profile, to let the story emerge naturally.

Before returning to San Fernando, Morel relayed the list of survivors, compiled by Arriagada, to the Colchagua regiment headquarters. Páez Vilaró was given the task of reading it out, by phone, to Montevideo's *Radio Carve*, his voice broadcast live across Uruguay. Not knowing yet whether his son was on the list, he couldn't bear to look, covering it instead with a sheet of paper, choosing to reveal one name at a time.

Back in Uruguay, parents, grandparents, sisters, brothers, aunts, uncles, cousins, girlfriends, schoolmates, and teammates gathered in various places to hear the news – in estancias, at home, in cars hastening back to Montevideo, or assembled outside Ponce de León's house, where the list would be relayed via loudspeaker. Other relatives had already travelled to Chile, where they would hear the news first-hand, or from the Uruguayan chargé-d'affaires in Santiago. Those listening to *Radio Carve* braced themselves as Páez Vilaró started to read:

- Eduardo Strauch Urioste...

---

[1] Small cookies

The broadcaster immediately interjected: *"Dos veces cada nombre por favor"* – *"Each name twice, please"*.

- ... Eduardo Strauch
- Antonio Vizintín, Antonio Vizintín
- Álvaro Mangino, Álvaro Mangino
- Daniel Fernández, Daniel Fernández

When he uncovered the next name, his eyes welled up with tears, but there was no discernible variation in his voice...

- ¡Carlitos Miguel Páez, mi hijo!, ¡Carlitos Miguel Páez, mi hijo![1]

Although he had persevered through many periods of self-doubt in his long search, he had increasingly sensed his son's return, and this was now unequivocally confirmed. He continued reading, without missing a beat.

- Fernando Parrado, Fernando Parrado
- Roberto Canessa, Roberto Canessa
- Adolfo Strauch, Adolfo Strauch
- Gustavo Zerbino, Gustavo Zerbino
- Pedrito Algorta, Pedrito Algorta
- Alfredo Delgado, Alfredo Delgado
- Roberto François, Roberto François
- Roy Harley, Roy Harley
- José Luis Inciarte, José Luis Inciarte
- Ramón Sabella, Ramón Sabella
- Javier Methol, Javier Methol

The longer list implied by this short list would forever mark the families; those who had lost, and those who had won. As private moments of despair and joy were taking place across Uruguay and Chile, the first batch of survivors were being flown to San Fernando. When the helicopters landed in the regimental compound, Páez Vilaró had to be restrained from rushing dangerously towards them in his eagerness to see his son, but the emotional reunion between 'el padre loco' and 'su cabro perdido en las montañas'[2] wasn't long delayed. Their joy contrasted with the grief of Mr Nicolich, who

---

[1] My son!

[2] The crazy father, and his kid lost in the mountains.

had turned up at the regiment a short time earlier, and had not yet heard the list. Daniel Fernández went up to him and broke the sad news. Later, Mr Nicolich spoke to Carlitos, who told him the full story, about the crash, the letters that Coco had written, and the avalanche.

The boys spent only a few minutes at the regiment before being taken to the nearby *San Juan de Dios* hospital, to be examined, bathed, and eventually given some solid food – meat and pasta. An impatient crowd of parents and relatives had gathered outside the hospital, anxious to be reunited with their sons and brothers. They were finally let in after Nando's sister Graciela, her emotions at bursting point after hearing the voice of her brother inside, put her aikido lessons into practice, and floored the policeman who was guarding the entrance. Fearing a riot, the hospital officials opened the doors, allowing the relatives in until 7:00 p.m. The helicopters, meanwhile, were flown back to their base at *Los Cerrillos*, where the team attended a short press conference about the rescue.

Fig. 87. Las Hijas de la Caridad *chapel in San Fernando*.

The next morning, at 10:30 a.m., the boys participated in their own brief press conference, before attending Catholic Mass in *Las Hijas de la Caridad* chapel, adjacent to the hospital. Afterwards, the survivors travelled to Santiago; Álvaro and Coche taken by ambulance to the *Posta Central* hospital, the others travelling with their families directly to the *Sheraton San Cristóbal*, where rooms had already been reserved.

The second batch of survivors, on being rescued, had stopped for just a short time in *Los Maitenes*, as there was no urgent need for them to eat immediately. But it was long enough for them to appreciate their new surroundings, and to luxuriate in the same sights and smells that their companions had experienced the previous day. Arriving in San Fernando, some of the boys were amazed to find their families there. They had naively imagined that, should they ever be rescued, they would just call their parents from Santiago, and then travel to Montevideo themselves. In their discussions on the mountain, they had planned that they would spend two or three days in Santiago, resting and recuperating, and then, to avoid flying, would take a train over the Andes to Mendoza. This would be followed by a bus to Buenos Aires, and, for the final leg, the ferry to Montevideo. So it was an intensely emotional moment when they spotted their parents and brothers during the brief stopover at the regiment, before flying on to the *Posta Central*. The families of Fito, Gustavo, Bobby, Roy, and Javier were all there, and several were allowed to join their sons in the helicopter flight to the hospital. The reunion of Moncho and his brother was delayed a bit longer, as the latter turned up by car just after the departure of the helicopters, and was faced with the long drive back to Santiago before the two could meet and embrace.

Arriving in the early afternoon, the reception at the hospital also took the boys by surprise. Landing on the roof of the *Posta Central*, they were greeted by people waving and clapping at the windows of the tall buildings surrounding the hospital. Once inside, they found the corridors lined with doctors, nurses, and other hospital workers – some crying and shouting out – all wanting to get a glimpse of them as they were ushered away from public view, to an area where they could shower and undergo a medical examination. Afterwards, there was a meal – steak with rice and stuffed tomato, followed by a dessert – and a Mass celebrated on a makeshift altar in the hospital's auditorium. The boys, all except for Álvaro, Coche, Javier, and Roy, who were kept in overnight for observation, were then discharged, arriving at the hotel in the late afternoon.

Moncho's brother had gone into town to buy clothes for many of the survivors, who had nothing to change into, and Gustavo had also managed to sneak out of the hospital before he was officially discharged, on a quest to find some new shoes. Leaving the hospital with a Chilean friend, Eduardo Cisternas, he coincidentally bumped into his father at the entrance. Mr Zerbino joined them on the shopping expedition, the three of them driving downtown in Eduardo's car. After buying the shoes, they wandered around the centre for a while, and, passing near the *Hotel Crillón* where the families of the non-survivors were staying, Jorge Zerbino asked his son if he wanted to greet them. Gustavo was keen to do so, and a meeting was hastily arranged in the lobby with Mr and Mrs

Nicolich, the fathers of Daniel Shaw and Rafael Echavarren, the brother of Juan Carlos Menéndez, an uncle of Marcelo Perez del Castillo, and several others. The relatives were surprised and gratified to find one of the survivors there within hours of his arrival in Santiago. Gustavo had an affectionate word for each of his companions who had remained on the mountain. He told Mr Echavarren about his son's constant optimism, and the spiritual strength with which he'd faced his difficulties. He talked to Marcelo's uncle about how fundamental the *Old Christians* captain had been for them. And he remembered Coco Nicolich fondly, returning to the *Crillón* later in the day to deliver to Mr and Mrs Nicolich the letters their son had written on the mountain. They contained the first indication for the bereaved parents of what the boys had done to survive.

Whilst those staying at the *Crillón* returned to Montevideo as soon as practical, most of the survivors and their families stayed on in Santiago for some rest and relaxation, only Daniel Fernández and Bobby François joining the bereaved families on the flight back home. The others spent their time poolside at the *Sheraton San Cristóbal*, enjoying the luxury of being able to eat what and when they wanted. Instantly recognizable by their sun-blackened faces and gaunt appearance, the survivors were met with a generous welcome on their occasional forays into town, hailed on the streets as heroes, and not allowed to pay for the new clothes they needed to fit their emaciated bodies.

Some of the boys readapted remarkably quickly to life in the real world. The *Grange Old Boys* organized a lunch for the survivors on the 24th December at the *Prince of Wales Country Club* next to the *Grange School*. *Old Boy* John Scott recalled:

> As it was summer it was held on the terrace. In those days the chairs were metal with cushions, but they were a bit hard, and they had to ask for more cushions, because they had no more flesh on their buttocks – they were all skin and bones, and full of sores and wounds. I was very struck by their physique, they were so skinny and weak. We had a kickabout with a football, and as it was summer, we all played without shirts. I remember Roberto, it was funny to watch him, he could barely run in his pitiful state. We couldn't believe that they could play ball after everything they'd been through.

Gustavo also played, and Bobby Jaugust. With a host of reporters sticking close to the boys, their every move was reported in the media, and several interviews were conducted that day, including one with a Uruguayan TV channel. That evening, there was a party at the Sheraton to celebrate the boys' return, and at noon the next day, the families attended a Mass of thanksgiving at the Catholic University. It was presided over by Father Rodríguez, a recently ordained Uruguayan Jesuit priest who had spent the previous four years there, studying theology. He was known to several of the boys – Gustavo, Moncho, and Rafael

Echavarren amongst others – having once taught them at the *Seminario* in Montevideo. He would prove to be a welcome ally in the storm that followed.

The first hint of something unusual, appeared in *La Prensa* on Christmas Day. Under the frontpage headline **NO HAY EXPLICACIÓN MEDICA[1]**, the newspaper printed the somewhat enigmatic statement of Dr Arriagada, who was well aware of the truth:

> As for the food eaten during this period, I can say very little about it, because it is a matter of secrecy. But the explanation of how they resisted in such an adverse environment must be sought elsewhere, outside the realm of medicine.

On the same day, a few thousand kilometres away in Lima, page 20 of Peruvian newspaper *CORREO* was more explicit:

> The dramatic situation of the Uruguayans isolated in the mountains forced them to consume human bodies, according to a confidential report from the Chilean Air Force Air Rescue Service (SAR), obtained here by newspaper and television correspondents from Buenos Aires.

The breaking news in Santiago the following morning prompted the weekly magazine *Revista Vea* to comment:

> And what had hitherto only been whispered about, was clearly written in block letters. For four days the journalists kept silent, even though they had no doubt about the dramatic truth. Then the inevitable happened.

The Chilean newspapers had headlines of varying sensationalism. On the morning of Tuesday 26th, *La Tercera* led with:

Macabre report of the survivors: THEY REVEAL THE ENIGMA THAT ALLOWED THEM TO LIVE

Puro Chile went with:

Chilling confession of the Charrúas: WE HAD TO EAT CADAVERS

---

[1] There is no medical explanation.

Perhaps the most distressing of the Chilean headlines appeared in the evening newspaper *La Segunda*:

May God forgive them! JUSTIFIED CANNIBALISM

The next day, *El Mercurio* had a milder lead:

THEY ACTED FORCED OUT OF NECESSITY

But it was accompanied by a front-page photograph showing some human remains next to the wrecked fuselage.

This public assault on what, for the boys, had been a private and justified decision taken after much soul-searching, upset them greatly. The guilt that they felt was due to the fact that they had survived whereas their friends had died, rather than to the decision to use their bodies. Fr Rodriguez assured them that they should feel no guilt on either account. That there could be no moral significance assigned to who died versus who lived, and that the Catholic Church accepted anthropophagy *in extremis*, the latter backed up by various pronouncements from higher-up authorities.

Under such intense and uncomfortable scrutiny, the boys were eager to get back home, where the media coverage had been muted and respectful. Nando, much sought after for interviews, stopped speaking to the press altogether after an Argentinian reporter started making defamatory insinuations. He and his family moved to another hotel, and from there to the house of some friends in Viña del Mar.

Despite the unwelcome attention from the media, public consensus was that the anthropophagy was justified, and the survivors continued to experience the warmth and generosity of the Chileans right to the end of their stay. On the day of their return to Montevideo, some of the boys had run out of cigarettes, and needed to replenish their supplies. With long queues everywhere in town due to rationing, and their departure time fast approaching, they asked one vendor if they could jump to the head of the queue because they had a plane to catch. When he wouldn't allow it, the man at the front of the line insisted that they take his cigarettes, and refused to accept any money from them. Finally, in the late afternoon of 28th December, ten of the survivors, accompanied by their families, took to the air in a LAN Chile Boeing 727, crossing the Andes with some trepidation on their way home.

V.   Telling the Story

RETURNING HOME

On the night of 21st December, *Old Christians* board member Connie Hughes was hosting a group of business school students at his house; members of the *Movimiento Universitario Nacionalista*, the student movement associated with the Wilsonista sector of the National Party. It was an end-of-year celebration for the group. As they were preparing a traditional *asado* on the warm summer day, one of the party suddenly shouted out some startling news: *"¡Han aparecido dos sobrevivientes!"* – "Two survivors have appeared!" Everyone stopped what they were doing, and crowded around the radio, disbelieving what they were hearing, as the breaking story rapidly filled the airways.

The next day, the names of the sixteen survivors were revealed in the tense and emotional broadcast by Carlos Páez Vilaró. A meeting of the board of the *Old Christians* was immediately convened, involving Connie, Adolfo Gelsi, and the president of the club, Daniel Juan. The trio formed a committee to manage the situation, inviting a fourth member to join them – Emilio Azambuja, a former classmate of Connie and Adolfo. Mindful that they had no experience of handling the press, Connie also contacted journalist Antonio 'Manino' Mercader, the husband of a classmate, to ask for his help and advice. Mercader, at the time, was editor of the evening newspaper *El Diario de la Noche*, but later he would go on to have an important role in government, becoming Minister of Education and Culture in the nineties.

Meeting with the committee the next morning, Mercader laid out a plan of action. A time and date were fixed for a press conference to take place at the school, arranged to coincide with the survivors' return from Chile. He then prepared an announcement and arranged for it to be sent to various press agencies, eliciting interest from around the world. The power of communication was soon brought home to the young committee when they started receiving phone calls from as far away as Japan, and questions began to pour in on the teleprinter at Mercader's office.

Meanwhile, the committee started working through the details and logistics of the press conference and the survivors' arrival. Connie's father, lawyer for the ONDA bus company, arranged for two coaches to drive up to the plane on arrival, and transport the boys directly to the school. And the committee coordinated with the Christian Brothers to ensure that the gymnasium was available to host the conference, and to prepare it for the large number of attendees that were anticipated.

Preparations were going smoothly until the foreign press broke the news about the anthropophagy, creating a new crisis for the young committee. Unsure of the truth of the claims, Connie called Gustavo Zerbino's father Jorge, who was still in Santiago, asking him whether the information they were receiving was correct, and if so, how he wanted them to handle the situation. Mr Zerbino told Connie that the boys had decided to appear as a group in the press conference, and that he should be confident that they would make a clear statement on the matter.

Fig. 88. *Stella Maris prefects, 1963. Conrado Hughes, Emilio Azambuja, Adolfo Gelsi, Marcelo Pérez de Castillo, Aldo Magri. A decade later, the first three would form part of the survivors' reception committee, and Marcelo and Aldo's brother Guido would both die in the Andes.*

As it turned out, the boys' return to Montevideo could hardly have gone more smoothly. The ten survivors who disembarked from the LAN Chile Boeing 727 at Carrasco airport on Thursday 28th December were welcomed by cheering crowds waving at them from the terminal's viewing balcony, and were met at the foot of the steps by a small greeting party, which included first lady Josefina Herrán and *Old Christians* president Daniel Juan. They boarded the buses, and set off towards Carrasco, the streets lined with people hoping to catch a glimpse of them as they drove past. First stop was *Colegio Sagrado Corazón*, the girl's school next door to *Stella Maris*, where a private meeting took place between the boys, Mr Zerbino, the committee, and the Christian Brothers, in preparation for the press conference.

Javier went home to be with his family whilst the other nine boys proceeded to the gym at their old school. Just after 8:00 p.m., they entered the auditorium, to prolonged applause from the packed audience of relatives, friends, and journalists from around the world. Local television stations were there to record the event, with live footage relayed by microwave to Buenos Aires and beyond. The boys took their seats at the front of a stage framed by the Uruguayan and Chilean flags. Friends and relatives followed them on, gathering around them. Sitting centre stage, with the survivors on either side of him, was Daniel Juan, the young president of the *Old Christians* and a contemporary of the boys from the class of '66, which had suffered the most losses in the tragedy. Juan acted as master of ceremonies, welcoming the boys, and then inviting each of them to speak in turn.

First up was Gustavo, who talked about the lead-up to the accident, and the time in Mendoza. Eduardo and Roberto followed, with the latter going on to describe the moment of the accident. Others talked about its aftermath, and their life on the mountain – making water, the sleeping arrangements, and saying the rosary. Carlitos talked about the moment they heard the search had been cancelled, and how Coco Nicolich had raised everyone's spirits. Fito described the sunglasses he had invented, and then went on to talk about the avalanche, crediting Roy with saving his life. Pancho spoke of how they had given a Christian burial to their friends who had died in the accident, and of how they had been convinced that they had been spotted by the search planes which had flown over them.

The account of the anthropophagy was left to the end, and it was Pancho's inspired statement that relieved the tense and expectant atmosphere in the auditorium. His spiritual explanation, although not theologically condoned by the Roman Catholic Church, conveyed the respect with which the boys had approached the matter on the mountain, and it had the effect of silencing the press from further questions, and bringing the session to an end.

I want to make it clear that when the moment came that we no longer had food, we thought that if Jesus at the Last Supper offered his body and blood to all his apostles, he was giving us to understand that we should do the same. ... And that was an intimate communion amongst all of us that helped us to subsist... We don't want this, which for us is an intimate, intimate thing, to be exploited or made light of in any way.

Fig. 89. *The press conference at Stella Maris College, 28ᵗʰ December 1972.*

The members of the *Old Christians* committee were eager to talk to the survivors as soon as possible about how the story would be handled in the coming weeks, and Mr Zerbino organized for all of them to meet in a school room immediately following the press conference. The committee started off by saying that they had spoken with the families, and with psychologists who had advised that the boys leave Montevideo for a couple of weeks, to escape the media frenzy and to recuperate. But as the interest of the international press was so heavy, they proposed that the survivors sign an agreement giving the committee the authority to handle all press relations, and to coordinate any interview requests. They suggested, moreover, that the first use of any money coming from any interviews should be used to help the families who had been particularly hard-hit by the tragedy. The boys concurred, and signed the agreement.

Connie was put in charge, and the interview requests soon came flooding in. The first approach was from a representative of the *Sunday Mainichi* (a Japanese weekly news magazine), who had travelled to Uruguay the moment news of the press conference had reached Japan. Connie charged him $3000 – around $20,000 in today's money – for an interview with Nando Parrado, to which the reporter immediately agreed, reaching into his pocket and pulling out the cash on the spot. The BBC were next in line, Connie charging them $2000 for an audience with Roberto Canessa.

With the interview money flowing in, Connie turned his attention to the family of his friend and former classmate, Julio Martínez Lamas. Julio had been the sole breadwinner in the family, who were now in desperate need of help. Connie and Adolfo Gelsi approached local estate agent Eduardo Blengio, asking him to recommend a two-bedroom apartment in downtown Carrasco that would suit Nené Martínez Lamas and her thirteen-year-old daughter Ana Inés. Meanwhile, Julio's colleagues at the bank had been contributing to a collection, which raised a further $4000. The combined funds were enough to purchase an apartment on Arocena Avenue, the main street of Carrasco, and, on 29th March 1973, the deed was signed over to the Martínez Lamas family, with both Blengio and the notaries waiving their fees, and with Connie Hughes and Roy Harley acting as witnesses and representatives of the *Old Christians* and the survivors.

Many more interviews took place over the following weeks, with Nando Parrado and Pancho Delgado topping the list, the former for his heroics on the mountain, the latter for his eloquence at the press conference. In the first week of January, the two of them received an invitation to appear on the biggest show on Brazilian TV – to be interviewed by controversial presenter Flávio Cavalcanti. The opportunity had come via Rafael Ponce de León rather than through the *Old Christians* committee, and the TV channel was keen to speak to the radio ham also, in order to get a perspective on events away from the mountain. Nando declined this particular request, as he had a conflicting interview with a European magazine. But for Rafael and Pancho, the thought of a few days in Rio was compelling, and they were eager to go. There was an immediate snag in that Pancho was reluctant to get on a plane again, as the flight home from Chile had been a nerve-wracking experience for him. So the two decided to travel by bus – a trip of almost 40 hours from Montevideo.

There was a lot of interest on their arrival in Rio, and intricate plans had been made to throw the pursuing press off the scent. The boys were dropped off at one hotel and then led through the kitchens to another waiting bus. After this manoeuvre had been repeated two or three times, the boys arrived at their final destination, where they holed up for a couple of days before being taken to the bright lights of the TV studio. After the monotony of the previous days, and the stress of a live TV interview, the boys felt that they'd earned the right to enjoy the beaches in Rio for a while before the gruelling bus ride home.

Choosing an Author

As the news broke around the world, an alert young editor-in-chief in New York, Ed Burlingame of *J.B. Lippincott Company*, was one of the earliest to see the possibilities of the story:

> *On the morning that the New York Times published its front page article about the miraculous reappearance of the sixteen Uruguayan boys, I was riding to work on the train. I was intrigued by the account, and thought these boys must have a fascinating tale to tell, so I decided to fly to Montevideo right after Christmas to meet the survivors and the families. My secretary booked the air tickets that same day, and it wasn't until I got home that evening that I discovered in an atlas exactly where Montevideo was!*

Burlingame spoke no Spanish, but a banker friend put him in touch with Gilberto Regules, a partner in *Guyer and Regules*, one of the top law firms in Montevideo. The lawyer, a cousin of the father of Gilberto 'Tito' Regules, agreed to represent Burlingame, and to make the necessary introductions. The meeting with the survivors took place soon after Burlingame's arrival, in the garden of one of the families. Sipping lemonade on the warm summer's day, a pleasant respite from the harsh New York winter, he chatted informally with the boys and their parents, grateful that most of them were proficient in English.

When asked to give his thoughts about the possibility of a book, Burlingame emphasized two points. The first was that, if they wanted their story to be told to the world, they would need to form themselves into a legally-binding entity, and to agree to cooperate exclusively with a single writer and publisher. The second was to be very careful in the choice of writer, the quality and reputation of whom would be the best guarantee of the success of any future book. This advice, unremarkable though it was, would work to Burlingame's advantage in the coming days, as rival publishers failed to give sufficient consideration to the matter.

Even before leaving New York, Burlingame had felt that the young English writer Piers Paul Read, son of poet and literary critic Sir Herbert Read, would be the best choice to tell the story, should the opportunity arise. The young Catholic author's literary output had been limited to fiction up to that point, but his recent novels had been published by Lippincott to considerable acclaim. *Monk Dawson*, awarded both the *Hawthornden Prize* and the *Somerset Maugham Award* for 1970, followed the lives of two friends who meet on their first day at a boarding school run by Benedictine monks. The narrative was closely informed by Read's experiences at *Ampleforth College*, which, like *Stella Maris*

College, was a Catholic rugby-playing private school, run by clergy. In a later interview with the Uruguayan leftist newspaper *Marcha*, Read reflected on his time at Ampleforth:

> *I irritated the monks a lot, and they irritated me. I annoyed them by repeating that St. Benedict would not approve of the best priests in England devoting all their energy to the exclusive education of the children of the rich! It was quite ironic that the survivors of the Andes belonged to Stella Maris, a school like mine.*

But more than this commonality, it was Read's low-key and thoughtful personality that Burlingame felt would reassure and win over the boys:

> *I told Piers of my plans, and asked if he might be interested. He was polite, but thought the idea quite mad. The other writer I considered was Peter Matthiessen, but Piers seemed to me the right age—younger than the parents, old enough to gain the boys' respect and trust, sort of an older brother in whom they could confide. Piers was a practicing and serious Catholic and, like Matthiessen, was a critically acclaimed and admired writer. As I had been working with Piers as his American editor, I understood the range of his gifts — at that point perhaps better than he did. I knew him to be an excellent listener and a very sympathetic man. I thought the boys would trust and like him.*

After meeting with the boys several more times, Burlingame was left in no doubt that their story would make a marvellous book, and set about convincing Read.

By this time, a formal solicitation for bids from book publishers had been released. Whilst many of the boys had escaped to the countryside or the beach for a couple of weeks of rest and relaxation, the *Old Christians* book committee of Hughes, Azambuja, Juan, and Gelsi, had been busy working through the details. Showing proficiency and ingenuity that belied their youth and inexperience, the four of them laid out the ground rules for the bidding process. And they asked Manino Mercader, who had trained as a lawyer as well as a journalist, to prepare the request for tender, which was then propagated internationally through his contacts at the *Associated Press*, *Agence France-Presse*, and other news agencies. Bidders were asked to propose a monetary offer, and to nominate an author.

Representatives from other US publishing houses had already begun arriving in Montevideo, meeting with the committee to discuss their ideas for the book, as well as talking to the survivors and their parents. By the time the formal bidding process started in the middle of January, four candidates had thrown their hats into the ring: *Lippincott*,

Harcourt Brace Jovanovic (HBJ), *Doubleday*, and *Reader's Digest*. The latter had a division at the time – *Reader's Digest Press* – which published full-length non-fiction books, but they also wanted to keep a close eye on the bidding process, so that they would be at hand to discuss serialization rights with the winning party. They came with Assistant Managing Editor Edward T. Thompson and writer Joseph Blank, "a veteran with the magazine who has handled many delicate subjects and big stories, with great experience in interviewing", according to a report filed by local journalist Eugenio Hintz.

Fig. 90. Connie Hughes and Emilio Azambuja, Jan 1973, members of the book committee.

The editor representing *Doubleday* was the bearded Walter I. Bradbury, 'Brad' for short. Intelligent, jocular, and with a lot of money to spend, he would, on introducing himself, always qualify his name with a disarming "...not Ray Bradbury!" Ironically, he had played a major role in launching the career of his namesake, having been the *Doubleday* Science Fiction editor responsible for the publication not only of Ray Bradbury's first novel, *The Martian Chronicles*, but also Isaac Asimov's first novel, *Pebble in the Sky*, both in the first half of 1950.

On the face of it, Doubleday's choice of writer was a compelling feature of their bid; by far the best known of all the proposed authors. Gay Talese was very much in the ascendancy, with two recent best-sellers: the 1969 *The Kingdom and the Power*, an insider's look at the *New York Times*, the newspaper where he had cut his teeth as a journalist; and the 1971 *Honor Thy Father*, about the Mafia in the USA. Brad explained to the committee that Talese wasn't present because he was actively researching his next book, the subject of which was the changing landscape of sexual practices in the USA, which would eventually appear in 1981 as *Thy Neighbour's Wife*. Early in the research, Gay Talese had spent some months at the famous Sandstone Retreat – a swingers' resort in Southern California. News of the nature of Talese's current project, and his hands-on approach to research, which soon spread through the community, didn't sit well with the Catholic parents. To make matters worse, Talese stated that he would come to Montevideo to meet the survivors only if and when he was chosen.

The *HBJ* editor Henry Raymont, a personal friend of future Uruguayan president Jorge Batlle, arrived with prominent lawyer Paul Gitlin, and Argentinian writer Luisa Valenzuela, who was little known in the English-speaking world at the time, but came highly recommended. Daughter of Argentinian writer Luisa Mercedes Levinson, she grew up surrounded by the literary elite of Buenos Aires, the family home frequented by a steady stream of Argentina's most celebrated authors. Jorge Luis Borges, in particular, was a close friend of the family and would visit regularly, his sharp intellect and mischievous humour in abundant supply. Like Read, Valenzuela was known only for her fiction, and, by January 1973, had published three books in Spanish. Raymont, who had been *New York Times* correspondent in Buenos Aires, and was familiar with her work, had proposed that *HBJ* publish translations of her first two books, *Hay que sonreír* and *Los heréticos*, and she had just returned from signing the contract in New York when the Andes story hit.

Despite objecting to the idea of the families having the right of chapter-by-chapter censorship over the final account, *HBJ* joined the others in submitting a substantial offer. Unwisely, Raymont distributed some copies of Valenzuela's books. Her eccentric and ingenious tales defying the established order were unlikely to have found favour within the community. The feeling was mutual; after speaking to the families, and being horrified by a couple of the stories that some of the survivors had told her, Valenzuela became disenchanted by the project, and cynical about the survivors' supposed status as 'envoys of God'. Had *HBJ* won the contract, it would have made for interesting reading. Valenzuela would go on to become one of the most prolific and widely translated of female and feminist Latin American authors, Carlos Fuentes proclaiming her 'the heiress of Latin American fiction'. One of her short stories, *El enviado* (*The envoy*), published in 1993, would use the anthropophagy in the Andes, and its subsequent justification, as a starting point. Developing the theme of a literal versus metaphorical interpretation of the 'body of Christ' to a point of absurdity, it was perhaps a reflection of the lingering distress aroused by her experience in Montevideo.

Burlingame knew that for *Lippincott* to have any chance of winning the rights, it was imperative that Read be personally present in advance of the first round of bidding, in order to meet with the families and the committee. He called Piers in London and urged him to get on the next plane to Montevideo, to buy a first class ticket for the long flight, as he'd be busy from the moment he arrived. Piers was unenthusiastic, feeling that any bid was doomed to failure, and protesting, "I'm a novelist, what has this got to do with me?" But Ed persisted, calling him again in the middle of the night, insisting that he was the right person to tell the story, and impressing on him the urgency of the opportunity. Piers reluctantly acquiesced, flying to Montevideo and checking in to the *Victoria Plaza*, where Ed and the other bidders were staying.

The hotel was, as Piers later recalled, "fizzing with scheming and intrigue". Having seen the competition, he continued to voice his pessimism about their chance of success. For him, it seemed inconceivable that *Lippincott*, a relatively small publisher advocating an author with no experience in writing non-fiction, could compete with the might of *Doubleday* and their best-selling non-fiction writer Gay Talese. Burlingame saw the competition quite differently. He realized that the main rivals had been unwise in their selection of authors, and was quietly confident of success.

The bidding process took place over two rounds, with the opportunity for each bidder to up their offer after the first-round results had been revealed. The committee made clear that offers would be evaluated against three criteria – monetary, concept, and writer, although not necessarily in that order. From a monetary perspective, the bids covered not only the amount of the advance, but importantly, how the advance and future payments would be divided between author and survivors. So whilst *Lippincott*'s offer was ostensibly the lowest (less than half of *Doubleday*'s proposed $500,000), their royalty split was much more favourable for the survivors, who would receive 75% of all income versus *Doubleday*'s 50%, including that from the sale of subsidiary rights – book club, paperback, foreign language, and film. *Lippincott* also scored highly in concept and writer, and by the end of the first round were in the lead, followed by *Reader's Digest*, *HBJ*, and *Doubleday*, in that order.

A second round of bidding, in which the publishers increased their offers, didn't change things significantly, and once the committee had collated all the information, they called a meeting with the survivors, to present the different offers. The sixteen of them, joined by Rafael Ponce de León, then took a vote, the result being a clear majority in favour of *Lippincott*. Reassured by Read's Catholic credentials, and persuaded that he would not write a sensationalist exposé, the survivors voted for the man, not the highest offer. Burlingame's choice of author had been vindicated.

The next day, 23rd January, Connie Hughes revealed the winning bid to the local press. Starting off by thanking the other three publishers, he continued:

> *Lippincott's offer was not the largest financially, but we felt it was the most serious, and the one which, from the outset, presented exactly the approach the 16 survivors were looking for. The English writer, Read, impressed us from the start. He will remain in close contact with all of us until he finishes the work.*

Connie then noted that the initial draft of the book would be delivered by September 1973, and that the funds raised from the book would be managed by a foundation made up of the survivors, with some of the proceeds going to the families of those who died, as needs dictated. He added that Antonio Mercader had been appointed by the survivors to help Read in his research.

Ed Burlingame also addressed the press, saying how pleased he and Piers Read were to win the contract, and adding:

> Piers Paul Read has already, this afternoon, started the work. It will be an arduous task for him. First of all, he will have to collect, weigh, and study all the data provided by the survivors. He will then have to research all the material he finds available on the case, which is considerable. Then, and only then, will he start writing the book.

True to Burlingame's statement, Read had immediately started making preparations, reviewing the main elements of the story, and collecting the initial contact details that would allow him to prepare a schedule of interviews with the boys. The day after the press announcement – Thursday, 25th January – he arrived at the Strauch residence, to interview Eduardo and Fito. The families of the two Strauch cousins occupied the first two floors of an elegant house in *Parque de los Aliados* (these days *Parque Batlle*). The third floor had been occupied by their Urioste grandfather, but was now rented out to a US family. The boys and Read chatted in the garden, joined by Eduardo's mother, Sara Urioste. The three spoke English well enough that Piers was able to conduct the interview without the need for an interpreter.

Fig. 91. *Eduardo Strauch and his mother Sara Urioste in their garden, January 1973.*

The next day, he visited Coche and his *novia* Soledad, both English speakers, although he conversed in French with Coche's mother. And at the weekend he moved from Montevideo to Punta del Este, where many of the families could be found in the summer months. Pancho Delgado and Carlitos Páez were both spending January in Punta Ballena, a few miles west of the main resort; Pancho staying with his fiancée's family, and Carlitos Páez at his father's studio in Casapueblo. An Argentinian journalist arranged to bring the two boys to meet with Piers for lunch, and later they went on to Casapueblo, where a pop concert – a 'homage to Chile' – was due to take place, and where he briefly met Carlos Páez Vilaró. He later recorded his impressions of Vilaró's eccentric edifice:

> *Casapueblo itself is a warren of whitewashed rooms connected by passages and opening onto terraces which overlook the sea. There are Miró-like creations everywhere, tapestries, plates, sculptures, etc... The sun sinks into the sea and at sunset the concert starts.*

The next day, he conducted a formal interview with Carlitos Páez, commenting in his notebook: "Frank and straightforward; each one seems to give away more than the last," although Read's progress was doubtless helped by his increasing familiarity with the story. As the interviews continued, he was able to use the information garnered from previous sessions to formulate more probing questions for the next, and his long interview with Roberto Canessa the following day was especially productive. He planned to speak to each survivor twice, so that he could cover any ground he missed the first time round.

There was time to conduct two more interviews – with Moncho Sabella and Pancho Delgado – before Read had to head off on a whirlwind tour of Argentina and Chile, recording his impressions along the way. The itinerary: Buenos Aires on 2nd February, then Mendoza, Santiago, San Fernando, and Santiago again before arriving back in Montevideo on 7th February. The leg from Mendoza to Santiago across the Andes was by car: "a stupendous drive on appalling roads – very exciting and very worthwhile."

The excitement of the return flight from Santiago to Montevideo was of a more alarming nature. The SAS DC8 was forced to return to *Pudahuel* airport after the undercarriage mechanism jammed. Read, his fear fuelled by a constant preoccupation with the book, was sure that they were going to crash. As he contemplated his imminent demise, his thoughts didn't turn to God; rather, he felt a desperate desire to see his family again, and a depression at the banality of dying in a plane crash. As it was, the plane landed safely, and he was soon on another flight, arriving back in Montevideo without incident. The next day, he resumed his interviews with the survivors, starting with Nando Parrado, whom he met in the office of the family hardware store, *La Casa del Tornillo*.

Read had gone to Chile with journalist Eugenio 'Gene' Hintz, a last-minute stand-in for the survivor-appointed Manino Mercader, whose wife Rosario Medero was due to give birth. Rosario, an accountant and university colleague of Connie Hughes, was the daughter of Benito Medero, the Minister of Agriculture in the Bordaberry government. The decision of Mercader to remain in Montevideo was a wise one, as the baby arrived on 3rd February, when Read and Hintz were still in Mendoza. The appearance of Hintz meant that Read now had two local experts to research those parts of the story that he would not have the time to investigate himself.

Mercader, an international correspondent, and editor at the *El Diario* newspaper, was 28 at the time, and had come to prominence three years earlier in 1969, as joint author of *Los Tupamaros*, an important historical snapshot of the urban guerrilla group at the zenith of their popular appeal. A member of the National party, and a supporter of

Wilson Ferreira Aldunate, Mercader would later go on to serve as Minister of Education and Culture of Uruguay in the governments of both Luis Alberto Lacalle and Jorge Batlle, his ministerial appointments sandwiching his post as Uruguayan ambassador to the Organization of American States. Born in Madrid in 1944, he had some notable relatives. His father was brother to Spanish film actress María Mercader, brother-in-law (through María) to acclaimed Italian director Vittorio De Sica, and cousin to Ramón Mercader, the ice-axe assassin of Leon Trotsky. Mercader's role would be to provide biographical information about the passengers, and to help Read to understand the sociocultural context of the story.

Antonio Mercader circa 1970

Eugenio Hintz at work, by renowned Uruguayan caricaturist Hermenegildo Sábat.

Fig. 92. *The journalists helping Piers Paul Read.*

Gene Hintz, 49, was an influential figure in the Uruguayan film community, founding the *Cine Club del Uruguay* and the *Cineteca del Cine Independiente*, and winning prizes for his documentary and scientific films. Later, he turned to journalism, joining *El País* in 1956, and acting as Uruguayan correspondent for various foreign newspapers such as the *New York Times* and the *Financial Times*. In 1967, he was sent by *El País* to Israel, as special correspondent and photographer, to cover the Arab-Israeli war. Hintz's remit in the Andes story was to provide a report on the Chilean side of things, and the accident itself, including any reports or analyses into its cause.

With the trip to Chile out of the way, and the two journalists embarking on their own research, Read continued with his main task of interviewing the survivors. All the interviews were taped, because he had decided that he would chronicle the story as it was, with no fictional embellishments, and no whitewashing of the events and interactions that took place on the mountain. Up to this point, the boys had been cordial with Read, but had remained quite distant, and hadn't opened up to him in a way that would allow him to craft a compelling narrative. This problem solved itself when Read asked the committee to recommend an interpreter. Adolfo Gelsi proposed his brother Pablo, whose English was fluent from a year in the USA, where he had won a scholarship to study at Princeton. Moreover, Pablo knew many of the passengers, having been in the same class as Fito Strauch, Gastón Costemalle, and Daniel Shaw, and he was a first cousin and friend of Guido Magri. As an added bonus, Pablo's field of study was psychology, and it was his reassuring presence in the interviews which helped the boys to open up and unburden themselves, with Read acting as confidante and father confessor. Such was the bond that developed, through Gelsi's mediation, between the survivors and Read, that they referred to him as 'the 17th survivor'.

Fig. 93. *Pablo Gelsi, in 1971 and 2019.*

Pablo would go on to become an eminent Jungian psychologist, but it was the unique experience of these interviews and his subsequent employment as the official school psychologist at *Stella Maris College* that would give him his first opportunity as a practitioner. The involvement of Adolfo and Pablo was not the only contribution of the Gelsi family. Their father Adolfo Gelsi Bidart was the personal choice of the boys as their legal representative, although formally the work was done under the umbrella of the legal practice of Zerbino and Rachetti, the former being Gustavo's father Jorge, who had played such a leading role in the search, and the survivors' return from Chile.

Interviews followed in quick succession, interspersed by social events at the weekends – an *asado* at the Fernández *estancia*, a party at the Sabellas, and lunch at the house of Pancho Delgado's fiancée in Punta Ballena. Read and Gelsi also met with radio ham Rafael Ponce de León, and with some of the parents whose sons had stayed on the mountain – the Valeta, Nicolich, Nogueira, and Platero families. The meeting with Roy Harley on Saturday 17th February marked the end of the first round of interviews, with all the survivors spoken to at least once.

It was around this time that Read received a late night visit from North American reporter Richard Cunningham, a feature writer and foreign correspondent for the Kansas City Star, whose intersection with the Andes story came from the Chilean side. Of Irish stock, Cunningham had grown up in Kansas on the wrong side of the tracks, spending two years in an orphanage despite the best efforts of his father to provide a loving home. But it was there that his potential was spotted by a nun, who nurtured in him a love of literature, a passion which eventually led to a Masters degree in Modern American Literature at the University of Kansas. In the course of doing his postgraduate work, he met the love of his life, a Chilean girl, Lucía Guerra, who was visiting on a Fulbright scholarship. Lucía would go on to become an eminent literary critic and author, teaching at the University of California where the couple later made their home. The trips to Santiago to visit Lucía's family marked a new start in Cunningham's life. He wrote of his first trip to Chile:

> *In this year of our Lord, 1970, I begin to live, I begin to fully enjoy life. I owe everything to Chile . . . Everyone here has treated me with great affection and friendship, from family to the boy in the street who shines my shoes. I feel like I've come to the exact place I always needed and was looking for . . . Long live Chile!*

In Santiago, it was inevitable that he would hear about the Andes story, and his journalistic interest and research for an article grew into a resolve to write a book. After conducting interviews with many of the protagonists in Chile, he headed to Montevideo in the hope of meeting some of the survivors. It was the discovery that they had signed an agreement to speak to no-one except Read that prompted Cunningham to visit the British author at the *Victoria Plaza* on 19th February. Cunningham wrote of the meeting in the introduction to his book:

He arrived at his hotel around midnight looking very tired, and we had a beer together. After a brief conversation, he mentioned that he was 'weak' on what had happened in Chile. He suggested that perhaps we could come to some agreement. To make matters brief, I was given a two-hour exclusive interview in return for a copy of my tapes.

Appearing in 1973, before Read's book, Cunningham's *The Place where the World Ends* features imagined diary entries recording the days on the mountain, interspersed by headlines which anchor it to a timeline of real world events. Strong on the Chilean side of the story, it also features a brief history of anthropophagy and cannibalism. Cunningham would go on to write two more books including the 2009 novel *Santiago Blues*, which gave a voice to the victims of the Chilean military government in 1973, a time of great terror on the streets of Santiago, with the worst violations occurring less than a year after the Andes survivors returned home.

Fig. 94. *A few of the 47 cassette tapes that Read brought back from Uruguay.*

By the time of Cunningham's visit, Read felt that he had a good enough grasp of events to start writing a longhand 4000-word synopsis of the story; an exercise that allowed him to explore the style in which the longer account might be written, and to hone his story-telling voice. Armed with a list of questions that had arisen from writing the story down, he and Gelsi embarked on the second round of interviews, clarifying statements as necessary, and digging deeper into various aspects of the tragedy. They finished the interviews with a group session involving the Strauch cousins, Daniel Fernández, Roberto Canessa, and Pedro Algorta. When he finally returned home in the first week of March, Read had amassed 85 hours of interviews, recorded on 47 cassette tapes.

Fig. 96. *Asado at the estancia of survivor Daniel Fernández, 11th February 1973.*

Fig. 95. *Group photo at the asado, with '17th survivor' Piers Paul Read. Only Tintín is missing.*
Back: Bobby, Pedro, Daniel, Roy, Pancho, Coche, Nando, Fito, Piers, Eduardo, Carlitos.
Front: Javier, Gustavo, Álvaro, Moncho, Roberto.

WRITING THE BOOK

Read's initial pessimism had long dissipated by the time he returned to London, and he was now enthused about the project, confident that he could do the story justice, and persuaded of the widespread fascination with it. From the moment Lippincott had won the bid, their foreign and subsidiary rights departments had gone into overdrive. Magazines, book clubs, and non-US publishers were queuing up to obtain serialization and translation rights. The experience of having worked in London for two years at the beginning of his career had given Burlingame the opportunity to form many lifetime friends and contacts in the publishing houses of Europe, and he personally set about arranging several of the deals.

First to get a call was Read's editor in the UK, Barley Alison, a particularly close friend, who had been responsible for bringing Ed and Piers together. Read's US publisher at the time had been less than enthusiastic about the manuscript of *Monk Dawson*, and a copy had been passed to Burlingame, who had read it and made an immediate offer, thus establishing Lippincott as Read's new Stateside publisher. Expedited by an already close working relationship, Burlingame soon engineered a deal with *Secker & Warburg*, who published Read's books in the UK under Barley's imprint, *Alison Press*. After obtaining exclusive rights for the UK and the Commonwealth, the British publishing house promptly more than recovered its outlay, by selling on exclusive prepublication serialization rights to the *Observer Magazine*.

By the end of March, rights for German, French, Slovene and Serbo-Croat language versions of the book had also been negotiated, with Spanish, Japanese, Italian, and others soon to follow. Read had got an early taste of this worldwide interest at first hand when he had been awoken in his hotel room in Montevideo by a 4:00 a.m. call from Munich; it had been the German magazine *Quick*, asking about serialization rights.

After spending a few days recuperating, and picking up on family life following his long absence, Read started the preparatory work for the book. The aim was to complete a polished draft within six months, which could then be reviewed by the survivors for accuracy. Read's first, by no means insignificant, task was to transcribe the tapes. It took him and an assistant until the middle of April to complete the work, the resulting transcripts half typewritten, half in Read's handwriting. By this time, Read had also received the materials from Mercader and Hintz, the only missing document being the Chilean Air Force report of the accident, and of the search and rescue efforts, which would eventually arrive in England two months later.

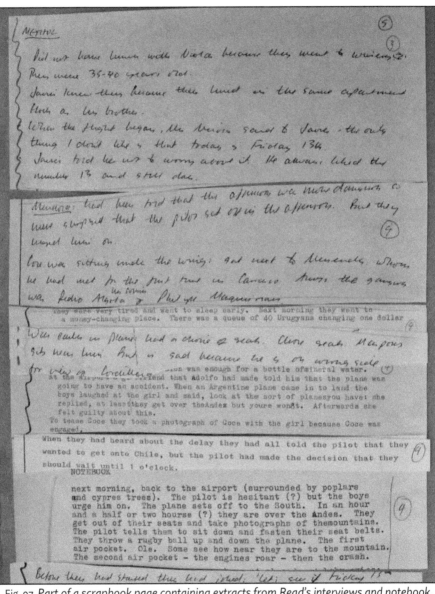

MENTOL ⑤

③

Did not have lunch with Nicola because they went to university...
They were 35-40 years old.
Javier knew them because they lived in the same apartment block as his brother.
When the flight began, the Nicola said to Javier - the only thing I don't like is that today is Friday 13th.
Javier told her not to worry about it. He always liked the number 13 and still does.

Marcelo had been told that the afternoon was more dangerous so were surprised that the pilot set off in the afternoon. But they wanted him on.

⑥

Coce was sitting under the wings. Sat next to Menendez, whom he had met for the first time in Caracas. His companion was Pedro Algorta & Phil ... Vizquerrain

⑦

they were very tired and went to sleep early. Next morning they went to a money-changing place. There was a queue of 40 Uruguyans changing one dollar

⑧

Will called in Plans had a choice of seats. Chose seats. Marpons sits next. But is sad because he is on wrong side for view of Cordillera. ...on was enough for a bottle of mineral water.
At the airport ... friend that Adolfo had made told him that the plane was going to have an accident. When an Argentine plane came in to land the boys laughed at the girl and said, look at the sort of planes you have: she replied, at least they get over the Andes but youre won8t. Afterwards she felt guilty about this.
To tease Coce they took a photograph of Coce with the girl because Coce was engaged.

⑦

When they had heard about the delay they had all told the pilot that they wanted to get onto Chile, but the pilot had made the decision that they should wait until 1 o'clock.
NOTEBOOK

⑨

next morning, back to the airport (surrounded by poplars and cypres trees). The pilot is hesitant (?) but the boys urge him on. The plane sets off to the South. In an hour and a half or two hourse (?) they are over the Andes. They get out of their seats and take photographs of themountains. The pilot tells them to sit down and fasten their seat belts. They throw a rugby ball up and down the plane. The first air pocket. Ole. Some see how near they are to the mountain. The second air pocket - the engines roar - then the crash.

④

Before they had started they had joked: 'let; see if Friday 13'

Fig. 97. Part of a scrapbook page containing extracts from Read's interviews and notebook.

With the source materials now largely in place, the task of organizing the disparate accounts into a cohesive whole was considerable. Read approached this problem in an ingenious way. After first making copies of all the transcripts, he drew a line down the left-hand margin of each page, the colour and the style of which indicated the particular source. Pedro Algorta was represented by a straight blue line; Roberto Canessa by a dashed green line; Javier Methol by a squiggly red line, and so on. Read then cut the transcripts into small sections, which he pasted into eighteen large scrapbooks, corresponding roughly to the planned chapters of the book. These scrapbooks, which also included extracts from his notebooks, and from the Mercader and Hintz reports, now provided a time-ordered resource, which became the primary reference from which to craft his narrative.

Fig. 98. *J.W. Lippincott and Ed Burlingame (third and fourth from right respectively) meeting with the foreign publishers from Spain, UK, France, Finland, and Italy.*

With scrapbooks to hand, Read started writing in earnest in the second week of May. His aim was to write 2000 words a day; a regimen to which he adhered religiously, though he later confided to fellow Catholic author Graham Greene: "Never again!" But on 17th August, Read sent the final 154 pages of the first draft to Ed Burlingame in New York, the complete manuscript running to 400 pages and 140,000 words. Despite the distraction of the publication of his latest book, *The Upstart*, which appeared on 3rd

September, and a trip to Holland to see Gerard Croiset, Read immediately set about revising the manuscript, based on feedback from Burlingame, simplifying the opening chapters, and ensuring a consistent style across the book.

Confident, now, of when the final draft would be ready, a detailed production schedule was put in place, with a publication date of 15th April 1974. Burlingame, on a trip to Europe to attend the Frankfurt bookfair at the beginning of October, took the opportunity to meet with the foreign publishers to coordinate international release dates. By the second week of October, a second draft had been completed, and copies sent to the *Observer Magazine* for the preparation of their serialization, and to Gilberto Regules to distribute to the survivors, to review before the arrival of Read and Burlingame in Montevideo on 23rd October.

When the contract was originally being drawn up, the boys' legal team had insisted that they should have the right to approve the final manuscript. Burlingame had explained to them that this was out of the question, that neither Read nor any writer of the calibre they wanted to tell their story would agree to such a condition. He had proposed that when Piers had completed a nearly final draft, copies would be given to the survivors. Then he and Read would return to Montevideo to meet with them, to hear any concerns they had, agreeing to correct any errors of fact, and promising to give good faith consideration to any other issues.

Even before leaving for Uruguay, Read had heard that the survivors were upset by the book, that they felt it didn't convey the mystical and spiritual aspects of their survival, and that the details in the book would not allow them to live side-by-side with the families of those who died. This reaction was reinforced by an emotional letter from Sara Urioste – the mother of Eduardo Strauch – which greeted Read on his arrival. She felt that Read had betrayed the trust of the boys, who had confided in him so openly, and she pleaded with him to emphasize the friendship and courage of the boys, rather than what they were forced to do.

Read, although stung by these negative reactions, was confident in his judgment, responding to Sara Urioste:

> My intention was to write the book in such a way that the reader lives those terrible seventy days with them, and with their parents down below. For this, it is important to let the facts speak for themselves; nothing would be worse than for their story to degenerate into pious sentimentality.

And justifying the inclusion of details about the anthropophagy, he added:

> I believe that the details should be included because they express most forcibly the terrible ordeal and dilemma that the boys went through. To remove the details is to weaken the story; to weaken the story is to dilute and denigrate the experience. It is also to leave open the door to rumour. No-one who reads the book as it stands can suspect that there is something that has been hidden. If we do hide the details, the reader will suspect it and will imagine far worse events up there on the mountain than those which took place.

Burlingame reserved a suite at the Victoria Plaza where he, Read, and the survivors met, the heated discussions stretching on into November, requiring significant diplomacy and sensitivity from Piers to help resolve the issues. One area of concern that remained was the survivors' dread of an adverse reaction from the bereaved relatives to the revelations in the book. Those fears were largely assuaged by a letter to Piers Read from Julio Martínez Lamas' sister Rosario, who wrote:

> They are not going to make us suffer more by telling us how they did what they did with details... Besides, we may all suppose that if those who died would have remained alive and vice versa, the same thing would have happened...They <u>cannot</u> feel guilty of what they did. If the church said it was right, if we love them as I love my dear brother, please let them know, let them get convinced that they <u>must</u> live happily from now on, that they must not feel they hurt us or have hurt us...

Read, who had encountered similar sentiments amongst the mothers of the *Biblioteca Nuestros Hijos*, showed the letter to the boys, who were sufficiently impressed that they asked for it to be included in the book. In the end, Read decided to express the sentiment rather than replicate the text of Rosario's letter, but it went a long way to dispelling the remaining anxiety amongst the survivors, and Read left Montevideo with his manuscript intact. Stopping in New York on the way back to England gave Read the chance to review the copy-edited version of the book.

Proofs were sent out to various individuals, evoking universal admiration at Read's skill. Especially gratifying was a quote from Graham Greene, who enthused:

> It is inconceivable to me that this story could have been better told. The concluding chapters in particular are a masterpiece of narrative.

Read even received a congratulatory letter from rival editor 'Brad' Bradbury of Doubleday, who, more than most, appreciated the work and skill that had gone into Read's accomplishment, and the difficulties that he'd had to overcome. Gratified by Brad's letter, Read admitted to Ed Burlingame:

> I was almost as anxious not to disappoint our rivals when writing the book as I was not to disappoint you and the boys.

The only blot in a profusion of glowing reviews would come later from William Golding, whose *Lord of the Flies* had touched on similar themes. Golding questioned the efforts that the boys had made to escape their situation, doubted whether their actions on the mountain merited admiration, and derided the spiritual justifications for the anthropophagy. Despite this, Golding praised the writing, conceding that Read's account of Canessa and Parrado's final expedition could not be bettered.

THE BOOK TOUR

With *ALIVE: The Story of the Andes Survivors* due to appear in the bookshops on April 15th, Lippincott opted for a 75,000 first-edition print run, and assigned it an advertising and promotion budget of $50,000 – close to $300,000 in today's money. As their salesmen started making the rounds of bookshops across the country, full-page ads were scheduled for dozens of top-tier newspapers, and glowing reviews started to appear. An early *New York Times* review was especially influential, calling it "A narrative of terrific and enduring significance", and stating: "In our century, perhaps the most arresting peacetime survival story yet told." But the main draw would be the presence of Nando Parrado and Roberto Canessa. A coast-to-coast itinerary was prepared, with TV and radio appearances in major cities across the USA.

The two boys flew in on 28th March, arriving early in order to see the sights of New York City. Ed Burlingame wrote to Piers Read:

> *The boys arrived last Thursday and are making a great hit with everyone. They spent the weekend with us and we gave several parties for them which seemed to be very successful. ... The tour starts on Thursday in Boston, and after that they are going to be very busy.*

The day before the tour, Lippincott arranged a reception for the editors of the paperback publishers and book clubs to meet the boys, with a preparatory eye on the lucrative sale of paperback rights once, as anticipated, the hardback edition hit the best-seller lists.

The tour itself proved to be an unqualified success, though it hit an early snag. The boys experienced a particularly turbulent flight from Boston to Washington, and were unnerved by it. As a result, their itinerary was rearranged to use train or road connections where possible, although some flying was inevitable. Accompanied by Lippincott publicist Dianitia Hutcheson, they made their way across the country towards the West Coast. Ed Burlingame kept Piers Read informed about their progress, enthusing on 11th April:

> *The boys are absolutely superb in promotion. They have won the hearts of everyone they met, and all of the hard-bitten television producers have called up afterwards – quite unheard of – to say they were bowled over by the two, and thought their program had been a huge success. They got nearly 10 or 15 minutes on "Today", a television program seen throughout the country and almost*

certainly the most important one for the promotion of a book. Tuesday night they taped an interview with David Susskind which will be broadcast this Sunday evening on television. He gave them more than ½ of his two hour program. Roberto is proving especially effective. He has not lost his habit of collaring the conversation but he is interesting, dynamic, and he throws himself fully into the spirit of the occasion.

15th April saw them in Detroit, 19th April in Chicago, and by the time they reached Los Angeles at the end of the month, *ALIVE* had entered the *New York Times* best-seller list. It would remain there for 30 weeks, reaching number two on the list on 15th September, pipped to the top spot only by *All the President's Men*, Bernstein and Woodward's Watergate exposé. The early success of the hardback edition generated an unprecedented response when the US paperback rights came up for sale in May, with Lippincott receiving four offers of over $1,000,000. The winning publisher, *Avon Books*, who secured the rights with a record bid of $1,200,000 for the paperback rights of a new book, announced the launch for the following year with a first edition of 1,800,000 copies.

The US leg of Nando and Roberto's grand tour came to an end at the beginning of May, when they flew from New York to Dublin, arriving on the morning of Saturday 4th May, and welcomed to Europe by a greeting party that included Piers Read and BBC representative Anne Tyerman. The plan was for the BBC Panorama team to film the boys as they went around the town over the weekend. On the Saturday night, there was an appearance on the *Late, Late Show* on Irish national TV. The next day, the boys would attend Mass at Dublin Cathedral and conclude their sight-seeing, before flying to London on Sunday evening. There, they would check into the recently opened *Gloucester Hotel* on Harrington Gardens in Kensington, in advance of a busy week of activities.

The plans for the week of 6th May had been shaping up for a couple of months. As early as February, Piers Read had confided to Ed:

Barley's plans for Parrado and Canessa grow more exotic by the hour, and now include receptions at the French Embassy and the House of Lords. I dare say that the two boys will be in a state of semi-exhaustion when they arrive anyway; the tour of fifty states may make their walk through the Andes seem like a piece of cake.

With her many high-profile professional and social contacts within and outside the publishing world, Barley was the ideal person to arrange events in London. Before entering the world of publishing, she had been in Special Operations in Algiers during World War II, after which she had had spells in the Diplomatic Service in Paris, and in the Foreign Office. In his biography of Roy Jenkins, with whom Barley had famously had an affair in the early fifties, John Campbell writes of her:

> In 1953 she left the Foreign Office and, after a short spell of travel and freelance journalism, went into publishing. She joined George Weidenfeld as his fiction editor and over the following years built up a remarkable list of authors including Saul Bellow, Vladimir Nabokov, Piers Paul Read and Margaret Drabble, until in 1967 she left (taking her authors with her) to set up her own imprint, the Alison Press, as part of Secker & Warburg. Their affair gradually petered out, but she and Jenkins remained good friends

Campbell goes on to add:

> She remained an extraordinarily original and vibrant figure on the London literary scene, famous both for her parties – she was never without a drink in one hand and a cigarette in the other – and for her devotion to her authors.

Barley had laid on a full programme for Roberto and Nando. The schedule for Monday was particularly busy:

09:00	Australian News Ltd + South African magazine.
10:15	World at One. BBC Broadcasting House.
11:00	Evening Standard Diary.
12:00	Press conference at Fleet Street Press Club.
13:00	Lunch with Piers Read and Christopher Ward of the Daily Mirror.
15:15	Radio London.
16:15	BBC.
18:00	Welcome drinks at Barley's house with editorial staff.

A review by George Gale, published in the next day's *Evening Standard* on the back of Monday's interview, drew a proprietorial response from the boys. In a letter to the editor, they challenged the reviewer's scepticism about the book's dedication, writing:

> We do not understand what Mr Gale means by "a note of improbable veracity signed by the survivors". Certainly it was signed by all 16 of us and it represents

what we believe to be the truth. Moreover, we feel that our ordeal could not have been better or more sensitively described... we and the other 14 survivors know that Piers Paul Read's book represents the truth and nothing but the truth.

Whilst the days were devoted to meetings with press and broadcasters, the evenings were filled with social events. On Tuesday there was a reception at the French Embassy, and, on Wednesday, drinks at the House of Lords, followed by dinner at the House of Commons, hosted by Barley's brother, Member of Parliament Michael Alison. On Thursday, there was a dinner at the exclusive *Garrick Club*, hosted by the literary editor of *Secker & Warburg*, David Farrer.

To cap things off, Barley had arranged one of her legendary drinks parties for 10:00 p.m. on Thursday evening, its invitation list a who's who of authors, literary critics, editors, academics, journalists, broadcasters, and MPs. Amongst the famous names were Margaret Drabble, Iris Murdoch, Kingsley Amis, Tom Stoppard, Antonia Fraser, Claire Tomalin, Jonathan Miller, Melvyn Bragg, and Roy Jenkins; the latter and his wife having remained close friends with Barley throughout. And with Nando in mind, invitations had been extended to racing magnate Bernie Ecclestone and Argentinian *Formula One* driver Carlos Reutemann.

By Friday, there was just a single appointment remaining – with Yorkshire Television – and then the boys were free from all commitments until Monday; a brief respite before the journalist-weary boys set off with Read on the next leg of their tour, boarding the 15:30 boat train to Paris.

The three were greeted on arrival at the *Gare du Nord* by Lippincott's literary agent in Paris, and a representative from Grasset, the French publishers. Promotional activities in France were well underway, and several reviews had already appeared, but the highest profile event was the appearance of Read and the two survivors on the French national television programme *Les Dossiers de l'écran*. The producers had been keen to also include the parents of a non-survivor, and, on the recommendation of Read, had invited Raquel and Gustavo Nicolich – the parents of Coco Nicolich. The couple had already given a number of press interviews in support of the survivors since their return from the mountain.

The programme attracted enormous public interest, with an estimated audience of 20 million, only the ongoing French presidential election competing for attention. As with many interviews, the main focus of discussion was the anthropophagy, and the question was thrown to the viewers: "What would you have done in their place?" The audience response was overwhelmingly positive, with 90% of the callers expressing their understanding of the reality of the situation, and supporting the decision. Several mentioned wartime parallels.

Canessa and Parrado, experienced by now in handling the media, expertly fielded the questions on anthropophagy. But it was the presence of Coco's parents that impressed everyone the most. They acknowledged that it was the only way to preserve life, and they referred to the letter that their son wrote on the mountain before he had died, in which he said he would willingly allow his body to be used if it could save somebody.

Fig. 99. *Piers Paul Read, Roberto Canessa, and Nando Parrado in Paris, May 1974.*

After a couple of days of sightseeing in Paris, the boys continued on their promotional tour, heading to Milan, where the Italian publishers *Spurling & Kupfer* were based. Read returned to England, but not before Roberto had played a parting practical joke on him. Inviting him to their room to say goodbye before he left for the train station, Roberto had rigged up a booby trap, and Read was greeted with a bagful of water on his head as he entered. Despite the unwelcome soaking, Read and the boys parted on good terms, and agreed to meet up again in June, the three of them invited by Barley Alison to her summer home on the *Costa de Almería*, for some rest and relaxation after the exertions of the previous months.

On Read's return to England, he wrote to Mecha Canessa to give her news of her son. He was full of praise for the way the two boys had handled themselves on the tour, writing:

> They have a real sincerity and joie de vivre that strikes everyone they meet – either directly or through television. In Paris, where I left them three days ago, all the people in the street shook hands with them after a big TV show. I can also say that even though they are heroes everywhere, it hasn't gone to their heads. They are, of course, deeply tired with all the journalists, etc., but have enough energy to enjoy London and Paris. Roberto is a tourist with the same determination he showed in the mountains.

The Paris leg of their tour propelled *Les Survivants,* as the book was titled in France, to the top of the best-seller list by the beginning of June. In the same week, sales were reported to have topped 100,000 in Japan, where the publishers were on their sixth printing, and in the USA, the book held a steady third place in the *New York Times* list through most of the summer. The rapid uptake around the world was not quite matched in Read's home territory as he ruefully observed in a letter to Regules: "...only in England, to my humiliation, is it stuck at number 5". A month later, he was still bemoaning the slow UK sales, writing to Ed Burlingame:

> The euphoria certainly continues on this side of the Atlantic – only slightly tempered by the book's disappointing progress here in England. I am afraid that the Observer serialization was too thorough.

Fig. 100. *The Observer ran a four-week pre-publication serialization of ALIVE.*

By this time, Roberto was back in Uruguay, and the only thing holding Nando in England was an upcoming course at the Jim Russell motor racing school at Snetterton in Norfolk. Until it began on 11th July, he was staying as a guest of Read and his family in London. Nando had enrolled in the course on the encouragement of Formula One champion Jackie Stewart, whom he had met at the Argentinian Grand Prix in January 1973. It would mark the start of Nando's competitive racing career, culminating in his selection as a driver for the Alfa Romeo team in the 1977 European Touring Car Championship.

The success of ALIVE, which would go on to sell more than five million copies, was a mixed blessing for Read. He didn't relish the fame and attention that it brought, and was considering a move out of the city, contemplating "some sort of country cottage in which I can escape the notoriety which pursues me in London, and get down to that improbable activity of writing another novel", as he wrote to Burlingame. On the other hand, the financial security that came with the success was what would allow him to pursue his career as a novelist without worry for the future.

He touched on this in his interview with *Marcha*:

> *I've been criticized for making too much money on this book. 'The Times' said I was a good novelist, and shouldn't do that sort of thing. Writers rightly complain that they can't survive, and then when someone manages to do so, they accuse him of selling out.*

Marcha was an influential newspaper that catered for a wide spectrum of left-wing views, and the interview caused quite a stir. Read had not known the political stance of the newspaper before the interview, but quickly became aware of it when the interviewer Marta D'Agostino praised him for having made it so clear that "the Uruguayan bourgeoisie have always been cannibalistic in the material sense". Read was forced onto the defensive ("he moves forward as if in a dark room full of vipers") as the meticulously-prepared D'Agostino continued to impose her own slant onto Read's account. Matters were not helped by some questionable translations, the rendering of 'straightforward' as 'primitivo' to describe Roberto and Nando being one of several examples. The storm blew over in the end, but it left a sour taste, and Read did not return to Uruguay that Christmas, as he had tentatively planned. As for *Marcha*, the 15th November 1974 edition in which the interview appeared would prove to be the penultimate issue, the publication shut down before the end of the month by the military dictatorship it had dared to criticize.

VI.   They Still Whisper in our Ears

Here I will lift the cover from a tomb,
And entering it, will in its farthest depths
Set thoughts alight that will illuminate
The solitude of its immensity.[1]

When, in December 1972, the list of the sixteen survivors from the lost Fairchild was broadcast by radio, it opened a deep chasm that cut across the close-knit community of friends and neighbours. Yet despite the grief of having lost their sons twice, many bereaved parents showed extraordinary generosity, going out of their way to provide moral support to the survivors, and justification for what they'd had to do. After the global attention died down, life had to continue, grieving families living side-by-side with those whose sons had been reborn, and although many friendships remained intact, it was easier, out of respect and for fear of causing distress, not to discuss the subject. Even within many families, any mention of the accident was taboo.

Twenty years later, the release of the film *ALIVE* acted as a catalyst for talking about the tragedy again, reopening old wounds, and accentuating the differences in fortune between the sixteen heroes of the Andes, and the families of those who died. From an international perspective, another period of quiet followed, until the release of Nando Parrado's memoir in 2006. Nando's account of his time on the mountain and his long trek through the Andes to safety is interspersed with memories and thoughts of his friends, including his mother and sister, who died on the mountain. It is an acknowledgment of the debt owed to those who died, and the inspiration he drew from them. But an article in the Mexican magazine *Gatopardo*, appearing in response to Parrado's book, was the first attempt to methodically interview the bereaved parents and siblings, and publish their thoughts on the tragedy.

The following years saw the survivors' profiles raised to new heights, with a proliferation of books, films, documentaries, and interviews. Many of the survivors became much in demand on the international conference circuit, providing lessons for how to overcome impossible odds by working together towards a common goal. The perennial attention on the survivors remained a burden for the whole community, and it wasn't until 2018 that a book appeared telling the story from the perspective of the bereaved families: *Del otro lado de la montaña* (2018), by the sister and niece of Marcelo Pérez del Castillo.

---

[1] Opening lines of *Tabaré* by Juan Zorrilla de San Martin, translation by Walter Owen.

The chapters which follow, born out of interviews and conversations with families and friends, are an attempt to further redress the imbalance, to record for history the stories of those who didn't return, and the impact on their families. In order for these to be self-contained, some descriptions from the general text are repeated here, often several times across the individual accounts. Conversely, some stories of general interest – such as the burial on the mountain, and the canoe accident – have been incorporated into the individual chapters.

In a few cases, the family has preferred to remain silent, or it has not been possible to establish a contact:

Daniel Shaw (21-Oct-1947 — 13-Oct-1972)
Numa Turcatti (28-Oct-1947 — 11-Dec-1972)
Graziela Augusto de Mariani (30-Dec-1928 — 14-Oct-1972)
Dante Lagurara (02-Feb-1931 — 13-Oct-1972)
Ramón Martínez (04-Dec-1942 — 13-Oct-1972)
Ovidio Ramírez (26-Jun-1946 — 13-Oct-1972)

In the months following the return of the survivors, the mothers of those who died would get together to share their grief. Out of these meetings grew a desire to do something positive in memory of their sons, and the idea of a library, dedicated to the literacy, education, and cultural development of kids from the poor neighbourhoods adjoining Carrasco, began to take shape, becoming a reality in August 1973. The *Biblioteca Nuestros Hijos* ("Our Sons' library") continues to this day, its mission as relevant now as fifty years ago.

The people you love die only on the day you forget them.
Javier Methol

Biblioteca Nuestros Hijos

The story of the Biblioteca was born from the grief of the mothers who lost their sons on the mountain. With no outlet for her pain at home, Selva Maquirriain, with the help of her friend Raquel Nogueira, started contacting the other mothers one-by-one, suggesting that they meet up to share the burden of their loss. Those first meetings acted as a powerful therapy, an opportunity to cry on each others' shoulders without restraint. It was the beginning of the healing process, but the mothers soon realized that it would not be enough; that to avoid drowning in their sorrows, it would be important to do something positive in memory of their sons.

One of the mothers, Agnes Valeta – a teacher – had seen a great need in the public school system, where poorer students did not have access to textbooks. She suggested that they could raise money to fulfil this need. Putting their heads together, the mothers evolved this idea, until the concept of a library emerged. Its income would come from subscriptions, with members – primarily drawn from the relatively well-off neighbourhood of Carrasco – able to borrow recreational books donated by the community. Schoolbooks would then be bought using the subscription money, and lent freely to schoolchildren in need, with the proviso that they be returned in good condition for the following year's crop of students.

The next question was where to house the library. Two of the mothers, Stella Pérez de Castillo and Raquel Nicolich, whose grandfather had been the founder of Carrasco, were long-time friends, with important connections throughout the community. One of their contacts, the mayor, used his authority to arrange for the use of a room in the iconic *Hotel Carrasco*. Despite some scepticism about the viability of the project, the mothers pressed ahead, some driving around the neighbourhood in a small truck with a loudspeaker, asking for people to donate books; others tasked with collecting subscriptions.

Alejandro Nicolich, brother of Coco, remembers helping his mother from the earliest days:

> *I knew the history of the Biblioteca because of all the books I'd transport. I took thousands of books from my house. My mother would tell me, 'You have to go to the centre to speak with so-and-so – he's going to give you 100 books to take to the hotel'. When I'd arrive at the hotel, all the mothers would be there, so I saw the growth of the library at first hand.*

Laura Methol, who had lost her own mother on the mountain, would often accompany her grandmother, whose job it was to collect subscriptions. She would relish those occasions when they had to stop by at the hotel; an opportunity to roam around the grand building, with its opulent salons, a great adventure for the eleven-year-old.

Fig. 101. *An early photograph of some of the founding mothers on Carrasco beach.*
Left to right: Helida Platero, Susana Magri, Agnes Valeta, Selva Maquirriain (seated),
Nené Martínez Lamas (seated), Raquel Nogueira, Stella de Pérez del Castillo, Raquel Nicolich.

Against all expectations, the library officially opened its doors on 1st August 1973, less than 9 months after the mothers had learned the fate of their sons. Its full name, chosen after much deliberation, was *Biblioteca Nuestros Hijos – Valor y Fe*[1], the last part drawing from the letters written by Arturo Nogueira and Coco Nicolich on the mountain in the days before they died.

With no experience of running such an organization, the mothers managed to solve the various problems as they arose, and together they oversaw its growth over the following decades, the responsibilities and roles changing over time as family circumstances

---

[1] 'Our Sons' Library – Courage and Faith.

allowed. But there was always someone to step up when needed. The official list of founders, all of whom played significant roles in the library, numbered thirteen:

Sara Vázquez de Echavarren	*Mother of Rafael*
María Susana Gelsi de Magri	*Mother of Guido*
Selva Ibarburu de Maquirriain	*Mother of Felipe*
Nené Caubarrère de Martínez Lamas	*Mother of Julio*
Gladys Rosso de Maspons	*Mother of Daniel*
Lita Petraglia de Navarro	*Mother of Liliana*
Raquel Arocena de Nicolich	*Mother of Coco*
Raquel Paullier de Nogueira	*Mother of Arturo*
Stella Ferreira de Pérez del Castillo	*Mother of Marcelo*
Hélida Riet de Platero	*Mother of Enrique*
Bimba Cornah de Storm	*Mother of Diego*
Agnes Vallendor de Valeta	*Mother of Carlos*
Ana Maria Nebel de Vázquez	*Mother of Fernando*

With books stored in every available space, including the bath and bidet, the library soon outgrew its original location. Raquel and Stella brought their influence to bear once more, securing a large room on the ground floor of the hotel. The extra space allowed the library to become a safe study area, where everyone was welcome, its mission clearly stated:

To keep alive the memory of those who did not return from the accident that occurred on 13th October 1972 in the Andes Mountains, their mothers founded this library. Every student, every reader, is received here in the name of our children.

These extraordinary mothers, with the help of a generous army of volunteers, continued to grow the reach and remit of the library over the following decades, staffing it in small groups, each pair of mothers assigned a particular day of the week. They were the focal point and the public face of the library; a draw for the many visitors. Their monthly meetings in one another's homes for coffee and cookies, and their shared work in the library, created a cohesion amongst them and a joy of life that had seemed impossible in the early days. They would get together socially and celebrate each other's family events.

One such occasion, the wedding of Felipe Maquirriain's sister Analia in July 1976, has an interesting anecdote attached to it, illustrating the reach of their project. The library had been contacted by a British couple, who wished to donate money on behalf of the wife's brother, who had died in that other great Uruguayan tragedy of 1972, the conflagration of the *Royston Grange*. The British cargo steamer had caught fire after a collision with an oil tanker in the River Plate, resulting in the loss of life of all 74 on board. As the library mother with the best command of English, Selva was asked to receive the couple, the meeting unavoidably arranged for noon on the day of her daughter's wedding. The benefactors turned out to be Robin Gibb of the *Bee Gees*, and his wife Molly Hullis, whose brother David had been a cabin boy aboard the ship. 1972 had been a bittersweet year for the couple, the death of Molly's brother followed by the birth of their first son, his middle name given in memory of his late uncle. By a strange coincidence, the Bee Gees single *Alive* (not to be confused with their later hit *Stayin' Alive*) had been released at the end of that year, when the boys were still lost on the mountain.

Fig. 102. *Some of the Biblioteca 'family' at the wedding of Analía Maquirriain in July 1976. Left to right: Mr and Mrs Valeta, Mrs and Mr Echavarren, Nené Martínez Lamas, Selva Maquirriain, Mr and Mrs Nicolich, Mr and Mrs Nogueira, and the groom and bride.*

Over time, the library served not only as a safe study space and a source of free textbooks, it also hosted free computer classes for children from nearby marginalised neighbourhoods, and began providing scholarships for disadvantaged children. But by the end of the millennium, it faced a threat to its existence. Because of the deterioration of the building, *Hotel Carrasco* was shut down (not to be reopened for another fifteen years), and the library lost its base of operations. Working out of temporary accommodation for three years, the library's future remained uncertain, until the city council offered it a permanent Carrasco home in the former studio of Uruguayan architect Juan Antonio Scasso.

Fig. 103. *The library's Information Technology classroom.*

Fig. 104. *Teresita Vázquez (sister of Fernando) in 2019 with her mural in the library's garden. The left-hand image of a male scribe at his desk (the original in the Bodleian library in Oxford) is complemented by a female scribe of Teresita's own design.*

In 2009, the founding mothers passed on the baton to the next generation, the sisters and sisters-in-law of those who died. Some had already been active in the library. Teresita Vázquez, sister of Fernando, the first of her generation to participate, had been working alongside the mothers when the library was still at the hotel. Stellita Pérez del Castillo soon followed, taking the leading role in guiding the transition from mothers to daughters. Her sister Claudia also joined the team, along with sisters and relatives of other victims – Rosario Maspons, Sandra Maquirriain, and Susana Danrée de Magri, amongst others. By 2016, Bimba Storm was the only one of the mothers still actively participating and attending meetings.

Fig. 105. *The founding mothers in 2012.*
Left to right: Bimba Storm, Raquel Nicolich, Sara Echavarren, Selva Maquirriain,
Hélida Platero, Gladys Maspons, Raquel Nogueira.

The library is now under the umbrella of the *Ad Astra Foundation* of *Stella Maris College*, an organization guided by the original mission of Christian Brothers' founder Edmund Rice, to teach disadvantaged youth. Sitting alongside the *Biblioteca Nuestros Hijos* in the *Ad Astra* network are the *Colegio Santa Margarita*, a state school under private management, for which the library provides books and scholarships, and *Los Tréboles*, an organization which uses sport as a unifying activity to guide and educate children.

A majority of the library's scholarships go to the children of *Colegio Sagrado Corazón* in the *barrio* of Paso Carrasco; a school with historic ties to the Carrasco community. Founded in 1964 in response to Vatican II, the school had been served by nuns from the school of the same name in Carrasco where many of the sisters of the Andes passengers had gone. Then, around the time of the accident, the nuns had moved out of Carrasco altogether, in order to dedicate themselves to the poorer community. Other scholarships are awarded through relationships with like-minded NGOs, such as *La Pascua*, a social organization in the *barrio* of La Cruz de Carrasco.

Fig. 106. *The 2016 fundraising tea in Hotel Carrasco (The Sofitel).*
Left to right: Cristina Cabral, Rosario Maspons (seated), Stellita Pérez del Castillo,
Sandra Maquirriain, Bimba Storm (seated), Teresita Vázquez, Susana Danrée de Magri.

The 120 scholarships, an ongoing supply of textbooks, the staffing of IT classes, and costs to transport students to and from the library, involve considerable outlay. Much of the income derives from the reading club subscriptions of several hundred members, and from the sponsorship of local companies, but there is constant need for donations. One such donor, who is much loved by the sisters of the library, is survivor Gustavo Zerbino. An enthusiastic member from the very beginning, he has continued to provide generous support, even donating proceeds of entire conferences to the library.

As the library approaches its fiftieth year, Raquel Nicolich is the only founding mother still alive, Selva Maquirriain having died in 2020. After Selva passed away, her daughter Analía started taking a prominent role in the library, calling up all the sisters to encourage them to continue their mothers' work, with Beatriz and Pilar Echavarren among the latest to take up the mantle. Together, they are expanding the work of the library with the same energy, commitment, and sisterhood that gave life and purpose to their mothers for almost four decades.

Fig. 107. *Raquel Nicolich, Selva Maquirriain, Bimba Storm, and Hélida Platero, the last surviving founding mothers of the* Biblioteca Nuestros Hijos *in 2015.*

Francisco 'Panchito' Abal
24-Jun-1951 — 14-Oct-1972

Don Francisco 'Pancho' Abal (father), a successful and well-connected businessman, was over fifty when he met María Luisa Guerault, a lady from Buenos Aires who would become his second wife. She was vacationing in Punta del Este, a beach resort popular with both Uruguayan and Argentinian holidaymakers escaping the heat of the city in the summer months. Nicknamed Malú from the initial letters of her names, she was more than twenty years his junior, but the couple fell in love, and tied the knot. Both had been married before, Don Pancho with one son Sergio, and Malú with two sons and two daughters – Alejandro and José Luis, and Silvia and María Luisa (Marilu). The new marriage yielded three more sons, with Francisco ('Panchito') born in June 1951, Fernando coming along a year later, and the youngest, Gonzalo, eight years after that.

Through hard work and a keen business mind, Don Pancho had prospered from the success of the family business, *Abal Hermanos*, at a time of unprecedented economic

Fig. 108. *The house in the botanical gardens.*

growth and opportunity in Uruguay. The post-war years in particular were a time of great prosperity, with the per-capita GDP on a par with most European countries, and a strong demand for Uruguayan exports. Under these favourable conditions, *Abal Hermanos*, established in 1877 by Don Pancho's father, had grown to become a major player in the tobacco and cigarette industry, supplying a third of the Uruguayan market. With his hard-earned wealth, Don Pancho had built a mansion inside the grounds of the botanical gardens in the beautiful Prado district of Montevideo. The house, a stone's throw from the official president's residence, was staffed with a cook, a gardener, a chauffeur, a couple of domestic helpers, and a trusted overseer called Atilio; so the childhood years of Panchito and Fernando were literally, and metaphorically, a walk in the park.

The two brothers shared a room in the mansion. Though close in age, the boys were opposites in temperament and appearance; Panchito calm, with blond good looks inherited from his mother, Fernando fiery and dark-haired, like his father. But they were inseparable, doing everything together, sharing friends and interests, and helping each other in any way they could. As children, the long hours playing with their electric train set would be interspersed with bouts of unrestrained wrestling; Silvia in the bedroom next door would hear crashing and banging against the wooden floor and the furniture, as they strove to get the better of each other.

Given the family business, it was perhaps inevitable that smoking was an integral feature of family life; part of the culture. Boxes of cigars and cigarettes and silver lighters were liberally strewn around the house. Everyone smoked, and even the children were inducted into the habit at an early age.

The summer months of December to February were spent in Punta del Este, where Panchito's parents had built a large house just across from *La Draga* beach – part of *Playa Brava* on the ocean side of the peninsular. The house, named Malú, and its garden, took up the whole block.

In July each year, taking advantage of the winter school break, the family would head over to Buenos Aires, to visit the maternal grandparents. They would take the night boat across the River Plate, either the *Ciudad de Montevideo* or the *Ciudad de Buenos Aires*,

Fig. 109. *Don Pancho and Malú relaxing in Punta del Este.*

leaving at 10:00 p.m. and arriving the next morning at 7:00 a.m. In another Uruguayan tragedy, the latter boat was hit by a North American freighter in August 1957, and sank with great loss of life; an event that shocked the whole country, and which must have been particularly disconcerting for those, who, like the Abal family, made regular use of the service at that time of year.

Earlier that year, when it was time for Panchito to go to primary school, it was decided that the benefits of the new bilingual school in Carrasco, *Stella Maris College*, outweighed the daily inconvenience of getting up in time to catch the early bus. So, in March 1957, Panchito entered the first year of *The Christian*, joining Pedro Algorta, Enrique Platero, and Arturo Nogueira in the class of '66. He was not the keenest of students, but he possessed a natural ability as a sportsman, and soon became one of the best rugby players in the school. By 1967, just a year after he had left, he was already in the *Old Christians* A team, playing their first season in the top division of Uruguayan rugby. He was renowned for his effortless speed and fluency playing on the wing. His teammates in that 1966 team included Daniel Shaw, Gastón Costemalle, Guido Magri, Marcelo Pérez del Castillo, and Nando Parrado. Of these, only Nando would survive the 1972 disaster.

It was around this time that Panchito's life took an abrupt turn for the worse, when his parents had a sudden and acrimonious separation. Panchito and Fernando took their father's side, and the three of them moved out of the house immediately, taking up residence in a two-bedroom apartment in Pocitos, a *pieds-à-terre* of one of Don Pancho's close friends, who spent most of the year at his *estancia* in the interior of the country. What began as a stopgap loan of the apartment became a prolonged tenancy as the bitter divorce proceedings, which precluded Don Pancho from buying a new apartment, stretched on with no end in sight. The complexities of the settlement would provide a team of lawyers with their livelihood for the next six years, and Don Pancho and his sons would still be living in the Pocitos apartment when Panchito set off on the 1972 trip.

The two brothers shared the apartment's small second bedroom. At the weekends, they would pick up Gonzalo in Prado, and he would stay over, sharing the main bedroom with his father. With the departure of his brothers and father, the family home had become a lonely place for 7-year-old Gonzalo, with only his mother and one domestic helper remaining, later to be joined by his grandmother. So the weekend trips to Pocitos were a welcome opportunity for him to get some attention from his older brothers, who would stage mini soccer games on the wide balcony overlooking the busy Avenida Brasil, much to the horror of the maid. Or, if it was raining, the boys would play cards. Either way, their high-spirited camaraderie would provide some compensation for the dullness of Gonzalo's weekdays.

The Prado mansion would see one more drama before it was finally sold. The Tupamaro urban guerrillas were becoming increasingly active by the turn of the decade, and the privilege exemplified by the Abal family made them a ready target. Early one afternoon, a small group of Tupamaros paid a visit to the house, tying up the grandmother and the maid before waking Malú from her siesta. They talked with her politely for a while but chose not to tie her up. One of the group, a well-spoken young woman armed with a small handgun, entered Gonzalo's room and told him to keep playing with his toys while she searched around. Before leaving, they tarred the walls and curtains with the Tupamaro emblem, and pocketed the key to one of the side doors. That same night they returned, and stole several items including the silver cutlery and most of Don Pancho's high-value paintings, one of which Silvia spotted many years later, for sale in a Buenos Aires art gallery.

Don Pancho made a brief appearance the next morning as the police were doing their crime scene investigation. It was the first time he had set foot in the house since the parting of ways with his wife, and he would never again return. He didn't see or speak to Malú, who was sedated, but he did remain at the house for a while, sitting in the large winter living room, staring blankly at the stained walls and curtains. Later, he arranged for a 24-hour police guard, which remained in place for the next six months.

Panchito and Fernando were deeply affected by the divorce. They had seen their idyllic and privileged childhood, and their family, precipitously demolished, and were left in the middle of a storm, the only personal channel of communication between their parents, who never spoke to each other again. Panchito lost his trust in people, and sought solace in the company of his closest friend, his rugby teammate Nando Parrado, in whom he felt able to confide. Rugby, parties, girlfriends, movies, motorbikes, and cars kept them busy, and helped to numb his pain. Panchito was very popular with the girls – sensitive, athletic, handsome, and stylishly dressed. He had been fashion-conscious from an early age, and would take advantage of the annual trips to Buenos Aires, to keep up with the latest trends. The fact that he had money and a sporty car – a Mini Cooper – only added to his playboy image.

He continued playing rugby, but mainly for enjoyment. And even though he was less than assiduous in his practice regime, his natural ability won him a place in the national squad, *Los Teros*. Such was his presence on the rugby field, that Fernando, fed up of sitting on the bench and being outrivalled by his brother, left the *Old Christians* to play for a rival club, *La Cachila*.

After *Stella Maris*, Panchito completed most of the preparatory work for entering university, where he planned to major in Economics, but, towards the end, he lost interest in academic work, and dropped out of school. Don Pancho had inherited his work ethic from his own father, who had immigrated to Uruguay from Galicia as a boy with just a letter of recommendation in his pocket. On hearing that Panchito had given up his studies, Don Pancho instructed him to turn up at *Abal Hermanos* headquarters the next Monday morning at 7:00 a.m. sharp – no lateness tolerated.

Fig. 110. *Los Teros, Panchito seated first from right.*

Panchito arrived on time in his best suit, expecting, as the owner's son, to be given a comfortable office job. Instead, he was sent directly to the factory floor, given a pair of blue overalls, and put to work cleaning one of the large machines – a job that took him all day. His father's attitude was, "If you can't finish secondary school, let's hope you are as good with the broom as you are with the rugby ball." Panchito turned out to be more than proficient with the broom, and after six months he was offered an entry-level white-collar position. But by this time, he felt more at home on the shop floor, familiar with every nut and bolt of every machine, and able to operate and maintain them with ease. The prospect of an office job no longer appealed to him, and he turned it down.

Working at the factory had a steadying effect on his lifestyle. The work day, combined with three hours rugby practice in the evenings, meant there was little time for other distractions. Panchito settled down from his playboy days, and by 1970 he started going steady with 'a nice girl from a suitable family', Raquelita. Panchito was constantly mindful of his youngest brother Gonzalo, whose family had disintegrated overnight, and who continued to suffer the loneliness of living in an almost empty mansion with its creaking floors and staircase. Realizing that he was in desperate need of family attention, Panchito and Raquelita 'adopted' the 11-year-old, allowing him to tag along on various outings – surfing or camping, or going to the amusement park. By 1972, the couple were making plans to get married, and Panchito signalled his commitment to the family business with plans for a trip abroad to gain further industry experience.

Abal Hermanos had its headquarters at 1780 Paraguay Street, across from the central railway station of Montevideo. *La Casa del Tornillo*, the first and foremost of the three hardware stores owned and run by Nando's parents, was three blocks away at 1610 Paraguay Street, a site strategically selected by Nando's grandfather to capture the footfall of the ranchers arriving at the station from the countryside. Nando had also started working in the family business, and so he and Panchito were within easy walking distance of each other and would get together every workday for lunch.

Fig. 111. *Plaque on Abal Hermanos headquarters. The company was sold to Philip Morris in 1997.*

Both Nando and Panchito had gone on the previous year's trip to Chile and were eager to go again. On the Monday before the trip, Panchito persuaded his cousin Javier Methol, fifteen years his senior, to go along with his wife Liliana. Javier was the son of Don Pancho's sister, and worked alongside Panchito at the family business. Panchito also asked his brother Fernando, but he had other plans, wanting to spend time with his girlfriend. A week was too long to be away from her, and, under pressure to go from both Panchito and Don Pancho, Fernando asked his sister Marilu to invite him to her home in the countryside, so that he would have a ready excuse to get out of the trip gracefully.

On the morning of the trip, Panchito was picked up early, sharing a ride to the airport with Moncho Sabella and Alexis Hounie, with Moncho's brother Mono driving. In Panchito's luggage were dozens of cartons of cigarettes. Someone had mentioned that the cigarettes in Santiago were not so good, so everyone was bringing Uruguayan varieties as gifts, but Panchito and his cousin Javier had free access to them from the factory. These cigarettes would be much coveted on the mountain.

Arriving at the airport, Panchito met up with Nando, and they sat together on the plane, close to Nando's mother, Eugenia, and sister, Susana. When the Fairchild unexpectedly stopped in Mendoza, the Parrados and Panchito checked in at the *Hotel Sussex*, half a block away from the large central square, *Plaza Independencia*, and a couple of blocks from the one of the main shopping streets, Avenida San Martín. Panchito and Nando shared a room and, in the afternoon, went to watch some stock car races they'd seen advertised in a local newspaper. Later that evening, they met up with Marcelo, Julio Martínez Lamas, and Álvaro Mangino to see *What's Up, Doc?* at a local cinema.

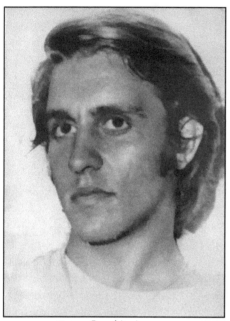

Fig. 112. *Panchito in 1972.*

The next morning, Panchito and the Parrados did some shopping, stopping at the *Farmacia del Águila* on Avenida San Martín to get some toiletries before taking a taxi to the airport, arriving around noon. The pilots didn't show up until an hour later, and there was another long delay before the Fairchild finally took off for Santiago. As on the previous day, Panchito and Nando sat together on the left-hand side of the plane, with Eugenia and Susana a couple of rows further forward, across the aisle. The time passed quickly for the two boys. They were discussing a new business idea, selling fibre-based cleaning cloths in the interior of the country. They were so engrossed in their conversation that Nando failed to fasten his seatbelt when the steward warned of turbulence ahead.

When the impact occurred and the base of the fuselage hit the slope, the seats broke loose from their bearings, and when the fuselage came to an abrupt halt at the end of its slide, Panchito's seat became airborne, propelled forward over the other seats, with Panchito still strapped in, and Nando alongside him. Both boys sustained serious head injuries as they hit the bulkhead, Panchito coming off the worse, and Nando perhaps saved by having his seatbelt unfastened.

In the devastation and chaos, there was little that could be done before the rapid onset of nightfall. The 'doctors' triaged the injured whilst others struggled to clear the tangled mass of seats. By the time darkness came, only a small space had been cleared for the thirty-five passengers to squeeze into for the night. Some of the seriously injured were still trapped in or under seats, but Panchito and Nando had ended up on top of the pile of seats and twisted metal. The two were moved to the back of the plane, along with Susana, who was also badly injured. Although they were lying on the floor of the fuselage, the side wall at the back right-hand side of the plane had been stripped off in the accident, and they were exposed to the elements, and in contact with the snow.

A small group of uninjured passengers – Marcelo, Roy Harley, Diego Storm, and Bobby François – were also braving the back of the plane, and stood across from the injured, with a little bit of protection provided by a makeshift wall of suitcases built by Roy. During the night, Diego sensed that Nando was perhaps not as badly injured as they first thought, and might survive. The boys brought him over to lie between them for warmth. Susana was heard crying out in the night about how cold she was, and when morning finally arrived, Panchito was found lying over her. He had died sometime in the early morning hours, but Susana was still breathing, and several of the boys credited him with saving her life. He may have been just seeking the solace and warmth of human contact, but Nando recalled in his memoir many years later how fiercely protective Panchito had always been of Susana. So perhaps, despite the cold and the confusion of his injury, he found the clarity or instinct in his last hours to try to save his best friend's sister.

Back in Montevideo on the evening of 13th October, reports of the accident were starting to come through. Silvia went to her mother's house, to be with her and Gonzalo, and Marilu went to Pocitos to be with Don Pancho and Fernando. Calls were made to Chile, to the house of the Uruguayan chargé-d'affaires, César Charlone, whose son, also named César, had been an *Old Christians* teammate of Panchito. Eventually, it became clear that the plane had disappeared. In the early hours of the morning, at about the time that Panchito was dying on the mountain, Malú suddenly woke up. She cried out that Panchito was dead, that she had seen it and knew for certain. She needed a heavy dose of tranquilizers to get back to sleep.

Despite the certainty of the vision, Malú's mind told her not to lose hope, that a miracle might occur, and the boys might appear. She kept in touch with the news about the search and rescue attempts, and with other families – the parents of Roberto Canessa, Coco Nicolich, and Arturo Nogueira; and Nando's father. Don Pancho, on the other hand, held out no hope from the beginning.

When reports of survivors hit the news just before Christmas, Malú and Fernando immediately took advantage of the plane provided by the Uruguayan Air Force to take families of the passengers to Chile. Don Pancho couldn't face the trip, and remained in Montevideo, joined at his apartment by Silvia and Gonzalo, and by a close friend of the family – eminent neurosurgeon Doctor Miguel Estable. He was convinced that his son would not be on the list of survivors. He just cried continuously, shaking his head, rejecting any possibility, despite the exhortations of those around him to retain some hope.

The final confirmation of Panchito's death had a devasting effect on the 75-year-old. The divorce and his heavy smoking had already taken a high toll on his health, and he had his first heart attack a few days after the list of survivors became known. He stopped working, and never returned to the factory. He kept a photo of Panchito on his nightstand, but he could find no consolation. Unable to fall asleep at night, he tried to keep the stress and distress at bay by reading cheap cowboy novels, and occasionally he managed to catch a few hours of sleep between dawn and noon. But in the end, the grief became too much for him to bear, and, in November 1973, less than a year after the survivors' return, he suffered a second, this time fatal, heart attack, dying in his sleep.

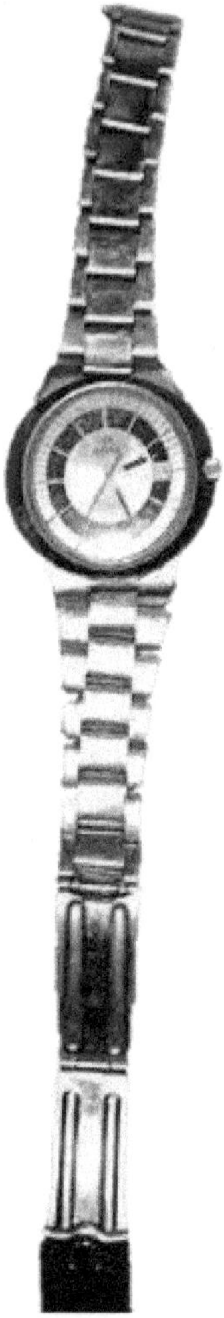

When Nando returned to Uruguay, he tried to see Panchito's father, but neither Don Pancho nor Fernando wanted to see him, despite the best efforts of Javier to bring them together. Nando did go to visit Malú, bringing her Panchito's chain, and his *Omega* watch, which Nando had worn on his trek through the Andes, even though it no longer worked. Gonzalo has that watch today – it is still stopped at 2:25 a.m., 14th October, the mechanism broken by the frigidity of that first night on the mountain, perhaps also marking the time when Panchito succumbed to his injuries and the cold.

The loss of Panchito, and the promise of a life cut short, left huge gaps in the lives of his family, and it was a long time before the wounds started to heal. Fernando and Gonzalo distanced themselves emotionally from the pain and horror of the tragedy, and have been reluctant to talk about it, even between themselves, with the rest of the family following their lead. The two brothers have had little contact with the survivors over the years, cynical about how some have made a business out of the tragedy, and how this one event has defined their lives.

Fig. 113. *Panchito's watch stopped at 2:25 a.m. on 14th October 1972.*

GASTÓN COSTEMALLE
11-DEC-1948 — 13-OCT-1972

Gastón Costemalle came from a family of lawyers. His father Julio César was an attorney for Uruguayan Customs, his mother, Blanca Jardi, a criminal prosecutor. Blanca's two sisters were also lawyers; one a top professor of procedural law, the other a legal counsel for the UN.

The Costemalle side of the family were of French-Basque lineage, originating in the southwest province of Béarn in the Pyrenees. Gastón's grandparents, who were second generation, had settled in the Trouville neighbourhood of Montevideo, in an apartment overlooking a pleasant balustraded square – Plaza Gomensoro – a stone's throw from Pocitos beach, and with an unobstructed view of the River Plate. The grandfather, Abel, an accountant and always impeccably dressed, the grandmother, Carmen, cultured and conversant with a wide range of topics. On summer evenings, she would sit on the balcony of their apartment tanning her legs, waiting to spot her husband returning from his office in the *Ciudad Vieja*, recognizable by his elegant straw boater as he got off the bus.

Fig. 114. *Costemalle y Cia. Corner of Zabala and 25 de Mayo in Montevideo's Old Town.*

Abel and his brother Raúl owned a construction company, *Costemalle y Cia*, with Raúl as the chief engineer, and Abel taking care of the finances. Amongst other projects, the company was involved in building Route 1, the main highway going west from Montevideo to Colonia; and in doing the excavations for the *Estadio Centenario* that was built to host the first football World Cup in 1930.

The grandchildren – Gastón, his brother Daniel, and their cousin Carlos, who was a few years older than Gastón – would often get together to play at the Plaza Gomensoro apartment. They all lived nearby in Pocitos, but they kept their bikes at their grandparents' place, where they enjoyed certain liberties, such as Coca-Cola in the fridge, which were frowned upon at home. Of the three of them, Carlos would be the only one to carry on the family name in Uruguay.

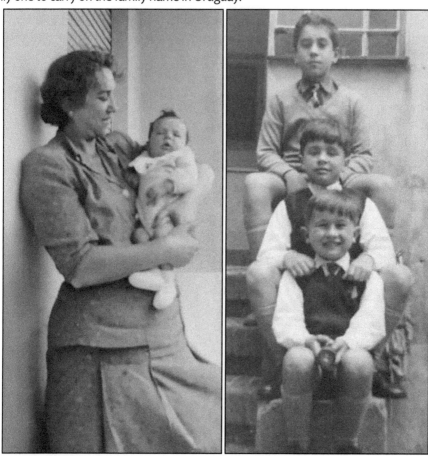

Fig. 115. *Left*: *Gastón and grandmother Carmen.*   ***Right***: *Carlos, Gastón, and Daniel.*

Gastón started primary school at the *Windsor School* (now the *Ivy Thomas Memorial School*), just around the corner from Plaza Gomensoro. There he met Coche Inciarte, who became his best friend; a friendship that would remain constant throughout his short life. But in 1957, Gastón transferred to *Stella Maris College*, where he became a classmate of Fito Strauch and Daniel Shaw in the class of '64. Gastón was a stand-out student, eventually becoming head of house and senior prefect. He also developed into an excellent rugby player, called up to play in the short-staffed *Old Christians* first team whilst still at *The Christian*. But a tragedy was to cast a shadow on his final year at the school. The unexpected and unresolved death of his father Julio César, occurring shortly after Abel and Carmen's

268

50th wedding anniversary, would be the first of three tragedies that would devastate the Costemalle family.

There had been rumours of an imminent contraband shipment from Paraguay to Uruguay, and Julio César, in his capacity as attorney for the Uruguayan Customs department, had travelled to Asunción to investigate. Attending an official dinner at the end of his trip, he died of a heart attack – at least, that was the story the authorities gave to his wife Blanca. It seemed suspicious. Julio César was an active sportsman, and a water polo champion, representing the Biguá club of Pocitos. Carlos has early memories of playing on the beach at Punta del Este, whilst his uncle did his daily 5 km swim to Gorriti island and back. Julio César also made the Uruguayan national swimming team, representing his country at the 1936 Berlin Olympics and the 1948 London Olympics. On hearing the news of her husband's death, Blanca travelled immediately to Paraguay, but on arrival she was not allowed to see his body, which had been placed in a sealed and locked coffin. There were suspicions and rumours that his death had been a consequence of his investigation into the shipment.

After *Stella Maris*, Gastón did the last two years of secondary school at the *Seminario*, studying law. Here he became classmates and friends with Pancho Delgado and Numa Turcatti. In 1965, he entered the Faculty of Law at the *Universidad de la República*. A disciplined and intelligent student, his interests went far beyond his studies. In 1967, he started side work as a journalist, visiting Bolivia and Chile in 1970 to write articles on current political affairs, and acting as the Uruguayan correspondent of the UK *Daily Express*. At the time of his death, he was also editor of the political weekly *Opinión Nacionalista* (the organ of the Wilsonista sector of the *Blancos*) and he was a leading activist in the MUN (*Movimiento Universitario Nacionalista*), the student movement associated with the sector. A week after the plane disappeared, when the MUN published a eulogy of its active members who had been lost in the Andes, Gastón was at the top of the list.

He was also an avid sportsman. He played tennis and football, and was a good swimmer like his father, but his great passion was rugby. A leader on and off the field, Gastón, along with Guido Magri and Marcelo Pérez del Castillo, played a key role in helping to establish the *Old Christians* as a successful club. He played on the first team for six years, some of them as captain. In 1967, he was selected to play for his country, and became the first *Old Christian* to represent Uruguay, playing as Prop against Chile in the Fifth South American Rugby championship. He would go on to make four international starts.

In 1969, a second tragedy struck the Costemalle family. On 27th May, a late autumn day in Montevideo, Gastón's younger brother Daniel – nicknamed Teco – had been studying at home in Pocitos when he got a call from his friend Eduardo Gelsi, inviting him to go canoeing. The outing had been planned the night before by José Luis Lombardero, who owned the canoe, and Jorge Camilloni as they sat chatting in García's, a popular bar in Carrasco. Lombardero invited Eduardo, who in turn had called Teco. The four were all friends and former classmates from *Stella Maris*, who had graduated together in 1966.

Fig. 116. *José Luis Lombardero, Eduardo Gelsi, Teco Costemalle at a class dinner in Oct. 1965.*

The invitation was a welcome diversion for Teco, and he headed to Carrasco with his study mate Jaime Comas, with whom he had been preparing for an upcoming Law exam. The boys gathered at Lombardero's home on Puyol street at around noon. The addition of Comas to the party meant that they already had a full quota for the canoe, and José Luis didn't bother calling Jorge, who was still asleep after a late night. The house was a popular meeting place, serving as a clubhouse for the Puyol Street 'gang', a group of friends – which included future Andes victims Arturo Nogueira and Enrique Platero – who all lived within a block or two of each other on this street which would have so many associations with the 1972 tragedy.

The boys set out, with scant attention to safety, without life jackets or proper bailing equipment, in a canoe that was better suited to just two people. After making steady progress, conditions started to get rough, and the canoe began taking on water faster than they could bail it out. Eventually, all four ended up in the water, with the canoe capsized and partially submerged. Hampered by the fierce wind that had suddenly picked up, the boys were unable to right it, and decided that their best option was to swim for the shore. They split into two groups, Lombardero – a swimming champion – pairing with Gelsi, who was a weaker swimmer, and Teco pairing with his study mate.

In the frigid waters, the boys experienced severe cramping and hypothermia, and of the four of them, only Jaime Comas made it ashore. According to Jaime's testimony, Teco had been struggling in the water behind him and at one point had cried out, but that had been the last time Comas had seen or heard him. Reaching the shoreline, Comas dragged himself up the beach to the *Rambla*, where he waved down a passing bus. It took him a couple of blocks to the nearby Naval Academy, where he raised the alarm. A sea-air search and rescue operation got underway immediately, and, as word spread, friends, families, and many others in the close-knit community gathered and searched along the beaches, continuing through the night and into the next day. Jorge Camilloni, who had been so close to being the fourth canoeist, rushed down to the beach on his motorbike as soon as he heard the news, although he had no idea that his friends were involved, or even that they had set out in the canoe that day. The initial reports erroneously referred to an accident involving fishermen in front of 'the former *Hotel Miramar*'. Jorge arrived at the beach to find his friend Enrique Platero already there. Enrique broke the tragic news to him.

Blanca, on hearing the news, rushed to a friend's house overlooking the beach, and stayed there for three days, remaining on her feet, staring out of the window and scanning the estuary in the desperate hope that her son might appear. Teco, like his father, had been an experienced swimmer with a life-guard diploma, and it was a surprise that he had not made it to land. A few days later, when his body washed ashore a few kilometres downstream on Solymar beach, it was Gastón, having hurriedly returned from a six-month trip to Europe with Eduardo Strauch, who went to identify him. A medical examination determined that Teco had not drowned, but had died of a heart attack brought on by his exertions in the frigid waters, possibly exacerbated by the after-effects of an anaesthetic he'd received the day before, for a wisdom tooth

---

[1] The *Hotel Miramar* was active from the mid-thirties to 1950 when it became a nursing school. In 1968, a year before the canoe accident, it became the home of Naval Academy.

extraction. The cry that Comas heard behind him as he swam towards the shore perhaps marked the onset of his friend's heart attack, but another explanation was suggested by a conversation, years later, between Diego Costemalle – son of Teco's cousin Carlos – and Leopoldo Fernández, the naval officer on duty that day and the first to the scene. The latter told Diego that one of the boys had gone back to help the others, so it is possible that the cry was Teco shouting out this intention. More likely, perhaps, the officer was referring to José Luis Lombardero, who, by himself, would most probably have made it to safety, but who refused to leave the side of his close friend Eduardo, the two of them dying together.

Gastón was devastated by his brother's death. But life had to continue. Gregarious and confident, he had many friends, but his inner circle came through his girlfriend Inés

Fig. 117. *Gastón and best friend Coche Inciarte.*

Clerc, whom he planned to marry in 1973. She was friends with Coche Inciarte's girlfriend Soledad González and Pancho Delgado's girlfriend Susana Sartori. The six of them would get together to socialize, or to go dancing in Pocitos. Gastón was a great joker with a mischievous sense of humour, and Soledad was his co-instigator. When she and Gastón decided to throw a fancy-dress party one year, they wrote out invitations, stipulating the costumes to be worn, and signing with fake names. Such was their reputation that everyone immediately guessed who the perpetrators were.

Gastón had gone on the 1971 trip to Chile, and although his rugby endeavours had tailed off since then, he was keen to return. His mother gave him the money for the trip. At a party thrown by Susana Sartori on the Saturday before departure, Gastón persuaded Pancho and Coche to travel, and Pancho, who was not an *Old Christian*, extended the invitation to his friend and Law Faculty colleague Numa Turcatti.

Gastón had largely lost touch with his cousin Carlos during the few years preceding the Andes flight, because the latter had married and left Montevideo to manage his wife's family farm in Rocha on her father's death. But in September 1972, the two cousins got together again with their grandparents, to celebrate a birthday. Carlos and his wife had just had their fourth child, and Carlos' parting and final words to Gastón as they hugged goodbye was, "The factory is closed, we've already got four kids, it's your turn now."

On the morning of the flight, Soledad picked up Pancho and Gastón, before stopping in Punta Gorda to collect Coche on the way to the airport. The image that Soledad had of Coche turning to wave and smile at her just before boarding the plane was a memory that would sustain her over the following weeks, and one that remains vivid to this day.

During the unanticipated stopover of the flight in Mendoza, Gastón and some of the older boys had lunch together, and arranged a hotel for the night – a guesthouse not yet officially opened, but owned by the proprietors of the restaurant at which they'd eaten. After a long siesta, Gastón, Pancho, and Eduardo Strauch wandered through the attractive tree-lined streets and squares of Mendoza and had dinner before heading back to the hotel. There, sleeping six to a room, Coche fondly remembers him jumping up and down on the beds until one of them gave way and split down the middle.

Fig. 118. *Gastón – always joking.*

The next day, the boys had breakfast and took a bus to the airport. Gastón sat down in the last row and as Coche boarded Gastón gestured to him to come and sit next to him. But Pancho Delgado, eager to sit in the back row due to a premonition that the plane would crash, sat there instead. Later, when the plane started to experience turbulence an hour into the flight, Gastón and Pancho had to vacate the back row, and it was Gastón, who, seeing the passenger-address microphone at the back of the plane, jokingly announced: "Attention everyone! Please put on your parachutes, the plane has developed a fault and we're going to have to jump."

Fifteen minutes later, the Fairchild hit the mountain, and the wings, and the tail section containing the galley, the lavatory and the rear luggage area separated from the main fuselage. Several of the seats at the back, including Gastón's, were pulled from their bearings by the decompression, and flew out of the gaping hole. In an expedition to the site of impact a few days later, Numa, Gustavo Zerbino, and Daniel Maspons found Gastón alongside Alexis Hounie, still strapped into their seats.

Inés Clerc and her brother-in-law Guillermo 'Sapo' Risso, a good friend of Gastón, travelled to Chile on 15th October with a group of friends and relatives of the passengers. A few days later, as hopes of finding the boys faded, they headed back. But Sapo returned to Chile on 31st October with Dr Jorge Zerbino, Gustavo's father, and Dr Luis Surraco, the father of Roberto Canessa's *novia*. After landing in Santiago, they drove to Talca to meet up with Carlos Páez Vilaró, who was leading the parents' efforts to find their sons after the official search was called off. Talca was the area erroneously suggested by seer Gerard Croiset as the location of the accident, and in the following days, they searched it thoroughly by helicopter, later making expeditions by foot into the mountains. They were supported and accompanied by a large contingent of volunteers, but after several days of fruitless searching, they decided to abandon their efforts in that area, and Sapo returned to Montevideo with Surraco and Zerbino.

Meanwhile, Inés and Soledad would go almost every day to Blanca's house. Even though she had lost her other son three years earlier in the canoe accident, it was she who would act as a calming influence over the girls, convinced that her son was still alive. The two girls were together when the reports came of two survivors, but when it transpired that they were Roberto Canessa and Nando Parrado, Inés immediately looked at Soledad and said, "Gastón is dead." "Why do you say that?" "Because if he were alive, he would have walked."

In Carrasco, *Old Christians* board member Connie Hughes had organized a barbecue at his parents' house for some MUN members to celebrate the end of the year; he had just given a speech about Gastón, remembering him and his contributions to the group, when they heard the astonishing news on the radio. On the farm in Rocha, Carlos was harvesting tomatoes when his wife came running and shouting: *"¡Aparecieron dos sobrevivientes!"* – "Two survivors have appeared!"

Later came the news that sixteen had survived, and the list was read out on *Radio Carve*. Gastón's name was missing. Blanca had lost her husband and her two sons within the space of ten years. In each of the three tragedies, she had been unable to see the body, but somehow she retained her spirit, integrity, and generosity. Gracious and well-presented, she was always ready with a smile. Coche and Pancho would often visit her after they got back; and when Coche got married in 1973, the first of the survivors to do so, Blanca offered him and Soledad her apartment in Punta del Este for their honeymoon, her sisters preparing it with flowers and balloons. Years later, when Disney offered the families money for the film *Alive*, Blanca would have nothing to do with it – there was no price that would compensate for the loss of her son.

Rafael 'El Vasco' Echavarren Vázquez
20-Aug-1950 – 18-Nov-1972

5:00 p.m. on 11th April 1973: A father looks on intently as his son's body is carefully lowered from the left rear door of a Uruguayan Air Force C-47 transport plane. Dozens more people are gathered nearby on the tarmac at Carrasco airport – family, friends, the boy's fiancée, the relatives of the victims of flight 571, and several survivors with their families. The body is transferred to a hearse, and, soon after, a funeral motorcade wends its way the fifteen kilometres to *Buceo Cemetery*. Some words of remembrance at the cemetery chapel, and then the burial in the family *pantheon*, the first of the family to be laid to rest there.

This scene marks the end of an extraordinary and protracted episode in the history of Flight 571. The boy was Rafael Echavarren, and he was the only fatality of the Andes tragedy to return from the mountain. It was an episode driven by Basque spirit and determination on the part of both Rafael and his father. On the mountain, Rafael – nicknamed 'El Vasco' (the Basque) – would daily declare his optimistic intention to return to Uruguay, despite the agony of a crippling injury which claimed his life after five weeks. His father, Ricardo, learning of his son's wishes, spent more than three months working tirelessly to fulfil them, grappling with authorities across three countries, making expeditions into the mountains, and even suffering arrest and detainment.

Rafael spent the first six years of his life on the family ranch, *Los Tapiales*, in Durazno, 250 km north of Montevideo. It was here that he gained a love of all things rural, riding from an early age, and helping out with small tasks given to him by his grandfather and father, his cheerful disposition and uncomplaining outlook evident from an early age. The family also had an apartment in the neighbourhood of Pocitos in Montevideo, and that's where he was based during his school years, educated by the Jesuits at the *Seminario* until the end of high school. Gregarious, with a sense of humour and camaraderie, Rafael was an incessant mimic, and it was the teachers at the school who were most frequent target of his impersonations.

On leaving high school, he studied Veterinary Science before specializing in dairy production at *Escuela Superior de Lechería* in Nueva Helvecia – a town 120 km north-west of Montevideo which had been settled by Swiss immigrants in the nineteenth century. The legacy of their cheese-making skills and traditions remained strong within the community, and it was cheese production that enthused Rafael. He started a small *tambo* – a dairy production facility – on the family *estancia*, in partnership with a friend, Walter Aguerre, who had graduated from the *Escuela de*

Lechería the previous year. His commitment was such that he requested money rather than gifts on his 21st birthday, so that he could add it to the fund his grandparents had given him to start the enterprise.

Fig. 119. *Estancia Los Tapiales.*

By the time of the trip to Chile, the *tambo* was already producing and selling cheese, and Rafael and Walter had plans to expand and diversify it. Rafael was planning to get married soon to his girlfriend Ana, whom he had known from an early age, and the *tambo* would be their livelihood. Away from his studies, he would spend time with Ana, visit his parents and grandparents, or head up to the *estancia*. Hard-working, generous, and fair, he was a popular person there, much loved by the staff and labourers.

He had a close relationship with his mother Sara ("Sarita"), with whom he would have long conversations, sipping *maté*, chatting about his progress at the *Escuela de Lechería*, or the Spanish furniture he and Ana had arranged to have made in preparation for their life together. With his mischievous good humour, he would charm all the women of the family, and conversations were usually punctuated by uncontrollable laughter. For his three sisters – Sara ('Sarucha'), Beatriz, and Pilar – he could do no wrong. They were all younger than him, but it was Sarucha who would be the one left in charge when the parents went away, discharging her responsibility conscientiously, whilst Rafael, who didn't take life too seriously, would spend the time joking around.

Pilar has fond memories of the time spent with her cheerful and affectionate brother, usually in the company of Ana:

> He always invited me to ride in his Land Rover, and on the way to pick up Ana, it was compulsory to stop at "Los Dominguez" to buy an almond chocolate bar as a gift for her. How I loved those adventures with them... for me, indelible memories of childhood.

The three would spend time at the beach, the park, or the *estancia*, where they would often be accompanied by some farm animal – a calf or sheep – in the back of the Land Rover.

Away from the *estancia*, Rafael played football for the Loyola club, and was a long-term member of *The Neptune* swimming club. He also dabbled in rugby. Along with his good friend Tito Regules, he was a member of *La Cachila*, a rugby club even younger than the *Old Christians*, whom they narrowly beat to win the first of five consecutive championships in 1971. Although not a strong player, nor a member of the first team, Rafael did enjoy playing, and the ethos of the game appealed to his sense of fair play. "I love it in my soul, because it's a sport without dissension", he once said to his mother.

Fig. 120. *The Seminario's Loyola football club. Rafael front row second from right.*

Rafael's presence on Flight 571 had little to do with rugby – it was, after all, an *Old Christians* trip. He found out about the trip shortly before the departure date, invited by his friend Tito Regules. Rafael was good company, and they needed to fill the plane.

When visiting the agricultural school in Sarandí Grande, he coincidentally bumped into Carlitos Páez, who also encouraged him to go. The idea of the trip appealed to Rafael, and he returned from the *estancia* to Montevideo on the day before departure in order to make the necessary arrangements. By evening, everything was in place, and he and Ana had a farewell dinner together with his whole family. It was one of his favourite meals – baked chicken with tomato salad, and, for dessert, a *dulce de leche* millefeuille with ice cream. He said goodbye to them that evening because he would be staying at his grandparents' house overnight. As he left, he lowered his head for his mother to make the sign of the cross over him and give him her blessing: "God bless you Rafo, have a good trip." Then she kissed him, and he left the house for the last time.

Arriving at the airport the next morning, driven by Ana, he discovered that his friend Tito was nowhere to be found. As the time of departure approached and all attempts

Fig. 121. *Rafael Echavarren Vázquez.*

to locate him failed, it became apparent that he would miss the flight. Fortunately, Rafael had other friends who were travelling to Chile: Carlitos, Bobby and the rest of 'the gang' – Coco Nicolich, Roy Harley, and Diego Storm – and Moncho, a former classmate from the *Seminario*. He sat with them during the flight, and during the unexpected stopover in Mendoza, the group stuck together, eating in the same restaurants, and staying at the same hotel, the *San Remo* on Avenida Godoy Cruz, where Rafael shared a room with Alexis Hounie. After a siesta to sleep off the wine from lunch, Rafael, Bobby, Alexis, and Moncho took a taxi to the top of the *Cerro de la Gloria*; the hill that overlooks the city. Afterwards the four met up with the rest of the gang. They wandered idly around the city, stopping to chat in a café, and all the while discussing their plans for Chile.

In the morning, they made a late start, their breakfast also serving as lunch. Rafael, true to his calling, bought a large Roquefort cheese with which they made sandwiches – their last meal before the accident. They then took a bus to the airport, and took turns weighing themselves on the airport scales while they waited for the announcement to board the plane.

On the flight, everyone was continually moving around in the plane, looking through the windows to see the mountains, or sitting down to chat with one or other of their friends.

For a while, Rafael was sitting next to Moncho, then with Bobby. Later, he moved forward and sat with Carlitos on the right-hand side. When the air pockets started, the boys started joking around, singing *Olé, Olé* at every bit of turbulence. Rafael swapped places with Carlitos so that he could take photos. When the second big air pocket came, they began to get scared. Seeing the rocks a few metres away, Carlitos asked his friend: "Is it normal to fly so close?" Rafael hardly had time to reply before they heard the engines revving at full power, pressing them back against their seatbacks as the plane desperately tried to gain altitude before making contact with the ridge.

When the tobogganing fuselage came to a halt, Rafael was eventually extricated from the twisted metal by Carlitos, Coco, and Diego who had all been able to get free relatively easily. After the three of them helped him out, they saw that his trouser leg had been ripped to shreds, and his calf horrendously torn, hanging loose from the bone. As an initial triage, they put it back in place, disinfecting it with eau de Cologne, and wrapping it with a shirt. Rafael bore it without complaint, telling them to see to those who were more seriously injured.

Back in Montevideo, initial reports of the accident were sketchy and inconclusive. Beatriz and Pilar were returning from Spanish dance class and had stopped by the house of their grandmother. She had heard mention of a plane disappearing, but hadn't connected it to the *Old Christians* flight, because of the assumption that the boys were already in Santiago. By the time the two girls arrived home, their mother, who had been there alone, had only just turned on the TV, and was seeing the reports for the first time. Her husband was away, as he and Sarucha had been at a cattle auction in Tacuarembó 350 km north of Montevideo. In desperation, Sarita started calling the parents of other boys on the flight; those that she knew – the fathers of Daniel Fernández and of Pancho Delgado, and the mother of Gustavo Zerbino. The lines were constantly busy, but finally she got through to Mr Fernández. "Can you tell me anything?" she asked him, "Ricardo is away from Montevideo but I heard on TV that there has been an accident. Could it be the boys?" "Don't worry, Sarita," he said, "It can't be them."

Meanwhile, Mr Echavarren and Sarucha had started the long drive back from Tacuarembó. Sarucha shared her father's love of the countryside, and would often accompany him on such trips. Although she didn't work with him on the *estancia* at the time, she would start doing so after the accident. On this particular trip to the interior, Sarucha was with her friend Inés, whose brother was the brother-in-law of Daniel Fernández. Not long after setting out, Mr Echavarren turned on the radio, and immediately they started hearing reports of a Uruguayan plane lost in the Andes. Unable to ascertain whether or not it was Rafael's plane, he turned the car around, and headed back to Tacuarembó, to the house of the cattle auctioneer Abayubá Valdez, a long-time friend of his. There, he was able to telephone Sarita, who told him that it was a possibility that it was the boys' plane, but that no-one knew for sure. Mr Valdez pressed them to stay overnight at his house, but Mr Echavarren was desperate to get back to his wife, and set off immediately with Sarucha and her friend. Outwardly calm, although with anxiety etched on his face, he spent the five-hour drive changing from one radio station to another, to keep abreast of the developing reports. By the time they arrived in Montevideo close to midnight, Mr Echavarren was sure that it was Rafael's plane that had been lost. As the family embraced each other in a heartfelt hug, Sarita still maintained some hope, telling her husband: "Ricardo, let's wait until it's officially confirmed." They didn't sleep that night, but all of them felt that Rafael was still alive.

In the following days, the family – optimistic by nature – was held together by the spiritual strength of their mother, and the physical presence and determination of their father. The girls were given no latitude to feel sorry for themselves, and on the next school-day they were expected to attend as usual, told that life must go on.

On the mountain, after the horrors of the crash and the first night, the boys started to get organized. The shortened fuselage, once cleared of twisted metal and seats, provided cramped floor space for the twenty-eight passengers to sleep at night, but the injured suffered every time someone moved. Roberto Canessa proposed building a hammock from the straps and poles designed to secure cargo, and, working with Daniel Maspons, he rigged up something secure and wide enough to hold two boys. As a result of their efforts, Rafael was able to sleep more comfortably, although it was considerably colder away from the warmth of the other boys, and in the path of the wind blowing through the fuselage.

In the early days, Álvaro Mangino would share the hammock with Rafael. Roberto had also rigged up a hanging seat, where Arturo Nogueira would lie, his feet resting on the hammock. Over the following weeks, Rafael and Arturo would spend a lot of time together in the fuselage. The two boys could not have been more different. Rafael, whose whole outlook was focussed on dairy production and the hard work and practicalities of day-to-day life on the family *estancia*; Arturo, an idealist and intellectual who thought deeply about the social injustices in Uruguayan society, and could argue persuasively about them. It was a pairing that could have led to fractious political arguments, but the two got along, and often the conversation was punctuated by laughter and swearing. More often than not, it would be the more mundane matters that they would fight over, such as the lack of blankets, or where one or other had positioned their feet.

Whereas Arturo often became morose and introspective, Rafael always remained optimistic, and was constantly lifting the mood of the group. He would make light of the difficulties they faced. He would pretend to hand out chocolates to everyone, ruefully remembering the occasions, at his grandmother's house, when she would open a box of chocolates she had bought, only to find that they were all gone, already eaten by Rafael. And when Canessa and Zerbino would do the rounds of the injured, he would always tell them to attend to the others first – that they were worse off than him.

Rafael's main topic of conversation was dairy production, and he taught the boys about the process of making cheese and yoghurt. He would talk business with his former classmate Moncho, whose family had an estancia near to Los Tapiales. Rafael would discuss his plans to expand and diversify his lechería, whereas Moncho would talk about fruit production on the family farm. On other occasions, Rafael taught the group some of the many folkloric songs he loved to sing back in Uruguay. He especially enjoyed the emotive songs of legendary Uruguayan singer Alfredo Zitarrosa, such as Zamba pa vos, Pa'l que se va, and Milonga para una niña, which he shared on the mountain along with other traditional songs such as Si vas para Chile and El Indio Muerto. The boys and Liliana Methol would all join in, happy to be briefly transported away from the desperation of their situation.

Fig. 122. *Rafael was a lover of folkloric songs, some of which he taught and sang on the mountain, though without guitar.*

Only once was Rafael a bit down. Gathering everyone together, he informed them that he was going to die, and that he wanted to leave his motorbike to his business partner Walter, and his Land Rover to Ana. The others joked with him, asking him if he could leave various of his possessions to each of them. They didn't believe he was close to dying, and in fact he survived a long time after that brief dip in his optimism.

After the avalanche, which he survived due to being on the hammock, Rafael started to deteriorate. The pain from his leg meant he always had it hanging out of the hammock, and he began to develop gangrene in both his legs. Despite his ongoing agony, Rafael would try rally those feeling despondent, daily stating his intention to return home. In the 1992 movie *Alive*, Rafael's name was changed to Federico Aranda, and he is one of the most memorable of all the cast. As he lies on his hammock in his red jacket, he grabs Canessa, who is dressing his wounds, and tells him, "My name is Federico Aranda, and I will return." The red jacket and his pronouncement are both accurate. Later in the film, the same jacket is seen on Carlitos as he sews the sleeping bag; another detail that matches reality. Carlitos wore that jacket after Rafael died, and brought it back from the mountain to give to the family. It is still in the possession of Rafael's sisters.

Fig. 123. *From right to left: Rafael's sisters Sarucha, Beatriz, Pilar, and Pilar's son Rafael in 2022. Beatriz is holding her brother's famous red jacket which came back from the mountain.*

On 17th November, at around the time Parrado, Canessa, and Vizintín were setting off on their first expedition to the east, a group of relatives arrived in Chile to continue the search, taking over from Carlos Páez Vilaró, who, after five weeks of searching, had needed to return to Montevideo and then São Paulo to prepare an art exhibit. Among the parents was Rafael's father. He was joined by the mother and brother of Marcelo

Pérez del Castillo, and the mother and great-uncle of Carlitos, the latter a commercial pilot for PLUNA, the Uruguayan national airline. They made expeditions deep into the mountains on muleback, concentrating their efforts on *Descabezado Grande*, the peak that most closely matched Gerard Croiset's visions. The land expeditions were supplemented by air searches, courtesy of the *Talca Aero club*. But the endeavour was doomed to failure; they were searching 100 km to the south of the actual crash site.

At the same time as Ricardo Echavarren was arriving in Chile to search for his son, Rafael was taking a sudden turn for the worse on the mountain. He started becoming delirious, believing himself to be on the *estancia*, talking with his sisters, and convinced that his father was outside the fuselage. Eventually, his breathing became laboured, exacerbated by the humidity in the plane, and despite the attempts of Gustavo and Carlitos to give him artificial respiration, he died a couple of hours later.

When the news came through that two boys from the plane had appeared in the Chilean *precordillera*, Rafael's parents and sisters were at the *estancia* in Durazno. They were convinced that one of them must be Rafael, because of his indomitable spirit. The whole family immediately returned to Montevideo, stopping in the El Prado home of a relative who had managed to secure, for Ricardo, the last ticket for the early morning flight to Santiago. Various unofficial lists were doing the rounds, muddling survivors and non-survivors, but the official list didn't get broadcast until the next afternoon, well after Ricardo arrived in Santiago. Many other relatives were on that flight with Ricardo Echavarren – Mecha Canessa, Raquel Nicolich whose husband was already in Chile, and the Strauch, François, Shaw and Hounie families, among others. Of these, only Mecha knew her son was alive. Raquel was optimistic, buoyed by an erroneous rumour that her son had survived. When they arrived in Santiago, some went straight down to San Fernando by taxi or in the cars of friends, while others went to the house of the Uruguayan chargé-d'affaires, where they heard the list of survivors.

In San Fernando, speaking to Daniel Fernández, Mr Nicolich learnt of his son's leading role on the mountain until his death in the avalanche, and Mr Echavarren learnt of his son's survival for more than five weeks. The parents were staying at the *Hotel Crillón* in Santiago, and Sarita Echavarren called there to speak to her husband. The concierge told her that he wasn't in, but he put her through to Mrs Zerbino, who informed her that Rafael had died. Sarita thanked her, grateful that she had had the courage to give her the news.

Ricardo Echavarren returned to Montevideo, and the whole family went to the press conference in the *Stella Maris College* gym a few days later. They sat silent during the various speeches, accepting what happened as the hand of God. Later, Daniel Fernández went to speak to the family to give them the full story of Rafael on the mountain. Daniel had marvelled over how it had always been Rafael who, despite his crippling and painful injury, would rally the other boys, stopping them from losing heart. When Rafael had died, Daniel had been worried that there would no longer be anyone to encourage them to keep fighting. Daniel told the parents about his injury, his courageous spirit, his optimistic outlook, his refusal to write any letters that could be passed on in the event of his death, and above all his daily declaration: "I am Rafael Echavarren, and I assure you that I will return". It also became apparent that, as one of the last to die, his body, though emaciated from his steady decline, could still be identified. Weighing all this up, Ricardo determined that he would whatever it took to recover his son's body from the mountain, and return it to Uruguay, and he headed back to Santiago.

TWO BURIALS

The general problem of what to do about the remains of the victims was an unprecedented one. The passengers were Uruguayan, their bodies were in Argentina, and the rescue had been from Chile. The anthropophagy, and the consequent difficulties in identifying the remains, significantly added to the complications. With the recovery of Rafael's body his foremost goal, Ricardo had a vested interest in these discussions, and based himself in Santiago for the duration, acting as a representative of the other parents. In the end, the families agreed upon, and signed, a declaration that the remains should be interred on the mountain, in a common grave. It took until the second week of January for the necessary authorizations to be put in place, the Argentinian authorities ceding, to their counterparts in Chile, the permissions to conduct the burial. The task would be carried out by the volunteer *Cuerpo de Socorro Andino* and the Chilean Air Force *Servicio Aéreo de Rescate*, accompanied by Captain Crosa of the Uruguayan Air Force and San Fernando parish priest Fr Iván Caviedes. The whole operation would be conducted with minimum publicity, in order to avoid any sensationalist media coverage.

From the beginning, Ricardo Echavarren had been clear with the other parents about his wish to recover his son's body. As he was not permitted to be present at the burial on the mountain, he prepared the way by approaching Sergio Díaz of the *Cuerpo de Socorro Andino*. He described what he planned to do, and gave him photos of Rafael, and instructions for how to identify him. He asked Díaz to locate his son's body, wrap it in a polythene bag, and bury it slightly apart from the other bodies, with a marker to indicate its location. Sarita Echavarren also wrote to Díaz from Montevideo:

Relying on your kindness and spirituality, which I know you have in abundance, I am sending you, via my husband, a small envelope containing a medal and a few words to my son Rafael. I would like you to place this envelope under his shirt, next to his body. I am also sending a handful of Uruguayan soil to put on the grave of all the Uruguayans who will be buried together, and another little bit to put on the body of my son Rafael, who was obsessed during his suffering on the mountain with the desire to return to his country. I think you will be able to understand the wishes of a mother who would like to go with you to the Andes at any cost. Thank you very much, Mr. Díaz. I will always be grateful to you for your kindness. All my appreciation, have a good trip and success!

At the time of the rescue, Díaz had been the first person to step out of the helicopter onto the glacier, to greet and hug the boys, their first contact with the outside world for 72 days. He had spent the night of the 22ⁿᵈ December chatting with them in the fuselage, and was aware more than any other outsider of the situation on the mountain. So he was sympathetic to the request of Rafael's parents.

The burial operation started early on the morning of 18ᵗʰ January 1973, with the establishment of an advance base at the spa town of Termas del Flaco, just 25 kilometres south of the crash site. Lieutenant Mario Ávila of the SAR, who had first gone to the site as the pilot of helicopter H-90 during the rescue on 23ʳᵈ December, recalled:

During the days of the burial, I must have made that trip from Termas del Flaco to the Valley of Tears at least ten times, because we had to move so many people – Andinistas, Chilean and Uruguayan Air Force personnel, forensic experts, and the priest – along with all their equipment.

The team spent the morning setting up camp, carefully positioning it to minimize the risk of being hit by an avalanche. Work began at 1:00 p.m. They worked slowly as they adjusted to the altitude. One patrol was tasked with separating out the bodies and remains from around the fuselage – which was, by now, balanced on a metre-high snow pedestal made by its own shadow – and placing them in polythene bags. Another team began work on the grave; they picked a spot on a ridge a few hundred metres away from the plane above the glacier; the only area not covered with snow.

It soon became apparent that the work would be fraught with danger. The unprecedented snowfall the previous winter, the hot afternoon sun, and the angle of slope had created perfect conditions for avalanches. At 2:15 p.m., the priest, and three CSA volunteers narrowly avoided being hit by one. Five minutes later, another avalanche brought down with it the wing of the plane, and two of the bodies that had been higher up the mountain. The wing came to rest 100 metres from the fuselage.

Fig. 124. *The burial team's camp on the mountain.*

The next day, work began at 7:30 a.m., with the gravedigging team continuing their efforts of the previous day, and the fuselage team beginning the difficult task of carrying the bodies and remains up to the burial site. Meanwhile, another patrol of three volunteers made their way up the slope towards the impact point, to recover the remaining bodies. An avalanche watch was set up, and within the space of one hour in the early afternoon, nineteen avalanches were counted in the areas where the work was going on, one of them bringing down with it the turbine that had been up near the wing. The ongoing danger to the CSA volunteers, who were risking their lives, gave an increased urgency to wrap up the work, and Captain Mario Jimenez of the SAR, made the decision that the recovery efforts could not continue beyond the end of the day.

The difficulty of digging to any great depth meant the grave covered a wide area – around 6 metres by 6 metres – but was only about a metre deep. The bodies and remains were placed there, and covered with soil and rocks. Sergio Díaz was successful in locating and identifying Rafael's body, and it was placed closest to the cross, its location indicated by a marker.

At 7:00 a.m. on the morning of 20th January, with everyone gathered around the grave, Fr Caviedes committed the victims to their final resting place with these words:

> *Before the grave of these Uruguayan brothers, we are celebrating the Lord's supper. God is here. And in the silence and the solitude of the Cordillera, they won't be left alone. We leave them a cross. It will keep them company. This cross will also bring to the world a message of hope and a message of brotherhood: NEARER OH GOD TO THEE... The cross that we'll leave in these mountains will also shout, insistently, through the winds and hurricanes, a second message; because on it can be read: THE WORLD TO ITS URUGUAYAN BROTHERS. A message of universal brotherhood, or fraternity, that is a struggle on behalf of each man, until justice and its fruit, which is peace, will come to be a reality. A struggle that is carried out with love, the only thing, when real, that is capable of transforming the world. Hope and brotherhood is the song that will be sung forever by this cross and this community of Uruguayans that rest beside it, until they will arise glorious. Its melody may be heard permanently by every man of good will, coming from the middle of the Cordillera de los Andes.*

Fig. 125. *Fr Ivan Caviedes celebrating the funeral Mass at the grave on the mountain.*

As a final act before leaving, the burial party doused the fuselage with fuel, and set it alight. At 9:00 a.m. the helicopters returned to pick them up. On their arrival back in Santiago, Sergio Díaz met with Ricardo Echavarren, giving him photographs of the burial site, and indicating where Rafael's body lay in the collective grave. Ricardo immediately put his own plan into motion. He hired an *arriero* – a Chilean muleteer – who was intimately familiar with the mountains on the Chilean side. They set off up the *Azufre* river to *Los Maitenes*, where Canessa and Parrado had appeared, and then up the

courses of the *Portillo* and *San José* rivers that had led the boys to safety. But by the time they reached the snowline, it became clear that the *arriero* did not know where the plane was, and they turned back.

Ricardo then decided that he would have to approach from the Argentinian side. His wife suggested he contact a friend, Enrique Franchetti, who lived in the town of San Rafael, quite close to the village of El Sosneado, the gateway to the part of the Andes where the fuselage was

Fig. 126. *Return of the burial party to Posta Central.*

located. The Echavarren and Franchetti families had met during a guided two-month tour of Europe in 1969. They had bonded through their common interests and background, the Echavarrens with a cattle *estancia* in Durazno in Uruguay, the Franchettis with one south of Córdoba in Argentina. They had kept in touch, exchanging Christmas cards with promises of visiting one another.

The Franchetti family had heard about the accident when it was in the news, and then again when the survivors had appeared, but they had no intimation that their friends' son had been a passenger. So it was a shock when Ricardo Echavarren contacted Enrique to tell him that Rafael had been one of the boys who had died. Ricardo asked him if he could help to find someone in the area who could guide him to the scene of the accident.

Enrique was a well-known local merchant with good knowledge of the region. He bought and sold cattle in the nearby town of Malargüe, and also did business there as a soft drinks manufacturer. Malargüe, being close to El Sosneado, was a good place to find contacts amongst the *puesteros*, the *gauchos* who lived in the mountains, breeding goats. Descended from indigenous people and Spanish settlers, the *puestero* families had a tradition going back hundreds of years. They maintained breeding posts and paddocks in the foothills of the *Cordillera*, spending the winters there or in Malargüe. In December, when the snow began to melt, they would take their livestock up to graze in the highlands.

Enrique contacted his soft drinks distributor in Malargüe, who introduced him to Paquito Fernández, a local representative of the *Los Andes* newspaper. Fernández knew the *puesteros* who lived in that part of the mountain, and introduced Franchetti to one of them, René Lima. At the time of the burial on the mountain, Lima had seen the helicopter activity in the distance while tending to his goats, and, with his intimate knowledge of the local topography, deduced where the fuselage must lie. With an introduction from Lima, Enrique went to visit another *puestero*, Antonio Araya, whose domain was the closest to the suspected crash site.

The trip to Araya's post involved a lengthy drive down a gravel road – *Provincial Route 220*. Branching off *National Route 40* at the village of El Sosneado, the road follows the course of the Atuel river upstream, eventually skirting the 5177-metre *El Sosneado* volcano, the mountain that the boys could see from the glacier, which had dissuaded them from heading east. After 60 kilometres, the road passes by the *Termas del Sosneado* – thermal pools warmed by the sulphurous waters of the nearby *Overo* volcano – and the hotel which, in its heyday, housed visitors to the spa. Today, the hotel is in ruin, although the pools still attract visitors, but even in 1972, the hotel had been closed for almost two decades, unable to sustain the business in so remote an area for so short a season. Two kilometres past the hotel is the *Puesto de Gendarmería*, the small police station active in 1972, but now abandoned, which served as a checkpoint for vehicles going to the *Sominar* sulphur refining plant 15 km further up the road. The sulphur mines themselves were a few dozen kilometres beyond the refinery, past the end of route 220, on the slopes of the *Overo* volcano. The mining operations, which closed down in 1978, were active over the summer months – December to February – of 1972/73.

Araya's post was located just past the police checkpoint, near where the wide delta of the *Lágrimas* river feeds into the *Atuel*. Looking west from there, you can see in the distance, 20 km away, the 4,600-metre-high mountain ridge that forms the border with Chile, and surrounds the valley in which the *Lágrimas* has its source: to the left, the slope that the fuselage of the Fairchild careered down on the afternoon of 13th October, to the right the mountain that Roberto Canessa, Fernando Parrado, and Antonio Vizintín climbed on their final expedition. It was from near the top of that mountain, on the evening of 13th December, that Canessa had debated with the other two whether or not the line he could make out in the distance was a road. In the end, they were unsure, and continued west. If by chance they had happened to spot the distant lights of a mining truck passing Araya's post on *Route 220* as they lay down to sleep that night, they would undoubtedly have aborted the expedition and headed east.

Having established that the *puesteros* had a good idea where the plane was, the Franchettis asked if they were willing to act as *baqueanos* – local guides – to reach the site, and recover Rafael's body. They agreed, but requested certain equipment for the horses – harnesses, horseshoes, and other tackle. Ricardo Echavarren arrived in San Rafael on 26th January, driving from Santiago. The two of them went to see the *puesteros* again, bringing them the equipment they asked for, and food for the expedition. Echavarren and Franchetti did not make it up the mountain on this occasion, but the *puesteros* were able to reach the site, coming across the tail first, then the fuselage and grave. Echavarren had given them instructions about where his son's body was, and the identification marker that had been left by Sergio Díaz. They confirmed all this, and reported back to Franchetti and Echavarren once they returned. However, they felt that conditions on the mountain were still too dangerous to be able to safely recover the body.

With that advice, Echavarren returned to Uruguay, determined to attempt the recovery immediately after the Argentinian elections in March, before the snows started again in the mountains. Back home, he was contacted by Coco Nicolich's father Gustavo, who also wanted to visit the site where his son was buried. They decided to join forces – Echavarren determined and impulsive, Nicolich more thoughtful and analytic. On hearing reports of a first snowfall in the Andes, the pair left for Argentina, Echavarren accompanied by his wife and daughters who would stay in San Rafael whilst the two fathers were on the mountain.

Enrique Franchetti had asked his 28-year-old son Ricardo to take his place on this expedition, but nevertheless travelled with them to Araya's post to see them off. He brought the *gendarmería* gifts, as he had met them on previous trips, with the story that he was there to buy cattle from the *puesteros*. The full expeditionary party consisted of the two fathers, Ricardo Franchetti, Lima and Araya, and journalist Juan Antonio Domínguez from Mendoza.

Fig. 127. *Nicolich, Echavarren and Franchetti at the tail after finding Coco's suitcase.*

The group set off with horses and mules on the afternoon of 21st March, crossing the *Atuel* river and the *Lágrimas* delta before ascending into the mountains. The first night, they reached the area of *Las Tres Lagunas*, at about 2,900 metres. It was a place where the *puesteros* took their livestock to graze in the summer. They stopped at a rudimentary shelter – a *pirca* – with a curved dry wall and corrugated iron roof, but otherwise open to the elements. Communication with the taciturn *baqueanos* had been infrequent as they had made their way up the mountain, but that night, over a meal of bread, salami, and cheese, Echavarren talked about his son, and the promise that he'd made to bring him home.

As the weather was good, the group slept outside, avoiding the discomfort of the cramped *pirca*. Getting up at first light the next morning, they made coffee, and then set off up the mountain again at 6:00 a.m., leaving some of their equipment at the *pirca* to collect on their return. Along the way, Echavarren and Nicolich stopped to pick some bunches of wildflowers to take to the grave – *clavelillos de la sierra* (small mountain carnations) and *orejas de gato* (cat's-eyes); the *baqueanos* also dismounted to lend a hand. Continuing up the mountain, the landscape became increasingly rugged and dangerous, with steep canyons and raging torrents, until they eventually reached the snowline.

Late in the morning, they came across the tail of the plane and stopped there for a while, to rest and explore. Amongst the scattered bags, they found Coco's combination-lock suitcase that his father had brought back as a gift from the US. It had been slit open and emptied, like all the other cases, by the four boys who had made the trips to the tail in November and December. They had been searching for food and clothing, and anything else that might help their survival, and they had arranged the most brightly coloured clothes in the form of a cross. Still visible was the message for any would-be rescuers that Parrado had penned on the tail before leaving it for the last time:

17 survivors further up in the fuselage. 7/12.

They continued for a while until the *baqueanos* asked them to dismount because of the danger of crevasses. The two parents, whose footwear wasn't designed for the mountains, were helped up the steep snow-covered slope by the *baqueanos*, using ropes. Approaching the area of the fuselage was a harrowing experience, as Ricardo Franchetti recalled with emotion almost fifty years later:

I was ahead of everybody. I was walking and suddenly I started to see things. I saw that there were human remains in the snow. At first I passed them by, but as I continued on, there were bigger things. I stopped and asked Echavarren, Nicolich, and the puesteros what we should do, whether or not we should keep going.

The burial team had cleared as much as possible in the two days available before the dangerous conditions had forced them to leave, but Araya and Lima had still seen unburied remains at the fuselage when they had reconnoitred the site at the end of January, a few days after the burial. Now, after almost two months of summer thaw, many more remains had been exposed, including two whole bodies. When the journalist took out a camera and started taking pictures, he was immediately confronted by Echavarren, who wanted full control over what photos were taken. He didn't want any sensationalist images to appear in the press. Domínguez agreed that he would only take photos with the explicit permission of Echavarren.

The first task was to deal with the two intact bodies. Hindered by the altitude, some minor avalanches, and extreme fatigue, Ricardo Franchetti somehow summoned up the strength to carry one of them the few hundred metres to the grave. The other was carried by one of the baqueanos, whilst Echavarren stayed with Domínguez at the fuselage. When Ricardo returned, Echavarren asked him to take photos of all the remains as a record for the authorities – to show that the job had not been completed in January.

Ricardo and the baqueanos then gathered up the remaining parts, and took them up to the grave for burial. There at the cross, after locating and removing the bag containing Rafael's remains, and burying all the remains found by the fuselage, Echavarren wanted to make absolutely sure that it was his son's body. There were three identifiers that he wanted to check. The first was a distinctive scar from a riding accident – Rafael had fallen off a horse and had cut his eye with barbed wire. Echavarren asked Ricardo to look at the body. Seeing that decomposition had started to set in, Ricardo revealed just enough of his face for Echavarren to confirm the scar. Again with Ricardo's help, Echavarren was also able to verify the wounded and gangrenous legs, and his son's hammer toe.

Convinced beyond a doubt that this was Rafael, Echavarren authorized the baqueanos to start taking the body down the mountain. They wrapped it in a tarpaulin, and started lowering it down the slope, to where they had left the horses and mules. Once there, they secured the body on to one of the animals, and, at about 4:00 p.m., the party started making its way down. A short time later, they were surprised to see, a few hundred metres down the mountain, a group of 20 or so people coming up towards them, on horseback. It turned out to be a group of Chileans, equipped with filming equipment, who were on their way up to the fuselage. They had taken a circuitous route over a pass used by muleteers – the Paso de las Damas, 25 kilometres to the south to the Fairchild – before heading north over lower mountains until they reached the Lágrimas river; and finally west up the valley towards the crash site.

Echavarren and company, relieved that they had done much to clean up the site before the Chileans had arrived, continued their way down the mountain, and decided to keep going the whole way to the bottom, stopping at the *pirca* only to pick up the equipment they had left there that morning. The going was more dangerous on the way down, because, by evening, the torrents had swollen significantly, and their slow descent meant that the *baqueanos* were well ahead of Echavarren, Nicolich, and Franchetti by the time they reached the bottom of the mountain, the three of them having had to rely on the horses to guide them back.

Fig. 128. *Guide Armando Araya flanked by Enri Franchetti, Rafael's sisters Pilar and Sarucha, cousin Eduardo, mother Sara, and aunt Lilly near the sulphur mines.*

Meanwhile, the *gendarmería* had got wind of what was happening. They had seen a funeral car drive past earlier in the day, and had demanded to know what was going on. As a consequence, when Rafael's body arrived back from the mountain, it was immediately taken into custody; and when the expeditionaries turned up, exhausted, at Araya's post, at 11:00 p.m., Echavarren had barely time to greet his family before he and his companions were arrested, and held at the police checkpoint.

It took several hours of questioning, and phone calls to the regional and national authorities, before they were released. The body was taken to Malargüe, and held there overnight before it was transported to San Rafael, where permission had been granted for it to rest in the Franchetti family tomb until its repatriation. While the Franchetti family and Nicolich were dealing with arrangements in San Rafael, Echavarren reported to the police station in Malargüe. There, he was questioned and fingerprinted, and put through various other formalities to verify his identity. Throughout the process, he had nothing but praise for the Argentinian authorities. At the foot of the mountain and in Malargüe, the police had treated him kindly, being understanding and supportive of what he had done as a father, but required to go through due process. The judge from San Rafael called several times to help expedite things, and a colonel arrived from the regional capital, Mendoza, expressly to assure Echavarren of the support of the national authorities.

Fig. 129. *Sons Coco Nicolich and Rafael Echavarren in Mendoza Oct 12, 1972 and mothers Raquel Arocena de Nicolich and Sarita Vázquez de Echavarren at the Biblioteca Nuestros Hijos 2012.*

The Foreign offices of Argentina and Uruguay still needed to follow the diplomatic procedures to effect the repatriation, and Nicolich travelled to Buenos Aires on the 25th March to deal with some of the formalities, returning to Montevideo early on the 27th. Echavarren and his family travelled back to Montevideo by car, arriving on the same day. They didn't have to wait long for the formal authorization. On 10th April, a Uruguayan Air Force plane left for San Rafael, and returned the next day with Rafael's body. Once on home territory, he was buried in the family *pantheon* in Buceo Cemetery.

The *pantheon* had been built recently. A couple of months before the fateful trip, Rafael had gone with his sister Pilar to have lunch at their grandparents' house. After the meal, his grandfather had said to him, "Rafael, come and look at these plans for the *pantheon*, I'm getting old, and I need somewhere to go. As the oldest grandson, tell me what you think." Rafael had leant over his grandfather, who was hard of hearing, and had said laughingly, "Take a closer look, you're going to be the one to inaugurate it!"

From the time of the accident, the family had gone to great lengths to shield Rafael's grandfather from the news. Afraid that reports of the accident would trigger a heart attack, his wife 'Queta' would tear out the pages of the newspapers, so that he wouldn't be able to see them. But he was always suspicious, because Rafael no longer came to visit. One day, walking with his goddaughter Pilar, he said to her, "I think something must have happened to Rafael." In deference to her grandmother, Pilar changed the subject.

In the end it was Rafael, the only fatality of *Flight 571* to return to Uruguay, who was the first to be buried in the family tomb, but his grandfather was not far behind, dying a few days after Rafael's body arrived back in Montevideo. By a strange coincidence, the number of the *pantheon* was 571.

Despite the pain of losing her son, Sarita Echavarren exhibited extraordinary faith and equanimity. When she knew for certain that he was dead, she would quote from the book of Job: "The Lord gave, and the Lord has taken away; blessed be the name of the Lord." She felt that God's justice was different from man's justice, and that God had taken him for some reason. And she didn't want to dwell on it, preferring to look forward, and to ensure that their home continued to be a joyful place. The girls never felt any reproach, and life continued as normal. The fact that they lived in Pocitos saved them from the constant reminders that persisted in Carrasco. They didn't like to talk about the subject with outsiders, and lived their lives as if it hadn't happened. But people would still treat them differently, and if someone happened to mention the subject to Beatriz, she would immediately cut them short.

Within the family, though, they always talked about Rafael, and in their hearts he was still alive. Invariably, they would alternate between tears and laughter, remembering his sense of humour

Fig. 130. *The Echavarren family pantheon in Buceo cemetery where Rafael is buried, plot number 571.*

and his antics, and the good times they had shared with him. Even when Beatriz went to the mountain in February 2018, her emotions vacillated as she stood by the grave of Rafael's companions, overlooking the glacier, crying one moment and laughing the next. Beatriz had planned to go one year earlier, on which occasion her mother had told her: "If you go on the trip, please don't tell me anything when you get back. At my age, the whole matter makes me very sad." As it turned out, the 2017 trip was postponed, and Sarita never knew of her daughter's trip the following year. She passed away on 5th June 2017.

Fig. 131. *Rafael's body is lowered from the FAU C-47 on arrival in Montevideo.*

JULIO CÉSAR FERRADÁS
24-JAN-1933 — 13-OCT-1972

Colonel Julio César Ferradás was considered one of the top pilots in the *Fuerza Aérea Uruguaya*. Graduating as a military pilot in December 1952, he was an experienced flight instructor, and had amassed more than 5000 hours flying a variety of planes, including the T-6 Texan Advanced Trainer, B-25 bomber, C-47, Fokker F-27 Friendship, and Fairchild FH-227. The latter three formed the backbone of the transport fleet, Group 3 consisting of 18 C-47s (serial numbers FAU 507 to FAU 524), and Group 4 including two each of the more modern aircraft (serial numbers FAU 560/561, and FAU 570/571). Ferradás was a specialist pilot in Group 4. Calm and methodical, he was a reassuring presence in the cockpit, respected by his crew, and his ready wit and jovial nature made him a popular member of the Air Force fraternity.

The two transport groups, part of Air Brigade 1, based at Air Base 1 in Carrasco, provided the aircraft and pilots for TAMU (*Transporte Aéreo Militar Uruguayo*), which ran regular passenger and mail services to the major towns in the interior of Uruguay, as well as monthly trips to the capitals of the closer South American countries. To raise additional funds, the organization also ran charter flights. The *Old Christians* trip was one of these, assigned FAU 571.

The two Fairchilds were the most recent additions to the fleet, just over a year old. Their purchase had been authorized in October 1970, and nine months later a delegation of pilots and technical staff had travelled to Hagerstown in Maryland for a month of theoretical coursework, followed by three weeks of flight training. The team then embarked on a six-day flight to bring the aircraft to Uruguay, with Chief of Mission Colonel Wilder Jackson commanding FAU 570, and Ferradás in charge of FAU 571. For these two experienced pilots, the transition from

Fig. 132. *Colonel Júlio César Ferradás.*

Fokker to Fairchild was straightforward, the latter being a stretch version of the former. The aircraft made overnight stops at Corpus Christi, Managua, Panama, and Lima, before crossing the Chilean Andes and landing in Mendoza on Thursday 12ᵗʰ August. As Ferradás boarded the Fairchild the next day for its final leg to Carrasco, he would have had little thought that fourteen months later, again on Friday 13ᵗʰ, he would be taking off from the same runway for the aircraft's final flight.

Fig. 133. *The FAU team flanked by their instructors in Hagerstown, Maryland, Aug. 1971. Wilder Jackson and Julio Ferradás are second and third from left respectively.*

Ferradás was married without children, but he was very close to his nieces and nephews: Virginia, Gabriela, and Héctor, the children of his sister María Elena; and Alicia and Alejandro, the children of his younger brother. The kids loved their uncle's good-natured and jocular personality and would always enjoy family visits to the open spaces near the lakes of Paso de Carrasco, where he and Tia Babi lived. Julio brought back gifts from Hagerstown, with Alejandro receiving a belated birthday present – a 1971 Mattel jack-in-the-box. Alejandro's father, Roberto, was also an FAU pilot, who graduated in December 1962. By a cruel twist of fate, the two brothers, despite their impeccable records, would both die in catastrophic accidents, the worst ever involving Uruguayan aircraft: the Andes accident of 13ᵗʰ October 1972, and the Artigas accident of 10ᵗʰ February 1978.

298

Chile was one of Julio's favourite destinations, and he had made the crossing of the Andes close to thirty times in each direction, sometimes by the *Cristo Redentor* pass, and at other times by the Planchón pass. His reputation and experience went some way towards assuaging the fear of some *Old Christian* parents, who doubted the military's competence to conduct civilian flights. Ferradás showed the requisite caution when making the decision to land in Mendoza on 12th October, rather than continue across the Andes in conditions of severe turbulence and icing. On the following day, Ferradás again made a conservative decision, flying over the safer Planchón pass, which necessitated a significant detour. Not feeling so well, Ferradás took over the navigational duties, and authorized second-in-command Dante Lagurara to pilot the plane.

Fig. 134.
The jack-in-the-box that flew back on FAU 571.

Taking off at 17:18 GMT (14:18 local time), the flight was initially uneventful, the Fairchild heading south for fifty minutes to Malargüe before heading west across the mountain range. At 18:21 GMT, Ferradás made first contact with the *Pudahuel* control tower in Santiago, and confirmed Visual Meteorological Conditions. Three minutes later, he claimed to be over Curicó; an impossibility. Changing course to head north, the Fairchild entered the clouds and started experiencing extreme turbulence, rapidly losing altitude in two deep air pockets. The last communication with *Pudahuel* was at 18:30 GMT:

SANTIAGO: Uruguayan 571 can you confirm your current level?
FAU 571:   Level 150...[1]
SANTIAGO: Received....

The Chilean Air Force later reported that all radio calls were made by Ferradás with his natural voice, with the exception of this last response which was made hastily. By this point, the Fairchild would have lost all instrument contact with the Maipú radio beacon in Santiago, and as they emerged out of the clouds, the pilots found themselves heading towards a 15,000 foot mountain ridge. Too late to change course, the pilots put the engines at full power, in an attempt to gain altitude, and aimed for a notch in the ridge. They were fractionally close to clearing it, and their actions combined to save at least some of the passengers. But Ferradás himself died

---

[1] 15,000 feet.

when the fuselage came to a halt, the cockpit crushed as it hit a mound of snow at the end of its slide down the other side of the mountain.

In August 1973, Roberto and his wife Elena named their new-born son, brother to Alicia and Alejandro, in memory of his uncle. The family lived in the neighbourhood of La Blanqueada, less than a hundred metres from the stadium of one of the two giants of Uruguayan football, *Club Nacional*. For the neighbours, the close proximity of 'la casa del piloto' must have created some unease in the years of the civil-military dictatorship, when anyone might get denounced for having the wrong associations. But they needn't have worried; the Ferradás home was a cultured and relaxed place, with little heed paid to the more officious strictures of the military government. Roberto was a great fan of music and the arts, with a large vinyl record collection, ranging from classical to the Beatles. He would listen to his albums whilst indulging his other passion, that of building 1/72 scale World War II model aircraft; an activity that would absorb him on Sunday mornings.

THE ARTIGAS ACCIDENT

Early on the morning of the accident that would take his life, a blue Air Force Ford pick-up stopped by Roberto's house as usual, to take him to Air Base 1. At the time, he was in transport Group 4, just as his brother had been, piloting Fokker and Fairchild aircraft. But his long previous experience with the C-47 made him an obvious stand-in, if, as was the case, Group 3 was suffering a temporary shortage of pilots due to annual leave.

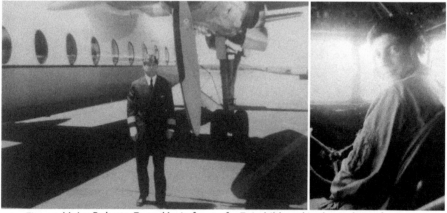

Fig. 135. *Major Roberto Ferradás, in front of a Fairchild, and in the cockpit of a C-47.*

His duty for 10th February 1978 was to pilot the fortnightly TAMU circular route of towns in the west of the country. Leaving Montevideo at 8:00 a.m., it would make stops at Paysandú and Salto, before arriving at Artigas in the extreme north of the country at 11:40. There it would stop for half an hour, before heading back to Montevideo, arriving at 15:15 after a brief stopover in Rivera. These flights connecting towns in the interior had been free in the early days, and even in 1978 they were still very affordable, and heavily utilised.

The particular aircraft assigned to the trip was FAU 511; a C-47 with a murky history, albeit unknown to the public at the time. Seventeen months previously, it had transported twenty-two political prisoners from Buenos Aires to Montevideo. Known as 'the second flight', the prisoners had disappeared, their fate unknown to this day. The pilot and crew had been ordered to stay in the cockpit for the duration of the flight.

On the day of the Artigas accident, the flights were uneventful, except that at Salto, Ferradás had not been able to start the right-hand engine, and it had had to be started manually. This procedure was achieved by means of a special rope sling, with two boots – each placed over the tip of one of the propellor blades. Then a tractor, Jeep, or team of men, would pull the rope, to rotate the blades in coordination with the pilot switching on the ignition. In order to avoid a similar problem in Artigas, the engine was left running as the passengers disembarked, and new ones boarded.

Fig. 136. *FAU 511, the C-47 involved in the 'second flight' and the Artigas crash.*

The leg from Artigas to Rivera was full, and not everyone was able to secure a place. One woman was asked to get off, to make place for a retired military officer. Another lady boarded with her two boys, and found that there was no place to sit. When offered a place at the back amongst the baggage, she declined, and disembarked, unwittingly saving the lives of herself and her children. She would later be referred to, sometimes with a hint of animosity, as 'the one who survived'.

The subsequent events were later recounted by the Air Force[1]:

> With everything ready and 38 passengers (23 adults and 15 minors) inside, including Sgt Nery Pereira[2] of the Air Force, it took off from Artigas towards Rivera at 12:18 from runway 10 (towards the city). Two minutes later and at an estimated eight hundred feet of altitude, the right engine failed, so the pilot feathered the propeller, proceeding to return to the airfield, flying with a single engine, making a transit to the right at low altitude, and skewed with the runway he intended to use, i.e. again runway 10. He lowered the landing gear, and then turned to the right to make the final approach, but overshot the headland and the runway axis, so he tightened the turn to the right trying to align with it, which brought the aircraft close to stall speed. When this occurred, the aircraft fell vertically and crashed, with the total loss of life of the 44 occupants, and the aircraft destroyed.

The decision to bank to the right, in order to return to the runway, took the plane away from the city, and Ferradás was praised for this in an article that appeared in *El País* later in the year:

> The pilot's heroism prevented what could have been an unprecedented catastrophe by preventing the plane – which he had lost control of, due to technical failures – from crashing into the town centre.

But later, air-crash investigator Colonel Ego Correa Luna suggested that a better option might have been to circle to the left, giving the pilot an unobstructed view of the runway, and keeping the turns on the same side as the good engine.

In terms of passenger and crew fatalities, the accident was, and still is, the deadliest involving a Uruguayan plane, and the second most deadly worldwide involving a DC-3/C-47. The large number of deaths reflected the common practice of parents travelling with children on their laps, and the commemorative plaque at Artigas airport shows instances

---

[1] *Historia de la Fuerza Aérea Uruguaya*, book 2, volume 1: 1953-2003 by 1st Lt Juan Maruri.

[2] Sgt Nery Pereira had been part of the crew of Julio Ferradás when delivering the FAU 571 in 1971, and can be seen fifth from the right in the Hagerstown photograph.

of names repeated many times, perhaps representing whole families who perished. The remains were taken to the municipal gymnasium, and the tragedy, witnessed by so many in this small town of 30,000 people, continues to live deep in its consciousness.

Outside Artigas, the tragedy is barely remembered, and receives much less attention than the Andes accident. But for the Ferradás family, it was a double tragedy. Roberto Ferradás had often speculated what must have gone through his brother's mind in the moments before the Fairchild accident. As he made that final tight turn, taking the split-second decision to try to make the runway and save everyone rather than crash-land, he had the misfortune to find out.

Flight crew		Technical crew
Major Roberto Ferradás		Corporal Ricardo Masollo
Captain Néstor Pimienta		Airman 1st class Mario de los Angeles
Sublieutenant Daniel Marchesano		Airman 1st class Julio César Rodríguez

Passengers		
Heber Mila		Eduardo B. Fernández
Ana Diaz de Mila	Robert Chua	Sgt. Nery Pereira
Yonny Marcelo Mila	Crescêncio Chua Aguirre	Adan Jaques
Ana Claudia Mila Diaz	Eulinda Diaz de Chua	Cap. (ret.) Américo Cardozo
Olga Techera de Castro	Elvira Chua	Sonia R. Lima
María Janir Castro	Richard Chua	Claudia M. Lima
María Emilia Castro	Eduardo Chua	Renee Beatriz Lima
Floreal Ramos	Edison Prado	José E. Libindo
Pablo Ferreira Ramos	Blanca Ester Romero de Pio	Alba Graciela Libindo
Romilda Pio de Ramos	Irma F. Moreira de Ferreira	Ramón Rodríguez
Adriana Ramos	Juan Diego Ferreira	Esmeralda Diaz de Bicudo
Wilson Ramos	Jhony Da Silva	Loreley Marinela Bicudo
Elvira de Mello Meladett	Juan C. Moreno	Julián B. Arébalo

The 38 passengers and 6 crew members who died in the FAU 511 crash on 10th February 1978.

JORGE ALEJO 'ALEXIS' HOUNIE SÉRÉ
31-JAN-1952 — 13-OCT-1972

In November 1833, Charles Darwin, awaiting repairs to *The Beagle* in Montevideo, took the opportunity to make a two-week excursion to explore the lands to the west. Travelling by horseback, he and his guide planned a circular route, taking them up the River Plate to Colonia, then north up the Uruguay River to Mercedes, before heading south-east back to Montevideo. A week into the trip, they stopped for three days at the *estancia* of an Englishman on the *Arroyo Bequelo*, west of Mercedes. Darwin recorded in his diary:

> One morning I rode with my host to the Sierra del Pedro Flaco[1], about twenty miles up the Rio Negro. Nearly the whole country was covered with good though coarse grass, which was as high as a horse's belly; yet there were square leagues without a single head of cattle. The province of Banda Oriental, if well stocked, would support an astonishing number of animals.

Twenty-seven years later, a young man named Juan Hounie emigrated to Uruguay from the province of Béarn in south-west France. Coming from a family of shepherds, Juan continued that work in his adopted country, and within 30 years he was owner of some of those lands noted by Darwin. Juan initially concentrated on sheep farming, the export of wool to Britain providing an important source of income. But over time he turned his attention to cattle, taking advantage of the salting houses in nearby Mercedes, and the Liebig factory across the river in Fray Bentos. By the time Juan died in 1903, refrigeration plants had taken over from the salting houses, triggering further expansion of the beef industry.

The French connection continued when Juan's son Alejo married a Basque woman, Jeanne Bidegain, who even travelled back to France for the birth of their son Roberto – the father of Alexis Hounie. Consequently, French was often spoken in the Hounie household, especially when the parents didn't want the children to understand what they were saying. And although Alexis' parents gave their three children Spanish names, they were always known by their French equivalents: Juan Pedro as Jean Pierre, Clara as Claire, and Jorge Alejo as Alexis.

---

[1] Referring to the *Arroyo Perico Flaco*.

The children spent their childhood on the family *estancia*, named *La Sorpresa*, a ranch of around 3000 hectares. Roberto was an expert in the field of cattle breeding, and the *estancia* contained a stud farm. He had started with Shorthorn cattle, and later added Aberdeen Angus. In 1962, he and his family travelled all the way to Perth in Scotland to attend a cattle show, where he invested in more of the latter to improve his existing herd.

Fig. 137. *Estancia La Sorpresa.*

When the children reached school age, Roberto decided that their studies should take place in Montevideo, almost 300 km to the south-east. As a child, Roberto had been sent to a private school in Buenos Aires, in the days when there had been a good boat service down the Uruguay river, but to become fluent in English, he had had the opportunity to spend a year or so in Southampton, on the south coast of England. He wanted his children to learn English also, and the promise of the new bilingual Catholic *Stella Maris College* in Carrasco led Roberto to throw his support behind its founding.

The choice of school involved considerable reorganization. The family moved to an apartment in the centre of Montevideo, close to Plaza Libertad, where the ONDA buses would arrive from the interior of the country. Roberto would share the school run with two other parents, allowing him to work at the *estancia* for half the week if needed. Once the school moved to its new premises in the early sixties, the boys were able to take public transport, rising at 6:00 a.m. and always the first to arrive due to the inconvenient bus schedule.

In contrast to Jean Pierre and Claire, who were more intellectual in their interests, Alexis lived for sports – football, tennis, and above all, rugby. A natural sportsman, he played in the pivotal position of scrumhalf. When Alexis left *Stella Maris* in 1967, he went on to play with the *Old Christians*, becoming captain of *Shannon*, one of the two B teams, the other – *St Patrick's* – led by Coco Nicolich. The two boys also had their chosen careers in common, both studying veterinary science at the *Universidad de la República*, albeit a year apart. By 1970, Alexis had made the first team, helping the *Old Christians* to win their second national championship, playing alongside Panchito Abal, Nando Parrado, and Arturo Nogueira, under the captaincy of Marcelo Pérez del Castillo. Brother Thomas O'Connell, who arrived at the school only a few months before the accident, still remembered him almost fifty years later as "a live wire on the rugby field, but neat and tidy with not a hair out of place".

Always joking when he was with his friends, Alexis put on a more serious face at home, and didn't speak much with his brother or sister. He wasn't an avid reader, but when he started becoming interested in girls, he went to Claire for advice. He confided in her that he had no idea of how to speak to them, and asked her which books he should read to impress them. Claire's suggestions, such as *One Hundred Years of Solitude* by Gabriel García Marquez, had the desired effect, and he soon became very popular with the opposite sex.

Fig. 138. *Alexis and Coco Nicolich, captains of the two Old Christians B teams, with referee Bobby Jaugust.*

The Hounie family were close-knit and always went on holiday together, once to the United States, and a couple of times to Europe, at a time when it was unusual for Uruguayan families to travel so far afield. Roberto would say that it was better to travel as a whole family, because if the plane crashed, they would all die together. The last holiday they spent together was at Bariloche, in the Argentinian lake district. The five of them, along with Claire's fiancé, gathered there for the parents' twenty-fifth wedding anniversary in January 1972. Before the end of the year, Alexis would be dead.

Early on the morning of 12th October 1972, Alexis was picked up at the family apartment by Moncho Sabella, who, like Alexis, lived downtown. With Moncho's brother Mono driving, they also stopped to collect Panchito Abal before continuing to the airport. The flight was uneventful until the unexpected stop in Mendoza. There, Alexis joined a group of the younger boys, who got a free lift into town in a station wagon. After a big lunch at a restaurant owned by a Uruguayan expat, who plied them with food and wine, they booked into the *Hotel San Remo* on Godoy Cruz Avenue, the eight of them splitting up into pairs to share rooms. On one floor, Alexis with Rafael Echavarren, and Moncho Sabella with Bobby François. On another floor, Coco Nicolich with Diego Storm, and Roy Harley with Carlitos Páez. After a siesta to sleep off the wine, Alexis, Rafael, Moncho, and Bobby set out to do some sightseeing, taking a taxi to the top of the *Cerro de la Gloria*, the hill overlooking Mendoza, crowned with a monument commemorating the Army of the Andes.

Fig. 139. *Alexis front right in the 1971 Old Christians first team.*

On their return, they met up with the others from the hotel and together they strolled around the centre, taking in the sights, and enjoying the relaxed atmosphere of the city late into the evening. When some of the boys decided to go dancing, staying out until the early hours of the morning, Alexis, along with Bobby, Coco, and Diego, headed back to the hotel for an early night. A late start the next morning meant that the group didn't eat until 11:00 a.m.; their meal – the last before the accident – serving as both breakfast and lunch.

When they boarded the plane later that afternoon, Alexis sat towards the back, near many of the other rugby players. The boys were constantly changing seats during the flight, but when the turbulence started and they were asked to return to their seats and buckle their seat belts, Alexis found himself sitting next to Gastón Costemalle at the back left-hand side. When the right wing of the plane hit the mountain ridge, it tore off the roof on the side of the fuselage before severing the tail cone. Within moments, the force of the decompression catapulted the boys' seat out of the gaping hole at the back. An expedition several days later by Gustavo Zerbino, Daniel Maspons, and Numa Turcatti, found their bodies high up on the mountain, near the point of impact. The two were next to each other, still in their seats and face-down in the snow, with no visible sign of injury.

When news of the accident started to come through, Alexis' father and brother were at the *estancia*. They left immediately to join the rest of the family in Montevideo. Claire, who worked during the day, had been downtown attending night school, training to become a social worker. After class, she and a friend had bought pizza, and had sat chatting in the car on the Rambla, oblivious of the news coming from Chile. She only realized something was amiss on arriving home in the early hours of the morning, to find her fiancé Juan waiting for her. Her mother, who had been alone when she heard the news of the plane's disappearance, had been unable to reach Claire, and had called Juan in desperation. He had gone over immediately, to keep her company, as Roberto and Jean Pierre wouldn't arrive until the next day.

The family followed the news of the search, but from a distance. Living downtown meant that they had little contact with the daily gatherings of parents that were taking place in Carrasco. For the most part, Alexis' parents and siblings stayed at home, receiving friends and well-wishers who came to keep them company. Mrs Hounie, recognizing that the evening hours were a difficult time of the day, developed a daily ritual. The family would get together at 5:00 p.m. for tea and pastries, brought fresh to the house each day by a cousin. The hour together would help the family compose themselves, and prepare them to receive their visitors between 6:00 p.m. and 9:00 p.m.

The Hounie family had been convinced, from the very first moment, that Alexis was dead, and had already mourned his loss. So it was a shock when the news came that two survivors had appeared. Jean Pierre immediately flew out to Chile with some of the other relatives, and went to the house of Uruguayan chargé-d'affaires César Charlone, to try to find out what had happened. When he arrived, no-one yet knew who had survived, but it was at Charlone's house that Jean Pierre heard the list confirming Alexis' death. He returned home with the other bereaved relatives, and he and Claire both attended the press conference and the Mass at *Stella Maris College* once the survivors arrived back in Uruguay. Their parents preferred to stay at home, mourning in private, and, by January, the whole family had returned to the *estancia*.

Alexis's death had an immediate practical impact on Jean Pierre. He was already doing many of the more onerous management tasks at *La Sorpresa* because of the health of his father, who had suffered two heart attacks. But after the accident, his father asked him to take over the full management of the *estancia*, which had a workforce of around 20 people. In the time before the accident, Jean Pierre had harboured the hope that it would be Alexis, who, once qualified, would take over the management. He saw Alexis as more practical and better suited to running the *estancia*, and he himself had dreams of a more academic career. In the end, circumstances dictated that he wasn't even able to complete his agronomy studies in Paysandú.

Two of Alexis' possessions, retrieved by Gustavo Zerbino from Alexis' body high on the mountain, eventually made their way back to the family: a jacket and a Rolex watch. Jean Pierre had an identical jacket and watch, bought on a family trip to Europe. The watches were passed down through the family to the next generation, to Claire's sons. Over the years since, there has been very little contact between the family and the survivors. The ties with the Carrasco families were not so strong from the beginning, and subsequently their lives were centred around the *estancia*, away from Montevideo.

The family have always taken the straightforward view that this was just a tragic accident of the sort that can happen to any family, such as a loved one dying in a car crash, and they accepted this destiny and didn't look beyond it. They didn't follow the survivors, or read any books about the tragedy, or watch the movies. Alexis' mother simply remembered how excited he had been to go to Chile, how she had packed his suitcase, and the look of happiness on his face the last time she had seen him. And she took some solace in the fact that he must have died immediately, or slipped away in the cold of the first night.

Fig. 140. *Alexis age 18.*

GUIDO MAGRI
20-FEB-1949 — 13-OCT-1972

On 24th September 1967, two young rugby players sat chatting in a hotel lounge in San Isidro, an affluent suburb of Buenos Aires. The occasion was the Fifth South America Rugby Union Championship. Ezequiel 'Chelin' Bolumburu, a Chilean whose home club was the *Grange Old Boys*, had made his national debut earlier that day, as Chile had edged close rivals Uruguay – *Los Teros* – in the opening game. The youngest player in the tournament, Chelin was discussing tactics with *Old Christian* Guido Magri, who was

still waiting for the chance to represent his country. The two boys were exchanging views on how to overcome the physically dominant Argentinians.

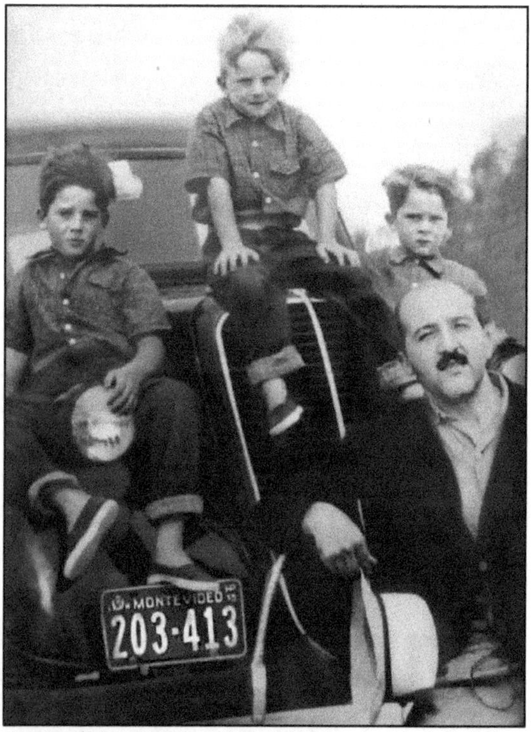

The conversation must have inspired Guido because, making his own debut three days later, he scored Uruguay's only try in an entertaining loss to Argentina played in thick mud. Chelin and Guido parted as friends, with the casual promise of keeping in touch and arranging a friendly match between their respective clubs. It was a promise that would have repercussions across the decades, leading to the fateful flight five years later, in which Guido died; and emerging out of that tragedy, an unbreakable bond between the two clubs celebrated by the

Fig. 141. *Aldo, Guido, and Gastón Magri with their father in front of the family Fordson, prior to a camping trip.*

annual *Copa de la Amistad (Friendship Cup)*, which continues to this day and has seen its own dramatic events.

Guido's leading role in the *Old Christians*, and in building the relationship with the *Grange Old Boys*, make him a major figure in the Andes story, even though he tragically died in the first few moments of the accident. He was the middle of five children, with twins Silvana and Aldo older than him, and Gastón and Vera coming after him. Their father. Ricardo Magri, was a doctor and a biology teacher, but of the boys, only Gastón followed in his father's profession. Aldo and Guido preferred life on the farm; a passion that came from the maternal side of the family. Their grandfather had three farms: an *estancia* in Tacuarembó (a department far north of Montevideo), one in Colonia, and a small farm in San José, quite close to Montevideo. It was the latter that had passed down to the family through their mother, Susana Gelsi. There was already a house on the farm, and they added a dairy, and concentrated their efforts on pig- and cattle-farming. At the time of the accident, Aldo was already working at the farm full-time, and Guido was all set to join his brother, once he'd finished his agronomy studies at Paysandú.

Fig. 142. *Guido (left) and brother Gastón.*

The Magri family holidays would usually be to far afield in places such as Rio, or Bariloche – the lake district of Argentina. But often the father and the boys would pack up their gear into their old Fordson E83W pickup, and head off to go camping. Either to the Atlantic coast, or to their grandfather's farm in Colonia, where they would ride horses, or help with the cattle and the sheep. They would invariably be joined by their Gelsi cousins – Adolfo, Pablo, and Eduardo – sons of Susana's brother.

The story of the three Gelsi boys is woven through the Andes tragedy. All of them, as *Stella Maris* pupils, had friends and classmates who were on the plane. The eldest, Adolfo, was an *Old Christians* club board member at the time of the accident, and part of the committee that managed the story and the reception of the survivors; he would also tragically die in the Andes, in a car accident three years later. The middle cousin, Pablo, having just graduated as a psychologist, his English-speaking skills honed from a year at Princeton, was chosen to be the interpreter for the interviews of the survivors conducted by author Piers Paul Read. And the youngest, Eduardo, died along with two friends – including Gastón Costemalle's brother Daniel – in a canoe accident off Carrasco beach, three years before the Andes accident; a harbinger of the later tragedy.

Guido was in the class of '65 at *Stella Maris College*, entering the school in 1956, a year after it opened. As Guido progressed through the school, he grew to love the game of rugby, embracing it with the tenacity and passion he gave to all his endeavours, hard work and determination paving the road to success. Strong, of medium height, cheerful, living life to the full, and always joking, he became a great friend of his long-term classmate and rugby teammate Nando Parrado. Nando, with his height and strength, played second row in the scrum, whereas Guido, with his speed and ball-handling skills, played as scrum-half, the crucial link between the forwards and backs.

On leaving *Stella Maris*, Guido's studies turned to agronomy, with a view to helping run the family farm, but he continued playing rugby with the *Old Christians*. Along with Marcelo Pérez del Castillo and Gastón Costemalle, he took a leading role in guiding the fledgling club to the first division in 1966, and he captained the team that won Uruguayan championship in 1968, the first of many titles for the club.

Fig. 143. *Guido releasing the ball from the scrum, 1967.*

Then came the 1967 South America cup, in which Guido and Gastón made their national debuts. True to their word, Guido and Chelin kept in touch after their chat in San Isidro, and met again in 1969, when Chile hosted the South America cup. As a result of their friendship, the *Old Christians*, captained by Guido, travelled to Chile in 1971 to play a game with the *Grange Old Boys*, and with a Chilean national selection.

By this time, Guido had other reasons to travel to Santiago. He had fallen in love with a Chilean girl, Angeles Mardones. She, along with the rest of her family, had spent many years in Uruguay in the sixties, as a result of her father's posting as a World Health Organization expert. It was Guido's friendship with her brother José Luis – a former classmate – which had brought him to the Mardones home in Santiago initially, but by 1969, Guido was looking for every opportunity to spend time with Angeles. On one occasion, during a one-month road trip to Peru, Ecuador, and Bolivia with close friends Eduardo 'Mincho' Deal and Alberto 'El Chileno' Rodríguez, Guido contrived a detour to Chile just so that he could see her. And Angeles would reciprocate, travelling to Uruguay as often as she could, spending time with Guido at the farm or the beach, and taking the opportunity to meet up with her old school friends.

The success of the 1971 rugby trip spawned plans for a repeat visit in October 1972, this time organized and captained by Marcelo. Guido and Angeles' wedding had been set for 14th December 1972, and there were still arrangements to be made, but Guido had not planned to go on the October trip. By then, he had stopped playing for the *Old Christians Club* because he was spending the year in Paysandú, completing his agricultural degree. He could ill-afford to take time off from his studies, but a strike at the college made him reconsider. He and 'El Chileno', who was also studying in Paysandú, returned to Montevideo, and stopped by Marcelo's house to see if there were any seats available. There were still a couple left, and Guido snapped one of them up. 'El Chileno', who would be attending the wedding a couple of months later, decided to forgo the October trip, but lent Guido the keys to his apartment in Santiago, a place where Guido had often stayed during his previous visits to see Angeles.

Fig. 144. *Angeles Mardones and Guido Magri at Carrasco Airport 1971.*

Angeles only learnt that Guido would be coming, shortly before the plane left Montevideo, but during the stopover in Mendoza, Guido was able to telephone her, and they had a long chat, reflecting on the short distance – less than 200 km – which now separated them. Guido, in his last-minute haste, was short of cash, and hotels in Mendoza were not cheap. He booked into one, but soon switched, after Gustavo Zerbino told him of the much cheaper place they had found; a soon-to-open *pensión* – *La Casa del Gobernador* – which was a third of the price of the standard hotels. A photograph taken on the streets of Mendoza, standing with friends at the corner of Avenida San Martín and Gutiérrez street on the morning of 13th October is the only other record of Guido's time in Mendoza. Coincidentally, Guido's aunt and uncle – the parents of the Gelsi cousins – were attending a conference there, and had bumped into some of the boys on the street, although there is no record that Guido met up with them.

On the afternoon of 13th October, Guido boarded the plane and sat down in the last-row-but-one of the Fairchild, in front of the law students, but near to many of the rugby players. The last recorded image we have of Guido, before the fasten-seatbelt sign caused everyone to sit down, is of him reading a popular Argentinian comic magazine, *Patoruzú*. A few minutes later, when the plane hit the mountain, severing the tail, Guido was sucked out into the frigid air, along with teammates Alexis Hounie and Gastón Costemalle, and two of the crew. In an expedition a few days later, Gustavo Zerbino, Numa Turcatti, and Daniel Maspons found their bodies on the slope near the impact point, with no visible signs of injury.

Meanwhile, at *Los Cerrillos* airport in Santiago, a small group had gathered to greet the Uruguayans. Angeles arrived with Chelin, and with Tito Regules, who had missed the chartered flight and had travelled instead on a commercial flight the previous day. The atmosphere was relaxed. Chelin and Tito would joke with Angeles whenever a plane appeared, telling her, "Look – there's Guido – waving to you from the third window." Time passed, and there was still no news of the flight. Eventually César Charlone, the Uruguayan chargé-d'affaires in Chile appeared, with his wife Belela. The Charlone family, although stationed in Santiago, were from the same community as the passengers, and well known to the families of Carrasco; one of the sons – César (now a famous cinematographer) – had been a *Stella Maris* classmate of Guido and of Angeles' brother José Luis, and the latter was now engaged to one of Charlone's daughters.

While her husband went to the control tower, Belela walked straight over to Angeles and hugged her, telling her the desperate news: "The plane is lost." When Angeles heard the news, she felt the blood drain from her, and she was left in shock. Later, she spoke by telephone to Guido's mother, and wanting to give her a little bit of hope, told her that the boys had landed in a small town and were safe, sure that they would eventually appear. Unfortunately, this private conversation gave rise to a rumour which rapidly spread amongst some of the parents, temporarily raising hopes. It was quickly scotched, however, first by César Charlone, and later by Rafael Ponce de León, who spoke directly to Angeles, a recording of their conversation broadcast on Radio Monte Carlo throughout the night of the 13th.

Once it was clear that the plane had been lost, the Magri parents immediately accepted that their son had died – that there could be no chance of surviving a plane crash in the Andes – and they were not among the families that took part in the search. Angeles still clung on to the hope that they might be found – that no news meant that there was still a chance.

When news started to filter through on 21st December of a note thrown across a mountain torrent to a cattle drover, by two boys claiming to be from the Uruguayan plane, Angeles, with her parents and brother Ricardo, immediately left for San Fernando, where the note was being examined by the authorities. They went directly to the town hall, where the quartermaster showed them the letter. Angeles had been convinced that it would be Guido's handwriting that she would see on the note, and it came as a big blow when it wasn't. The four of them stayed in San Fernando that night to await the arrival of the survivors the next day, which Angeles later recalled:

> I arrived at the hospital and several people were already hospitalised. I remember seeing Carlitos, Nando, and then Eduardo Strauch who was very burnt and skinny. Ricardo, my brother, was with him. When I came in, he said to me on the verge of tears, "Flaquita, I don't want to make anyone suffer". And then he spoke to me about Guido.

Back in Montevideo, Guido's brother Aldo was at the farm in San José, preparing the pork for Christmas, when the list of survivors was read out on the radio on 22nd December. He was working with his friends 'El Chileno' Rodríguez and 'Mincho' Deal. In his heart, Aldo already felt that Guido must have died, because he knew that his brother would have been the one to walk out with his friend Nando, had he been alive. Bracing himself for the worst, Aldo silently counted in his head as the list was read out. When the sixteenth and final name was announced, Aldo showed no outward emotion and just continued working. But he made a promise to himself that there would always be a Magri in the *Old Christians*. He kept his word, helping the club survive and grow after the tragedy, and acting as first team coach from 1974 to 1989. Today, there is a plaque in honour of Aldo in front of the main *Old Christians* rugby pitch for his services to the club.

Fig. 145. *Aldo Magri, Oct 2019, by the plaque honouring his contributions to the club. The field and trees behind are testament to his hard work.*

Sometime after the accident, Adolfo Gelsi started going out with Angeles. Sensitive to Aldo's feelings, and not wanting to appear to supplant Guido, Adolfo turned up at his cousin's farm one day to ask his permission to marry Angeles. Aldo told him that he didn't need to ask, and that of course he gave his permission. The marriage took place on 2nd September 1974 in Montevideo. By the end of 1975, their first child had arrived, and Adolfo had rented offices near those of his father, planning to work with him as a lawyer. But tragedy was to strike again in the Andes.

In April 1976, Adolfo and Angeles made plans to travel to Chile, to show the baby to Angeles' family. Adolfo, not keen to cross the Andes by plane, asked his good friend Ricardo, Angeles' brother, to come and meet them in Mendoza, and they would drive across the *cordillera*. Route 60 from the top of the *Cristo Redentor* pass towards Los Andes in Chile, was, and still is, a treacherous road to navigate, especially in winter conditions. Just below *El Portillo* ski resort, there are twenty-nine tight switchbacks, and at the very first of these – curve 29 – the car came off the road, ending up 100 metres below. Ricardo and Adolfo, who were in the front, died immediately. Holding her baby, Angeles, who was sitting in the back with one of her brothers, was thrown out of the car on impact. Tragically, her baby died, but Angeles and her brother survived, and, although badly injured, the latter managed to make his way to the road and alert the emergency services.

Angeles, who must have thought that her life was doomed after these two Andean tragedies, did eventually recover, marrying again and starting a family. She had a career at the Craighouse school in Santiago, where she cofounded and ran the playgroup for three- to four-year-olds. She is still in close contact with her former school friends in Montevideo, but doesn't like to talk about the Andes, which have been so cruel to her. These days, her life revolves around her many grandchildren.

The Magri family have always taken a philosophical view of the Andes accident. They have never asked the survivors any details about what occurred on the mountain – they felt that this was something private to the sixteen. They have also not talked publicly about the tragedy, feeling that it was a story about the survivors; but their involvement with the *Old Christians Club* has enabled them to maintain close ties with other families caught up in the tragedy. Guido's mother Susana was one of the founding mothers, in August 1973, of the *Biblioteca Nuestros Hijos*; and the wife of Guido's brother Gastón, also Susana, continues the work today.

FELIPE 'PHILLIP' HORACIO MAQUIRRIAIN
31-JUL-1950 — D. 13-OCT-1972

When the Andes accident occurred, Felipe (Phillip at home) was 22 years old. He was in his third year in the School of Economics at the *Universidad de la República*, together with Pedro Algorta and Arturo Nogueira. The three of them had been classmates at *Stella Maris College* some ten years before, and although their lives had taken different paths since then, it was a natural and amicable reunion when they formed a study group, meeting at each other's homes to escape the disruption of the student unrest downtown.

Arturo was an important member of the *Old Christians* first fifteen, and it was he who suggested that Phillip and Pedro join him on the rugby team's trip to Chile. The ticket on the chartered Air Force plane would be inexpensive, provided they could gather together sufficient numbers of passengers. With the prospect of a welcome break from their studies over the extended weekend, and the excitement of a trip away from home with friends and peers, Phillip and Pedro decided to sign up.

The decision, made so easily, and without any premonition of disaster, would have very different consequences for the three friends. Pedro would return after seventy-two days on the mountain. Arturo would suffer for thirty-three days before dying in Pedro's arms. And Phillip, sitting next to Pedro as the plane hit the mountain, would die within a few hours, comforted at the end by another former classmate, Enrique Platero.

Phillip, born on the 31st July 1950, was the eldest of four siblings. He was followed by Melisa (1951), Analía (1953), and Sandra (1956). His father, Felipe Maquirriain, was Argentinian, and married to Selva Ibarburu, a Uruguayan. Starting their married life in Buenos Aires, where Phillip and Melisa were born, they moved to Montevideo in 1953, where Mr Maquirriain was in the process of establishing a new business with a North American partner. For a while, he found himself separated from his family who were unavoidably stuck in Buenos Aires, after Argentine president Juan Domingo Perón chose to close the borders between Argentina and Uruguay. Desperate to reunite the family, Selva bought plane tickets for a flight to Rio de Janeiro, with a stopover in Montevideo. Travelling with her two children, and pregnant with a third, 27-year-old Selva was allowed to disembark in her home country, and, reunited once more, the family embarked on their new life in Uruguay.

Mr Maquirriain was a great admirer of the USA. Having lost his father as a three-year-old, he had spent much of his childhood and adolescence living with his widowed mother and brother in Oklahoma, and he loved the enterprise and the can-do attitude of the people there. Returning with his mother to Buenos Aires in his late teens, he embarked on his working life, his impeccable English a valuable asset in the job market. After a stint in the banking industry, he took a position at *Pan Am*; a job which he enjoyed immensely, and had no thoughts of leaving, until a customer who owned a large Buenos Aires dry-cleaning operation proposed a business opportunity. He offered Maquirriain several times his *Pan Am* salary to expand the business – *Tintorería Sandoz* – across the River Plate to Montevideo. The offer was too compelling to refuse, and Felipe took on the challenge, and became an entrepreneur.

Selva Ibarburu was a country girl from Soriano, a department in the interior of Uruguay, famed for its grazing land. Daughter of rancher, she was the youngest of three children. Growing up on an *estancia*, in the embrace of a loving and supportive family, made for a carefree upbringing. Once the three siblings were of school age, the family settled in the small nearby town of Mercedes, the capital of Soriano, where life was equally idyllic, though with the added opportunity to expand their circle of friends. Alongside their academic studies, music became a big part of family life, with the children studying piano throughout their school years, and Selva's sister going on to achieve considerable success as a concert pianist. When the time came for university, the three siblings moved to Montevideo, the challenge of leaving friends and home and adapting to life in the big city made easier by the presence of a large extended family. Both the Ibarburu on their father's side and the Samacoitz on their mother's side came from sizeable Basque families, who had stuck together in the new world, bound by shared principles of honour, honesty, and hard work.

Mr Maquirriain also had Basque ancestry, so when he and Selva met at a summer resort in Uruguay, falling in love at first sight, their common heritage only served to strengthen their bond, and ease the passage to their marriage the following year. Already strong and self-motivated as individuals, together they made a formidable team, and the challenge of moving the family to Montevideo energized them, as they sought to establish themselves financially and socially in their new environment.

Mr Maquirriain had been part of the Methodist Church in Buenos Aires; an Anglo-Argentine community, so it was natural to move close to a similar community in Montevideo, and the family initially rented a house near the *San Pablo* Methodist church and its associated school, the *Crandon Institute*. The location had the added benefit of being just fifteen minutes away from the family business. The three older children all started their schooling at the *Crandon*, but, by the end of the decade, Mr Maquirriain, wanting his children to become fully bilingual, moved them to the recently opened *Uruguayan-American* school, where they would be taught directly by US teachers, alongside US pupils. Although further from home, the school was, at the time, directly adjacent to Mr Maquirriain's second home

– the prestigious *Club de Golf del Uruguay* in Punta Carretas. The children rapidly became fluent in English, and Phillip stayed on there, after completing his six years of primary education. All four children were at the school when JFK was shot; a moment which, amplified by their environment, lived long in their memories.

Fig. 146. *The house on Mar Antartico,*
Plaza Virgilio across the street, and a sunset viewed from the balcony.

As the parents sought to accommodate their growing family, they rented a succession of houses in different districts, until, in 1961, they bought their dream house. It was in *Punta Gorda*, an attractive *barrio*, protruding into the estuary like the prow of a ship. Their house was in prime position, at the apex of the neighbourhood, across the street from a sloped, tree-lined park, *Plaza Virgilio*. Its uninterrupted views over the sea were enriched by spectacular sunrises and sunsets. They would live there for 23 years. The spacious and welcoming home, so emblematic of the family, became a natural meeting place for the children's circle of friends.

By then, Phillip was eleven, and although he had excelled in his first year of secondary school at the *Uruguayan-American*, achieving the top student award, he had few Uruguayan classmates, and his parents decided to seek out a bilingual school closer to their new home. They opted for the boys-only *Stella Maris College* in Carrasco, run by the Irish Christian Brothers, which also had high standards of English teaching. The three girls

went to the rival *British School*, which was equally blessed with a strong academic curriculum, and an extensive program of sports and other activities.

The strong emphasis that *Stella Maris* placed on rugby didn't appeal to Phillip, who was not a keen sportsman, and had probably never seen a rugby ball in his life when he entered the school. Nevertheless, like every other boy at the college, he learnt the game under the

Fig. 147. *The Maquirriain children in the garden, at the end of a school day at the Uruguay-American school.*

tutelage of the Christian Brothers, and it must have made an impression, because one night whilst sleepwalking, he attempted to rugby-tackle his mother. Whereas rugby was an unavoidable part of school life, he willingly took to golf. Following in his father's footsteps, he would often be found on the golf course at the weekends, and achieved some success, winning one 72-hole tournament by eleven shots in his handicap category.

Phillip entered the school in 1964, a member of the class of '66, which included Arturo and Pedro, with whom he would renew a

Fig. 148. *Phillip (right) with friend and Stella Maris classmate Tomás Linn, and Klaus the dog.*

friendship some years later. It was difficult to integrate into a new environment, where existing friendships stretched back seven years to the beginning of primary school, but he soon formed a close friendship with a boy who lived nearby, Tomás Linn, with whom he shared much in common. Both of them intellectual, analytic, and well-read, they would spend hours at each other's houses, talking about politics and debating the significant issues of the day. Tomás would go on to become a noted journalist and writer, a deep thinker, and a political voice in Uruguay.

Outside school, Phillip made another lifelong friend: Antonio Dieste, the fourth of eleven children of internationally-renowned architect and engineer, Eladio Dieste, who lived close by, on the same street. Phillip found a kindred spirit in Antonio, whose Roman Catholic family's principles and intellect mirrored those of his own. He considered Antonio the brother he never had, and they would head off together in the summer, to the Atlantic coast, sometimes by car, sometimes hitchhiking. Those carefree days camping with the Dieste family in La Pedrera were amongst the happiest of his life.

Fig. 149. *Eladio Dieste's Church of Atlántida, a UNESCO World Heritage site.*

After leaving *Stella Maris*, Phillip finished his secondary education in the *Lycée Français*, near to the university. The bus journey downtown added an hour each way to his day, but he relished the diversity of his new environment: students from different social, political, and religious backgrounds; long coffee shop discussions; openness to fresh ideas, all in a rich cultural milieu near the university. This varied upbringing, and the example of his father – a self-made man who had lived and travelled abroad – encouraged Phillip to set high standards for himself. But any hard ambition was tempered by the warmth of the family home where he was doted on by the women of the house. Selva was a woman who was eternally positive, and it was from her that Phillip got his amiable and empathetic nature. Any favouritism she showed towards her son was overlooked by his three young sisters, on whom Phillip lavished his affection and attention – although perhaps teaching 12-year-old Sandra to drive was a step too far. It was a home life to be envied, and it was little surprise that Phillip developed a stable and relaxed temperament.

Fig. 150. *The Maquirriain family at home. Phillip 18, Melisa 17, Analía 15, Sandra 12.*

A voracious reader, Phillip would often have two books on the go, one placed over the other, equally at ease reading in English, Spanish or occasionally French. His wide exposure to different ideas and cultures led him to become the family's encyclopaedia; a role he relished, although he would always share his knowledge in an engaging manner – unassuming rather than dogmatic.

But his main passion was drawing, and his sketchbook and graphite pencil were always at hand. He had been very struck by a film about Toulouse Lautrec, showing the artist frenetically sketching on paper napkins in the dance halls of Paris. An adept cartoonist, Phillip would use rapid, thick strokes to quickly capture a scene, often to humorous effect. On 13th October, as the boys were waiting to board their ill-fated flight in Mendoza, Phillip spotted a plump lady, eccentrically dressed in a carnival-like manner, with a voluminous skirt, multi-coloured stockings, and a small hat. She was a perfect subject for one of his caricatures. Seeing how accurately Phillip had portrayed the lady, Gustavo Zerbino couldn't resist showing it to her. She was delighted, and even more so when Gustavo presented it to her, and she insisted on a photo with the boys.

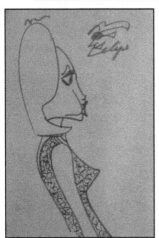

Fig. 151. *A few of Phillip's rapid sketches.*

In those days, there were limited career paths for an artist or graphic designer, and Phillip took the practical decision to study accounting at university rather than art, which was his passion. He joined the Faculty of Economics at the *Universidad de la República* in 1969, his entry allowing him to get an exemption from Argentinian military service. In the first couple of years, he hung out with a group of Roman Catholic students, and it was amongst this circle of friends that he met his future *novia*, Mercedes. They started studying together, and she became a regular visitor to the Maquirriain home, treated by everyone as one of the family. Her parents lived permanently at their ranch, located in Tacuarembó, several hundred kilometres north of Montevideo, so she lived by herself in an apartment in Pocitos, and relished the visits to her second family.

By the third year of university, Phillip had started studying regularly with Pedro and Arturo. Phillip hadn't known Arturo so well at *The Christian*, but they immediately took to each other, sharing a mutual respect and admiration. The three would often meet at Phillip's home in Punta Gorda, away from the unrest and the confrontations between students and police that were happening downtown. Phillip's sister Sandra, 16 at the time, remembers those study sessions; Pedro quiet and well-mannered, Arturo warm and brotherly. They would break to have tea with Selva, who took great pleasure in their company and conversation.

The three students, all independent thinkers, got on well, despite differences in political views. The revolutionary movements that were sweeping throughout Latin America obliged students to take a stance at a time of heightened political awareness. Some held communist views, pointing to Cuba, China, or the Soviet Union; others favoured more direct action and joined the Tupamaro guerrillas; a few became Catholic priests, and many, particularly amongst the Carrasco families, were inspired by the charismatic leadership of Wilson Ferreira Aldunate, an uncle of Marcelo Pérez del Castillo and head of the Liberal faction of the *Blancos*. In the Economics Faculty, almost everyone leaned strongly to the left. Pedro actively worked for the *Frente Amplio* – the broad alliance of leftist parties – in the 1971 elections. Arturo, too, had socialist views, although he remained unaligned to any faction, speaking out against the violence that was being espoused by some students. Almost alone amongst his faculty colleagues, Phillip resisted these ideological pressures, keeping an open mind, although respecting the arguments of his peers. His willingness to stand up for his own opinion was illustrated at an early age. When he had first arrived from Buenos Aires, aged four, a neighbourhood kid had asked him: "Which do you like best – Peñarol or Nacional?" Believing that they were talking about ice-cream flavours rather than the rivalry between the two top Uruguayan football teams, Phillip answered, "I like strawberry!"

It was inevitable that Phillip would hear about the trip to Chile, given his regular contact with Arturo, who, like all the passengers, was tasked with helping to fill the plane. His parents were not keen on the idea of him going to Chile, but Phillip, having never been on a long trip before, felt it would be a good opportunity to experience a different culture. There was a scare the month before departure, when his sister

Sandra's school trip to Córdoba in Argentina had almost gone tragically wrong. The bus driver had made a misjudgement, attempting to cross a bridge that was partly submerged by an overflowing river. With the water deeper than anticipated, the bus had started floating and sinking. Fortunately, it had stayed upright, and with the help of the teachers, the students had been able to escape through the emergency windows to the roof, and await rescue. Everyone back home was shocked; especially Phillip, who was dismayed at the thought of almost losing his kid sister.

However, the scare didn't dissuade him from going ahead with his plans for Chile. He wrote to his sister Analía, who was in Europe, of his excitement about the upcoming trip; about what an adventure it would be, and how much he was looking forward to the freedom of a trip with his peers. In the days leading up to departure, he and Pedro turned up at rugby practice a couple of times to make themselves known to the rest of the passengers, as neither of them played the game anymore.

Mr Maquirriain and Phillip arose at the crack of dawn on the morning of 12th October, unaware that outside the house Sandra was just returning from a night out dancing with her friends at the *Ton Ton* nightclub. Seeing the light on in her parents' bathroom, and

Fig. 152. *Phillip Maquirriain.*

scared that her father would be angry at her for coming home so late, she crept silently upstairs and slipped into bed, missing a last opportunity to hug her brother goodbye.

Phillip and his father left at 6:00 a.m., stopping fifteen minutes later at Carlos Sáez street in the heart of Carrasco to pick up Pedro from his uncle's house, and arriving at the airport by 6:30 a.m., one-and-a-half hours before the plane was due to depart. With plenty of time to spare, they went upstairs to the airport restaurant for a leisurely breakfast. Afterwards, they chatted to some of the boys who had started to gather in the crowded terminal, including Rafael Echavarren, conspicuous in his distinctive red jacket, whom they knew because he lived in the same apartment building as Mercedes.

While Phillip went off to telephone his *novia* for a last goodbye, Mr Maquirriain approached the TAMU counter to enquire as to who would pilot the *Old Christians* flight. His reluctance for his son to travel was in part based on the fact that it was an Air Force flight rather than a commercial one. But he was reassured when they told him that the pilot was Julio Ferradás; one of the best and most experienced in the FAU.

Phillip and Pedro sat next to each other on the flight, and stayed together during the stopover in Mendoza. They shared a room with their former classmate Enrique Platero, at the *Hotel Horizonte* on Gutiérrez street, 50 metres from *Plaza Chile*. Arturo stayed at the same hotel, sharing with Carlos Valeta and Antonio Vizintín. The next morning, Phillip and Pedro took the opportunity to visit the faculty of Economic Sciences at the local university. Arriving at around 11:00 a.m., they were greeted by a Professor Mora, who showed them around before driving them to the airport.

When they finally boarded, Pedro and Phillip sat together again, making the ill-fated decision to sit on the right-hand side. Across the aisle sat Coche Inciarte, who, although not blood-related to Pedro, shared an uncle in common with him. The flight south was uneventful. At one point, Pedro pointed out to Phillip the salt flats below, but he has no other memories of the flight, having suffered amnesia after being severely concussed in the accident. Phillip fared much worse, sustaining both external and internal injuries that caused blood to flow from his mouth. Prioritizing the injuries of the various passengers, the 'doctors' – Roberto Canessa and Gustavo Zerbino – felt that there was little they could do for Phillip in the immediate aftermath of the accident. It was not possible to free him from the wreckage in the limited daylight that remained, and it was left to Enrique Platero – who had shared a room with Phillip the previous night, and who had his own frightening injury – to care for him in his last hours. Largely unconscious, Phillip died sometime in the night, and his body was carried outside the next morning.

Back in Montevideo, Mr Maquirriain was attending a board meeting at the *Club de Golf del Uruguay*, where he was the treasurer. It had been a tough year for the club. In the early hours of 22nd December 1971, a group of five Tupamaro guerrillas had burst into the clubhouse, overpowering the night watchman. They had dowsed everything with fuel and set fire to the premises before making a rapid getaway. The action was part of an ongoing campaign against the 'oligarchy'. The fire destroyed almost all the facilities on the upper floor of the building – the dining room, the bar, the reading room and library, the kitchen, the boardroom, and the billiard room, along with many of the club's memorabilia from past Uruguayan champions. How to finance the rebuilding had become a major preoccupation for Mr Maquirriain, and with damages estimated at around $70,000, he was instrumental in encouraging the members to become life partners to help meet the cost.

The board meeting on 13th October was about the upcoming biennial World Amateur Team Championship – the 1972 *Eisenhower Trophy*. The club, taking advantage of it being hosted in nearby Buenos Aires, was entering a four-man team to represent Uruguay. The meeting was interrupted by an urgent call for Mr Maquirriain, alerting him to news of the accident. Excusing himself to his fellow board members, he set about finding out more, first calling the Air Force where he drew a blank, and then the *Hotel Kent* in Santiago, where some of the boys had planned to stay. There, he got through to Bobby Jaugust, who had travelled by commercial flight. The conversation was brief:

"Do you know what's happened to the Rugby Team?"
      "They're here, of course."
"Are you sure?"
      "I'll find out and call you back."

Mr Maquirriain didn't hear back from Bobby, and in the absence of any definitive information, most people assumed that it was the Fairchild returning from Chile, after dropping off its passengers in Santiago. Later, when the rumour went around that the boys had landed safely in Curicó, he was invited to celebrate at the house of a friend, the father of *Old Christians* president Daniel Juan. But the rumour was soon scotched, and when confirmation came through that it was, in fact, the boys' plane, no-one in the Maquirriain family had any hope that there would be survivors. Having had a recent operation on his leg, Mr Maquirriain didn't travel to Chile to take part in the parents' search efforts, instead opting to contribute money, and attending the meeting between the parents and FAU after the search had been called off.

When news of survivors hit the news channels two-and-a-half months later, it was Analía – recently back from Europe – who went to Ponce de León's house to hear the list, and who returned home with the sad news. The family suffered Phillip's loss for a second time, but unlike many families, they had never held out any hope that Phillip might be still alive. And despite the tragedy of losing him, they were thankful at least for the return of the survivors, who were able to tell them about what had happened to Phillip, and to return his personal belongings.

Mercedes suggested to Sandra that the two of them should visit one of the survivors to find out more. She had been like an older sister to Sandra during the ordeal, and the friendship, made stronger by the shared loss, would continue to stand the test of time, lasting until her death in 2019. Such was Mercedes' closeness to the family, that when she started going steady with another boy five years after losing Phillip, she introduced her new *novio* to them before she brought him to meet her own parents.

There were two survivors – Nando Parrado and Coche Inciarte – who lived close by in Punta Gorda. Nando was already a celebrity, his house packed with journalists and friends, so Mercedes and Sandra went to Coche's house. There they were received with great warmth by Coche's mother, who led them through the house to her son. They were shocked by what they saw. Emaciated, with deep-set eyes, and a faraway expression on his face, Coche nonetheless greeted them with affection. He told them what he could about Phillip, how he had died soon after the accident, and about the great respect the survivors had accorded those who had died at the beginning. He described the scene after the crash; how six bodies had been laid next to the plane, and how the survivors had given them a Christian burial, and had gathered around them to pray. The appearance of that exact scene in the film *ALIVE*, twenty years, later gave great comfort to the family.

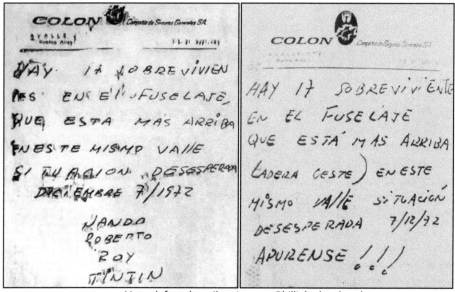

Fig. 153. *Notes left at the tail, written on Phillip's sketchpad.*

The family got another reminder of Phillip at the end of March 1973. The parents of Rafael Echavarren and Coco Nicolich, in their trip to the mountain to repatriate Rafael's body, had found two notes left at the tail, both with the same plea: that there were seventeen survivors further up the valley and that their situation was desperate. The notes had been left by the four boys after their unsuccessful expedition to the tail to hook up the plane's radio to the batteries. When one of the notes appeared in the newspapers, the letterhead, that of Buenos Aires based insurance company *COLON*, was immediately recognized by the daughter of the owner. Phillip, a friend of the family, had been to visit their home a few days before the trip. He had done some sketches for them on a company notepad, which he had then taken back with him, planning to use it in Chile. The notes are not as well-known as the one thrown over the river to Sergio Catalán, but had the search planes spotted the cross at the tail, they might have been of vital importance.

Fig. 154. *A dinner with other members of the Biblioteca 'family'.*
Ana María Vázquez, Sarita Echavarren, Mr and Mrs Valeta, and Mr and Mrs Maquirriain.

Mr Maquirriain told the family that if Phillip had come back, then he would have been no different from all the other survivors. As his son hadn't returned, Mr Maquirriain made it clear that he didn't want a word spoken about the accident in their home. It was Selva who held the family together during the long healing process, and helped them to smile again, although it would be another twenty years before grief finally turned to acceptance. As with all the survivors and non-survivors, life had to continue under the long shadow of the accident. The family never imagined that the story would receive such prolonged, worldwide attention, unabated fifty years later. The loss of Phillip brought the family closer together over the following years, although there would be another loss twelve years later, when Phillip's sister Melisa died of cancer.

Selva's initiative in bringing the bereaved mothers together to share their grief and look to the future not only brought about the *Biblioteca Nuestros Hijos*, but also fostered a close and supportive circle of friends who would get together socially, their lives intertwined and bound by the shared tragedy.

Fifty years after the accident, with the library now under the stewardship of the sisters. Sandra and Analía have both served on the board of directors, the latter joining after the death in May 2020 of Selva, one of the longest-lived of the mothers. In recent years, as the pain of the tragedy recedes into the past, there has been more communication between the families on the two sides of the divide, with some of the survivors actively working to promote the library. Gustavo Zerbino has been particularly generous with his time and support, donating the proceeds of conferences given entirely on the library's behalf.

Back in December 1972, it was Gustavo who brought Phillip's wallet back from the mountain, and presented it to the family. After Selva died, it was another survivor, Álvaro Mangino, who brought a more evocative keepsake to Sandra – the frames of Phillip's glasses, which had been found on an expedition to the mountain a few years before.

Fig. 155. *Phillip's glasses frames were found on the mountain and returned to Sandra by Álvaro Mangino in 2020.*

Julio Martínez Lamas
31-Oct-1947 – 13-Oct-1972

Julio Martínez Lamas is instantly recognizable in the photographs of the boys during their stopover in Mendoza. Tall and lean, he stands a head above everyone else, and, with his well-groomed beard and his jacket and tie, he looks mature beyond his years. Although he was one of the older *Old Christians* – from the *Stella Maris* class of '63, with classmates Marcelo Pérez del Castillo, Eduardo Strauch, Connie Hughes, and others – he had had to shoulder the responsibility of providing for his family from an early age.

When he was ten, his father – also called Julio, and a lawyer – died of a heart attack. Connie remembers the moment at school when the class heard the news, the shock to their young minds to hear of a parent dying, and Julio's strength in coping with it. It was the middle of three tragedies for Julio's mother, María Esther 'Nené' Caubarrere. A year previously, she had given birth to a son Marcelo, but he had died after just three days; and a year later, Nené's mother, who had been living in the house, also passed away.

Fig. 156. *Rosario and Julio at Carrasco beach.*

A month after her husband died, Nené gave birth to a daughter, Ana Inés. There were now three children – Rosario, the eldest; Julio, who was 16 months younger, and Ana Inés – and there was no source of income. To make matters worse, Nené contracted hepatitis when Ana Inés was still a baby. The family struggled by for some time, with the help of friends and relatives. But when Julio was 15 and had completed the *Liceo* – the first stage of secondary education – he left school and started an apprenticeship at the national bank, the *Banco de la República*, becoming the family's breadwinner. It was a responsibility he would take very seriously over the coming years, taking care of his mother and young sister, and forgoing the possibility of a girlfriend, and the full social life that his contemporaries enjoyed.

It was at the beginning of *Liceo* that his classmates discovered his full name. Julio, along with Connie and Marcelo, had been taken by the latter's mother to pick up their entrance exam certificates. Connie happened to glance at Julio's as it was handed to him, and saw to his astonishment the name on the official document: Julio M. M. M. M. Martínez Lamas. Connie said to him: *Julito, ¿Tú cómo te llamas?* "Is that your name or did they make a mistake?" *¡No digas a nadie!* – "Don't tell anyone!" *¿Cómo no?* Julio went on to explain that his father had given him the name Julio Martín Marcelo Maximiliano Marcial Martínez Lamas as a precaution, so that he would never get legally misidentified as someone else having the very common name of Julio Martínez.

Connie said to him, *Julito, les tengo que contar* – "I must tell our classmates." Julio good-naturedly acquiesced. He was a well-liked boy at school, and such was his popularity and standing, that, although he spoke with a slight lisp, he was never teased about it. He took it in his stride when his classmates started calling him Maximiliano. Years later, his sister

Fig. 157. *Julio, Nené, and Ana Inés.*

Ana Inés would give the name Maximiliano to one of her sons.

The years after leaving *Stella Maris College* were filled with Julio's banking career, looking after the family, and rugby at the weekends. By necessity, the work at the bank took priority, and he rose steadily through the ranks. As he strode out to the bus stop each morning, he would always call out and wave goodbye to Ana Inés and her friends. And if he had to do a double shift at the bank, he would have lunch with his other sister, Rosario, who was married

by then, and living downtown. By the time of the accident, Julio, who worked in the industrial credit department of the bank, was a well-known and sought-after contact in Carrasco, due to his knowledge and expertise. And because of this and his support for the National party, he became a trusted friend of Wilson Ferreira Aldunate, the charismatic young *Blanco* leader, who had won more votes than any other candidate in the 1971 election. Years later, Ana Inés would visit Ferreira and his wife Susana when they were in exile in London, from where they were coordinating the campaign against the military regime.

In the years before the 1973 dictatorship, the army had been authorized to deal with the unrest in the country – the Tupamaro guerrillas, but also the labour unrest, and the numerous strikes called by the unions. Bank employees were one of the targeted groups, and on one occasion the military entered the headquarters of the *Banco de la República*, an imposing building in the Old City, where Julio was working. It was known that the military would not apprehend anyone singing the national anthem, and so as the soldiers came up the steps, the employees started singing it en masse. As individuals began to tire, they were taken away, and Julio disappeared for a few days, along with dozens of others.

It was a couple of days before a colleague heard news of what had happened to them. Speaking to someone in *La Mascota* – a popular bar and meeting place in Carrasco – he discovered that they were being held in a large house in the Florida department of Uruguay, and he scribbled a hurried note on some scraps of paper for the contact to deliver:

> *Dear companion, it was only this evening that we found out where you had been taken. To put your mind at ease, we have been in contact with your mother and reassured her that you are well. The same day that you were taken, we all went to the 9th Cavalry section, but they released us at 1 am. Your family are all well, but there isn't time for your mother to write to you right now as she is at home in Carrasco. She says to stay calm and she will send you news as soon as possible. I think that a friend of mine, Prego, is with you. I only found out last night that he was also on the list of 150. I'm sending 6 boxes of cigarettes just in case you can't buy them there. Ask Prego to say if he needs anything and give him some cigarettes too. See you soon.*

Julio did receive the note and the cigarettes, but it turned out that he and his colleagues were being held under mild conditions and had been able to play football and cards with one another. The abduction had been a scare tactic to discourage bank workers from going on strike, and Julio and his colleagues were released without harm or consequence.

Julio had never been selected for the rugby teams representing *Stella Maris College*, but he loved the game and had become an enthusiastic and active member of the *Old Christians Club*. He worked hard at improving his rugby game, and by the end of the decade, he was captaining *Shannon*, one of the two B teams of the *Old Christians*. Playing with blue jerseys, the side included Connie and several other former classmates of Julio.

Fig. 158. *On the touchline.*
Adults left to right: Marcelo Pérez, Eddie Suarez, Julio Martínez Lamas, Br. 'Chato' O'Donnell, Nando Parrado.

The other B team *St. Patrick* played in white and, at the time, was captained by a young Gustavo Zerbino, in the years before he got promoted to the first fifteen.

Julio was a great fan of the first team. He and Gustavo were the most vocal of all the supporters on the touchline, heard and appreciated by all the players. He was also a great ambassador and activist for the club. He had been on the 1971 trip, and was keen to go again; it was a welcome opportunity for a short, inexpensive holiday, away from work and responsibilities. As most of the money he earned went to the family upkeep, the *Old Christians* offered him a loan to cover any shortfall for the trip.

Marcelo Pérez del Castillo asked Julio and another classmate, Pepe Pollak, to help him recruit passengers, but by Sunday 8th October, the go/no go deadline, there were still places that needed to be filled. Marcelo, throwing caution to the wind, informed his Chilean counterparts they would be there, that the trip was on. He and Julio then set about the task of persuading the last few people to sign up.

The day before the trip, Nené, Julio, and Ana Inés went out to eat at *Dackel* – a traditional German restaurant in Carrasco. Ana Inés, who knew that Julio believed he would die young, had a sudden sense of the meal being a final farewell. Her mother reacted in alarm when Ana Inés voiced this thought, beseeching her not to say such a thing. After dinner, the three of them walked home, stopping at Dr Pancho Nicola's house on the way, as Ana Inés was experiencing an earache. They stayed a while after he had examined her, Ana Inés throwing a rugby ball around with the Nicola kids in the garden, whilst Julio discussed arrangements to get to the airport the next morning. The Nicolas were planning to take a taxi, and offered to stop by to pick up Julio. Later that evening, Julio phoned Rosario to say goodbye. She asked her brother to bring back both a left-wing and a right-wing newspaper from Chile, so she could get a balanced sense of how the country was reacting to the recently-elected Allende government.

When the plane stopped over in Mendoza, Julio got together with Marcelo and Álvaro Mangino, to find a hotel for the night. Álvaro was not an *Old Christian* – he had done his early schooling at the *Deutsche Schule* and part of his secondary schooling at the *Seminario* – but Marcelo's brother was married to the sister of Álvaro's *novia*, so the two boys knew each other. Álvaro had been one of the last-minute invitees from the previous Sunday, persuaded to travel by club president Daniel Juan. The three boys joined other passengers at the *Casa del Gobernador*, a pension where they slept six or seven to a room.

The three of them ate at a small Spanish restaurant, before heading back to the hotel for a siesta to sleep off the wine. Refreshed from their nap, they took a bus around Mendoza, hoping to stop off and watch some stock car races they'd seen advertised, but they arrived too late. One of the things they chatted about as they toured around the town was the possibility of renting a car in

Fig. 159. *Julio on the 1971 trip, Andes in the background.*

Chile and doing a bit of skiing, since, ironically as it would turn out, some of them had never seen snow.

After stopping for tea, the three of them joined Nando Parrado and Panchito Abal at the cinema, to watch the popular 1972 comedy *What's Up, Doc?* Then dinner and an early night. The next morning, they met up with some of the other boys for breakfast, in the main shopping area of Mendoza. A famous photo from the time shows Julio and Álvaro amongst others at the corner of Avenida San Martín and Gutiérrez street. Then, with Marcelo mindful of his responsibility as organizer of the trip, the three of them headed out to the airport with Enrique Platero, the first of the passengers to arrive there.

Julio sat towards the front of the plane, on the right-hand side. The impact and the slide down the mountainside caused the seats to break loose, and when the plane came to a halt, the seats flew forward, crashing into each other, trapping and crushing the passengers, or propelling them against the bulkhead. Julio survived for a few hours, but succumbed to his injuries during the first night.

Rosario was preparing dinner for her children when the news came about the accident. She had just switched off the television, and they were about to sit down to eat when a

friend called: "Have you seen the news? Julio's plane has crashed." Rosario immediately started thinking about what to do, because Nené and Ana Inés had gone to see a film downtown. Leaving her children with her husband, she ran to each of the cinemas in turn, explaining the emergency so that they would let her enter to check all the rows. Not spotting them anywhere, she took a taxi to the family home in Carrasco, arriving ahead of her mother and sister, who had taken a bus. They had heard about the accident en route, and when they arrived at the house, they found not only Rosario, but a crowd of neighbours and friends, who had come to give their support.

Fig. 160. *Julio sporting a beard.*

During the uncertain seventy-two days that followed, Ana Inés accompanied her mother everywhere – to the houses of Canessa and Ponce de León, and to the daily Masses being offered for the boys. In Ana Inés' school, *Sagrado Corazón*, there were many connections with the passengers, many girls whose brothers had been *Old Christians*. In her class alone, were Gustavo Nicolich's sister Raquelina, Gustavo Zerbino's sister Rosina, and Maria Marta, the sister of Soledad González, Coche Inciarte's *novia*.

Ana Inés was comforted by the daily communications with Chile, and by the faith and optimism of some of the mothers, but Nené did not believe her son to be alive, and every night she would caution her daughter: "There's no cause for optimism, we need to just wait and see what happens." Rosario was of the same frame of mind as her mother, and preferred not to maintain any false hope.

On 21st December, Rosario was with her husband and children, staying at one of her father-in-law's properties in the summer resort of Villa Serrana, 150 km north-east of Montevideo, near the town of Minas. Due to the rural location, the house was not connected to the grid, and communications were difficult, but after ten weeks of no news, they were not expecting any developments over the Christmas period. It was an unexpected visit by a favourite aunt of Rosario that led to them hearing the news of possible survivors. The aunt had turned up with her daughter one day, arriving and leaving by taxi. After she left, they discovered she'd forgotten her small transistor radio, and when examining it, they turned it on just as the early reports of possible survivors were starting to come through.

Rosario and her husband looked at each other in disbelief. They made the decision to leave for Montevideo immediately. They walked to the nearest main road, taking a shortcut across the land, their five children in tow, Rosario carrying the youngest and holding tightly onto the hand of her second-youngest – not yet three – who was running alongside her. Once at the road, they were able to flag down a bus to take them into Minas. There was another wait for a bus to Montevideo, and eventually they arrived home late at night. Leaving the children with her husband, Rosario immediately took a taxi to Carrasco, to be with her mother and sister.

The next day, while her mother was waiting for an official phone call that never came, Rosario listened to the list of survivors broadcast on the radio, and heard the news that her brother was not coming back.

Ana Inés was thirteen at the time she lost her big brother, who had been like a father to her. The father she had never known had died when Rosario was twelve. And Nené had also lost her father at a similar age. Many years later, Ana Inés would feel a certain trepidation when her own daughter approached her teenage years.

A few days later, the family attended the press conference. The survivors, just returned from Chile, were up on stage in the *Stella Maris* gym, and when Gustavo Zerbino caught sight of Nené in the front row, he leapt down from the stage to give her a hug. Ana Inés was busy pointing out to a journalist the names of the different boys on the stage, and she missed the significance of Pancho Delgado's words, so when they got home, Rosario explained to her how they had survived; something the family never had any issue with.

The family had lost not only a son and a brother, but also their breadwinner. After the press conference, it was agreed that the *Old Christians* committee would act to coordinate all the requests for interviews from around the world, and act as a buffer to the survivors. It was also decided that money from those interviews would go to help the families who had been particularly hard hit by the tragedy – the Martínez Lamas family, and the Nicola family, with four orphaned boys. On the mountain, the boys had talked about writing a book if they survived, to try to transmit the great unity they felt there; and they had thought that the profits from the book might be used to help those families. But money from the interviews came in much faster.

Connie Hughes was put in charge, and requests for interviews arrived thick and fast from around the world. The first came from Japan's *Sunday Mainichi* magazine for an interview with Nando Parrado, the second from the BBC for one with Roberto Canessa. These two interviews alone raised $5000; a considerable sum in those days. Julio's bank also had a collection, generously contributed to by his colleagues, which raised $4000. The combined funds were enough to purchase an apartment on Arocena Avenue, the main street of Carrasco, and, on 29th March 1973, the deed was signed over to the Martínez Lamas family, with estate agent and notaries waiving their fees, and with Roy Harley and Connie acting as witnesses and representatives of the *Old Christians*. By a strange twist of fate, the fourth-floor apartment was directly above *Dackel*, the restaurant where Julio had eaten with his mother and sister on the eve of his departure.

Later, Julio's friend and former classmate, Pepe Pollak, acted as the family's legal counsel in a case against the Uruguayan Air Force, the body deemed to be responsible for the loss of the family's income, and this was settled out of court.

Towards the end of 1973, when the first draft of Piers Paul Read's book was circulating amongst the survivors and their families, there was consternation that the book had too much in the way of detail, and would make it impossible for the survivors to live in the close-knit community, side-by-side with the families of those who hadn't returned. In response, Rosario wrote an extraordinary letter to Read, reflecting the widespread generosity of spirit of the bereaved families towards the survivors, and assuaging the boys' fears about how the book would be received:

> "They are not going to make us suffer more by telling us how they did what they did with details... Besides, we may all suppose that if those who died would have remained alive and vice versa, the same thing would have happened...They cannot feel guilty of what they did. If the church said it was right, if we love them as I love my dear brother, please let them know, let them get convinced that they must live happily from now on, that they must not feel they hurt us or have hurt us..."

This was the view of Nené also. Generous-hearted and accepting, despite the difficulties she'd had to face, she was one of the founding mothers, in August 1973, of the *Biblioteca Nuestros Hijos*. In 1975, she and Ana Inés went to Chile by bus, and had to pass through the Andes. Nené had been reluctant to look at the mountains as they drove across the *Cristo Redentor* pass between Argentina and Chile, but, once there, she was so struck by the beauty of the mountains, that she exclaimed her son could not be resting in a better place. Years later, after Nené had died, Ana Inés went to the Valley of Tears with Coche Inciarte and Álvaro Mangino. Ana Inés had bumped into

Coche at a wedding, and had mentioned her wish to go one day with her three children to visit the grave of her brother. Coche made her promise to go, and a week later, four tickets appeared.

As with many relatives who visit the grave on the mountain, the experience had an emotional and cathartic effect. Feeling his presence in the majesty and quietude of the mountain, she finally felt able to release the suppressed emotions of so many years, to talk to her brother about what she had made of her life, and about her children, and to imagine the pride he would have had in his kid sister.

Fig. 161. *Ana Inés visiting Wilson Ferreira Aldunate and his wife Susana in exile in London. Wilson, the great liberal hope of the National Party, won the most votes in the 1971 elections, but was forced to flee the dictatorship in 1973. Popular with many of the Carrasco boys and a cousin of the mother of Marcelo Pérez del Castillo, he was a personal friend of Julio.*

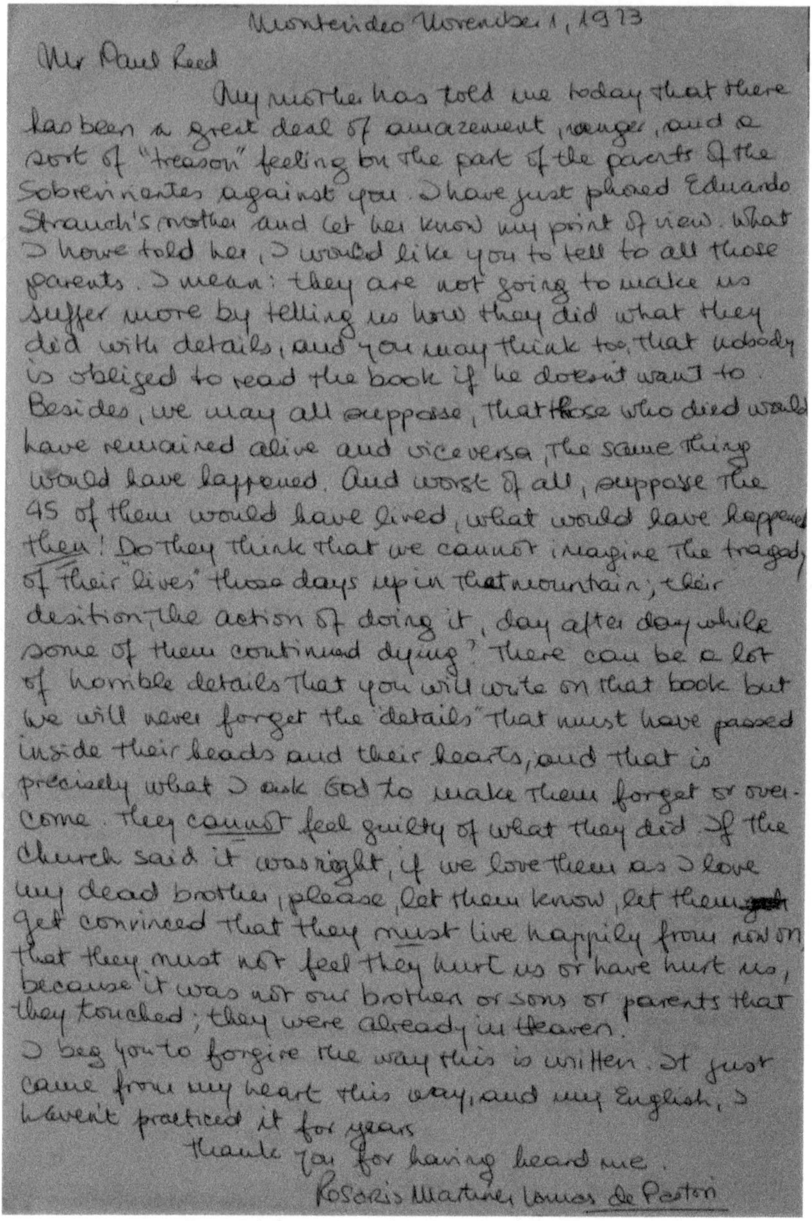

Montevideo November 1, 1973

Mr Paul Read

My mother has told me today that there has been a great deal of amazement, anger, and a sort of "treason" feeling on the part of the parents of the Sobrevivientes against you. I have just phoned Eduardo Strauch's mother and let her know my point of view. What I have told her, I would like you to tell to all those parents. I mean: they are not going to make us suffer more by telling us how they did what they did with details, and you may think too, that nobody is obliged to read the book if he doesn't want to. Besides, we may all suppose, that those who died would have remained alive and viceversa. The same thing would have happened. And worst of all, suppose the 45 of them would have lived, what would have happened then! Do they think that we cannot imagine the tragedy of their 'lives' those days up in that mountain; their desition, the action of doing it, day after day while some of them continued dying? There can be a lot of horrible details that you will write on that book but we will never forget the 'details' that must have passed inside their heads and their hearts, and that is precisely what I ask God to make them forget or overcome. They cannot feel guilty of what they did. If the Church said it was right, if we love them as I love my dead brother, please, let them know, let them get convinced that they must live happily from now on, that they must not feel they hurt us or have hurt us, because it was not our brother or sons or parents that they touched; they were already in Heaven.

I beg you to forgive the way this is written. It just came from my heart this way, and my English, I haven't practiced it for years.

Thank you for having heard me.

Rosario Martínez Lamas de Pastín

Fig. 162. Rosario's letter to author Piers Paul Read, Nov 1, 1973.

DANIEL AGUSTIN MASPONS
20-AUG-1952 — 29-OCT-1972

The Maspons family home on Mones Roses street in Carrasco was a popular place to be, with Gladys, the mother of the family – affectionately known as Mamama throughout the neighbourhood – at its core. She managed to balance the disparate elements of the large household, her joyful disposition making for an open and relaxed home, where laughter and joking were in abundance. The children who grew up in this chaos loved it as much as their friends, who were constantly visiting.

It was the father, Sergio, who was the serious one of the family. He was the owner of the family business *Maspons S.A.*, a well-known company established in the early 1920s by his father Agustin, who had immigrated from Spain. The business dealt in local and imported fabrics, specializing in fine English cashmeres, with a retail shop located downtown, at 839 Uruguay Avenue, near its intersection with Andes Street.

Fig. 163. *Maspons S.A. newspaper advertisement in a 1960 edition of* El Bien Público.

There were five children – four daughters and a son – Rosario, Isabel, Pilar, Daniel, and Amparo. Rosario, as the eldest, had watched all her siblings grow up, and had been especially close to Daniel in his formative years. Spurning traditional pastimes such as playing with dolls, Rosario preferred the rough and tumble of climbing trees and playing football, and she was always sparring with her young brother. The fights were friendly, although on one occasion Daniel broke his wrist, catching the wall as he swung a punch at her. Rosario would also play football with Daniel, and later, when she learnt to play tennis, he became her on-court sparring partner.

The two of them were jealously supportive of each other. In later years, when Daniel started excelling at rugby, it was Rosario who was his most vocal fan on the touchline. And when Rosario and Isabel achieved good success as part of a four-person folk group – winning several awards and appearing on television – it was Daniel who would applaud the most enthusiastically.

Isabel was the calm one in the family, her equanimity acting as a balance to Rosario's exuberance. Like her mother, Isabel was an accomplished cook, but whereas Mamama was famed for her savoury dishes – her semolina gnocchi being a particular favourite of Daniel – Isabel excelled in creating delicious desserts.

The family had originally lived in Punta Carretas, opposite the infamous prison from where, in the early hours of 6th September 1971, a hundred Tupamaro guerrillas had escaped; among them Pepe Mujica – future president of Uruguay. But by that time the family had moved to Carrasco, where Daniel was already attending *Stella Maris College*, having switched from a private English school closer to home. One of his new classmates was Roberto Canessa, with whom he would become firm friends.

Fig. 164. *A family meal out: Mamama, Amparo, Isabel, Rosario, Sergio, Pilar, and Daniel.*

Like many Carrasco families, the Maspons had a second house in Punta del Este. Sergio would drop them off there at the beginning of summer, and they would spend the whole three months at the resort, Sergio joining them when work permitted. Mamama would take the five children to the beach every morning, requiring them to learn how to swim. She would teach them one at a time, the others having to wait patiently for their turn. After lunch, the children would sometimes head off to the end of the marina, where, using shrimp as bait, they would spend the afternoon fishing for *pejerrey* – the Argentinian silverside so common in the River Plate estuary.

Daniel preferred sports to academic pursuits, and, as he grew older, soccer, tennis, and basketball increasingly gave way to rugby. He learnt the game under the tutelage of the Christian Brothers, becoming a member of the school team, and travelling to Buenos Aires for the annual match against *Cardinal Newman* college. Later, he became an active member of the *Old Christians Club*, going on to captain one of the B teams in 1971, and being appointed to the committee in 1972. He played as wing forward, and his disciplined training regime paid off when he made the first team, shortly before the 1972 trip to Chile.

Fig. 165. *A day at the beach.*

Not only was Rosario a great fan of the team, but her son Alejandro became their mascot, and when her second son was born, Alejandro suggested the name Marcelo for his baby brother, after his hero Marcelo Pérez del Castillo, the captain of the team. The games were often refereed by the legendary Brother 'El Chato' O'Donnell, but occasionally a young referee, Willy Davies, would be in charge. Willy was educated at the *British School*, arch-rivals of *The Christian*, and so Rosario would shout out from the touchline "*¡juez chorro!*" – "the referee's a cheat!" – not suspecting that fifteen years later, after the breakdown of her first marriage, Willy would become the love of her life, and would become like a father to Alejandro and Marcelo. It was a measure of the rivalry between the British and Irish Brothers' schools that when Rosario and Willy got married, they jokingly considered it more of an impediment to their union than their opposing support for the two national football rivals, Rosario for Peñarol, and Willy for Nacional.

Willy had turned to refereeing after a career-ending injury on the rugby field, although it wasn't until 1978 that a formal body (the Association of Referees) was formed, with Willy as an inaugural member. Although he didn't know Daniel personally, Willy's fairness as a referee made him a much-loved figure in that generation of *Old Christians*, who, to this day, recognize and greet him in the street. Willy went on to have further success as a manager, taking charge of the second team in the 1982 South American Jaguars tour of South Africa, which included a famous 21-12 victory over the Springboks at Bloemfontein.

In the years that Daniel was playing rugby with the *Old Christians*, Rosario was living with her first husband, and had moved out of the family home. With Isabel also married, and living in Argentina, Daniel became closer to Pilar and Amparo. Like her brother who was two years younger than her, Pilar was a keen athlete, though favouring gymnastics and dance over team sports. In later years, she became a Pilates expert, teaching for many years at the Carrasco Lawn Tennis Club, which had sent her to train in the US. And in 1983, she became host of a keep-fit programme on national television.

Amparo, three years younger than her brother, went to *Jesús María* school, where one of her best friends was Adriana Canessa, Roberto's sister. With the girls in *Jesús María* keen to spend time with the *Old Christian* boys, and vice versa, Amparo and Daniel put aside their sibling squabbles, and became allies. Amparo got to know all of Daniel's friends, and Daniel – good-looking, stylishly dressed, and with a laid-back and straightforward personality – proved popular among her circle of friends, and for a while he went steady with her best friend.

After leaving *The Christian*, Daniel continued his friendship with his old classmate and rugby teammate Roberto Canessa, and when rugby and studies permitted, the two of them would get together with other friends and former classmates, to go dancing at one of the popular nightclubs of the time – *Zum-Zum* in Pocitos, or the distinctive *Lancelot*, whose building resembled a castle. The fathers of the two boys were also friends, and would get together to play poker on Saturdays; part of a wider group that included Arturo Nogueira's father.

With only one Maspons family in Uruguay, and only one son to carry on the family name, a heavy burden of expectation rested on Daniel's shoulders, although being the only boy meant that he was indulged to some extent. It was assumed that he would join the family firm and carry it forward when his father retired. To that end, he began taking his studies more seriously, starting pre-university courses in Economics in 1969. Needing to repeat some maths courses in 1971, for university admission, he gained experience working at *Maspons S.A.* alongside his father, with whom he was good friends. Finally, in 1972 he was accepted into the Faculty of Economics at the university.

When Daniel was invited to travel to Chile, Sergio's first reaction was that his son should not accept, that he should concentrate on his studies, as it was the middle of the university term. Rosario, standing next to her father on the touchline one Sunday, pleaded with him to reconsider, to understand what an enjoyable experience it would be for Daniel. Roberto, along with trip organizers Marcelo Pérez del Castillo and Julio Martínez Lamas, also spoke to him, telling him that Daniel was needed to make up a full team. Sergio, proud of his son playing for the first fifteen, finally relented, and gave his son the money for the ticket.

Pilar, hearing her brother discussing the trip with his father, and discovering that there were seats to fill on the plane, told them that she would like to go along also, with a group of her friends. Daniel ridiculed her suggestion, telling her that the trip was for boys, not for girls. So, when it was time for Daniel's mother to take him to the airport, he and Pilar were still not speaking to each other, and she missed the opportunity to say goodbye to him. Rosario, however, stopped by on the eve of the trip to say her farewell, as she would be heading into work early the next morning with her father. As she had often done in the past, she slipped her brother some extra spending money.

Fig. 166. *Daniel on the rugby field and on the dance floor.*

345

On the plane, Daniel sat next to Roberto, and when they were unexpectedly forced to stop over in Mendoza, the two of them, along with Fernando Vázquez, stuck together and found a three-person room at the *Hotel Horizonte* on Gutiérrez street, where many of the other boys were staying. In the morning, they walked around the town, stopping for some lunch before heading out to the airport.

On the second leg, Daniel and Roberto sat together once more, in the third row, behind Liliana and Javier Methol; Daniel by the window, and Roberto on the aisle across from Fernando. It was a fortuitous choice with the two boys miraculously escaping any injury in the accident. Once the plane came to a halt, Roberto managed to get out of his seat immediately, and, with the help of Gustavo Zerbino, was able to free Daniel, who was trapped under a seat. The three of them, the first on their feet, feared for a brief moment that everyone else had died. Then came the cries and the moans from the wreckage, and they set about freeing as many of the other passengers as they could; most of whom, if not injured, were dazed and in shock.

Daniel was in good physical shape from his rugby training, and on the mountain he was one of the hardest-working boys; uncomplaining and optimistic, sensitive and sympathetic. As the group started to organize itself after the chaos and trauma of the initial accident, Daniel did double duty, working both on the cabin team and the water-making team. Disregarding the scepticism of the others, he helped Roberto rig up the hammock, the hanging seat, and the hanging door, which allowed the injured to sleep away from the crowded floor, where any small movement would cause paroxysms of agony. And when the decision came to use the bodies of the dead, Daniel was one of the main advocates, supporting Fito Strauch, Gustavo, and Roberto in persuading the other boys, and participating in the initial breaking of the taboo.

Once the boys heard the news that the search had been called off, they decided that a group should set out without delay, to try to climb up the track of the fuselage towards the impact point, in order to get a better view of the surrounding mountains, and to look for the tail, which contained the plane's batteries. Daniel immediately volunteered, and set off up the mountain with Numa Turcatti and Gustavo. When nightfall came, they were still some distance from the top, and, reluctant to cede the height that had been so arduously gained, they decided to risk spending the night outside. Hitting each other with their fists all night to keep their circulation going, for what seemed like an eternity, they managed to hang on until the first rays of sunlight hit them, and they were able to thaw out. Much weakened, they continued their climb. Eventually, they came across the bodies of their friends and the two crew members, who had fallen out of the back of the plane. But the tail was nowhere to be seen, and, more worryingly, the surrounding mountains seemed to offer no escape route. Not wanting to get caught out for another night, they hastened back down the mountain, Daniel losing a shoe at one point. His recovery owed much to the boys back at the fuselage, who massaged his feet over the following days.

On the night of the avalanche, Daniel was sleeping on the right-hand side of the fuselage, with Roberto opposite him, Nando Parrado to his left, and Enrique Platero to his right. Due to the angle of the plane, those on the right-hand side of the fuselage were much lower than those on the left, and so when the avalanche swept through the cabin, they found themselves immobilized, under several feet of snow. Nando was the only survivor out of a contiguous group of six on the right-hand side. Roberto, less deeply buried, was nonetheless trapped, with a heavy weight of snow on his chest, and he had to wait his turn before Roy Harley was able to free him. Roberto immediately started digging for his friend, clawing frantically at the compacted snow with his bare hands, but by the time he reached him, it was too late. When he finally uncovered his dead friend's face, it appeared to Roberto as though Daniel were just sleeping.

When Sergio Maspons heard the news of the accident on the radio on the evening of 13th October, he was in despair, not forgiving himself for having allowed Daniel to travel. And for Isabel, living in the small town of Vicuña Mackenna, 300 km south of Córdoba in Argentina, it was particularly difficult, her distress compounded by the separation from her parents and sisters. Communications were rudimentary, and phone calls had to be relayed by word of mouth, so Isabel left for Montevideo as soon as the news reached her.

With the exception of Rosario, the family had no hope that he was alive, or that anyone could have survived such an accident. Rosario alone believed that there was hope. Every day after work, she would leave her kids with their bikes, and go to Ponce de León's house, gathering with Mecha Canessa, Stella Pérez del Castillo, and other relatives, to hear the news relayed by ham radio from Chile. Meanwhile, the Christian Brothers from the school would visit the Maspons household, to lend their support. When news came that there were sixteen survivors, Sergio and Mamama joined their daughter outside Ponce de León's house, to hear the list being broadcast. Rosario was sure that Daniel's name would be on the list, that her faith and her prayers over the previous 72 days would be justified. As she listened to the diminishing list of names, she kept saying to herself – "Next will be Daniel, next will be Daniel."

In the following days, the family escaped to Punta del Este, to get away from the swarm of reporters and the news coverage. As well as the sensationalism of the tabloid press, the news was coloured by the political climate. The boys had been from a privileged sector of Uruguayan society, and there was little sympathy for the families in some quarters. After the immediate scrutiny had died down, the subject became taboo in the

Maspons household. Sergio preferred not to talk about the accident, and forbade his daughters to discuss it. But Daniel's absence at Peñarol games, now attended by Sergio and Rosario alone, was a bitter reminder of the tragedy for both father and sister.

Mamama found solace in her grandchildren. After just one son among four daughters, her grandchildren were predominantly male, and she would see something of Daniel in them, compensating in a small way for his loss. The oldest grandson, Alejandro, whose

Fig. 167. *Mamama with Isabel and her children.*

second name was Daniel after his uncle, called his grandfather Tototo, mimicking the sound of the family car – a DKW – which would alert Alejandro to the visit of his grandparents. But for Tototo, things started to unravel. He lost interest in the family business now that Daniel wasn't going to carry it on, and in the end, he lost everything. The family's standard of living, which had been good before the accident, declined precipitously. Eventually, the foundation set up by the survivors helped the family out with an apartment. The parents lived there until they died, after which it passed to one of the other families.

Mamama, however, always liked to be active, and she used her cooking skills to good effect to sustain the household income. She and Rosario started catering for *Stella Maris College*. It started off small, the two of them selling a dozen or so packed lunches from their car outside the school. Encouraged by Brother Kelly, the business grew rapidly, and they were soon providing lunch for the majority of the students, and for the Brothers themselves. This continued for three or four years, until the College, which had become their second home, established a more permanent catering solution. Mother and daughter then switched their services to the *British School* canteen, where they would serve meals to 400 students; and on Saturdays, they would provide catering for *Montevideo Cricket Club*.

When Mamama, who was never allowed to speak of the tragedy at home, heard about the library that was being planned in memory of those who hadn't returned from the mountain, she expressed interest, and became one of the thirteen founders. For many mothers, the library became a place to share their grief, to talk about their sons, and to cry. Mamama didn't like it when that happened, but she did take solace in the presence of Brother 'El Chato' O'Donnell, who would visit the library every afternoon. In recent years, Rosario has been helping out at the library.

Fig. 168. *Amparo, Rosario, and Pilar in October 2019.*

Gustavo Zerbino – who is much loved by the family – returned Daniel's watch and medallions to them. And over the years, he has stayed in touch, encouraging the sisters to consider him a brother. Another survivor who has had contact with the family is Roberto Canessa, who accompanied Rosario's son Marcelo and a group of friends to the mountain in 2004. It gave Marcelo the opportunity to spend time with Roberto, who spoke at length about Daniel, about his calm presence and courage on the mountain. Marcelo was very moved by the whole experience, developing a close feeling of kinship with Roberto. When he returned, he relayed everything to his grandparents, and to his mother, to reassure them of the great respect and gratitude that the survivors had for those who hadn't made it back.

In the early years, it was difficult for the survivors to stay close to the parents of those who had lost their sons. Roberto, who had made an attempt to speak to Daniel's mother in the months after his return from the mountain, reflected on this in *Stranded*, a documentary by Uruguayan director Gonzalo Arijon:

> I think they're in the air, they float all around us. I think they are here with us. Otherwise their families wouldn't be at peace and we wouldn't love each other so much. At first their presence was so powerful it was if they were screaming at us. And so we couldn't be with their mothers. They've learned to be spirits. Or maybe we've learned that they are invisible, and yet, they still whisper in our ears.

The *Stranded* film crew had gone to the mountain two years after Marcelo's trip, in March 2006. Arijon was accompanied by four survivors – Roberto Canessa, Gustavo Zerbino, Moncho Sabella, and Fito Strauch – who brought along their children. Also present were Juan Pedro Nicola – son of Pancho Nicola and Esther Horta, who had both died in the first moments of the accident – and Uruguayan author Pablo Vierci, making his first trip to the site. Vierci was a friend of many of the survivors, and a former classmate of Nando Parrado and Guido Magri from *Stella Maris College*. He had started writing an account of the tragedy in 1973, but the choice of British writer Piers Paul Read as the official chronicler had put an end to that. Now, after being contacted by Arijon and encouraged by the survivors, he had finally embarked on writing the book that had been forming in his mind for the past thirty-three years. It would appear two years later with the title *Sociedad de la Nieve*; a book interleaving an account of the tragedy with personal testimonies of all sixteen of the survivors.

The person with overall responsibility for the expeditionaries was Mario Peréz, who had, for several years, been the head guide for Edgardo Barrios, the businessman who had pioneered commercial trips to the site. A veteran of dozens of expeditions to the glacier, Mario had first gone there in 1988, age 17. Three months before the current visit to the site, he had made a crossing of the Andes as part of a *National Geographic* expedition; the first to follow the route that Nando and Roberto had taken in 1972.

For Mario, the mountains were, and still are, a place of peace and spirituality, where he most feels the presence of his own son who died age 16. The grave of the Andes victims is a place of particular reverence for him, and it retains an aura that strikes many who make the pilgrimage to the site of the accident each summer. The arrival at the memorial after a two-day trek on horseback is always an emotional moment, and as the four survivors and their families gathered around the grave, the strong gust of wind that welcomed them seemed to confirm the presence of their lost friends.

The next couple of days were taken up with the filming on the glacier, which Mario had helped to secure with lifelines to make it safe for the documentary team. Between takes, Mario had the opportunity to spend many hours chatting with the survivors, learning first-hand about their time on the mountain. On the last night, Mario bid everyone goodnight as usual and made his way up to where he always slept, some distance away from the main group, on a ridge closer to the grave, and overlooking the glacier. Mario's preference is to sleep under the stars, his down sleeping bag placed over the sheepskin saddle of his mountain horse. From where he lay, he could enjoy the night-time grandeur of the mountains and glacier, whilst, at the same time, keeping an eye on the main camp, alert to the sound of any rockfall that might endanger the expeditionaries.

As he drifted off to sleep that night, an extraordinary phenomenon started to occur. He felt his feet being lifted up, pivoted rigidly at an angle from his neck, only his head on the ground. Scared, he opened his eyes. The cold, strong wind blowing against his face convinced him that he was not asleep. Petrified, he started praying, and as he felt his feet lowering to the ground, he was struck with sudden force by a name: **DANIEL MASPONS, DANIEL MASPONS**. It seemed to him as if it were being branded on his forehead, and he instinctively covered his face. Uncovering it a few moments later, and looking out towards the glacier, he suddenly became aware of a young woman with a beautiful face and long fair hair, sitting on a nearby rock, her hands in her lap. She was staring out towards the glacier. He would later realize, on seeing a photograph, that it was the face of Susana Parrado, who had died eight days after the accident. Terrified, he buried his face in his sleeping bag, afraid to look any more, but the name of Daniel Maspons continued to reverberate around his head.

Mario didn't dare to tell anyone about this vision for many years, for fear of being ridiculed. He had seen Daniel Maspons' name along with the others on the recently constructed memorial obelisk near the grave, and he knew that Daniel had been a close friend of Roberto, but otherwise there was no special connection. Over the years, however, the name kept resonating in his mind, and he felt compelled to contact Daniel's family. Eventually, after meeting one of Daniel's relatives on a 2014 expedition, he obtained Rosario's email address and wrote to her about his enigmatic vision.

Fig. 169. *The glacier at dusk, close to where Mario Peréz had his vision. The grave is to the left.*

That night in March 2006, Mario had been tempted to run for the companionship of the main camp. But he reasoned that if he let his fear get the better of him, he would never be able to return there. After a while, he was filled with a sense of calm, and he fell into a deep sleep, not waking until daybreak.

JUAN CARLOS MENÉNDEZ
06-APR-1950 — 29-OCT-1972

Juan Carlos Menéndez is the forgotten passenger of the Andes tragedy. He was not an *Old Christian*, nor associated with the community in Carrasco, nor a close friend of any of the passengers, although he was acquainted with some of the law students on the plane. And after the survivors returned from the mountain, his mother had some initial contact with the other mothers who lost sons, but over the years, the connection was lost. Any personal memories of Juan Carlos' life before the trip come from his close university friend, Daniel Bruno:

I met him in 1968 at the Faculty of Law and Social Sciences at the Universidad de la República *and we formed an unforgettable study group, sharing trips to the interior and all kinds of wonderful experiences, both sporting and otherwise. As for his personality, I have to say that he was a quiet, humble boy, a friend and unconditional companion, thin, a smoker like me, and of prodigious intelligence – a single reading of a study text was enough for him to sit an exam. His words were always measured, and he was friendly and congenial.*

Juan Carlos – 'Carlitos' to his family, 'El Flaco' to his friends – was the younger of two brothers. His aspiration was to become a public notary. Coming from a traditional middle-class Catholic family, which had moved from the interior and settled in Montevideo, he and his brother were the first generation of the family to study for professional careers, evoking the theme of a famous play *M'hijo el Dotor* by Uruguayan playwright Florencio Sánchez, which presents a generational clash between a rural father – named Olegario, like Juan Carlos' own father – and his son, who moves to the city to study medicine.

The members of the close-knit study group would meet at each other's houses, sometimes at the Menéndez home in Pocitos, at the corner of Avenida Luis Alberto de Herrera and Echevarriarza street, and sometimes at Daniel's house in Punta Gorda. Early in the group's formation, someone had given Daniel a statue of Pai Joaquim das Matas – a wise old black man, revered in Umbanda tradition – and the study group developed a light-hearted ritual of asking Pai Joaquim to give them luck the day before any exam. When the group met at Juan Carlos' house, his mother would be very welcoming and attentive, providing them with a steady flow of ham-and-cheese sandwiches to fuel their studies. His father wasn't so much in evidence, but when he did appear, his wife would always address him with the formal 'Don Olegario'.

Meeting in the different homes created a familial bond between the members of the group. Daniel remembers Juan Carlos and the others teaching his young nephew to take his first steps. And it was at Daniel's house that the subject of the trip to Chile came up:

We were studying at my father's house in Punta Gorda when a friend of mine, Daniel Freiría, told us that he had a place on the charter flight to Chile with the Old Christian boys, and that he was unable to go. Well, the study group – made up of Daniel Queijo, Washington Angiolini, Juan Carlos, and me – came to an agreement. Daniel and Washington did not want to go, and my father would not allow me to travel, thus saving my life. Unfortunately that left just Juan Carlos who would die in the avalanche that swept through the fuselage. Of course we talked about how much fun he was going to have on the trip with the guys from the Old Christians, whom he didn't know. I did know one or two of them but they were acquaintances more than friends. I often wondered how he adapted to that group, and what his experiences were, because he was somewhat shy, a man of few words. Very little was said about him afterwards – only that he had died in the avalanche.

Fig. 170. *In front of the Fairchild at El Plumerillo airport in Mendoza.* **Back left**: *Carlos Roque.* **Foreground**: *Juan Carlos Menéndez, Pancho Delgado, Gastón Costemalle, Felipe Maquirriain.*

Juan Carlos would have the company, at least, of his law faculty colleagues, two of whom – Pancho Delgado and Numa Turcatti – were soccer players like himself, and not so tightly integrated into the rugby group. Soccer was a passion for Juan Carlos, and he and Daniel played for the same team in the University Soccer League – *Club Soriano* – which had been formed in the first half of the nineteenth century by natives of Soriano, who had come to work or study in Montevideo.

On the flight to Mendoza, the 'lawyers' stuck together at the back of the plane, and in Mendoza, the three stayed at the *La Casa del Gobernador,* along with several others, including the fourth law student, Gastón Costemalle. Juan Carlos and Numa went out walking in the town on the evening of 12th October, along with Antonio Vizintín. They stopped for a drink at a bar, where they met three Mendocinian girls, who took them on an extensive sight-seeing tour around the city, including to the *Cerro de la Gloria.* By way of a thank you for their hospitality, the three boys invited their guides to a late dinner, before saying their goodbyes and heading back to their hotels.

Boarding the plane the next day, Juan Carlos sat on the left-hand side, a few rows from the back, and was joined by Coche Inciarte – also a soccer player. Coche remembers little of

the conversation they had, only that when the plane turned north, they talked of their surprise as to how quickly they had passed over the Andes. Juan Carlos, like Coche, was uninjured in the accident, although he was initially trapped in his seat, and had to be released by Gustavo Zerbino and others. That night, Gustavo and Juan Carlos found themselves next to each other in the crowded fuselage, and kept each other warm, massaging one another throughout the night to keep their circulation flowing. Gustavo, who would often sleep opposite Juan Carlos in the nights that followed, remembered him as a kind-hearted, uncomplicated boy, who was anxious to get back to his family.

Fig. 171. *Lighter used by Canessa and Parrado on the final trek. The monogram suggests it may have belonged to Juan Carlos Menéndez.*

Juan Carlos' spirits dipped low when he heard that the search had been called off, and, like many of the boys stressed by their impossible situation, he became somewhat irascible. His frustration at finding himself sleeping at the cold end of the fuselage more than his fair share provoked him to reprove the leaders and organizers, for monopolising the warmer places in the plane. Whether or not it was a fair criticism, Juan Carlos was again positioned by the back wall of the fuselage on the night of 29th October, with Carlos Roque to his right, and Pancho and Numa in front of him. When the avalanche swept in that evening, he and Roque had no chance – they were hit by the collapsing wall, and the full impact of the snow. It would be many days before they could be dug out.

Back in Montevideo, the members of the study group were in shock, as the news of the accident spread through the community. Assuming the worst, they went to Juan Carlos' house, to comfort his mother. The absence of any definitive news only prolonged the pain and sadness of losing their friend, and the hopes momentarily raised by news of survivors were soon dashed, although it at least brought some finality to the uncertainty of the previous months. Even so, it was difficult to accept that he was finally gone, and Daniel vividly remembers Juan Carlos' mother, in a state of shock, saying over and over, "Carlitos is coming today, Carlitos is coming today."

There was some solace in the appearance of the survivors, who could provide information about his last days, but, being peripheral to the group, Juan Carlos was rarely mentioned, and Daniel later reflected:

> It has been a long time since I have seen my friends from the study group, and after the emotional shock we received – very traumatic for all of us who loved him – we stopped talking about the accident, with many questions still unanswered. What I wonder – though I don't question – is to know how Juan Carlos integrated into the group before and after the accident, if he was accepted as one more member, and why on that stormy night he was sitting in a place which received the full force of the avalanche. The truth is that very little was said about him and I would have liked not only an explanation but also more detailed information.

Daniel Bruno firmly believes that the events on the mountain – from the survival of the initial accident through to the appearance of the muleteer – were miraculous, supported by faith, culture, a code of conduct, and the Uruguayan trait of *garra charrúa*. He sees it as an affirmation of life, and a confirmation that anything is possible.

LILIANA NAVARRO DE METHOL AND JAVIER METHOL
07-FEB-1938 — 29-OCT-1972, 11-DEC-1935 — 04-JUN-2015

Javier Methol heard about the trip to Chile on the Monday before departure. His cousin Panchito Abal, a colleague at the *Abal Hermanos* cigarette factory, mentioned to him that there were still a few places left to fill on the charter flight, and encouraged him to come along with his wife, Liliana. Javier broached the idea with Liliana, whose immediate reaction was, "You're crazy – today is Monday, and you want to travel on Thursday!?" But more importantly, she was reluctant to go because she was due to start a course that day, picking up on her studies to become a notary, which she'd put on hold since the arrival of her first child. But when she turned up at the faculty that afternoon, she found that all classes were cancelled. The students had started striking against an Education bill designed to give the state more control over secondary and university education, which had been largely autonomous to that point. It threatened to be a prolonged strike, so when Liliana got home, she agreed to go on the trip.

Javier had led a charmed life up to that point, surviving a succession of accidents and illnesses; so much so that his reappearance, after 72 days in the Andes, didn't completely surprise his family, and caused one brother to exclaim to their mother, "You didn't have a son, you had a cat!"

The first incident happened twenty-one years to the day before he and Liliana set off on that fateful trip to Chile. He had recently turned fifteen, and was on his way to meet his girlfriend. Freshly bathed, hair gelled, cologne liberally applied, he was riding his moped at breakneck speed in his eagerness to see her, when a car hit his rear wheel. He remembered being hurled towards the kerb, and his head smashing against a lamppost, then nothing. He was rushed to the hospital, where he lay unresponsive in a coma, his parents at his side, distraught and wracked with guilt for having allowed him to have a moped. The doctor told them to prepare for the worst, and a priest was called in to administer the last rites. Then, against all expectations, he awoke from the coma on day five, although he would spend another ten days in critical condition. Finally, his family's anxious vigil was rewarded, when Javier opened his eyes to find them gathered around him.

Even at that early age, Javier attributed the hand of God to his miraculous recovery. He would say that he had made the trip to Heaven, but, since it was full, they had sent him back. However, it had come at a cost. The blow had cut an optic nerve, and he would never see out of his right eye again. He also began to experience difficulty in memorizing things; something that hampered his career, although he would learn to compensate over time, and it didn't prevent him from joining the family business at age 18. Started in

1877 by Javier's maternal grandfather Narciso Abal, a poor immigrant from Galicia, *Abal Hermanos* had grown to become a major player in the tobacco and cigarette industry, supplying a third of the Uruguayan market. Starting at the bottom, Javier worked his way up to the position of deputy general accountant.

In July 1957, at the age of twenty-one, he embarked on a study tour of Cuba and the USA, to learn about tobacco cultivation and marketing. The trip to Cuba, on the invitation of *H. Duys & Co.*, brought him into close contact with the Cuban revolution, which was coming to a head. He spent two months in the small town of Cabaiguán, where, on his tours of the tobacco plantations, he observed, at first-hand, the clashes between Fidel Castro's guerrilla force, and the soldiers of US-backed dictator Fulgencio Batista.

From Cuba, Javier went on to Wilson, North Carolina, where the *James I Miller* corporation was based. He had been there only a month when he had his second brush with death. He was diagnosed with tuberculosis and was advised not to return to Uruguay, as he was in no condition to endure the trip. By good fortune, the sanatorium in Wilson was reputed to be one of the best in the country for treating tuberculosis, and Javier was hospitalized there for five months. Away from his family and friends, and alone in a hospital bed in a foreign country, he wasn't even able to while away the time by reading, thanks to his visual impairment. But within a month, he learned to speak English, conversing with nurses and doctors in the hospital, and he adopted the philosophy to always see the good side of things, to maintain hope and optimism, even in the presence of pain and death,

Fig. 172. *Javier and Liliana.*

and to trust entirely in those who could save him. It was a philosophy that would stand him in good stead in the Andes.

Returning to Montevideo in February 1958, it would take another four months before he completely recovered, but he now had the support of his family and his *novia* Liliana, whom he had met in 1955. The two got engaged on Javier's 24th birthday, and they married six months later; a grand wedding, with 600 guests. They honeymooned in Rio de Janeiro, after an earthquake had scuppered their plans to visit Chile's lake district. Javier had been promising a trip abroad as an anniversary present, and so the opportunity to go to Chile fulfilled that promise, resonating with their missed opportunity twelve years previously, although on this trip they would only have time to visit Santiago and the seaside town of Viña del Mar.

Javier considered himself the happiest man alive, to be marrying such a wonderful woman; but his series of misfortunes didn't stop after the wedding. Three years later, Javier suffered a third serious episode, this time contracting a severe case of hepatitis, which consigned him to bed for several months. But Javier rode out this episode with the same equanimity and positivity as the previous incidents.

By the time of the trip, the couple had four children – María Laura, Pablo, Anna Inés, and Marie Noel, aged 10, 9, 5, and 3. The family had originally lived in an apartment in Pocitos, but a curious incident had led to them buying their house on Puyol Street in Carrasco a few years before the accident. Javier's father had noticed the house up for sale at auction,

Fig. 173. *Liliana and María Laura.*

and had told Javier's brother, "We must buy that house for Javier." They were his last words to the family, because he died later that evening, after having driven up to the family farm north of Montevideo. At the funeral, the brother told Javier of his father's last wish, and insisted that they should act on it, encouraging Javier to go to the auction the following day. Javier was reluctant, so his brother went instead, and placed the winning bid for the house, paying more for it than Javier would have been willing to spend. However, a lengthy legal delay, on the seller's side, allowed Javier ample time to get the finances together.

Liliana loved the new house, and it gave them the indoor and outdoor space they needed for a growing family. When they reached school age, María Laura started at *Colegio Jesús María*, and Pablo at *The Christian*. Liliana would help out a few hours a week at her daughter's school, which was a dozen or so blocks from the house, doing administrative or teaching-related work. The married couple complemented one another – Javier's calm temperament meant that any flashes of anger or frustration on Liliana's part would wash over him and quickly dissipate, and on the rare occasion when Javier got angry, Liliana would know how to deal with it. Their lives were centred around the home, and even their hobbies were domestic; Liliana's sewing skills were applied to making dresses for her daughters, and Javier spent his spare time in his workshop, fashioning toys for the children, or shelves and tables for the house.

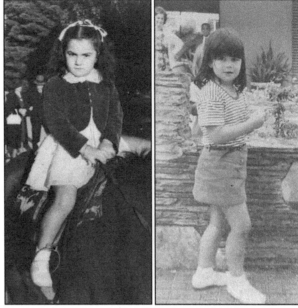

Fig. 174. *Liliana (left) and María Laura (right), age 5.*

Javier's mother owned a house in the seaside resort of Punta del Este, and made it available every summer for the use of her children and their families. Half of the season would be reserved for Javier's eldest brother Pedro and his family, and the other half for the families of Javier and his other brother Juan José, whose children were closer in age.

Another popular destination was the Methol family farm in the department of Florida, near Sarandí del Yi, around 200 km north of Montevideo. The farm was usually too hot during the summer months, although the installation of a swimming pool made it bearable. It had belonged to Javier's father, and was now jointly owned by his children – the three brothers and a sister. Pedro (informally known as Perucho) and Javier both went into the Abal cigarette business, and it was left to Juan José to run the farm. Typical of many families who owned a farm, he would work there through the week, and then join his family at the weekend in Montevideo, or they would all head out to the farm for the weekend.

With little time to prepare for the trip to Chile, Liliana made hasty arrangements for her parents, who lived in Pocitos with her sister, to stay in the family home in Carrasco and look after the children while she and Javier were away. Early on the morning of 12ᵗʰ October, the extended family arrived at the airport in two cars, to see off the couple. With the airport near to Carrasco, the children were allowed the rare treat of riding in the back of the pickup truck. At the terminal, Javier and Liliana met up with Panchito Abal, who had invited them on the trip, and who now introduced them to some of the passengers. Living in the tightly connected neighbourhood of Carrasco, there were inevitably some that they already knew: Nando Parrado, who was Panchito's best friend; Gustavo Zerbino, who lived two blocks away, and whose godmother was Javier's sister, and Arturo Nogueira, who lived on the same street as the Methols. Some years previously, they had also met Pancho Nicola and his wife Esther Horta – the other couple on the trip with four young children – who had once lived in the same apartment block as Javier's brother in Pocitos.

On the flight, Liliana and Javier made the acquaintance of Eugenia and Susana Parrado; and when the plane unexpectedly stopped over in Mendoza, the four of them had lunch together in town, inviting Graziela Augusto de Mariani to join them. They all checked into the upmarket *Hotel Sussex*, half a block from *Plaza Independencia*, the main central square of Mendoza, along with Nando, Panchito Abal, and the Nicola couple. Graziela, who didn't know any of the other passengers, asked Javier and Liliana if she could accompany them if they went sight-seeing. So that afternoon, the three of them took a bus to the *Cerro de la Gloria*, the hill in the *Parque General San Martín* with panoramic views over the city.

The next morning, Javier and Liliana stayed near the hotel, unsure of when they would need to go to the airport. Eventually, discovering that they wouldn't be flying until the afternoon, they had some sandwiches in town before heading to the terminal. They arrived with Graziela around mid-day, only to find that everything was closed, and they would have to wait another couple of hours before flying. Javier took several photos to while away the time, but his camera and the photos were destined to be lost in the Andes. One of the photos he did take was a group shot of the boys with an eccentric plump woman who frequented the airport. She wore clothes that gave her an almost carnival appearance, with a voluminous skirt and multi-coloured socks, and she claimed to be godmother to the pilots. Felipe Maquirriain sketched a perfect caricature of her, which Gustavo Zerbino presented to the woman. She was so delighted that she requested a photo with all of them. Javier had planned to send it to her after the trip, care of the airport.

When they boarded the plane, Liliana and Javier sat in the second row on the left of the aisle, with Liliana by the window. Graziela was by herself in the row in front of them, and across the aisle from Javier were Esther Horta and Pancho Nicola. Esther was quite superstitious, and voiced her fear about flying on Friday 13th. Javier reassured her, telling her that he liked the number thirteen. The flight south to Malargüe, and then west towards Curicó, was smooth and uneventful, but once it turned north and started its descent, the plane entered into the clouds, and started to move around some more. A first deep air pocket drew chants of *Conga, Conga* from the boys at the front, but after the second air pocket they could see the snow and rocks close by, and Javier took Liliana's hand. They started to pray aloud the *Our Father*. Javier closed his eyes, and then heard a crash, followed by two more. Then a rush of air, the plane sliding down the mountain, and finally an abrupt stop. Javier looked to his left and saw that Liliana was alive and conscious, but when he looked to the other side, there was devastation – the seats had all piled to the front of the cabin, killing or badly injuring the passengers there.

The pair of seats in which Javier and Liliana had been sitting had shifted only slightly, and their injuries were minor in comparison to those of the others – bruising and cuts to Liliana's face, and a cracked rib for Javier. Liliana stood up, and asked Javier to try to do the same, but he felt quite incapacitated, as though he had a fever and bad headache. He was suffering from severe altitude sickness – something that he had experienced once before in a stopover at La Paz airport, 4,000 metres above sea level. But at the time it seemed an unlikely explanation, as they believed that they must be in the Chilean *precordillera* at around 1,500 metres. In fact, they were closer to 4,000 metres.

As Javier tried to take stock of the situation, he became aware of a boy lying by his side; Javier helped him up, and allowed him to rest on his leg, the blood from the boy's wound seeping over Javier. The cries and shouts of the injured, in the tangle of seats, prompted Javier into further action. Two immediate tasks were to help extricate people, and to take the seats out of the plane, to make more space in the fuselage as darkness descended. That bitterly cold first night, Javier and Liliana were separated as she was afforded a place, along with the injured, in the warmest part of the plane, behind the pilot's cabin. Graziela Augusto, whose company the Methols had enjoyed the previous day, was still trapped when night came, and passed the night in agony. She died the next morning, just at the point at which the boys were finally able to release her.

Javier's cousin Panchito died during the first night, but his friend Nando, for whom there initially seemed to be no hope, survived. Javier had heard that Nando was still alive, but hadn't seen him since the accident. It was days later when he realized that the boy lying next to the injured Susana Parrado was actually Nando, unrecognizable with his bloodied and swollen face.

As the survivors started to get organized, Liliana became somewhat of a mother to the boys, actively working to keep their spirits up, helping the 'doctors' do their rounds of the injured, and tending to Javier. She promised the boys that when they got out of there, she would invite them to her house, and cook some special dishes for them. Her tenderness and affection contrasted with the brashness of the boys, but she refused to be treated differently from anyone else, doing her full quota of work – whether making water or sewing gloves using the material from the seat-back pockets. She also did her rotation in the coldest part of the plane without complaint. The only concession she agreed to was a screened-off seat the boys placed outside the front of the plane for her to use as a toilet.

The effects of altitude sickness may have made Javier slow-moving and lethargic, but the optimism born out of his previous trials meant that he never had any doubt that he would return from the mountain. Not even the news that the rescue efforts had been suspended dampened his outlook. If any of the boys became sad thinking of their family or their *novia*, he would tell them not to worry; that if they were still alive, it was because they were going to get out of there.

As the days passed without sign of rescue, and their small stash of supplies dwindled, the more proactive of the boys broached the likely necessity of having to use the bodies of their dead friends for food before they got too weak to do anything. Eight or nine days after the accident, a few of them cut some slivers of meat from one of the bodies and each ate a piece; proof that the taboo could be overcome, and an encouragement to the others. Only a few ate that day. The next day, when they heard the news that the search had been abandoned, most of the other boys started eating, but Javier and Liliana held out. Although they supported the decision, they felt unable to participate.

Javier waited another day or two before succumbing to his hunger. He reasoned religiously that surviving the plane crash was impossible, but God had let them live. It was impossible to live in the Andes, but God had given them the fuselage for shelter. The only way to continue to survive was to use the food that God had given them – the bodies of those who had died. When he balked at the prospect of taking that first piece, Marcelo Pérez del Castillo came to talk to him, and encouraged him to think of it as a communion, relaying a comment that Pedro Algorta had made on the first day of eating. After the horrific effort needed to swallow that first piece, Javier quickly became immune to it, but he never considered it as food; it was purely a means of survival. Liliana continued to hold out until the last piece of chocolate was gone, until she too was persuaded by Marcelo that it was the only way to survive, and that it was something that she would have to do if she wanted to return to her children.

The children were a constant and bittersweet preoccupation for Liliana and Javier. They would talk fondly of the good times, but at the same time worry about what was happening to them. Javier would reassure Liliana with the knowledge that her parents would be looking after them, and they made the decision that when they got back, they would invite her parents to move in with them. They discussed which room would be set aside for them, and how they would decorate it. They also resolved to have another baby. Liliana had previously been advised by a doctor that giving birth again might greatly exacerbate a problem she had with her spine. But a recent consultation with an orthopaedic specialist had dismissed that concern.

Another worry for Liliana was what would happen if they didn't return, or if only she returned. She had no knowledge of Javier's business affairs, but again Javier reassured her that his brothers would take care of everything, and she would live as well as if he were there beside her. Liliana started writing these things down in a letter to the family; also mentioning how wonderful all the boys were. She gave the unfinished letter to Javier for safe-keeping.

The boys were conscious of the danger of avalanches, and Javier had even proposed building a shelter away from the slope behind them, but the idea was dismissed as impractical. On the night of the avalanche – 29th October – the boys trooped into the fuselage in sleeping order. Liliana took her position about halfway along on the right-hand side, with Javier opposite her, their feet on each other's chests. She had Diego Storm to the left of her and Nando Parrado to the right, and Javier was sandwiched between Roberto Canessa and Roy Harley. As Javier was drifting off to sleep, he heard a sudden whoosh to his right, and for a brief instance, saw the snow entering the back of the fuselage. He was completely engulfed except for one of his hands, which he could move just enough to allow him to uncover his face. Next to him, Roy, who had leapt up and had escaped being buried, started to dig out some of the others. Because Javier's face was free, and he was not in immediate danger of dying, those digging bypassed him as they sought to uncover other faces. Unable to move, all Javier could do was to shout to Liliana beneath the snow to hold on, that someone would come soon. He implored the others to dig for Liliana, but the heads of those on the right-hand side were half a metre under the surface of the hardening snow, and it was a matter of luck as to whom could be found. Eventually, Gustavo Zerbino dug Javier out, and together they dug for Liliana. But it was too late – and only Nando was saved from the row of boys on either side of her.

The days following the avalanche were horrendous for everyone, trapped inside a small space in the fuselage, with their dead friends lying half-buried beside them. Javier had lost, in an instance, the dearest thing he had in the world, and, in the pain of the moment, he didn't believe he could ever recover. It was only his desire to return to his children, and his unshakeable faith in God, that helped him to bear it.

There was no doubt in his mind that the moment she had died, she had flown up to heaven, and he prayed that God would allow her to be his guardian angel.

Once the boys had escaped from the fuselage after three days buried, the fittest of them started organizing again, digging out the bodies buried in the snow, preparing the food, and planning the expeditions. There was little that Javier could do in the way of strenuous work, but he realized that if he got too weak, he would die, so he tried to keep himself active by making water, or sharpening knives. Javier's penknife, which had a screwdriver as well as a blade, was one of three that the group used to cut the meat. Two of the lighters also came courtesy of Javier, as did the large supply of cigarettes found at the tail, which he and his cousin had brought along as gifts for their hosts in Chile, where good cigarettes were reputed to be in short supply.

The boys would sometimes make fun of Javier, who often seemed to be in a world of his own, and who would talk and move frustratingly slowly. Whenever he carefully made his way back from collecting fresh snow to make water, each mis-step or stumble would elicit an 'Olé' from the watching boys. Javier good-naturedly went along with the ribbing, knowing it was good for their spirits, and thankful for these boys who would be his salvation.

A popular topic of conversation for the group was food, and here Javier had the advantage over everyone else, with years of experience sampling the many restaurants in Montevideo. He could talk for hours about their different dishes and specialities, and Coche recorded these in a notebook that had belonged to Coco Nicolich. Javier was also an accomplished cook, and promised to teach Tintín how to make *chupín de pescado*, a traditional fisherman's dish made over an open fire with potatoes and tomatoes. Numa Turcatti, who overheard this conversation, shyly asked Javier whether he could come along too. Numa would always address Javier formally, to a point where Javier threatened to stop speaking to him if he didn't start using his first name. Numa's gentle nature endeared him to Javier, and his rapid decline and subsequent death on 11th December affected Javier deeply.

Another of the boys Javier became especially attached to was Álvaro Mangino. In the first days after the accident, Javier had found Álvaro particularly spoilt, telling him that if he had been his father, he would have given him a sharp reprimand. But as the days passed, he became increasingly impressed with Álvaro's rapid maturation and change of behaviour. After the avalanche, the two of them paired up as sleeping partners. Álvaro was particularly difficult to sleep opposite, because his broken leg caused him to move it often, but the even-tempered Javier was quite tolerant of this, allowing him to position his leg where he wanted.

As the survivors prepared for the final expedition to the west, Javier helped where he could, participating in the sewing of the sleeping bag and, on his better days, doing his small part to dig holes in the snow to cover or uncover bodies. The days of waiting that followed the expeditionaries' departure were long and listless, and as time passed with no news, Fito Strauch and the other leaders started considering a further expedition. But the sudden news on the 21st December that Canessa and Parrado had reached civilization changed all that, and brought their time on the mountain to a rapid conclusion.

The helicopters arrived at around midday, dropping three members of the *Socorro Andino*, and an army nurse. They brought with them warm clothes, foods, tents, and cooking equipment. Six of the boys were immediately evacuated, and the remaining survivors awaited the helicopters' return. As evening approached with still no sign of them, the boys resigned themselves to spending another night on the mountain.

In retrospect, Javier – seeing the positive in everything as always – was happy not to have left the mountain on the first day of the rescue. He heard later that the helicopter flights for the first batch of evacuees had been terrifying; and besides, the extra night had allowed him to experience the hospitality of the volunteer *Cuerpo Socorro Andino*. They first set about dressing any wounds that needed attention, including Javier's hands, which had been giving him a lot of pain. They then prepared a variety of food, singing as they worked. There were butter-fried steak sandwiches, soups of various flavours – chicken, Scandinavian, and onion – and *Pan de Pascua*. To drink, there were juices, coffee, tea, and *yerba maté*.

When the helicopters picked them up the next day at 10:00 a.m., Javier travelled with Roy, Pancho, and Tintín. There was a brief stop at *Los Maitenes*, where Javier experienced the joy of seeing greenery and flowers for the first time in seventy-two days. Then, a short layover in San Fernando, where, although he was not allowed to leave the helicopter, he was briefly able to see and greet his brother Perucho, who had flown out immediately on hearing the news. Finally, the helicopter took them to the *Posta Central* hospital in Santiago.

Javier was the first of the arrivals to enter the hospital. He was overwhelmed by the reception they got from the people lining the corridors, and the constant attention they received from the doctors and nurses. After a bath and a shower, he was put in a ward with Coche, Álvaro, and Roy– the survivors who most needed medical attention, and who had lost the most weight. Javier had lost 25 kilos on the mountain, whereas Roy had lost 40 kilos; almost half his weight. The boys demanded food, and after some initial resistance by the medical staff, they were brought cheese and biscuits. Later, they had a supper of steak and mashed potato. And late in the evening, the nurses brought them a chocolate cake with cream. It didn't sit well with them, and gave Roy and Javier a terrible diarrhoea. The next morning, Javier felt too ill to eat his breakfast, but he was eager to get out of the hospital, and was released with his ward-mates at 10:00 a.m., joining the other survivors at the *Sheraton San Cristóbal*.

At the beginning of the odyssey, the families in Montevideo had started to hear the news of the disappearance of the plane from various sources: a friend of Javier's who had contacts in Mendoza, the fiancé of the Methols' maid who was a corporal in the Air Force, and the initial sketchy news reports. On the Friday evening, the house on Puyol street was full of relatives and friends, but the status of the flight was still unclear. On the Saturday, the directors of the *Stella Maris* and *Jesús María* colleges arrived at the house, and after a meeting with the relatives behind closed doors, it was Javier's sister, Marta, and Liliana's sister, Graciela, who emerged to break the news to Laura and Pablo.

Soon after the accident, Javier's sisters-in law, Raquel and Yinyú, found out about a rhabdomancer, Claudino Frigeiro, who lived in the poor neighbourhood of Maroñas, and who claimed to know the whereabouts of the plane. They paid him a visit, as later recalled by Raquel's daughter, Raquelita:

> After the crash, my mother, Raquel Donamari, and my aunt, Yinyú Servetto, wife of my uncle Juan José, said that they had heard of a rhabdomancer in the Curva de Maroñas who claimed to know where the plane was, and that there were survivors. My father, Pedro, and my uncle, Juan José, said that they were crazy, that it was impossible for anyone to have survived, and that they did not plan to visit him. So my mother, my aunt, and I went alone.

> When we arrived at the place, the man told us that we needed to bring a map to mark the place. So we went back to Pocitos, to my uncle Juan José's apartment, where my aunt Yinyú found an atlas, and we returned with it to Maroñas. I will never forget the moment when the rhabdomancer put his divining rod over the map, drew a circle, and said: "there are survivors"; it was very exciting.

> From there, the three of us went to Rafael Ponce de León's house so that he could radio Carlos Páez Vilaró and have them search in that place. We went there every day to hear the news. But Páez Vilaró's response was that they had already searched that area without success and that they were now looking elsewhere.

The place that Frigeiro had circled was a point 20 km north of Termas del Flaco on the Chilean-Argentinian border, near the *Tinguiririca* volcano, his pen-stroke starting and ending on the exact spot where the boys were. But the news that the Chilean air rescue service had already searched the area thoroughly meant that the matter was dropped, and attention turned to the pronouncements of Dutch clairvoyant, Gerard Croiset, which indicated a different place. Later, after the rescue had taken place and the rhabdomancer had been proved correct, Juan José went back to visit and reward him.

After this initial flurry of activity and optimism, there began a long period of uncertainty. After the official search ended, the unofficial sorties continued, and the Methol relatives contributed money to these efforts, but didn't take part in them. The highest priority was the children. For the first month and a half, they continued living at their own house in Carrasco with their maternal grandparents, but all their relatives stayed close, caring for them, and showering them with presents. When it became apparent that their parents wouldn't be returning, it was decided that Juan José and Yinyú were the best people to adopt them, as their own children were the closest in age, with Gabriela just six months younger than Laura. All the family on the father's side lived in Pocitos, most of them in the same apartment building, and that's where the children moved. The three youngest stayed in their schools for the time being, but Laura changed from *Jesús María* to her cousins' school in Pocitos. With their family now swelled to seven, Juan José decided to buy a new house in Pocitos, near the Panamericano building which towers above Buceo bay. They were just at the point of exchanging contracts when the news came of the appearance of Nando Parrado and Roberto Canessa.

The children were at the farm at the time. Laura and Pablo were sitting in their uncle's Jeep, along with Gabriela, listening to the radio as the names of the survivors were read out. As the list neared the end, their hopes started to fade, but the sixteenth and final name was Javier Methol. Laura and Pablo couldn't contain their happiness. The unexpected joy of having one parent return from the dead overwhelmed the sadness of having lost a mother for whom they had already grieved. Gabriela, on the other hand, was in tears at having lost her aunt and godmother.

They returned to Montevideo and stayed at their grandmother's apartment in front of the Kibón, from where they called their father in the hospital in Santiago. In the absence of Javier at Christmas, it was Laura who dressed up as *Papa Noel* that year. When the survivors returned on 28th December, the children went with their relatives to the school, joining the other families to await the arrival of the buses from the airport. As the gaunt and bearded survivors, almost messianic in appearance, emerged from the buses one by one, the children had difficulty distinguishing which one was their father.

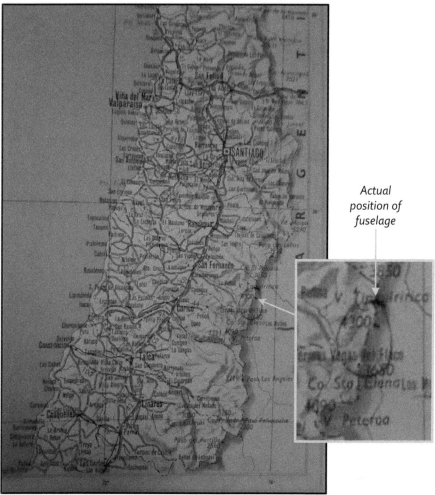

Fig. 175. *Position of plane marked on the atlas by rhabdomancer Claudino Frigeiro.*

After the joyful reunion, Javier decided not to go to the press conference, and he slipped away with his family. Everyone had cautioned the younger children not to talk to their father about their mother as he was very sad, and had gone through a very difficult situation. But as soon as they got into the car, three-year-old Marie Noel couldn't help blurting out: "Where's Mamá?" Javier explained that she was with God. A few days later, they all went to the grandmother's house in Punta del Este, spending the summer there because the family home in Carrasco had been rented out to a friend before news of the survivors had emerged. One day that summer, Javier was walking hand-in-hand with Marie Noel, who had been unusually quiet all day. Suddenly, she looked at her father and said, "Papá, you came back from the sky, but when is Mamá coming back?" Javier responded, "Mamá was so very nice that God needs her in the sky. She is so important that she is living with God. She's always looking at you from the sky." Marie Noel didn't ask any more after that, but she would always speak about her mother in the present tense.

Javier was, and continued to be, perhaps the most religious of the survivors, never losing his faith despite the loss of Liliana. He thanked God for keeping him alive for his children, and he believed that much of what had happened was miraculous. But he felt fortunate that the accident happened with that group of boys from *The Christian*, because he felt they would not have survived without the discipline, leadership, and teamwork that the boys had learnt at the school.

Fig. 176. *Javier in the kitchen.*

After spending the summer in Punta del Este, Javier and his children moved back into their former home, and, fulfilling one of Liliana's last wishes, her parents moved in to help look after the children. At the time, Javier felt that he would never get married again, because the memory of Liliana would compromise his happiness; but after four years he started courting Ana María, his cousin's daughter, whom he had known since she was born, and whose family lived in Buenos Aires. Javier and his children would visit them regularly, and they, in turn, would spend every summer in Punta del Este. The two got married a year later, exactly five years after the rescue from the mountain, and Javier went on to father four more children with her.

Talk about the mountain was off-limits within the family in the years after the accident, and they didn't read the books about the tragedy. It wasn't until the movie *Alive* came out in 1993 that Javier began to talk about some things. In March 1995, Javier travelled back to the mountain with twelve other survivors, spending the night near the grave

where Liliana was buried. He was struck by how the positive lessons of the story had transcended the individual tragedies. He reflected that whilst Liliana's body remained on the mountain, her love had stayed alive in him, and through him, in his children.

Two years later, Javier travelled to San Fernando with his children and their families, joining a large

Fig. 177. *Javier enjoying a maté.*

contingent from Uruguay to commemorate the twenty-fifth anniversary of the tragedy. The visit ended with the opening of a permanent exhibit about the Andes story at the local *Museo Lircunlauta*. The Uruguayans were amazed to find not only the museum authorities there, but hundreds of people from the local community, who welcomed them with the same affection that they had shown at the time of the rescue. Javier said of the warm reception: "There are two words that describe the Chileans: fraternity and friendship." The day was rounded off with a celebration featuring a traditional *cueca*, the Chilean national dance.

In later years, after he retired from the family business, which had by then been bought up by Philip Morris, Javier started telling his story more widely, speaking in workshops on teamwork, hosted by the Franklin Covey consulting company.

On Liliana's side of the family, her mother, Lita Petraglia de Navarro, became one of the founding members of the *Biblioteca Nuestros Hijos*. When the work took her to the *Hotel Carrasco* – the library's first home – Laura would tag along, eager to explore the grand hotel by herself whilst her grandmother went about library business. Laura never felt the calling to carry on her grandmother's work in the library, but she pursued similar goals through her volunteer social work. Even as a schoolgirl at *Jesús María*, she would work with the nuns in the nearby *asentamiento* (slum) of *Barrio C*. In later years, after her son started at *The Christian*, Laura began volunteering with the *Madres de la Cruz*, an association dedicated to support the education and development of kids in the *asentamiento* of *La Cruz de Carrasco*. It had been started by the last two Christian Brothers on leaving the school.

Unlike her husband and children, Laura has never read any of the books about the tragedy. She has preferred to hear about her mother directly from the survivors; from Coche, Pancho, Gustavo, and Roberto. They tell her about the great esteem in which Liliana was held on the mountain, her maternal role, her optimism, and her resolute strength.

On 4th June 2015, Javier became the first of the sixteen survivors to die, succumbing to cancer. He is buried in Buceo cemetery, where his fellow passenger Rafael Echavarren is also laid to rest. Like Rafael, Javier's part in this extraordinary story is commemorated with a plaque placed on his tomb by the *Re Viven* group.

A saying on his memorial card expresses his simple outlook on life:

Don't complain about what you lack
Be grateful for what you have
And never, never stop fighting for what you want.

Fig. 178. *Last family photograph before Javier's death in June 2015.*

Francisco 'Pancho' Nicola and Esther Horta de Nicola
08-Aug-1932 — 13-Oct-1972, 15-Aug-1932 — 13-Oct-1972

On the evening of 31st May 1932, thirty-year-old paediatrician Dr Francisco Nicola Reyes had just finished his day's work at the Pereira Rossell Hospital in Montevideo, when a nurse asked him to urgently attend to a young boy with tuberculous meningitis who had taken a life-threatening turn for the worse. Although the boy was not his patient, Nicola Reyes hurried over to his bed and called for oxygen to help relieve his distress. Moments later, the boy's father arrived, a civil servant who had lost his wife some years previously. Seeing the agony that his son was experiencing, and hearing the doctor's prognosis, the distraught father drew a gun, firing two shots at Dr Nicola Reyes and one at his son before turning the gun on himself. The boy died immediately, but the doctor clung on to life, one bullet having grazed his heart, the other permanently lodged in his spine. When he finally emerged from hospital in January 1933, paralysed from the waist down after an arduous eight-month struggle for survival, his wife Marita Brusco took over his fulltime care.

Confined to a wheelchair, and unable to continue as a paediatrician, he became a ham radio aficionado, transmitting under call sign CX3CN, quickly establishing himself as an indispensable medical resource, nationally and internationally. Keeping up to date with the medical state of the art, he would advise, diagnose, and even guide operations in remote regions, or at sea. In the latter years of the second world war, when amateur radio was prohibited in most countries in the world, Dr Nicola Reyes was given special dispensation to continue transmitting, due to his humanitarian contributions. QST, the US amateur radio publication, reported in its March 1945 edition:

> To those of you who think ham radio is completely shut down around this war-ridden earth, it will be welcome news that a few, a very few, amateurs are still operating in a very few places. Information reaches us from OA4D in Miraflores, Peru, ... that he has a 'sked' every Saturday at 4:00 p.m. Peruvian time (21:00 GMT) with CX3CN in Montevideo, the only Uruguayan ham permitted to operate in his country.

The brief report concluded, somewhat patronisingly, that the doctor had only been granted this privilege because he was bed-ridden, and radio was his only diversion. In fact, when the weather and his radio commitments permitted, he would spend the afternoon sitting in his wheelchair on the promenade overlooking Pocitos beach, close to his home in the first block of Brasil Avenue. There he was a well-recognized and popular figure, and many passers-by would stop to greet him, and chat with him.

The satisfaction that Dr Nicola Reyes garnered from being able to save lives remotely was surpassed only by his delight in watching his son grow up. Francisco had been born three months after the shooting tragedy, and in the same hospital, at a time when his father's life had been in the balance. As is common in Spanish, Francisco went by the standard nickname of Panchito when he was young, which later became Pancho once his own son was born.

Dr Nicola Reyes had been an avid sportsman in earlier days, playing as a defender for the Intermediate Division *Oriental Pocitos* football team. Now he participated vicariously through his son, who, by the age of 12, had become a junior swimming champion, representing the Biguá club where the fathers of Gastón Costemalle and Coco Nicolich were already members. Later, like them, he represented Uruguay in the South American swimming championships, taking part in the freestyle events at the 1949 championship in Montevideo and the 1952 championship in Lima.

Panchito also excelled on the rugby field, playing for local team Trouville – the 'reds' of Pocitos – in the Uruguayan first division, and getting selected for the national team, *Los Teros*, in the first South America Rugby Championship in Buenos Aires in 1951. He played as a centre three-quarter in all three games, helping *Los Teros* to a creditable second place, losing only to Argentina. Not very tall, but strong and agile, Pancho's tackling in the low-scoring win against Chile led to his moniker "the Uruguayan who tackled the entire Chilean three-quarter line".

As well as being an accomplished sportsman, Pancho was a top student, and was studying to become a paediatrician like his father. But by the early fifties, Dr Nicola Reyes' health was beginning to deteriorate, and he died in May 1954, not surviving to see his son qualify as a doctor. Pancho 's mother Marita also died prematurely, in June 1959, just before his final exams, but she did live to see the birth of his first child in November 1958 – a boy named Francisco like his father and grandfather before him.

Pancho's wife, Esther Horta, was the oldest of six daughters and four sons, the large family matching that of her father who was the penultimate of ten children. Esther's great-grandfather Félix Evaristo José Horta was the younger of two Catalan brothers who had emigrated to Uruguay in the mid-nineteenth century. They had settled in Paysandú and joined forces in business, becoming important figures in local industry and international commerce. Félix later became a successful financier and an agricultural landowner. His farmlands were passed down through the family, although the acreage diminished over the generations, as parts were sold off. The farm in Paysandú was familiar territory for the Horta siblings, and in later years, Esther's children and their cousins would spend a month in the summer visiting their aunt Ana who lived there. But Esther's father administered a

44,000 hectare farm in the department of Florida, closer to Montevideo, and Esther would spend the summer months there where she and Pancho, to whom she was engaged by this time, would look after her younger siblings.

Fig. 179. *Horta family. From back, left to right: Adela, Ana, Esther, Graciela; Félix, Señora Esther with baby Gonzalo, José Alberto; Cristina, Diego, María*

After the couple got married, they settled in Pocitos, Pancho working to establish himself as a paediatrician, and Esther turning her attention to raising their growing family, which, by the mid-sixties consisted of four boys: Francisco ('Pancho'), José Luis ('Pepe'), Juan Pedro ('JuanPe'), and Marcelo ('Marce'). By the time JuanPe was born, the apartment in Pocitos had become too small, and the family moved to Carrasco. Pancho was by now well-established in his profession and they rented an attractive detached house on Avenida Blanes Viale that was more commensurate with his status. The sons were to go to *Stella Maris College*, with its unique combination of Catholic and bilingual education and, as an added bonus, rugby – the game at which Pancho had excelled long before the school had been conceived of.

The older two boys started playing rugby at school, and it wasn't long before their father found himself getting involved with the *Old Christians* also. He responded to a plea from Brother 'Chato' O'Donnell who was the prime mover of all things related to the club. Chato desperately needed people to help share the load, and had made an appeal to parents of children in the school. With his knowledge of the game and experience as a player, Pancho was a godsend, and he was appointed youth team manager, and assistant coach. He became an ardent supporter of the first fifteen, and he and his sons would watch all the games, which, at that time, were still being played at the school.

Fig. 180. *The house on Avenida Blanes Viale.*

Outside school and rugby, there were trips to one or other of the *estancias*, or, in the summer, to the beach in Punta del Este. At weekends, when rugby permitted, a popular past-time was water-skiing. The husband of Esther's sister Cristina had a motor-boat, and the two couples and the children would spend the day at *Lake Calcagno* in Carrasco. They would often be joined by Esther's sister Adela and her children.

When the opportunity arose to go to Chile, Pancho jumped at it – he fondly remembered his international game against Chile in which he had won such acclaim, and it was a good opportunity to get away for a few days, and to support and manage the team. Esther was not so sure. She had a great fear of flying, and was worried about leaving her children for a few days. Her sister María Laura was recently married, and while she and her husband were waiting for their apartment to be ready, they were staying in an annex at Esther and Pancho's house, and would be able to look after the boys for a few days. But Esther was worried about what would happen if she didn't return. She called Cristina to tell her that she hadn't prepared for the eventuality of not coming back, asking her to promise not to separate the boys, and to look after them should the worst happen. She reinforced the message when, three days before the flight, she went to Cristina's home downtown for a farewell dinner with her father who was living in his daughter's house, the mother having died in 1967. Esther also spoke to one of the Brothers at the school, to ask him to take special care of her youngest son who was just starting there.

Fig. 181. *Esther Horta and Pancho Nicola with sons JuanPe, Francisco, Marce and Pepe.*

Despite Esther's misgivings, she set off with her husband on the morning of 12th October, and it was an uneventful flight until bad weather over the Andes forced a stopover in Mendoza. Whereas, for most of the passengers, this was a frustrating delay that would take time away from their few days in Chile, it was, for Esther, a serendipitous turn of events, as it afforded her the unexpected opportunity to spend time with her sister Adela and her family. Adela's husband, Alberto Koninckx, was a biologist, and, in 1970, he had been offered a research position in Mendoza. For a year, he had lived away from his family, but on the couple of occasions that Adela had visited her husband, the four children would stay back in Montevideo with Esther, swelling her household to eight children. By 1971, it was clear that this would be a long-term position for Alberto, and the whole family moved to Mendoza, settling three or four kilometres north of the town centre. Esther hadn't seen her sister since the move.

After checking in to the *Hotel Sussex*, half a block from *Plaza Independencia*, Esther and Pancho headed to Adela's house. Finding no-one there, they spoke to a neighbour who directed them to the local sports club, the *Club Social y Deportivo General San Martín* – the *Pacific club* for short – on Perú street. Adela and husband were taking advantage of the national holiday and the sunny weather to play a game of tennis, and the kids had gone with them to practise their roller skating.

Fig. 182. *Koninckx children Jeannine (10), Alain (11), Denise (9), Ghislain (7), and Baloo the dog soon after the unexpected appearance of their aunt and uncle Esther and Pancho.*

The children had been very close to their aunt and uncle when the family had lived in Montevideo, enjoying days at the beach together, or water skiing. Their school had been nearer to Esther's house than to their own and they would often end up there after school, which gave them the opportunity to spend time with their cousins. So, despite the excitement of moving to a new place, they sorely missed their extended family. Denise – nine years old at the time – later recalled the moment when their aunt and uncle had appeared:

377

I was with my siblings skating when all of a sudden I saw two familiar individuals crossing the rink, approaching us with a broad smile. I did a double take and could hardly believe my eyes; but it was them, my aunt and uncle standing in front of us, they were real! When the euphoria passed and we were able to catch our breath, we learnt that they were flying to Chile when the pilot decided to land in Mendoza because of bad weather conditions.

Adela and Alberto wanted to take full advantage of the short time Esther and Pancho would spend in Mendoza and were eager to show them some of the places that the family had discovered and enjoyed over the previous year. They arranged to leave the children at

home and set off by car, following the road north out of Mendoza into the foothills to visit the thermal springs at Villavicencio where they spent the afternoon. Despite enjoying the sights, the mountains provoked a certain disquiet in Esther, more used to the sea and the low rolling hills of Uruguay.

They returned to Mendoza in time for dinner at the house of their neighbours Teodoro and Elena Martínez who had become firm friends with Adela and Alberto from the moment the family had moved in. They had been busy preparing a special meal in

Fig. 183. *Adela and Esther at Villavicencio 12th October 1972.*

honour of the visitors. Chatting late into the evening, the joy of this unexpected visit prompted a plea for them to stay for a few more days, rather than continue on to Chile. Esther and Pancho were tempted, but felt an obligation to their *Old Christian* friends who had invited them along on the trip. Driving them back to the hotel that evening, the two couples stopped off briefly at *Parque General San Martín*, stopping to admire the ornate gates at the entrance, and to stroll down the lakeside rose-garden promenade. Esther was especially taken by the lingering fragrance of the roses and the tranquil view over the lake by night.

The next morning, Adela and Alberto picked up Esther and Pancho at the hotel and drove them to the airport where they mingled with the other passengers waiting to hear whether they could continue their trip. There were still doubts because of the weather. Esther was so nervous that she approached the pilot, telling him that she had four children at home, that she wanted to get back safely, and she pleaded with them not to fly if conditions weren't right. The pilots reassured her. Adding to Esther's worries was the fact that it was now Friday 13th, a date on which she would never have arranged to fly. Javier Methol told her not to worry, that for him, thirteen was a lucky number. Esther was not convinced, and asked Adela to accompany her to the ladies' room, where she took a sedative to quell her anxiety.

Eventually the decision was made. Based on information from a meat-carrying cargo plane travelling in the opposite direction, which had landed at the airport shortly before, they would fly a different route, over the Planchón pass further to the south rather than over the higher but more direct *Cristo Redentor* pass. Copilot Dante Lagurara would be at the helm, since the captain, Julio Ferradás, was feeling unwell.

Boarding the plane, Esther and Pancho sat down in the second row on the right-hand side of the plane, Esther by the aisle, and Pancho by the window. There they took a photograph of Adela and Alberto who were waving goodbye. Across the aisle from Esther were the Methols who had also left four children at home, Javier on the aisle, and Liliana by the window. The flight went smoothly until they started hitting the air pockets. The boys seated further back were putting on a brave face and singing rugby chants. Pancho Nicola turned around and joined in with the team members throwing a rugby ball around. The second big air pocket caused more alarm. Roberto Canessa, who was sitting behind Javier, diagonally across from Esther, asked her if she was afraid. She barely had time to answer "Yes!", when rocks appeared a couple of metres outside the window, followed by a series of crashes. A great rush of cold air filled the fuselage, as the stricken plane landed on its belly, and started tobogganing down the mountainside. When it came to a halt, the seats on the right-hand side, loosened by the impact and the crumpled floor, all piled forward. Javier, on the left-hand side was unscathed. After checking that Liliana was all right, he looked across the aisle. Esther had been crushed by the seats moving forward, and Pancho had been thrown forward, his head hitting against the bulkhead. Both had died immediately.

In Mendoza, Alberto Koninckx was working in his lab where the radio was on when he heard the chilling report that Uruguayan Air Force Flight 571 had disappeared. For the Koninckx family, the devastating news contrasted starkly against the joy of the previous day, and the fond farewell at the airport just a few hours earlier. Listening to the developing news over the following days became an agony which would reduce Adela to tears, and she would light candles in every room of the house to keep a flicker of hope alive. Alberto and Adela tried everything possible to participate in the search and rescue effort, but to no avail, and were horrified and incredulous when the search was called off after eight days. With the help of their neighbour Teodoro, who was a ham radio operator, they at least found some solace in keeping in regular contact with their relatives in Montevideo at a time when the cost of an international phone call was prohibitive.

When the news had broken in Montevideo, there had been uncertainty and disbelief that the reports could be referring to the *Old Christians* flight. Cristina heard the news from her father when she got home from work, but her immediate reaction was that it was impossible, that they would have arrived in Chile the previous day, but eventually it became clear that it was their plane. Amidst the confusion and uncertainty of the news, Rosario Martínez Lamas, distraught about her brother Julio who was on the flight, called Dr Nicola, her children's paediatrician. To her shock she discovered that he and his wife were on the same plane.

In the days following the flight, Esther's brothers and sisters came to the conclusion that everyone had died, and, apart from the efforts of Adela and her husband in Mendoza, didn't participate in the search. Only the sons held out hope that they might still be alive, and Francisco, who was thirteen at the time, often went to Ponce de León's house to keep abreast of the search efforts. Francisco and Pepe, who was eleven, both knew what was going on, but the younger ones, seven and six years old, were shielded from any talk of what might have happened. Nevertheless they deeply felt the absence of their parents, and JuanPe had many nightmares over that period. The two older brothers felt a responsibility towards the younger boys, and went to every one of their rugby and football games in place of their parents.

When the news came through that there were survivors, there was renewed hope. Although there was doubt as to whether Esther might have survived such an ordeal, it was felt that Pancho, who was a great leader and an athlete in good physical condition, would have every chance of making it. This hope turned to optimism when there were reports of a 'doctor' amongst the passengers who had cured the injured, and the only doctor on the flight was Pancho. Everyone was convinced that he must have orchestrated the boys' survival on the mountain. On the back of this conviction, Esther's two youngest brothers, Gonzalo and Diego, travelled immediately to Chile. There they heard the bad news when the survivor list was broadcast. A false story was circulating that Pancho had survived for five days, and had prepped the boys on survival techniques before he died, but the survivors soon scotched that rumour, confirming that the couple had died immediately. Gonzalo and Diego returned to Montevideo.

Despite the shock and grief at the final confirmation, there was some comfort that at least sixteen families had received good news. There remained the pressing practical issue of what to do about the four children. During the seventy-two days of no news, they had been staying at the house on Blanes Viale with María Laura and her husband. Francisco promised his young brothers that they would not be split up, the same sentiment that Esther had made clear in the days before the trip. But the sudden burden of care and expense for four extra children was not easily mitigated. The family decided that the four boys should continue living at their parents' house under the immediate care of María Laura and her husband. María Laura – the youngest of the sisters – had previously entered a convent in preparation for becoming a nun, but later she had left the religious life, and had studied to become a social worker. At the time of the accident she was recently married, and expecting a baby.

Cristina was made the children's legal guardian and she helped out in every spare hour. Like María Laura and Graciela, Cristina had a fulltime job in Montevideo. Adela was in Mendoza and there was little she could do, but Ana took care of the children over the summer at the farm in Paysandú. Then there was the issue of school fees. In view of the extraordinary circumstances, the Brothers decided to give the boys full scholarships for the duration of their time at *Stella Maris*, and made a special effort to watch over them, to console them at those moments when the realization of their situation would suddenly hit them. Brother Chato O'Donnell, in particular, acted as a father figure, nurturing them through school and on the rugby field.

After two years with María Laura, the children spent a year or so with an uncle – José. By this time, royalties from the book *ALIVE* were starting to come through, and the survivors clubbed together to buy the boys a house on Ferrari Avenue in Carrasco where they could live by themselves. Initially two ladies would come every day to cook and clean, and the boys' aunts would help at the weekend or during the week when work permitted. But eventually, Cristina found a lady with a young son who was happy to take up the position of a full-time live-in helper, to deal with the day-to-day running of the household.

Life was very difficult for the first 15 years. The disparity between what they had had before, compared to what they had after, was a stark lesson about what could happen in life. One positive thing that helped them to cope with their adversity was the development of an unbreakable bond with the *Old Christians*. JuanPe later recalled:

> *1284 Ferrari Avenue became almost like a clubhouse. Roberto, Nando, and Gustavo would always be coming over to see us. We would sing rugby songs, and they would hold meetings there and conduct club business. And if ever any one of us fell ill, Pepe would bring Roberto home to attend to us.*

Gustavo and Roberto also made sure that the boys had the mementos of their parents that the two of them had brought back from the mountain – their mother's rings, and their father's *Omega* watch which Roberto had worn on the final expedition.

Fig. 184. *JuanPe Nicola in 2019 outside the house bought for them by the survivors in the mid-seventies.*

Rugby became an increasingly important part of the boys' lives, with the discipline and team spirit learnt on the field providing them with a code of conduct for how to live their lives off the field. Francisco, who would go on to become a paediatrician like his father and grandfather before him, was part of the great *Old Christians* team of the second half of the seventies, which won five successive Uruguayan championships; a team that included Roberto, Gustavo, Tintín, Alejandro Nicolich (Coco's brother), and Bobby Jaugust who had been on the 1972 trip, but had flown by commercial airline. It was a team coached by Aldo Magri (Guido's brother), and moulded around their iconic long-term captain Jorge Zerbino (Gustavo's brother) who represented his country twenty-seven times.

Pepe, a strong and intelligent player, who played centre three-quarter like his brother, also became part of that team, and rapidly sprang to the notice of the national selectors. He made his international debut in a 48-0 defeat of Brazil at the 1979 South American Rugby Championship, and went on to represent *Los Teros* six times, scoring a total of 7 tries – all of them coming in the 1981 championships in Montevideo, in which Uruguay finished top. But his international career was cut short by the diagnosis, that year, of *Lupus Nephritis*, a disease that attacked his joints and would eventually result in him needing a new kidney.

The *Old Christians* immediately organised a fundraiser to try to get him the best possible care. Pepe travelled with Roberto Canessa to Stanford University Hospital in California, one of the top medical centres in the world. The trip not only provided the medical care that Pepe needed, it also triggered a pivotal change in Roberto's career. As he later recalled in his memoir *I Had to Survive*, it was the conversations he had in Stanford with Dr Norman Shumway – the first doctor to perform a heart transplant in the USA – that led to an interest in echocardiography and to his subsequent career as a paediatric heart surgeon.

Despite the blow to his rugby career, Pepe stayed active within the *Old Christians Club*, working on various committees or on the board, and there was a last hurrah on the rugby field. It was in a 1984 championship-deciding game against *Carrasco Polo* which the *Old Christians* were losing with minutes to go. Pepe, whose knee was racked with pain from the effects of the lupus, came on and led the drive to win the game in the dying moments. He was carried off on a stretcher. That year was the start of another period of great success for the *Old Christians* who won back-to-back championships from 1984 to 1989.

By the end of the decade, Pepe had got to the point where he was in critical need of a kidney transplant. His aunt María Laura, who had looked after him in the first couple of years after his parents died, travelled with him to São Paulo and became his living donor. Sadly, three or four years later, María Laura died of cancer, but her kidney lived on in Pepe. In 2005, he made a trip to the mountain with Chato O'Donnell who had been such an important figure in his life, along with several of his former classmates, amongst them his lifelong friend Pepe Lestido. And when Pepe Nicola needed another transplant a few years later, it was Lestido – a family man with five children – who, in an act of extraordinary love and generosity, offered one of his own kidneys to Pepe. Through all this, Pepe continued to work tirelessly for the *Old Christians Club*, becoming president in 2009, and continuing for several years, a popular and respected presence at the club. Another of his classmates who had gone on the 2005 Andes trip was Arturo Nogueira's brother Gabriel ('Pulun') who observed of him: "Pepe is, for our generation especially, a symbol of courage, integrity, and approachability, with all the good qualities a person can have."

Of the two younger brothers, it was Marce who excelled on the rugby field, the seed sown by Pepe in those early years after their parents died, when Marce was only 6 or 7 years old. Pepe would spend hours practising with his young brother in the garden of the house on Blanes Viale. Setting up an old tyre, he would get Marce to repeatedly pass the ball through it to improve his accuracy. That early coaching paid off, as Marce would go on to be the most successful of the four brothers on the rugby field, playing fullback for Uruguay twenty-one times between 1989 and 1995, and becoming one of the most prolific scorers in the history of *Los Teros*, with a career total of 209 points. He captained the *Old Christians* over that period, becoming their coach when his playing days were over, and, in 2001, he became assistant coach of the national team, helping to take them to the 2003 Rugby World Cup in Australia.

Fig. 185. *Pepe Lestido, Chato O'Donnell, Pepe Nicola in the Valley of Tears, summer 2005.*

The 2005 expedition was not the first trip Pepe had made to the mountain. The four brothers had made a trip together as early as 1997, the twenty-fifth anniversary of the tragedy. They were invited by five of the survivors – Roberto, Gustavo, Nando, Coche, and Moncho, and were joined by Coco Nicolich's brother Alejandro. It was a trip that was sponsored and documented by the *Universidad Católica de Chile*.

Approaching from the Chilean side, they followed the courses of the *Portillo* and *San José* rivers upstream, reversing the route that Nando and Roberto had taken in 1972. Once they reached the snowline and progress became too difficult, they dismounted and continued on foot for a while, far enough to reach the foot of the steep gully that it had taken Roberto and Nando two days to make their way down.

Later, two prearranged helicopters picked up the four brothers, along with Roberto and Gustavo, and, following the route that the rescue corps had flown in 1972, they dropped them on a safe part of the glacier. As in 1972, there had been a heavier than usual snowfall that year, and they saw their surroundings much as they had been twenty five years previously. The group spent an emotional 30 minutes on the mountain. The conditions made the grave inaccessible, so they erected a cross, and, gathering around it, they paused to pray and remember. Then there was time for a quick game of touch rugby before the helicopters picked them up.

In 2002, the brothers travelled to Chile again, though not to the mountain this time. They were part of a group of close to 200 Chileans and Uruguayans – *Grange Old Boys* and *Old Christians* – who gathered for the annual *Copa de la Amistad*, the *Friendship Cup*. All four brothers played in the symbolic five-minute memorial match before younger club members took over. Pepe scored the try that clinched the draw.

There have been many other trips to the mountain. JuanPe has been three times. In 2006 he went with his son Mateo and four of the survivors, Roberto, Gustavo, Fito, and Moncho. It was the first time JuanPe had been able to stand at the graveside. That expedition had also included Uruguayan author Pablo Vierci, and Uruguayan director Gonzalo Arijon, who was filming the documentary *Stranded*. Another time, accompanied by family and friends, he went with Gustavo and a group of Argentinian boys from *Rugby Sin Fronteras* – Rugby without Borders – the foundation cofounded by Gustavo.

In the early years after the accident, JuanPe stayed silent about the tragedy, bottling up his pain inside, and he only started to open up when, at age 16, he met his future wife, Carolina. But in recent years, JuanPe, an IT manager and an amateur pilot, has been one of the most active proponents of the story. He believes that, in Uruguay, not enough is being done to spread it to future generations, that it is a rich story of humanity and love, with many life lessons. He feels that the community in Carrasco, centred around *Stella Maris College* and the British school, was transformed by the story to focus their lives on the service of others, that the human values deriving from those of rugby are of universal importance.

One place where the story has made a difference in Uruguay is in the area of organ transplants. Uruguay was the first country in the region to have legislation on transplants, approved in 1971. Despite the fact that Uruguayan donor rates were some of the highest in Latin America, there was still an acute shortage of organs. In September 2010, the *Fundación Viven*, set up by the survivors in 2006, with Coche Inciarte as president, launched a campaign to get more Uruguayans to donate their organs. Coche explained:

> *Emulating the pact of life that we made up there in the Andes Mountains, in which we donated our entire bodies each to the other, the* Fundación Viven *has decided to make a new pact of life, but this time between all Uruguayans, through an awareness campaign.*

JuanPe worked actively in the campaign, championing the cause on the radio. The focus on the issue had the desired effect, resulting, in 2013, in new legislation that made all Uruguayans donors by default.

This was one of several humanitarian projects carried out by the *Fundación Viven*, which was set up in memory of those who didn't return. In 2012, on the fortieth anniversary of the tragedy, they presented a tribute to the families of their dead friends:

> *They are the real heroes of this story.*
> *Their courage and generosity was what allowed us to return to the love of our families.*
> *Because at the end of the day, what always remains and what is always valuable is love...*
> *Love of life itself...*

Gustavo 'Coco' Nicolich
03-Aug-1952 — 29-Oct-1972

By the second week of May 1974, Nando Parrado and Roberto Canessa were embarking on the last leg of their marathon tour to promote the book *ALIVE*, the official account of the tragedy. An intense month of local and national media appearances in 20 cities across the US had been followed by ten days of the same in Ireland and the UK, interspersed with numerous social events attended by politicians, nobility, literati, and other eminent members of British society, all eager to meet the Andes heroes. The promotional tour had now moved to mainland Europe, where the boys were due to appear on the French national television programme, *Les Dossiers de l'écran*.

The producers were keen to have a parent of a non-survivor for the programme, and *ALIVE* author Piers Paul Read had recommended Raquel and Gustavo Nicolich, parents of Coco. Despite their ongoing grief, they felt an imperative to support the survivors, and had never closed the door to reporters. Much to the appreciation of Nando and Roberto, they agreed to fly to Paris especially for the show, which aired live on Tuesday 14th May.

As with many interviews, the main focus of discussion was the anthropophagy, and the question was thrown to the viewers: "What would you have done in their place?" The programme attracted enormous public interest, with an estimated audience of 20 million, with only the ongoing French presidential election competing for attention. The audience response was overwhelmingly positive, with 90% of callers expressing their understanding of the situation, and supporting the decision. Several mentioned wartime parallels.

Canessa and Parrado, experienced by now in handling the media, expertly fielded the questions, which ranged from the morbidly curious, "What does human flesh taste like?" to the tendentious, "What about rumours that the boys hastened the death of some passengers?" Canessa talked about the terrible decision they had had to take, and the role he had shared in convincing the other boys to break the taboo. Parrado confirmed that in identical circumstances they would make the same decision again. But it was the presence of Coco's parents that impressed everyone the most. They acknowledged that the anthropophagy was the only way possible to preserve life.

Referring to a letter that Coco had written on the mountain before he died, Raquel said: "We are proud of this tribute of friendship made by our son, and we support the decision taken by Roberto and Fernando. We are trying to help them overcome this ordeal." The letter included an explicit confirmation of Coco's part in the pact that the boys had made on the mountain:

One thing that will seem incredible to you – it also seems so to me – today we started to cut the dead in order to eat them, there is nothing else to do. As for me, I asked God in all that is possible that this day would never come, but it came, and we have to face it with courage and with faith. Faith because I came to the conclusion that the bodies are there because God put them there, and as the only thing that matters is the soul, I don't have any remorse – and if the day came and I could save someone with my body, I would gladly do so.

After the interview, as Nando and Roberto continued their European tour, Raquel and Gustavo returned to Uruguay, to their beautiful family home on Divina Comedia street in Carrasco. The house, designed by Gustavo and decorated by Raquel, had been a popular place for Coco and his friends to gather, especially on Saturdays,

Fig. 186. *Coco in primary school.*

when they would get together to play cards and discuss politics, with gin and tonic to lubricate the rowdy interchange of opinions. The absence of those lively gatherings only served to accentuate the sadness that now pervaded the family home.

The group of friends, known as 'the gang', consisted of Coco, Diego Storm, Roy Harley and his brother Walter, Carlitos Páez, Tito Regules, Bobby François, and Pablo Fonseca whose father was a cousin of Mr Nicolich. The Fonsecas and the Harleys lived on the same street as Coco, and the others all lived within walking distance, close to the beach and the main streets of Carrasco. The families formed a close social circle going back many years, with parties, shared dinners, barbecues, days on the beach, and get-togethers at one or other *estancia*.

Coco, tall with dark curly hair, extroverted, self-confident, and with a good sense of humour, was the oldest of the Nicolich children, his younger brother Alejandro sandwiched by sisters Mónica and Raquelina. The Nicolich boys were known as the 'Cocoliches' at *Stella Maris College*, where all the gang had gone, Cocoliche being a pidgin language spoken by early Italian immigrants to Uruguay: from *Nicolich* to *Cocoliche* to *Coco*, a name that would later be inherited by Alejandro.

Fig. 187. *Clockwise: Carlitos Páez (in foreground), Coco Nicolich, Diego Storm, Pablo Fonseca.*

The gang would get together regularly after school, to chat or plan their activities. On Friday nights, they would meet at Diego's house, for an evening of reflection with Fr Faget, a young priest from the community, discussing the problems and difficulties of everyday life. On Sundays, there was rugby for those that played. Coco, though not the fastest of players, was a natural leader, and captained one of the *Old Christian* B teams, *St Patrick's*. He played fullback; a position ably filled in the first team by Eddie Suarez, so it was only when Eddie was unable to play that Coco would make an appearance in the first fifteen.

Like Diego, Coco loved to travel, and the two of them hitchhiked the 2,500 km to Rio de Janeiro in January 1970. They were joined by Pablo Fonseca, and by Juan Francisco Garcia-Austt, the boyfriend and future husband of Coco's sister Mónica. On their return, the boys were interviewed about their adventure by journalist Jimmy Arocena – an uncle of Coco. In a photo of the interview, the boys are looking on intently at Arocena as he makes detailed notes, Coco leaning forward in his denim suit; a gift from a friend of his father, which earned him the nickname 'Mr Levi'.

Fig. 188. *Hitchhiking trip.* **Left**: *Pablo, Juan Francisco, and Coco in Rio.* **Right**: *Juan Francisco, Coco, Pablo, and Diego being interviewed by reporter Jimmy Arocena on their return.*

Coco had not gone on the 1971 trip to Chile, and was keen to go in 1972, but it was only a couple of weeks before the trip that he managed to get together the money for the ticket and the $10 per day that the Chilean government required all visitors to bring into the country. He also had his studies to worry about. He was doing a degree in veterinary science at the university, and was active in student politics, being a delegate of the *Movimiento Universitario Nacionalista*. His immediate problem was that he was due to sit an exam on the Wednesday after the trip. But he was a good student, and he reckoned that he'd have enough time after his return to do some final revision.

The evening before the trip, Coco and his novia, Rosina, spent some time with their friends at a disco in the popular *Ton Ton Metek* nightclub, overlooking Lake Caleta, a few kilometres east of Carrasco. By chance, Alejandro also turned up there with his own girlfriend and circle of friends. Spotting Coco across the dance floor, Alejandro went over to speak to his brother, to wish him good luck for the trip.

Later that night at home, the atmosphere was not so cordial. Chatting with Rosina and Diego, Coco was getting ready for the trip. Tidiness didn't rank high amongst his qualities, and so it was Rosina who was organizing his clothes, folding and packing his shirts. And not just his own. Coco had asked her to pack Alejandro's favourite shirts also; some that their father had brought back from the USA a couple of months previously.

Feeling aggrieved, Alejandro angrily appealed to Rosina, suggesting that Coco was just taking them to attract the girls in Chile. His entreaties fell on deaf ears.

This was one of the things on Coco's mind when he wrote to Rosina from the mountain:

> I remember when you helped me pack my suitcase and when you sorted my clothes... I also remember Juan and Mónica and Ale's trip to Tom Tom. Poor Ale, tell him that his shirts are lost, but I promise to bring him as many as I can.

The suitcase would later be found at the tail by Coco's father in March 1973.

On the morning of 12th October, Diego and Roy, driven by Diego's mother Bimba, stopped by Coco's house to pick him up on the way to the airport. The gang assembled at Carrasco airport minus Tito, who had overslept and was nowhere to be seen. They were joined by Rafael Echavarren and Moncho Sabella who had been invited by various members of the gang. On boarding the plane, the group commandeered two rows of seats near the front of the cabin. A famous photo, which appeared in the book *ALIVE*, shows the two rows of passengers, Coco in the aisle with his arm around Roy, with Moncho and Rafael, and Bobby and Carlitos, seated across the aisle.

Fig. 189. *Rosina and Coco.*

The boys were constantly moving around during the flight, swapping places, and going to the pilot's cabin. After a while, Coco went to play cards with a group at the back of the plane, and then stayed there a while, reading comics. When the plane stopped in Mendoza, the group of friends got a lift into town in a station wagon, and, after eating at a restaurant coincidentally owned by a Uruguayan expat, they checked into the *Hotel San Remo* on Godoy Cruz Avenue, Coco sharing a room with Diego. After a siesta, they headed out on foot to explore the town, Coco walking in his distinctive manner, with a slight stoop. As they strolled through the wide, tree-lined boulevards and pleasant plazas of Mendoza, Coco kept getting distracted by the pretty girls they met – Alejandro's prediction not so far off the mark –

and the others teased him about it, knowing his commitment to Rosina. But he wasn't tempted to go dancing with the others, and he headed back to the hotel with Diego, Bobby, and Alexis Hounie for an early night.

The next morning, after a late breakfast which also served as their lunch, the group made their way to the airport. There, they spent the last of their Argentinian money, and passed the time weighing themselves on the airport scales before boarding the plane a second time.

When the accident came, Coco was sitting with Diego in the fourth row, behind Daniel Maspons and Roberto Canessa. He described the crash in his letter to Rosina nine days later:

> The crash was unbelievable, I was sitting near the front with Diego who was next to the window, and I didn't even have time to panic because the instance Diego told me to look out the window, the tail hit the mountain and the wings flew off at the same moment. The plane immediately started to slide down the mountain and at the same time snow was coming in through the gaps and we started freezing bit by bit until suddenly it stopped. Diego and I were trapped upside down in our seats (as the plane had tilted in the meantime). What most of us found unbelievable was that the first thing we all did was to call out for each other: Carlitos, Gordo, Diego, Roy, Moncho, Gordo Echavarren, that is all of us plus two boys we'd gone around with in Mendoza. We were lucky that God wanted us all to be there. The ones who were free – Roberto Canessa, Gustavo Zerbino, Daniel Maspons, and Marcelo Pérez – immediately began helping everyone else. I was able to get out quite quicky and I immediately helped Diego. Then together we extricated Gordo Echavarren and soon, almost all of us were free.

Other than a cut on his chin, Coco was uninjured, and once free, he worked with the others to try to bring some semblance of order in what remained of the fuselage. It was impossible to get out all the seats before nightfall, and some passengers were still trapped. Worst of all was Graziela Augusto who had been sitting in the very first row at the time of the accident. When the seats all piled up at the front of the cabin, her legs got trapped in the twisted metal, and the boys were not able to free her. She spent the night crying out in pain, isolated amongst these boys she didn't know. Coco and Moncho spent the night next to her, doing their best to comfort her whilst struggling to survive the cold themselves. Eventually her cries died away, and in the morning she died just as the boys released her.

Coco was strong, both physically and mentally, and acted as a big brother to the younger boys – those in the gang and beyond – looking out for them, getting them up in the morning, and keeping up their morale. He was in charge of the cabin group, tidying up after the boys had gone out of the fuselage in the morning, and preparing it at night. The job had its perks. One day, as Coco was arranging things in the cabin, he noticed a strong smell of alcohol in the area at the front right of the fuselage. He called Roy over. Using the plane's axe, the two of them broke down the partition between the pilot's cabin and the compartment holding the communication equipment, and found a bottle of whisky, three small jars of jam, and a few small pieces of dried fruit. They ate the latter, but the rest they saved for the group. The following day, Coco found a pen and some paper, and resolved to write a letter.

It was ten days after the accident when Marcelo and Roy heard the news on their small transistor radio that the search had been called off, but it was Coco who saved the group from sinking into despair. He went inside the fuselage, and announced, "I have good and bad news. The bad news is that they are not looking for us anymore; the good news is that now we have to get out of here on our own." Coco felt that it was a call to action, to stop sitting around waiting, and instead to take active steps to save themselves. He was one of a group of a dozen or so, including the gang, Enrique Platero, Tintín, and others, who were planning an early expedition.

The gang had escaped the accident unscathed, and had the advantage of each other's company to prevent them from becoming depressed. Coco, Roy, and Diego would often chat about things back home, imagining what was happening in each other's houses, and reminiscing about the good times. As the survivors settled down to sleep on the evening of 29th October, Coco lay down on the right-hand side of the fuselage next to Roy, and opposite Carlitos Páez and Moncho Sabella, with whom he had become great friends since the night of the accident. Coco confided in Roy about how much he regretted not spending more time with his girlfriend and her family, how he had sometimes treated them badly, and how he was longing to see them again. Diego, who was lying opposite Roy, interrupted their conversation, asking Roy if he would swap positions with him so he could sleep sitting up, thereby alleviating a sore on his tailbone. Roy agreed, and Diego settled down next to Coco. When the avalanche swept in a few minutes later, Coco and Diego were among those buried the deepest, disadvantaged by the slant of the fuselage. Despite the best efforts of Roy and Carlitos, the two friends were dead by the time the latter uncovered their faces. Coco was much mourned by the boys, and Roy in particular was devastated at the sudden loss of his close friend.

Coco's positive frame of mind on the mountain, his optimism and humour, and his retrospective appreciation for his family, friends, and girlfriend were preserved in the two letters he wrote a few days before the avalanche. Others of his possessions were also retrieved and utilized by the group. When Coche found Coco's notebook, the group used it to make a list of all the restaurants they knew in Montevideo, and to record the bets that they made as to what day the expeditionaries would reach civilization. The supply of lighter fuel that Coco had brought along allowed the boys to smoke throughout the ordeal. The red lining of his raincoat had served in the first few days as a means to try to attract the attention of passing planes. And, with the approval of the group, Tintín took Coco's boots after the avalanche, and made good use of them in the various expeditions.

Back in Montevideo, the family were trying to come to terms with the tragedy which had occurred on Raquel's birthday. Coco's *novia* Rosina and Álvaro Mangino's girlfriend Margarita Arocena Storm, were in Punta del Este when they heard of the accident. They were both obsessed with the thought that their boyfriends were alive, repeating to each other, "How cold it must be for Gustavo and Álvaro." But Mr Nicolich had no doubts that his son was dead; that he couldn't have survived a crash in the Andes. Alejandro remembers walking with his father and his uncle Jimmy Arocena a few days after the crash:

> We went walking to the beach. It was night-time, and as we walked, my father said to me: "Well, your brother is dead, now you have to be the head of the family." My uncle tried to soften the effect of his words, but I started to cry. After that I began trying to take the place of my brother, but I believe that it was more complex than that – I was trying to stop the suffering of my parents. I remember after the announcement of the survivors, I would always go out of the house to cry. It was very difficult in those days, very difficult. But, time heals everything.

On 5th December, Mr Nicolich got together with some of the other fathers, to try to persuade the Uruguayan Air Force to resume the search. The Chilean authorities had already ruled out further sorties before February 1973 – after all, it was impossible that there could be any survivors. Even though the fathers believed their sons to be dead, the unresolved questions remained, and they wanted to turn their attention back to the original search area marked out by the SAR, the *Servicio Aéreo de Rescate*. The fathers were not happy with the influence of parapsychologist Gerard Croiset, which had led to a month of fruitless combing of the Talca region, actually 100 km from the crash site.

The group met with Brigadier José Pérez Caldas at the *Boiso Lanza* Air Force base in the north of Montevideo. The Brigadier was sympathetic to their request, and not only made available a C-47 – a military version of the DC3 – but also authorized the participation of a limited number of the parents to act as observers on the flights. It was decided that Gustavo Nicolich, Juan Carlos Canessa, and Walter Harley would go to Chile, whilst the wider group of parents would provide monetary and logistical help, relying on Rafael Ponce de León's ham radio expertise for communications support.

On 10th December, there was a long meeting at Mr Nicolich's house. The three going to Chile were joined by Luis Surraco – the father of Roberto Canessa's *novia* Lauri – and two experienced pilots. Alejandro recalls that day:

> *I remember huge maps laid out on the dining room table, and two pilots scrutinizing them. One was Rodriguez Escalada, a professional pilot, and the other one the father of a friend of mine. They were taking into account the SAR reports, the flight data, and the weather conditions to narrow the search area.*

Rodriguez Escalada – the great uncle of Carlitos Páez – had already been active in various search efforts, and was going to accompany the fathers to Chile. Each person gathered around the table was given to analytic thinking – Canessa and Surraco were doctors, Nicolich an architect, and Harley an engineer. With the pilots, they methodically went through all the data, and came to the conclusion that the plane must lie between the *Tinguiririca* and the *Sosneado* volcanoes.

After a delay due to an engine failure, the C-47 flights got going on 13th December, with Nicolich and Rodríguez Escalada on board – a four-hour early morning flight over the Planchón pass. On 15th December, there was a false alarm as Nicolich spotted a cross on the Santa Elena mountain, below the expected route of the Fairchild. Photos were taken and analysed, but it turned out to be part of a geological survey. After several more flights over the following days, they interrupted the search to spend time with their families over Christmas. Although they had not found the Fairchild, their actions had convinced the Chilean rescue services to resume their search efforts also.

On 20th December, Nicolich, Canessa and Harley boarded the C-47 to return to Montevideo, but it experienced yet another engine failure, and they were forced to make an emergency landing in San Rafael, on the Argentinian side of the Andes, where they spent the night. The next day, Canessa took a bus to Buenos Aires, but Nicolich and Harley decided to wait for the repair of the C-47, whose pilots were friends of the Fairchild crew. Late that night, communicating with Ponce de León via ham radio, the two heard the startling news that two boys had appeared in the Chilean *precordillera*, claiming to be from the Uruguayan plane. They left right away for Mendoza, driven by the local ham radio operator in the mayor's car. From Mendoza, they hitched a ride to Santiago on a cargo plane, and then took a taxi, reaching San Fernando just before the helicopters arrived with the first batch of survivors. Mrs Nicolich was not far behind. Back in Montevideo, she had heard an erroneous rumour that her son was among the survivors, and had flown with several other parents on the first possible flight to Santiago, before taking a taxi to San Fernando.

As the helicopters landed, and the boys stepped out, it was Daniel Fernández who spotted Mr Nicolich and told him the news that his son wouldn't be returning. Later, Mr Nicolich went to the military hospital to speak to Carlitos, who told him the full story, about the crash, the letters that Coco had written, and the avalanche. Back in Santiago the next day, Gustavo Zerbino went to the *Hotel Crillón* where Mr Nicolich was staying, and gave him the two letters. They provided some comfort and insight into his son's last days, and the leading role he had played on the mountain, but the knowledge that Coco had been alive and unharmed for so long provoked a flood of anger against Gerard Croiset, who had lost them several weeks searching in the wrong area. The next day, 23rd December, they travelled back to Montevideo, met by Alejandro and one of his sisters at Carrasco airport. It was the first time Alejandro had seen his father in such distress, the first time he had seen him crying.

Despite their grief, Coco's parents gave their immediate support to the survivors. Their son's letters gave them a personal insight into the difficult decisions that had been made on

Fig. 190. *Raquel Nicolich with Moncho.*

the mountain. The full text of one of the letters appeared in the *El País* and *El Diario* newspapers on 27th December. A few days later, *El País* published a photo of a smiling Raquel Nicolich embracing an emotional Moncho Sabella, the close friend that Coco had made on the trip, whose warmth had helped him survive the first night.

In March, Gustavo Nicolich travelled to Argentina with Rafael Echavarren's father, who was making the trip to recover his son's body. Mr Nicolich was under no illusion about the possibility of repatriating the remains of his own son, who had been explicit in his letter that he would be glad for his body to be used in the event of his death. But he did want to see where Coco had lived out the last two weeks of his life, and where he was buried. The two set off up the mountain on 21st March with the *baqueanos* and two others, reaching the site on the morning of the 22nd. The summer thaw had exposed many remains that had not been visible at the time of the burial, and Nicolich saw the full horror of what the boys had had to go through, and understood the extent of their suffering. He came back a changed man.

Although Coco's parents, in support of the survivors, talked extensively about the tragedy to the media over the years, things were different at home, where the subject was off-limits. It was especially difficult for Alejandro, who had no opportunity to express his emotions. With his brother's shadow always hanging over him, someone to be compared to whenever he fell short, Alejandro subconsciously sought to take his place. His brother had always had the better marks, but now Alejandro set about studying harder, and ended up surpassing Coco's success. And over time, he became known as 'Coco' to his friends. When it came time for university, Alejandro blindly followed his brother's course of studies. Later in life, he reflected that veterinary science wasn't his true vocation; that he would have preferred to pursue a career in architecture, like his father.

Alejandro also exceeded Coco's achievements on the rugby field, getting selected for the national under-18 team, and, in the second half of the seventies, making six starts for the full national team in the Number Eight position. In the same period, he was part of the legendary *Old Christians* team, captained by Jorge Zerbino, that won the Uruguayan championship five years in a row; a team resurrected from the devastation of the Andes, which included Roberto, Gustavo, 'Tintín', Bobby Jaugust, and Pancho and Pepe Nicola, the sons of Pancho Nicola and Esther Horta.

The club became Alejandro's second home. He was there constantly, working to improve the field and the clubhouse, and helping to install the changing rooms. His leadership saw the building of the barbecue area; with tiles decorated with *gaucho* scenes by his mother, it became the focus of the club's social gatherings. His friends were mainly from the club – including those teammates who returned from the mountain – Roy, Tintín, Roberto, Gustavo, and Nando – and the relatives of those who didn't – Guido Magri's brother Aldo, Enrique Platero's brother Zika, and the Nicola boys. In later years, his son Santiago has continued the Nicolich involvement in the club.

In the years after the accident, Alejandro had felt a great need to know about his brother's life on the mountain, but it had been difficult to communicate with the survivors. Their families had been protective, and had discouraged them from talking, wanting them to forget about the horror they'd endured. This changed in December 1997, when Alejandro and the four Nicola brothers were invited to go to the mountain with five survivors – Roberto, Gustavo, Nando, Coche, and Moncho. It was a trip that was sponsored and documented by the *Universidad Católica de Chile*.

Approaching from the Chilean side, they followed the courses of the *Portillo* and *San José* rivers upstream, reversing the route of Nando and Roberto. With just the sound of the horses' hooves against the loose rock to break the silence, it was a time for contemplation as they slowly made their way up the mountain. In evenings around the campfire, survivors and 'non-survivors' talked at length, and the memories and suppressed emotions poured out. When they reached the snowline and progress became too difficult, they dismounted and continued on foot for a while, travelling far enough to reach the foot of the steep gully that had taken Roberto and Nando two days to make their way down.

Later, two prearranged helicopters picked up the Nicola brothers, along with Roberto and Gustavo, and dropped them on the glacier, following the route that the rescue

Fig. 191. *Alejandro Nicolich, November 2019.*

corps had flown in 1972. Although Alejandro did not reach the site on that occasion, the trip was a revelation to him. He no longer had the burning questions from twenty-five years previously, but he understood for the first time the suffering of the survivors, and the guilt they felt at having survived when their friends had died. As with his father, the experience of being on the mountain brought home the reality, and he came back a changed man.

Over the years, Gustavo continued to invite Alejandro to the mountain, but it wasn't until 40 years after the accident that he finally accepted. The trip was with a group of 30 Argentinian boys from *Rugby Sin Fronteras* – Rugby without Borders – an organization cofounded by Gustavo, which uses rugby as a means to promote friendship and peace across borders. For Alejandro, it was another intense and emotional experience, his first visit to the glacier and the grave, and finally a chance to see where his brother had spent his last days, to say goodbye to him, and to tell him how much he missed him.

Alejandro had always spoken to his children about his brother, and his wish to immerse them deeper in the story found expression in a family trip to the mountain in February 2017. His sisters Mónica and Raquelina joined them. On the way up to the site, they unexpectedly passed Rafael Echavarren's sister Beatriz, who was on her way down; an evocation of the trip their fathers had made forty-four years earlier. As before, the experience of the mountain surfaced hidden emotions in everyone, and the tears flowed freely on their return as they reflected on the trip in a hotel room in Malargüe. That trip marked the end of the story for Alejandro; the final lifting of a burden he'd been carrying since 1972.

Although the tragedy was never discussed in the house, not even between Coco's parents, Raquel had an outlet for her emotions in the *Biblioteca Nuestros Hijos*. She had been one of the founding mothers, and had come up with the scheme for how to finance it. She enlisted Alejandro to collect the thousands of books that were being donated and take them to the library's first home in *Hotel Carrasco*.

In an interview in 2017, Raquel, still going strong at ninety, reflected on the forty-five years of the library, and how it had brought together the mothers, creating a protective shell around them, allowing the wounds to heal. Included in the library's collection are the many books about the tragedy – the general accounts and the memoirs – and Raquel, the last surviving of the founding mothers, has read them all, finding, in each one, something new about this story which has been so much a part of her life.

Fig. 192. *Raquel Nicolich on 14ᵗʰ October 2022, the day after her ninety-sixth birthday.*

ARTURO NOGUEIRA
19-APR-1951 — 15-NOV-1972

A few months before the Andes trip, Arturo Nogueira was sitting with his mother looking at some photographs when he turned to her and said, "Mum, don't forget that I'm 21 now." He was referring to his premonition that he would die at that age. Perhaps similar to the thoughts that many young people have, but Arturo wasn't someone to say things lightly. His mother remonstrated with him, not believing in such things, and told him that he still had a lot of things to do in his life, and to think of his young brothers, Gabriel (known as 'Pulun') and Diego, who so looked up to him. Aged 12 and 10 at the time, they were the youngest of a family of seven, with Raquel the oldest, followed by Arturo, Cristina, Daniel, and Selina.

Fig. 193. **Left**: *Arturo with sisters Cristina and Raquel.*   **Right**: *Parents Arturo and Raquel.*

Raquel and Arturo were named after their parents. Arturo senior was the owner of an import/export company dealing in paper, wood, and hardboard, and representing mills in Chile. The family had originally lived in the Prado neighbourhood of Montevideo before moving to Carrasco in the early fifties, where they settled in a house on Puyol street. By the time Arturo was of school age in 1957, *Stella Maris* had opened its doors two blocks away on the same street, and Arturo entered the school in the same year as Panchito Abal, Pedro Algorta, and Enrique Platero, with Felipe Maquirriain joining their class some years later.

Arturo excelled both as a student and as a rugby player. On the academic side, he was repeatedly selected to represent his class in the nationally-televised *Student Olympiad*, not getting a single question wrong in his four years of participation. On the rugby field, he was a stand-out fly-half, playing for the *Old Christians Club* from 1968. A strong, individualistic player, he soon made the first team, and was a member of the *Old Christians* side that won the Uruguayan championship in 1970 under the captaincy of Marcelo Pérez del Castillo, playing alongside several of the boys who would be on flight 571 – Panchito Abal, Nando Parrado, and Alexis Hounie. An insight into Arturo's character is provided by an incident on the rugby field in a key game against rivals *La Cachila*. The *Old Christians* were losing 3-6 in the final minute of the game when they were awarded a penalty kick 40 yards out, on the left touchline. From that side of the field, the choice of kicker was between Arturo and Roberto, the former having the greater accuracy, the latter the ability to kick further. As this needed both skills, it was a toss-up as to who should take it, but the captain went with Roberto, who calmly converted, tying up the game and keeping the team in with a chance to win the championship.

Fig. 194. Arturo in the 1971 *First Team*.

Justifying his decision later, Marcelo explained that Arturo would never have forgiven himself if he had attempted the kick and missed, whereas it wouldn't have bothered Roberto at all; a viewpoint with which both kickers concurred.

Like many of his *Stella Maris* classmates, Arturo went on to the *Seminario* for his pre-university preparation. At the time, he was still religious, and would attend Mass and take Holy Communion. He especially enjoyed singing the *Misa Criolla*, the Creole Folk Mass that had become popular in South America after the Second Vatican Council had allowed vernacular languages to replace the Latin. He had an exceptional voice. When younger, he had enjoyed performing *gaucho* folksongs, accompanying himself on guitar, even winning a local competition in his early teens which earned him the moniker 'The singing kid of Carrasco'. He continued his singing in his later teens as part of a folk group, with Enrique Platero and other classmates. Arturo put his beliefs into practice, his religious and social conscience forged by his active service in the slums of Montevideo. As part of the Jesuit *Castores de Emaús* movement, he would help to build houses, and play football with the kids from the poor neighbourhoods; an experience that would later inform his political views.

In May 1969, Arturo suffered a tragedy with the loss of three of his classmates: Teco Costemalle, Eduardo Gelsi, and José Luis Lombardero – the brother of Arturo's *novia*

Inés. They had set out with another boy, Jaime Comas, in a canoe from the beach at the end of Arturo's street, aiming to reach some rocks, *Las Pipas*, a couple of kilometres from the shore. The canoe had started to take on water and had eventually submerged in the cold and choppy late autumn waters. Only Comas made it back to land. No other class in the school would be hit by tragedy so hard as the class of 1966. Three and a half years later a further four, including Arturo, would be lost in the Andes.

Arturo told his mother after the canoe accident that he would only accept his friends as dead once it was confirmed. It was an attitude that Mrs. Nogueira would remember when the plane disappeared in the Andes. In the case of the canoeists, it was their boat which was found first, a few kilometres downstream, at Shangrilá beach. The bodies appeared later, one by one, over the following days. The tragedy weighed heavily on his mind. He had been thinking of joining them in the canoe, and he told his father that he regretted not being with them to share their fate. When the Andes accident happened,

Fig. 195. *Arturo playing and singing in his folk group.*

Mr Nogueira reflected that if anyone were to come back from the mountain, and Arturo was amongst them, he could never be happy again because of the friends left behind.

1969 was also the year that Arturo entered the Faculty of Economics at the *Universidad de la República*, where Arturo's concern for social problems led him to become active in student politics. He gravitated towards the left, sharing the views of many students of the time, although atypical of those from Carrasco. He considered himself a socialist ideologically and idealistically, but he preferred not to align himself with any particular political group. He would act as a calming influence over his fellow activists, arguing persuasively against any form of violence, maintaining that nothing could be gained by it. His sense of social justice made him react against the privileges of high society, and, with little interest in money and business, and no time for frivolities such as parties and dances, he felt a calling to work more directly for the benefit of society.

Fig. 196. *Arturo surrounded by his brothers and sisters.*
Left to right: *Diego, Cristina, Selina, Daniel, Raquel, and Pulun.*

Arturo and his sister Raquel would have long discussions with their father, who, like Mrs Nogueira, was a Batlle supporter. Despite their disagreements, they respected one another's views. Before the 1971 election, Raquel and Arturo were part of a group of young people invited to meet presidential candidate Jorge Batlle at a friend's house. When the presidential candidate spoke about the economy, Arturo was outspoken, interrupting him several times; something that rattled Batlle, who later confided to Mrs Nogueira that although both her children were very intelligent, Arturo was a touch arrogant. Mrs Nogueira wouldn't tolerate anyone misrepresenting her children, and she told Arturo that she would no longer vote for Batlle. Her son, however, convinced her that she should vote according to her conscience.

Despite his involvement in politics, Arturo continued to study hard, aided by the neat and copious revision notes he made for all of his courses. He became reacquainted with

Pedro Algorta and Felipe Maquirriain, who had been classmates at *Stella Maris* and who were now also studying economics at the university. The three, all intellectuals and independent thinkers, would study together, enjoying each other's company despite their different aspirations and viewpoints. They would often meet at Felipe's home in Punta Gorda, away from the unrest and the confrontations between students and police that were happening downtown. When studying there, they would break to have tea with Felipe's mother Selva, who took great pleasure in their company and conversation. On one occasion, Arturo got into a detailed conversation with Felipe's sixteen-year-old sister Sandra about the Russian Revolution. Impressed by how knowledgeable she was, he admitted to her, "Your oligarch school must be quite good"; rare praise that had Sandra, still in school uniform, glowing with pride.

Arturo had gone on the 1971 trip and was keen to go again in 1972, but his father told him that it was Daniel's turn; the cost of raising a family of seven, and putting them all through private schooling, meant that finances were tight, and Mr Nogueira would only countenance funding one of his sons for the trip. Arturo and Daniel had not been especially close; even though they had rugby practice together at the club, the three or four years that separated them meant that they had a different circle of friends. But in the months before the trip, they became much closer. Arturo had suggested they start a joint record collection, as they both had the same taste in music. And Daniel had the opportunity to do a favour for his older brother when a girl Arturo had met in Chile on the 1971 trip turned up in Punta del Este, and contacted him. Arturo, who had no wish to compromise his relationship with Inés, made himself scarce, and asked Daniel to meet the girl in his place. Daniel spent the afternoon with her and her friend on the beach, making excuses for Arturo not showing up.

Daniel considered signing up for the trip, but none of his classmates were going, and he had some important exams in his final year of university preparation that he could ill-afford to miss. So when Arturo forced the issue, asking him to make a decision as to whether he was going or not, Daniel said no. Arturo immediately claimed the place on the plane. Through Arturo, his study mates Pedro and Felipe learned about the trip, and they also signed up.

The night before departure, Arturo said his goodbyes to Inés, swapping the cross that he wore around his neck with the medal and cross that she wore; keepsakes that had belonged to her brother José Luis, who had died in the canoe accident. The next morning, Mr Nogueira dropped his son off at the airport. There, Arturo mingled with his rugby teammates whilst waiting for the boarding announcement, chatting with Nando Parrado, and with Tintín and his father.

In the stopover in Mendoza, Arturo stayed at the *Hotel Horizonte* on Gutiérrez street; the same hotel as his friends Pedro, Felipe, and Enrique Platero. Those three were sharing a room, so Arturo shared instead with Tintín and Carlos Valeta. There is no record or memory of Arturo's time in Mendoza. Whilst Felipe and Pedro went to visit Cuyo University on the morning of the 13th, it is possible that Arturo joined Enrique, Carlos, and others who walked to the main street, San Martín Avenue, in search of breakfast.

In the accident, Arturo was caught up in the mass of twisted metal and seats at the front of the fuselage. As Roberto and Gustavo removed the seats and uncovered him, he shouted out, "Look, I'm all right!" But his foot was twisted, and he had sustained a broken leg. They put him on the luggage shelf at the front left of the plane, Tintín above, and Arturo below. Later, Roberto and Daniel Maspons made a hammock and a hanging seat for the injured, making use of the poles and straps designed to secure cargo. Rafael Echavarren and Álvaro Mangino would lie on the hammock, and Arturo would use the hanging seat, his feet resting on the hammock.

In the early days on the mountain, Arturo would involve himself in group activities, crawling outside to help make water, and taking part in the conversations. In the discussion about favourite foods, in which each boy contributed a favourite dish, he described a dessert of *dulce de leche* with meringue and cream. And when Carlitos Páez decided that they should pray the rosary together each evening, it was Arturo who, despite a lapse in faith, had to remind them how to do it.

Later, Arturo's conversation became more politically charged. No one else had much appetite for political discussions, because they invariably led to arguments, and Arturo's abrasive interjections only served to alienate him from the others. As a young boy, Arturo had been open and chatty, talking to his mother about everything, but in later years he had become more guarded and introvert. He had a close group of friends, amongst whom he felt comfortable and confident, and to whom he was extremely loyal. But outside that circle, he could sometimes appear brusque and unsympathetic, belying his inner sensitivity. On one occasion, Carlitos was taking the boys' minds away from their dire situation by telling stories about Casapueblo, and about the famous people who had come to visit his father, such as Brigitte Bardot. Arturo reacted strongly against these descriptions of what he saw as a lifestyle which placed materialism over concern for one's fellow human being. Carlitos was taken aback by his vehemence, and Roberto took Arturo to task, telling him he had no right to treat Carlitos that way, that Carlitos had a good heart. Arturo immediately regretted his reaction, agreeing that he had been in the wrong, and asking to be forgiven.

In the accident, Arturo had lost his friends Panchito Abal and Felipe Maquirriain, and in the avalanche he lost his close friend and neighbour Enrique. Of his former classmates, only Pedro Algorta remained. Pedro would try to take Arturo's mind away from their predicament by chatting about life back home, and about the exams they would take. On 27th October, two days before the avalanche, Pedro and Arturo recalled the day, exactly 15 years previously, on which they had made their first Holy Communion together. Arturo had lapsed in his faith since he had left the *Seminario*, and had stopped going to Mass, but towards the end, he experienced something of a conversion. He asked to lead the rosary one evening, and impressed them all with the sincere and profound way he introduced each mystery, articulating the unspoken thoughts of his companions. Afterwards, he cried from the emotion of it all, telling Pedro that it was the first time he had felt God again since his loss of faith.

Later, he confirmed his renewed faith in a letter to his parents and *novia*, written on the back of his packing list, his neat handwriting reduced to a scrawl: *I've never suffered as now, physically and morally, though I never believed in Him so much as now.* He addressed

Fig. 197. *Be strong! Life is hard but it is worth living, even in suffering. Courage!*

his mother and father with the affectionate *papito y mamita*, words he had never used in person, apologizing to them for the way he had behaved towards them, for the way he had neglected to express any feelings for them. But the bulk of the letter was addressed to Inés, his *negrita* as he affectionately called her, ending with the exhortation: *Be strong! Life is hard but it is worth living, even in suffering. Courage!* Mrs Nogueira had plates made with her son's last words to give to her friends. The letter, which was found in Arturo's wallet and delivered to the family by Gustavo Zerbino, was framed, and remained in Mrs Nogueira's possession until her death in August 2018, at which point the family passed it on to Inés.

Despite the maxim with which Arturo had concluded his letter, his conviction that he would die at age 21 convinced him that he would not be returning from the mountain. He became increasingly introspective and isolated from the rest of the group. He stopped making the effort to go outside, and spent the day lying in the dank fuselage, poring over aeronautical maps in an attempt to pinpoint their location. Arturo's teammate Nando would care for him by arranging his bed and adjusting his socks, but when he brought him food, Arturo would refuse it. His revulsion for the raw meat had caused him to stop eating altogether. Nando tried hard to convince him to remain optimistic, and to fight to live, promising to have him out of there by his girlfriend's birthday in the last week of November, but it was to no avail.

Soon after, Arturo took a turn for the worse, starting to shiver uncontrollably, his breathing becoming more laboured – perhaps the onset of pneumonia. In his delirium, he was convinced there was a farmer arriving in a truck to deliver milk to them. Another time, he shouted out that someone was trying to kill him. But he also remembered Inés during this time, speaking fondly of the Sundays they had spent together.

During the last three nights, Pedro slept with him in the hanging seat, hugging him to stop him from climbing down, and giving him tranquilizers to calm him. On the last night, they took Arturo down onto the floor, where Pedro held him to comfort him and keep him warm. Pedro woke in the night to find Arturo stiff in his arms. Gustavo tried to revive him, but Pedro knew he was dead, and he wept over the loss of his friend. The next day, the boys took Arturo's body out of the fuselage and laid it with the other bodies. Pedro, with the consent of the others, took Arturo's *Old Christians* jacket with its shamrock emblem.

Back in Montevideo, when news of the accident broke on 13th October, Selina was home with her sister Cristina, who had hepatitis. Their mother was attending her Friday appointment at the hairdresser. The first inkling Selina had that something might be amiss was when a friend of her father called and asked, "Where is Arturito?" "He went to Chile yesterday." "Are you sure?" "Yes!" Twenty minutes later, her father returned home with the news.

Daniel had a special maths class that evening at the *Seminario* in the lead-up to the university entrance exams. At 7:00 p.m. he had to step out of the class for a short time to attend a class delegates' meeting. There he was approached by a girl:

> *"Have you heard of what happened with the* Old Christians' *plane?"*
>> "No."
> *"It came down."*
>> "When did it happen?"
> *"Today."*
>> "No, it can't be their plane. They flew yesterday."

When he returned to the maths class, Daniel repeated the conversation to his teacher, who, knowing Chile's reputation for good cheap wine, responded flippantly, "They'll all be drunk in Santiago by now, so don't worry."

Daniel thought no more about it, and took a bus with a friend back to Carrasco. They would usually get off at the same bus stop on the *Rambla* and then walk home in different directions, as they lived four blocks apart. That evening, however, the friend insisted on accompanying Daniel home. Arriving there to find a large number of cars parked outside, and a house full of people, Daniel realized that the reports must be true.

From the very beginning, neither Mr Nogueira, nor Daniel, held any hope that Arturo could have survived a crash in the Andes. But a rumour circulating later that evening, that the boys were safe and had landed elsewhere in Chile, had caused Mr Nogueira to reconsider. The rumour had originated in a private conversation between Guido Magri's *novia* Angeles Mardones, and Guido's family. Contacted by Rafael Ponce de León via ham radio, Angeles had immediately scotched this rumour. Rafael recorded their conversation, and made it available to the local media. Walking home from his father's house later that night, Rafael passed Mr Nogueira outside his house and had to convince him that there was no truth to the rumour.

Despite being a close friend and neighbour of the Ponce de León family, Mrs Nogueira, unlike many of the mothers, didn't initially attend Rafael's evening ham radio calls to Chile. But several weeks after the boys' disappearance, she turned up at the house to explain the reason for her absence: "I know that you've been asking why I've not been here. The reason was that I didn't want to get my hopes up, but if you don't mind, I'll start coming every day." Rafael told her that she shouldn't feel obliged, but reassured her that the door was always open. Mr and Mrs Nogueira then started turning up every evening, finding it helpful, as there was always news to look forward to.

Although Mrs Nogueira was generally pessimistic about Arturo's survival, she did retain a glimmer of hope, remembering her son's attitude after the canoe accident, before the bodies of his friends had been recovered. Arturo had had several other brushes with death – a blood condition at six months, a polio scare at age five, and an accident at age fourteen when a car had ploughed into his bike, putting him in hospital for several weeks. She was a great believer in praying to the dead, feeling that those who had died were close by, and had seen the face of God. She would ask her dead parents to help Arturo, whether he was dead or alive, and would also ask for help from the three friends who had died in the canoe.

Sometimes, her hopes were briefly raised by the parents' search trips, or some statement from Croiset, but these would soon be dashed. On one occasion, Mecha Canessa, while visiting the Nogueira home, called up a noted local clairvoyant who operated out of the *Palacio Salvo*. The seer, who used cards to make her predictions, had been uncannily accurate in the past when consulted on domestic matters. She informed Mrs Canessa not to look for the boys, that they would get out by themselves. She also mentioned that she saw uniforms around the plane; something that convinced Mrs Canessa that the boys were alive, and were being held by the Tupamaros. Although a faint possibility, it was not beyond reason that a group of privileged boys be kidnapped at the height of the military campaign against the Tupamaros. But it did seem implausible, given that no ransom had been demanded.

Despite the distress and uncertainty of Arturo's disappearance, his parents decided that Christmas should be celebrated, like any other year. On 21st December, Mrs Nogueira, Cristina, Selina, and Inés drove downtown in the family Morris to do some Christmas shopping. On the way back, they made a detour to the *carnicería* across the *Puente Carrasco*, to buy meat for the holidays. As they were chatting over the counter, the owner commented, "Oh, Mrs Nogueira, did you hear about the plane that disappeared...?" Stunned by the news, they drove back home immediately, to find a crowd of people waiting at the house.

The next day, Mrs Nogueira went to Ponce de León's house, where everyone had gathered to hear the list of survivors, relayed from Chile by ham radio. But the tense atmosphere there persuaded her to retreat to the privacy of her own home, where she made herself some soup to help relax. Daniel was already at home, standing on the balcony and chatting with Enrique's brother Zika, who lived across the street, but the two boys joined their respective families to hear the list. After the sixteenth and final name was announced, Mrs Nogueira couldn't help but feel happy for Mrs Sabella, who had called her up in distress so many times. She also reflected that the loss of Arturo's good friends Panchito Abal and Enrique Platero would have been an enormous blow for Arturo had he survived.

Four of the survivors came to see her in the days following their return to Uruguay – Gustavo, Roberto, Pedro, and Coche. She felt great calm and peace when she was able to speak to them, and she and her husband felt fortunate to be able to hear about Arturo's last days, despite feeling anguish for his prolonged suffering. Gustavo brought back Arturo's *Old Christians* jacket, and Inés' cross and medal, which Arturo had been wearing on the mountain. He also presented them with Arturo's letter, which gave Mrs Nogueira great solace, proving to her that Arturo had regained his faith on the mountain, and that his suffering may not have been in vain.

For Inés, a shy eighteen-year-old, the letter was also a source of great comfort. She had suffered a lot over the previous three years, with the divorce of her parents, the death of her brother in the canoe tragedy, and now the loss of her fiancé. After the accident, she had become part of the family, and now that Arturo's death was confirmed, Mrs

Nogueira felt a special bond with her, and was determined to help her recover from these blows. She told her that life had to go on, and that one day she would find someone else, that Arturo would help her in that choice.

Mrs Nogueira reflected later that she didn't want the Andes story to leave people with a sense of sadness, but rather one of happiness. She liked to talk of 'those who stayed on the mountain', feeling it was better that they stayed there together in that majestic place. Unlike some mothers, she didn't think of the survival of the boys who returned as a miracle; rather, it was a heroic adventure. For her, the real miracle was the attitude of her husband, who, although he had no religious belief, had taken his son's loss with so much peace and equanimity. On 2nd January, a week after the survivors had returned to Montevideo, he felt compelled to write a letter to the newspaper on behalf of his family, exhorting the public to learn from the lessons of the Andes:

> These brief lines, born out of an inescapable imperative of our hearts, wish to publicly pay tribute in admiration and recognition of the 16 young heroes who survived the tragedy of the Andes. Admiration because such is our feeling in the face of the many proofs of solidarity, faith, courage, and serenity which they faced and overcame. Deep and eternal recognition for the constant care they gave to our dear son and brother Arturo until his death many days after the accident. We invite all the citizens of our country to a few minutes of meditation on the immense lesson of solidarity, courage, and discipline provided to us by these boys, and may it serve us all to learn to put aside petty egotism, unbridled ambition, and lack of concern for our fellow man. A final word of thanks to Stella Maris College, whose brothers and teachers have formed so many generations of students, sportsmen, and fundamentally MEN for our country.

Mrs Nogueira realized that it was difficult for the parents of the survivors to speak to the bereaved parents, burdened by the guilt of their children having survived. Her friend Mecha Canessa had paid an early visit with her husband, but had stayed only for a few minutes. Raquel was determined that things should return to normal, and one day at the beach, she sought out Mecha and told her, "You and I didn't decide who would live and who would die, it was the hand of God. Things between us should return to how they were before."

Later that year, Arturo's mother became one of the founding members of the *Biblioteca Nuestros Hijos*, the library formed by the bereaved mothers to help underprivileged children and to keep alive the memories of their sons. She was also one of the longest-lived mothers, dying in August 2018. But despite her faith, she never got over the loss of her son, nor did she ever make the trip to the mountain. Arturo's brothers did go to the site of the accident, with guide Edgardo Barrios in 2004. Standing in front of the grave, and looking over the glacier, where their brother had spent so many days suffering, brought home the reality of his death, and served as an opportunity to say goodbye.

Fig. 198. *Daniel and Selina, November 2019.*

EUGENIA DOLGAY DE PARRADO AND SUSANA PARRADO
07-DEC-1921 — 13-OCT-1972, 29-MAY-1952 — 21-OCT-1972

When Clodomiro Parrado opened his saddlery business in Montevideo in 1932, he strategically situated it two blocks away from the *Estación Central General Artigas*, the main terminus of the Uruguayan railway network. As ranch workers arrived at this primary entry point to Montevideo and made their way downtown, they would inevitably pass by his store, and the business began to prosper. But as buses started to take over from trains as the favoured mode of transport, and as motorized farm machinery increasingly replaced horse-drawn equipment, the initial demand started to wane. In response, Clodomiro's son Seler, who had taken over from his father, expanded the business to include screws, bolts, and other fixings. These hardware items rapidly took over from the riding equipment as the primary offering, and Seler rebranded the store at 1610 Paraguay street as *La Casa del Tornillo*.

Fig. 199. *Zenia and Seler Parrado.*

In 1945, Seler married his blue-eyed *novia* Eugenia Dolgay. She had emigrated with her family from Ukraine at the beginning of the Second World War. Highly intelligent, 'Zenia' had a job in a medical laboratory, but she would help out at the store in her spare time. Together, through hard work and a single-minded determination, the couple brought the store into profitability, allowing Zenia to leave her job at the lab to concentrate on the business and to start a family. Graciela ('Ciela') was the first to arrive, in 1948, followed by Fernando ('Nando') a year later, and finally Susana ('Susy'), in 1952. In the early years, the family lived in a house across the street from the store, but when the children were still very young, the family moved, living first in Prado, then in Malvín, before fulfilling a dream of Zenia's by moving to the peninsula of Punta Gorda, to a beautiful house with views over the estuary.

The children were raised with the same work ethic that had underpinned their parents' success. Zenia was constantly active, whether it was raising the family, running the business, making school uniforms, or pickling the produce from the family vegetable patch, the latter a project of Zenia's mother. An irrepressibly happy person, Zenia never allowed circumstances to get the better of her, and she expected her children to have the same philosophy. If any of the children once complained that they were bored, they would never say it again, as they would be put to work immediately.

With Carrasco close by, the children now had the opportunity to start attending the excellent schools in the area, Ciela and Susy at *Colegio Jesús María*, and Nando at *The Christian*. Ciela, intelligent and driven like her mother, excelled at school and, at age 14, won a scholarship to study in Rome. Accompanied by her mother, she travelled there by ship, the Costa Line *Enrico C*; a journey lasting 20 days, with stops at Buenos Aires, Santos, Rio de Janeiro, Tenerife, Lisbon, Barcelona, Cannes, and Genoa. Ciela was already very close to her mother, but it was a good opportunity for them to spend uninterrupted time together, away from Zenia's busy everyday life. Once they arrived, Zenia started to have second thoughts about leaving her teenage daughter in a foreign city 11,000 kilometres from home. She had thought the college would be run like a traditional convent school, but the nuns had a liberal outlook, and gave the girls free rein to explore the city on their own, the only restriction being that they had to be back by 10:00 p.m. Despite her trepidation, Zenia told Ciela that she trusted her to behave responsibly; a confidence justified by Ciela, who, though living the experience to the full, never strayed far from her studies. It was an international school, with girls from around the world, one from each country, and Ciela shared a large bedroom with an Indian girl and one from Mexico. She would later look back on it as the best year of her life, studying languages and anthropology, subjects would continue to inspire her later in life. The year was capped off by a trip with her classmates and the nuns to Lake Geneva.

Ciela's extended time away from home during her siblings' formative years meant that she missed out on sharing the strong bond that developed between Nando and Susy. Nando, quiet, responsible, good-humoured, and a bit introverted, was in the class of '65 at *The Christian*. He was a classmate and close friend of Guido Magri, and of Pablo Vierci who would later write *La Sociedad de la Nieve*, a book which gave voice to the personal accounts and memories of each of the survivors. For Pablo, rugby was just a pastime, but for Nando and Guido it became an important part of their lives. Nando, with his height and strength, played second row in the scrum, whereas Guido, with his speed and ball-handling skills, played as scrumhalf, the crucial link between the forwards and backs. Guido would go on to play for his country, one of the first *Old Christians* to do so, and it would be Guido who would forge the ties with the *Grange Old Boys* in Chile, conceiving of and organizing the inaugural trip to Santiago in 1971, and captaining the team.

Fig. 200. *The Enrico C, and Zenia on deck at the moment the boat crossed the equator.*

Nando's other great friend was Panchito Abal, from the class below, with whom he shared a love of rugby, cars, and girls. Nando had developed his interest in cars and engines at an early age from his father, who had worked as a mechanic before taking over the family business, and who had been one of the founding members of the *Asociación Uruguaya de Volantes* – the Uruguayan Race Car Drivers' Association. In later years, Nando's friendship with Panchito had been strengthened by the proximity of their workplaces, and their common interest in business. They had both joined their respective family firms, Nando having a managerial role at *La Casa del Tornillo*, and Panchito joining the *Abal Hermanos* tobacco company, three blocks away on the same street. They would meet every day for lunch, and then spend the weekends together when rugby, parties, movies, motorbikes, and cars would keep them entertained.

In 1967, before working at *La Casa del Tornillo*, and after completing his two years of university preparation at the *Institute Alfredo Vázquez Acevedo* downtown, Nando spent eight months in the United States with the *Youth for Understanding* exchange programme. Staying with a family in Saginaw, Michigan, he experienced snow for the first time, one of the few boys to have done so before their sojourn in the Andes. As well as attending high school over the year, he managed to visit 32 of the 50 states. The US way of life appealed to him, and he came back feeling that the different perspective had matured him and made him more capable of making decisions. On his return, he gave up thoughts of university, and started working with his father, supplementing his work with practical courses at the polytechnic.

Susy followed in Nando's footsteps two years later, participating in the same exchange programme. Like Nando, she thoroughly enjoyed her time in the USA, and had thoughts about applying to university there. Affectionate and outgoing, Susy was tall with long blonde hair, and was exceptionally intelligent, like her sister Graciela. After graduating from the *Crandon Institute* in Montevideo with top honours, she became, at age 20, one of the youngest instructors in higher education, teaching English and economics at the Uruguayan American School. Nando had been very protective of his younger sister as she was growing up, always chaperoning her to parties, and watching out for her. But despite her good looks and pleasant personality, she did not have a steady boyfriend, not wanting to be tied down at this time in her life, when there was so much to achieve and explore.

Meanwhile, Ciela had returned from Europe, and had started studying medicine at university, with a view to becoming a surgeon. At age 19, she met her future husband Juan Berger, at a party in Buenos Aires. Very much in love, he quit his architecture degree

Fig. 201. *Susy at her 15ᵗʰ birthday party with her best friend Lila, and sister Graciela.*

and left Argentina to be with Ciela in Montevideo, where he started working for the family business. The two got married and started a family, a son Gaston coming in 1970. To supplement the family income whilst she was studying, Ciela also had a part-time job, working as a secretary in the Channel 4 TV station, and her busy life left her little time to spend with her brother and sister.

However, when Nando suggested that his sisters and parents should accompany him to Chile, Ciela thought it would be a good opportunity to get away for a few days and spend time with the family. Nando had thoroughly enjoyed the previous year's trip; he and Panchito had met some girls at Viña del Mar, and they planned to meet up again. Zenia also had friends in Chile whom she was eager to see. So the whole family signed up, with the exception of Seler, who had injured his toe playing tennis.

Fig. 202. *Zenia and Susy.*

A few days before the trip, a lawyer for Channel 4, who also represented a fur business, turned up at the studio with some fur-lined antelope-skin coats. Ciela immediately bought one and Susy, after seeing her sister wear it, decided to buy one also, using the money from her first pay cheque as a teacher. Having bought the coat, Ciela started to have second thoughts about going to Chile. Finances were tight in the family, and having spent all her spare money on the coat, she decided that she couldn't justify the additional expense of the trip, and returned her ticket.

On the day of the trip, Seler drove Zenia, Nando, and Susy in the family's olive-green Rover to the airport. On the way, they stopped by the house of a friend who had asked them to hand-deliver a letter to a daughter who was living in Chile. Nando would keep that letter throughout the ordeal, and it would accompany him on his trek through the mountains, until he was finally able to deliver it to her at the hospital in San Fernando. Once the Parrados arrived at the airport, they had breakfast together upstairs, in the terminal building restaurant, and then mingled with the other passengers until departure time.

On the plane, Nando sat with Panchito, and Zenia with Susy. Although Nando knew Javier Methol through Panchito, it was the first time that Zenia and Susy had met him and his wife; and when the plane unexpectedly landed in Mendoza, the Parrados and the Methols joined the Nicolas and Graziela Augusto de Mariani in checking in to the upmarket *Hotel Sussex*, half a block from *Plaza Independencia*, the central square in the town. With the exception of Panchito, who was sharing a room with Nando, the rest of the boys, who had been dropped at the hotel by the free taxi service, set off into the town to find cheaper accommodation.

With the Nicolas taking the opportunity to visit Esther's sister, who had moved to Mendoza with her family the previous year, Zenia and Susy joined the Methols and Graziela for both lunch and dinner. In between, Zenia and Susy went to explore the town and do some shopping, whilst the others took a bus to the *Cerro de la Gloria*, the hill in the *Parque General San Martín* that overlooks Mendoza. Nando and Panchito had their own agenda, going to watch the stock car races on the outskirts of the town before meeting up in the centre with Marcelo, Julio, and Álvaro to see *What's Up, Doc?*.

In the morning, after breakfast, the Parrados and Panchito headed to the main shopping area. There, they stopped in the *Farmacia del Águila* on Avenida San Martín, where they stocked up on some pharmacy supplies, several of which were difficult to find in Uruguay at the time. The two-page receipt shows lip gloss, toothpaste, talcum powder, stain remover, and various make-up items. The first two of these would prove essential on the mountain, the lip gloss giving valuable protection against the harsh sun reflecting off the snow, and the toothpaste serving as a dessert 'better than caviar', as Eduardo Strauch would later describe it. The Parrados also stopped at a shoe store half a block away, where Zenia bought some little red tennis shoes for Graciela's son, Gaston. The shoes would feature – most prominently in the movie *Alive* – in a much-related anecdote, in which Nando split up the pair before setting off on the final expedition. Taking one with him and leaving the other at the fuselage, he told the boys, "When I come back for you, we'll have a pair again." The shoe store, *Creaciones DAISY*, no longer exists at Avenida San Martin 1346, but there is another one in its place.

With no real idea of when the plane would leave, the four of them then took a taxi to the airport, arriving around noon. There, they mingled with the rest of the passengers, waiting for the pilots to arrive, and for the immigration and customs desks to open. As they stood around that warm Mendoza spring day, some of Nando's friends started kidding his mother for wearing a blue and black madras around her shoulders, but the square blanket would later contribute to Nando's survival on the mountain, accompanying him on all his expeditions. Susy's new coat would also serve him well; before travelling, she had asked Nando whether he thought she would need it, and he had advised her to bring it along just in case.

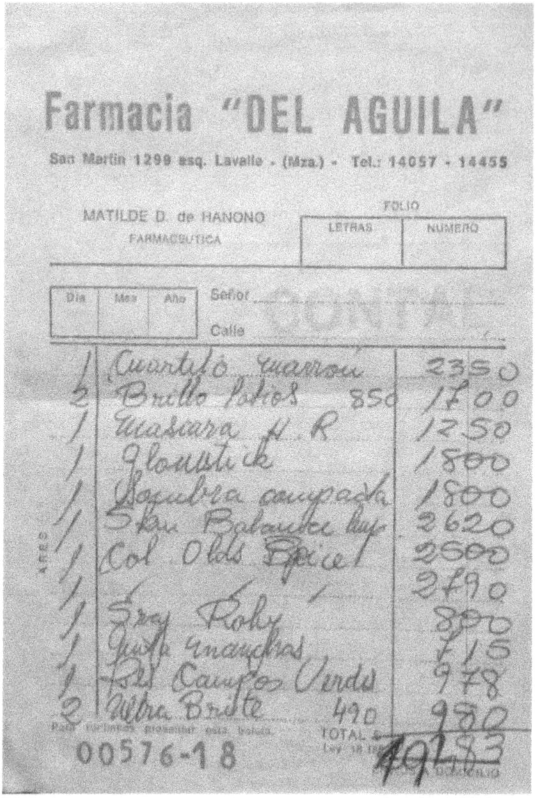
Farmacia "DEL AGUILA"
San Martín 1299 esq. Lavalle - (Mza.) - Tel.: 14057 - 14455
MATILDE D. de HANONO
FARMACEUTICA
FOLIO
LETRAS | NUMERO
Día | Mes | Año
Señor
Calle
2350
850 1700
1250
1800
1800
2620
2500
2790
800
715
978
490 980
TOTAL
00576-18

Fig. 203. *First page of the receipt for a long list of pharmacy items bought by the Parrados on the morning of 13th October.*

When they boarded the plane, Nando and Panchito sat in adjoining seats towards the back, on the left-hand side, close to Guido Magri and other rugby team-mates. Zenia and Susy found seats a bit further forward, across the aisle. The flight went smoothly for the first hour. Gustavo Zerbino, walking up and down the cabin before the seatbelt lights came on, noticed Zenia with her glasses on, reading a book – perhaps the recently-published *Mujer Piloto*[1] by Robert J. Serling, which was found later in the broken fuselage. Nando and Panchito were engrossed in a discussion about a joint business venture they were contemplating, selling fibre-based cleaning cloths in the interior of the country. Not even the increasingly alarming turbulence could distract them from

[1] The retitled Spanish translation of *She'll Never Get off the Ground.*

their conversation, and Nando, after swapping seats with Panchito, neglected to refasten his seatbelt.

The accident came swiftly. They descended out of the clouds and saw the mountains almost within touching distance. The sudden acceleration and angling of the plane, the frantic screams from the cockpit for more power, the sound of the wing impacting against the ridge, and the sudden exposure to the snow and cold as the roof and tail were ripped off; these were the last things Nando could remember before he lost consciousness. Their friends behind them had disappeared out of the tail, and the joined seats in which he and Panchito were sitting were propelled forward over the other passengers, colliding with the bulkhead at the front of the cabin. They both sustained near-fatal blows to the head. When the fuselage came to a sudden stop, the other seats, loosened by the depressurization, broke free from their bearings, piling up against each other at the front of the cabin. Those on the right bore the brunt of the impact, and Zenia and Susy were amongst the worst hit, Zenia dying immediately, crushed by the impact of the seats behind her, and thrown to the floor, and Susy sustaining internal injuries and a cut to her head, resulting in a flow of blood over her eyes and face, which Roberto Canessa, one of the 'doctors', wiped away as best he could.

By some perverse twist of fate, and despite sitting at different places in the plane, almost all the passengers who had stayed at the *Hotel Sussex* the previous night sustained injuries that would prove to be fatal. Like Zenia, the Nicolas, who had been sitting in the second row on the right, died immediately. Graziela Augusto, who was sitting at the front left, was trapped by the seats with her legs broken, and would die the next morning. Only the Methols escaped almost injury-free. And of the others, only Nando would survive.

As the able-bodied boys attended to the injured, and started clearing the fuselage in the short time left before darkness descended, Nando, Susy, and Panchito were placed on the floor at the back of the plane; a place open to the elements, where the roof had been ripped off. Their injuries seemed too extreme for them to survive. Nando was completely unconscious. Panchito, who had a horrific wound to his head, was semi-conscious, but couldn't see. He was comforted by Álvaro, who, with a broken leg, had been placed next to him. Susy was also semi-conscious, asking for her mother. As darkness came, and the temperature rapidly dropped to 30° below, precious little space had been cleared in the wrecked fuselage, and whilst the surviving passengers crowded inside, Nando, Panchito, and Susy were left where they had been initially placed, exposed to the cold, the wind, and the snow.

Close by were Marcelo, and a group of friends from the gang – Carlitos, Bobby, Roy, and Diego – huddled together for warmth. At one point, Diego sensed that Nando, despite being unconscious, wasn't as badly injured as they'd first thought, and they pulled him into the middle of the group; an intervention that would be crucial in the weeks to come. Panchito and Susy were left in the cold. During the endless night, Susy could be heard constantly calling for her mother: "Mamá, mamá, vámonos de acá. Vámonos a casa, mamá." Another time, she was heard praying the *Hail Mary* in English.

When morning finally arrived, Panchito was found lying over Susy. He was dead, but she was still breathing, and several of the boys credited him with saving her life. Perhaps he was just seeking the solace and warmth of human contact, but Nando reflected in his memoir many years later on Panchito's faithfulness as a friend, and the fierce way in which he would always protect Susy. So perhaps, despite the cold and the confusion of his injury, he found the clarity or instinct to try to save his best friend's sister, in a final act of loyalty.

Although Susy was breathing, she was still in a very bad way. To add to her existing injuries, her feet had become frozen. Roberto immediately moved her to the 'hospital wing' at the front of the fuselage; the warmest part of the plane. There the doctors spent hours massaging her feet which had turned black and violet. The next day, Nando awoke from his coma. Struggling to comprehend what had happened, he managed to process the fact that his mother had died, and that Susy was critically injured. He took over from the doctors in caring for his sister, giving her water and chocolate, holding her through the night, and caring for her feet – constantly massaging them and keeping them wrapped in his mother's blanket. He would talk to her, but though conscious, she could only respond with a nod of her head. One night, eight days after the crash, he awoke in the early hours of the morning to find her dead. He tried to give her mouth-to-mouth resuscitation, but to no avail. He stayed embracing her until the next morning. Then the other boys took her out and laid her by her mother.

Nando didn't allow himself to grieve. His single-minded focus was now to escape from the mountain, and return to his father. Nando's time on the mountain, his unifying presence, and his famous ten-day trek into the unknown with Roberto Canessa have been well documented, not least in Nando's acclaimed 2006 memoir *Miracle in the Andes*, the first of the survivor accounts to be published in English. Whenever he felt like giving up, he would take inspiration from the story his father had told about the last desperate moments of a rowing race, in which he had been neck-and-neck with an Argentinian rival. Seler, who at the time was one of the best competitive rowers in Uruguay, had been about to give up and concede defeat, but seeing the same look of agony on his opponent's face that he felt on his own, he kept going, persevering through the pain, and winning the race.

But for Seler, the loss of most his family was a challenge too far. On 13th October, Ciela had been at a rugby game with her husband Juan and son Gaston. Planning to spend the holiday weekend at Seler's house, they arrived there after the game to find him sitting on his bed, sipping *maté*, and watching the news about a Uruguayan plane that

had gone missing in the Andes. Initial reports on the television were vague, not even mentioning a rugby team. Ciela immediately called Channel 4, to find out more from her colleagues. A newsman at the station told her, "It's a plane with some guys who were going to play rugby in Chile." She replied, "My whole family was on that plane."

Ciela made the immediate decision to stay with her father, moving with Gaston into Nando's room. Later that day, when a rumour started circulating that the boys were safe, she didn't celebrate with her father, who was drinking champagne with his friends. She realized that if they had

Fig. 204. A young Seler (middle) at rowing practise. Nando took inspiration from his father's rowing exploits during his Andes trek.

genuinely been safe, her mother would have called at the first opportunity. When the bad news was confirmed, Seler was one of a group of 20 relatives to travel to Santiago on 15th October to find out more about the search and rescue efforts. After they were abandoned a few days later, and the unofficial sorties into the mountains conducted by the parents came to nothing, he became despairing, resigned to the idea that his wife and two of his children were dead. With nothing left to work for, Seler sat Ciela down in front of him and told her that the business was all hers, that he didn't want to carry on. Ciela, wanting to pursue her medical career, told him she had no interest in taking over, and advised him to sell everything, but her husband Juan intervened, saying that he would keep the business alive.

The next weeks were chaotic, with crowds gathering daily at Ponce de León's house to get updates on the unofficial search, and regular pronouncements from Gerard Croiset temporarily raising hopes before they would be dashed again. Ciela decided she had to escape the emotionally-charged atmosphere of Carrasco, and moved with her son to the family's apartment in Punta del Este. She was quite sure in her own mind that everyone had died in the accident, and she needed the time and space to think things through. Her fifteen-year-old sister-in-law, Elizabeth Berger, came from Buenos Aires especially to keep her company. It wasn't long after Ciela had moved there, that a friend of hers appeared one evening with her father, a Uruguayan Air Force Brigadier. He told Ciela about the note that had been thrown across the river in the Chilean *precordillera*, claiming that there were sixteen survivors. On hearing the news, Ciela confided to her friend: "Marie, if there's anybody alive, they must have had to eat each other." Her friend was shocked, but Ciela knew that there was no other way they could have survived.

Later that night, after Ciela had gone to bed, her sister-in-law woke her up excitedly, to tell her the news that her brother was alive. At three in the morning, her father called to confirm it, and to tell them that Juan was already on his way to Punta, to pick them all up. The three were waiting downstairs when he arrived, and they drove directly to Carrasco airport, where, with just the clothes they were wearing, they and Seler boarded a plane to Santiago, along with several of the other parents. Only Elizabeth stayed behind, to look after Gaston while his mother was away. The flight to Chile was very tense. The only sure information was that Nando and Roberto had survived, but there were rumours going around about the other survivors. Seler was convinced his wife was alive, telling Mrs Nicolich that if so many had survived, it must be due to Zenia's presence on the mountain.

When they arrived in Santiago, they were met at the airport and driven straightaway to San Fernando, 150 km to the south, where Nando, Roberto, and the first crop of survivors were being attended to by the doctors at the *San Juan de Dios* hospital. When they arrived, the front of the hospital was crowded with journalists, cameramen, and antennas. Ciela by this time was so tense that her hands were bleeding from digging her nails into her palms. They reached the door, but the doctors wouldn't allow them to enter, and a policeman was guarding the way in. Nando, who was in the room closest to the door, heard Ciela remonstrating, "But I want to go in. My brother's in there." He immediately shouted out to her, "Ciela, I'm here!" Ciela, unwilling to wait any longer to see her brother, reached breaking point. An aikido student at the time, she lashed out and floored the policeman. General chaos ensued, with shouts going back and forth between Nando and his father, others jostling to get in, and Ciela, after being restrained by the doctors, sitting down on the ground in an attempt to calm herself. The doctors, assessing the mood of the crowd, decided it would be more prudent to let the families in.

Ciela was the first to enter the hospital. She rushed into her brother's room, and they embraced. "How thin you are!" she exclaimed, and began crying. Juan and Seler followed close behind. Nando, despite having lost 26 kilos in the Andes, lifted his father into the air as he embraced him. "Mamá? Susy?" Seler asked. Nando shook his head. They stayed together chatting until 7:00 p.m., when all visitors were asked to leave. They returned at 9:00 a.m. the next morning, continuing where they had left off. At 10:30 a.m., there was a brief press conference, followed at 11:00 a.m. by a Catholic Mass in the *Las Hijas de la Caridad* chapel, adjacent to the hospital. After Mass, a friend of the family took them to lunch, before driving them to Santiago. Rooms had been reserved for the survivors and their families at the *Sheraton San Cristóbal*, and they went directly there, bypassing Santiago's *Posta Central* hospital, where the other survivors were taken to be checked over.

After showering, Nando, accompanied by Juan, took a taxi into the centre to buy some clothes. Everywhere he went, he was instantly recognized, and none of the shops would accept money from him. Unable to find a taxi, they walked back to the hotel. The chance for Nando to enjoy his fill of food after the deprivations of the mountain, and to relax with his family by the hotel swimming pool, was frustrated by the steady stream of journalists, who followed him everywhere. When the story leaked about the anthropophagy, their questioning became even more intrusive, and after an Argentinian reporter started making defamatory insinuations, Nando stopped speaking to the press altogether, and the family escaped to the *Hotel Carrera* to seek some respite from the onslaught.

A flight had been arranged for all the survivors and their families to return to Montevideo on Thursday 28th December, but the Parrados were invited to Viña del Mar by some friends of Zenia. They took up the offer, and spent a couple of days relaxing at the friends' villa, undisturbed by the press. On 29th December, they returned to Santiago, where they arranged a flight for the next day. Coincidentally, the *Iberia* flight crew were staying at the same hotel that night, and realizing that Nando would have some trepidation about the flight, they assured him that they would take good care of him. When the family boarded the plane the next day, they found that they would be flying alone in first class, assisted by two dedicated flight attendants. Keeping the blinds down, Nando only got nervous when the flight experienced some turbulence coming in to land.

The control tower at Carrasco Airport asked that the Parrado family be allowed to disembark first, as there were cars waiting for them on the tarmac. They were excused the need to go through customs. A large crowd had gathered on the airport viewing gallery to await Nando's arrival, and they waved and cheered as they saw him emerge from the plane. His friends were gathered at the bottom of the aeroplane steps, and he stopped to have a quick chat with them, before getting into the *Porsche 911* belonging to one of them. Seler followed close behind in his brother's car, accompanied by Ciela. More crowds were waiting to greet Nando at the airport exit, waving and throwing flowers at the car as it drove by. There was no let-up when he got home, with a large number of friends, relatives, and neighbours already gathered at his house, and a steady stream of cars arriving throughout the day. But the most lavish welcome came from his dog Jimmy, about which Nando wrote in his memoir:

He had been fast asleep, and now hearing us enter, he opened his eyes wearily without lifting his big square head from his paws. He gave me a curious glance, then his ears perked and he sat up and cocked his head as if in disbelief. For a long moment he studied me, then, with a happy yelp, he launched himself towards me so fast that at first he ran in place as his paws scrabbled on the slippery tile. I hugged him as he leaped into my arms, and let him lick my face with his warm, wet tongue... For me it was a fine welcome home.

Fig. 205. *Nando greeted by dog Jimmy on his return home. Looking on is Ciela's sister-in-law Elizabeth Berger.*

The next few weeks were hectic for Nando. He and Pancho Delgado, who had spoken so eloquently at the press conference, were the most sought-after for interviews by the local and international press. Nando's heroics on the mountain had made him a public figure, and very popular with the girls. He spent the summer in fashionable Punta del Este, living the life of a playboy, and appearing regularly in the social columns of the local newspapers, until his fellow survivors called for a stop to it. In January 1973, Nando headed across the estuary to Buenos Aires, to see the Argentinian Formula One Grand Prix. There, to his amazement, his boyhood hero Jackie Stewart – who had been fascinated by the Andes story – asked to meet him, and the two became firm friends. It was the start of a change of direction for Nando, who, encouraged by Stewart, started racing competitively, working his way up through the ranks until, by 1977, with the help of racing magnate Bernie Ecclestone, he was driving for the Alfa Romeo team in the European Touring Car Championship.

Seler, gaining a new lease of life with Nando's return, poured his energies once again into *La Casa del Tornillo*. With Zenia no longer there to help, and Nando embarking on his racing career, Ciela gave up her dream of becoming a surgeon and started working full-time alongside her husband and her father at the family business. It would be another five years before Nando, newly married, would give up his racing career to join them. Together, they built up *La Casa del Tornillo* to become one of the largest chains of hardware stores in the country. In later years, they were joined by Ciela's son Gaston, who, after the rescue in December 1972, had become the recipient of the famous little red shoes, one of the pair carried by his uncle Nando on his ten-day trek, the other brought back from the mountain by Carlitos Páez.

Nando's time was divided between the business and a second career as a TV producer and host on Uruguayan television; a role he shared with his wife Veronique. And twenty years after the accident, he became the first of the survivors to present a conference talking about his experiences on the mountain. The

Fig. 206. *Gaston, recipient of the little red shoes, in 2019.*

reaction of the audience, their emotional response and gratitude, overwhelmed him, and took him by surprise, making him realize that the Andes story had a universal message of love and perseverance through hardship. Over the years, he has continued to give conferences around the world, and many of the other survivors have followed his lead.

Ciela has always been a bit of a workaholic, devoting long hours to running and growing the family business until she and Nando finally sold it in 2021. She has an energy and vitality that belie her age; her youthful complexion a tribute to the secret face-cream recipe brought by her grandmother from Ukraine. Since retirement, she has moved out of Carrasco, now spending most of the year in Punta del Este. She and Nando have had little time to talk over the years, Ciela busy with the business, Nando in constant demand wherever he goes. When they do talk, it is never about Zenia and Susy. They have mourned separately, Nando finding expression through his book and his conferences, Ciela grieving in solitude, and more recently through her involvement with the *Museo Andes 1972*, established to honour the memory of all the passengers. Both

Nando and Ciela have been to visit the grave on the mountain on several occasions. In the early years, before the route through the ravines and across the torrents had been established, it was a hazardous and arduous journey, but for their father it was a regular pilgrimage. He made the trip seventeen times and, in 2012, he returned to the mountain to stay, Ciela bringing his ashes to join the remains of her mother and sister.

Fig. 207. A portrait of Seler Parrado overlooking Ciela and Nando on the day the family business was sold in 2021.

Marcelo Pérez del Castillo
26-Mar-1947 — 29-Oct-1972

Marcelo Pérez de Castillo first became captain of the *Old Christians* in 1967-1968, and would continue to play a leading role in the club until his death in the Andes in October 1972. Tito Virginella, who had just taken on the role of physical trainer at the beginning of the seventies, despite knowing little about rugby, later acknowledged Marcelo's importance in the foundation of the *Old Christians* as a dominant force in Uruguayan rugby:

> It was in the seventies, with Ricardo Moore-Davie as coach, who a month later went to live in the United States. I was stunned – left on my own thirty days after starting! Then a solution emerged: Marcelo Pérez del Castillo, the captain; Guido Magri, a tremendous leader, and Gastón Costemalle, a gentleman, formed a triumvirate that met with me to put together the team. Those were my first steps in rugby, the year the Old Christians were promoted to the first division and we became champions.

Marcelo's involvement in running the club stretched back to its incorporation in 1964 when he had become one of its first directors, and at the time of the accident he was not only captain of the team, but also vice-president of the *Old Christians Club*. The ethos of rugby – its values of integrity, discipline, and respect – resonated deeply with him, and he demanded the highest standards from his players. Brother O'Connell, who had joined the community in March 1972, remembers being struck by an on-field incident when a member of the team had questioned a refereeing decision; for Marcelo, this was unthinkable, and he immediately asked the player to leave the field. But this strictness was tempered by a concern for his teammates, as recalled by a young Antonio Vizintín in 1973:

> He was a great team captain. Once I injured my leg and he came to pick me up at home on a Sunday morning to take me to the doctor. He cared a lot about all the players. When there were problems, he would talk about them up front. A friend to everyone, he knew how to get serious when he had to.

This combination of authority and humanity was forged in the family home. His mother, Stella Ferreira, exerted a school-like discipline to mould her children's behaviour. When their conduct fell short, she would give them lines to write out – 'I must not eat with my mouth open', or 'I must not spill the water', to be repeated a hundred or more times. But Marcelo always managed to defuse the situation with his humour, resorting to old schoolboy tricks such as tying several pencils together, or preparing ahead of time by writing 'I must not' multiple times. His mother soon cottoned on to the latter, after discovering his stash of partially written lines, and was a bit less formulaic the next time she meted out the punishment. Marcelo's good-humoured rebellion against his mother's dictates showed itself in other ways. When his parents went away on a trip, they asked him to write to them (in the days before electronic communication). "What should I put?" asked Marcelo. "Well, you take paper and pencil, and you think 'what could I put'." The first letter he sent began, "Dear Mum and Dad," and continued, "What shall I put? What shall I put?" for another three pages.

Fig. 208. **Standing**: *Juan Manuel, Manolo, Marcelo.*
Seated: *Stellita, Stella, Claudia, Álvaro.*

His father, affectionate and attentive, was more relaxed about discipline, especially when it came to Claudia, the baby of the family, who could do little wrong. Manuel, known to everyone as Manolo, was an architect. He and Stella had been early adopters of the idea of Carrasco as a residential neighbourhood, where Manolo had designed an elegant and spacious house for his family. Influenced by contacts in the *Christian Family Movement*, the two of them had also been leading proponents of the formation of *Stella Maris College*, travelling to Dublin in person to convince the Irish Christian Brothers to open a college in Montevideo. Manolo was on the first board of directors of the school, along with his good friend Eduardo Strauch, father of the Andes passenger of the same name. The Pérez del Castillo and Strauch families were very close, the two couples even having honeymooned together, and they were prominent in the fundraising efforts for the new school building, also designed by Manolo.

Marcelo and Eduardo (son) were equally close, having been classmates at *Stella Maris* before going on to study together in the Faculty of Architecture at the *Universidad de la República*. It had been a difficult decision for Marcelo, as to whether to follow his father into architecture, or to go into agronomy like his two brothers – Juan Manuel, who was two years older, and Álvaro, three years his junior. He loved the countryside, and the family had a 4000-hectare *estancia*, *El Sauce*, located in the Rocha department, and another half that size in the Maldonado department, so there was ample opportunity to pursue a career there. But Marcelo's mathematical skills and draughtsmanship persuaded him to choose architecture. He got a lot of enjoyment from drawing, and would often illustrate his letters with amusing pictograms.

El Sauce had been passed down through the Ferreira side of the family, and in 1968, Juan Manuel was already working there full-time, when tragedy struck. Manolo had travelled to Brazil for a routine operation on his aorta, but had died from complications a few days later. It was a devastating blow to the family, and their ability to recover was largely due to Marcelo. With Juan Manuel and Álvaro both living in the interior, the latter studying in Paysandú, it was left to Marcelo to hold the family together, and he became a father figure for his younger sisters. As kind and devoted as Manolo had been, he would see them off to school in the morning, listen to the account of their day when they got home, and tuck them into bed at night. But he was also strict when necessary. His sister Stellita remembers an occasion when, due to the heavy rain that day, she decided to skip her German class. Marcelo would have none of that, and insisted that she go. Such was his authority, that, even at age eighteen, she obeyed without argument.

Marcelo decided not to carry on with his father's prestigious architecture business, preferring instead to start from scratch. He and Eduardo joined forces, working out of Manolo's old office in the family home. Many of their architectural projects were in

Rocha, making use of Marcelo's ties to the area. The two boys would often get together socially also, meeting up with Stellita and her group of friends.

Outside of architecture and rugby, Marcelo enjoyed fishing and camping. Every Easter, he would ask Juan Manuel for the loan of the farm truck, to go camping with his friends in the *Santa Teresa National Park* in Rocha. The two brothers, separated by only two years, had been close friends from childhood, playing together as toddlers with tin soldiers and cars. One Easter, the old farm truck wouldn't start, causing Marcelo to exclaim to his brother: "We have to change this piece of junk!" Juan Manuel flippantly retorted, "No problem, just exchange it for a zero-mileage cattle truck." To the older brother's great surprise, a new vehicle arrived at the ranch a few days later with an accompanying note reading, 'Enclosed with this letter, I'm sending you the truck you requested.'

Fig. 209. *Juan Manuel (left) and Marcelo (right) had been great friends from childhood.*

This facility for getting things done made Marcelo the ideal person to arrange the trip to Chile. He had travelled the year before, under the captaincy of Guido Magri, and in 1972 he took the initiative to organize it himself, enlisting the help of some former classmates, Rafael Ponce de León, Julio Martínez Lamas, and Pepe Pollak. Rafael marshalled the communications with their Chilean hosts, whilst the others set about signing up sufficient numbers of rugby-playing *Old Christians* to assemble a competitive team. Marcelo arranged the charter with the Uruguayan Air Force, which, with a full complement of forty passengers, would ensure a per-ticket price of $40. Anyone already signed up was tasked with recruiting friends and family members. As the deadline approached, Marcelo redoubled his efforts to fill the plane, even using the occasion of his brother Álvaro's wedding party on 25th September to spread the word. A final push in the week before departure brought the number of passengers to forty, amongst them Juan Manuel's future brother-in-law Álvaro Mangino.

Marcelo drove himself to the airport on the morning of 12th October, making a small detour to pick up young teammates Roberto Canessa and Gustavo Zerbino along the way. The boys had no premonition of the upcoming disaster and its immediate aftermath, in which the three of them would play the leading roles. Marcelo sat with Álvaro on the plane, and in Mendoza, the two of them walked around with Julio, eating lunch together at a Spanish restaurant, before joining Nando Parrado and Panchito Abal to watch What's Up, Doc! in the evening.

Fig. 210. *Panchito Abal and Marcelo at a friend's wedding in May 1972.*

In the accident, the three boys who had shared a ride to Carrasco airport the previous morning were the first to emerge from their seats, despite having been seated in different parts of the plane. Each of them was left relatively unscathed, Marcelo being the worst off, with a twisted ankle and pains in his chest. Remarkably, they were also the three best suited to deal with the immediate aftermath. Marcelo immediately used his authority to start organizing the other boys, many of whom were in shock, directing them in the task of clearing the fuselage and helping to release those who were trapped. Roberto and Gustavo, meanwhile, used their rudimentary medical knowledge to start triaging the injured.

Marcelo's leadership continued through the evening and into the night. When Carlos Valeta was spotted floundering down the mountainside, it was Marcelo along with Bobby François who jumped into the snow to try to reach him, sinking to their thighs before realizing it was a hopeless cause. During the night, Marcelo took the coldest spot in the plane, along with Roy Harley and others in the gang, directing the building of a rudimentary wall to keep out the wind. And as people shouted out during the night, he would try to calm the hysteria. The next morning, Marcelo arranged for the bodies of those who had died to be taken outside and laid to rest at the side of the plane.

Over the following days, he took the leading role in organizing their makeshift home, rationing the food, and keeping people occupied. Naturally optimistic, he would encourage the others to stay positive, and to expect that rescue was on its way. One of the ways he raised spirits was by singing; something he had always enjoyed. At age 18, he had been involved in a bad car accident in Punta del Este with four friends, but even with his arm in a cast and his jaw wired shut for forty days, he had amused everyone by continuing to sing throughout, albeit with a severely compromised enunciation. Now on the mountain, he sang songs from his teenage years, favourites such as the upbeat doo-wop hit *Blue Moon*.

Fig. 211. *The 1971 Trip*
Above: J Cazet, Eduardo Viera, Adolfo Gelsi.
Below: Zika Platero, Marcelo, Guido Magri.

As the days passed with no rescue in sight, thoughts turned to what they might have to do to survive. The use of their friends' bodies had not yet occurred to Marcelo when Roberto and Fito separately broached the subject with him. His initial reaction was to rebel against the idea of something so unthinkable. But after considering it further, he admitted that the arguments were sound. Once the decision had been made, and the taboo broken, he resumed the captain's mantle and made the daily distributions of the meat to the boys, ensuring that everyone had their fair share, going short himself if necessary to keep the peace. He also took it upon himself to gently persuade those who were still holding out – Coche Inciarte, and Javier and Liliana Methol – likening the act to that of communion.

The weight of responsibility took a heavy toll on Marcelo psychologically. He would constantly blame himself for getting everyone into this predicament, despite their protestation. After hearing news of the search being called off, he continued to put on a brave face during the daytime, outwardly optimistic and still fulfilling his role as the leader of the group. But at night, his emotions would overcome him, and he would become depressed, thinking about his family back home, worrying about how his mother and sisters would cope if he didn't return, and upset by the thought of Álvaro's honeymoon being ruined. Eduardo, who would sometimes sleep next to him, would hear him crying in his sleep.

Sleeping side-by-side again on the night of the avalanche, the two friends were completely buried and immobilized by the inrush of snow, powerless to rescue themselves. Fito Strauch, on the other side of Eduardo, was one of the first to break free, with the help of Roy Harley. He immediately set to work, freeing his two cousins before moving on up the line to Marcelo. Digging with the help of Eduardo and Tintín, he found Marcelo already dead, a look of resignation on his face. The date was 29th October, four years to the day his father had died.

Two weeks earlier, when the news had broken in Uruguay about the plane's disappearance, the Pérez del Castillo family had been scattered in different places. The two girls had been in Montevideo, Stellita hearing the news from her *novio* Gustavo Perrier, and Claudia called into the principal's office at school and sent home. The two had waited alone in the house for the return of their mother, who, in deep shock, was being driven home from the *estancia* by her brother-in-law and sister. Juan Manuel, attending a cattle show in the town of Minas, had been alerted to the news by friends; he left for Montevideo immediately on hearing the reports. Álvaro, on honeymoon in Brazil, had been informed by a cousin who lived locally and who, due to the difficulty of obtaining ready funds, arranged a collection to buy tickets for the next flight back.

As everyone converged on the family home, the news was still unclear, and hopes were briefly raised by the unfounded rumour that the boys had landed safely. But by the next day, it became clear that the plane was lost, and that a search was underway. Over the following weeks, many meetings were held in the family home, taking place in the large upstairs room, which had been the domain of Marcelo and his brothers. Manolo, when designing the house, had included a side entrance with easy access to the uncarpeted upper room, so that the boys could enter after football or rugby without tracking mud through the main part of the house. Marcelo, in recent years, had used it for *Old Christians* gatherings, conducting team meetings there or social get-togethers, often accompanied by an *asado*. The boys' bedrooms, jokingly referred to as 'elevators' by Marcelo due to their small size, all led off the main room.

The area, equipped with a round table, chairs, some shelves and a telephone, was now repurposed as a place to hear and discuss the latest search news from Chile. Stella, sensing that her son was still alive, was in frequent communication with Dutch clairvoyant Gerard Croiset, the connection enabled by ham radio. Stella would place a call to Rafael Ponce de León, who would patch it through to a ham radio operator in the Netherlands, who would in turn relay it to Croiset by means of another local call. Croiset's calculations, which had pinpointed an area in the Chilean Andes east of Talca, convinced Stella to personally make a trip to search for Marcelo. She was joined by her son Juan

Manuel, Rafael Echavarren's father, and the mother and great-uncle of Carlitos Páez, the latter a commercial pilot for PLUNA, the national airline. They spent three days making expeditions deep into the mountains on muleback, concentrating their efforts on *Descabezado Grande*, the peak that most closely matched Gerard Croiset's visions. But it was to no avail, they were 100 km south of where the fuselage lay.

The news of the appearance of two boys in the Chilean *precordillera* initially brought hope, but when it was learnt that the boys were Nando and Roberto, Stella knew right away that Marcelo hadn't made it; that he would have walked out if he had been alive. This was soon confirmed by the list of survivors, shared with Stella, ahead of the radio announcement, by her cousin Wilson Ferreira, leader of the *Blanco* party, who had been given advance notice.

When the boys returned from the mountain, Marcelo's two brothers each went to visit a survivor to get first-hand information about his time on the mountain. Juan Manuel spoke to Álvaro Mangino, the *novio* of his wife's sister, whereas Álvaro went to visit his great friend Coche, recalling later:

> I went immediately to Coche's house to congratulate his family on the news. I will never forget the silence when I entered.... but I will never forget the hug we exchanged with Marta, his mother, a divine woman who always remembered the event.

Álvaro's wife Teresa Favaro and Coche's *novia* and soon-to-be-wife Soledad Gonzalez had been classmates and close friends for ten years at the *Sagrado Corazón* school. Reflecting on the two-and-a-half months of uncertainty before the survivors appeared, Álvaro acknowledged the importance of this friendship:

> My memory of the 72 days of waiting is of having shared the anguish with Soledad and other friends of Teresa whose boyfriends were on the plane: I especially remember Gastón Costemalle's girlfriend Inés, who was also a childhood friend of Teresa and Soledad.

The two couples remain firm friends to the present day, and Teresa and Álvaro's first son, named Marcelo after the uncle he never knew, is godfather to one of Soledad and Coche's grandsons. Friendships and social interactions with the survivors have continued through the years, and have passed down to the next generations, who are often unaware of the global significance of the story which had so impacted the lives of their elders.

434

Stella made the decision not to talk about the tragedy any more at home. She eventually found solace and companionship within the group of bereaved mothers who gathered to meet in the months after the return of the survivors. Under the leadership of Selva Maquirriain and the inspiration of Agnes Valeta, the idea of the *Biblioteca Nuestros Hijos* was born; a project in honour of their children that allowed them to find new purpose and to escape the grief by doing something positive for the community. In recent years, Stellita and Claudia have continued the work, providing the transition from the mothers to the next generation, and leading the library's mission to promote literacy, education, and cultural development in poorer neighbourhoods around Carrasco.

Forty-five years after her brother's death, Claudia found expression for the suppressed emotions of a lifetime, working with her niece María del Carmen Perrier Pérez del Castillo – daughter of Stellita – to tell the story of those days. The resulting book, *Del otro lado de la montaña*[1], which appeared in 2018, talks not only of Manolo and Marcelo, but also touches on the lives of the other bereaved families, and on the foundation of the library. It was the first book on the Andes tragedy to tell the story from the perspective of those who didn't return.

---

[1] *From the other side of the mountain.*

ENRIQUE PLATERO
21-JUL-1950 — 29-OCT-1972

On the afternoon of 13th October 1972, Zika Platero was having a snack in the dining room of the family home on Puyol street in Carrasco when he distinctly heard the voice of his brother Enrique saying, "Mamá." Zika's mother Eita, across the table, looked at him and asked, "Did you hear that?" "Yes!" They didn't know what to think. Enrique should have been in Chile by then, having travelled the day before. Later that evening, they heard the news about the accident, but the episode in the dining room convinced Eita that her son was alive.

Enrique was the oldest of the three children – all boys – of Enrique and Hélida 'Eita' Platero. Francisco, three years younger than Enrique, was nicknamed Zika by his parents after the dwarf Zikali in the Rider Haggard *Zulu* trilogy, books they'd been reading at the time of his birth. The youngest brother Fernando, also known as Pimpo, followed five years later. The family owned a 250-hectare farm 50 km from Carrasco, off Route 8, where the family had a dairy herd. Their lands also included a large forest,

which served the family firewood business. As a result, Enrique grew up in the countryside, and it was only when he was of school age that he started to spend time in Carrasco, entering *Stella Maris College* in 1957.

From an early age, Enrique had shown an independent spirit. Forging his own way as he grew into his teens, he rebelled against his father's

Fig. 212. *Enrique's parents: Enrique and Hélida 'Eita'.*

strict ideas of how he should conduct his life. His reluctance to study, or to do a full quota of work on the family farm, exasperated his father to such a degree that he eventually told his son to leave home, telling him that he didn't want to support him anymore. Enrique simply refused, retorting, "No, this is my home, and I'm going to stay." This enmity created an imbalance in the family. Whereas Zika, who lived up to his father's expectations, would always receive a nice birthday present, such as a bike or a Rolex watch, Enrique would get nothing. Pimpo quietly observed all this, and also moulded his own behaviour to comply with his father's wishes. In retrospect, Pimpo was grateful for the lessons taught by his father's strict regime, but Zika couldn't help but feel that it was wrong of his parents to compromise their love for their children with such an overt display of favouritism.

Despite Zika's good behaviour on the farm and with his schoolwork, he would frequently get into fights with boys at school, to such an extent that Enrique nicknamed his brother 'Lucifer'. A contemporary of Carlos Valeta and Gustavo Zerbino, Zika would normally scrap with boys more or less his own age, but when he got into a fight with an older boy, his brother might have to intervene. Self-assured and strong, Enrique never needed to fight for himself, and the only circumstance in which he would get involved would be in defence of his brother.

The battles within the Platero household were more of an argumentative nature, the family facetiously referring to their home as the 'Middle East'. Enrique would observe: "I have a tough father and a soft mother and I'm in between the two." He would call his mother *mija*, a term of endearment coalesced from *mi hija* – my daughter. But Eita, living with four rough men, learnt to be tough also, and could hold her own against them. And when the boys would ask awkward questions during their adolescence, Mr Platero would hurry off to the farm, leaving it for his wife to explain. Enrique the son was taciturn in nature; a man of few words, who rarely laughed out loud, but his keen sense of justice is illustrated by an anecdote from the farm. An impoverished elderly couple had settled, with permission, in a hut on the family's lands. Mrs Platero would give them milk from the dairy each day, along with a cheap cut of meat. One day, after collecting his provisions, the old man met Enrique at the gate as he was leaving, and mentioned that it was his birthday. Enrique immediately went to his mother and demanded the best cut of meat, along with some wine and fruit which he took as a gift to the man, galloping after him on horseback.

At the farm, Mr Platero was a hard man. When friends José Luis Lombardero and Jorge Camilloni came to visit Enrique there, Mr Platero greeted them dismissively: "You Carrasco boys don't know how to do hard work." Eager to prove him wrong, the two boys worked non-stop over the next couple of days, both of them ending up with painfully raw hands. They been classmates of Enrique at Stella Maris, and Enrique would often go canoeing with them on the River Plate estuary. The canoe belonged to Lombardero and was kept at his house, also on Puyol street, but closer to the beach than that of Enrique. In May 1969, tragedy struck when Lombardero drowned a kilometre or so off the shore after the canoe capsized in choppy waters. Enrique and Camilloni were not in the canoe that day, their places taken by two other former classmates who also died – Eduardo Gelsi, and Teco Costemalle – the younger brother of future Andes victim Gastón Costemalle.

The loss of three boys from the *Stella Maris* class of '66 was a tragedy which would be compounded three-and-a-half-years later by the deaths, in the Andes, of four more classmates – Enrique himself, alongside Panchito Abal, Felipe Maquirriain, and Arturo Nogueira.

In their mid to late teens, Enrique and Arturo, who lived across the street from one another, both played guitar and sang as part of a five-man musical group, along with Eduardo Gelsi and two other classmates. They would perform Argentinian folk music classics, such as *Zamba de Mi Esperanza* and *La López Pereyra*, Enrique's voice evoking the rich tones of legendary Uruguayan zamba singer Alfredo Zitarrosa.

Fig. 213. Classmates Jóse Barreiro, Arturo Nogueira, Eduardo Gelsi, Álvaro Jaume, and Enrique Platero.

On the rugby field, Enrique's combination of strength and speed made him the ideal Rugby Sevens player, and he was a member of the under-20 *Old Christians* team that won a national championship in 1968. As with his folk group, he was surrounded by former classmates – his near-neighbour Arturo, Teco Costemalle who played fly-half, Jorge Camilloni and Vladimir Jaugust, who were fellow canoeists, and Daniel Juan, who would go on to become president of the *Old Christians* by the time of the Andes accident. Enrique also became a member of the *Old Christians* first fifteen, his solid build and strength used to best effect in the front row of the scrum, where he played prop. His best friend Eddy Suarez, yet another former classmate, played full-back for the team, and the two could often be seen at Garcia's on Arocena avenue after a game, sharing a drink with their teammates.

Fig. 214. *Friends from the class of '66: Arturo Nogueira, Daniel Juan, and Vladimir Jaugust; Jorge Camilloni, Teco Costemalle, and Enrique Platero.*

Fig. 215. *The same group of friends as 1968 U20 National Sevens Champions: Nogueira, Juan, Platero, Costemalle, Jaugust, Caubarrere, Camilloni.*

Zika, a prop like his brother, also rapidly developed into a first-team player, in direct competition with him. On one occasion, after Enrique had been called up to the national squad, the coach of *Los Teros* telephoned, revealing that the wrong Platero had inadvertently been selected. Zika refused to take Enrique's place until the selectors agreed that both would be part of the squad. Except for when they were young boys, the two brothers hadn't been particularly close. Zika didn't like to share a room, so Enrique slept in the same bedroom as Pimpo. He would always be joking with his young brother, on one occasion persuading him to smoke some dubious substance, which resulted in a two-day coughing fit. But the year before the trip saw a warming in the relationship between the two older brothers. The turning point was in March 1971, when Enrique and Zika sat together to watch the boxing match between Joe Frazier and Muhammad Ali – billed as the 'Fight of the Century'. Both were supporting Ali, and although it would turn out to be Ali's first-ever loss, the two boys continued chatting into the early hours of the morning, until they finally fell asleep. They became firm friends after that, and the year before the accident was a great time for the two of them, as they had both fallen in love.

The steadying effect of a *novia* produced a marked change in Enrique's behaviour. He no longer shirked his responsibilities at the farm, working hard throughout the summer, cutting and hauling wood. During term-time also, he would help out at the weekends, making the long trip down from Paysandú, where he was studying Agronomy, specializing in Forestry and Cattle.

Despite Enrique's change of attitude, when the opportunity to travel to Chile came up, Mr Platero was against the idea, and wouldn't provide any funds. In the end, it was Enrique's teammate Nando Parrado who lent him the money. Zika, who had been on the 1971 trip, decided not to go this time, because he had an exam at the university on the day after the trip. Later, after he learnt of Enrique's death in the avalanche, Zika regretted not going, feeling that had he accompanied his brother, the two of them would have been sleeping opposite each other, and one would have immediately started digging for the other.

Several of Enrique's former classmates were on the trip, and during the unplanned stopover in Mendoza, he shared a room with two of them, Felipe Maquirriain and Pedro Algorta, staying at the *Hotel Horizonte* on Gutiérrez street. The next morning, as Felipe and Pedro went to visit Cuyo University, Enrique strolled with some of the other boys to San Martin Avenue in search of breakfast. There, on the corner of Gutiérrez street, he posed with some of his fellow travellers for a photograph, before heading out to the airport, the first to arrive, along with Marcelo Pérez del Castillo, Julio Martínez Lamas, and Álvaro Mangino.

In the plane that afternoon, the boys were moving around constantly, but at the time of the accident, Enrique was sitting next to Roy Harley. They were on the left side of the plane under the wings, and could see the propellers close by. After the two air pockets, Harley saw the rocks about 5 metres away and asked Enrique if it was normal to be flying so close – they seemed to be flying through some sort of corridor. Soon after, the wing hit the mountain, followed rapidly by the severing of the tail, and the impact of the belly of the plane on the mountain. The damage to the floor caused the seats to run free, and as the fuselage tobogganed down the mountain, the seats started to slide forward and to the right, culminating in a pile-up at the front of the cabin when the plane finally came to an abrupt halt, trapping and injuring many of the passengers.

Gustavo Zerbino and Roberto Canessa, the two 'doctors', were amongst the first to get free and act to release the others. As they pulled up the seats, Enrique appeared from beneath one, and when he stood up, Gustavo was shocked to see that his belly had been impaled by an iron rod. Gustavo controlled his immediate panic, and told Enrique that he was fine, remembering from a medical psychology course the importance of reassuring the patient. Enrique looked at him incredulously, sceptical about the assessment: "Do you really think so?" Gustavo drew from another recent medical course to further reassure him: "Don't worry, that's smooth muscle tissue, it doesn't hurt like other muscle tissue. Come on, you're strong, help me to get the others out."

As Enrique turned to go and help the others, Gustavo wrenched out the rod. "Ouch!" "Don't be a sissy – think about those who are much more seriously injured." Several centimetres of intestine or peritoneum had come out with the rod. Seeing a small cut in the protruding tissue, and worried about the possibility of peritonitis, Gustavo didn't try to push it back into the wound; instead, as a temporary measure, he wrapped it against the outside of Enrique's stomach with a clean shirt. Enrique then set to work without complaint, attending to Felipe Maquirriain, with whom he had shared a hotel room the previous night. But there was little he could do other than provide comfort; Felipe's injuries would prove fatal, and he would die before the night was out.

The next day, Gustavo examined his patient's wound in more detail, making a small cut where the length of intestine was attached to the peritoneal membrane, in order to more easily effect a repair. He still didn't feel that it was safe to push it back in. A few days later, when Gustavo was on an expedition with Daniel Maspons and Numa Turcatti, Enrique came to Roberto and asked him to take a look. By this time, the protruding tissue had healed, and much of it had retracted into his wound, but there were still a few centimetres visible. Roberto lay his patient horizontally on a hanging door he had rigged up a couple of days earlier for Enrique to sleep on. The protuberance looked dry, but Roberto was concerned as to whether it was part of the intestine, or part of the membrane. Making sure he had clean shirts, needle and thread, and a razorblade close by, he washed his hands and started operating. Carefully cutting away what appeared to be dead tissue, he eventually reached a point where he could push the remaining protuberance back inside the wound. Roberto, worried about possible infection from stitches and wanting to avoid further pain for his patient, felt that it would be better not to sew up the wound, and bound it instead with the shirts he'd set aside.

Enrique was elated by the result, telling Roberto that he was now ready to go on an expedition. He had been very active over the first few days, working hard without complaint, despite his injury. Before the water production system was in place, he and Gustavo had made the first litre of water, filling a bottle with snow, and shaking it for long periods. It took the better part of a day for it to become fully liquid, but Enrique didn't drink any of it, leaving it all for the sick and the wounded. Tintín also worked with Enrique to produce water in this way, and, as they went about their task, the two of them discussed the idea of an early expedition to walk out of there. Enrique felt that it was madness to wait until mid-November, as proposed by Fito Strauch and Marcelo. He wanted to leave as soon as possible. Enrique was supported by Tintín and Bobby François, and after the news that the search for the boys had been abandoned, the three started working actively to make it a reality. On 29th October, mindful of how Gustavo had been affected by snow-blindness on his trek a few days previously, they spent the day making dark glasses for their own expedition, cutting and filing some plastic material that they had found.

As they settled down to sleep that night, Enrique was by now well enough to sleep on the floor of the plane with the others, and the hanging door had been removed. Enrique settled on the right-hand side of the fuselage with his back against the sloping wall, and his legs angling up along the floor, lying opposite Marcelo and Pedro. The tilt of the plane meant that when the avalanche swept in, Enrique and the others on the right were buried more deeply, with a metre of snow above them. Of the five to Enrique's left, only Nando survived, his face fortuitously uncovered by Roy's hand digging down deep.

Back in Montevideo, Zika and Pimpo were convinced that their brother was alive, and their mother felt the same way, telling herself throughout the seventy-two days that her son was okay. When, on one occasion, Croiset was shown a photo of the rugby team, Enrique was among the boys he pointed out as being alive. These pronouncements would help to keep Eita's hopes up, and, every evening, she would walk the fifty metres to Ponce de León's house, to hear the news from Chile. Eventually, though, she stopped listening to the various reports, emotionally drained by the false hopes, and the lack of any concrete progress.

When the news arrived on 21st December that two survivors from the Fairchild had appeared in the Chilean *precordillera*, Eita, her husband, and Zika were staying at the farm. The news came on the radio, but Mr Platero turned it off, telling her, "That'll be another false report, promise me that you won't turn it on again." At 5:00 a.m. the next day, Mr Platero got up to vaccinate the livestock. Eita waited until 8:00 a.m. before her urge to turn on the radio became too strong. Immediately, it was clear that the reports were true, the news programmes were talking about nothing else.

The family left for Carrasco, where Eita immediately packed a bag in preparation for going to Chile. Zika, sure that his brother would be alive because of his strength and determination, also made preparations, arranging for the cash that would be needed for the hastily planned trip. The three of them gathered to hear the list. When the sixteenth name had been read, Eita couldn't accept it immediately, insisting that Enrique could still be alive. For Zika, the experience of hearing the list was terrible – not only the loss of his brother, but also the sight of his parents, particularly his father, weeping uncontrollably. He was angry with the authorities for the way they had allowed the list to be publicly broadcast before informing the bereaved. Eita eventually accepted that her son had died. She had experienced the pain of having lost her son twice, but the appearance of the survivors at least brought some finality after the months of uncertainty.

Pimpo, meanwhile, was 300 kilometres away, at the farm of some friends of his parents; a place where news travelled slowly. They were sitting down to a meal when they heard the list being broadcast. Only a few names had been read before the owner of the farm turned off the radio. Pimpo immediately exclaimed, "Why did you turn it off? We need to keep listening!". The owner made the excuse that the battery was dead. Thirteen-year-old Pimpo didn't believe this for one moment, but there was nothing he could do. Arriving back in Carrasco, he still believed his brother to be alive. When his family told them that Enrique had died, he couldn't believe it, saying that God had assured him that his brother was alive and well in San Fernando.

That first Christmas, a couple of days after they learnt of Enrique's death, was a sombre occasion. The family didn't prepare anything, but neighbours rallied round and brought them all the usual Christmas fare – food and champagne. Mr Platero, devastated by the loss of his son, went over to the fireplace where there was a photo of Enrique. He stood there pondering a while, then he raised his glass to his son. That moment of sad acceptance was etched permanently onto Zika's memory; a low point balanced only by the birth of his own son years later, when, for the first time since the accident, he saw his father laugh again, happy at the arrival of his first grandson.

In the days and weeks after the survivors returned, Gustavo, Roberto, and Nando each went separately to visit the Platero family. Nando arrived with Enrique's belongings – his coat, chain, and watch, which Gustavo had collected on the mountain. Handing them over, he told them, "These belonged to a guy we love, then and now." The watch, which displayed both time and date, was stopped at 4:00 p.m. on 13th October, the exact moment that Zika and his mother had heard Enrique's voice in the dining room.

Nando also talked a bit about Enrique's life on the mountain. Zika, remembering that Nando had given Enrique the money for the trip, wanted to repay him, but Nando wouldn't hear of it. There was some initial resentment about the way Nando had been conducting himself at the time, riding his motorcycle and being photographed with a succession of girls, whilst other families were suffering. But Nando remonstrated that the motorcycle had always been his passion – that he didn't do it to attract girls; and he pointed out that he also had lost his mother and his sister in the accident. This helped to put things in perspective, and Nando left on good terms.

Eita drew great comfort from such visits. She had maintained her faith throughout, believing that the human mind cannot fathom God's mind, and that it wasn't her place to question God. She felt that Enrique and the survivors had a common destiny, that they maintained something of her son in them, and her intention was to help them achieve some peace after their ordeal. She felt that the mothers of those who died were better equipped than anyone to help the survivors, better than their parents or psychiatrists, because their only objective was love. And she refuted any criticism of what they had been forced to do, saying: "They need to know that we don't see any shame about what they did – I'd have done the same, and Enrique also had to do it before he died. If Enrique had survived, I'd have liked the mothers of the victims to understand my son, and that's why I do the same." Another consolation for Eita was the presence of *Old Christian* Diego Insiburo, who went a small way towards filling the void left by Enrique's death. A university friend of Zika, Diego went from being an occasional visitor to becoming almost a full-time member of the family.

When Piers Paul Read came to interview Eita in February 1973, she gave him an equally warm welcome, happy to talk about her son, and to give her thoughts on the story. They had been talking for just thirty-five minutes when Mr Platero arrived home from the farm with Pimpo. Eita, emotional from her reminiscences, introduced Read to her husband. But Mr Platero would have none of it. He told the young English author to stand up and leave immediately. The families had been initially told by the *Old Christian* committee that the money from the book that Read was writing would be divided into three equal amounts – for the survivors, the families of non-survivors, and the club. But later they were informed that only the survivors would receive money. When the book did come out in early 1974, they didn't read it, having no confidence that it would reflect reality, adamant that no one could make a judgment about what had happened on the mountain.

The following months and years were very difficult for the Platero family. The brothers saw that their father, whom they had always thought of as a hard man, was vulnerable and emotional. He regretted that he had been so hard with his oldest son, especially in the year before the accident, when Enrique had changed his ways. After the accident, Pimpo started spending more time with his father on the farm, working beside him and getting to know him much better. And Zika took the load off him when it came to the family finances. The interest on the loans that Mr Platero had taken out for farm and school had spiralled out of control, and the bank was demanding payment. Mr Platero was in no state of mind to deal with it, so Zika took it in hand. He worked with the bank to solve the problems, to consolidate and refinance the debt. The skills he learnt along the way were to prove essential later in life, when he was elected mayor of a large municipality in Montevideo, El Municipio E.

Despite her faith, Eita also had her problems. She became increasingly dependent on alcohol in the dozen or so years after the accident, until it reached a breaking point. Zika and Pimpo gave her an ultimatum, telling her that they would not be able to bring her grandchildren to visit if it continued; that it wouldn't be safe to leave them with her. That served as a persuasive and decisive incentive. She immediately called up a friend of hers, a doctor, telling him that she wanted to be cured. He gave her the number of Alcoholics Anonymous, where she went that same evening, and continued to go, never touching a drop after that.

Despite those difficulties, Eita felt a compulsion to transform her pain into something positive, and she found expression as one of the founding mothers of the Biblioteca Nuestros Hijos, helping people and spreading her wisdom well into her eighties. Fernando Vázquez's sister Teresita, who worked in the library from the days when it was still in the Hotel Carrasco, reflected later, "I enjoyed talking with Eita Platero so much, she was always so wise. I loved to chat with her, and I still miss her."

Over the years, the subject of the Andes wasn't spoken about within the family. Even to this day, Zika and Pimpo rarely talk about their brother, although he is never far from their thoughts. When Zika prays in time of difficulty, he will often invoke the help of Enrique and his friends – Arturo Nogueira and Panchito Abal. But when Pimpo's son, who would like to visit the site of the accident, asks his father why they never speak about it, he shrugs his shoulders and says, " We just don't know – we don't speak about it and we don't know the reason."

The brothers maintain a good relationship with several of those involved in the tragedy. Guido Magri's brother Aldo has been a close friend. Aldo became head coach of the *Old Christians* in 1974, a position that he held until 1989, and it is through the club that many friendships were formed and sustained. In 1973, a difficult year of rebuilding, after so many had been lost in the Andes, Zika played in the first team alongside Nando, Tintín, Roberto, and Gustavo. Remarkably, the *Old Christians* shared the championship that year with *La Cachila*. A few years later, Pimpo also played for the club, bucking family tradition by playing fullback.

Fig. 216. *Pimpo and Zika Platero, October 2019.*

The family have maintained a close relationship with Roberto. When one of Sergio Catalán's sons came to Uruguay to seek his fortune a few years after the accident, it was the Platero family who responded to Canessa's request to find him work, giving him a job on the family farm, chopping and loading wood. But Zika's friendship with Roberto almost didn't survive when the latter remarked to him one day, "Zika, you have to understand that this story is about survival – anyone can die, the great thing is to survive." Whilst he accepted the truth of what Roberto had said, it caused a rift in their friendship, and he stopped speaking to him. An event years later was to change all that, when Zika got an urgent phone call from Pimpo.

His brother had been working on the farm with Santiago, the second of Zika's three sons. Santiago had fallen off his horse and had sustained a spinal cord injury, and Pimpo exhorted his brother to come to the ranch immediately, as it looked like Santiago might not survive. Desperate, and not knowing what to do, Zika called Roberto, who immediately sprang into action. Within the two minutes it took for Zika to get to Roberto's house, Roberto was already making phone calls, trying to arrange for a helicopter. When the two of them arrived at the farm, Roberto took control to ensure that the correct procedures were followed, and marshalled Santiago's safe transfer to the intensive care unit. Over the next few days, Roberto dedicated his time to helping

Santiago, researching the latest treatment, and using his contacts to get in touch with world-renowned neurosurgeon Dr Barth Green in Miami, a leading specialist in spinal cord injuries. He then managed to secure a course of prednisolone, a treatment option for such injuries, through Gustavo Zerbino's pharmaceutical company.

Later, Roberto accompanied Zika and his son to the Jackson Memorial Hospital in Miami, where they met other families involved in the Miami Project, a programme to research cures and improve quality of life for spinal injury victims. There was some amazement that Santiago had managed to receive prednisolone in Uruguay, so far from the centre of the research programme. Although Santiago needed a wheelchair after that, he was able to continue to ride his horse, and to work on the farm, but his main activity today is as the production manager of the Platero group – the family business that now supplies wood for the pulp, construction, and energy sectors.

When Zika was diagnosed in early 2019 with motor neurone disease, he contacted a handful of his closest *Old Christians* friends to let them know the bad news. This time, it was Nando who responded immediately: "Come on Zika, we'll climb this mountain together."

CARLOS ROQUE
10-FEB-1948 — 29-OCT-1972

By rights, **Carlos Roque** should not have been on the *Old Christians* plane. Crew assignments for FAU charter flights were done on a strict rota basis, as they were an opportunity to earn extra money, each crew member being paid a per diem in dollars for the duration of the trip. Carlos had travelled on the preceding charter flight a couple of weeks earlier, one carrying a group of retirees to Paraguay. The itinerary had included a side-trip to the Iguazú Falls, and a visit to a reserve on the west bank of the Paraguay river, which was home to the indigenous Maká people. Hugo Igenes, a navigator and good friend of Carlos, had accompanied him on that trip, and the two of them had taken several photos of each other with Hugo's recently-purchased camera, some of the last images of both Carlos and the aircraft.

Fig. 217. Carlos Roque in his mechanic's overalls in front of the Fairchild, two weeks before the fatal trip.

Having returned from Paraguay, Carlos had no expectation of another charter trip anytime soon, and was relaxing at home with his family, drinking *maté*, when there was a knock at the door. It was a neighbour relaying a message at a time when few had phones in their houses. The mechanic assigned to the *Old Christians* trip didn't want to miss his child's first birthday, and was offering his place to Carlos. Being the father of a 1½ year old himself, Carlos understood the importance of such family occasions, and he readily agreed to cover for his colleague.

Fascinated by aircraft, Carlos had joined the *Fuerza Aérea Uruguaya* in 1968, after studying electronics and electrical engineering at the *Universidad del Trabajo del Uruguay*. Enrolling in the FAU's Technical School of Aeronautics, he pursued his goal of becoming an Air Force mechanic, reaching the rank of Mechanic Airman First Class by the time of the accident. The next step in his education would be a study course in Panama, a place to which the FAU sent their mechanics to extend their skills. Hugo remembers him as a consummate professional dedicated to his job.

Fig. 218. *The charter trip to Paraguay, two weeks before the Andes accident.*
Left: *The steward, Carlos Roque, and Navigator Hugo Igenes at the entrance to the Gran Hotel Paraguay in Asunción, the Uruguayan flag flown as a welcome to crew and passengers.*
Right: *Visiting the Maká reserve: Pilot Orique, Igenes, Copilot Cuadrado, Roque, and steward.*

Carlos' parents had tried to discourage him in his choice of career, but he had been determined to follow what he saw as his vocation. His father Juan Carlos was a machinist in a wood factory, his mother Dominga Gonzalez a dressmaker, and he had a younger sister Elizabeth, who doted on him:

> My brother was everything to me, my idol, confidant, friend, accomplice in some pranks even though he was ten years older than me, and he protected me from everything and everyone. He was a person with a noble heart, humble, and always willing to help others.

Fig. 219. **Top:** Wedding of Sonia and Carlos, with his parents and sister Elizabeth. **Bottom:** Carlos with Alejandro at Parque Rodó (left) and on his first birthday (right).

In the year after joining the Air Force, he married Sonia Medina, and on 4th May 1971, they became the proud parents of Alejandro Daniel. Quiet and good-natured, Carlos was very much a family man, his adoration of his son evident from the few photos that survive. Later, on the mountain, the survivors were moved by how he'd constantly talk about Alejandro, distraught at the thought of not being there for him. Elizabeth recalled almost fifty years after the accident:

> What a great father my brother was! The adoration he had for his son was mutual because when his father came home from work, Alejandro's joy was immense. Carlos devoted as much time as possible to his son, and he loved playing with him. Alejandro was everything to him. If he were alive today he would be so proud of his son, of the beautiful person he is, the excellent professional he has become, and the wonderful family he has formed.

A few months before the *Old Christians* flight, Carlos' mother had been much disturbed by a cargo plane accident in the Andes. The aircraft had been a Canadair CL-44, operated by Argentinian airline AER (*Aerotransportes Entre Ríos*). It had left Carrasco airport at noon on 20th July, loaded with 86 live cattle, its destination *Pudahuel* airport in Santiago. A few hours later, on entering the mountain range, it had disappeared from the radar screen, losing all contact with the *El Plumerillo* control tower in Mendoza. Heavy snowfall and dipping temperatures had hampered the search effort, which was abandoned after ten days, the six members of its Uruguayan crew presumed dead.

Commenting to her son about how terrible it was, Dominga expressed her hope that they would be found alive. Carlos responded, "Mamá, if you could see the nature and immensity of those snow-covered mountains, you would understand that they couldn't possibly have survived. If one day I fall into the *cordillera*, don't wait for me, because nobody ever gets out." It must have preyed on her mind. Elizabeth would be turning 15 on 10th January 1973, an important milestone in Latin American culture that is widely celebrated. But, almost as though she had a premonition, Dominga told her husband that she was going to hold off on making preparations for her daughter's birthday party, because something might happen which would lead to it being cancelled.

There is little record of Carlos' activity over the two legs of the *Old Christians* trip, or during the stopover in Mendoza, where he headed into town with the other crew members to seek food and accommodation. When a crew needed to stay overnight en route, the hotel would be paid for by the Air Force rather than coming out of their per diem, but it is not known where they stayed that night, and other than occasionally spotting each other walking around Mendoza, crew and passengers kept apart. Only one photograph on the morning of the accident gives a brief glimpse of Carlos going about his duties at *El Plumerillo* airport.

During the accident, Carlos was sitting on the cockpit's jump seat, in close proximity to the pilots, a situation described by a former *Piedmont Airlines* captain:

> *The FH-227 had a small cockpit and very little room for a jump seat. However, regulations require all aircraft used in airline service to have jump seats for check pilots and/or FAA inspectors. The captain and copilot seats backed up to the circuit breaker panels and the only place for the jump seat was just inside the cockpit. The cockpit door served as the seatback, with the 'seat' wedged between the circuit breaker panels. When riding jump seat on the FH-227, the 'rider' was almost shoulder-to-shoulder with the two pilots (just slightly aft) and very aware of the actions taking place in the cockpit.*

Fig. 220. A *glimpse of Carlos in Mendoza.*

The view from the cockpit when they descended out of the clouds must have been chilling, as they found themselves on a direct collision course with a 4,500-metre mountain ridge. In a desperate attempt to clear it, the engines were set to full throttle, the screams of the pilot for more power heard clearly in the passenger cabin. Carlos later told the boys that he had been the one pushing forward the thrust levers, to accelerate the plane. The impact was followed by the terrifying slide of the fuselage down the other side of the mountain, the crew in the cockpit again unavoidably having a front-seat view. With Julio Ferradás and Dante Lagurara crushed by the control panels – the former dying immediately, and the latter in the night – Carlos was the only crew member to survive. A blow on the head, and the terror of witnessing the accident at first hand had caused him to go into shock; a condition further exacerbated by Eduardo Strauch sitting on his head in the confusion of the first night, believing it to be a cushion.

Carlos immediately reverted to military mode, asking Eduardo to identify himself and show his papers.

The days following the accident were difficult for Carlos. Weighed down by the responsibility of being the only surviving crew member, he felt the need to assert some authority, telling the boys that once they got out, they should not say anything to the press about the accident, that he would deal with it. For their part, they quizzed him about food supplies on the plane (there were none except for coffee and *yerba maté*), about the batteries in the tail, and about the possibility of rescue. Carlos was optimistic that they'd soon be found by the search planes, and when, on the Sunday, three of them flew over without giving any sign of having spotted them, he reassured them that it was because they couldn't make sharp turns in the mountains. His optimism seemed justified when a fourth and final plane made a low pass and wiggled its wings, convincing many of the survivors that a rescue would soon be underway.

When they heard the news, on day ten, that the search had been abandoned, Carlos was one of those most devastated, lamenting that he would never see his son again. The boys tried to console and encourage him, to persuade him that they would all escape from the mountains, but his isolation was accentuated by the cohesion of this privileged group of boys, with their shared cultural and educational background.

Another boy almost as isolated was Juan Carlos Menéndez, two years younger than Carlos. Although a colleague of law students Pancho Delgado and Numa Turcatti, he didn't know them well, and had no shared social background with the boys of Carrasco. Like Carlos, he had despaired over the news that the search had been called off. The two would share the same fate. Sleeping next to each other at the back of the plane on the night of the avalanche, they were hit by its full force, instantaneously buried in a wall of snow. It would be weeks before they were eventually dug out, Carlos found with his arms above his head.

Back in Montevideo, Carlos' wife Sonia, who had been informed by the FAU soon after the plane's disappearance, called her in-laws late on the afternoon of 13th October. Elizabeth later recalled:

> That was the moment our nightmare began. We immediately went to my brother's house to be with my sister-in-law and my nephew, then other family members began to arrive, joining us to wait for news of what had happened to the plane. There were endless hours, days and nights waiting for them to be found alive, never giving up hope. Air Force personnel – senior officers and

colleagues – came regularly to inform us of what was happening with the search, but there was never any good news. We clung to what we heard, that they might be in one place or another, until ten days later the search was called off.

Sonia, one of four widows of the Andes tragedy, went several times with Alejandro to the military base to try to get more information, but she had little contact with other families, because she lived some distance from Carrasco. However, when the family found out about the nightly communications with Chile from Ponce de León's house in Carrasco, they began going there, holding out hope that they would be found alive.

Remembering what her son had said about the Andes, Dominga had been doubtful about his survival from the beginning, but one night, a couple of weeks after the accident, she had a dream that convinced her to stop hoping. On waking, she told her family: "Carlitos is not coming back, he is dead. I saw him buried in the snow, sticking out his hands and telling me 'Mamá, help me.'" Another day, Elizabeth had a vision of her own:

> I don't know if it was a dream or reality, I can't explain it. I was sitting in the kitchen of our house when through the window I saw a white light appear and it became more and more intense. In it I saw my brother in his Air Force uniform and I told him "Carlitos!, You've come back! You've come back! You're alive!". I wanted to hug him and kiss him but he told me "No, I came to say goodbye, I am fine" and just as he came he was lost in that bright white light and disappeared. I never dreamt of him or saw him again, because to this day, fifty years later, I don't know if it was a dream or a reality.

In time, the family had to return to living their everyday lives, and this continued until 22nd December when hopes were raised once more with news of survivors. Carlos' father immediately went to his employer to ask for financial help to enable him to travel to Chile. But having secured the funds, he arrived home to hear the bad news. Elizabeth recalled:

> At home, my mother and I knelt at the radio and listened to the names of the survivors until the list ended, and my brother was not there. My father came home happy because we could travel to Chile to look for him, but when my mother told him that he was not alive, the three of us hugged and cried. It is indescribable what we felt at that moment: rage, impotence, hatred for those who were alive, and we asked ourselves only one question: Why not him? From that moment on we began to process our grief. Life went on, but it was not the

same, the void my brother left was never filled. In our house we stopped celebrating Christmas and birthdays for many years.

It wasn't until sometime after the sixteen returned to Montevideo that the family found out he had survived the accident and had died in the avalanche sixteen days later, buried in the snow with his arms outstretched just as his mother had dreamt about him. The revelation caused even greater pain, because they realized that if the search and rescue effort had been successful, he would have returned to them alive.

In the following weeks, his parents went several times to the Air Force to ask them to bring back his remains for burial in Montevideo, so as to have a place where they could go to take flowers, but the impossibility of fulfilling their request was evident in the reply they would always get from the heads of FAU Transport Group 4: "Do you want us to give you a box full of stones?"

The only contact the family had with the boys who survived was when they saw them in person at the press conference held on 28th December at *Stella Maris College*, and sometime later Gustavo Zerbino contacted them to return some of Carlos' belongings. As time went by, the families of those who hadn't returned were forgotten, and there was only talk about the survivors. Elizabeth recalled those difficult years after the accident:

And so we went on living with our pain without anyone caring. I watched my parents waste away every day. In my house we didn't talk about the accident, only when my parents died did I start to talk about it with my nephew Alejandro.

Alejandro knew his father had died in a plane crash in the Andes, but not much more than that. The devotion bestowed on him by his mother ensured that he had a happy childhood, and it was only in his adolescent years that he started to feel more acutely the absence of his father. The first inkling he had that there was something special about the accident was when he was eight or nine years old. He had been playing with some friends who had started speaking about it, mentioning the eating of the dead bodies. Alejandro had no idea what they were talking about, and thought they must be referring to a different incident, so when he got home, he asked his mother. She told him yes, it was the accident his father had been in, and she spoke to him more about it. Thereafter, whenever he heard someone talking about the accident – often jokingly – he would keep quiet about who he was.

In his teenage years, Alejandro had frequently seen Roberto Canessa and Nando Parrado talking about the accident on television, something that had kindled in him a desire to speak to the survivors, to ask them about his father on the mountain. One day, seeing Canessa being interviewed on TV once more, a cousin who was with him asked Alejandro why he didn't make contact. He replied that he had no idea of how to get in touch with him. His cousin dismissed his objection, saying that, as a doctor, Canessa would certainly be in the phone book. Alejandro was too shy to call, but his cousin dialled the number, and when Roberto answered, he handed over the phone to Alejandro. The first thing that Alejandro asked was, "Do you remember my father?" "Of course!" replied Canessa, who immediately invited him to his house to meet his family. Through Canessa, Alejandro started to meet other survivors – Nando, Gustavo Zerbino, and others. These connections to the story prompted him to pick up the book *ALIVE*, which he read attentively up to the point of the avalanche, before losing interest. A couple of years later when the movie came out, he went to see it by himself, forewarned by Canessa that it had portrayed his father as being a bit crazy on the mountain.

Having heard about his father from the survivors, Alejandro still felt the need to speak to former Air Force colleagues, to get their memories. But when he visited the base, asking to be put in contact with them, he was told that it was very difficult to get hold of anyone who would have known his father, because they had all retired. His despondency at not being able to make a connection was short-lived. Not too long after, he coincidentally and unexpectedly received a phone call at work: "Alejandro, you don't know me, but I was a colleague and friend of your father." "What?!!" Alejandro couldn't contain his excitement. It was Hugo Igenes, Carlos' companion from the Paraguay trip.

Hugo had an interesting end to his career in the *Fuerza Aérea Uruguaya*. In November 1971, he had graduated from flight school as a navigating officer, missing out on becoming a pilot. The official designation was NDR – *Navegante con Diversos Roles*[1] – although jokingly they would say *No Dio Resultado*[2]. Unhappy with the dictatorship that had been established in Uruguay in 1973, and eager to be with his Argentinian girlfriend, he made a rash decision. Rather than ask for a discharge, he decided to steal a plane, setting course for Buenos Aires, early on the morning of 16th August 1974, in a single-engine Cessna T-41D trainer (serial number FAU 605). After a bumpy landing at *Jorge Newbery* airfield, he taxied up to the attached military base, and presented himself to the base commander, requesting asylum. It was the start of a long period of exile for

---

[1] Navigator with Diverse Roles.

[2] It Didn't Work Out.

Hugo, who was helped to get established by a generous collection from former colleagues in the FAU, and the connections of a retired Uruguayan military officer who worked in Argentina.

Hugo, who had obtained Alejandro's phone number through the *Re-Viven* social media group, travelled from Buenos Aires to Montevideo in 2006, especially to meet him. As well as the opportunity for Alejandro to hear about his father from a close colleague, it was the start of a friendship, and the first link in a chain of events that would lead to him visiting his father's grave on the mountain, a year later. Encouraged by his wife, he joined a *Re-Viven* expedition led by Andes guide Juan Ulloa. Alejandro later reflected on his feelings as he approached the site:

I was filled with conflicting emotions, struck by the beauty of the mountains, but at the same time unable to forget that it was a place which had brought so much sadness. When I reached the grave in which my father is buried, I started crying uncontrollably, and I deeply sensed his presence. In all the years since the accident I had never felt closer to him.

The night spent at the crash site, where, like his father, he experienced altitude sickness, gave him a small glimpse of what it must have been like living on the mountain.

These days, Alejandro has come to terms with what happened, helped by his contact with the survivors and his friendship with Hugo, but most of all by the support of his wife Ana, who encouraged him to open up and talk about it. Sensitive and kind-hearted, Alejandro is a family man in the same mould as his father. Overcoming his early setback, he is a self-made man who worked hard to put himself through computer school, pursuing a career as a systems analyst. He and Ana have two daughters, Camila and Sabrina, who are both interested in the Andes story. Unlike their father, who would always keep quiet in his younger years whenever someone mentioned the accident, they are not afraid to speak up. On one occasion, the subject was being discussed in a Christian Education class, when, to Camila's surprise, another girl told the teacher, "I am a niece of someone who didn't survive." The two girls then started talking and became friends, the story passing to a new generation.

Fig. 221. **Left**: *Carlos Roque's entry into the FAU.* **Right**: *His son Alejandro and sister Elizabeth at a tribute by the FAU who named the 2021 Technical Aeronautics graduating class after Carlos.*

Fig. 222. *Alejandro in 2022, with his wife Ana and two daughters Sabrina (left) and Camila (right).*

DIEGO STORM
30-AUG-1952 — 29-OCT-1972

On the evening of 11th October 1972, Diego met up with his cousin Margarita Montes to celebrate the birthday of a mutual friend, Elisa Levrero. Amongst the guests were several of the passengers who would be flying to Chile the next day, and their trip was the focus of the conversation, the boys unable to stop talking about it. In the midst of all the excitement, Margarita put a bit of a damper on the evening, saying out loud: "Diego, please don't travel on that plane! Who knows what kind of condition it's in or if it's even properly maintained?" Diego, remaining in high spirits, jokingly replied: "They'll take me out with the cattle when the thaw comes!" He was referring to the much talked-about crash of a Uruguayan-crewed cargo plane carrying 86 live cattle, which had been lost in the Andes less than three months previously. The search had been called off after ten days, postponed until the summer thaw. When Carlitos Páez returned from the Andes, the first thing he said to Margarita was that, on the mountain, Diego had remembered her comment from Elisa's party.

Fig. 223. **Left**: *Juancito, Margarita, and Diego.* **Right**: *Margarita and Diego at Areranguá.*

Diego and Margarita were particularly close as cousins. Born only five days apart, they grew up together, and were more like brother and sister. They had spent their early years in the Durazno countryside, living on neighbouring *estancias*, two of three rented and managed by their grandfather, Enrique Storm. When the children were of school age, the two families moved to the city, settling in Carrasco. There was no problem fitting in. They had often spent the summers in the neighbourhood, and the parents had a close circle of friends there, among them: Raquel and Gustavo Nicolich, Marta and Pepe Fonseca, Madelón and Carlitos Páez, and Isabel and Carlos 'Buby' Regules. Their children went to the local schools – the boys to *Stella Maris College*, the girls to the adjacent *Colegio Sagrado Corazón* – forming close friendships forged by the shared experience of growing up in an idyllic neighbourhood.

One particularly close group of friends emerged from this social circle: 'the gang', consisting of Diego, Coco Nicolich, Carlitos Páez, Walter and Roy Harley, Bobby

François, Pablo Fonseca, and Tito Regules. Roughly the same age, but from different years in *The Christian*, the boys had remained friends after they left school, and would get together to drink *maté* and play cards, listen to music, or just to chat. At weekends, they would go dancing, or to the cinema. Some of them, Roy and Coco in particular, were keen rugby players, and during the season their Sundays were taken up with that. And because of their parents' long-term friendship, Coco and the Fonseca brothers were regular guests of Diego at *Los Molles* – the *estancia* in Durazno.

The other *estancia* run by Diego's grandfather was in *Arerunguá* in the department of Salto. It was too far away to entice his friends, requiring an overnight train journey in sleeper coaches to Tacuarembó, followed by a two-hour drive on poor roads in chauffeur-driven rental cars. But the two cousins would often go there in the

Fig. 224. *Baby Diego with his mother Bimba.*

winter or spring holidays, Margarita with her mother and sister, Diego with his two brothers Juancito and Enrique, the latter nine years his junior. Margarita later recalled those long train journeys:

> *Diego, who had no fear, would go outside onto the steps of the train while it was moving, leaning out to feel the wind on his face. The guards would rush up to my mother, asking her to order him back inside, but he would just move on to a different carriage and do it again. The same when we went to Buenos Aires with our grandmother on the overnight 'Vapor de la Carrera' across the River Plate. He loved to be in the prow of the boat – Titanic-style – when we were*

approaching the city. It was forbidden, of course, but the crew's interventions were usually in vain.

The trips to *Arerunguá* were an occasion to relax and enjoy life in the countryside and to go riding. But for Juancito, who would eventually take over the day-to-day running of the *estancia* under the supervision of his grandfather, the time would be spent working with the cattle and sheep, or hunting for pigeon or fox.

Grandfather Enrique would visit *Estancia Arerunguá* once a month or so, often with his brother, taking the train from *Los Molles* to Tacuarembó. The railways were in his blood, his father Johan Storm (a Norwegian immigrant who had changed his name from Torgersen on arrival) having been a civil engineer who had helped to build the railway network, culminating in his appointment in 1933 as head of Uruguayan railways. At the Tacuarembó end of Enrique's monthly trip, there was no option other than to suffer the two-hour car ride, but at *Los Molles* the connection was easy, with a station nearby. In fact, the railway tracks ran almost through the garden of the *estancia*, and the cousins would often play on them, alerted to approaching trains by the vibrations in the ground, but standing up close as they trundled by, exhilarated by the proximity of the powerful locomotives.

The lands around *Arerunguá* have a special place in Uruguayan history for their connection to José Artigas, the father of the nation, who, according to some sources, had an *estancia* of 105,000 hectares in that area. Author William Katra, wrote of him[1]:

> *After his rapid abandonment of the second siege of Montevideo in 1813, Charrúas were a constant presence with the armies commanded by himself and his lieutenants throughout the Banda Oriental. One testimony of his force at Arerunguá (his personal landholding in the north) counted 1,300 'hijos del país' – his gauchos – along with 300 Indians and 200 soldiers who had deserted from Buenos Aires ranks.*

The Uruguayan countryside served as inspiration for Diego's father Juan, who, once the family had moved to Montevideo, had given up any idea of following in his own father's footsteps as an *estanciero*, concentrating instead on his art. Starting at age thirty-three, he had learned his craft at the Torres-Garcia workshop, but later he had broken with the *Constructivism* of the founding master, instead forging his own unique style. He

---

[1] In *José Artigas and the Federal League in Uruguay's War of Independence (1810-1820)*.

would go on to gain international recognition for his emblematic depictions of the Uruguayan landscape, with its *gaucho*-inhabited pampas and expansive skies. Juan had grown up on *Los Molles* and continued visiting the estancia there until the mid-sixties, when the rental contract expired, and although he hadn't visited *Arerunguá* for many years, the rural scenes at both *estancias* were deeply embedded in his memory.

Fig. 225. *Diego's father, Uruguayan artist Juan Storm, and his painting Poncho Amarillo (1987).*

As much as Diego loved the countryside, he was drawn to life in the city. Meticulous in his appearance, he would personally iron his blue-and-beige Lee jeans – the height of fashion at the time – and polish his leather moccasins purchased at *Guido*, a trendy Argentinian shoe store. His good looks, slim build, and sense of style made him highly popular with the girls. Music was also fundamental to his life. A fan of the Beatles from the early days, when few in Uruguay knew about them, he soon got Margarita hooked, and the two of them would spend hours listening to their vinyl records, singing along to 'She loves you' and other classics. His tastes extended to other popular music of the day – the Rolling Stones, and the Bossa nova hits emerging from Rio de Janeiro.

The summers would be spent in Punta del Este, where Diego and Margarita's grandmother would rent an apartment across from the Emir beach on the Atlantic side of the peninsula, nowadays much diminished, with only a small area of sand remaining, and the water almost up to the street. For Diego, it was an opportunity to swim out to the wreck of the *Santa María de Luján*; a cargo ship which had been carrying Brazilian pine from Porto Alegre to Buenos Aires when it had struck the rocks 150 metres offshore in the dense fog of 21st July 1965. As Diego clambered up onto what was left of the deck, he would be watched with concern by his cousin and grandmother on the shore, who would make frantic signs for him to return. Diego's sense of adventure made him game

462

for anything, and in January 1970 he set out hitchhiking with Pablo, Coco, and another friend, making it the whole way to Rio, a 2,500 km trip up the Atlantic coast.

Fig. 226. *A close circle of friends enjoying summer in Punta.*
Left to right: *Diego. Bimba, Juan, Juancito, Marta Fonseca, and Carlos 'Buby' Regules.*

Although not a rugby player, his love of travel made him one of the earliest to sign up for the trip to Chile. He, Coco, and Roy had almost gone the previous year, and those who had made the trip spoke so enthusiastically about the experience that the friends were determined to go in 1972. Between them, they encouraged the rest of the gang to travel, including a reluctant Bobby, whose natural inclination was to stay close to home. In the end, only Pablo and Roy's brother Walter declined to go, the latter unable to spare the money, and concerned that he had already missed too many classes at his agricultural school. Diego, Coco, and Roy would also miss classes, but were confident they could make them up. They had all started at the *Universidad de la República* in 1972, Diego the first in his family to study Medicine.

463

The night before the trip, Roy stayed over at Diego's house on Arocena Avenue, and early the next morning, Diego's mother Bimba drove them to the airport, stopping to pick up Coco on Divina Comedia street. They passed by Tito's house on Pedro Figari street, but seeing his mother's car in the driveway outside the garage, they assumed that she had already driven him to the airport. In fact, Tito had been staying overnight at his father's house in *Parque de los Aliados* 10 km away and was still fast asleep; perhaps the consequence of having stayed too late at the Casino the previous night. When, at the airport, it became apparent that Tito was not going to make the flight, the rest of them joked about how the plane would now crash, and Tito would be saved.

On the flight, the gang commandeered two rows of seats towards the front of the plane. They were joined by Rafael Echavarren, whom Tito had invited, and Moncho Sabella, who had been invited by Bobby and Carlitos. One of the topics of discussion was the idea of renting a car and exploring the areas around Santiago – Viña del Mar and the ski resort of *El Portillo*.

On landing in Mendoza, the seven of them, along with Alexis Hounie, who was a classmate of Bobby, got a ride into town in a station wagon. The first order of business was to eat, and they found a restaurant owned by a Uruguayan expat, where they had a large lunch washed down with liberal amounts of Mendocino wine. The eight of them then checked into the *Hotel San Remo* on Godoy Cruz Avenue, Diego sharing a room with Coco. They slept off the wine in the heat of the afternoon, and in the evening they went exploring the town, with its beautiful plazas and vibrant atmosphere. Some of the group went dancing late into the night, but Diego and Coco, along with Bobby and Alexis, went back to the hotel for an early night. In the morning, after a late breakfast in a café, they headed out to the airport.

The gang again took over two rows of seats near the front of the plane, and were constantly moving around and swapping with each other. At the time of the accident, Diego was sitting next to Coco, four rows from the front on the left. The sudden deceleration that brought the seats crashing to the front of the plane left him tightly trapped. Moncho and Bobby managed to free him and, remarkably, he was uninjured, except for bloodshot eyes and a swollen and bruised face.

After the initial shock of the accident, the medical students started to attend to the injured, but Diego, who was the first of his family to pursue a medical career and had only just started his studies, took a back seat to Roberto Canessa and Gustavo Zerbino. He did, however, perform one vital act that would prove to be instrumental in the group's survival. As darkness rapidly fell, there was little time to clear the mangled seats to make room in the fuselage. Diego, along with other members of the gang, and rugby captain Marcelo Pérez del Castillo, spent the night by the open gap at the back of the fuselage. Near them, and even more exposed, were Nando and Susy Parrado, and Nando's friend Panchito Abal. No-one believed that the three would survive, and besides, there was no room elsewhere. During the night, however, Diego decided that Nando might not be as badly injured as originally thought, and he pulled him in to the midst of the tightly-huddled group, to give him some warmth. Later, when Nando finally regained consciousness, he opened his eyes to see the three 'doctors' gazing at him. Diego 's alertness had saved Nando.

As the boys worked to get organized in the days following the crash, Diego was active in the cabin team, working with Coco and Carlitos to clear it, and to keep it tidy. Not as strong and fit as the rugby players, and suffering from the harsh conditions, he nevertheless stayed optimistic, confident that they would get out of there, and he would try to cheer up his friend Roy, who would often go around with a pessimistic look on his face. At night, Diego, Roy, and Coco would play a game in which they took turns to imagine and describe what would be going on in their homes in Carrasco at that exact moment.

On the evening of 29th October, the weather on the mountain took a turn for the worse. A snowstorm was brewing and a strong wind raging, forcing its way in through the various holes in the fuselage, and the makeshift wall at the back. Diego was lying on the left-hand side of the plane, his back flat against the floor, his feet on the chest of Roy sleeping opposite him.

Fig. 227. *Four close friends: Diego, Roy, Carlitos, and Coco. They would be sleeping next to and opposite each other on the night of the avalanche. Only two would survive.*

Bothered by a sore on his tailbone, and convinced that he would be more comfortable sleeping in a sitting position, Diego asked his friend to swap places with him. Minutes later, alerted by a vibration, Roy leapt to his feet a split second before the avalanche

465

engulfed the plane. Overcoming his initial panic and fear of being the only one left alive, he started to dig frantically, releasing Carlitos to his side, before trying to find Diego opposite him. Unable to locate him, and desperate that he and Carlitos were the only ones free, Roy briefly turned his attention to Fito Strauch, whose hand he saw sticking out of the snow, releasing him whilst Carlitos started digging for Coco. Searching for his friend again, Roy's hand uncovered Nando's face, Diego thus unwittingly and this time indirectly contributing to the future expeditionary's second escape from death. The two to the right of Nando and the three to the left of him, including Diego and Coco, all died, deeply buried due to the slant of the fuselage.

Fig. 228. *Carlos Páez Vilaró (left), Madelón Rodriguez (centre), and Bimba Storm (right) at the Talca Aero Club in the last week of October 1972.*

One hundred kilometres to the south, Bimba and her friend Madelón Rodriguez – Carlitos' mother – were at the end of a five-day trip to Chile. On the day of the accident, Bimba had had a vivid dream about Diego – one that matched reality, as his friends later confirmed – seeing him with a bruised face, but otherwise uninjured. Convinced like Madelón that her son was alive, and refusing to accept the official assessment that there could no longer be any survivors, they joined Madelón's ex-husband Carlos Páez Vilaró in Chile, spending some days flying over the mountains east of Talca in a small plane, courtesy of the *Talca Aero Club*. They also managed to secure the services of private company *HelicopServices*, who were willing to rent out their helicopter at a reduced rate, although it would not be available until 1st November.

On the day of the avalanche, the mothers were sitting in their hotel room, reflecting on their search, and preparing to leave the next day. The weather, as in the Valley of Tears, had become unsettled, turning grey and rainy. All day long, Bimba felt inexplicably sad, unable to stop crying. Returning to Montevideo the next day, she told Madelón that, for her, the search was over, and in the following months, she no longer showed any interest in talking or hearing about it.

Back in October, Margarita had been the first of her family to process the news about the accident:

On 13th October, my mother and I were returning to Carrasco from the centre at around 7:00 p.m., driving down the Rambla in our VW Beetle. I was fiddling with the radio dial trying to find some good music when suddenly I caught a news report about a plane that had disappeared en route to Chile... I turned up the volume, and immediately I knew it was Diego's plane... My mother said that it was impossible because the Fairchild had left on the 12th... I began insisting louder and louder that it was his plane and I begged my mother to drive faster so that we could find out more at home. But the rest of our family merely echoed my mother's opinion. My grandfather told me that I was just fond of catastrophic news, and forbade me to speak to Bimba, saying it was already too late to call her. I went to sleep knowing inside that it was Diego's plane, and when I awoke next morning, that terrible news was confirmed.

Now, at the end of the odyssey, Margarita was with her uncle when the list was read:

The list was communicated by radio: Diego's father and I listened to it alone with the door closed, my uncle with his head resting on his arms on the dining room table... Diego's name was not on the list. My uncle and I remained in a deathly silence that seemed to last for ever. Then we left the dining room, going into the living room where my aunt Bimba was. There was no need to say a single word... we all remained silent.

Unlike his mother, Enrique had been convinced that his brother was alive. Just eleven at the time, he would jump onto his bike every evening and head over to Ponce de León's house to hear the latest reports. But he was at the *estancia* with Juancito when the news of survivors broke. By 1972, the railways were in decline, and the fastest way back was by bus. They took the first one possible, setting off for Montevideo without waiting to hear the list of names. Arriving several hours later, they were greeted at the bus station by their mother, who told them that Diego was not among the sixteen.

When the survivors returned to Montevideo, Bobby and Roy both went to see the mother of their friend on several occasions. But the visits were too painful for Bimba; she would question herself as to why her son, who had had so much promise and to whom she was so close, had died when his friends had lived. In the end, she asked them not to visit anymore. Juancito and Enrique both knew that Diego had been her favourite son, and understood what a devastating blow it had been for her.

Fig. 229. *Juan Storm, brothers Enrique and Juancito, and Juancito's wife Magdalena.*

Juancito continued his work as an *estanciero* in *Arerunguá*, somewhat isolated due to the distance, and only able to visit Montevideo every few months. Enrique continued living with his mother on Arocena Avenue until age 20, when, seeking adventure, he joined a ship transporting 40,000 live lambs to Libya, working in the galley to pay for the sixteen-day passage. He had the opportunity to continue on to Australia, but decided to spend some time in Spain. The five months he had originally envisaged turned into a lifetime, as he made the decision to settle there permanently, realizing his destiny lay outside Uruguay.

Bimba and Juan separated sometime after the accident – something they'd decided on much earlier – but not before the family spent one last summer together at Punta. Bimba did find some solace as one of the founding members of the *Biblioteca Nuestros Hijos*. There, the mothers didn't dwell on the accident or the survivors, but they supported each other in their grief, and focused their energies on making the library a success, helping the children in the poorer areas around Carrasco. Bimba continued to be an iconic figure at the library throughout her life, the last of the mothers actively working there, until her death in September 2018. But even towards the end of her life, when Uruguayan businessman Jörg Thomsen founded *Museo Andes 1972*, with its mission to represent all those caught up in the tragedy, she never wanted to get involved.

Fig. 230. *Bimba in later years.*

Carlos Valeta
14-Feb-1954 — 13-Oct-1972

At 3:30 in the afternoon of 13th October 1972, Agnes Valeta had a terrible premonition; she saw a plane falling. She tried to dismiss the feeling, but it persisted, and by 5:30 she felt that her son Carlos was dead. When she told her daughter, she paid little attention to it, because Carlos had flown the previous day. News of the stopover in Mendoza hadn't yet reached them.

It wasn't the first time that Agnes had experienced an accurate premonition about a family death. Ten years earlier, she had had a vivid dream about her mother – that she had left this world and gone to a paradise. When a priest came to see Agnes the next day to break the news that her mother had died whilst travelling in Germany, she already knew the purpose of his visit. And it was her mother who came to her in a dream soon after the Andes accident, to tell her that Carlos was with her, and to show her his face, covered with a small amount of blood. Agnes took it as confirmation that her vision had been correct and that her son was dead. When, five days after the accident, Agnes went with her husband to the funeral of a friend's grandmother, the friend was touched that they had come, given the circumstances; but Agnes put her at ease, saying, "I'm at peace, I saw his face and I know. I'm at peace."

Fig. 231. *Teresa, Carlos, Agnes, and Inés.*

Agnes was one of the few mothers who worked outside the home. She had wanted to become a doctor, but her family had discouraged that, and she had trained as a natural history teacher instead. She initially taught in a private school in Carrasco, later switching to a public school. Her husband Helios was a gynaecologist, who would go on to play an important role in calming the sensationalist and sometimes hostile reactions to the anthropophagy.

Carlos was the youngest of the three children, with two older sisters, Inés and Teresa. The family lived in Carrasco, a few houses down from the family of Julio Martínez

Lamas. When Julio's father died in 1958, the family had gone from being comfortably well-off to being without income, and Julio, after completing *Liceo*, started an apprenticeship at the National bank, becoming the family's breadwinner. Julio's sister Rosario supplemented the income by tutoring neighbourhood children in English, the Valeta children amongst them. The extra practice in English was helpful for Carlos, who had started attending the bilingual *Stella Maris College*, starting in the same year as Gustavo Zerbino, Roy Harley, Carlos Páez, and Tintín.

Fig. 232. *Carlos riding his first horse Tobiano.*

Carlos always favoured the academic side of school. He was not a rugby player, but he was a skilful footballer, and he loved the outdoors, learning to ride at an early age, and developing a passion for fishing. He caught his first freshwater fish – a toadfish – from the pier in the village of Nuevo Berlin, on the banks of the Uruguay river. Like his catch,

he was hooked, and he talked about little else for months after. The children would go every February to their great-aunt's ranch in Nuevo Berlin. Sometimes she would come to Montevideo to collect them, staying in town a couple of weeks before accompanying them by bus to Nuevo Berlin, travelling the last couple of kilometres to the ranch by taxi. On other occasions, their parents would drive. It was a long and sometimes difficult

Fig. 233. *Carlos with his sisters, showing an early interest in fishing.*

trip in those days, often taking eight hours or more, especially if heavy rain had caused flooding and deep mud on the dirt roads. For many years, there was not even a bridge over the Rio Negro, and they would need to take a ferry. Inspired by his first success,

Carlos continued to fish on the banks of the Uruguay, and often the family would take a boat out into the river, angling for catfish and rays.

The family had their summer home in Portezuelo, near Punta del Este, situated at the mouth of the River Plate estuary, where water was salty from the ocean. There, Carlos would go spin fishing for silversides, often going to the beach after dark with a lantern. Also at night, he would go flyfishing for wolf fish in the lagoon near Portezuelo, and sometimes Carlos and his father would take a boat out into the Atlantic ocean off Punta del Este, where sea bass were plentiful. When he was older, Carlos would spend time with his friends, angling amongst the rocks in nearby Punta Ballena and José Ignacio, at the time sparsely populated communities, but now upmarket summer destinations.

Within the family, Carlos was the most talkative of the children, with an opinion, fact, or joke on any subject. Teresa called him a parrot, a scarlet macaw, because of his incessant chatter. But he had good values, and a social conscience. He and his sisters would go to a *cantegril* – a shanty town – in the neighbourhood of La Cruz de Carrasco, to teach various skills. On one occasion, a tornado had wreaked destruction on the flimsy houses, and they had gone to help rebuild and restore them.

Fig. 234. *Carlos, Teresa, Inés, Agnes, and Helios, March 1972.*

On leaving *Stella Maris*, Carlos, like many of his classmates, went on to the *Seminario* for his pre-university years. Always an excellent student, he got into the *Universidad de la República* to study medicine. His father, who was immensely proud of his son's achievements, had hopes of him becoming a surgeon, but Carlos was more drawn towards psychiatry. He started at the university in March 1972, at the same time as Gustavo Zerbino. Gustavo had been his classmate for a while during primary school at *Stella Maris* and again at the *Seminario* for pre-university. Reunited once more by a common course of study, it was Gustavo who invited Carlos to sign up for the *Old Christians* trip.

Eight months earlier, the month before university started, Carlos had gone travelling with a group of friends to Córdoba in Argentina, visiting the towns and the surrounding mountains. Passing through Cosquín, he spotted a two-foot-high wooden carving for sale – a striking bust of Martin Fierro, the archetypal *gaucho* who is the eponymous hero of Argentina's most famous epic poem. The excitement of finding the perfect gift for his father outweighed the inconvenience of this unwieldy addition to his luggage, and it came back with him by bus to Montevideo.

Fig. 235. *Carlos (left) and friends near Córdoba, Feb 1972, and the carving of Martin Fierro he brought back as a gift for his father.*

The weekend before the trip, Carlos had a party in his house for some friends from the faculty, which lasted into the early hours. One of the guests missing from the party was his *novia*. Carlos, slim, with fair hair and an open nature, had always been popular with the girls, and he would fall in love easily, but a few months before the trip, he had met someone special in his university class, and they had been going steady ever since, and she became his official *novia*. But at the time of the trip, she was visiting Europe, so there was no opportunity to say goodbye.

Early on the morning of Thursday 12th October, Carlos' parents drove him to the airport, and dropped him off. There, he coincidentally met another classmate from the faculty of medicine, Miguel Martínez, who was on his way to Salto. Miguel was the last of Carlos' friends or family back home to see him alive.

Stopping over in Mendoza, Carlos was one of a group of twelve boys who stayed at the *Hotel Horizonte* on Gutiérrez street, close to Plaza Chile. He shared a room with Arturo Nogueira and Tintín. In the morning, he went with several of the boys to the main shopping street, Avenida San Martín, to have breakfast. There, they bumped into Gustavo and others, who had stayed at a different hotel. A photograph from that morning shows the group of boys at the corner of Avenida San Martín and Gutiérrez street.

On the second leg of the flight, the only recorded statement about Carlos comes from the moment of the accident. Gustavo was sitting close to his friend, and saw Carlos swept out of the back, still in his seat. Gustavo was sitting approximately in the middle of the plane,

Fig. 236. *Carlos, 1972.*

and so it is likely that this happened in the slide down the mountain, rather than at the first impact when the group of passengers and crew in the last two rows of the plane had been sucked out. The floor of the plane had been mangled by the impact and the slide, and many of the seats had broken free of their bearings. When the fuselage came to an abrupt halt at the end of the slide, they were propelled forward by their momentum, causing most of the serious injuries and deaths, especially on the right-hand side of the plane. It seems plausible that Carlos' seat broke free sufficiently that it detached during the slide down the mountain.

It was soon after the fuselage came to a stop that the first boys to emerge from the back of the plane saw a figure half striding, half falling down the slope in the track of the fuselage. The figure was sufficiently close that they could see it was Carlos. His proximity is further evidence that he became separated from the plane a long time after the initial impact. Marcelo Pérez del Castillo and Bobby François tried to make their way towards him, but they sank to their waists in the snow, and any upward progress was impossible. The boys then started calling out to him to direct him to where they were. "To the left, to the left!" But at one point he stumbled, and started snowballing down the slope, finally disappearing in the snow. In December, after Nando Parrado and Roberto Canessa had set off on their final expedition and the thaw had set in, Carlitos Páez and Pedro Algorta found Carlos' body downhill from the fuselage.

Back in Montevideo, when the news came through that the plane had crashed, Inés had been studying downtown with a friend. It was late, and she called her father from a restaurant, asking him to come and collect her. Once she was in the car, he told her the news, "The plane has crashed, and we don't know what's happening." Inés wouldn't believe him: "No, it can't be true, he's in Chile." He told her, "Please don't talk when we get home, your mother is very sad. Just be quiet, and don't say anything." He was quite certain his son would be dead – if not from the crash, then from the cold.

Despite her certainty that her son had died, Agnes still went every evening to Rafael Ponce de León's ham radio shack in the basement of his father's house on Puyol street. She wanted to be with the other mothers, and to hear the news from Chile. And although the Valeta family didn't take part in the search, they did contribute money, when, at the beginning of December, the fathers of Roberto Canessa, Coco Nicolich, and Roy Harley joined Carlos Páez Vilaró in Chile to renew the search.

When the news came through that there were survivors, Helios gathered together his wife and daughters. As a doctor, he knew that the only way they could have survived would be to have used the bodies for food. He told his family this, and then he asked them to decide right there and then – before they knew who had survived – what position they were going to take. If they would approve of Carlos surviving by using the bodies of his friends, then they should not blame the others if Carlos hadn't survived.

When the story of the anthropophagy broke later in the foreign newspapers, he took his daughter Inés aside, and showed the sensationalist photos of body parts that had appeared in the Brazilian magazine *Manchete*, to show her the reality, and to make her aware of the upcoming storm. He knew that Inés, as a medical student, would see it for what it was. But the shock to Inés was only made bearable by the presence and comfort of her husband-to-be, Jorge Lucian Mena, who put into words what her father was showing her.

A few days later, the family were at *Stella Maris College* to greet the returning survivors. After Pancho Delgado had brought the press conference to its conclusion with his inspired speech about the anthropophagy, Dr Helios Valeta spoke to the press:

> *I came with my family, because we wanted to see all those who were friends of my son and because we are sincerely happy to have them among us again. What is more, we are glad the 45 were there, because that helped at least 16 to return.*

I'd like to say that what has been confirmed today, I knew from the very first moment. As a doctor, I understood immediately that no-one can survive in such a barren place without appealing to courageous decisions. Now that I have certainty of what happened, I reiterate: thank God that the 45 were there so that 16 homes were able to regain their children.

His statement helped to diffuse a difficult situation, releasing the psychological pressure on the survivors and their families, and earning him their undying gratitude. The parents of Eduardo Strauch expressed their appreciation in a letter to Dr Valeta after the appearance of the book ALIVE:

We owe you and your family a debt we can never forget. The nobility and understanding that you showed by being present when the survivors returned from the mountain range, and your statements to the newspaper El País are of unusual magnanimity.

Your attitude, especially your justification of what happened on the mountain, was, in our view, of great importance for public opinion to begin to understand the real dimension of the drama experienced by the boys. And no less important was it in helping them to overcome the trauma produced by such a tremendous experience.

In those days we made a resolution to visit you to thank you personally for your generosity. If we did not do so, it was because we thought that our presence might add to your grief.

Now, on reading the book, which has renewed all the emotions we experienced then, we feel the need to express our deep gratitude to you with these lines.

To you Dr Valeta and your noble family, thank you, thank you very much.

Discovering, from the survivors, that Carlos had died in a way very much aligned to Agnes' vision, the family took solace in the thought that he had slipped away slowly in the cold, a calm and peaceful death. Dr Valeta, talking to the press about his son, reflected:

From the very first moment, all of us, my daughters, my wife, and I were resigned. Inexplicably, I had a sort of certitude that my son had died in the accident. Now that his friends have told me how it happened, I can confirm it. It's better that way; at least I know he was not suffering a long agony.

Agnes, like many of the mothers, found purpose and solace in the work and companionship of the *Biblioteca Nuestros Hijos*, acting as its president for many years. The idea of a library had been born out of the need that she had personally encountered when teaching in the public schools.

A year after the accident, Dr Helios Valeta went to the site of the accident with his brother-in-law Lino Bensich. He was following the precedent of Rafael Echavarren's father, who had gone there a couple of months after the accident to retrieve his son's body. Echavarren had been helped by some Argentinian friends, the Franchetti family, who found mountain guides René Lima and Antonio Araya to take them to the crash site. Dr Valeta asked for the Franchetti's help to put him in touch with the same guides. As an amateur photographer, Helios took many pictures of the site, and shared them freely, though anonymously, with the local newspaper *El País*.

Having regained some peace of mind from his visit to the mountain, Helios decided that the family should start a new life, and distance themselves from the tragedy. He moved them from Carrasco to Buceo, to a flat with a nice view over the River Plate estuary. They had never lived in an apartment before, and didn't know if they would adapt, but it turned out to be a great decision, allowing them to regain some happiness. They also sold their summer home in Portezuelo, replacing it with one in Punta del Diablo, a couple of hundred kilometres up the coast, near the Brazilian border.

For Inés, it was more difficult to forget about it. She had been in the same class in medical school as Roberto Canessa and Fernando Vázquez. When Canessa first came back, he had come up to her as they were going down the stairs in the lecture hall and had given her a big hug, and there had been no ill feeling. But also, at the university, she would often hear, "She's the sister, she's the sister."

Gustavo Zerbino, who had invited Carlos on the trip, brought back his medal and chain from the mountain. His kindness was much appreciated by the family, and he provided a lot of support for Agnes. He is still in touch with the sisters today. Another item of interest to the family was discovered on the mountain in 2011 by Ariel Osvaldo Torres, who was exploring the glacier with ex-FAU navigator Hugo Igenes. Ariel spotted a bit of plastic sticking out from the snow, and, on examining it, saw it was a luggage tag with 'H. Valeta' on it. In December 2012, Ariel met with the Valeta family at the house of Alfonso Guerrina Valeta, Teresa's son. Alfonso and his family were gathered there with Teresa, and with Inés and her daughters. Agnes had died the previous year. The sisters confirmed that it was from the family suitcase, with their address at the time.

A month later, in January 2013, Alfonso travelled to the site of the accident; the first family member to visit the glacier since his grandfather 40 years previously. He joined the annual expedition run by Ricardo Peña, the Mexico-American mountaineer who found Eduardo Strauch's jacket high up at the impact point in 2005. Alfonso's father, who had been at school with many of the passengers, also signed up for the trip. Alfonso carried with him a plaque, commemorating his uncle, which he placed on the common grave. Ricardo and Eduardo, who also goes on these expeditions, then led the group out onto the glacier, and pointed out to Alfonso and his father where Carlos had disappeared into the snow.

Fig. 237. **Left:** Dr Helios Valeta on his way to Argentina to visit his son's grave, January 1974. **Right:** Alfonso Guerrina placing a plaque on his uncle's grave, January 2013.

Over the years, Inés and Teresa have tried not to get too immersed in the story. After graduating, Inés pursued a professional career as a microbiologist and as a clinical lab director. A well-respected practitioner in her field, she has represented Uruguay as an observer on an international standards committee for improving the analysis of clinical lab results. During her career, she has never felt she wanted to bring the subject up with her work colleagues, and those of them who know her connection to the story have been respectful of that. But she hates the fact that it is always there, that there is no end to the tragedy. When people find out who she is, the subject will usually come up.

Teresa has had an even more impressive career. She was one of a small team that established the first *Tata Consultancy Services* office in Uruguay, and has acted as chief financial officer for the global giant in both Uruguay and Chile. In Santiago, she was president of an informatics company for several years, whilst being simultaneously responsible for the TCS offices in Peru and Ecuador. On several occasions, she has flown to India to meet the chairman of *Tata and sons*. When living in Santiago, Teresa would fly back to Montevideo for a couple of days each month, but Agnes would never visit her there. She was worried about the flights over the Andes, and would always say "The *Cordillera* will take two children."

Fig. 238. *Inés, her daughter Ana, and Teresa, November 2019.*

The two sisters are reluctant to mention their careers, but feel it is important to convey the message to those who have suffered a great sorrow, that it is possible to move on from the pain, to raise a family, and to have a successful professional career. Teresa's preference is to stay away from the story, but, like Inés, she will occasionally visit the *Museo Andes 1972* or the *Biblioteca Nuestros Hijos,* to show her support. Neither sister has read much of what has been written about the story. Just the original book, *ALIVE;* the 2015 account of expeditions to the mountain, *Hacia el avión de los uruguayos* by Ariel Osvaldo Torres; and the 2018 *Del otro lado de la montaña* by Marcelo Pérez del Castillo's sister and niece, giving the perspective of the families of the boys who didn't return.

Now that the generation of mothers has mostly passed away, several of the sisters of those who died stay in regular touch with one another through the 'Andes' chat group set up by Ana Inés Martínez Lamas. A group of them, Teresa and Inés included, have started getting together more regularly, in person. Their inaugural meeting was at the Hemingway restaurant in Punta Gorda, overlooking the estuary, and they have continued to meet either at a restaurant, or in one or another of their homes. They talk about their loved ones and about the Andes, and call themselves *las hermanas del alma*.

FERNANDO VÁZQUEZ
20-AUG-1952 — 13-OCT-1972

In an early attempt to fly across the Andes in 1929, French aviator Jean Mermoz was forced to make an emergency landing on a plateau at 4000 metres, about the same altitude at which the *Flight 571* passengers would be stranded several decades later. Spending two nights in frigid temperatures, with no food and without hope of rescue, he and his mechanic patched up the damaged Latécoère 25, and in a series of hops and dives, managed to get airborne again, and return to safety. This exploratory flight had been one of many that Mermoz had made to establish new routes for the fledgling *Aeroposta Argentina* airline, whose director was fellow aviator and famed author Antoine de Saint-Exupéry.

A few years later, Mermoz pioneered the Dakar to Natal to Buenos Aires transatlantic route, helping to establish the weekly Air France *Croix-du-Sud* mail run. In December 1936, four hours after Mermoz set off on the first leg of what had now become a routine flight, he ran into difficulties, and a terse final message was heard: "cutting right rear engine"; then silence. The plane and its crew were never found, despite pleas by Saint-Exupéry to continue the search for his friend.

One of the important mail packages that went down with the plane was a bid from a British consortium to build the first hydroelectric power plant on the Rio Negro; the major river that divides the northern and southern regions of Uruguay. Without competition from the British, the tender was won by a German consortium, beating out the only other bid from Czechoslovakian company Škoda. A few years later, a Uruguayan investigative commission concluded that the Air France flight had been sabotaged by Nazi operatives, to ensure the success of the German bid.

The power station, the first of three, was to be located at a place called Rincón del Bonete, a few kilometres upstream of *Paso de los Toros*, one of the main crossing points of the river. Work started in 1937 with a planned completion date of 1942, and even when World War II broke out, work continued for a while, due to Uruguay's neutrality. Very soon, however, the battle of the Atlantic made it impossible to continue trading with Europe. The residents of Montevideo even had a front row seat at the culmination of the first major naval engagement of the war, the battle of the River Plate, when Captain Langsdorff, commander of the German pocket battleship, the *Admiral Graf Spee*, made the decision to scuttle his ship in Montevideo harbour. By 1941, all trade with Germany was banned, and the contract was terminated, with the plant still lacking its turbines, generators, and transmission lines.

The departure of the German engineers, and their knowhow, turned into an opportunity for five young Uruguayan engineers, the pick of graduates from the new Industrial Engineering programme at the *Universidad de la República*, who were selected to spend two years in the United States. The goal was for them to gain the necessary experience and skills to finish the project, using US technology. One of these graduates was 27-year-old Franco Vázquez; a young man with engineering in his blood, whose father had been a senior engineer working with the British to build the railway network in Uruguay.

Spending time with the *Tennessee Valley Authority* and other big hydroelectric enterprises in the US, Franco and his colleagues returned in 1944, equipped with the knowledge to manage and train the engineering workforce in Uruguay to complete the project. He was struck by how motivated people were, and how eager they were to learn, when they were enthused by a shared ambitious goal. His expertise would stand him and his country in good stead. For the next 35 years, he acted as the chief electrical

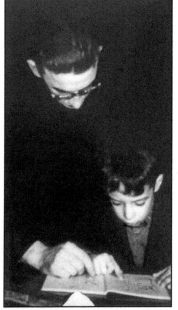

engineer for the entire high voltage power network of Uruguay, and taught at the university as a professor of Electrical Power Systems, becoming Emeritus Professor on his retirement.

In 1951, Franco married Ana María Nebel, and children soon followed, with Fernando born in August 1952, and Teresita two years later. Like many professional families, they lived in Carrasco, and Fernando went to school at *Stella Maris College*. He was in the same year as Roberto Canessa and Daniel Maspons, but unlike many of his classmates, Fernando took little interest in sports, preferring to concentrate his efforts on his studies. A standout and diligent student from the start, his intelligence and reasoned opinions earned him the respect of his friends and schoolmates.

Fig. 239. *Fernando Vázquez school yearbook photo with Br. McCaig.*

Franco's profession took him around the world, and 1962 found him in Paris, working as a consultant for *Electricité de France*. When the summer vacation began, the family joined him there, and it would lead to a lifelong friendship with the Pinter family, whose two children, Silvia and Patrick, were the same age as Fernando and Teresita. Franco and Ana María would visit France each year to stay with the parents, and the children would exchange letters and sometimes a gift; Saint-Exupéry's *Citadelle*, sent by Silvia, was especially treasured. Years later, when Roberto Canessa and Nando Parrado passed through Paris on the 1974 book tour for *ALIVE*, they met up with Silvia, having found her address in Fernando's notebook, recovered from the mountain by Roberto.

With their father often away from home, working in the interior or further afield on one of the hydro-electric projects, life for the children would revolve around their mother. Literate and knowledgeable, Ana María was Teresita's closest companion and confidante. The two siblings were also close, with Fernando endeavouring to look out for his younger sister, although he would join in when his friends would tease her about her dolls, snatching them away and hanging them on trees in the garden. In later years, however, as Fernando and his friends became interested in parties and girls, Teresita and her friends were sought-after company.

Like many from that era, Fernando had a large collection of vinyl records – singles and LPs – and he was always knowledgeable about current releases. He and Teresita had the advantage of a father who travelled often to Europe and the US, and they were among the first in Montevideo to own Beatles singles. When Franco brought back *A Hard Day's Night* shortly after its release in 1964, the Vázquez house was a popular place to be.

When Fernando finished at *Stella Maris*, most of his friends and schoolmates went on to private institutions such as the *Seminario* or the *IUDEP* (*Instituto Uruguayo de Estudios Preparatorios*) to prepare for university, but he had made up his mind to go to a state school. He felt that he had been living in a bubble, in a privileged environment where people didn't face any real problems. He wanted to know the real world, and he enrolled in the *Instituto Alfredo Vásquez Acevedo*, the large and well-regarded high school downtown, but one with a radical reputation, whose students had played a prominent role in the 1968 demonstrations.

The school calendar in Uruguay runs from March to December, and Fernando successfully completed his first year, 1969. But before the beginning of the following year, the Pacheco government, in an attempt to stamp out radicalism and impose order on the public school system, created a commission with the authority to intervene at will. After a fractious year of strikes and unrest, things came to a head at the end of August, when the commission shut down the public schools for the remaining three months of the academic year.

Ana María, desperate for her son not to lose a year due to this disruption, called the director of the *Seminario*, Padre Aguerre, begging him to take Fernando for the remainder of the school year. Such a request would typically be doomed to failure, as even at the beginning of the school year, competition for a place in the school meant that there was always a waiting list. But such was Fernando's reputation, that after a few minutes talking to his counterpart, Padre Montes, at *Stella Maris College*, Aguerre called Ana María back, asking for her son to turn up at the school the following Monday.

Three months later, after the final examinations, Fernando received the *Seminario's* Gold Medal, the award for the student with the top marks in the school. But it was a bittersweet achievement for him. He had recently lost one of his dearest friends, Guzmán Fleitas, whom he had known from his days at *Stella Maris*. Guzmán had suffered from a heart condition, and had died unexpectedly during an intervention. Fernando and Teresita were shocked at the suddenness and finality of it; Teresita, unable to stop crying, was able to express her emotions outwardly, but Fernando held his grief inside. Guzmán had been a brilliant student, and so, to honour him, Fernando gave the gold medal to his friend's father.

Fig. 240. *Fernando with his father Franco.*

Interested in politics and in making a difference in society, Fernando became an active member of the JDC (*Juventud Demócrata Cristiana*), the youth wing of the PDC (*Partido Demócrata Cristiana*), a left-of-centre organization founded on principles of Christian humanism. In 1971, the PDC was one of the parties making up the *Frente Amplio*, the broad front on the left of Uruguayan politics. Fernando and his friends from the *PDC* put their beliefs into practice by working in Barrio Marconi, one of the poorest neighbourhoods of Montevideo.

Despite the fact that Franco, who had inherited a love of trains from his own father, would bring back a *Marklin's* model engine or railway carriage for his son whenever he travelled to Europe, Fernando showed little interest in following the engineering careers of his father and grandfather. Instead, he chose to study medicine at the *Universidad de la República* with a special interest in psychiatry. Roberto Canessa was in the same year, and they attended the same lectures, so whilst they had known each other at *Stella Maris*, it was university that cemented their friendship, and they would study together every day.

When time permitted, Fernando would head over to Buenos Aires. He was a good friend of the son of the Uruguayan ambassador in Argentina, Julio Lacarte Muró, but more importantly, his girlfriend Corina lived there. Fernando would always fly to Buenos Aires, but when Corina visited Montevideo, she preferred to come by boat, not keen to board an aeroplane. When she came to Carrasco in the days before the trip, she expressed her fear of him flying over the Andes. Fernando's father was more concerned that it was the Uruguayan Air Force who would be conducting the flight. He didn't trust their expertise to make such a trip, and would have preferred Fernando to travel by commercial airline. Bobby Jaugust, another good friend of Fernando, who was often to be found at the house, was going on a scheduled

Fig. 241. *Fernando with his girlfriend Corina.*

commercial flight, as his father was the KLM representative in Uruguay. Franco said to his son, "Why don't you go with Bobby Jaugust? I'll pay for the trip. Please go with Bobby." But Fernando was adamant that it would be more in the spirit of the trip and more fun to fly together as a group. Franco never forgave himself for not insisting.

It was Roberto who had encouraged Fernando to go to Chile, and together they had requested permission to miss an upcoming exam; permission that was granted due to their excellent academic standing. For Fernando, the trip was an opportunity to travel, something he loved to do, and a prelude to a trip to Europe that he'd been saving up for. He had never been to Chile, and, as he was not a rugby player, he had no special plans.

He was just going along to have fun, to be with his friends, and see a new country. On the day before the trip, he had dinner with Corina and Teresita, and joked that the plane would crash and he would survive, returning a hero. That evening, Corina helped him to pack, and early the next morning, Fernando went into Teresita's room, which she was sharing with Corina during her visit, and kissed his sister and girlfriend goodbye, before heading off to the airport. That was the last time they saw him.

In the plane, he sat near Roberto and Daniel Maspons, and when they stopped over in Mendoza, the three of them shared a room at the *Hotel Horizonte* on Gutiérrez street. The three of them sat together again on the second leg, Daniel and Roberto sitting in the third row on the left-hand side, Fernando across the aisle from Roberto. When the accident happened, all three of them survived the impact, and Roberto and Daniel were two of the first to get free from their seats. Roberto spoke briefly to Fernando to check that he was alright, and then went on to help the more visibly wounded. But a major artery in Fernando's leg had been severed in the accident, and he died from loss of blood a short time later, in the rapidly fading light.

Back in Montevideo, Teresita was at the Crandon Institute that day, studying for her secretarial qualifications. Around the time of the accident, she had been chatting with a friend about the worries her parents had of Fernando working in the poor neighbourhoods, fearing that something might happen to him because of the Tupamaros, and the unrest on the streets. She arrived home to find her boyfriend waiting, wanting to know if she'd heard anything. Sent by Teresita's mother to fetch something at the pharmacy, the two of them soon found that the whole neighbourhood was talking about the accident. Ana María called her husband who was in Córdoba, working with his Argentinian counterparts on the plans for the joint *Salto Grande* hydroelectric project. Franco returned immediately, arriving that evening amidst a confusion of reports. At 9:00 p.m., a rumour was circulating that the Fairchild was in Chile and the boys were all alive, but by the next morning it was clear that the plane had disappeared.

In the following weeks, the house saw a steady flow of people through the day, coming to pay their respects, to give their condolences, and to provide support. From the beginning, both Franco and Ana María thought it impossible that anyone could have survived, and they never went to Ponce de León's house, where many families gathered every evening to listen to the news from Chile. They knew other families, such as those of Felipe Maquirriain and Coco Nicolich, but they preferred to stay at home. Even so, it was impossible to avoid the subject in Carrasco, where everyone had some connection, through family or friend, neighbour or schoolmate, or through church or rugby club. The main contact for the Vázquez family was Mecha Canessa, Roberto's mother, who would visit them regularly. She would say, "Ana María, they're alive, they're alive. Don't lose hope," to which Ana María would respond, "No, it's not possible."

Unlike her parents, Teresita couldn't admit to herself that Fernando was gone. Ana María recognized that, and wanting her to face up to reality, told her to go to her brother's room and start clearing it out. It was a terrible task for Teresita, but one of the items she found was a poem, *El camino de un hombre* – The way of a man – that Fernando had written on some scraps of paper. The last verse of the poem was remarkably prescient of his final resting place in the Valley of Tears:

El camino es el surco de las lágrimas	*His path is a furrow of tears*
una lápida o no	*a tombstone or not*
una tumba que no existe	*a grave that doesn't exist*
un cadáver olvidado	*a forgotten corpse*
un nombre en el viento	*a name in the wind*
el olor esfumado	*a faded smell*
las letras viejas	*old letters*
los recuerdos de familia	*family memories*
palabras solo palabras	*words only words*
y el sentimiento que perdura.	*and a sadness that endures.*

The poem was published in its entirety on 14th November, a month after the accident, in *Ahora*, the organ of the *PDC* that would be shut down two years later by the military dictatorship. The brief obituary accompanying it, written by his friends in the party, reflects the esteem in which they held him:

He was 20 years old and a bundle of energy, joy, and vitality. He had barely glimpsed life and had already mastered his destiny: self-confident, brilliantly oriented in his medical career, he seemed to sense his brief earthly transit. And he lived fast, he lived intensely. He cultivated affections that will never be forgotten: in the "Young Christian Democrats", in the circle of the "Christian Brothers", in his Faculty, and among his family and friends. But more than that, and above all, he was a thinker, a budding philosopher, a secret poet, hidden, inexplicably caught up in the exuberance of his twenty years.

After a while, people stopped coming to the house, and Teresita made a conscious effort to stop dwelling on it, training herself not to be sad. But on 22nd December, it started again. The family went to bed that night with the startling news that the boys may have been found. They didn't give the report too much credence, as there had been several false hopes in the previous weeks. But Teresita awoke the next morning to hear her mother crying and shouting. Ana María's mother had phoned, saying that Fernando was alive. For a few brief seconds, they dared to hope, but once they turned on the news, they realized that it was Fernando Parrado everyone was talking about. The grandmother had just heard 'Roberto Canessa and Fernando', and in her excitement, she had blocked out the surname. She was so used to seeing Roberto and Fernando together – every day they would stop by at her house to study, as Pocitos was closer to the university than Carrasco.

Fig. 242. Fernando's poem published in Ahora 14-Nov-1972.

Later in the day, the names of the other survivors were broadcast on *Radio Carve*. As the list was read out, a ghastly Russian roulette, Teresita and Ana María counted off the names, and finally had confirmation of what they had assumed from the start, that Fernando wouldn't be coming back. Before the list was read, Franco had told them that the only way they would have been able to survive was by using the bodies of the dead. The family never once felt this was wrong, and Teresita felt angry when certain elements of the press criticized the survivors. Despite Teresita's sadness, she was happy for the others to have come back. They had already mourned Fernando, and this was sixteen deaths less. Many years later, when Roberto Canessa's son Hilario had his own son, Teresita was overcome by an immense happiness that her brother had contributed to this continuation of life.

After the confirmation of the list, the visits of condolence and support started again. Gustavo Zerbino visited to give them Fernando's Fabre-Leuba watch – crushed in the accident – which he had brought back from the mountain. It had been a gift from the Uruguayan ambassador in Argentina, who had brought it back from Switzerland. But the grief of Franco and Ana María was unbearable, and they decided to sell the house in Carrasco and move to Pocitos. Ana María continued to be reminded of Fernando as she went around the house, and she felt that she would go crazy if she stayed there. They found an apartment that overlooked the gardens of the Spanish embassy on one side, and had a distant view of the beach on the other. After the move to Pocitos, the family immediately headed off to the United States for five months, putting further distance between themselves and the tragedy.

Franco had been working on the Salto Grande project to build a 1,890 MW hydroelectric plant on the Rio Uruguay that forms the western border of the country, separating it from Argentina. It was the largest such project in Uruguay. By then, Franco was working privately for a consulting firm, alongside internationally famed engineer Eladio Dieste. The company, in partnership with an Argentinian consortium and US company Chas. T. Main, had won the contract. The project team assembled at the Chas. T. Main headquarters in the south-east tower of Boston's recently built Prudential Center.

Teresita, who had finished her secretarial studies, acted as a translator on the project. The work helped take their minds off the tragedy, but one day Teresita saw and bought the first unauthorized account of the story to appear in the States. She was shocked by the sensationalist account and the photographs of the remains.

The authorized account *ALIVE* came out the following year, when the family was back in Uruguay, and Teresita read and loved that book. Now that the family were living in Pocitos, Teresita saw the other families involved in the tragedy less frequently than before. And although she still visited her friends in Carrasco, she started a new life, working full-time with her father, and getting involved in other social activities. Over the years, people have always been kind to her, wanting to know more once they learn about her connection to the tragedy. But on occasion, she has also overheard people talking jokingly and disrespectfully about the event, not knowing that she is nearby.

Fig. 243. *Sarita Echavarren and Ana María Vázquez, January 1983.*

Although Ana María was one of the founding mothers of the *Biblioteca Nuestros Hijos*, she didn't like to talk about the accident, and didn't spend much time there. But she would help out whenever she was asked, and she remained firm friends with several of the mothers – Sarita Echavarren, Inés Valeta, and Selva Maquirriain in particular. Uniquely among her generation, Teresita became actively involved with the library when it was still at its original location in the *Hotel Carrasco*. She enjoyed getting to know and chatting with the founding mothers, forming a special bond with Eita Platero, whose wisdom she greatly admired, and with Selva Maquirriain and Inés Valeta.

Roberto Canessa has stayed in touch with the family over the years, and gave a copy of *ALIVE* to Teresita's son Carlos when he turned eighteen, inscribing it: *Para Carlos, en recuerdo de un muy buen amigo que perdí en el accidente de los Andes ... Fernando Vázquez ... buen estudiante, buen amigo, y que disfrutó la música y la vida* – 'For Carlos, in memory of a very good friend whom I lost in the Andes accident... Fernando Vázquez... good student and good friend, who enjoyed music and life'. According to both Roberto and Teresita, Carlos bore a striking resemblance to his uncle at the same age.

Roberto had made plans to take his children to the site of the accident in February 2002, and Teresita asked if he would take another 'son', Carlos. Roberto agreed. Two years later, Carlos went a second time, this time accompanying his mother and his sister Verónica. With Roberto again organizing everything, Teresita took her mother's ashes with her. After spending the night on the mountain, Roberto woke the family early the next morning, before the other expeditionaries were up, and they assembled at the graveside for a private ceremony. As the priest who had accompanied them said a blessing, Teresita laid down her mother's ashes and then placed a plaque over them:

> Ana María Nebel
>
> 29.12.25 – 13.12.01
>
> My beloved Fernando, my mother's ashes will remain with you until the end of time, as will my love and admiration for both of you. And if today you see me smiling, it is because your joy has always been contagious...
>
> Don't be surprised if when you read this plaque you hear music in your heart.
>
> Tere (sister of Fernando Vázquez Nebel, 20.08.52 - 13.10.72)
>
> With all our love from your son-in-law Carlos and your two grandchildren Carlos Alfredo and Verónica Palma.

VII. Fifty Years

THE OLD CHRISTIANS

Just three months after the survivors returned from the mountain, fifty people turned up to the first practice session of the 1973 season, a foretaste of the determination with which the club would strive to recover from the tragedy of the Andes. Having lost three great leaders (Magri, Pérez del Castillo, and Costemalle) and many other regular or occasional first-team players (Abal, Hounie, Nogueira, Platero, Shaw, Maspons, and Nicolich), it would have been understandable for the club to abandon any short-term ambition to remain competitive. But not only did the *Old Christians* share the championship with *La Cachila* in 1973, their third in eight years, the team would go on to win five successive Uruguayan championships in the second half of the decade, the first club in Uruguay to achieve such a record. And even greater successes would follow in the eighties.

Fig. 244. *Key individuals who helped lead the recovery of the club after the accident.*
Left: *Tito Virginella, Jorge Zerbino, Brother 'El Chato' O'Donnell (below)*. **Inset**: *Daniel Juan.*
Right: *Johnny Bird, Aldo Magri, Hugo de Saugy at the Grange Old Boys La Dehesa field (1974).*

The 1973 team included four of the survivors – Roberto, Nando, Tintín, and Gustavo – and Zika Platero, the brother of Andes victim Enrique Platero. Of the former, Nando would continue to play for only a couple more years, but the rugby careers of the other three, regulars in the *Old Christians* first team, would go from strength to strength, with multiple call-ups to the national team. Tintín represented his country ten times between 1975 and 1981, playing as prop; Roberto played for *Los Teros* eight times as wing-three-quarter; and Gustavo got the call-up five times, playing in a variety of positions. The Uruguayan squad which competed in the tenth South American Rugby championship – finishing second to Argentina – saw all three survivors playing on the same team exactly five years after they had been stranded on the mountain. The captain of *Los Teros* that day was, as on numerous occasions, Gustavo's brother Jorge – one of Uruguay's most successful players, who racked up 153 points playing as flanker in an international career that stretched from 1973 to 1985.

At the time of the accident, Jorge had been more interested in pursuing a football career, so his offer of unconditional support to the *Old Christians* was as surprising as it was generous. His approach to the club was recalled years later in the July 2011 edition of the OCC magazine:

> *Days after the accident, Jorge knocked on the Club's door and said: "I've come to help". We are talking about a young man who had lost his brother in the Andes. Daniel Juan was the Club's president and remembers the context. "Everything was a big mess, the plane was missing, people were talking about nothing else, and the Club's directors were trying not to despair. In the midst of it all, the approach of a shy and anguished young man, who offered to bear his pain, was a noble gesture and very much his own."*

He would become the mainstay and leader of the first fifteen for many years to come, spearheading a golden era in the history of the club. The roots of that success lay in the hard work of a few visionaries, first and foremost amongst whom was Brother Eamonn 'El Chato' O'Donnell, who believed that rugby taught values for life. Gustavo Zerbino, certainly, had no doubt that the lessons learned from rugby were instrumental in their escape from the mountain. The respect in which the community held El Chato is reflected in these excerpts from the longer eulogy written by Gustavo on the Christian Brother's death in April 2021:

> *You were a person with a unique charisma, who formed a personal and unbreakable relationship with everyone you met. You always transmitted values to make a difference – humility, friendship, loyalty, and solidarity; with the example of giving everything for others.*

493

You allotted, with perfection, a time and moment for everything. A time to work, to study, to practise or to enjoy with family or friends, or to do something for others. You taught us what a vocation of service is, and to live life with joy and passion, to be consistent in and committed to what one wants, and if it goes wrong, to try again with more strength than before.

You were always present, attentive to what was going on around you, your eyes shone, they were complicit, they were supportive. You practised unconditional love, compassion, you laughed with those who laughed and cried with those who cried, no one was indifferent to you. With just your presence or a glance you would impose authority when necessary or a sense of humour if a difficult situation had to be defused.

You left your beloved country, Ireland, and adopted Uruguay as your second homeland. You arrived here with the name Eamonn O'Donnell in 1961 at the age of 24, and you knew only two words in Spanish, "adiós" and "amigo", which sums up exactly the reason for this message, to say ADIÓS AMIGO, we will never forget you, Chato, for all the love and affection you sowed in all those who knew you.

You were our coach before, during, and after the cordillera, and your stoic attitude gave us the strength to carry on, with a lot of pain, but as if nothing had happened, treating us all equally, survivors, brothers or relatives of friends who died, and players in general. We were very few, and it was very difficult, severe, but in that year 1973, with your support and the effort of all of us, we were champions in honour of our friends who stayed on the mountain.

In 1974, as Director of the school, you gave us an ultimatum, telling us that it was the last year we would play at the school. You encouraged us to grow, to be autonomous, and, with the Board of Directors chaired by Hugo de Saugy, we bought the land where San Patricio is today, the official headquarters of the Club.

Today again, 60 years after your arrival in Uruguay, we find ourselves, once again, facing the triumph of life over death, of the essential over the secondary, because our dear Chato, from now on, is immortal and will live forever in our hearts full of the love and gratitude inspired by him.

During these years of transition, 1973 and 1974, El Chato was supported by Tito Virginella, who acted as fitness trainer, and Daniel Juan, who was president of the club. Juan's treasurer was Hugues Frossard de Saugy, of Swiss heritage, who in Uruguay was always known as Hugo. He had been part of the *Stella Maris* class of '63, a close friend of Marcelo. Hugo later recalled:

> *In November 1972, after the search for survivors had been called off, I had a dream in which Marcelo asked me to help the board of the Club, as our class was the second to graduate from Stella Maris, and in the best position to rebuild the future first team and the club. Later François Manchoulas, who was the treasurer of the committee, told me he wanted to leave the board and asked if I wanted to take his place for 1973. Daniel Juan told me he would be glad for me to accept, and so I did.*

In response to Chato's ultimatum, Hugo and others set about finding land where the club could be based. An initial suggestion, from the Zerbino family, was for the land opposite the Naval Academy in Carrasco, but it faced legal hurdles that couldn't be overcome. Eventually Hugo found a small farm eleven kilometres from *Stella Maris College*, east of the airport. It consisted of four hectares and a driveway. The club bought the land and, anticipating that it would need space for future expansion, the survivors purchased another few adjacent hectares. The location was known as San Patricio. The board then commissioned a study for the design of the new clubhouse, selecting Eduardo Strauch and Guillermo Hughes as architects.

At the end of 1974, Daniel Juan retired as president of the club, and Hugo took over, with Gustavo Zerbino as his vice-president. Hugo asked Aldo Magri – Guido's brother – and Dicky Moor-Davie to take over the coaching responsibilities. Moor-Davie was a former international player, who had captained *Los Teros* on several occasions, including the games in which Gastón Costemalle and Guido Magri had made their debuts. Aldo had participated in the very first season of the *Old Christians*, playing alongside Andes passengers Daniel Fernández, Marcelo Pérez del Castillo, Eduardo Strauch, Gastón Costemalle and Daniel Shaw. He remembered when they first chose the club's jersey:

> *With no place to buy them in Montevideo, we got cheap tickets on the ferry to Buenos Aires, because the owner's son played for the Old Christians. We bought the blue and white jerseys of the Buenos Aires Rugby Club. Guido got the material for the shamrocks and cut them out for the mothers to sew on.*

By the early seventies, Aldo had stopped playing rugby, but returned after the accident to lend his support, taking to the field as a member of the B team whilst the club tried to rebuild the first-team squad. When his brother died in the accident, Aldo had made a pledge that, while it was within his power, there would always be a Magri at the *Old Christians*, and the coaching job gave him the opportunity to fulfil that promise.

Despite Moor-Davie leaving partway through the first season, Aldo, with no previous experience of coaching, flourished in his new role. His partnership with team captain Jorge Zerbino would result in twelve national championships over the following sixteen years. With Aldo concentrating on the first team, the important job of nurturing and bringing through boys from the junior teams fell to a group of first team players, all of whom would be regulars, not only in the successful *Old Christians* side of the late seventies, but also in the national team of the same period: props Antonio Vizintín and Johnny Bird (a lifelong friend of Aldo), and backs Eduardo Viera and Abel Vivo.

Fig. 245. **Left:** *Aldo Magri's original Old Christians jersey (missing its shamrock).* **Right:** *The jersey that Gustavo Zerbino wore for 72 days on the mountain.*

With the new location needing a lot of work before it was fit for purpose, Aldo's early years on the job involved a lot more than coaching, as he later recalled:

> I brought the seeds and the fertilizer for the field in my pick-up truck, along with the sowing and spreading machines. And all the trees around the field were planted by my wife and myself. We would go out to buy them, bring them to San Patricio in my truck, and plant them one-by-one. One of the good things I did when I started coaching, was to involve the wives and girlfriends. They went on to form close friendships and it brought a lot of unity to the club.

> In the beginning, we had to level the ground. The contractors we used didn't do a proper job. They left a dip in the middle of the field where the water would collect, creating a terrible mudbath. We had to start bringing in loads of sand. We would arrive early on Saturday morning and use the boys of the rugby team to spread it. Then we would have a training session for the match.

From early on, the coaching was heavily influenced by the attacking style of French rugby, with its emphasis on fluid movement and skilful ball-handling. Paradoxically, this came about through the fame of the Andes story. The same tragedy that had decimated the club also created the opportunities for its future growth and success. It was on the back of the club's renown that Albert Ferrasse, the long-term president of the *Fédération Française de Rugby* (FFR), was persuaded to make a side trip to Montevideo whilst on tour with *Les Bleus* in Argentina. He visited the school, attending an *asado* and providing Aldo with technical books and practice routines used by the French team. The FFR also sent tapes of the six-nations tournament (not readily available at the time) so that Aldo could get tips on how the professional international teams played.

Later, the club worked with experienced FFR coach Jean Pierre Juanchich. He had originally arrived in Santiago in 1974, before settling there permanently in 1978. His mission was to grow the game of rugby in Chile, a goal that he would achieve with remarkable success, his vision and grass-roots work leading to a tenfold increase in the number of Chilean clubs. Despite his focus being west of the Andes, Juanchich had a good relationship with the *Old Christians* and would help out whenever he could. Hugo de Saugy recalled:

> With his help, our coaches were able to deepen their tactical knowledge, and we also had the help of the experience gained in Argentinian rugby by brothers Cisco and Bobby Jaugust. In order for the young team to gain the necessary experience, several matches were organised, from the end of 1974, with Argentinian teams such as CASI, Cardenal Newman, San Luis de La Plata, Jockey Club de Cordoba, as well as the return to Chile, this time by train, invited by the Grange Old Boys.

The club received more international attention when Juanchich interviewed Saugy for the January 1977 issue of the FFR rugby review. The title of the piece was *Rugby in Uruguay*, but the emphasis was very much on the *Old Christians*:

> This year the club won all four official tournaments, in the 1st division and the two reserve tournaments. In the 3rd division (juniors A), the team finished in second place. The junior B and cadets won the respective national championships. These results clearly show the effectiveness of the work undertaken after the tragic plane crash in 1972 in the Andes Mountains, south of Santiago de Chile.

> In addition to the 14 senior players selected for the Uruguayan national team and the 14 juniors who took part in the South American championship in Santiago de Chile last July, the club can add to the list of achievements. Uruguay won the

*runner-up title after being beaten in the final by Argentina's "pumitas" in front of...
4000 enthusiastic spectators.*

*Rugby is still new and very young in Uruguay, as the Federation (URU) has just
celebrated its twenty-fifth anniversary. The average age of the players in the 1st
division is 21 and this fact is worth noting. At 25, the captain Jorge Zerbino, the
team's top scorer, can be considered... an old man! He is also the captain of the
national team. Two other survivors of the Andean tragedy also play for the
national team: Roberto Canessa, who scored 22 tries in 1975, holding the
Uruguayan record, and prop Antonio Vizintín (known as "Tintín").*

The article didn't mention Andes survivor Gustavo Zerbino, who was also active during
those golden years, and in fact the book *Rugby in Uruguay*[1] remarks on the unique
presence of the Zerbino family – father and sons– within the club:

"The Prophet" Jorge Zerbino[2] *would give his voice of encouragement and
advice from the touchline, and even opened up his home for the post-match
meetings. His sons – Jorge (the 'great captain'), Gustavo, Rafael, Daniel and
Enrique – all played for the Old Christians. On 22 April 1978 all five were
together on the rugby field when they faced Carrasco Polo in a first division
match. And on 30 April and 21 May of the same year, they played together
against Trouville and Los Cuervos respectively.*

The team of the second half of the seventies also included Alejandro Nicolich, who
adopted the name 'Coco' after his brother died on the mountain, and Pancho and Pepe
Nicola. Pepe would go on to become president of the club from 2009 to 2012, and
Nicolich took over the reins as the club approached the fiftieth anniversary of the Andes
tragedy. The youngest Nicola – Marce – would join the team in the eighties, the most
successful rugby player of the four brothers, playing fullback for Uruguay 21 times from
1989 to 1995, and becoming one of the most prolific scorers in the history of *Los Teros*.
He captained the *Old Christians* over that period, becoming their coach when his playing
days were over, and in 2001 he became assistant coach of the national team, taking
them to the 2003 Rugby World Cup in Australia.

---

[1] *El Rugby en Uruguay* (2001) by Gonzalo Etcheverry Campomar and Luis Ignacio Ubilla Schauricht.

[2] Jorge Zerbino (father) had an imposing and charismatic presence, and his motivational team talks
before a game gave him the aura of a prophet.

Fig. 246. **1977 Old Christians team.**

Back: Hugo de Saugy (president), Jorge Zerbino (captain), Alejandro Nicolich, Francisco Platero, Guillermo Mateos, Alberto Uría, Álvaro Alonso, Rafael Zerbino, Alberto Gari, Antonio Vizintín, Vladimir Jaugust, Johnny Bird, Bobby Jaugust, Aldo Magri (coach).
Front: Jean-Pierre Juanchich (FFR), Ricardo Piñerúa (fitness trainer), Andrés Gianoli, Antonio Grasso, Eduardo Viera, Ignacio Amorim, Rafael Ubilla, Abel Vivo, Jose Ubilla, Daniel Mutio, Roberto Canessa, Enrique Zerbino, Gustavo Zerbino.

Uruguay has always punched above its weight on the international scene, having qualified for five Rugby World Cups. Tintín (2004-2005) and Gustavo Zerbino (2008-2011) have both had stints as presidents of the *Uruguayan Rugby Union*. And it was Aldo Magri, after his retirement as coach, who found a home for *Los Teros*:

> *The Charrúa stadium was built during the dictatorship when the military authorities decided the country needed a second football stadium. But nobody wanted to play there – there was not much capacity, and it was becoming dilapidated. In 1993 or '95, I was working for the* Intendencia Montevideo *at the same time as I was coaching the national team. As the stadium was lying empty, I asked my superiors, "Can you give me access?" They answered: "Here are the keys... do what you want..." [laughs].*

> *We prepared the field for the South American Championship and we held the whole event there, and then we received France who had been playing Argentina in Buenos Aires. Afterwards, I gave back the keys, and it stayed empty. Then the authorities offered it as a permanent home for Uruguayan rugby, but the rent they wanted to charge was too much. Eventually, they just decided: "It's better that it's in your hands as nobody else is using it." That's how we got the lease. Now everybody wants it back!*

The 14,000-capacity stadium is perfect for Uruguayan rugby, and gets filled to capacity for important international matches. The club championships are also held there, the games played out in front of passionate and partisan supporters. The *Old Christians* have continued to compete at the top of Uruguayan club rugby, going through a lean period in the nineties and the noughties, but winning four championships since 2015, the most recent in 2019, when they comprehensively beat the British School *Old Boys* 43-13 in what was the end of an era for Uruguayan Rugby. That year saw the formation of the first professional rugby union team in Uruguay. *Peñarol* (*Club Atlético Peñarol de Rugby* in full), assembled with players from the top teams, including many *Old Christians*, has been competing with some success in the *Superliga Americana de Rugby*. After being runners-up in 2021, the team won the 2022 championship.

The *Old Christians* did suffer from the loss of so many players to the Superliga, but the club is still thriving, with hockey and football teams also long-established, the introduction of the former in response to *Colegio Stella Maris* going coeducational in the mid-eighties. The number of playing fields at San Patricio has grown to accommodate the increase in activity and membership, with four for rugby, three for football, and one for hockey.

From the beginning, the *Old Christians* travelled abroad to play games. In the early years, there were trips to Buenos Aires to play the old boys of *Instituto Cardenal Newman* and other teams in the capital. Later, they travelled further afield in Argentina, taking advantage of the Easter weekend to visit Rosario, Cordoba, or Mendoza. By the 1980s, with their fame preceding them, there were tours outside the continent – in 1980/81 to Europe, in 1982 to Bloemfontein, and in 1988 to the UK. But the one consistent thread that has run through the years since the Andes accident is the annual match with the *Grange Old Boys* of Santiago, *La Copa de la Amistad* (the Friendship Cup).

Fig. 247. *2019 Uruguayan Rugby Club final in the Charrúa stadium.*
Above: *Colourful scenes before the start of the game.* **Below:** *The Old Christians (playing left to right) look to add to their score against the Old Boys.*

A CUP OF FRIENDSHIP

In October 1967, two young men – Ezequiel 'Chelin' Bolumburu from the *Grange Old Boys* of Santiago and Guido Magri of the *Old Christians* – had their first call-ups to their national teams. The occasion was the Fifth South America Rugby Union Championship in Buenos Aires. Only three teams were competing: *Los Pumas*, *Los Teros*, and *Los Cóndores* – the national Rugby Union teams of Argentina, Uruguay, and Chile respectively. The two boys were the youngest in the competition, and, as half-backs, were both small in stature, especially when compared to the towering Argentinians. *Los Pumas* were a cut above the other national teams in South America, having achieved recent success in a tour of South Africa and Rhodesia which included a famous victory over the *Junior Springboks*.

Their similar circumstances made for a natural alliance between the two boys as Chelin later recalled:

> *Guido approached me in the lobby and we hit it off immediately. He was very nice and friendly, a typical Uruguayan. In those conversations he told me that they were planning to grow the* Stella Maris *alumni club where he played, and I told him about our history with the* Grange School *and the Old Boys. We realised that we were quite similar in many ways. Guido was very interested in how we had managed to set up the club, motivating the people from the school to continue playing, and how we did all the administrative and organisational side of things. You could see that he was very interested in making his club grow.*

The *Grange School* was, and still is, a private college in Santiago, located in the neighbourhood of La Reina. A school of choice for the Chilean elite, its graduates are well-represented in positions of leadership around the country, especially within the business world. Like many 'British' schools in Chile, Rugby Union formed an important part of the curriculum, and the alumni organization – the *Old Grangonians Club* – continued the tradition. Popularly known as *Old Boys*, the club had, by 1972, already achieved considerable success in the *Torneo Nacional de Clubes*, with six championships to its name, second only to the *Prince of Wales Country Club* (PWCC). The latter was adjacent to the Grange School, and was a convenient and popular place to gather for *Grange* alumni, many of whom were members. When the *Old Christians* visited in 1971, one of the two games they played took place on the PWCC field against a Chilean national team which included several *Old Boys* – amongst them Chelin and his contemporary Claudio 'Cachula' Cabrera. The other game was played against the *Old*

Boys at their headquarters which were much further afield – in the suburb of La Dehesa in the far north-east of the city. Cachula recalled the difficulties of getting there:

> *Getting to La Dehesa was like going to the moon! We would all meet at the Elkika restaurant at the corner of Tobalaba and Providencia, and those with cars would take the rest. There was also a bus that stopped at that corner and went all the way up there.*

But the distance served to cement the camaraderie and spirit of the club. John Scott, who was a member of the *Old Boys* 1971 and 1972 teams, and who would later become president of the club, paints the picture:

> *The club was the continuity of the passion we had for rugby, from school to the club, and in those days, usually 20 or 30% of the first team would go on to play at the club. There you would meet up with your school mates and friends and play the sport you were passionate about. The Old Boys' headquarters in La Dehesa was a very cosy club house where every weekend there was something going on. And whether it was a match with Country[1] or Stade[2], there was always a 'third half'[3]. Across the road was St Andrés Rugby Club which had some excellent players.*

As with the *Old Christians,* the *Old Boys* First XV sometimes relied on exceptional players from the school to make up the numbers, and Chelin and Cachula both got an early call-up to the alumni team. Nevertheless, when Chelin met Guido in 1967, he was still relatively new to the club, so when Guido suggested that they keep in touch and try to organize a tour, Chelin was thrilled:

> *I was very happy, I was just joining the club, and to arrive with a proposal like that, serious and concrete, was something important. We started to write to each other, but in those days the exchanges took months, everything was very slow, letters came and went until the next South American Championship in 1969 when*

---

[1] *Prince of Wales Country Club.*

[2] *Stade Français* – another prominent club based in Santiago.

[3] The traditional post-game social fraternization.

we met again, but this time in Chile. We played in Viña del Mar[1], so I couldn't show him very deeply what the club was like. But it was an unforgettable South American championship, a lot of fun, and we had a great time. We were older now and we formally realised the long-awaited plan of the tour. It was to be held on the 12 October bank holiday weekend in two years' time.

By 1971, Chelin was president of the club, and the task of organizing everything fell to him and Cachula. Chelin and Guido sent many letters back and forth to each other, but by the time the preparations had to be finalized, the country was in a difficult situation:

It was hard to find supplies, and we had to receive a whole delegation and organize hotels. All the logistics were complicated. Bread and drinks were hard to come by. A friend who owned a shop managed to get us some Coca-Cola, and the assistants at the school lent us all the tables, chairs, pots and pans etc. without the knowledge of the authorities. My dad lent me his van and we took everything to La Dehesa, where, with the help of a couple who lived there, we made all the preparations to create a welcoming atmosphere. In the end we made hotdogs, which were a real challenge to get because of the shortage.

The warm welcome helped to make the visit of the *Old Christians* an unqualified success, both on and off the field:

They stayed in a well-located hotel in the centre and flirted with all the women, who were amazed by them – it was quite funny, they seemed like rockstars. We had a party at the club and they invited a lot of women whom they had just met when strolling around the streets of Santiago.

Ironically, Chelin and Cachula, who had worked so hard to make the tour a reality, were unable to play in the match between the two clubs, and don't appear in photographs of the event. They, along several other teammates, had been called up to the national squad, preparing for the upcoming 1971 South American Championship due to be held in Montevideo. Short of several key players, the *Old Boys* team was supplemented by players from the *Country Club*.

---

[1] Chile-Uruguay was played at the Sausalito stadium in Viña del Mar, the games against Argentina were played at the Prince of Wales Country Club.

1971

OLD CHRISTIANS

Standing, left to right
Eduardo 'Mincho' Deal
Fernando 'Nando' Parrado
Gastón Costemalle
Francisco 'Zika' Platero
François Manchoulas
Roberto 'Bobby' Jaugust
Roberto 'Musculo' Canessa
Marcelo Pérez del Castillo

Below, left to right
Arturo Nogueira
Adolfo Gelsi
Alberto Villamil
Guido Magri
Eduardo 'Canario' Viera
Juan Villamil
Francisco 'Pancho' Abal

OLD GRANGONIANS

Standing, left to right
Charles Cunliffe
Juan Carlos Arriagada
Cristian Brautigam
Claudio Zamorano
John Scott
Rafael Ruíz
Gerardo Moro
German Armas
Felipe Jugo

Below, left to right
Ian Steel
Alfredo Alvarez
Michael Scott
Ronald Roberts
Roberto Harriqalde
Enrique Karich

Fig. 248. *1971 Old Christians and Old Boys teams.*

When Chelin said goodbye to Guido at the airport, it was with the promise to meet again the following year, this time in Uruguay. It was the last time Chelin would see Guido in person, but they kept in touch by phone, and a call from Guido led to a change of plans:

> He told me that they wanted to return to Chile instead, that they had had a great time and that the exchange rate was very favourable for them. He gave me no alternative, he was quite categorical about it: "We're going!" On the other hand, it was very expensive for us to travel at that point in time, with the situation in the country and the price of the dollar[1], so we were quite happy to agree. They also had this cheap plane. The problem of organizing everything like the previous year came back, but now it was much more complicated and it was almost impossible to get everything together. To this day we still make jokes about all the hot dogs we had to eat because of them getting lost in the Andes.

Up until the point of the accident, there had been no special bond between the two clubs other than the personal friendship between Guido and Chelin, but by virtue of them having toured the previous year, there was more organization in place in 1972 to give them a warm welcome on their return. Whilst most of the Old Boys congregated in the club to await their arrival, Chelin and team captain Cachula went to greet the Old Christians delegation in person at the airport. Waiting alongside the two Old Boys were Chelin's girlfriend and future wife Gabriela, Guido Magri's fiancée Angeles Mardones, and the two Uruguayans who had flown separately – Tito Regules and Bobby Jaugust. The plane was due to arrive at 4:00 p.m. and the group spent the afternoon chatting and joking as they waited on the viewing terrace, watching the planes come in. When the Fairchild didn't appear, Cachula and Chelin went up to the control tower, and were told that it was delayed, that it would arrive in ten more minutes. They continued to wait, but as time went by and there was still no sign of it, their anxiety started to rise. Their attention was suddenly grabbed by the screech of brakes as a car pulled up outside the control tower. It was the Uruguayan chargé-d'affaires César Charlone, who could be seen hurrying towards the entrance. Chelin followed fast on his heels:

> I went to the tower and they wouldn't let me in. I explained the situation, that we are the hosts, they are our friends, there is a girlfriend here, we are the Old Boys; and they told me "OK, sir, come on in". I went in by myself and I saw how they explained everything to Charlone, that the plane was lost. They had some big

---

[1] The Chilean escudo had almost halved in value since the previous year.

tables with maps and they started to show us that at this point at such and such a time, contact had been lost and that according to their calculations they could be in this area, the Tinguiririca area.

Chelin and the others who had been waiting at the airport were invited back to Charlone's house – a large ambassador's residence in the El Golf neighbourhood of the city. There, the first calls from Charlone to the Uruguayan authorities began, and a connection was established with the radio ham operators:

We stayed all night in the house, in the living room. The process of calling and receiving calls from relatives began. We were helping as much as we could, but it was a very sad night. It was a terrible shock for me to think about Guido, that I had just spoken to him and now he was dead.

Meanwhile, news had filtered through to the other *Old Boys* waiting to welcome the delegation at the clubhouse. Alfredo 'Perico' Alvarez, a future president of the club, was in charge of hospitality, as he had been the previous year:

At that time there were no mobile phones, but someone called the club phone and we were told that the plane was lost. Maybe they diverted further south, but we didn't know. The fact was that they had lost contact with the plane that took off from Mendoza, and that was the information we were given. In situations like that, time is relentless, hours go by and there is no news because something tragic has happened.

On the Friday, there was still hope that the plane might turn up, but by Saturday, when the information about the pilot's last communications became known, it was clear that the Fairchild had crashed. The *Old Boys* gathered again at the club, as John Scott recalls:

The match had been scheduled for Saturday, and the right thing to do was to be at the club. The whole team got together on the pitch. We were all very upset and sad... We got together, with the initiative of players, directors and friends, to organize searches in the hope of finding something. We were all convinced that there were no survivors, that there had been an accident and they had all died.

In the days following the accident, the team helped to set in motion various initiatives making use of contacts in the *Old Boys* network, coordinating private search flights, setting up radio ham communication channels, arranging and participating in the Catholic Masses that were being held for the passengers, and meeting with the families.

Although the Chileans didn't believe anyone could have survived, they empathized with the parents and their need to not lose hope. The news on 21st December of the appearance of two survivors was therefore an extraordinary and unexpected turn of events. Several of the *Old Boys* – Chelin, Cachula, and Perico amongst them – immediately made their way down to San Fernando, where the first batch of survivors had arrived, and were convalescing in a private wing of the hospital.

It was difficult to gain access, and only Chelin managed to see Roberto and Nando that day, but was unable to speak to them. He was shocked at how emaciated they were. Cachula saw them the next day at the Mass in the chapel adjacent to the hospital:

> As they were leaving, I greeted them one by one. That was what marked me. I don't remember much about what happened before and after, but for me it was very shocking to see someone, whom you had thought was missing and then dead, alive and in such extreme physical condition. We were sportsmen, but I remember the big guy Vizintín who was down to his bones, burnt and damaged. The inclemency of the weather was brutal to them.

Later, there was a get-together at the *Sheraton San Cristóbal*, and again at the *Prince of Wales Country Club*, where the *Old Boys* hosted a lunch. It was the beginning of a lifelong bond between the boys of the two teams. The *Old Boys* were quietly supportive on the issue of anthropophagy, and, out of respect and affection, nobody made any comments about it.

In 1974, the *Old Boys* invited the *Old Christians* to visit once again. In the process of rebuilding and in need of games to restore the club to normality, the team readily accepted, though this time the boys chose to travel by train. It was the start of what would become an annual tradition, continuing to this day, alternating between Santiago and Montevideo. As new generations of players have come to the forefront, the game between the old-timers has become largely symbolic, played for a few minutes before the younger club members take to the field. Over time, the rugby match became known as the *Copa de la Amistad*, even receiving international recognition when the *Old Christians* won the 2002 International Rugby Board's *Spirit of Rugby* award. Gustavo and Roberto travelled to London to attend the awards ceremony which took place at the Landmark hotel. Considering the *Old Boys'* participation to be of equal importance, the *Old Christians* had a replica of the trophy made to present to them.

2002 was a landmark year in another way. It was the occasion of the 30th anniversary of the tragedy, and Perico Alvarez, by then the president of the club, had not only conceived of a spectacular commemoration of the event, but had also managed to keep it a secret. Only the participants and fellow organizer John Scott were in the know. Perico and John, who had been members of the 1971 and 1972 teams, were both strongly connected with the story, and Perico had the idea of enacting a living account of the rescue. He secured an appointment with the Chilean Air Force to request their participation, and was invited to visit their offices, where, coincidentally, he was met by Mario Ávila, now a general and Vice-Commander-in-Chief. Perico was completely unaware of Ávila's role in the original rescue:

> I begin to explain that I am the President of Old Boys and that we plan to make this commemoration of life and the Andes rescue. I explain to him about the Copa de la Amistad, I tell him that we had already spoken to Don Sergio Catalán and that he was going to participate. The plan was that he would come on horseback from the mountains[1] and that Canessa would go out to meet him. I formally ask if he can help us with the presence of a helicopter at the ceremony. The plan was that Nando Parrado descends in the helicopter with a little red shoe, and Carlitos Páez comes out to meet him, and then the Copa de la Amistad begins.

> The general gets up, I see his eyes watering and he asks me if I want a coffee. I accept, and he goes to the coffee machine and excitedly he tells me: "I was one of those pilots!" We had coffee, he told me his story and promised to be present at the commemoration.

With the participation of Ávila and Catalán, Perico's vision became a reality:

> It was very exciting, because the survivors didn't know anything about it, they started to hear the noise of the blades and the helicopters appeared from below and started to circle the field. They got up excited and hugged each other, it's a special connection between them and the helicopters. One UH remains in the air and one lands on the pitch, from where Nando Parrado disembarks, carrying the Copa de la Amistad in his hands. He is joined by Roberto and Don Sergio on his horse, and the three of them hand over the Cup.

For many, this particular Copa has never been surpassed, the appearance of Catalán and the sound of the helicopters bringing tears to the eyes of the 151 Uruguayan visitors.

---

[1] By 2002, the Old Boys had moved their headquarters from La Dehesa to Peñalolén, a commune high in the foothills west of Santiago. In 2010, the club moved to its current location in Chamisero, the Peñalolén land now the site of the iconic Bahai Temple of South America.

The occasion was made more poignant by the participation of the four Nicola brothers in the game, with Pepe scoring the equalizing try.

By the fortieth anniversary, John Scott was president of the club, and he and Perico organized a similarly memorable event. The large Uruguayan delegation was received by the president of Chile, Sebastián Piñera. With Ávila's help and contacts, Perico arranged for an Air Force plane to fly over the club and drop sixteen parachutists (one for each survivor) onto the rugby field where they were met by Nando, Roberto, and Sergio Catalán. The occasion was also notable for the return of Susy Parrado's notebook to Nando. He had dropped it in *Los Maitenes*, and it was later found by Vicente Espinoza Muñoz, the carabinero who had shared his horse with Nando on the morning of December 22nd. It had remained in the Espinoza family for forty years, before being returned by Vicente's daughter Helen.

Fig. 249. *Meeting the visiting delegation is an important ritual: Old Boys Chelin Bolumburu, Perico Alvarez, club president John Scott, and Roberto Haritçalde greet the arrival of Nando Parrado (third from left) and Old Christians president Julio Lestido (right) for the 2012 Copa.*

The previous year had seen the first Grange *Old Boy* go to the mountain. Francisco Planella, an international fly-half who has attended every *Copa*, accompanied Gustavo Zerbino, Alejandro Nicolich, and a group of boys from *Rugby Sin Fronteras* to the site, where they played a symbolic game of rugby. Planella's reflections on that experience underline the importance that the *Old Boys* attach to the Andes story and their relationship with the *Old Christians*:

> *Gustavo brought along shirts. Alejandro was the captain of the blues, I was captain of the whites. For me it was the most relevant game I played in my life. The fact that I played for Chile for many years makes no difference, it was the most important game I ever played. It was incredible to participate in that.*

Fig. 250. *Estancia La Rábida in the hours before the 2017 tragedy.* **Above:** *Preparing the asado.* **Below:** *Survivors' group photo: Roy, Roberto, Coche, Gustavo, Eduardo, Álvaro, Tintín.*

The *Copa* has seen its share of drama. In 2010 in Santiago, Old Christian Daniel 'Peti' Mutio suffered a heart attack during the match. Mutio, a scrumhalf who had played in the 1971 game against the *Grange Old Boys*, was part of the successful *Old Christians* team of the late seventies and made many starts for the national team in that period. John Scott was right next to him when he collapsed. He saw that Mutio was swallowing his tongue, and, in the process of trying to stop that, he managed to knock out one of his teeth. Mutio was unconscious for some time before he was resuscitated by nearby doctors who were participating in the event. When he came to, he wanted to know where his tooth was. It was never found, but his friends obtained a horse tooth and framed it, presenting it to him as his missing tooth at the following year's *Copa*.

One of the doctors who performed CPR on Mutio and helped save his life that day was *Old Boy* Fernando 'Feñuca' González Foretic. Aged fifty-five, he was a specialist in sports injuries who taught traumatology at a couple of the private universities in Santiago, and served as the doctor for the Chilean national rugby team. But more than anything, he was a passionate member of the *Old Boys* club as his daughter Paula, a *Grange Old Girls* hockey player, recalls:

> *My dad enjoyed playing rugby, loved being with his friends at the club, loved the school and the* Old Grangonians *family. Every Saturday we had an early lunch because my dad had to go to the club. He didn't miss a game. He went both to enjoy the rugby, and as the doctor in charge. And always with a barbecue afterwards. They are pure alumni, generations of friends who have carried the club forward. Their sense of belonging is very strong. For my dad, getting together with them and staying for dinner at the club was the best thing. Every Thursday he would go there to share with his friends and eat "lomo a lo pobre", which we didn't make at home. The club was part of our family life from the very beginning, but even more so after 2012 when it moved to Chamisero and, for the first time, rugby and hockey came together at the same location.*

Feñuca was invariably present at the *Copa de la Amistad*, and the forty-fifth anniversary get-together in Montevideo in 2017 was no exception. In recent years, his children had often accompanied him to Uruguay, an occasion to share the experience and bond with them, but this year, events had conspired so that none of his children were there with him. Paula, twenty-three at the time, would later rue her absence at what would be her father's last days on earth. He had invited her and offered to pay for her, but she had just been selected for the Chilean national touch rugby team, and had flown out to California the same day that Feñuca had left for Uruguay.

As was customary, the rugby matches were played on the Saturday, with the following day providing an opportunity for the older club members to get together to socialize. The *Old Boys* were invited by the *Old Christians* to a traditional Uruguayan *asado*. The setting was *La Rábida*, an *estancia* located in the San José department, fifty kilometres north-west of Montevideo on the banks of the River Plate.

The warm spring afternoon, the idyllic surroundings, and the exceptional food and drink made for a relaxed and jovial atmosphere. Group photos were taken, and after the meal, there were speeches from *Old Christians* president Julio Lestido, Andes survivor Gustavo Zerbino, and *Old Boy* Rafa Ruiz, the latter having the audience in almost continuous fits of laughter with an uninterrupted series of jokes. It was against this backdrop of conviviality that a tragedy was about to unfold. After the speeches, guests were invited to go down to the private beach, a couple of kilometres from the ranch house, to enjoy the sunset. As they arrived at the unspoilt stretch of sand, they were greeted by a small bright yellow aeroplane – a Piper J3 – flying low and coming in to land. The pilot, fifty-five-year-old Rodrigo Artagaveytia, son of the owner of the *estancia*, taxied back along the beach. When *Old Christian* Alejandro Bauer climbed out of the passenger seat, there was no lack of guests wanting to take his place for a brief ride, but it was Feñuca who got there first, just ahead of John Scott.

The plane needed only a short stretch of beach to take off, and once airborne, the pilot veered around to the right over the river, making a 180-degree turn so that it was heading back towards the spectators. As it banked again slightly towards the shore, the right wing touched the surface of the water and, almost as in slow motion, the plane flopped down into the estuary about 200 metres offshore. The impact was gentle and the initial shock of everyone watching turned to relief when two heads could be seen bobbing in the water near the partially-submerged plane. Rather than stay with the plane, Rodrigo and Feñuca started swimming towards the shore, and several of the guests – Peti Mutio among them – stripped down to their underwear and started swimming to meet them. Relief turned to alarm again when one of the bobbing heads seemed to disappear.

Eventually, the first swimmers from the shore reached the pilot, and the news quickly spread that Feñuca had drowned, struggling to remove his boots and trousers. A later medical report, issued after his body had been found downstream, revealed that there were no injuries from the crash. Perico Alvarez reflected later:

> *Many returned to Chile that night. I, together with Cachula Cabrera and Gustavo Zerbino, stayed there until very late. Fernando was a very well-liked guy, very committed to the club. As a traumatologist, he was the club's official doctor – everyone went to see him. John Scott had to go and pick up the parents the next*

day, and he had to inform them that the body had turned up. There was a private meeting between the pilot, the wife, the children and Fernando's parents. A personal friend of the family – German Garib – took care of all the legal formalities. The Uruguayans made things very easy. It was very tragic, another accident, another plane, but now it was our turn to lose one of us. We lost a man who was very dear to all the people at the club.

Fig. 251. Old Christians *and* Old Boys *swim out to the wreck in the moments after the accident. Roberto Canessa can be seen on the right with his hands on his head.*

Feñuca's brother and his twenty-six-year-old son Sebastián left immediately for Uruguay on hearing the news. On arrival, they went straight to La Rábida, although by that time, it was dark and raining heavily, and little could be done. Feñuca's wife Paula and daughter Isabel – also a doctor – arrived the same evening; and his parents flew in the next day, picked up by John Scott at the airport just as news was breaking that his body had been found washed up downstream. Only daughter Paula was missing from the family gathered in Uruguay:

I was in San Francisco when I heard about it. I was out of signal, at the Golden Gate Bridge, and one of my team received a lot of messages telling me to check my mobile phone. I got on Wi-Fi at a McDonald's and my phone exploded. I didn't understand what all the "Cheer up" and "I love you so much" messages were about. I realized that it was something to do with my dad, and I went into the "family" chat group where they asked me to call them. I didn't understand much, because I had messages from my dad from just two hours previously, where he was sending me photos of the barbecue and of the beach. I was able to get in touch with my family and they told me. My dad still hadn't turned up. I went to the hotel, grabbed my things and went to the airport, bought the ticket at the counter, like in the movies. I flew with a friend to Uruguay, it took me 30 hours. I had a stopover in Panama and there they told me that they had found my father. I had boarded the plane in San Francisco thinking that he might turn up and I was still holding out hope. I remember that I fell to the ground and cried. I arrived in Uruguay on Tuesday at about 1:00 a.m.

The family stayed all week in Montevideo, taken care of by the *Old Christians* and several of the *Old Boys* who had changed their return tickets in order to support the family. On the Friday, the family received Feñuca's ashes, and they flew home the same day. The two daughters, Isabel and Paula, accompanied by several friends, returned to Uruguay two years later, for the last *Copa de La Amistad* before the pandemic. They were taken care of by Peti Mutio, whose life had been saved by their father all those years previously. Mutio took them out to *La Rábida*:

We met with the family who owned the estancia and shared some yerba maté with them. We spent time with the pilot. He had been left with a tremendous guilt and we went to tell him that we did not blame him for what happened and that the tragedy was an accident, that he should be at peace, that there is no hatred towards them in our family. I hope this has helped him, I put myself in his shoes and it must be terrible. We knew that they were very upset with everything that had happened, and we went to empathize with them.

This more recent tragedy has only served to strengthen the relationship between the two clubs, just as the original tragedy had forged the initial ties. With the 2022 *Copa* approaching, John Scott reflected on the fifty years since that fateful day in 1972:

What I have learned is that sport allows us to generate these bonds of friendship, which could have been generated without having this accident in the middle, but it was the accident that was the catalyst that forced this relationship. And now we are going to be fifty years old and soon the grandchildren will be playing and there will be three generations already. The union of two institutions and the homage to the fallen is manifested today in the ceremony of the olive tree, which is our symbol, our union, and our homage to the fallen.

Fig. 252. *Feñuca with wife Paula, and children Isabel, Sebastián, and Paula.*

Fig. 253. *Team captains John Scott and Roy Harley reflect on their fallen comrades during the Olive Tree ceremony at the 2012* Copa de la Amistad *in Chile.*

TITO'S STORY

In any fatal plane crash, there are stories of passengers missing the flight, and the *Old Christians* trip was no exception. A series of small events, each insignificant in isolation, conspired to prevent Gilberto 'Tito' Regules – one of the 'gang' – from boarding the Fairchild FAU 571 on the morning of 12th October 1972.

The first of these was Tito's decision to sleep at his father's house in *Parque de los Aliados* on the eve of departure, twenty minutes' drive from his friends in Carrasco. His divorced parents would vie to spend time with their six children, and as Mr Regules had paid for Tito's ticket, he felt it was only right that his son stay over that night. Tito planned to get up early the following day and head over to Carrasco to share a ride to the airport with his close friends Bobby François and Carlitos Páez, both of whom lived within a couple of blocks of his mother's house. When Tito was nowhere to be seen the next morning, they assumed that he had decided to make his own arrangements to get to the terminal.

Then there was the strange malfunctioning of the phone in his father's house. In the somewhat antiquated system of the time, there was a switch that had to be manually set to cause the upstairs phone to ring. This worked perfectly when Tito's prearranged 5:30 a.m. wake-up call came through, a service provided by the national phone company. It woke up his sister Carmen, who, knowing Tito to be a heavy sleeper, had promised to make sure he was fully awake. Satisfied that she had fulfilled her duty when he had sat up and spoken to her, she went back to bed and fell asleep again. Unfortunately, so did Tito. It was then that the upstairs phone inexplicably stopped working. Despite the increasingly desperate calls from his friends, the household remained undisturbed, blissfully unaware of the consternation that Tito's absence was causing at the airport.

There was one more chance to salvage the situation. Eduardo Strauch, on reaching the airport, realized that he'd left his travel documents at home, and he sent his brother Ricardo back to fetch them. As the Strauch family lived just a couple of blocks from Mr Regules' house, Tito's friends asked Ricardo to stop by there to check on him. After racing the 20 km back to *Parque de los Aliados* and finding his brother's identity papers, there was little time to spare. Approaching Tito's house, Ricardo saw that the long iron gate, always closed at night, was now open and the car in the driveway. Taking it as a sure sign that Mr Regules must have already dropped his son off at the airport, he sped on by. In fact, it was a third unfortunate coincidence; a rare oversight had led to the gate remaining open all night.

By the time Mr Regules awoke at 9:00 a.m., it was well past departure time, and he was somewhat aggrieved that his son had not bothered saying good-bye before he left.

Only then did he realized that Tito was still asleep in his room. They desperately called the airport on the off-chance that the flight had been delayed, but it had departed on time. As Tito's friends had boarded the plane without him, they had starting joking that the plane would now crash, and he alone would be saved.

Back home, Tito was facing his father's wrath:

How can you be so stupid!?
    Dad, there's a commercial flight I can take to Santiago this evening.
Come on Tito, you must be nuts if you think I'm going to pay for another ticket when you've been so careless. Do you think I'm made of money?
    But if I don't fly today, the money you spent on the return flight will be wasted!

Mr Regules' anger didn't last long. His own father having died when he was a baby, he loved his children with a passion, and was accustomed to spoiling them, and that evening Tito boarded an *Iberia* flight to Chile. He later recalled: "It was raining in Santiago when I arrived and I remember that when, according to my estimation, we were passing over the *cordillera*, I felt a turbulence that shook the plane. It was very dark, and I couldn't see anything outside." Arriving after midnight, he called the Mardones family, and found out from Guido Magri's *novia* Angeles that the Fairchild had stopped over in Mendoza and might have to return to Montevideo. Tito then headed into town to his hotel. The next morning, after speaking to the family again, and calling *Los Cerrillos* – the destination airport for the Fairchild – he finally got confirmation that the flight had been given the go-ahead, and his friends would be arriving around 14:30 local time.

He made his way to the airport where he waited with Angeles and *Old Boys* Chelin Bolumburu and Cachula Cabrera. Standing on the viewing terrace overlooking the runway, the group spent the time joking around, imagining the arrival of every plane to be that of the *Old Christians*. As time went by with no sign of them, they started getting anxious, but it was only when Uruguayan chargé-d'affaires César Charlone arrived with his wife and hurried towards the control tower that everyone realized that something was seriously amiss.

The news quickly spread that the plane had gone missing. Tito stayed around with Mr Charlone and others to await further developments, and they were soon joined by *Old Christian* Bobby Jaugust, who had only just arrived in Santiago. With his father head of KLM in Uruguay, Bobby had taken a commercial flight, arriving at *Pudahuel* mid-afternoon before making his way to the *Hotel Kent*. Unaware of the drama that was unfolding, his first inkling that something was wrong was a telephone call to the hotel soon after his arrival.

On the line was Felipe Maquirriain's father in Montevideo, wanting to know if the boys had arrived in Santiago. Not knowing about the disappearance of the Fairchild, Bobby at first had answered 'yes, of course' before Mr Maquirriain had sowed doubt in his mind.

Tito couldn't accept that there had been an accident, preferring to believe that they must have been diverted somewhere else. After waiting around for another couple of hours, he and the others were invited back to the ambassador's house by Charlone, and spent the night awake there in the living room as communications with the Uruguayan authorities were initiated. The next morning, Tito and Bobby took the weekly KLM flight back to Montevideo, stopping to give a brief press conference on their arrival.

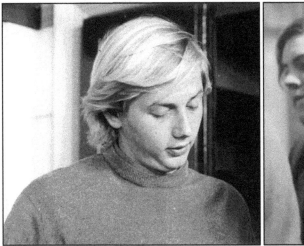 

Fig. 254. *Bobby Jaugust and Tito Regules on their return from Santiago.*

During the seventy-two days, life had to continue, and Tito returned to the agricultural school in Durazno where he had been studying with Bobby. Cut off from news of the search, he was kept in touch by his girlfriend Eleonora Braga, who would write detailed letters about how the search was progressing:

> *Madelón and Bimba left today for Chile. You know that the two Dutch seers (who didn't know each other) and another one from Cordoba gave the same position for the plane. Bimba and Madelón were going to meet the Cordoban at the Hotel Crillón in Santiago, but at the last minute the man said he couldn't go because his herd had been hit by an outbreak of foot-and-mouth disease.*

When news came of survivors, Tito accompanied Carlitos' mother, Madelón Rodriguez, to Santiago. On arrival, they were picked up by some relatives and driven to San Fernando, where they spotted Páez Vilaró with a preoccupied look on his face. Fearing the worst, Tito called out to him. He came over to them and gave them the good news: "I give you Carlitos as a present." He had arrived by helicopter 15 minutes earlier. From Carlitos, Tito learnt that of his two best friends, Bobby was still alive and waiting to be rescued from the mountain, but Diego Storm had died, along with two other close friends, Coco Nicolich and Rafael Echavarren. Tito lived for many years with the guilt of having convinced Rafael to travel.

The two boys had known each other because their *novias* were close friends, and although Rafael already knew some of the other passengers and immediately integrated into the group, it was Tito who had painted the picture of what a great time they would have together in Chile.

Having survived the accident in the Andes, it was only a matter of time before fate would catch up with Tito. Charismatic and much-loved by his many friends and girlfriends, he was also reckless, living life on the edge. He would drink hard, drive fast, and throw himself into new projects with little regard for practicalities. His father, who doted on him, was the opposite. Ordered and pragmatic, he would try to temper his son's excesses, providing sound advice and caution to steer him away from unwise decisions. One business venture, which almost led to Tito's death in June 1977, was a stint working with the owner of one of the big slaughterhouses in Uruguay, who had asked Tito to go to a cattle auction in Salto.

Fig. 255. Tito at the estancia in gaucho gear.

Tito had been prepared to fly, ticket in hand, when at the last minute something had come up and he had been reassigned to a task closer to home. The TAMU Embraer Bandeirante, registration FAU-584, in which he had been due to fly, crashed on approach to Salto, striking trees in an orange grove, and killing most of those aboard.

Tito's charmed life finally came to an end on the 22nd February 1991. By this time, he was married to a Spanish woman, and had a son, Diego (named after his friend Diego Storm) who was just six months old. His wife's family were visiting, and when the father-in-law expressed a wish to exchange his rental car for an automatic, Tito offered to go and pick up the new car. Driving along a country road, he was blinded by the headlights of an oncoming vehicle, and crashed straight into another car, abandoned in the middle of the road with no lights, invisible in the dark. He died immediately in the violent collision.

TRIPS TO THE MOUNTAIN

Fifty years after the accident, there is a steady stream of visitors to the glacier each summer. They make the journey for a variety of reasons. For some, such as the families of those who died, it is an intensely personal pilgramage. Others, with a strong interest in the story, come to see and explore the place where the seventy-two days played out, and to pay their respect to those who remained there. On occasion, documentary teams have made the trip accompanied by some of the survivors, most of whom have also made many personal trips, either with their companions of the mountain, or with their families.

One such occasion was in October 1997. A large group of survivors, their families, and those of the victims, arrived in Chile to commemorate the twenty-fifth anniversary of the tragedy. The Colchagua regiment set up a camp for the Uruguayans in *La Huertecilla* near *Los Maitenes*. An expedition had been organised for some of them to retrace the route taken by Nando and Roberto in 1972. The two survivors, joined by Coche, Gustavo, and Moncho, were part of the twenty-seven strong cavalcade which set off up the *Portillo* valley. Led by Sergio Catalán, the group included the four Nicola brothers, and Alejandro Nicolich.

The progress of the expeditionaries, and the discussions around the nightly campfires were filmed by a documentary team from the *Universidad Católica de Chile*, who were sponsoring the event. When the team got to the snowline, they had to dismount and proceed on foot, but were only able to reach a point where they could see the mountain gully down which Nando and Roberto had descended in December 1972. Later, Roberto and Gustavo and the four Nicola brothers were flown by helicopter to a point in the mountains near to where the survivors had spent the seventy-two days. There, they erected a cross and gathered around it to pray and remember.

When the expeditionaries returned, they joined the others for a Mass, which was celebrated by Father Andrés Rojas, who, in 1972 had been the first to minister to the boys in the hospital at San Fernando after their rescue from the mountain. The whole party then returned to San Fernando, where they attended the opening of a permanent exhibit about the Andes tragedy at the local *Museo Lircunlauta*. The day was rounded off with a celebration featuring a traditional *cueca*, the Chilean national dance.

The rare approaches to the *Valle de las Lágrimas* from the Chilean side more typically cross into Argentina at *Paso de Las Damas*, twenty-five kilometres south of the crash site, near Termas del Flaco. But the majority of trips to the site start from the Argentinian side, at one of the horse posts near the abandoned *Hotel Termas El Sosneado* on *Provincial Route 220*.

Fig. 256. The 1997 expedition.
Top: Heading up the Portillo Valley towards El Brujo. **Left**: Reaching the snowline.
Right: José Luis, Marcelo, Francisco, and Juan Pedro Nicola flanked by Roberto Canessa
and Gustavo Zerbino in front of the cross they erected on the mountain.

Many details of various expeditions have been recounted in the 2015 book *HACIA EL AVIÓN DE LOS URUGUAYOS*[1] by Argentinian author Ariel Osvaldo Torres. In the introduction, Torres reflects on his own reasons for his annual pilgrimage:

I cannot say that I felt the presence of God on the ten occasions that I was in the Valley of Tears, but I can say that this place and this particular story changed my perspective on life... When I am in the mountains I feel that nature nourishes me and acts as a purifier; there I am able to get rid of the negative burden of civilization, which I sometimes carry with me. And then I return to society feeling refreshed, focused on the things that I know make me happy, and fortunately there are many of them. Definitely, those trips have left me with the legacy that every minute of life should be enjoyed, and, as much as possible, lived with intensity.

Fig. 257. *Horse and cattle post – the usual starting point for any trek into the mountains.*

---

[1] Towards the Uruguayan plane.

The route is the same one pioneered by Lima and Araya in 1973. The first difficulty is the crossing of the wide *Atuel* river, which must be done on horseback. Further up, there are other torrents to cross, including *El Barroso* and *Las Lágrimas*. The flat land at the confluence of these two creeks make it a perfect location for a base camp – *Campamento El Barroso* – now a popular overnight stop. In the early years, the journey to the site was a hazardous undertaking, with the paths through the ravines and across the creeks not yet established. But over time, the route has become well-trodden and more widely used. Whilst some expeditions and individuals choose to trek to the site on foot, most make the trip on horseback. The slow wending approach to the glacier over two days has the effect of detaching riders from their everyday lives, entering them into a world where time seems to slow down. It is a sensation heightened by the anticipation of arriving at a site of such historic resonance, where this dramatic survival story was played out. Many who make the pilgrimage to the mountain feel a strong spiritual presence up there, and it is a common sight to see visitors weeping openly by the side of the grave. It is rare for anyone to leave unchanged.

The pioneer of commercial trips to the mountain was businessman Edgardo Barrios, who, in the early nineties, leased some buildings in the small village of El Sosneado from mining company *Sominar SA*. The buildings had originally served as accommodation for workers at the Sominar Sulphur mines and refinery 75 kilometres to the north, along *Provincial Route 220*. He repurposed the accommodation as the *Hostería Sosneado*, and it became the base of his adventure tourism business, although, at the time, he didn't yet know the story of the Uruguayan plane. Later, after learning about it, he organized a couple of private trips to the site, working with the local *puesteros* and guides, but it was only after a 1995 trip with twelve of the survivors – organized by Roy Harley and led by mountaineer Gabriel Cabrera – that he started to commercialize the trips.

Edgardo worked with many guides over the years, including René Lima, but increasingly came to rely on experienced guide Mario Peréz. Born in 1965, Mario had first been to the site as a teenager, hiking with some friends, but it was later expeditions with the survivors that has given him a unique perspective on the story, hearing the memories of their ordeal in person. He joined Barrios at the turn of the millennium, starting off in a logistical role, but soon assuming entire responsibility for the expeditions, as his boss started devoting more time to the promotional side of things.

Hostería El Sosneado
Alojamiento de Montaña

Ruta 143 - El Sosneado
San Rafael - Mendoza - Argentina
RESERVAS: (02627) 15660623
E-mail: elsosneado@infovia.com.ar

EXPEDICIÓN AL AVIÓN DE LOS URUGUAYOS

DIA 1: Recepción en la Hostería El Sosneado, alojamiento, cena. Charla con los guías y preparativos para la partida.

DIA 2: Desayuno y salida en vehículo 4 x 4 hasta el destacamento limítrofe de Gendarmería Nacional; almuerzo en puesto ganadero típico de los Andes (Araya), iniciamos la cabalgata que comienza con el cruce del Río Atuel. Al atardecer montamos nuestro campamento en el paraje denominado El Real. Cena. Noche.

DIA 3: Desayuno y partida hacia el Glaciar Las Lágrimas, la jornada de este día será muy dura ya que tras cuatro horas de cabalgata; alcanzamos los 3.700 m/s/n/m arribando al sitio donde se encuentran los restos del avión, sobre el límite entre Argentina y Chile. Rendiremos en silencio nuestro homenaje a las víctimas, para luego hacer un reconocimiento del lugar. Almuerzo. Descenso hasta el campamento El Real. Cena. Noche.

DIA 4: Desayuno y desarme del campamento. Cabalgamos de regreso al Puesto Araya. Almuerzo. Regreso en vehículo 4 x 4 hasta la Hostería, tomando en el camino un baño termal en el viejo Hotel. Despedida en la Hostería. Fin de nuestros servicios.

SERVICIOS INCLUIDOS

01 (una) noche de alojamiento en la Hostería El Sosneado. Traslados en vehículos 4 x 4 (Hostería El Sosneado / Puesto Araya / Hostería). 02 (dos) noches de campamento con pensión completa y refrigerios. Equipo completo de montaña para pernoctar y acampar. Mulas para transporte de cargas. Equipo de primeros auxilios. Guías y baqueanos. Seguro médico.

SERVICIOS NO INCLUIDOS

Bolsa de dormir.

DURACION Cuatro (04) días / tres (03) noches
OPERABLE De diciembre a marzo
DIFICULTAD Moderado - Principiantes y expertos
EDAD MINIMA 18 años - Menores acompañados por padre o tutor
SALIDAS Consultar

EQUIPO NECESARIO

Sugerimos tener en cuenta los siguientes elementos personales: Bolsa de dormir, sombrero ala ancha, cortaviento, pantalones tipo bombacha de gaucho, zapatillas deportivas, zapatillas de trekking, buzo de abrigo, chaqueta impermeable, pañuelo para el cuello, protector solar, anteojos de sol, faja, riñonera.

TARIFA POR PERSONA:	$ 350,-

Fig. 258. A 2001 *web page for the Barrios expedition.*

In February 2005, Peréz was involved in a remarkable discovery high above the glacier. He had recently returned from the mountain when he was asked by Barrios to speak to Mexican-American mountaineer Ricardo Peña, who had been guiding on Aconcagua and had a few days to spare before returning to the US. Ricardo was interested in exploring the crash site, having been enthralled by the story from an early age after watching the Mexican movie *Survive*. Mario agreed to guide him up there, and after exploring the area around the grave and memorial, they made the arduous climb up the mountain towards the impact point. Mario takes up the story as they approached the top:

> We stopped to take a rest – to eat and to rehydrate. As I was gazing across the slope, I caught sight of a patch of blue in the snow. I called out, "Ricardo, are you seeing what I'm seeing?", and I pointed it out to him. We went closer and saw that it was a piece of cloth buried in the snow. We were a bit wary of picking it up because we thought that it might contain human remains. But we took courage and when we examined it, we found it was a jacket. I told Ricardo to look at the buttons, to see if it was perhaps a military jacket because of its colour. But inside, we found Eduardo Strauch's documents. It was a very emotional and intimate moment.

The jacket, which contained a wallet and ID documents, had been bought by Eduardo especially for the trip. Flying over the Andes, the passenger cabin had been uncomfortably warm and he had taken it off and placed it on the overhead luggage rack. When the tail had broken off, it had disappeared out of the back along with everything else that was unsecured. Peña and Peréz left the jacket on the mountain, to be retrieved at a later date, but its contents made their way back to Eduardo via Barrios and Álvaro Mangino, and the news of the find spread quickly. Such was the interest that Ricardo and *National Geographic* writer James Vlahos won a grant from the magazine to organize an expedition to follow Parrado and Canessa's route over the Andes, the first time it had been attempted since their original trek. The successful crossing took place in December 2005, with Mario Peréz accompanying Peña and Vlahos.

Three months later, Peréz and Peña were part of the March 2006 expedition, responsible amongst other things for the safety of survivors and film crew during the making of the *Stranded* documentary. March 2006 also saw a new monument erected; a black granite monolith taken to the site in pieces and erected west of the grave, with logistics again provided by Barrios. Showing the names of survivors on one side and those who died on the other, the monument was commissioned and approved by Mr Tan Sri A. P. Arumugam, the Malaysian businessman who owns the Argentinian territory where the accident occurred, part of a much larger swathe of land that includes the *Las Leñas* ski resort.

Barrios finally moved on to other business ventures when the lease on the *Hostería Sosneado* ended in 2008, but Mario, who has made close to 150 trips to the site, has continued working and still leads regular trips to the mountain, most recently through his tourist agency *Baruma EVT* based in San Rafael.

The discovery of the jacket in 2005 led to a close friendship between Ricardo and Eduardo, and the start of an annual expedition to the site, through Ricardo's Colorado-based company *Alpine Expeditions*. Assembling in the beautiful provincial capital of Mendoza, the expeditionaries, who come from around the world, get to meet Eduardo, spending the next

six days with him as he accompanies them to the mountain. The arrival at the memorial is an emotional moment as Eduardo is given time alone at the graveside to reflect on his fallen friends. Ricardo is an accomplished mountaineer, guiding in the Rockies, the Andes, the Himalayas, and elsewhere. In 2022, Eduardo joined him again on one of *Alpine Expeditions'* most recent adventures, a successful trek to the summit of Kilimanjaro.

Another guide who has led many expeditions to the Andes crash site is Juan Ulloa, whose company *Valle Verde Expediciones* is based in

Fig. 259. *Eduardo Strauch on Peña's 2015 expedition.*

Malargüe. Ulloa first visited the site in 1987, trekking alone on foot, but it was only in 2007 that he started leading expeditions. In an interview that appears in *HACIA EL AVIÓN DE LOS URUGUAYOS*, Ulloa says of the trips that he leads:

> There are two groups that stand out from the rest... Those groups are Rugby sin Fronteras *and* Re-Viven. *Both do their tributes with a feeling I have never seen before. In the case of the* Re-Viven *group, they do it with increasing fervour and enthusiasm.*

Fig. 260. *Expedition scenes.*

Rugby Sin Fronteras, the first of the two groups highlighted by Ulloa, is an organization founded in December 2009, whose purpose is to use the values and the game of rugby to promote peace and good-will across international borders. Amongst other achievements, the foundation has brought together young people from Palestine and Israel, and, on another occasion, veterans from the two sides of the Malvinas/Falklands conflict. Gustavo Zerbino was one of the co-founders, and the story of the Andes resonates strongly with the organization's ethos. One of the memorable trips made by members of *Rugby Sin Fronteras* was a fortieth anniversary expedition which included a rugby game played at the Barroso base camp on a specially constructed field. The following day, Ulloa led the 45-strong contingent up to the memorial.

Fig. 261. *December 2015 crossing of the Andes, following in Parrado and Canessa's footsteps.*
Left: *Roberto Ramallo high on the headwall, ahead of Mariana Lay and Juan Ulloa.*
Right: *Aito Cardozo, Mariana Lay, and Federico Sanguinetti at the summit of Mount Seler.*

Re-Viven is a social media group formed in 2004, originally hosted in *MSN Groups*, but in recent years, a *Facebook* group. Even before it came into existence, the friends (including Torres) who would later become the first members of the community, would get together for trips to the site. These annual expeditions, led by Barrios in the early years, and later by Ulloa, have yielded many artefacts discovered on the mountain. And in December 2015, four of the group – Federico Sanguinetti, Gerardo 'Aito' Cardozo, Mariana Lay, and Roberto Ramallo – joined Ulloa in making a crossing of the Andes at the same time of year as Parrado and Canessa's original trek.

The person responsible for the creation of *Re-Viven* was a young Argentinian, Alexis Scarantino, who can also claim credit for having created, in 1997, the first web page and online community dedicated to the story.

ONLINE

Alexis Scarantino, born in 1983, was eight or nine years old when he first heard about the Andes story. His brother, Gustavo, had mentioned it on returning from a friend's house, where he had seen the book *ALIVE*. Their father, who had avidly read Piers Paul Read's account when it had first been published, outlined the main aspects of the story for his sons, awakening in Alexis an insatiable interest:

> When my father started talking about it, I started to create some images in my mind that stayed there for months. One day, still a child, I went to the video store and rented the movie Alive. It was incredible – the first movie I watched with subtitles. I was hooked, and within a few weeks, I was reading the book. When I finished that, I still craved more and more information. Being a child, I really didn't know why I liked this story so much, and I felt a bit alone as I couldn't imagine that there could be any other person who would share such an intense interest.

Over time he read several books about the tragedy, and, partly as typing practice, he started writing up summaries of various episodes. When, after some years, he got access to the internet – soon after the World Wide Web came into common use in the mid-nineties – Alexis started searching for web pages about the accident. Entering queries such as "Andes Crashes", "Tragedia de los Andes", and "Milagro de los Andes", he found virtually nothing – just a bit about the book and movie, and an interview in Portuguese with Nando Parrado.

Around the same time, he read an account of the twenty-fifth anniversary trip to Chile which had seen many survivors and families of the passengers gather in San Fernando and *Los Maitenes*, with some of them flown by helicopter to a location near the Valley of Tears. In the article, which appeared in *Viva*, the Sunday magazine of the Argentinian national newspaper *Clarín*, Roberto Canessa lamented the fact that he didn't receive as many letters from the public as he had done in the early days. When the magazine published Canessa's address in the next issue, Alexis sent him a letter, asking him, amongst other things, whether a website existed. Receiving only a general reply, he wrote again, but this time addressing it to Roberto's assistant Alejandra Campeas. She replied that she knew of no online resource dedicated to the story.

Not knowing much about computers or the internet, Alexis, with some help from his brother, embarked on creating such a website. At the time, it was not so straightforward, with everything needing to be done in code, and little in the way of supporting software. He used the *GeoCities* hosting service – one of the few options for building a community-based website at the time. The earliest manifestation of the site consisted of just a main page with three links to some of the summaries he had written.

Alexis' initial aim had been just to satisfy his own interest, and to create something for the survivors and the families of those who died. He had no expectation that anyone would contact him. But when he put his email address on the website, people started writing – from Argentina, Chile, Uruguay, and Mexico. The first emails he received were about technical issues such as links not working, but over time, there grew a demand for more content:

> People started asking me for more information and photos. So, over the years, I started putting in a lot more links, to make the story complete. I would scour the book-seller stands in the parks and street markets for old books and magazines. Every week I would go out, sometimes twice a week. Also the national library. I remember whole winter holidays that I spent in the national library poring over large books of old newspapers or skimming through microfilmed archives. You couldn't take photographs or make photocopies, so I would read and copy out the articles by hand, and then I would go back to my house and upload my notes to the site.

As Alexis continued to add new material, the number of visitors grew rapidly, numbering in the thousands. News of the website reached the survivors, as Alexis discovered in 1999. He had learnt that four of them – Roberto Canessa, Roy Harley, Carlitos Páez, and Gustavo Zerbino – were coming to Buenos Aires to appear on the popular TV chat show *Almorzando con Mirtha Legrand* (Having lunch with Mirtha Legrand). He contacted the programme to see if he could attend in person, but he was told it wasn't possible, that the studio was too small. On hearing this, Gustavo, who was older and less shy, called up again, speaking in place of his brother. He confidently stated that his name was Alexis Scarantino, that he was a personal friend of Canessa, and that he had built the website for the survivors. This did the trick, and Alexis was invited to be part of the audience. After the filming, he went straight up to Laura Surraco, Roberto's wife, and introduced himself. Laura immediately called her husband over, saying, "Look Roberto, this is Alexis Scarantino, the boy who's doing the website." Alexis recalled later:

> I was ecstatic to meet Roberto. He introduced me to the other survivors. It was incredible. I remember that day like a dream. I felt like I was floating on a cloud.

The best was yet to come. Alexis had read in a magazine that the survivors had made a trip to the Valley, something that he hadn't realized was even possible. He was determined to go to the site himself, and the opportunity arose in 2001 when his uncle contacted Edgardo Barrios to make the necessary arrangements.

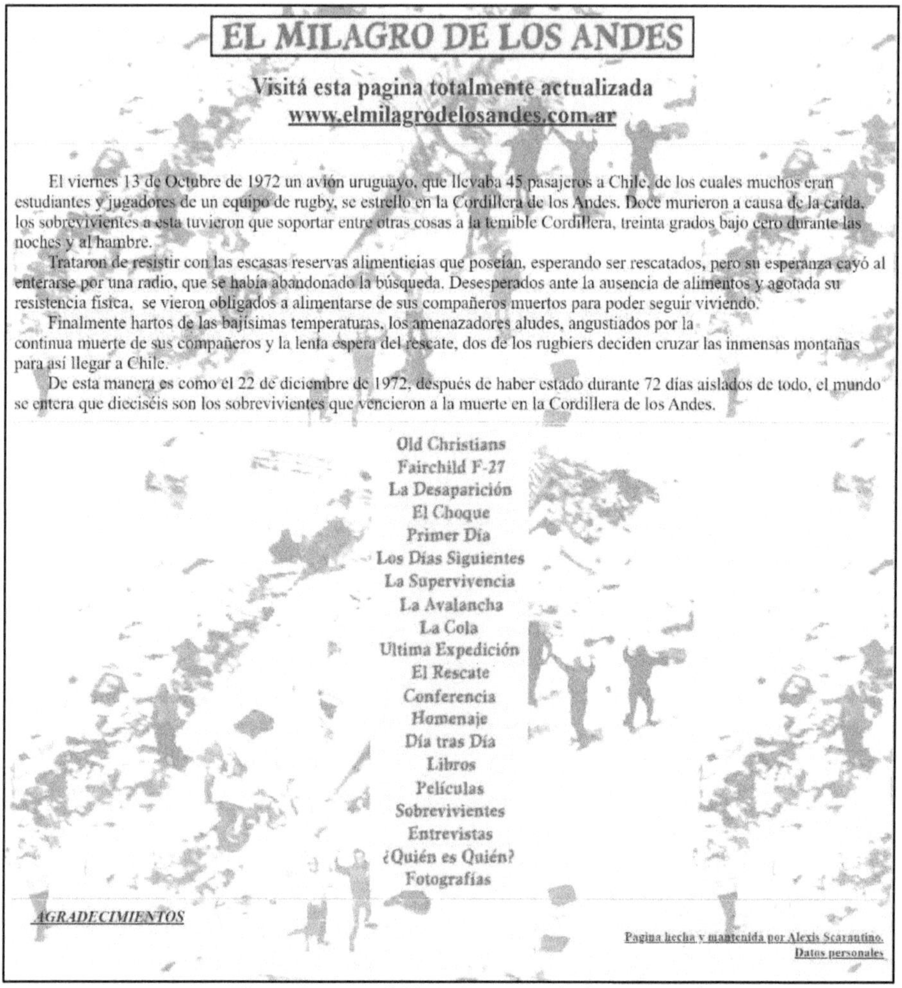

EL MILAGRO DE LOS ANDES

Visitá esta pagina totalmente actualizada
www.elmilagrodelosandes.com.ar

El viernes 13 de Octubre de 1972 un avión uruguayo, que llevaba 45 pasajeros a Chile, de los cuales muchos eran estudiantes y jugadores de un equipo de rugby, se estrelló en la Cordillera de los Andes. Doce murieron a causa de la caída, los sobrevivientes a esta tuvieron que soportar entre otras cosas a la temible Cordillera, treinta grados bajo cero durante las noches y al hambre.

Trataron de resistir con las escasas reservas alimenticias que poseían, esperando ser rescatados, pero su esperanza cayó al enterarse por una radio, que se había abandonado la búsqueda. Desesperados ante la ausencia de alimentos y agotada su resistencia física, se vieron obligados a alimentarse de sus compañeros muertos para poder seguir viviendo.

Finalmente hartos de las bajísimas temperaturas, los amenazadores aludes, angustiados por la continua muerte de sus compañeros y la lenta espera del rescate, dos de los rugbiers deciden cruzar las inmensas montañas para así llegar a Chile.

De esta manera es como el 22 de diciembre de 1972, después de haber estado durante 72 días aislados de todo, el mundo se entera que dieciséis son los sobrevivientes que vencieron a la muerte en la Cordillera de los Andes.

Old Christians
Fairchild F-27
La Desaparición
El Choque
Primer Día
Los Días Siguientes
La Supervivencia
La Avalancha
La Cola
Ultima Expedición
El Rescate
Conferencia
Homenaje
Día tras Día
Libros
Películas
Sobrevivientes
Entrevistas
¿Quién es Quién?
Fotografías

AGRADECIMIENTOS

Pagina hecha y mantenida por Alexis Scarantino.
Datos personales

Fig. 262. *The main page of Alexis Scarantino's Geocities website.*

Chatting with Barrios at *Hostería El Sosneado* on the day before the trip, Alexis saw a van pull up in front of them, and a group of English-speaking boys pour out of it:

I asked Edgardo what was happening, but the next moment I saw another van pull up with Roberto Canessa. I said, "That's Roberto Canessa". Edgardo answered, "No, he's just a friend who looks like him" "No, no, I'm sure it's Roberto. I know him!" Then Edgardo said, "Come with me, I'll introduce you." Well, I already knew Roberto from his trip to Buenos Aires, but to meet him there was very special. Roberto said to me: "Oh, what a pity you've just arrived. We've just returned from the valley." But it was a little lie to hide the surprise that had been arranged, because the next day we started going up to the valley together. It was the fulfilment of another dream. I told Roberto that I had dreamed many times about knowing the survivors, and also about visiting the site, but never in my wildest dreams had I imagined that I could go to the valley with him.

Fig. 263. *Seventeen-year-old Alexis Scarantino with Roberto Canessa on a trip to the site, February 2001.*

Alexis placed a link to Barrios' website on the *GeoCities* site, and in the following years, increasing numbers would join him on what became an annual pilgrimage. In 2002, he went with Ariel Osvaldo Torres, and met Roy Harley and Antonio Vizintín; although the survivors were on another expedition, their stays in the *Hostería El Sosneado* and on the mountain coincided with those of Alexis' expedition. Another time, he went with Coche Inciarte and Álvaro Mangino, and he would continue going until 2007, when his summer job as a lifeguard precluded him from going any more.

In 2002, the survivors decided to form their own website, www.viven.com.uy, and contracted a company to produce it. The web-building team took much of the content verbatim from Alexis's site, initially without permission or acknowledgment, although later his name appeared in the credits. But for Alexis, it was an endorsement for all his hard work, an honour that his content was now the basis for the official site. It did mean, however, that Alexis lost the motivation to continue improving the *GeoCities* site, eventually losing it altogether when he stopped paying for the server, and an attempt to incorporate it as a subsite of Carlitos' Páez website failed.

The appearance of the official website was a watershed event for the survivors, as Daniel Fernández later reflected in *Sociedad de La Nieve*:

> *During all these years some of us had closed ourselves to silence. We had not talked about the accident or what happened in the Andes. The reason is quite simple. We lived very close to the families of those who remained in the mountains. If we lived in another country, or in a larger country, it would be different, but here we not only lived in the same territory, but also in the same city and even in the same neighbourhood, Carrasco. So, we were very sensitive not to cause any unnecessary pain...*

> *The turning point, which happened to many of us, occurred thirty years after the accident. Among other things, in 2002 we set up the Viven website... When I started to read the emails that we received every day on the website, I discovered something that I had not imagined: the need that many people have to know about this kind of experience. So I said to myself: "There's a reason I went through this. If what I say is useful to someone, the least I can do if I am saved, is to talk to whoever asks me. This story does not belong to me".*

For Alexis, who had made such a seminal contribution, the greatest regret was that he was no longer making contact with fans of the story from around the world, who now flocked to the survivors' website, millions of them signing the guest book. He was pondering this one night when lying in bed:

> *I had almost fallen asleep when suddenly ... ping ... I realized that the solution was to form an MSN Group. I immediately got up, turned on my computer and created the group. I then sent an email to all the friends who had been members of the GeoCities community, "Check out this group that I'm starting. You can upload your photos and news there". When I had made the original website, I hadn't been sure that it would be successful, but I had no doubt that this group would work.*

It was 30th August 2004, and this invitation marked the birth of the *Re-Viven* group, a community of aficionados of the story. *MSN Groups* allowed members to contribute to message boards, so it became an important means of communication, and a repository for the many documents, articles, and photos that members collected and posted over the years. Survivor Pedro Algorta said of the group in his memoir *INTO THE MOUNTAINS*:

> *They form a virtual group and are our most loyal followers. They forgive us everything and follow us everywhere. They know more about our story than we do because they've taken on the task of cross-checking all our accounts, they travel every summer to explore the site where we crashed in the Andes, and every 13th October they travel to Uruguay or to Chile to attend the match that the Old Christians play with the Chileans... They are a very special group, our most faithful fan club.*

In the early years, the group would meet up at Alexis' home. He recalled later:

> *We would eat asados, and spend the time talking about the Andes. I would show them all the material I had collected, and share out one or two folders at a time for people to take home and return at the next meeting. Even though the first contact was always the internet, we would instantly become friends on meeting in person because everyone felt the same. The group would travel every year to the Andes, and to the Copa del Amistad in Montevideo and in Santiago. And we would even do other trips unrelated to the Andes just for fun. We spent a lot of time together.*

When *MSN Groups* closed down in February 2009, Alexis migrated the group to another platform, *Multiply*, before it finally transitioned into the Facebook *Re-Viven* group in 2009, the popular platform giving rise to a tenfold increase in membership. Some of the intimacy and personal interaction of the early years has been lost, but the interest in the story has continued unabated.

Alexis is still a prominent member of the *Re-Viven* community, but his interests have diversified over the years. When he is not working as a lifeguard – in Argentina during the austral summer, and in Spain throughout the boreal summer – he concentrates on his music – playing guitar, harmonica, and drums. And when he has free time, he returns to the Andes story.

Fig. 264. *Alexis Scarantino at home, November 2019.*

MUSEO ANDES 1972

The *Museo Andes 1972* sits on a quiet side street in the Old City of Montevideo, diagonally across *Plaza Constitución* from the Cathedral. Its location is easily missed, but for those who do find their way there, few leave dissatisfied or unmoved. The museum is consistently rated amongst the top few attractions in the city, with comments such as "Absolutely the best thing I did in Montevideo". It houses an impressive set of artefacts, some recovered from the mountain, others donated by the survivors and the families of those who died, and the detailed panels tell the story of the ordeal in Spanish and English. Visitors often have the good fortune to meet and chat with owner and curator Jörg P. A. Thomsen, who is equally at ease speaking Spanish, German, Portuguese, or English as he expounds and expands on the different aspects of the tragedy.

Fig. 265. *The main hall of the Museo Andes 1972.*

Jörg was a teenager at the time of the accident, and grew up in the same neighbourhood as many of the passengers. When talking about the accident, he stresses the importance of understanding the political context of the time:

Those times were complicated locally and internationally. 1972 started with a lot of dead people due to the Tupamaros. In retrospect it is clear that that the 'war' was won by the armed forces, but at the time, you never knew what might happen. You could be walking down the street and be hit by a bomb blast, or you could be kidnapped. It was a big question mark every day. My house was raided by the military three times in that period. I was suspicious not only because I was a teenager, but because everybody was a target of suspicion. I never knew in those days who was a friend and who was an enemy, and everybody was cautious to talk. It's important to perceive this in order to understand that when the plane disappeared, the first thing everyone thought was that it had been hijacked, especially because there were some relatives of the former President on board.

And he vividly remembers the moment he heard the news of the disappearance of the *Old Christians* plane:

I can describe the car. I can describe the weather. I can describe the ride home with my classmate when his father switched on the car radio. In those days, I did double hours at school Monday to Saturday, enrolled in both a German programme and the Uruguayan one. It was Saturday 14th October and we were on the Rambla approaching Punta Gorda. I still remember hearing the long, long list of passengers. The two reporters took it in turns to read out the names – many well-known to me, others not so much. We were almost home by the time the list was finished.

One of the most important reasons that drove Jörg to create the museum was the idea of justice. Everybody was talking about the survivors only – the authorized book on the story was called *ALIVE*, and people spoke only about the 'miracle in the Andes'. He felt it was important to tell the whole story, that society should remember the victims also, many of whom were still alive when the search was abandoned after eight days. His way of thinking had its roots in the stories he had been told about members of his own family who had gone missing during the Soviet occupation of East Germany in World War II.

At age nine, Jörg personally experienced the loss of someone close to him. Phillip August Rossel – his father's sixty-year-old business partner, and Jörg's godfather – died, along with his wife, in the LAN Chile 107 flight disaster of 6th February 1965. In what is still the deadliest accident in Chilean aviation history, the Douglas DC-6B flew into a mountainside in the Maipú Canyon when crossing the Andes. All eighty-seven passengers and crew died on impact, including twenty-two players and staff of Santiago's *Antonio Varas* football team who were travelling to play a game in Montevideo. Jörg's memories of those hours of uncertainty after the accident were brought into sharp focus again by the news of the Fairchild's disappearance in October 1972:

> When my Godfather died in the LAN Chile flight, it was a hot February day. I was sitting in the garden, on the terrace with my mother. She was knitting, and I was playing, when my father appeared, saying that the plane had crashed. For the next long hours, there were all sorts of contradictory reports: "the plane is presumed to be in Mendoza", "the plane is still in Santiago", and so on. It must have been similar to what all the relatives experienced in those days of October 1972. On that evening of Saturday 14th, I remember going to Garcia's in Carrasco to buy a pizza, and I passed by the church and saw it crowded with people. I felt sure, from what I had experienced with my Godfather's accident, that there could be no survivors, that those who were searching for the plane were just wasting their time.

Fig. 266. *Relatives and survivors at the inauguration of statue of Sergio Catalán in the museum.*
Back: *Teresa and Inés Valeta (sisters of Carlos), Álvaro Mangino, Coche Inciarte, Nando Parrado, statue of Sergio Catalán, Roberto Canessa, Gustavo Zerbino, Roy Harley.*
Front: *Raquel Nicolich (mother of Coco), Ana Inés Martínez Lamas (sister of Julio), Juan Pedro Nicola (son of Pancho Nicola and Esther Horta), Paula and Daniela Catalán (twin daughters of Sergio).*

Then in 1988 Jörg experienced his own near disaster when travelling with his family on an international night flight. Shortly after take-off, a fire started under one of the wings of the Jumbo Jet, the cabin blacked out, and the plane started shuddering and losing altitude. In the face of impending doom, Jörg's primary reaction was regret that he hadn't done more in his life to make a difference. In the following years, one area where he thought he might be able to contribute was in politics, and in 1994, he joined forces with Roberto Canessa and others to form a new political party – the *Partido Azul* (Blue Party).

In the national elections that year, they campaigned respectively as senatorial and presidential candidates:

We wanted to make a political party, not because we had any wish to be president or a senator, but because we wanted to kick things forward. If you ask people to change, they are not happy to do so. For instance, the idea of one computer per child was formed by our party. Now it's Plan Ceibal, introduced by the Frente Amplio. Another thing we wanted to do was to downsize parliament. Why do we need ninety-nine people with their salary and personal assistants and all the free things they get? The parties vote as a block, so why do we need so many? We made the suggestion to reduce it to twenty-one. We had wonderful ideas, aggressive ideas because we love our country.

The new party had negligible success in the 1994 elections, but Thomsen never regretted this foray into politics. It was an eye-opener for him, showing him the self-serving reality of Uruguayan political life. It was another of the reasons he created the museum – to promote the values of leadership and responsibility, teamwork and decision-making that had been present on the mountain, to teach that setting goals and persevering towards them in a spirit of optimism and cooperation was a better way to bring about change.

With these different threads percolating through his mind, Jörg had been struck by a visit to the *Peenemünde* museum when travelling in Germany, impressed by the way they presented the history of the *Vergeltungswaffen* – the V-weapons of World War II. He envisaged a similar museum, albeit on a smaller scale, telling the full story of the Andes. But when he spoke to one of the survivors about it, suggesting that they make such a museum, their sharp retort was that he should establish one himself. He took up the challenge. That same day, he started looking for a model of a Fairchild FH-227, and, finding that no such thing existed, he commissioned one to be custom-made by a specialist model-maker, Victor Porta. The 1/72-scale replica became an inspirational focal point as he set about laying the groundwork for the museum.

He then started looking around for a suitable building. His original intention had been that it could be in Carrasco, close to his home, but after months of proposals and delayed responses, no reasonable options opened up. However, having lunch one day with his daughter at the *Tajamar* (an iconic thatched-roof structure in Carrasco, designed by architect Juan Antonio Scasso), and seeing how under-utilized the space was, he suggested to the concessionaire, Virginia Robinson, that they could mount a temporary exhibition there, something to commemorate the fortieth anniversary of the tragedy. To his surprise, she readily agreed, and arranged for a one-month slot to be available in three weeks' time. Caught unprepared, and despite heavy work commitments, Thomsen hastily assembled a small team, which included his son Niels, and Roberto Canessa as technical adviser, to construct the cabinets and gather the exhibits in time for the opening. The attendance was disappointing, with not many more than a thousand visitors over the period of the exhibition from 23rd August to 22nd September 2012.

Fig. 267. **From Left:** *The author, Paula and Virginia Catalán (daughter and wife of Sergio), and museum owner and curator Jörg Thomsen holding the original Collins antenna of the Fairchild.* **Background:** *Painting (from actual photo) of the boys in the Fairchild (artist: Fabián Varietti).*

Follow-up exhibitions in Punta del Este at the height of summer yielded significantly fewer visitors. As Thomsen wrote in TOUCHED: *The Story Behind the Museum of the Andes 1972 Ordeal:*

> *Despite the enormous effort and dedication of time and money, the exhibitions were unfortunately very disappointing experiences. But because of my nature, the disappointments did not demotivate me or deter me, on the contrary, they fired my spirit.*

Meanwhile, a possibility opened up to permanently house the exhibits in a historic nineteenth-century building in the *Ciudad Vieja*. Owned by Jörg's uncle, Harald Görke, it had housed a restaurant until 2008, but was now lying empty and derelict, with little prospect of new tenants. Thomsen visited the building with various people associated with the story – Antonio Mercader, Pablo Vierci, the Strauches, and Canessa. He also

invited ministers, ex-ministers, and other high-ranking people. Harald, impressed by the initiative shown by his nephew and his commitment to the story, offered to be his first sponsor, and encouraged him to base the museum in the building, waiving the first year's rent, and putting in place a beneficial ongoing rental contract. Buoyed by the support of his uncle, and failing to find a further sponsor, Jörg decided to fund the museum from his own resources. He and his partner in the venture, Andrea Prada, worked around the clock to get the building ready for the opening of the museum on 5th October 2013 – heritage day.

Harald continued to provide support and advice to his nephew over the following years, a constant presence at the museum, who could often be seen sitting in one of the seats near the entrance, before his death in 2019.

Fig. 268. *Harald Görke (2018) waving a greeting from his customary spot at the front of the museum.*

In the first week or two of October each year, visitor numbers are swelled by the presence of survivors and families of non-survivors gathering to celebrate the museum's anniversary and to commemorate the tragedy. The museum hosts several other special events throughout the year, but on a normal day, the atmosphere is muted and respectful as the visitors absorb the extraordinary story told by the exhibits. There have been some difficult years in which the cost of running the museum has far exceeded the income from visitors, but Jörg remains committed and undeterred, and continues to put his own money into the project. He has been convinced by the frequent testimonies from visitors that the museum serves as an essential place of healing for people who have undergone tragic events in their lives.

Fiftieth Anniversary Commemoration

The fiftieth anniversary of the accident gave rise to many tributes. On Friday 7th October 2022, there was the unveiling of both a new commemorative stamp, issued that day, and a commemorative coin to be released in 2023. The event took place in the *Museo Andes 1972* with Uruguayan president, Luis Lacalle Pou, joining the many survivors and families in attendance.

The following day, a horse parade took place in the old city in honour of Sergio Catalán, a tribute organized by Jorge R. Diaz, the president of the Uruguayan Union of Traditionalist Societies. The riders included survivors Gustavo Zerbino and Roberto Canessa, and relatives Ana Inés Martínez Lamas, Raquelina Nicolich, and JuanPe Nicola, with many others in attendance, including the Uruguayan culture secretary, and the Mayor of San Fernando. The cavalcade was led by Katja Thomsen, holding the Uruguayan flag. Katja, daughter of Jörg Thomsen, is a well-known face in Uruguay, most famously for having represented the country in the 2000 Miss World competition, finishing in the top five. Those who died in the Andes were represented by twenty-nine unsaddled white horses; a thirtieth, representing Sergio Catalán, was draped with a Chilean flag.

On 13th October, there was a Catholic Mass at *Stella Maris College*, attended by the survivors and families of the dead, many of whom took an active role in the celebration. Notable amongst the attendees was Raquel Nicolich on her ninety-sixth birthday. The Mass, presided over by the bishop, was graced by a personal letter from Pope Francis who invited the community to remember those who had remained on the mountain, and their families: "Let their memory be a source of inspiration, like that which moved those mothers to create the *Biblioteca Nuestros Hijos*."

The Mass was also attended by the 220 Chileans who made the trip for four days of events. The *Copa de la Amistad* took place on 15th October at the *Old Christians Club*, with Luis Lacalle Pou again in attendance alongside Bill Beaumont, head of world rugby, who gave a speech stressing the importance of rugby in promoting social cohesion within local communities. The Uruguayan Air Force arranged a flyover, and three parachutists, flying the flags of Chile, Uruguay, and the two clubs, were dropped onto the rugby field before the games. Many of the survivors and the 1972 *Grange Old Boys* team kitted up for the ceremonial five-minute game. The unusually competitive game finished with one try apiece before the younger club members took over. The weekend was rounded off with the traditional invitation-only *asado* on the Sunday.

Santa Marta, 10 de octubre de 2022

Sr. Gustavo Zerbino
Presente

Querido hermano,

Gracias por la invitación que me realizó a unirme en la eucaristía que celebrarán el próximo 13 de octubre con motivo de la conmemoración de los 50 años del accidente que vivieron en los Andes. Celebrar la eucaristía es la invitación del Señor a hacer memoria, memoria agradecida de su paso en nuestra vida y en nuestra historia. Con este espíritu, en primer lugar, me gustaría hacer memoria e invitarlos a rezar especialmente por los chicos y los familiares que no volvieron; recemos por ellos, por sus familiares y dejemos que su recuerdo sea fuente de inspiración como ese que movilizó a esas madres a crear la Biblioteca Nuestros Hijos. Un dolor maternal desgarrador que, vivido en clave pascual, fue capaz de trascenderse y hacerse signo de una vida de servicio por amor. Mi saludo y gratitud por el ejemplo y testimonio.

Ustedes tuvieron que enfrentar situaciones extremadamente difíciles, trágicas me animaría a decir, donde la hostilidad y la incertidumbre, la soledad y el abandono, el sinsentido y la privación, entre tantas otras cosas, se apoderaba de vuestras jornadas poniéndolos continuamente a prueba. En esta situación de despojo y de carestía total pudieron, sin embargo, hacer memoria y apelar a lo aprendido desde niños en vuestras casas y en la educación recibida: se tenían entre Ustedes — eran un equipo — y tenían la fuerza y el sostén de la oración. Se aferraron a lo más valioso que podían tener junto al deseo y a la voluntad de mirar hacia adelante y seguir viviendo. Experimentaron, no como un slogan, que nadie se salva solo, que se necesitaban unos a otros y que la oración, como me dice, les daba mucha contención y fortaleza.

También el de Ustedes es un testimonio pascual, donde el dolor y la incomprensión de lo vivido se transforma, para muchos, en signo de vida y esperanza. Gracias.

Los invito a que sigan siendo artífices y profetas de esperanza. Que este *hacer memoria* ayude a abrir puertas de futuro, coraje y compromiso principalmente en aquellas zonas y situaciones donde las personas viven situaciones adversas; que vuestro testimonio despierte al compromiso e invite a mancomunar esfuerzos para forjar un futuro mejor. Es cierto, no son pocas las veces que tenemos que enfrentar situaciones límites pero, en comunidad y con la oración, ayudemos a que podamos abrirnos a la esperanza.

El jueves 13 rezaré la eucaristía por todos Ustedes. Que Jesús los bendiga y la Virgen Santa los cuide; y, por favor, no se olviden de rezar por mí que también tengo "mis montañas" que atravesar.

Fraternalmente

Francisco

Fig. 269. *Letter from Pope Francis to Gustavo Zerbino on the fiftieth anniversary of the accident.*

THE SURVIVORS

Every 22nd December, the sixteen (more recently the fifteen) get together to celebrate the anniversary of their escape from the mountain, although usually one or two are missing. Only in 1995, when the group gathered in Buenos Aires at Pedro Algorta's house, was there a full complement of survivors. It is a personal time for them to reflect on their odyssey, away from the glare of publicity, although invariably a photograph of the event makes it to social media.

The public spotlight on the survivors has been relentless, especially in recent years. They have been the subject of numerous accounts on paper and on film, and many of them have given and continue to give conferences and motivational seminars worldwide, propagating the values learnt on the mountain. To report on their individual lives over that period with the same level of detail afforded the non-survivors would unreasonably lengthen this already sizeable history. More crucially, it would undermine one of its primary rationales, which is to rebalance the account of the tragedy. On the other hand, it would be odd to neglect the survivors altogether. So in this, the final chapter of the book, many of them have taken up my offer to contribute some words and thoughts.

For readers wanting to know more about individual survivors, the 2006 book *La Sociedad de La Nieve* (*The Snow Society*) is based on extensive interviews with each of them. Written by their former classmate, Uruguayan author Pablo Vierci, it records their very personal memories and thoughts on the story. Even more detailed accounts can be found in the memoirs of seven of the sixteen, each of which give a unique perspective of their odyssey in the mountain, their lives after their return, and their fellow survivors.

Nando Parrado	MILAGRO EN LOS ANDES (2006)	MIRACLE IN THE ANDES (2006)
Carlitos Páez	Después del día 10 (2007)	AFTER THE TENTH DAY (2019)
	DESDE LA CORDILLERA DEL ALMA (2015)	
Daniel Fernández	REGRESO A LA MONTAÑA (2012)	
Eduardo Strauch	Desde el Silencio (2012)	OUT OF THE SILENCE (2019)
Pedro Algorta	LAS MONTAÑAS SIGUEN ALLÍ (2014)	INTO THE MOUNTAINS (2016)
Roberto Canessa	TENÍA QUE SOBREVIVIR (2016)	I HAD TO SURVIVE (2016)
Coche Inciarte	Memorias de los Andes (2017)	Memories of the Andes (2020)

Describe your life since your return from the mountain.

I have lived an ordinary life. After the accident I returned to Argentina and for thirty years, I didn't talk about the accident. The people in the environments in which I moved did not know that I was a survivor of the Andes. When I reached the age of fifty, I realised that something had happened in my life, and that for others, my survival was a testimony that there are situations in life that you can overcome and then live a normal life. I didn't realise it and I was surprised by the effect it had on others when I told our story of survival. From then on, I started to open up my mountain, to talk about it, to remember and learn from everything that had happened to me. I was able to talk and I wrote a book in which I synthesised that path of rediscovering my mountain and its meaning. This book has been translated into English by my friend John Guiver.

What have your interactions been with the families of the non-survivors?

Because I have lived abroad for a long time, I have not had much contact with the families of survivors. I have kept in touch with Felipe Maquirriain's sister Sandra and sporadically with the families of other survivors. Sometimes I wonder if I shouldn't have been more proactive in the reunions.

What lesson from the story would you pass on to your grandchildren?

Simply that life has to be lived and that it is hard. There are no easy roads, but no matter how many difficulties we encounter, we can always get up and keep walking. I have three children and two grandchildren.

Describe your life since your return from the mountain.

The first thing I had to do when I got back was to talk to the relatives of the dead, to visit their homes, and tell them how sad it had been. I remember, when visiting Raquel Nogueira to talk about Arturo, feeling how fortunate I was to be alive, both for me and my mother. I felt that I had to lead a dignified life, in honour of the twenty-nine who died. I couldn't just sit back and enjoy life, I returned with an extra responsibility to lead a worthwhile life, otherwise how could I look their relatives in the eye. I felt that I had to dedicate a good part of my life to others, and there was no better way to do that than to continue my chosen career of medicine. In time I became a paediatric cardiologist, working with children who are born with congenital heart disease.

I married my *novia* Lauri Surraco in June 1976. Her sister Cecilia is married to Roy Harley, so the Andes is a family subject. Lauri and I have three children. When I went to the mountain with them, my daughter told me "The feeling of this place is very sad, but at the same time, very strong". But my greatest joy right now is being a grandfather. My grandchildren are already asking about the plane crash, about what happened and where we were.

On the rugby field I continued playing for the *Old Christians*, being top try scorer for several seasons in the National Championship, and between 1971 to 1979 I played for the National Rugby Team. I was president of the *Old Christians Club* for eight years, and during my tenure, Daniel Juan, who had been president at the time of the accident, said to me: "We have achieved what we wanted on the rugby field and in the rugby club, but what about the social achievements? We are also meant to be a social club, and we must do something to help society." In this way two programmes were born, *Los Tréboles*, and *Quebracho*, which are the club's commitment to helping less privileged communities. At *Stella Maris*, where my grandchildren go, they are already helping with that social work.

What have your interactions been with the families of the non-survivors?

My interaction with the families happened very soon because we had to rebuild the club. I remember Alejandro Nicolich, brother of Coco, playing in the first team, and the gym teacher of the school, Tito Virginella, helping us and saying it's going to take five years to recover to where we were. But at the end of that first season, we were champions again, and I remember Arturo Nogueira's father giving me a big hug, saying to me "my son is not here, but you are here".

Also, I felt very sorry for the Nicola family, those four kids who became orphans. So I used to go to visit them a lot. JuanPe very much enjoyed riding on my motorcycle, and then Pepe had kidney trouble... I was very close to them, and helped in any way I could. I am very proud, now, of the way they have raised their own families.

Then there was the *Biblioteca Nuestra Hijos*. For those mothers who wanted my support I was very happy to give it, and if not, I respected that also.

What lesson from the story would you pass on to your grandchildren?

Never tire of doing good. We complain that things are not getting better, but before complaining, ask yourself.... what can you do to make things better? We all have something to contribute, to give.

Fig. 270. *Roberto Canessa and family, September 2022.*

Describe your life since your return from the mountain.

As soon as I recovered physically, I continued with my engineering studies and rugby. I met Cecilia Surraco in September 1973 and we got married in May 1976. In 1980, I graduated as a Mechanical Industrial Engineer, and our three children arrived, Carolina (1978), Eloisa (1981) and Alejandro (1986).

I started working soon after getting married, involved in various activities until 1987 when I joined Imperial Chemical Industries (ICI) as Site Manager. My children finished their studies, Carolina as a Chemical Pharmaceutical Engineer, Eloisa as a Nutritionist, and Alejandro as a Civil Engineer. In 2009 ICI was acquired by AkzoNobel (Dutch) and I became Site Manager River Plate (Uruguay and Argentina) for the last six years of my career.

These days, I am dedicated to transmitting the message of the seventy-two days in the mountains (decision-making, tolerance to frustration, adaptation to change, leadership, etc.) together with my experience in all these years of working in large international companies.

Today what gives meaning to my life is my children, their corresponding partners and the 6 grandchildren they have given me, Carolina and Guillermo (Alfonso (14), Candelaria (12) and Ramon (8)), and Eloisa and Rodrigo (Sofia (6), Isabel (4) and Santiago (1)). I have a lot of fun getting together and going for walks with the family that Cecilia and I have made.

I consider myself grateful for life, it has given me so much more than what it put me through in 1972.

What have your interactions been with the families of the non-survivors?

I have more contact with some than with others. I am very good friends with the whole Nicolich family, and Cecilia and I have a great friendship with Mónica, Gustavo's sister.

I also have a close friendship with Daniel Turcatti, Numa's brother, and in 2012 I accompanied him to the *cordillera* to the site of the accident.

What lesson from the story would you pass on to your grandchildren?

To value and enjoy life, that we are fortunate for everything we have.

To value the most important thing we have in life which is our family and friends.

To be respectful of people and to be independent, not to depend on anyone in every sense.

Fig. 271. *Roy Harley (seated centre) and family, Christmas 2021.*

Describe your life since your return from the mountain.

I got married after eight months with my novia Soledad. I felt the urgency to start my own family. I had three children and today I have nine grandchildren. I lived and raised my children in the countryside, milking cows and sending the milk to *Conaprole*, the national cooperative of milk producers of which I was director for ten years. These days, now retired, I enjoy the pleasure of living as a family with my beloved Soledad, my three children, and my nine grandchildren.

What have your interactions been with the families of the non-survivors?

I get on with some of them very well (most of them), and with a few others badly! These don't love us and can't stand to see us, still alive despite the fifty years that have passed.

What lesson from the story would you pass on to your grandchildren?

I speak to them about happiness and how you have to merit it and thus find Peace in Life, and not just the abyss of death. Living in peace ensures health, and you become free and live without fear and live in truth! This is the meaning of life and it starts with giving and giving yourself to others and then you will be worthy of happiness!

Fig. 272. *Coche Inciarte (seated centre) and family, Easter 2022.*

ÁLVARO MANGINO

Describe your life since your return from the mountain.

For a long time I dealt with the situation very internally, a little bit at a time with my family. For 30 years I talked to almost no-one about what had happened to me; and even when *ALIVE* was written, Piers Paul Read, when he interviewed me, tried many times to get me to talk about things that, for me, were very much my own, things that it didn't make much sense to tell him, such as whether we had fought or not. I kept to myself, and for a long time I didn't talk. I started to talk when we went to the Andes, twelve out of the sixteen of us, to mourn our dead friends. Somehow, that opened my head a bit, and from that moment I started to feel more responsible for what had happened to me. Coche and I, who began giving talks together, started to look into why, and for what purpose, this ordeal had happened to us. I think that the answer to that question, which we all asked ourselves for so many years, is in something that Coche and I always say in our lectures, which is that in life you have to be happy, and to be happy, you have to understand how much more important it is to give than to receive. So, today, I feel very good when I talk about it. I think we bring values and principles that were fundamental to our survival, and which are a bit lacking in the normal life of people today. That makes us very proud of the public's response, to be able to transmit to people this sensibility we have for what happened to us.

What have your interactions been with the families of the non-survivors?

It was better and easier with some than with others. We had to respect the parents of the boys who didn't return, because the story was very intense for them. In a way, they suffered a lot, because to this day, new things continue to emerge, such as you writing this book, or in films, with sensitivities that were very hard for them because they had to be reminded all the time of what had happened to their children. I was very respectful. I had more affinity with some parents than others. With some we had very little connection, but with many I had a good connection because they were relatives of my wife Margarita. We had good relations and we were, in a way, trying to overcome the pain that these people had because of the death of their children.

What lesson from the story would you pass on to your grandchildren?

I would tell my grandchildren that in life you can always get where you want to go, you just have to have the attitude, which is what we had in order to get out of the *Cordillera*. I think that word sums up a lot of what our long seventy-two days in the *Cordillera* were like. The attitude that we had to get through it, based on getting back to our family and our loved ones, which was our biggest motivation during those 72 days. I think that value and those principles that we pass on to our grandchildren, of the importance of family, is the best gift we can leave them.

Fig. 273. *Álvaro Mangino (second from left) and family, on a pre-pandemic trip to Rio.*

CARLITOS PÁEZ

Although ours is a very dramatic story, it is one that, in the end, has a positive connotation, since life triumphed. Today there are many more of us – together we have more than one hundred children and grandchildren, so I believe it is a story that was worth it. Our passion, our attitude, our hopes were all worth it, and it was worthwhile to have worked together to enable life to triumph. In short, I believe that it is a story of struggle against denial, and it is a struggle of homage to life.

St. Francis of Assisi said: "Start by doing what is necessary, then what is possible, and suddenly you are doing the impossible." And that is exactly what we did. We conformed entirely to that process: we began with what was necessary, then what was possible, and we ended up doing the impossible in this incredible story of struggle for life; the struggle of human beings who had the ability to evolve, transform and move forward.

ADOLFO 'FITO' STRAUCH

This story has two very opposite aspects... on one side the tragedy, the deaths, all a great sadness... on the other side there is a look at the values that arose from the desperation to survive... my lesson was to learn to see this other side and it was thanks to my brothers of the Andes who helped me to see it...

EDUARDO STRAUCH

Describe your life since your return from the mountain.

My life has been a normal life, enriched by the lessons learned in the Andes. This odyssey gave me some opportunities that I would not have had otherwise. I have five children and two granddaughters.

What have your interactions been with the families of the non-survivors?

They were scarce with some, and different with each one. With some it was fluid, with great affection and respect, with others it was more difficult, and over the years that interaction, when there is any, is sympathetic and respectful.

What lesson from the story would you pass on to your grandchildren?

I would convey to them that to love is power and that love is powerful, it moves mountains.

Describe your life since your return from the mountain.

When I came back from the mountains I was met by my brother in the *Posta Central* hospital in Santiago, and we spent Christmas in Chile together before returning to Montevideo. Being reunited with my family and friends was very emotional, and I took a few days holiday with the whole family in Punta del Este. Then I went back to normal life. I had been working from a young age in the family business, managing part of the cattle and fruit farm, and I returned to that. The Andes became a thing of the past. We revisited the story for meetings and interviews, but my life, which has been very intense, ran in a different direction.

I am a restless person, very active, constantly developing businesses both in Uruguay and abroad. I lived in Brazil where I set up a factory, and in Paraguay where I am a property developer. I became accustomed to travelling at an early age, going around the world with my nine year old brother, on school trips, with thirteen, fourteen, and fifteen year olds. It gave me a lot of experience and independence.

My parents taught us to always be very supportive. They were always taking food to the elderly, and helping people in various ways. Through their example, I learned many important values which I have applied in my life. I have worked long hours, fighting for principles, values, solidarity, and justice; injustice is one thing I cannot stand. Today the world has changed a lot, and some values have been lost. Many kids today are going down the wrong path. I try to help with the issue of drugs, and also with the food banks here in Montevideo.

What have your interactions been with the families of the non-survivors?

I went to the *Seminario* rather than *The Christian*, so I knew almost none of the relatives of those who died on the mountain. The ordeal certainly created a strong bond with my fellow survivors, and I became good friends with their parents. But when I returned to Uruguay, I didn't want to bother the families of those who died, although I was always available to give information should they want to know.

A couple of days after I arrived back in Montevideo, Coco Nicolich's parents called me, wanting to meet me, because of the letter that their son had written on the mountain, talking about his great friendship with me that had arisen on the first night when I lay on top of him to keep him warm. A very strong relationship developed with the Nicolich family, which has continued to this day.

I did have some relations with other families because of the *Biblioteca Nuestros Hijos*. But I was a person who never wanted to talk much here in Uruguay, out of respect for them. I never wanted to appear in the press, except in a few situations, because I felt that talking about the story of the Andes in the Uruguayan media had the effect of stirring up the subject for them, and I didn't want to cause them pain. That's why I stayed respectful and perhaps a little distant, but there is a very strong affection for them, and we embrace whenever we see each other.

In 1997, I went with the Nicola boys and Alejandro Nicolich to the mountains, riding on horseback from the Chilean side with Sergio Catalán. We spent an intense four or five days in the mountains, during which time they were able to ask me all kinds of questions about what happened. It was very emotional. Somehow they were reassured, knowing where they were, in that impressive place, at that incredible cross on the mountain, which has a very special life, despite being full of death. It is a place filled with a very special energy that produces impressive effects on the people who go there.

What lesson from the story would you pass on to your grandchildren?

The society that we built on the mountain was one of great solidarity and creativity, where egos didn't exist, unlike in the real world where they can be very destructive. Up there, when you had a good idea, everyone came out to applaud it, whereas down here, when someone has a good idea, people have a tendency to sabotage it.

Even though I don't have grandchildren, I would pass on to them humility and solidarity, and encourage them to leave egos aside, and know the boundaries between one's individual rights and those of the wider society. This is something that I am trying to do with the children in schools, not to leave issues pending, to know that effort is the basis of everything. Effort, work and education are fundamental to any society. The world today has become totally unbalanced; important principles and values have been lost, and we need to rebuild them, starting with children at school.

The most important thing is family. Everything we did and fought for on the mountains, everything we suffered – the cold, the thirst, the hunger – we did so to stop the suffering of our families. We all presumed that they must have given us up for dead, although I found out later that my mother had always believed I was alive. I wanted to return home to stop the suffering of my parents, grandparents and friends; that was the driving force that kept us fighting, and prevented us from giving up.

GUSTAVO ZERBINO

Describe your life since your return from the mountain.

I felt a great joy to be able to return to my country and to see my family again.

I fulfilled the promise I made to Marcelo on the mountain when he asked me not to abandon the *Old Christians* after the accident.

I played rugby for twelve years in the club, where I was a director for almost forty years, President for seven and Vice President for five.

Ten months after losing forty kilos, I played for the Uruguayan national team in the South American Rugby Championship in São Paulo in October 1973.

I was fifteen years Director of the Uruguayan Rugby Union, and four years President.

I got married and have six wonderful children: four boys Gustavo (35), Sebastian (33), Lucas (31) and Martin (26), all of whom played Rugby at the Club; and two girls Luma (23) and Guadalupe (16), who also went to the school, and play Hockey at the Club.

I have been a director for forty years of *Cibeles* in the Pharmaceutical industry and I am President of the Chamber of Multinational Laboratories of Uruguay. I am a very happy person, with a great vocation of service and grateful for all the things that life has given me.

What have your interactions been with the families of the non-survivors?

The first thing I did when I arrived in Montevideo was to spend a month going day-by-day, house-by-house to tell them how they had died and how brave they had been while they were alive, and to take to all the people (mothers, brothers, girlfriends) who had lost a relative, a souvenir of my friends who died in the mountains. During the seventy-three days, I collected for them: watches, medals, crosses, documents, wallets, and letters written to them; so that they could get through their grief better. I have an excellent relationship with everyone, as they are my family too.

I have been a member from the first day and am a godfather to the *Biblioteca Nuestros Hijos*, which the mothers made in memory of their children. We see each other all the time and they know that they can count on me for anything they need and I know that I can count on them.

Some mothers, when they were left alone, I supported in every way I could and visited them or invited them to dinner until the day they died.

I felt it was what they would have done if they were alive.

557

What lesson from the story would you pass on to your grandchildren?

I am about to be a grandfather for the first time of two grandchildren. Antonio, son of Sebastian who is to born at the end of August and Leon, son of Lucas who is due the first week of September. It will be something totally new for me.

I would tell my grandchildren that the greatest energy that exists is love, which is what kept us alive.

That we come to life to be happy, that they should not be afraid to make mistakes, that mistakes and failure do not exist, only the lesson you learn about the way it doesn't work. That in life you have to get up only once more than you fall down.

That you have to connect with your heart and with your sincere desire and go after your dreams to make them come true and ask God for the strength to make them possible. That hope is the younger sister of faith, and that you have to keep your hope and humility always alive. That alone, you get there faster, but accompanied, you go further.

That they should be good people, good friends and in solidarity that God is always present if they open their hearts. That every day before getting up they should be grateful that they have a new day to enjoy and be the best version of themselves.

Fig. 274. *Gustavo Zerbino (standing centre) and family.*

Sources

Photo Credits

The portraits of the passengers in Part II of the book are by artist Daniel Vera and are copyright © Museo Andes 1972.

Fig. 1.	Fairchild FAU 572.	Author's personal archive.
Fig. 2.	Departure Terminal.	http://bibliotecadigital.bibna.gub.uy:8080/jspui/. Id 71212.
Fig. 3.	Ponce de León's House.	Author's personal archive.
Fig. 4.	Stella Maris College 1955.	From the book '50 años del Colegio Stella Maris'.
Fig. 5.	Hotel Carrasco 1980.	http://bibliotecadigital.bibna.gub.uy:8080/jspui/. Id 18627.
Fig. 6.	Rambla, Malvin and Buceo.	http://bibliotecadigital.bibna.gub.uy:8080/jspui/. Id 18505.
Fig. 7.	Buceo cemetery.	Author's personal archive.
Fig. 8.	Zum Zum nightclub.	https://enlanoche1985.blogspot.com/.
Fig. 9.	Kibon accident.	https://montevideoantiguo.net/.
Fig. 10.	Pocitos 1970.	http://bibliotecadigital.bibna.gub.uy:8080/jspui/. Id 19071.
Fig. 11.	Punta Carretas prison.	https://montevideoantiguo.net/.
Fig. 12.	Plaza Independencia.	https://commons.wikimedia.org/wiki/File:0577FMHA.jpg.
Fig. 13.	1970's Montevideo.	http://bibliotecadigital.bibna.gub.uy:8080/jspui/. Id 5645.
Fig. 14.	Zorrilla de San Martín.	Courtesy Francisca Zorrilla de San Martín.
Fig. 15.	The Last Charrúas.	Author's personal archive.
Fig. 16.	Department of Rio Negro.	1899 map of Rio Negro. Courtesy Cecilia Regules.
Fig. 17.	José Batlle y Ordóñez.	Eugenio Hintz archive, courtesy Sergio Hintz.
Fig. 18.	'Evelyn' Jackson.	El Diario, 9th January 1971.
Fig. 19.	Pacheco and Bordaberry.	Eugenio Hintz archive, courtesy Sergio Hintz.
Fig. 20.	Wilson Ferreira Aldunate.	Eugenio Hintz archive, courtesy Sergio Hintz.
Fig. 21.	General Seregni.	Eugenio Hintz archive, courtesy Sergio Hintz.
Fig. 22.	Stop and Search.	Eugenio Hintz archive, courtesy Sergio Hintz.
Fig. 23.	Navy Blockade.	Eugenio Hintz archive, courtesy Sergio Hintz.
Fig. 24.	1930's Carrasco.	http://bibliotecadigital.bibna.gub.uy:8080/jspui/. Id 18408.
Fig. 25.	1950's Carrasco.	http://bibliotecadigital.bibna.gub.uy:8080/jspui/. Id 18427.
Fig. 26.	Stella Maris Church.	Author's personal archive.
Fig. 26.	Hotel Carrasco.	Jimmy Baikovicius (https://www.flickr.com/photos/jikatu/).
Fig. 27.	Break time at Stella Maris.	Colegio Stella Maris 1964 yearbook.
Fig. 28.	1955 school photo.	Courtesy Conrado Hughes.
Fig. 29.	1920's-themed party.	Courtesy Cecilia Regules.
Fig. 30.	Easter at Las Cañadas.	Courtesy Cecilia Regules.
Fig. 31	Goodbye to the Tena boys.	Courtesy Alejandro Nicolich (Photo Margarita Montes).
Fig. 32.	The Gang.	Courtesy Roy Harley.
Fig. 33.	Eduardo at Casapueblo.	Author's personal archive.
Fig. 34.	Arturo's list of passengers.	Courtesy Daniel Nogueira.
Fig. 35.	Passenger manifest.	Archives IV Brigada Aérea Mendoza, courtesy Horacio Bollati.
Fig. 36.	Departments of Uruguay.	https://www.uruguayxxi.gub.uy/mapadigitaluruguay/.
Fig. 37.	Fairchild configuration.	Fairchild Pilot's Handbook, courtesy Pablo Vierci and FAU.
Fig. 38.	Pilot's seat and main cabin.	Courtesy Guillermo Scott.
Fig. 39.	Painting of boys in plane.	Artist Fabián Varietti. Property of Museo Andes 1972.
Fig. 40.	Passengers at El Plumerillo.	Courtesy Alejandro Nicolich.
Fig. 41.	Scenes of Mendoza.	Author's personal archive.
Fig. 42.	Ex-Hotel Sussex.	Copyright © Federico Sanguinetti.
Fig. 43.	Casa de la Gobernador.	Copyright © Federico Sanguinetti.
Fig. 44.	Hotel San Remo.	Copyright © Federico Sanguinetti.

ARCHIVES

Piers Paul Read archive, Brotherton Library Special Collection, Leeds.
Notebooks, scrapbooks, and other source materials for ALIVE. Also correspondence relating to the publication of the book, letters from readers, and film scripts.

Clair Blair papers, American Heritage Center, University of Wyoming.
Background material on passengers, burial on the mountain, military crew, rescue personnel, and interviews with families of non-survivors.

Eugenio Hintz archive.
Private archive of Uruguayan journalist Eugenio Hintz. Background on the Chilean side of things – the rescue and the events that followed it – and the accident itself. News reports and photographs unrelated to the accident, filed by Hintz in his years as a journalist and foreign correspondent.

Antonio Mercader archive.
Private archive of Uruguayan journalist Antonio Mercader. Detailed background material on all the passengers.

Guillermo Scott archive.
Private archive of Chilean researcher Guillermo Scott. In-depth interviews with Chilean protagonists: Air Force and Army personnel, Andinistas, journalists, rugby players, and others. Chilean and Peruvian newspaper articles from the time.

Universidad Diego Portales archive, Cenfoto Department, Santiago.
Photos from the time of the rescue, bought from *Vea Magazine* by *Cenfoto*.

Francisco Cuadra archive.
Private archive of retired Colonel Francisco Cuadra. High-definition colour photos from the time of the rescue.

Federico Sanguinetti archive.
Private archive of architect and mountaineer Federico Sanguinetti. Uruguayan newspaper articles (October 1972 to April 1973) from *Acción, Ahora, El Diario, El Oriental, El País*, and *El Popular*. Also high definition photographs from the December 2015 expedition to cross the Andes.

Roberto Canessa archive.
Private archive of survivor Roberto Canessa and his wife Lauri Surraco. Newspaper clippings and photographs including those taken by Dr Luis Surraco during the parents' search.

BOOKS ON THE ANDES TRAGEDY

This list is not comprehensive, and only Spanish- and English-language versions are shown.

Serge Soiret (1973) LA VERDAD SOBRE "EL MILAGRO DE LOS ANDES". Montevideo:Ediciones America Nueva.

Alfonso Alcalde (1973) VIVIR O MORIR. Chile:Editorial Nacional Quimantú.

Oscar Vega (1973) SAN FERNANDO, CHILE, URGENTE. Santiago:Pineda libros..

Hector Suanes (1973) EL MILAGRO DE LOS ANDES. Buenos Aires:Emecé editores.

Clay Blair, Jr.(1973) SURVIVE! New York:Berkley Publishing Corporation.

Clay Blair, Jr.(1974) SUPERVIVIENTES DE LOS ANDES. Mexico City:Editorial Diana..

Rodolfo Martinez Ugarte (1973) PARA QUE OTROS PUEDAN VIVIR. Santiago:Editorial Nascimiento.

Enrique Hank Lopez (1973) THEY LIVED ON HUMAN FLESH. New York:Pocket Books.

Enrique Hank Lopez (1973) THE HIGHEST HELL. London: Sidgwick & Jackson Ltd.

Richard Cunningham (1973) THE PLACE WHERE THE WORLD ENDS. New York:Sheed and Ward.

Piers Paul Read (1974) ALIVE. Philadelphia and New York:J.B.Lippincott Company.

Piers Paul Read (1974) ALIVE. London:The Alison Press/Martin Secker & Warburg Ltd.

Piers Paul Read (1974) ¡VIVEN! LA TRAGEDIA DE LOS ANDES. Uruguay:Barreiro y Ramos.

Carlos Páez Vilaró (1982) ENTRE MI HIJO Y YO, LA LUNA. Argentina:Espacio Editora S.A.

Carlitos Páez (2007) DESPUÉS DEL DÍA 10.

Carlitos Páez (2019) AFTER THE TENTH DAY.

Fernando Parrado (2006) MILAGRO EN LOS ANDES. Editorial Planeta.

Fernando Parrado (2006) MIRACLE IN THE ANDES. New York:Crown Publishers.

Pablo Vierci (2009) LA SOCIEDAD DE LA NIEVE. Buenos Aires:Editorial Sudamericana.

Pablo Vierci (2023) THE SNOW SOCIETY. Little Brown Paperbacks (A&C).

Madelón Rodríguez (2009) EL ROSARIO DE LOS ANDES. Punta del Este:Mar y Sol Ediciones.

Daniel Fernández Strauch (2012) REGRESO A LA MONTAÑA. Montevideo:Ediciones B.

Eduardo Strauch Urioste/Mireya Soriano (2012) DESDE EL SILENCIO: CUARENTA AÑOS DESPUÉS. Editorial Sudamericana.

Eduardo Strauch Urioste/Mireya Soriano (2012) DESDE EL SILENCIO: CUARENTA AÑOS DESPUÉS. Madrid: Ediciones Desnivel.

Eduardo Strauch (2019) OUT OF THE SILENCE: AFTER THE CRASH. Seattle:AmazonCrossing.

Matt J. Rossano (2013) MORTAL RITUALS. Columbia University Press.

Pedro Algorta (2014) LAS MONTAÑAS SIGUE ALLÍ. Buenos Aires:Editorial Sudamericana.

Pedro Algorta (2014) LAS MONTAÑAS SIGUE ALLÍ. Madrid:LID Editorial Empresarial.

Pedro Algorta (2016) INTO THE MOUNTAINS. London:LID Publishing.

Carlitos Páez (2015) DESDE LA CORDILLERA DEL ALMA. Montevideo:Editorial Planeta.

Ariel Osvaldo Torres (2015) HACIA EL AVIÓN DE LOS URUGUAYOS. San Andrés:Ariel Osvaldo Torres.

Roberto Canessa/Pablo Vierci (2016) TENÍA QUE SOBREVIVIR. Editorial Alrevés.

Roberto Canessa/Pablo Vierci (2016) I HAD TO SURVIVE. United States:Atria Books.

Roberto Canessa/Pablo Vierci (2016) I HAD TO SURVIVE. Great Britain:Constable.

Ignacio Martínez (2016) UNA VEZ EN LOS ANDES. Montevideo:Editorial Planeta.

Coche Inciarte (2017) MEMORIAS DE LOS ANDES:45 AÑOS DESPUÉS. Montevideo: Editorial Sudamericana.

Coche Inciarte (2020) MEMORIES OF THE ANDES. Heddon Publishing.

María del Carmen Perrier (2018) DEL OTRO LADO DE LA MONTAÑA. Penguin Random House Grupo Editorial.

María del Carmen Perrier (2022) ON THE OTHER SIDE OF THE MOUNTAIN. Editorial Sudamericana.

Francisca Vogt (2018) MAÑKE. Ediciones UC/ Museo Andes 1972.

Ariel Osvaldo Torres (2020) CORAZÓN DE ARRIERO. San Andrés:Ariel Osvaldo Torres.

Jörg P.A. Thomsen and Patricia Maher-Affeldt (2020): TOUCHED. Museo Andes 1972.

OTHER SOURCES

A large part of this book is based on many hours of interviews with families and friends those didn't return from the mountain, and with many others connected to the tragedy in Uruguay, Argentina, and Chile. A detailed list of participants is given in the Acknowledgements section.

Below is a list of some of the more general references used to inform various parts of the book. It is by no means comprehensive, and doesn't include the many newspaper and magazine articles consulted.

Luis Bértola (2016) EL PIB PER CÁPITA DE URUGUAY 1870-2015: UNA RECONSTRUCCIÓN. Documentos de trabajo
      (Programa de Historia Económica y Social, Unidad Multidisciplinaria, Facultad de Cienc. Sociales, Univ. Repúb).
Julio Cerda Pino (1972) INVESTIGACIÓN PERICIAL. FUERZA AÉREA DE CHILE.
Lindsey Churchill (2014) BECOMING THE TUPAMAROS. Vanderbilt University Press.
Charles Darwin (1839) THE VOYAGE OF THE BEAGLE.
Jennifer Ann Dufau (2017) TAINTED IDEALS: THE RISE AND FALL OF THE TUPAMAROS. Senior Project, Bard College.
Gonzalo Etcheverry Campomar and Luis Ignacio Ubilla Schauricht (2001) EL RUGBY EN URUGUAY. URU.
Lucía Guerra MEMORIES OF SORROW. Unpublished manuscript.
Eugenio Hintz (1973) HINTZ REPORT. Private archive of Eugenio Hintz, courtesy Sergio Hintz.
Rex A. Hudson and Sandra W. Meditz, editors. (1992) URUGUAY: A COUNTRY STUDY. US:G.P.O.
Juan Ivanovic (1972) OPSAR REPORT 13-72: BÚSQUEDA Y SALVAMENTO DE LA AERONAVE DE LA FAU 571 F-227. FACH.
Geoffrey Jackson (1974) SURVIVING THE LONG NIGHT. New York:Vanguard Press.
William Katra (2017) JOSÉ ARTIGAS AND THE FEDERAL LEAGUE IN URUGUAY'S WAR OF INDEPENDENCE (1810-1820).
                                                                    Fairleigh Dickinson University Press.
Edy Kaufman (1979) URUGUAY IN TRANSITION: FROM CIVILIAN TO MILITARY RULE. Routledge.
A.J. Langguth (2018) HIDDEN TERRORS: THE TRUTH ABOUT U.S. POLICE OPERATIONS IN LATIN AMERICA. US:Open Road Media.
Vania Markarian (2005) LEFT IN TRANSFORMATION. New York:Routledge.
Vania Markarian (2016) URUGUAY, 1968. University of California Press.
Juan Maruri (1995-2010) HISTORIA DE LA FUERZA AÉREA URUGUAYA, SEGUNDO TOMO, VOLUMEN 1, 1953-2003. Uruguay.
Antonio Mercader and Jorge de Vera (1969) LOS TUPAMAROS: ESTRATEGIA Y ACCIÓN. Barcelona:Editorial Anagrama (1970).
Mendoza, Montaner, and Llosa (2001). GUIDE TO THE PERFECT LATIN AMERICAN IDIOT. Madison Books.
Sonia Montecino (2010) EL RÍO DE LAS LÁGRIMAS. Article in Anales de la Universidad de Chile.
Thomas O. Moore (1978) THE TUPAMAROS: URUGUAY'S URBAN GUERRILLAS. M.A. Thesis, Texas Tech University.
Enrique Morel Donoso (1972) INFORME RELACIONADO CON EL RESCATE DEL AVIÓN URUGUAYO. Ejercito de Chile.
Daniel Nole (2005) NUMERALES DE LOS AVIONES FAU. Online document.
Cristina Peri Rossi (2008) STATE OF EXILE. SAN FRANCISCO. City Lights Books.
Adriana Piñeyrúa (2014). HISTORIA DE LOS 50 AÑOS DEL COLEGIO SAGRADO CORAZÓN DE PASO CARRASCO. Online doc.
Stella Maris College YEAR BOOK 1964-1965. Montevideo.
John W. R. Taylor (1970) JANE'S ALL THE WORLD'S AIRCRAFT 1969-70. Sampson Low, Marston & Co.
Maria Tena (2019) NADA QUE NO SEPAS. Spain:Tusquets Editores.
Louisa Valenzuela (1993) SIMETRÍAS. Editorial Sudamericano. (English edition (1998) SYMMETRIES. Serpent's Tail.)
Amílcar Vasconcellos (1973) FEBRERO AMARGO. Montevideo:Junta Departamental de Montevideo (2009).
Javier de Viana (1925) LA BIBLIA GAUCHA. Montevideo:Editiones Tauro (1967).
Pablo Vierci (2005) 50 AÑOS DE COLEGIO STELLA MARIS – CHRISTIAN BROTHERS. Ad Astra.
Juan Zorrilla de San Martin (1888) TABARÉ (Walter Owen (1956) Translation into English verse, UNESCO.)

Acknowledgements

The completion of this book has relied on the goodwill and support of many people. My greatest debt of gratitude is to those who granted me interviews; mainly the families and friends of those who died on the mountain, but many others also. Without exception, they were courteous, hospitable, and generous with their time, often going far beyond the call of duty. I hope they feel that this book is worthy of the great trust they placed in me. They are: Gonzalo Abal, Martin Aguirre Regules, Pedro Algorta, Johnny Bird, Ezequiel 'Chelin' Bolumburu, Daniel Bruno, Jorge Camilloni, Carlos Costemalle, Diego Costemalle, Silvia Cuadrado, Willy Davis, María Beatriz Echavarren, Sarucha Echavarren, María de Pilar Echavarren, Chela Etcheverria, Alejandro Ferradás, Ricardo Franchetti, Enrique Gadola, Pablo Gelsi, Soledad González, Roy Harley, Sergio Hintz, Cristina Horta, Claire Hounie, Jean Pierre Hounie, Connie Hughes, Hugo Igenes, Coche Inciarte, Denise Koninckx, Mariana Lay, Aldo Magri, Sandra Maquirriain, Angeles Mardones, Rosario Martínez Lamas, Ana Inés Martinez Lamas, Rosario Maspons, Isabel Maspons, Pilar Maspons, Amparo Maspons, Rosario Medero, Laura Methol, Margarita Montes, Lita Muñoz, JuanPe Nicola, Alejandro Nicolich, Daniel Nogueira, Selina Nogueira, Brother Thomas O'Connell, Graciela Parrado, Mario Peréz, Stella Pérez del Castillo, Claudia Pérez del Castillo, Juan Manuel Pérez del Castillo, Álvaro Pérez del Castillo, Francisco Planella, Francisco 'Zika' Platero, Fernando 'Pimpo' Platero, José Pedro 'Pepe' Pollak, Rafael Ponce de León, Cecilia Regules, Alejandro Roque, Elizabeth Roque, Hugues Frossard de Saugy, Alexis Scarantino, John Scott, Enrique Storm, Jörg P. A. Thomsen, Ariel Osvaldo Torres, Inés Valeta, Teresa Valeta, Teresita Vázquez Nebel, and Pablo Vierci.

Most of my interviews were conducted in English, but on occasion I needed a helping hand. So thank you to my interpreters, all of whom provided their services for free: Willy Davis, Malvina Eterović, Rafael Ferrés Echavarren, Betty Franchetti, Fernando Franchetti, Ignacio López, Federico Sanguinetti, Guillermo Sentoni, and George Staudohar.

Thanks also to those who helped with access to archives: Piers Read was supportive and encouraging at all times, and Sarah Prescott was ever at hand to facilitate things at the Brotherton Library; James Hedeen did a comprehensive job in providing copies of the University of Wyoming materials; Sergio Hintz searched through his late father's papers and located many items of interest for me; Rosario Medero entrusted me with the only copy of the archive of her late husband Antonio Mercader; Guillermo Scott granted me access not only to his interviews, but also to the Francisco Cuadra archive, the *Cenfoto* images from the *Universidad Diego Portales* archive, the Chilean Air Force and Army reports, and copies of the Chilean and Peruvian newspaper articles from the time of the rescue; Roberto Canessa and Lauri Surraco gave me the freedom of their house, leaving me undisturbed to explore, photograph, and scan their very extensive collection of photographs and press clippings; and Federico Sanguinetti was one of the early contacts I made in Uruguay, and the first to share his personal archive.

The testimonies from the interviews conducted by Guillermo Scott in Chile contributed much to the book, so I am most grateful to the participants: Alfredo 'Perico' Alvarez, Claudio 'Cachula' Cabrera, Claudio Lucero, Eduardo Arriagada, Ezequiel 'Chelin' Bolumburu, John Scott, Juan Carlos Polverelli, Mario Ávila, Osvaldo Villegas, Paula González, Ramón Canales, and Wilma Koch.

I am indebted to all those who provided the many photographs and images that illustrate this book. In all but a handful of cases, permissions were granted free of charge. A detailed list of photo credits is given on pages 560-565.

Many others, not mentioned above, have helped me in various ways: Margarita Arocena, Alejandro Bauer, Heather Briley, Ed Burlingame, Alejandra Campeas, the Catalán family, Laura Ferreiro de Nava, Lucía Guerra-Cunningham, Alfonso Guerrina Valeta, Karen Anne Higgs, Gemma Lockie, Cnel. (Nav.) Marcelo Lorenze, Wally Lusiardo, Álvaro Mangino, Charlotte McGuinness of Bishy Barnabee Photography, Leandro Mendaro, Juan José Methol, Pablo Methol, Raquelita Methol Donamari, Gabriel 'Pulun' Nogueira, Carlitos Páez, Carlos Palma Vázquez, Alejandro Parodi, Marcelo Parodi, Pancho Perrier, Cnel. (FAU) Mariano Rodrigo, Moncho Sabella, Adolfo Strauch, Eduardo Strauch, María Tena, Luisa Valenzuela, Gustavo Zerbino, and the team at the Museo Andes 1972: Jörg P. A. Thomsen, Harald Görke, Henriette Görke, Valentina Calero, Lucía Gordillo Corbo, and Jaime E. Fernández.

My thanks go, of course, to my long-suffering family, all of whom have been supportive and tolerant. My wife Dona has barely seen me over the course of the last couple of years as, almost daily, I would disappear into my study in the early hours and rarely emerge before evening. My stepson Max was my companion in 1993 as I did the rounds of the local cinemas when the movie *Alive* first appeared, and he later obtained for me an original film poster which has hung in our home ever since. My daughter Julie took an early interest in the story, doing a report on the subject when in middle school, and receiving top marks for her diligent research; I am following in her footsteps. My son James joined me on an expedition to the site of the accident in 2015, followed by a trip to Montevideo; there we were given a personal tour by Eduardo Strauch who took us to many interesting places connected with his childhood, and even introduced us to Josefina Herrán, the former first lady of Uruguay, and sister of Eduardo's aunt. My youngest daughter Maria joined me in Montevideo in November 2019, where she was able to meet some of the people I had had the privilege of interviewing in the previous weeks. After a rapid tour of Montevideo, Punta del Este, and Casapueblo, we headed up the River Plate estuary to the beautiful historic town of Colonia. From there we crossed to Argentina, spending time in Buenos Aires before flying south to Patagonia, where we shared some memorable hikes amongst the spectacular mountains and glaciers of the southern Andes.

Only two things diverted me from the task of completing this book. The first was a regular dose of tennis which kept me sane and passably fit, although my coach, Callum Forsyth, often had to bear the brunt of my frustrations when I was grappling with a particularly difficult section of the book. So, my thanks to him and to my many wonderful companions of the tennis court for continuing to provide such enjoyable respite from my labours. The second was the opportunity to visit my grandson Luke. Many of the survivors and siblings of non-survivors will attest to the fact that being a grandparent is an incomparable joy; one in which you get to experience all the precious moments of watching a child grow up, with few of the onerous responsibilities of parenthood. I hope that my grandson and his generation will draw inspiration from this story which speaks about what it is to be human.

Finally, a word of gratitude to my editor, Katharine Smith, for accepting this book for publication under the Heddon banner, whilst at the same time giving me full editorial control over the content, thus enabling me to fulfil a pledge I made to those I interviewed. It has been a great pleasure to work with her.

Overleaf: 2022 Memorial 'Milagro en Los Andes' by US Sculptor Jeffrey Breslow. Located in the Sculpture Park of the Pablo Atchugarry Foundation in Punta del Este. The 45 stones represent the passengers, those who survived resting on solid ground, those who stayed on the mountain shown as spirits in the air which sway with the wind.

Milton Keynes UK
Ingram Content Group UK Ltd.
UKHW051415050224
437301UK00016B/356